JOHN DEWEY

*Religious Faith and
Democratic Humanism*

ʼJOHN DEWEY,

Religious Faith and Democratic Humanism

STEVEN C. ROCKEFELLER

COLUMBIA UNIVERSITY PRESS
New York

Columbia University Press

New York   Oxford

Copyright © 1991 Columbia University Press

All rights reserved

Library of Congress Cataloging-in-Publication Data

Rockefeller, Steven C., 1936–
    John Dewey : Religious faith and democratic human-
ism / Steven C. Rockefeller.
        p.   cm.
    Includes bibliographical references and index.
    ISBN 0–231–07348–8
        1. Dewey, John, 1859–1952—Religion.   2. Dewey,
John, 1859–1952—Political and social views.   I. Title.
B945.D44R57 1991
191—dc20   90–28619
                                                                   CIP

∞

Casebound editions of Columbia University Press books
are Smyth-sewn and printed on permanent and durable
acid-free paper

Printed in the United States of America

c 10 9 8 7 6 5 4 3 2 1

Government, business, art, religion, all social institutions have a meaning, a purpose. That purpose is
to set free and to develop the capacities of human
individuals without respect to race, sex, class or
economic status. And this is all one with saying that
the test of their value is the extent to which they
educate every individual into the full stature of his
possibility.   —John Dewey
                              Reconstruction in Philosophy

We who now live are parts of a humanity that
extends into the remote past, a humanity that has
interacted with nature. The things in civilization
we most prize are not of ourselves. They exist by
grace of the doings and sufferings of the continuous
human community in which we are a link. Ours is
the responsibility of conserving, transmitting, recti-
fying and expanding the heritage of values we have
received that those who come after us may receive
it more solid and secure, more widely accessible and
more generously shared than we have received it.
                                    —John Dewey
                                    A Common Faith

Contents

Preface

THE STORY of the life and thought of John Dewey (1859–1952) is one of those critical narratives in the history of a people that can help them to clarify their shared identity and the meaning of their life together. It is the purpose of this book to retrieve for our time the intellectual, moral, and religious traditions associated with the John Dewey story. A rediscovery and critical reappraisal of the deeper enduring significance of Dewey's work is important not only for Americans, but also for all those throughout the world today who love freedom and seek to pursue the democratic way of life.

At the height of his career during the early decades of the twentieth century, Dewey exerted a major influence on American culture and his ideas also had an impact overseas. However, by the 1950s the earlier wide interest in his writings was on the wane. In part this was due to the emergence of a new generation whose thinking was shaped by the more pessimistic and conservative mood of the Great Depression, the Second World War, and the Cold War. Analytic philosophy, existentialism, Marxism, neo-orthodox theology, and other movements became popular in the universities, and in most quarters Dewey's blend of naturalism, experimentalism, and democratic humanism fell into disfavor. However, a small band of philosophers and scholars continued to assert the importance of various aspects of Dewey's thought. In addition, in a major scholarly undertaking begun in the 1960s and requiring twenty-five years of patient research and editing, Dewey's works, including hundreds of essays and over thirty books, were collected, annotated, and published by the Center for Dewey Studies and Southern Illinois University Press. During the 1980s, there was a reawakening to the value of classical American philosophical traditions, involving an intensification of Dewey scholarship. A major revival of interest in Dewey is now in the making, and in this connection Thomas M. Alexander, Raymond Boisvert, Larry A. Hickman, Richard Rorty, R.W. Sleeper, Robert B. Westbrook, and Cornel West have published important new studies of his philosophy. In these works, his thought is examined in the light of the history of American pragmatism and from the perspective of his logic, philosophy of language, metaphysics, social thought, and theory of art. Other important research involving biography as well as philosophical analysis is under way.

It is hoped that this book will advance the process of reevaluating Dewey by viewing his career as a distinctively American democratic quest for the ideal and by offering a critical examination of his life and work from the perspective of its religious significance. Earlier essays dealing with Dewey's contributions as a religious thinker, including Bruce Kuklick's book *Churchmen and Philosophers: From Jonathan Edwards to John Dewey* (1985), have been limited in scope, exploring only certain aspects of the larger complex story. This study also emphasizes the close connection between Dewey's life experience and his thought and seeks to call attention to the power of his philosophical vision taken as a whole. Approaching Dewey's thought from the perspective of its religious meaning and value provides a particularly effective way of entering into an appreciative understanding of the larger unified vision toward which Dewey was working throughout his career. To arrive at a point in one's work on Dewey when that comprehensive philosophical vision begins to come into view is the most rewarding experience granted those who persist in Dewey studies.

It seems that the time is right for giving Dewey a fresh hearing.

Ours is a time of moral confusion, spiritual search, and crisis in the relation of civilization and nature, and it is also one of renewed hope in the creation of a free world united by commitment to democratic values. In America, the twentieth century began with a confidence that democracy would soon be embraced by peoples everywhere and the full creative potential of civilization would be realized. Since World War I, however, humanity has lost its way again and again, falling into self-destructive patterns of war, oppression, genocide, and the abuse of the natural environment. Nevertheless, as the century comes to a close, the revolts against Communist totalitarianism in the Soviet Union and Eastern Europe, the opening of the Berlin Wall, the dismantling of apartheid in South Africa, and the worldwide awakening to environmental issues signal that democratic hopes and aspirations have spread extensively in the world and may yet be fulfilled in spite of formidable obstacles. At this time it may be possible to listen again with new appreciation to the voices of those men and women from the nineteenth and early twentieth centuries who developed creative philosophies of freedom informed by deep moral and religious faith and a keen sense of the interdependence of the human spirit and nature. One will not find ready-made or simple solutions to our complex social, environmental, and religious problems in the works of these earlier thinkers, but there is much wisdom in their understanding of the world and the human search for well-being. The philosophy of John Dewey is certainly one which merits careful study, keeping always in mind, of course, his own critical experimental approach to all ideas, old or new.

The writing of this volume would not have been possible without the assistance and support of a number of institutions and many men and women with whom it has been my privilege to be associated. It is not possible to mention all their names here, but I do wish to express my gratitude to those who have been especially helpful. First of all, I am deeply grateful to my teachers Daniel Day Williams and John Herman Randall, Jr., who introduced me as a graduate student at Union Theological Seminary and Columbia University to the tradition of American naturalism and the thought of John Dewey. Conversations with Joseph L. Blau, Lawrence A. Cremin, and George Dykhuizen during the earlier phases of my research and writing were very helpful. Dykhuizen's *The Life and Mind of John Dewey* (1969) was the first substantial scholarly attempt to look at Dewey's life as a whole, and it remains an invaluable resource to anyone interested in Dewey biography. I wish to express deep thanks to Jo Ann Boydston, the Director of the Center for Dewey Studies and the editor of *The Works of John Dewey,* for the countless ways in which she and her staff have thoughtfully assisted my research and for her comments on the manuscript. I have benefitted from exchanges with Malcolm David Eckel, Robert L. Ferm, John Macquarrie, Reuben Rainey, and Ralph W. Sleeper, pertaining to my Dewey work. I warmly thank James A. Martin, Jr., William Newell, and Bruce Wilshire for their very helpful critiques of my manuscript as well as their encouragement.

I wish to thank Middlebury College for providing leave opportunities that enabled me to advance my research at critical times. Acknowledgment must also be made of the cooperation received from the Morris Library at Southern Illinois University; Special Collections, Butler Library, at Columbia University; Special Collections, Bailey/Howe Library, at the University of Vermont; the Michigan Historical Collections at the University of Michigan; the Manuscript Division of the Library of Congress; and Starr Library at Middlebury College. I would also like to thank Southern Illinois University Press for permission to use many quotations from *The Works of John Dewey* and *The Poems of John Dewey.*

For many years Janet Winkler has typed and helped to proofread countless pages of Dewey material as my research and writing progressed, and I am very grateful for her kind and thoughtful assistance. Claire Wilson has patiently entered the entire book into the word processor, adding innumerable revisions, and has tirelessly helped with research, the correction of footnotes, and proofreading, and I extend to her my very deep thanks. I wish to thank Louise Waller, Ann Miller, and Leslie Bialler at Columbia University Press for the care and thought they have given my manuscript during the publication process.

The affection and understanding of the members of my family have sustained me in my research and writing over the years. I am particularly grateful to Laura Chasin, whose love and companionship helped me grow as a child, whose understanding of Dewey deepened my own, and whose careful critique of chapters of this book was invaluable in improving my work. For hours of good conversation about Dewey and American culture, for comments on the manuscript, and for her love and support, my heart is full of gratitude to Barbara Bellows Rockefeller.

Note

In each chapter, initial note references to books or essays contained in the bibliographies will include author, full title and page but no publication data. (For works in *The Works of John Dewey,* see below.) Where appropriate, subsequent references to author and title will be in shortened form. Initial references to those sources not cited in the bibliographies will include full publication data.

In each chapter, initial references to works by John Dewey and others that are contained in the thirty-seven volumes of *The Early Works of John Dewey, 1882–1898, The Middle Works of John Dewey, 1899–1924,* and *The Later Works of John Dewey, 1925–1953* (Carbondale, Illinois: Southern Illinois University Press), Jo Ann Boydston, editor, will cite author and title followed by Southern Illinois University Press's short form, e.g., EW 3:9–18 (Early Works, Volume 3, pages 9–18). Subsequent references to books and essays contained in *The Works of John Dewey* will cite author and title followed by page numbers only.

Initial references to works by John Dewey and others contained in *The Works of John Dewey* but not listed in the bibliographies will include information on the original publication only when it seems that such information may be of special interest.

JOHN DEWEY

Religious Faith and
Democratic Humanism

Prologue

> The next religious prophet who will have a permanent and real influence on men's lives will be the man who succeeds in pointing out the religious meaning of democracy, the ultimate religious value to be found in the normal flow of life itself. It is the question of doing what Jesus did for his time. —John Dewey, 1892

JOHN DEWEY was born in the late fall of 1859 and raised in the bustling town of Burlington, Vermont. Set in a great valley surrounded by mountains and lakes of awe-inspiring beauty, Burlington was a place where the challenge and freedom of pioneer days still lingered in the air and town meetings were the heart of lively democratic self-government. Here also men and women endured long harsh winters, relied on Puritan morals to discipline their desires, and believed in the Calvinistic dualisms of God and the world, spirit and flesh, heaven and hell. The nation into which Dewey was born was soon to be engulfed in a horribly destructive civil war. The war separated Dewey's father from his family home for five and a half long years. Shortly after the war between the North and the South had been concluded, America found itself plunged into another disruptive conflict with far-reaching implications. It was in 1859 that Charles Darwin published *Origin of Species By Means of Natural Selection,* and his theory of biological evolution would dramatically intensify the battle between science and religion, leaving large numbers of Americans feeling a confusing split in their psyche between the head and the heart. There were many positive dimensions to Dewey's boyhood experience, but the world in which he grew up was also one of sharp contrasts, unhappy separations, and threatening conflicts and divisions.

By nature young Dewey was a sensitive boy with a gentle compassionate disposition. There also emerged in him quite early a rare ability to think widely and coherently. Given these capacities and the many divisions in his world, it is not surprising that he developed a passionate craving for unity and that in time he became a philosopher dedicated to overcoming dualisms, that is, all those splits and separations in human experience that oppress life, restrict growth, and obstruct social progress, causing conflict and suffering. His philosophical labors are one long sustained endeavor to break down such dualisms as that between subject and object, experience and nature, mind and body, duty and desire, the individual and society, the school and society, the child and the curriculum, means and ends, moral values and science, the religious and the secular, the spiritual and the material, God and the world. In these divisions Dewey found the heart of what he viewed as the pressing social and intellectual problems of the age. Overcoming these separations became for him both the way of individual freedom and growth and the road to social justice.

Employing the neo-Hegelian philosophical language current in his day, Dewey conceptualized the most comprehensive dualism afflicting life as the dualism of the ideal and the actual (or real). Accordingly he defined the fundamental problem facing an individual and society as the problem of unifying the ideal and the actual. This is the general terminology Dewey used to discuss the problem of human values and the conflict between good and evil. Finding the way to unify the ideal and the actual—that is, to realize the ideal or to idealize the world—in contemporary democratic technological culture is Dewey's central concern as a thinker. It is for him the way to unification of self and self and world leading to freedom and community. The full significance of his various technical philosophical interests is appreciated only when they are seen in relation to this governing objective.

Even though Dewey's prose is often dry and difficult, his attack on dualisms was successful in conceptualizing the problems that troubled large numbers of Americans and in generating an inspiring vision of the ideal possibilities of life in the new world. As a result, few philosophers have had such a wide impact on their time. Together with Charles Sanders Peirce and William James he founded the revolutionary American philosophical movement known as pragmatism, and by the end of his career he was being honored at home and abroad as the foremost American philosopher. However, Dewey was much more than an innovative philosopher who had mastered an academic discipline. The formative period in Dewey's life coincides with those years at the end of the nineteenth century and the beginning of the twentieth century that generated the American progressive mind, and he became the philosophical voice of the Progressive Era. It was a time when America experienced the vanishing of the frontier and woke up to the seriousness of the social and economic problems accompanying rapid industrialization and urbanization. It was also a time of high ideals and hopes, when large numbers of men and women rededicated themselves with characteristic American confidence to realizing the promise of democracy for the common person. Dewey was in the vanguard of this movement. His thought was shaped under the influence of its best dreams and enthusiasms, and it found in him its most influential intellectual leader. He became both social critic and prophet of hope.

Dewey championed the cause of progressive education and the new social sciences as the most effective instruments of human growth and social progress in a democratic society. His writings on education earned him a worldwide reputation as a liberator of children, and he counselled governments on the subject and lectured in Japan, Mexico, Russia, South Africa, and Turkey, as well as in China where he lived for two years. Dewey recognized the scientific method as the most potent force shaping the modern world, and he saw the dangers posed by modern technology. His response was an endeavor to humanize the creative power of science and thereby to gain control of the future. For fifty years he persistently worked to transform the scientific method of knowledge into an instrument of individual moral guidance and enlightened social planning. This is the principal concern of his philosophical pragmatism. It is first and foremost a strategy and method for idealizing the world—for breaking down the dualism of fact and value, real and ideal. As he developed his philosophical, educational, and social thinking, he reconstructed and defended those ideas and values that constitute the core of twentieth century American social liberalism.

Dewey is often recognized for his achievements as a philosophical pragmatist, progressive educator, and liberal reformer, but the full and deeper meaning of his quest for unity and freedom is not appreciated until he is also seen as the prophet of a new spiritual attitude and way of being—what one might call a distinctively American democratic form of spirituality. In this regard, Dewey envisioned the most thoroughgoing and radical unification of the ideal and the real of any American thinker. He endeavored to reconstruct the intellectual, moral, and religious traditions of his time so as to eradicate the root causes of the forces that deny to everyday existence effective moral direction and a sense of inherent meaning and value. Dewey recognized early in his career that this problem had been greatly exacerbated by the rise of science and the process of secularization, leaving men and women painfully confused in their intellectual and spiritual loyalties. In an effort to resolve the problem, he worked persistently to break down completely the dualisms of the spiritual and the natural, religious values and science, the sacred and the secular, Christianity and democracy. His goal was to integrate fully the religious life with the American democratic life, transforming the religious life into a way of practical liberation for the individual and society and the democratic life into a way of religious self-realization and social unification. According to Dewey, nothing short of such a radical reconciliation between humanity's spiritual values and their everyday existence will bring wholeness to the modern psyche. Overcoming the dualism of religious values and modern culture has been central to the agenda of nineteenth- and twentieth-century religious liberals, but Dewey developed this agenda in a more complete and concrete fashion than any other liberal, tirelessly working out its meaning for psychology, pedagogy, epistemology, metaphysics, aesthetics, morals, social theory, and religion.

It is the purpose of this study to approach Dewey's life and thought from the perspective of its religious meaning and value, focusing on the ways in which he wrestled with the problems of faith and doubt, science and values, and the relation of religious life and everyday life in western secular society. This involves inquiring into the origin and nature of his own religious thinking, and it entails exploring the ways the latter is intimately connected with the other dimensions of his philosophy and expresses the deeper meaning and value of the whole. This task is undertaken in the conviction that the greatest relevance of Dewey's philosophy to the dilemmas of contemporary American society and the emerging global community is to be found just here in the way in which he endeavored to address the intellectual, social, and religious problems of the age by holding them together and thinking them through together. Only such an approach, believed Dewey, will achieve the freedom, community, and world peace that are the aspiration of modern men and women and the promise of democratic technological civilization. To enter deeply into Dewey's life and thought is to experience the soul of American culture wrestling with its meaning and destiny in one of its most profound expressions.

The Nineteenth-Century Setting

There is a logic to the religious thinking associated with Dewey's mature philosophical outlook, but to grasp it one must understand the evolution of his thinking as a whole from its earliest beginnings. His thought has a history and to appreciate its meaning it is important to know this history. In this regard, it is necessary to locate Dewey's early thinking in relation to the major intellectual currents at work in the nineteenth-century American world in which he was educated and to trace the ways in which his outlook is transformed over time in response to new ideas. It is useful, therefore, by way of introduction to our story to note very briefly some of the major characteristics of the American philosophical situation as it had developed in relation to religious and moral issues up through the 1870s when Dewey entered the University of Vermont as a college student. Following that a few further introductory comments will be made about the approach taken in this study to understanding the evolution of Dewey's own philosophy and religious thinking.

First of all, philosophers and theologians in the nineteenth century found themselves in a time of great intellectual and social change. The development of natural science, the spread of the Enlightenment faith in reason and nature, the rise of the middle class, and the emergence of democracy were forces dramatically altering the way men and women lived and looked at the human situation. These great forces of social transformation were causing a gradual shift in spiritual attitude or orientation that is particularly noteworthy. Growing numbers of people turned their attention and hope from the other world to this world, from the supernatural to the natural, from the sacred to the secular, from the transcendent to the immanent, from divine intervention to human invention. Especially in democratic America, with its vast frontier and resources and its great vision of freedom and opportunity, the common person could nurture a faith in progress and dream of earthly well-being in a fashion never before possible. This shifting of the focus of human concern and aspiration left thoughtful men and women pondering how to reconcile their religious beliefs and moral values, which had been inherited from a prescientific feudal culture, with modern ways of living and thinking. Some concluded that reconciliation was impossible and that a person must choose between traditional religion and modern culture. Others sought to reconcile religion and modern culture by radically reconstructing the idea of God and the idea of what it means to be a religious person.

At the end of the eighteenth and the beginning of the nineteenth century, the intellectual debate over the truth of traditional religious beliefs tended to focus on the meaning of the new science. Newtonian physics, with its vision of the world as a great machine operating according to strict mathematical laws, did away with all references to supernatural causes and final causes. Everything was to be explained in terms of natural mechanical causes. Science seemed to tell people that they lived in a material and mechanical world and that the values of truth, beauty, and goodness had no existence in this world outside the heads and hearts of human beings. Newton, of course, had retained the idea of God as the first cause, the watchmaker or master machinist who made the world, but it did not take reflective men and women long to begin wondering whether a God so remote actually existed and whether God is really necessary or legitimate as a scientific hypothesis. The new science seemed to mean a universe made up of matter in motion involving no God, no ultimate purpose or meaning, and no objective moral standards.

When philosophers wrestled with the questions raised by Newton-ian science, their inquiries centered on the problem of the method of knowledge and particularly on the question of the validity of the empiricist theory of knowledge formulated by the seventeenth-cen-tury British philosopher John Locke. In the eighteenth century the influence of Locke and British empiricism in America had been very strong in centers of philosophical and theological learning. It was the philosophy that Protestant theologians most often drew upon in their attempts to offer an intellectual defense of traditional religious beliefs. However, the Scottish philosopher David Hume demonstrated to the satisfaction of many that a rigorous application of the empiricist theory of knowledge, which assumes a radical dualism of subject and object, mind and external reality, leads to skepticism regarding knowledge of a necessary causal connection between events and of the existence of an external world, a self, God, and objective moral values. Even though Hume's skepticism raised doubts about the truth of the new science itself, what impressed and disturbed most of his readers was that it seemed to confirm the most negative implications of the new science for morals and religion. The way in which the new science and Hume's skepticism could be used to justify agnosti-cism, atheism, and moral relativism constituted the most serious challenge to theology and religious faith in the latter half of the eighteenth century.

One reaction in Europe was the development of what came to be known as Scottish commonsense realism. Its founders, Thomas Reid and Dugald Stewart, attempted to revise the Lockean tradition of empiricism so as to avoid Hume's skepticism and the materialism associated with it. Scottish realism taught that all empirical knowl-edge is founded upon certain self-evident truths or principles of common sense and that the basic principles of the moral order are self-evident to the moral sense or conscience. No philosophical skepticism, it was argued, can undermine the truth of the principles of common sense and moral sense, which are known directly in clear intuitions apart from sense experience and discursive reason. The Scottish philosophers went on to develop what they considered to be reasonable common sense arguments for accepting the supernatural revelations of Christianity.

The Reverend John Witherspoon, who came to America from Scotland in 1768 to become president of Princeton, was the first major champion of the Scottish philosophy in the new world. Presbyterian Princeton continued to be a center for study of Scottish realism down to Dewey's day when President James McCosh defended it as the best philosophical foundation for a defense of religion and the most appropriate philosophy for Americans with their practical bent of mind.[1] The influence of commonsense realism was not limited to Presbyterian theologians, however. It also became a major philosophical force shaping the thinking of Unitarians, Congregationalists, Episcopalians, and others. Sidney Ahlstrom writes that "during the first two-thirds of the nineteenth century, at least, it was ... among American Protestants the chief philosophical support to theological and apologetical enterprises."[2] According to Dewey its influence was strong at the University of Vermont during his student days.

A much more profound attempt to defend moral and religious values against Hume's skepticism and scientific materialism developed with the philosophies of Immanuel Kant and the post-Kantian German idealists. These philosophies emerged during the late eighteenth and early nineteenth centuries as major philosophical expressions of what is often rather loosely called the Romantic reaction to the rationalism and scientific materialism of the eighteenth century. On the one hand, Kant himself had a profound respect for science and part of his purpose was to show that despite some of Hume's skeptical objections the scientific method of knowledge does arrive at a universal and objective knowledge of the truth. On the other hand, Kant was much concerned to provide the moral values of European civilization with a firm foundation, and he also wished to provide a defense of religious faith in God. In short his aim was to reconcile science with morals and religion without denying the validity of either, and his strategy was to achieve this by separating them into two utterly distinct spheres of human experience, both of which are necessary and valid.

In his *Critique of Pure Reason* (1781) Kant undertook an extensive inquiry into how persons know and what they do know and have the capability to know. Kant did not deny that real knowledge involves sense impressions and that the reach of knowledge is limited by what is given in experience. However, he rejected the empiricist notions that sense impressions constitute the sole source of knowledge and the mind is a passive faculty or *tabula rasa* upon which sensations play. Presenting a theory that altered the course of modern philosophy, he argued that the mind is an active organ which organizes and synthesizes sense perceptions according to certain unchanging structures or a priori conditions. In other words, there is an ideal or transcendental structure derived from the activity of mind itself in all experience and knowledge. These a priori conditions include the space and time structure, which governs sense perception, and twelve concepts or logical categories, according to which the human understanding (*Verstand*) universally and necessarily organizes the objects derived from sense experience. Kant identified the concept of causality as one of these twelve a priori categories, and with this theory he was able to defend scientific knowledge against Hume's skeptical attack. Since the laws of science are constituted by the concepts of the understanding, they have an objective and necessary validity for the objects of all possible human experience. However, in Kant's solution there remains a problematic subjectivism and dualism. He insisted that in sense experience and scientific knowledge all we know are phcnomcna, the appearances of things, and not noumena, things-in-themselves, which remain an impenetrable mystery.

Pursuing the implications of his view that knowledge cannot transcend experience, Kant presented carefully constructed arguments to show that a rational demonstration of the existence of God is not possible. However, he came to the rescue of religious faith with his theory of practical reason. Practical reason, explained Kant, is an aspect of what he called Reason or pure reason (*Vernuft*), which he distinguished from the understanding (*Verstand*). In his *Critique of Practical Reason* (1788) he argued that practical reason operates in the sphere of the will and practical action as a source of moral law and religious faith. The essence of the moral law is found in the idea of reason itself, which includes the idea of universal law. The human being is a spiritual being whose nature is reason and will. The freedom and perfection of human nature is found, therefore, in a life of reason, or, more specifically, in obedience to universal law. Moral obligation is simply the unconditional obligation of human beings to obey the law of their own nature, the universal law of reason. Kant summed up the meaning of the moral law in a purely formal or a priori moral directive which he called the categorical imperative: act at all times in such a way that you could also will that the maxim of your action serve as a universal law governing all persons, or, as Kant also states it, act so that you treat every person always as an end and never as a means only. The good person is one who acts purely for the sake of duty, that is, out of respect for reason, law, the categorical imperative. A person who acts out of a sense of duty is not influenced by natural desires or by the consequence of his or her action. Kant's moral theory culminated with the vision of an ideal society of free and rational wills in which each is the autonomous author of a common system of universal laws derived from practical reason and the categorical imperative.

What Kant has done in his vision of the ideal society is to rationalize the Christian notion of the kingdom of God and to replace the will of God with the voice of practical reason. In short, he founded morality on reason and the essential nature of the human being rather than on the will of a transcendent God. In the final analysis, however, Kant did identify practical reason with the will of God, but instead of trying to found morality on religious faith he did the reverse. He argued that humanity's moral experience implies the existence of a soul (a free and responsible will), immortality, and God. In other words, starting with the fact of an unconditional obligation to obey the law of reason, Kant tried to develop a reasonable ground for belief in free will, eternal life, and God. However, he was careful to insist that these postulates of practical reason are a matter of faith pertaining to realities in the noumenal world and not of scientific or theoretical knowledge, which is limited to the phenomenal world. Kant's philosophy endeavored to reconcile science with morality and religion, then, by clearly separating the realm of empirical fact governed by the law of causality, which is apprehended by scientific knowledge, from the realm of free will, moral obligation, and God, which is apprehended by faith.

Beginning with Fichte, the post-Kantian German idealists argued that the philosophical reconstruction which Kant had begun was not completed by Kant himself. They were particularly dissatisfied with the subjectivism and dualism in his thought, especially the distinction between the phenomenal and the noumenal. They, therefore, set about developing Kant's thought in the direction of a thoroughgoing objective idealism. They rejected his concept of a thing-in-itself and identified what he had described as the subjective or ideal structure imposed by the mind on all objects of experience with the objective structure of reality itself. In brief, they argued that the world of reality is to be regarded as the manifestation or expression of a universal mind and absolute will, and that the philosophical discipline practiced by Kant of reflecting on the constitution and laws of the human mind is actually a process whereby the universal mind becomes aware of itself. The door was thus opened to attributing to Kant's transcendental ideas and practical reason a power of real knowledge of spiritual realities that Kant would never agree was possible.

Dissatisfied with both Locke and Scottish realism a small number of American thinkers began during the late 1820s and 1830s to turn to Kant and German idealism. Among the very first was the Reverend James Marsh, President of the University of Vermont and professor of philosophy. Of particular significance was his publication in 1829 of an American edition of Samuel Taylor Coleridge's *Aids to Reflections*. The book is prefaced by a forty-five page "Preliminary Essay" in which Marsh urged his American readers to adopt the synthesis of seventeenth-century Cambridge Platonism, Kant, and German idealism proposed by the English poet, literary critic, and philosopher. Marsh, who was a Congregationalist with deep roots in in the theological traditions of Calvin and Jonathan Edwards, found Coleridge's philosophy far more conducive to fostering personal religious experience and a vital Christian faith than Locke's empiricism and Scottish realism. In time this book was to have an important influence on Dewey. Its immediate effect was to help launch the movement known as New England Transcendentalism.[3] During the 1830s and 1840s Marsh's enthusiasm for Coleridge and post-Kantian German idealism spread rapidly among young men such as Emerson, Theodore Parker, Bronson Alcott, and Frederick H. Hedge. The consequences went far beyond anything Marsh had intended. A major reaction against Calvinism and conventionalism generally as well as Locke and Scottish realism erupted in New England. The thought of Kant, Schleiermacher, Jacobi, Fichte, Schelling, and Hegel soon became popular. However, there were few American scholars who actually read the German originals. Most relied on interpreters like Coleridge and Carlyle.

In German idealism, these American Transcendentalists seemed to find a worldview that satisfied an intense interest in both individual self-realization and a spiritual or religious conception of human nature and the universe. Most of them were not especially interested in scientific methods of knowing, and most were not primarily concerned with cultivating the logical powers of their discursive understanding. It was their belief that sense experience and discursive reason cannot disclose the spiritual meaning, the supreme ideals, that govern the universe and constitute the perfection of the soul; and spiritual truth and the soul is what interested them. They followed Coleridge and Marsh, therefore, in making a basic distinction between the natural understanding and the higher reason or some intuitive spiritual power of direct moral and religious insight. With this emphasis on some higher rational power of intuition, usually closely associated with the heart, feeling, and conscience, their philosophizing tended to be more prophetic and poetic vision than carefully reasoned argument.

One idea especially appealed to the Transcendentalists in their search for a spiritual conception of the nature of the universe. In opposition to the Newtonian mechanical metaphor of the clock, the Transcendentalists adopted the organic metaphor of the idealists, which asserts the ultimate unity of mind and the world and views reality as a dynamic and creative process of growth. The world, they taught, is an organic unity in process of development, and its source is a single divine mind and will. Further, this divine reason is immanent in nature and in the soul of each person. In "The Over-Soul" Emerson writes of:

> that Unity, that Over-soul, within which every man's particular being is contained and made one with all other; that common heart of which all sincere conversation is the worship, to which all right action is submission. . . . We live in succession, in division, in parts, in particles. Meantime within man is the soul of the whole; the wise silence; the universal beauty, to which every part and particle is equally related; the eternal One. And this deep power in which we exist and whose beatitude is all accessible to us, is not only self-sufficing and perfect in every hour, but the act of seeing and the thing seen, the seer and the spectacle, the subject and the object, are one.[4]

In this fashion Emerson and his followers sought to unify, or interrelate, humanity and God, humanity and nature, subject and object, the real and the ideal, and the individual and the community. There was a strong tendency towards pantheism among many transcendentalists, especially in the case of Emerson, but some of them endeavored to maintain a theism that appreciated the transcendence as well as the immanence of God.

Even though they emphasized the unity of the individual and the universal, the Transcendentalists stressed that each individual is a unique, infinitely significant manifestation of the universal. They championed the individualism of the Romantic movement and attacked whatever institutions and customs seemed to obstruct their freedom and creativity. Many, like Emerson, left the institutional church as too authoritarian and superstitious and as lacking a vital spiritual life. Along with a concern for a direct personal religious experience they emphasized the value of self-knowledge, self-reliance, joyful self-affirmation, and creative self-expression. The stress on individual self-realization and the anti-institutional emphasis among many transcendentalists led most of them to be little interested in the process of history and not greatly concerned with social action. Nevertheless, some Transcendentalists were outspoken in their support of abolition and women's rights, and they had their utopian visions and experiments.

By the time of the Civil War the influence of New England Transcendentalism was on the wane. The year Dewey entered college Octavius Brooks Frothingham was completing his classic history of *Transcendentalism in New England,* and he described it largely as an event of the past. However, Frothingham pointed out that American interest in German philosophical idealism is not dead. He writes that the idealist tradition in America "has taken refuge in St. Louis, and there comes to surprising life in *The Journal of Speculative Philosophy* conducted by William T. Harris an accomplished thinker and educator, who keeps alive the interest in German thought in the West. Through him and his little band of helpers the names of Kant, Schelling, and Hegel are made illustrious again."[5] Harris and his associates like Denton T. Snider and Henry Brokmeyer were largely Hegelians, and it was through *The Journal of Speculative Philosophy,* which was the first American journal to be devoted primarily to philosophy as distinct from theology, that Dewey was introduced to the American neo-Hegelian movement. There was some cooperation between the old leaders of New England Transcendentalism and the midwestern Hegelians. Alcott and Harris organized the Concord Summer School of Philosophy, which operated for about a decade between 1879 and 1887. However, among the Hegelians the mood had changed and the intellectual focus was somewhat different. The American neo-Hegelians were generally less radical and more sober-minded, more interested in science, schools, history, and democracy, and more systematic as thinkers. They did, of course, share with the earlier Transcendentalists certain basic convictions regarding the immanence of the divine in the human, the unity of thought and being, and the applicability of the organic metaphor to reality.

Like most of the New England Transcendentalists, the St. Louis Hegelians were philosophers working without academic positions in the universities, and in the final analysis this limited the extent and duration of their influence. However, a new generation of scholars was beginning to emerge who went to Germany to study and who would establish Hegelian philosophy in the universities. By the 1860s and 1870s a reaction had set in against Hegel in Germany, but in England at this time German philosophy from Kant to Hegel was being discovered with fresh enthusiasm. J.H. Stirling, T.H. Green,

F.H. Bradley, Edward Caird, John Caird, and William Wallace were in the process of launching the British neo-Hegelian movement. Typical of the new generation of young American philosophers was George Sylvester Morris. After a year-and-a-half at Union Theological Seminary in New York, he gave up a career in the ministry to study philosophy in Germany during the late 1860s and then brought British neo-Hegelian idealism to the University of Michigan and Johns Hopkins University where Dewey would eventually encounter him.[6]

A good part of the story of modern philosophy is an account of the ways in which philosophers have adjusted or reconstructed their ideas in the light of the discoveries of the sciences. No scientist in the nineteenth century had a greater impact on philosophy than Charles Darwin. The general idea of evolution was not a new one. Historians, philosophers, and geologists had been developing and speculating about the notion in one form or another for more than a century. For example, Hegel's philosophy was a theory of social and spiritual evolution. However, Darwin's theory of biological evolution brought the authority of modern science fully behind the concept in such a way that it became the most influential idea of the nineteenth century, causing impassioned reactions and eventually leading to far-reaching intellectual reconstructions.

Led by Professor Asa Gray of Harvard, the American scientific community began to unite behind Darwin's theory by the end of the 1860s despite the opposition of Louis Agassiz, the famed paleontologist. Soon Darwin's theory was being taught widely in colleges and universities. In England an influential group of scientists and philosophers including Thomas Henry Huxley, John Tyndall, George Henry Lewes, and Herbert Spencer set about popularizing Darwin and exploring some of the more radical implications of his thought for religion and philosophy. The essays and books of these authors were widely read in intellectual circles in America and did much to focus the discussion.

During the Civil War the church had paid little attention to the scientific debate, but in the 1870s the controversy over evolution erupted in full force. Darwin's teaching on natural selection contradicted the Biblical doctrine of creation. In the place of the comforting notion that a divine intelligence and will had specially created each and every life form and imposed a beneficent design on the natural world, there was the doctrine of evolution by blind forces of natural selection involving a brutal bloody struggle for survival of the fittest. Chance replaced design. The rejection of the Biblical account of creation in turn cast radical doubts on the whole theory of Biblical inspiration and revelation. Darwin's theory that the human species had actually evolved from animal origins, which was published in *The Descent of Man* (1871), challenged the orthodox Christian doctrine of the Fall and original sin. In general the Darwinian view of human evolution seemed so thoroughly to naturalize human nature as to strip it of its moral and religious character. For all these reasons Darwin precipitated a major crisis in the church and posed substantive problems for philosophy.

The initial reaction of most Christians was to agree with Professor Charles Hodge, a leading Presbyterian theologian from Princeton Theological Seminary, who argued in the 1870s that Darwinism is an atheistic attack on Christianity. However, in the colleges and universities and among the liberal clergy there soon began to appear theologians and philosophers who endeavored to reconcile evolutionary theory and the Christian faith. During the 1870s President Charles Eliot of Harvard gave his support to Professor Gray, who himself speculated about how to adapt Christian theism to Darwin, and President James McCosh of Princeton encouraged college presidents to become voices of compromise and reconciliation. Some, like George Sylvester Morris, used Hegel's evolutionary metaphysics to try to reconcile Darwinian biology and Christianity. During the 1880s Henry Ward Beecher, Theodore T. Munger, and Lyman Abbott became the first prominent evangelical preachers to popularize "the New Theology" in which evolutionary theory is accepted.[7] No serious young American intellectual in the 1870s and 1880s could ignore Darwin and the implications of his theories for an understanding of the natural world, human nature, morals, and religion.

At Harvard in the 1870s William James was just beginning his career as a psychologist and philosopher. Widely travelled, cosmopolitan in outlook, and trained as a scientist, James was drawn to a pluralistic world view and he had no use for Hegelian absolutism and a monistic metaphysics. He was entering upon reflections on evolutionary biology and the human mind that would eventually transform American psychology and philosophy. His approach is typical of a new group of philosophers who turned to Darwinian biology rather than Newtonian mechanics as the key to an understanding of their world, and in this way they sought to escape the limitations and problems of mechanistic materialism without rejecting science.

Occasionally there gathered in James' office a group that called itself the Metaphysical Club. It was headed by a brilliant younger man named Charles Sanders Peirce, who had a special interest in the interpretation of scientific logic and the relation of ideas to practice.[8] At an early meeting of the Metaphysical Club, Peirce presented a paper on what he called the pragmatic maxim, and the paper was published in 1878. Twenty years later in 1898 James would identify this paper as having set him on the path of pragmatism, which he and Dewey were at this time rapidly developing into a new American philosophy.[9]

One of James' first graduate students in the mid-1870s was G. Stanley Hall. Inspired by the example of G.S. Morris, he had interrupted his theological education at Union Theological Seminary to study philosophy in Germany. When he arrived at Harvard some years later, James convinced him to give up his interest in Hegel and to consider the more radical implications of Darwinian biology and the emerging field of experimental psychology. He sent Hall back to Germany to study with Wilhelm Wundt and Hermann von Helmholtz, leaders in the field of the new psychology and pedagogy. In 1882 Hall joined Morris and C.S. Peirce in the philosophy department at Johns Hopkins.[10] That same year Dewey enrolled as a graduate student in their department.

The American intellectual world into which young Dewey would plunge himself as an aspiring philosopher was, then, one that had been shaped in diverse ways by Calvin, Edwards, Locke, Reid, Kant, and Coleridge, and it was one being transformed by Hegel, Darwin and the new sciences generally. However, the intellectual ferment of the age was caused not only by the challenge of the new science but also by the forces of democratic social change, economic growth, and advancing secularization. It was a time that called out for new intellectual syntheses and fresh imaginative visions of the moral and religious meaning of the human venture.

Understanding the Religious Dimension of Dewey's Thought

In addition to recognizing the connections of Dewey's philosophy with certain nineteenth-century intellectual traditions, it is also important to keep several other factors in mind when trying to understand the religious dimension of his thought. First of all, the latter reflects the strong influence of his own life experience. For example, a knowledge of what Dewey went through in the course of his own quest for unity and the ideal does much to clarify the meaning of his philosophy of religious experience. The importance of biography for understanding Dewey's philosophy is underscored by the following comment made at the end of his career: "Upon the whole the forces that have influenced me have come from persons and from situations more than from books."[11] It is useful, therefore, to search for the origins of some of his attitudes and ideas in his childhood experience. In addition, this study will consider those personal relationships and events that at critical moments during his career exercised a significant influence on his emotional, intellectual, social, and religious development. In the course of these explorations some occurrences familiar to students of Dewey's life will be discussed yet again, but they are considered from a fresh perspective that often leads to new facts and meanings. Since Dewey's evolving thought and his life experience are closely related at each stage of his career, it has been thought best to consider them together throughout the story rather than to present the biographical and historical material separately at the outset.

Second, as has been indicated, the religious dimension of Dewey's thought cannot be understood apart from his philosophy as a whole. His religious thought gives expression to ideals or values that pervade his entire philosophy of social reconstruction and individual liberation, and an appreciation of the real meaning of these values requires a knowledge of the role they play in this larger system of thought. In addition, at each stage in his intellectual development, Dewey's philosophy culminates with a theory of religious experience and faith that completes his vision of the way to unification of the ideal and the real. The full meaning of his religious thought can only be grasped by seeing its continuity or organic connection with the way in which he wrestles with the problem of the ideal and the real all along the line in the other aspects of his philosophy including especially his psychology, theory of education, epistemology, metaphysics, ethics, and social theory.

Dewey's career is usually divided into two main periods by scholars, and in this connection reference is made to his early and later thought. The early period includes Dewey's childhood, his college years in Vermont, his graduate training at Johns Hopkins University, and the decade he spent teaching as a member of the philosophy department at the University of Michigan. During most of the Michigan years (1884–1894), he was closely associated with the tradition of neo-Hegelian idealism. The early period extends from 1859 to 1894. The second period begins with Dewey's move to the University of Chicago, which roughly speaking marks the time in his career when, having abandoned the neo-Hegelian system, he began constructing his own new philosophy of pragmatism and humanistic naturalism. The later period includes Dewey's ten years in Chicago (1894–1904), his long tenure at Columbia University (1904–1939), and his final years. It extends, then, from 1894 to 1952. The distinction between the early and later Dewey is a useful one provided it is recognized that there are important continuities as well as differences between the two. The roots of important aspects of Dewey's later thought may be traced back into the early period and his later thought is a reconstruction of his early philosophy. This is especially true of his religious thought. Part 1 of this book explores the early Dewey, and part 2 is concerned with the later Dewey.

The evolution of Dewey's religious thinking may be broken down into six phases or stages, the first four of which fall in Dewey's early period. The first stage involves his childhood years when he is under the strong influence of Vermont Congregationalism and his mother's rather sentimental and moralistic brand of evangelical pietism. The second stage encompasses his college years and the three years thereafter before he went to graduate school. At this point in his life Dewey was heavily influenced by the tradition of Vermont Transcendentalism that originated with James Marsh in the 1830s. This Vermont philosophy involves a blend of the New England theology, Kant, and Coleridge. The poetry of Wordsworth was also a vital inspiration to Dewey at this juncture. Exposure to these traditions provided Dewey with a lifelong appreciation of the value of religious experience. These first two stages are considered in chapter 1.

The third stage in Dewey's religious thinking begins with his exposure as a graduate student at Johns Hopkins University (1882–1884) to the philosophy of Hegel and his adoption of the neo-Hegelian absolute idealism of George Sylvester Morris, T.H. Green, and Edward Caird. From very early Dewey was drawn to philosophy rather than theology even though as a young man he maintained a Christian belief in God. Methods of knowledge based on supernatural historical revelations or dogmatic authorities had no appeal. He was inclined to put his trust in reason, intelligence. He was also early on impressed by the scientific method of knowledge, and as a philosopher he felt the attraction of a method that derives knowledge from experience. However, the unifying power of Hegel's ideas proved irresistible, and in his early philosophy he attempted to work out a synthesis of Hegelian rationalism and scientific experimentalism. This is the subject of chapter 2.

During the initial phase of Dewey's years as an absolute idealist, he was especially concerned with metaphysics and with what he later called "the quest for certainty," that is, the search for an intellectual or logical demonstration that the ideal and the real are one in spite of all appearances to the contrary. However, this phase did not last very long and gave way to a fourth phase in his development. A change in the focus of Dewey's thought began to occur when under the influence of developing social interests, romance, and reformers, the sensitive moral conscience that had been fostered in him by Vermont Congregationalism was transformed into the conscience of a social activist. Accordingly his absolute idealism was developed into what from the Christian theological point of view one might call a radical version of the Social Gospel or a form of liberation theology. Hegel tried to reconstruct Christianity so as to reconcile it with modern culture, transforming the transcendent God of Biblical theism into an immanent God whose being is realized in and through social struggle and the progressive evolution of world history. During the 1880s and early 1890s Dewey (like the St. Louis Hegelians and Walt Whitman before him) endeavored to adopt and apply Hegel to the America of his day. This meant to Dewey dissolving the separations between God and the world, the spiritual and the material, religion and science, and Christianity and democracy. His early philosophy emerged as an American brand of ethical idealism heavily influenced by liberal Protestant Christian values, social democracy, and science including the findings of evolutionary biology and the new psychology. Gradually the emphasis in his thought shifted from the purely theoretical identification of the ideal and the real to development of strategies for their practical unification. This story along with an account of his activities as a liberal Congregationalist in Ann Arbor is told in chapter 3.

Chapter 4 examines the ongoing political radicalization of Dewey under the impact of the *Thought News* affair and his relations with various progressive reformers. It considers how these experiences influenced his religious thinking and led him to search for a way of applying the experimental method of science to the processes of moral valuation and social planning. The chapter completes the account of how Dewey rationalized and naturalized traditional Christian teaching as he moved through his idealist period and then began shifting from idealism to humanistic naturalism. This concludes part 1.

The period covering Dewey's later thought involves a fifth and then a final phase in the development of his philosophy of the religious dimension of experience. The beginning of the fifth stage (1894–1928) coincides with his break with the institutional church and with the emergence of his mature philosophical position involving a new naturalistic process philosophy and democratic humanism. For almost three and a half decades his efforts as a philosopher were concentrated largely on such issues as problems in logic, pedagogy, ethics, and social reconstruction. With the exception of only a few essays, religious issues tended to recede into the background in his published works and were given rather brief treatment. The careful reader familiar with the evolution of Dewey's religious thought at the University of Michigan will find in his writings from this period some thoughtful explorations of elements of a new religious humanism, including some moving expressions of natural piety. However, these writings do not contain a fully developed naturalistic theory of religious experience. This situation began to change with the writing of his Gifford Lectures, which were published in 1929 as *The Quest for Certainty,* and mark the beginning of the final phase (1929–1952) in the evolution of his religious outlook. By the late twenties Dewey was ready intellectually to complete his philosophical vision with a coherent new theory of the religious life consistent with his naturalism and democratic humanism. A deep concern to unify the moral faith of Americans and to focus their reform efforts in the face of the social crises of the times impelled him to undertake this task, which culminated in the writing of *A Common Faith* (1934).

In Dewey's mature religious thinking, as in his entire philosophy of humanistic naturalism, he endeavored to find a middle way between what James called a tough-minded and a tender-minded world view. He rejected supernaturalism, theism, absolutism, and metaphysical idealism, but he continued to affirm the importance of religious values and religious experience. In seeking a middle way in religious and moral matters, Dewey tried to find a means of getting beyond the old splits between the head and the heart, reason and faith, materialist and romanticist, naturalist and idealist, philosophy and theology, relativist and absolutist, that have left contemporary culture confused and divided. His way of addressing these problems is not easily comprehended, in part because it runs counter to traditional ways of thinking. However, when it is understood, it emerges as a convincing and profound expression of one of the major alternative ways of being religious open to modern men or women. In brief, Dewey's philosophy as a whole, as well as his religious life and thought, is an effort to clarify and realize the religious and moral values inherent in natural experience and democratic culture.

Chapters 5 through 12, which make up part 2, examine the Chicago and Columbia years (1894–1939) and Dewey's mature naturalistic philosophy of religion and the larger philosophic vision with which it is intimately related. Chapters 5 to 9 are concerned with the main outlines of Dewey's naturalism and humanism and with some important aspects of his religious thinking as it was expressed during the fifth phase in its evolution. The various aspects of Dewey's philosophy are developed in and through a complex process that extends over many decades, and no attempt is made to provide a detailed chronological account of these developments with the one important exception of his religious thought. In the case of those parts of his larger philosophy, such as his theory of education, epistemology, metaphysics, and ethics, which are of basic importance for an understanding of his religious outlook, the effort has been made to give a straightforward account that pulls together the main lines of his thinking at an appropriate place in our story. For example, at the University of Chicago, Dewey's social and intellectual interests came to a focus around the school and the theory of education, and, therefore, his philosophy of democracy and education and its relation to his religious thought will be discussed in chapter 5, which gives special attention to the Chicago period. In discussing education in this chapter, some of his later thinking on the subject will also be considered. The full development of Dewey's metaphysics did not occur until the 1920s and the refinements in his theory of valuation and ethics appeared quite late so extensive treatment of these subjects is reserved until the later chapters.

The First World War put Dewey's deepest values, moral philosophy, and social leadership to a severe test, and this (including his debates with the pacifists) is the subject of chapter 6. During the war years Dewey found himself dealing with a crisis in his own personal life, and he sought solace and renewal in the writing of poetry and letters, the study of painting, a new method of psychophysical therapy, and a short-lived love affair. These matters throw light on Dewey's psychological development and personal religious experience as well as on the evolution of his philosophy of religion. They are explored in chapter 7.

In chapter 8 the epistemology and metaphysics of Dewey's evolutionary naturalism are described. This aspect of his philosophy provides the intellectual framework for understanding the significance of his theory of morals and his views on the ideal, the real, and God. Dewey's philosophy of the religious life is closely connected with his moral philosophy, and chapter 9 is devoted to an account of his theory of the moral life including his pragmatist or instrumentalist theory of moral valuation. In this discussion of the moral life special attention is given to the way he used the concept of growth to tie together his psychology, educational theory, moral theory, and social theory. The chapter concludes with further clarification of Dewey's understanding of the great unifying moral ideals that inspire his philosophy and in which he puts a religious faith.

Chapters 10 and 11 give an account of the final phase of Dewey's development as a religious thinker and explore the emergence in his mature thought of a coherent naturalistic interpretation of the religious dimension of experience. Keeping in mind the close links between Dewey's social and religious thinking, special attention is given to his concepts of the religious quality of experience, faith, natural piety, mystical intuition, the idea of God, and the role of ultimate meaning. The debates in the 1930s between Dewey and religious thinkers such as Reinhold Niebuhr are discussed. The volume concludes with a final chapter that gives a brief account of Dewey's last years and some reflections on the meaning of his philosophy from the religious perspective.

The written record of Dewey's religious thought is far more extensive than is generally recognized, and his naturalistic philosophy of religion involves a coherent and well-developed position. However, with the exception of only one small book of three lectures delivered towards the end of his career, *A Common Faith* (1934), his reflections on this subject are found in sections of books, isolated essays, lectures, poems, and private letters. Furthermore, in no one book or essay does Dewey himself pull all the strands of his religious thinking together. This fact, coupled with the complex evolution of Dewey's philosophical thought and the vastness of the Dewey corpus, helps explain why earlier scholarship has not succeeded in giving a complete exposition of the nature and significance of his views on the religious dimension of experience. In what follows the objective is to apprehend the connections between the early and later Dewey and to present the various aspects of his religious thought as interrelated parts of a developing whole that is closely interconnected with his personal experience, social concerns, and larger philosophical vision.

In conclusion, it has been suggested that Dewey's fundamental concern as both a social reformer and thinker was unification of the ideal and the real, and this study of Dewey's life and thought from the perspective of its religious significance gives special attention to this theme. From early in his career he identified the religious life with a quest for the ideal, and his own philosophy of the religious life is controlled by his understanding of the relation between the ideal and the real. Toward the end of his career in his Gifford Lectures, which were published in *The Quest for Certainty* (1929), Dewey briefly summarizes what his own life experience and philosophical explorations had taught him about the ways in which a person may endeavor to unify the ideal and the real, or to idealize the world, as he often puts it.

> There are three ways of idealizing the world. There is idealization through purely intellectual and logical processes, in which reasoning alone attempts to prove that the world has characters that satisfy our highest aspirations. There are, again, moments of intense emotional appreciation when, through a happy conjunction of the state of the self and of the surrounding world, the beauty and harmony of existence is disclosed in experiences which are the immediate consummation of all for which we long. Then there is an idealization through actions that are directed by thought, such as are manifested in the works of fine art and in all human relations perfected by loving care. The first path has been taken by many philosophies. The second while it lasts is the most engaging. It sets the measure of our ideas of possibilities that are to be realized by intelligent endeavor. But its objects depend upon fortune and are insecure. The third method represents the way of deliberate quest for security of the values that are enjoyed by grace in our happy moments.[12]

The first way involves "the quest for certainty," which preoccupied Dewey at the very beginning of his career as a philosopher. However, while he was still a neo-Hegelian idealist he began losing interest in "the quest for certainty" and moving towards the third way. Nevertheless, philosophy as imaginative intellectual vision always retained a certain unifying religious power for Dewey. The second way exercised a profound influence on Dewey's vision of the ideal throughout his career. His quest for the ideal was inspired by "moments of intense emotional appreciation" that were generated by experiences with nature, art, and poetry and by mystical intuitions, romantic relationships, a compassionate openness to others, and shared social life. It is, however, the third way, which endeavors to integrate the emotional and the intellectual by connecting both with a life of practical action in devotion to the ideal, that became the central concern of his life's work. As a mature thinker he reconstructed the idea of the religious life so that it is identified with the deeper spiritual dynamics and meaning of this third way. The result is Dewey's vision of the continuity of the natural and the spiritual, which harmonizes religious faith and democratic humanism.

PART I

The Democratic Reconstruction of Christianity

A Quest for Unity

IN THE SPRING of 1882 at the age of twenty-three, John Dewey departed from the world of his boyhood in Vermont and journeyed to Johns Hopkins University to prepare himself for a career as a philosopher. As he set out on this adventure his thoughts were on the future and there was much in his Vermont experience that he wished to set behind him. However, his mind and heart were in the grip of certain strong emotions, convictions, and interests, which had been engendered by the experience of his first twenty-three years, and which would go far in determining the teachers and ideas that would attract his attention at Johns Hopkins and the way his religious and philosophical thought would develop throughout his career. For example, Dewey left Vermont with a strong, even if largely unexamined, belief in the soundness of the democratic way of life. This faith in the democratic ideal early gained important moral and religious significance in his thought. His Vermont experience also developed in him during adolescence an intense emotional craving for unification, that is, for integration of personality and for social adjustment. Furthermore, this craving had become fused with a religious and philosophical quest for God and for the unification of the actual with the ideal.

To understand and appreciate these and other matters fully, it is necessary to explore young Dewey's life in Vermont between 1859 and 1882, considering the way his own sense of self emerged in interaction with the democratic and Christian culture in which he was reared. In addition to the influences of home, town, church and school, our story must include the influence of such figures as Kant, Coleridge, and Wordsworth and the tradition of Vermont Transcendentalism.

Democracy and Christianity in Vermont

The town of Burlington where Dewey lived and learned during his early years is located on a hillside that overlooks a large bay on the eastern shore of Lake Champlain. Across this great lake to the west the skyline is dominated by the rugged peaks of the Adirondack Mountains and behind the town several miles to the east rise Mount Mansfield and the Green Mountains. The first settlers had arrived in Burlington in 1773, and by 1859 the town had grown to a population of almost 8,000. Their dwellings were scattered over an area which extended about a mile along the lake. Surrounding the town were many farms spread out across the broad expanse of the fertile Champlain valley. Economically the most important enterprise, however, was the lumber business, which relied heavily on both the lake and the railroad. Burlington was the connecting link between the Canadian lumber industry and the cities of New England. As an increasing number of fine homes testified, the town had its wealthy citizens. It also had its dilapidated tenements where poverty and the social ills of the larger cities were beginning to manifest themselves. However, for most of its citizens, Burlington was a place of modest prosperity and the opportunities it offered insured a growing population.[1]

On the crest of the hill overlooking the town stood the main building of the University of Vermont, a long brick edifice "surmounted by a blazing gilt dome, visible on a sunny day from White Hall to Montreal."[2] The university, which had a fine reputation and included a medical school and agricultural college, was the special pride of the town. The location of the university and the respect given to its president and faculty would not go unnoticed by a bright young boy. The only other large buildings whose architecture would catch the eye of a visitor were a few of the many churches in town. The Congregationalists were the largest single church denomination in Burlington as well as in the state of Vermont, and the University was closely allied with Congregational religious traditions. There was a large Roman Catholic church that supported a growing French Canadian and Irish immigrant population, and the Baptists, Episcopalians, and Unitarians each had a church.[3] Learning, religion, farming, lumber, and related small town businesses were the interests that occupied most Burlington citizens, who were generally a plain, hardworking, frugal, and devout people.

Democratic self-government was also a major concern of Vermonters, and towards the end of his career Dewey outlined the nature of the democratic political and social values his Vermont experience taught him to respect.

> I shall never cease to be grateful that I was born at a time and a place where the earlier ideal of liberty and the self-governing community of citizens still sufficiently prevailed, so that I unconsciously imbibed a sense of its meaning. In Vermont, perhaps even more than elsewhere, there was embodied in the spirit of the people the conviction that governments were like the houses we live in, made to contribute to human welfare, and that those who lived in them were as free to change and extend the one as they were the other, when developing needs of the human family called for such alterations and modifications.

This idea of a "community of free self-governing individuals" was the "original American ideal," argues Dewey. It involved neither an antisocial individualism nor a view of the state as having value and sanctity in and of itself. "Its working ideal was neighborliness and mutual service. It did not deny the claims of government and law, but it held them in subordination to the needs of a changing and developing society of individuals." Throughout his life Dewey was guided by faith in this American democratic ideal of a community of free self-governing individuals, and his own social philosophy became an endeavor to understand anew the meaning of this ideal for modern industrial society.[4]

The democratic ideal meant more to Dewey than just a theory of government in the strictly political sense. Early in his career as a philosopher, he came to regard the idea of democracy as a great liberating ethical ideal with deep religious as well as social and psychological meaning. It involved for him attitudes toward the individual and the community that should govern all human relations and all institutions—the family, school, and factory as well as the town meeting and governor's office. The origins of this appreciation of democracy as a way of life lie in the traditions of Dewey's family and in his social experience and religious training in Vermont. Dewey's family had deep roots in New England and in its democratic traditions. Ever since the seventeenth century, his ancestors had been farmers, wheelwrights, and blacksmiths in Connecticut, Massachusetts, and Vermont. His mother's grandfather had been a congressman from Vermont and her father was a Vermont assemblyman and lay judge.[5]

Burlington made possible an unusually broad social experience for a Vermont town and in the midst of considerable cultural diversity life remained markedly democratic. The population could be roughly divided into two groups. There were the descendants of the original settlers in the Burlington area and other old New England families such as the Deweys. The members of these old American families largely controlled Burlington's economic, political, and cultural life. In addition, there was a large Irish and French Canadian immigrant group that by 1870 made up almost half of Burlington's population, which by then had grown to over 14,000.[6] Almost all children, regardless of the social status of their family, attended the public schools. About the quality of life in Burlington, Dewey's daughter writes: "In spite of the especial prestige of the few first families, life was democratic—not consciously, but in that deeper sense in which equality and absence of class distinctions are taken for granted."[7]

This statement by Jane Dewey may exaggerate the absence of class distinctions in Burlington, but life in this community did teach Dewey a profound respect for the principles of equality and freedom of opportunity. He had firsthand experience with the different facets of life in Burlington and the surrounding area. He lived in an "old American" residential community, joined the Congregational Church, went to the public school, learned French from the immigrant children, worked in the lumber yards, delivered an afternoon daily newspaper, had frequent contact with Burlington's intellectual elite, spent many summer months on his grandfather's farm, and eventually attended the University of Vermont.[8] The attitudes and values that Dewey absorbed from his social environment are summarized by Sidney Hook when he writes that the Vermont of Dewey's boyhood lived on in him in the form of "habits, deep preferences, and an ingrained democratic bias" evident "in his simplicity of manner, his basic courtesy, freedom from every variety of snobbishness, and matter-of-fact respect for the rights of everyone in America as a human being and a citizen."[9]

It is noteworthy that the Congregational Church, which young Dewey regularly attended, proclaimed social ideals that could only have deepened an earnest young boy's sense of the ethical and religious import of the democratic way of life. In church Dewey heard a preacher who taught that "no man finds completeness in himself. We come to the perfect man, to the perfect stature in Christ, only in our associate life. Men must be won to a common life and built up together in it."[10] It became a basic principle of Dewey's philosophy that fulfillment for the individual is found in and through wholehearted participation in those relationships that make up the life of the community. President Matthew Buckham, who taught Dewey political theory at the University of Vermont, also forcefully urged upon his students Christian values with democratic social implications. At his graduation Dewey heard Buckham state that "the great Christian doctrines of individual responsibility and personal worth, culminating in the sublime truth of the equality and brotherhood of man, have ennobled men in their own eyes, have given them courage to know and maintain their rights, have pulled down the mighty from their seats and exalted them of low degree, so that we may boldly say that simply and only in consequence of what Christ has taught and done, Christian political institutions . . . are rapidly spreading over the globe."[11] For Buckham democratic social institutions governed by the principles of equality and freedom are a product of

Christianity, and he looked to church-led social reforms rather than violent revolution for the improvement of American society. He also taught that "thinking men are not now looking in the direction of a further developed individualism for the bettering of man's estate, but in the direction of solidarity of interests, mutuality of service, union of hearts leading to a co-operation of hands."[12] Such Christian social idealism had a lasting influence on Dewey's outlook.

Shortly after Dewey's birth the peacefulness of daily life in Burlington was disturbed by the outbreak of the Civil War and President Lincoln's call for Union Army volunteers. A heavy majority in the town strongly backed Lincoln's policies, and Dewey's father, Archibald Sprague Dewey, who was then fifty, promptly sold his grocery business and joined the army as quartermaster for the First Vermont Cavalry.[13] It was almost six years before Archibald was settled again with his wife and three sons in Burlington. During that time young John and his older brother Davis and younger brother Charles seldom saw their father except for one winter which they spent at an army headquarters in a devastated district of northern Virginia.[14]

The man Dewey gradually came to know as his father was a handsome, easygoing, friendly older man. Born in the early decades of the new republic, he enjoyed telling the boys stories about his youth, the War of 1812, and the Civil War. "He read Shakespeare and Milton, not for culture, but because of his enjoyment of their words and turns of speech. He often quoted Milton while he worked, rolling with delight the unusual and euphonious phrases. Through an associate he learned the Scottish dialect and he took delight in reciting long passages from Burns to his children, finding satisfaction in Burns' type of humor."[15] People in town enjoyed the clever, amusing rhymes that Archibald invented for advertising his store goods. However, he was not particularly ambitious for himself or his sons, and "he was said to sell more goods and collect fewer bills than any merchant in town."[16] His views on politics and religion were rather conventional and conservative.

Even though Dewey became a person very different from his father, his personality shows certain similar traits. He retained his father's delight in poetry, which became for him a source of spiritual insight, and he himself later in his life tried his hand at writing poetry. Also, like the father who found it difficult to collect his bills, Dewey "was always fearful of hurting others" and often created the impression of being ill-at-ease in situations involving direct personal encounters.[17] On the whole Dewey's relations with his father seem to have been quite pleasant, but the long absence of his father during the war must have left him with some painful feelings of abandonment. Sidney Hook tells a story that reveals the depth of his attachment to his father, and it underscores the difficulty he would have as a young man in freeing himself from his Vermont background. Dewey "once told me," explains Hook, "that next to the religious issues he went through in relation to his mother, the most lacerating emotional crisis was a political one with his father—a veteran of the Army of the Potomac—when he and his brother announced they were voting for Grover Cleveland, a Democrat, the first Democrat to be elected to the Presidency after the Civil War. To John Dewey's father, this was tantamount to betrayal of the great cause for which he had fought."[18]

As a result of Archibald's military commitment Dewey was brought up during the first eight years of his life largely by his mother, Lucina Artemisia Rich Dewey, and it was Lucina who remained the dominant authority figure throughout John's childhood. Lucina was twenty years younger than Archibald. She was also a far more intense person and had higher aspirations for her children than her husband. Under Lucina's care the life of John and his brothers was "simple and healthful," and the early interest that John and his older brother, Davis, showed in books was strongly encouraged. Lucina's brothers had attended college, unlike Archibald, and "it was largely due to her influence that the boys ... obtained a college education."[19] Her greatest interest was religion. She had been raised a Universalist, but as a young woman she was converted in a revival meeting to the kind of evangelical pietism that was widespread in many parts of the country in the mid-nineteenth century. As a result she abandoned the central Universalist belief that God will eventually save all from sin and damnation, and she joined the Congregational Church.[20] Thereafter her personal faith centered around belief in the holiness and goodness of God, the problem of sin, and the doctrine that only those who experience a supernatural regeneration in and through God's grace as revealed in Jesus Christ will be redeemed. The emphasis fell on salvation of the individual soul and the cultivation of holy affections that purge the heart of base desires and demonstrate the workings of grace.

In Burlington at the First Congregational Church Lucina became known for her devoutness and missionary zeal. She taught in the Sunday school and became President of the Women's Home Mission Society.[21] Her piety also included an element of social activism. She worked in the Adam's Mission House, which was a church-supported settlement house in Burlington. One fellow church member writes of Lucina: "She gave her last thought to the problems which are still pressing on our philanthropists. 'How can we make Burlington a temperate and moral city, a safe, clean place for young men, a city of virtuous and happy homes?' Especially solicitous was she for the protection of the homes of the poor and unfortunate."[22] Sarah P. Torrey, the wife of Dewey's college philosophy professor, describes Lucina as "the idealist." "Her thought was always reaching to something beyond, something which might be done for those who needed help in body or soul." Sarah Torrey adds that Lucina "was always looking forward from things as they are, to what they ought to be, and might be."[23]

In caring for her children Lucina was constantly concerned about keeping them out of sin and intent upon instilling in them a pious devotion to God and Jesus Christ. Jane Dewey, in her biographical sketch of her father, concedes that Lucina exerted entirely too much "moralistic emotional pressure on the boys."[24] In the case of John especially this caused some trying emotional problems. Lucina's extremes in this matter may in part be explained by the shadow of war and death that lay over the Dewey household. In 1858 the Deweys' first son died a cruel death at the age of two-and-a-half in an accident at home caused largely by Lucina's negligence. John was born just ten months after the accident and given the same first name as his ill-fated older brother. Then came the war and Lucina was left alone to care for three boys. During the war years her sister died, and she took on the added responsibility of helping to care for her sister's son, John Rich. It is probable that guilt over her first son's death, a desire to atone, and the strain of having to raise four boys with little assistance all contributed to Lucina's excesses in the religious training of her children.[25]

When they were small, Lucina taught the boys to pray, read them the Bible, regularly took them to church, and eventually sent them to Sunday school where they were required to memorize the Ten Commandments, the Lord's Prayer, and the Apostles' Creed.[26] When John was eleven, she persuaded him to join the church and wrote the following statement for him to take to church requesting membership.

> I think I love Christ and want to obey Him. I have thought for some time I should like to unite with the Church. Now, I want to more, for it seems one way to confess Him, and I should like to remember Him at communion.[27]

Dewey recalls that the religion of his childhood "centered about sin and being good" and on the love of Jesus Christ "as savior from sin." There was little emphasis on articles of belief or theological doctrine; "belief was largely an emotional matter."[28] The image of God at work in Dewey's childhood was that of a rather remote supernatural monarchical figure who served as the Creator and the all-powerful authority behind the moral law.[29]

As the boys grew older, Lucina made a ceaseless effort to insure that they were not going astray and were properly fulfilling their moral and spiritual obligations. Frequently, she would anxiously ask, "Are you right with Jesus? Have you prayed to God for forgiveness?" and examine them about their activities, sometimes in front of other people.[30] Among the forbidden activities were dancing, cards, pool, billiards, drinking, gambling, and playing ball or marbles on Sunday, against which there was also a town ordinance.[31] The kind of over-scrupulous approach employed by his mother is indicated in the following comments that Dewey made in 1886 about religious emotion:

> Religious feeling is unhealthy when it is watched and analyzed to see if it exists, if it is right, if it is growing. It is fatal to be forever observing our own religious moods and experiences, as it is to pull up a seed from the ground to see if it is growing.[32]

Late in his life Dewey could still recall that his mother's habit of examining his conscience and that of his brothers "tended to induce in us a sense of guilt and at the same time irritation because of the triviality of the occasions on which she questioned us."[33]

Probably with the memory of his own childhood experience in mind, Dewey in 1903 vigorously attacked the idea "that the spiritual and emotional experiences of the adult are the proper measures of all religious life; so that, if the child is to have any religious life at all, he must have it in terms of the same consciousness of sin, repentance, redemption, etc., which are familiar to the adult."[34] Such an approach fails to appreciate and respect the nature of the religious experience that is natural to children and does violence to the natural process of growth, argues Dewey. Due to his mother's oppressive approach to his moral and religious upbringing, which was the source of painful emotional difficulties during his adolescence, his relation with her was never a particularly happy one. His strong reaction against the intense evangelical pietism that she represented may be viewed as one source of Dewey's lifelong hostility to dogmatism and his aversion to moral thinking that is preoccupied with introspection, feelings, and inner purity. However, there is in Dewey's philosophy a certain visionary moral idealism that reflects the influence of his mother's example as well as that of others in the Burlington church community.[35]

As far as most outward appearances were concerned, Lucina did succeed in making John conform to her ideal. He seemed to enjoy his play, but he was generally quiet and reserved. In school he was polite and friendly toward the teachers and worked hard even though he was often bored.[36] He also participated regularly in the life of the church. Having "nominally accepted the religious teachings in which he was brought up" and making a great effort to be sincere in his religious beliefs, he participated regularly in the life of the Congregational church.[37] During his sophomore year in college at the age of sixteen he underwent confirmation and formally joined the church as a young adult "with sincere religious feeling, but with no profound experience of conversion."[38] Thereafter he taught Sunday school and in 1881 became president of the young people's group called the Christian Endeavor.[39]

To a certain degree the First Congregational Church, which was located after 1842 in an impressive building of classic Georgian architecture, reinforced Lucina's discipline and teachings, but in the church community Dewey was free of her extremes. The Reverend Lewis O. Brastow, who served as minister of the First Church from 1873 to 1884 and eventually became Professor of Homiletics at Yale, was a man who preached a liberal evangelism that did not insist on a literal interpretation of the Bible. However, Brastow also believed that a preacher should "bear himself as one who means to have a hearing" and that he should be one who "does not patter with uncertainties."[40] In the words of Archibald Dewey, his sermons were "calculated to inspire deep and earnest self-examination,"[41] and they did contain some hard doctrines for the ears of an earnest young boy. Brastow taught that "men need to be delivered from the dominating lower life of the flesh, to be rescued to the higher life of the spirit, and to be shaped into a spiritual manhood."[42] The ideal according to which the church should reconstruct humanity, he summarized as follows:

> For the individual man this ideal, this pattern, this standard is the perfection of Christ ... for the community of individuals, for the church, for humanity collectively, the ideal is the Kingdom of God. The final purpose of the church is the realization of the ideal of a divine society; i.e., the building together of humanity into a social organism, after the pattern of a heavenly society.[43]

Young Dewey took the dualism of flesh and spirit and the ideal of Christ's perfection to heart, and together with Lucina's teachings, it eventually caused him to experience some trying difficulties in his social relations. Partly in an effort to work through some of these problems, Dewey during the first decade of his philosophical career spent considerable time trying to reconstruct and to rationalize the Christian ideals of the perfection of Christ and the kingdom of God.

In 1875, at the age of fifteen, Dewey entered the University of Vermont in Burlington. There were twenty-five students in his freshman class. Most of them came from Vermont, but several were from New York and one came from Illinois. In the previous year, the university became the first New England institution to award a bachelor's degree to a woman, and there was one woman among the eighteen students who graduated in Dewey's class in 1879.[44] The faculty of arts consisted of eight men, among whom Dewey found some excellent teachers—especially Matthew Buckham, the President and Professor of Political and Social Philosophy, and Henry A.P. Torrey, the Professor of Philosophy. During his years at the University he did discover some liberating philosophical and religious thinking, especially in the writings of Kant, Coleridge, and James Marsh, which will be considered shortly. However, the moral and religious values of the University were in most respects consistent with those of the First Congregational Church.[45]

At least three members of the faculty, John Goodrich, Henry Torrey, and President Buckham, were ordained ministers and active members of the First Church as well as old friends of Dewey's parents. One student from this period recalls that these three men "formed an educational triumvirate that dominated the polity of the University."[46] Goodrich, who had been the chaplain of Archibald Dewey's regiment during the Civil War and superintendent of the First Church Sunday school during Dewey's childhood, served as university librarian as well as professor of Latin and Greek. According to Davis Dewey, Goodrich felt obligated to oversee and censor the Dewey boys' choice of reading material.[47] Torrey, who had known Dewey as a boy and introduced him to philosophy, was a devout Congregationalist with a Puritan moral character. Buckham comments that while Torrey was usually a "gentle and placid" man he "had inherited from a long line of Puritan ancestors" a "power of severe and overwhelming rebuke," "the spirit of resentment against wrong, an aggressive and militant attitude toward what is evil and unworthy."[48]

Buckham gave freshmen private moral instruction, and some of the things which he and Torrey regarded as deserving of severe rebuke in students are mentioned in Buckham's 1878 baccalaureate sermon: "profanity," "untruthfulness," "the love of low company," and "the absence of all worthy ambition."[49] And even though Buckham encouraged students to think for themselves he found religious skepticism among young men "deplorable." He taught that "Man needs God. His nature has a divine element in it. The man who lives as though God were not, or as though God's being were no concern of his, not only forfeits part of his manhood, and the noblest part, but is engaged in a perpetual endeavor to thwart and subvert his own nature."[50] It was also Buckham's belief that "religion alone can furnish the sufficient motive to a high order of morality."[51] "Practical religion is morality," he explained, "not cold and abstract as it is in itself, but touched, warmed with an emotion which has its spring and its object in God."[52] At their graduation Dewey and his classmates rose from their seats to hear Buckham, who had just explained that Jesus is a "Savior" and not just a prophet, say the following in his final words to them as a class: "Young friends, the sum of our desires for you is that Christ shall draw you unto Himself. . . . Unless your lives are thus centered on Jesus Christ, they will be feeble, at worst wrecks. . . . You cannot be your best, or do your best without Christian faith and a Christian purpose."[53]

From childhood through college, then, Dewey was consistently under a strong moral and religious influence that ranged from a sentimental evangelical pietism to a more liberal brand of New England Calvinism. During his adolescence he inwardly rebelled against the attitude and behavior of his mother. In the course of his college career, he began to question privately whatever seemed arbitrary in the moral laws imposed on him, and doubts about Calvinist Christian teachings were growing. However, the place of authority accorded the Christian faith and the church by all those whom he loved and respected during his youth made such a deep impression on him that he could not at this point in his life seriously entertain breaking with New England religious traditions. Furthermore, during his college years the larger religious community in which he lived and studied offered him a more satisfactory approach to the Christian religious life than he had encountered at home, and this made it easier to be an exemplary young church member. He was generally well-behaved at college and rarely risked provoking the rebuke of men like Buckham and Torrey. The minutes of faculty meetings show that Dewey received demerits for helping to lock an instructor in a classroom and for being consistently absent from the required weekly military drill, which probably reveals some rebellious attitudes toward his father.[54] However, in 1883 Torrey could write that

"Mr. Dewey has always sustained an irreproachable moral character. . . . Sincerity and depth of conviction rather than emotion have characterized his religious life—He is thoroughly trustworthy in these respects."[55] Buckham agreed with Torrey's evaluation and writes at this time that Dewey "is sound and sweet all through—is true and loyal in matters of religion, and without any crotchets or drawbacks of any kind, so far as I know."[56]

A Craving for Unification

Neither Torrey nor Buckham perceived the spiritual turmoil that young Dewey was actually going through. In his autobiographical essay, "From Absolutism to Experimentalism" (1930), Dewey briefly describes the emotional crisis with which he struggled during his adolescence. He recounts that under the impact of Vermont culture he experienced painful feelings of being isolated and inwardly divided and that as a result he was possessed by an intense emotional craving for unification. He also points out that this passion for unity became intimately connected with his interest in philosophy and led him eventually to Hegel, whose inclusive philosophical vision he discovered in graduate school.

> There were, however, also "subjective" reasons for the appeal that Hegel's thought made to me; it supplied a demand for unification that was doubtless an intense emotional craving and yet was a hunger that only an intellectualized subject matter could satisfy. It is more than difficult, it is impossible, to recover that early mood. But the sense of divisions and separations that were, I suppose, borne in upon me as a consequence of a heritage of New England culture, divisions by way of isolation of self from the world, of soul from body, of nature from God, brought a painful oppression—or, rather, they were an inward laceration.[57]

Dewey explains that the dualisms to which he refers in this statement "were not so much intellectually formulated as they were emotionally felt . . . they were an emotional sense of restrictions and barriers."[58] The emotional craving for unification that resulted supplied the passion behind Dewey's philosophical and religious quest and profoundly influenced the direction it took. It is, therefore, important to understand further what Dewey means by the "isolation of self from the world, of soul from body, of nature from God."

When Dewey refers to New England cultural traditions as the source of his own inner conflicts and alienation as a young man, he is referring primarily to the sentimental pietism and Puritanism in his background. The chief source of the problem is his mother's excessive zeal in trying to control his religious feelings, beliefs and behavior. Even though the Congregational Church offered young Dewey a freer environment in which to grow, to some degree it had the effect of reinforcing the repressive and divisive factors at work in Lucina's approach. It is very likely also the case that the war and the long separation from his father contributed to Dewey's "sense of divisions and separations." His father's absence may have left him angry, even if unconscious of the fact, and also unsure of his father's love. Both of these factors may have intensified his efforts as a boy to be very good and to repress contrary impulses. Be that as it may, as a result of his early religious training, Dewey did become excessively self-conscious as a boy and was burdened with a relentless overdeveloped conscience, which he seems to have closely linked in his imagination with God. This oppressive conscience was so deeply ingrained in his personality that he would still be struggling to free himself from it as a man in his fifties.[59] The inner conflict, repression, and guilt generated by this conscience appear to be at the core of the "inward laceration" with which young Dewey struggled.

Sexual repression became a big part of the problem. As an adolescent he took to heart the church's notion of "the higher life of the spirit" exemplified perfectly by Christ and set in opposition to "the lower life of the flesh." As a boy, Dewey formed a warm and lasting friendship with his brother Davis and seems to have gotten on well with several other boys including James and John Buckham, whose father was president of the university. However, in his social life, Dewey from an early age evidenced bashfulness with girls; and even though he led a healthy outdoor life often involving fishing and camping trips, he began during adolescence to retreat more and more into the world of books.[60] He early gained the reputation of being a bookworm, and President Gilman saw fit to warn him at Johns

Hopkins about his "seclusive and bookish habits."[61] The evidence further indicates that he never developed a close personal relationship with a girl until he had reached his mid-twenties and had finished his graduate studies. Shortly thereafter, he met and married one of his early students, Alice Chipman. Dewey is reported by Max Eastman to have commented: "I tried to work up a little affair with my cousin when I was nineteen. I thought something ought to be done. But I couldn't do it. I was too bashful. I was abnormally bashful."[62] In summary, throughout his youth and into the early years of his teaching career, Dewey submitted to the demands of a stern moral code that caused him outwardly to become reserved and shy and inwardly to suffer the guilt and loneliness of those who deny themselves.

He repressed not only sexual desire, but also the early stirrings of autonomous reason. In this regard Dewey writes: "the conflict of traditional religious beliefs with opinions that I could myself honestly entertain was the source of a trying personal crisis."[63] Motivated by a "desire to be in harmony with his mother's wishes and the worthy recipient of her love," he had unconsciously made a great effort as a boy to overcome his lack of ardent feeling in religious matters.[64] Then gradually he woke up to the fact that he had been "passively accepting and reproducing ideas and feelings" which were not a vital part of his own being.[65] As his strong intellect and an equally strong impulse toward autonomy began to emerge, he found himself torn between two conflicting wishes. On the one hand, he was still attached to and dependent upon his mother and various church authorities, and he wanted very much to please them by conforming his behavior to their ideals. On the other hand, he experienced a growing desire to respect his own sincere feelings and began inwardly to resist what seemed oppressive, externally imposed, and arbitrary. This inner conflict probably intensified his feelings of guilt and alienation. Dewey's younger brother Charles acted out his rebellion so openly that he was suspended from college for a year.[66] However, being an especially earnest young man Dewey bottled up the problem inside of himself and suffered with it alone.

Struggling with these various inner conflicts Dewey's conscience told him that he was responsible for having failed humbly to surrender his will to "that perfect and living will of God as made known to us in Christ."[67] In his first book, which not surprisingly was a *Psychology* (1887), he calls this burden-some feeling of moral failure remorse: "Remorse is the feeling of the chasm existing between this ideal and our own actual state through some act of our own. We feel that we ought to have realized our own being, and that we could have done so, but that we have not. The feeling of this split, this dualism, in our nature constitutes remorse."[68] Living in this experience of sin and guilt Dewey found himself estranged from both the ideal self and his world, and he yearned for liberation from estrangement, for a harmony between the actual and the ideal self that would bring inner peace and a more satisfying social adjustment.

In describing the dualisms that oppressed him, Dewey also mentions the separation of God and the world. The idea of a great gulf separating God and humanity, the realms of nature and grace, was a major theme in New England Congregational theology. It involved the idea of God as a transcendent supernatural ideal being standing in judgment of a fallen, sinful world utterly dependent on his mercy and grace for salvation. For young Dewey this dualism of God and the world became a major symbol of the dualism of the spiritual and the natural, the ideal and the actual, with which he struggled in himself and in his relations with others. It intensified those feelings of guilt and isolation that afflicted his young heart and filled him with a craving for unity. In other words, the religious supernaturalism that located God outside the everyday world of nature and human relations gave symbolic expression to what disturbed Dewey most about himself and his world: the absence of the divine, that is, of harmony, self-acceptance, intimacy, and real community.

In the light of the factors considered, it is clear that young Dewey's craving for unification was a quest for what he later came to describe as a deep enduring adjustment of self and world involving integration of personality, a satisfying social adjustment, and a sense of belonging to the larger whole. In the language of his later philosophy the heart of the problem concerned unifying the ideal and the actual. This meant first of all finding for himself a liberating concept of the ideal. This ideal would have to be an ethical ideal that would lead him into authentic relationships with other persons and society. However, most importantly, it would have to be an ideal that as an autonomous person he could wholeheartedly choose as a guide to self-realization, for only in and through such an act of self-determination would he realize the personal sense of identity and unification of self that he craved. As a young man Dewey did not question the identification of the ideal with God, and for this reason his quest for unification was initially an explicitly religious quest pursued within a Christian intellectual framework. In the course of his college years, this quest also became a philosophical quest. As this study has suggested, dualism was the dominant note in Dewey's Vermont experience, but it must be added that he found in certain Vermont intellectual traditions some glimmers of light that gave him hope and direction intensifying his search for the promised land. This involves the story of the awakening of Dewey's intellectual powers and his encounter with the thought of Thomas Huxley, Kant, Coleridge, James Marsh, and Wordsworth.

The Awakening of the Philosophic Spirit

During his high school and college years, Dewey retreated more and more into the realm of ideas that he discovered in books. His philosophy teacher, H.A.P. Torrey, made this observation about him: "From early youth he manifested a deeply reflective turn of mind, accompanied by the reticence which often attends it."[69] It is probable that the deeper significance of Dewey's withdrawal into the world of books and thought is that it was the primary tactic which he instinctively used in order to escape from a frustrating environment and to protect the integrity of his emerging individuality until he could decide for himself who he was and what he honestly felt and thought. It appears that he was drawn to intellectual activity as one whose being senses without any clear understanding that by reading and learning to think for himself he might find his freedom and identity.

In 1887, in his *Psychology*, Dewey makes the following observation about the feeling associated with the possession of knowledge.

> Normally, it is a feeling that we *possess ourselves;* that we have become masters of ourselves instead of being controlled by external impres-

sions. It is a feeling of having come into possession of our own
birthright. It has been said that the great advantage of education is the
sense which it gives us of not being dupes. This is another way of
stating the truth that the emotion which arises from the organization
of knowledge into self is one of self ownership, of freedom.[70]

Dewey also writes in the *Psychology* that "the mainspring of our
cognitive experiences is the more or less conscious feeling that things
have meaning." In other words, the human endeavor to know is
founded upon a feeling of confidence that the world is intelligible.
"The very tendency towards knowledge," explains Dewey, "presupposes that there is no such thing as an isolated fact in the universe,
but that all are connected with each other as members of a common
whole."[71] Such an assumption seems to have been at work in Dewey's
early intellectual experience. Further, if the world has a coherent
rational structure and thus is thoroughly understandable, then,
knowledge can provide the self with control and freedom.

It seems, then, that from an early age Dewey was possessed by an
instinctive faith in reason or intelligence, that is, an intuition that the
world and human existence are intelligible and that by reflecting on
his own experience and by freeing his mind to think clearly, he could
understand himself and his world and thereby realize his own autonomy and individuality. There was, in other words, a strong element
of Emersonian self-reliance in Dewey that in his case involved a
confidence in reason and experience as the best method for understanding his world and for clarifying the nature of the unity of the
ideal and the actual.

In his *Psychology,* Dewey makes a distinction between the scientific
and the artistic temperament, and this distinction is useful in further
appreciating the nature of his own young mind. Persons of artistic
temperaments, he explains, "proceed by analogy, the striking simile,
and the quick metaphor. They express in a single sentence what years
of reflective study may not exhaust, the subtle and hidden connections, the points of identity with the whole framework of truth are so
many and so deep." Persons "of scientific turn of mind, of a reflective
and deliberative power" are concerned to know and to formulate
these connections and points of identity.[72] Using these meanings, the

dominant tendency of Dewey's mind was the scientific as distinct from the artistic. He was first and foremost a knower.

However, Dewey never had any intention of devoting himself to one particular science. Like many persons of scientific temperament before him, there was something of the poet in him in the sense that he had a profound yearning for unifying experience. It was the combination of his intellectual proclivities and this craving for unity that led him into philosophy. His craving for unity became "a hunger only an intellectualized subject matter could satisfy."[73] He could not rest content with poetic images and intuitions of unity; he wanted an intellectual vision of it. He found himself intellectually fascinated with the "schematic and formally logical,"[74] and he aspired to grasp the principles of order and interconnection governing all things. As a young man Dewey believed that this was the task of philosophy. In 1887 he defines "the distinctively philosophical instinct" as the desire "to see the universe and all phases of life as a whole."[75] "Science is the attempt to reduce the world to a unity, by seeing all the factors of the world as members of one common system," writes young Dewey, and "philosophy, as complete science, aims to do this fully."[76]

During his late adolescence Dewey's aspiration for a comprehensive philosophical understanding became the primary way in which he set out to achieve unification of the ideal and the actual. In other words, his religious quest for God was to a large extent channeled into a philosophic quest. The significance of philosophy for Dewey in this regard can be further explained by considering his own account of his first awakening to what he calls "a distinctive philosophic interest" under the influence of the idea of organic unity.[77]

What first brought Dewey's philosophic interest to life was his readings in Thomas Henry Huxley's *Lessons in Elementary Physiology*, which he was assigned in a college course during his junior year. Huxley was one of the most gifted and influential scientist-philosophers of the age and a champion of Darwinian theory and agnosticism, but what especially impressed young Dewey was Huxley's description of the human organism. From it he gained "a sense of interdependence and interrelated unity that gave form to intellectual stirrings that had been previously inchoate, and created a kind of type or model of a view of things to which material in any field ought to conform." Dewey had no interest in pursuing the study of physiology further, but from that time on, the idea of an organism or organic unity became for him a metaphor and a symbol for all that his divided soul craved. He recalls that: "Subconsciously, at least, I was led to desire a world and a life that would have the same properties as had the human organism in the picture of it derived from study of Huxley's treatment."[78]

The idea of organic unity had fascinated romantic poets and idealist philosophers for over a hundred years, and it eventually would lead Dewey to discover these traditions. No idea had a greater hold on his imagination as a young man. In Huxley's physiological concept he found the germ of the notion that the intelligible structure of reality is identical with an organic unity. It would take another four or five years of intellectual exploration and the study of Hegel at Johns Hopkins University before Dewey would be able to begin clearly articulating the significance that this notion contained for him. However, when he reached this point his psychology, epistemology, political theory, and metaphysics would all become a concentrated effort to spell out the meaning of the idea of organic unity conceived as the basic metaphor for the nature of the self, society, and the universe. The idea of organic unity symbolized the integrated self and the harmonious community for which he longed. More than that, Huxley's writings aroused in Dewey intellectual aspirations, which could only be satisfied by a vision of the entire universe as one great interrelated whole in which each person and all things are bound together by one common purpose and in which each person and thing has its special place and unique function.

In summary, under the influence of the symbolic power of the idea of organic unity, Dewey's emotional craving for unification fused with an instinctive feeling of confidence in his mind and the scientific bent of his gifted intellect. From that time onward he was possessed by "the philosophic spirit, the instinct for unity and generality," "the hunger for a harmonious and unified mental world."[79] For Dewey the idea of organic unity had all the attractive power of a great and beautiful sacred symbol. It awakened in his young mind and heart the passion of Plato's *eros* and led him into his own "quest for certainty."

It is significant that Dewey's early encounter with science led him to fasten onto the biological idea of organic unity rather than the notion of mechanistic materialism. During his junior year he took courses in geology, physics, and zoology as well as physiology, and he received a sympathetic introduction to Darwinian evolutionary theory. The university library subscribed to several English periodicals which Dewey read with considerable interest, and there he found essays that championed the scientific method, defended natural evolution, and promoted scientific materialism.[80] He was also led to read Harriet Martineau's book on Comte, and Dewey recalls that Comte's "idea of the disorganized character of Western modern culture, due to a disintegrative 'individualism' and his idea of a synthesis of science that should be a regulative method of an organized social life, impressed me deeply."[81] The explorations of scientific thinking encouraged in Dewey his own faith in intelligence, but it did not lead him to embrace a philosophy of mechanistic materialism or seriously tempt him to adopt an attitude of skepticism and despair. Throughout his career, Dewey's writings evidence an optimistic attitude which is grounded in what he termed in 1889 "belief in the meaning and worthiness of experience."[82] His early faith in intelligence and fascination with the idea of organic unity are indications of this deeply ingrained optimism involving a trust in the meaning and value of life.

Dewey, of course, was raised in a Christian culture and taught from very early that life has a moral purpose and enduring meaning. The idea of God was a potent symbol of the supreme reality of the ideal and of the ultimate meaning of existence. The evidence indicates that during the Vermont years Dewey did not seriously consider abandoning his faith in God and moral idealism even though he did ponder alternative ways of thinking about the nature of God and of God's relationship to the world. This is not to deny that in the late 1870s and early 1880s Dewey went through times when confusion and doubt shook his faith and hope. He may have had his own situation in mind when in a lecture on the psychology of religious education in 1903 he made the following observation:

> It is a serious moment when an earnest soul wakes up to the fact that it has been passively accepting and reproducing ideas and feelings which it now recognizes are not a vital part of its own being. Losing

its hold on the form in which the spiritual truths have been embodied, their very substance seems also to be slipping away. The person is plunged into doubt and bitterness regarding the reality of all things which lie beyond his senses, or regarding the very worth of life itself.[83]

What helped Dewey himself get through the "shock and upheaval" involved in an experience such as he describes was his faith in intelligence, intimation of the organic unity of the world, and the philosophic spirit. A faith in intelligence such as possessed young Dewey involves the notion of a rational world, and, as Socrates originally made clear in Plato's *Phaedo,* the first principle of intelligibility in a universe that is rational and makes sense from a human point of view is the idea of the good. It is the idea of a supreme ideal or good purpose for which the world exists and toward which it strives that gives to life intelligibility, meaning, and value in the final analysis. Dewey's early trust in intelligence and hope in the organic unity of the world implies just such a notion. This trust and hope were strong enough in him so that he was not overwhelmed by the forces of doubt and disbelief with which he had at times to wrestle.

In the long term Dewey's faith in intelligence would prove to be a dangerous rival to his faith in the Christ of Congregational theology. However, as a young man he tried to reconcile religious faith and reason, Christian theology and philosophy, and he remained a churchmember as long as he believed that this is possible. His philosophy studies at the University of Vermont helped him to pursue this objective.

Kant, Coleridge, and Marsh on Practical Reason

In the year 1881 the philosophy of Immanuel Kant was the center of much attention in philosophical circles in America. It was the centennial of the publication of his *Critique of Pure Reason.* Special lectures were delivered, books and essays were written, and at Saratoga and Concord scholars and students gathered to honor the Koenigsburg thinker. At the University of Vermont Henry A.P. Torrey, who taught Dewey philosophy in college and tutored him privately several years later in philosophy and philosophical German, enthusiastically endorsed the idea of the centennial, commenting: "I am the more interested because the philosophy which has been taught at

Burlington since the days of President James Marsh has been so largely derived from the metaphysical writings of German philosophers, particularly from Kant."[84] At the University of Vermont, then, as well as elsewhere in America, Kant was very much in the forefront of philosophical discussion when Dewey began to study philosophy.

Toward the end of his career Dewey recalled that Torrey's teaching was heavily influenced by the Scottish school of commonsense realism,[85] but in a letter he wrote to Torrey in 1883 he clearly indicates that Torrey's teaching remained a part of the James Marsh tradition with an emphasis on Kant and that his study of Kant with Torrey had a profound impact on his thought. Writing from Johns Hopkins University about his studies with Professor George Sylvester Morris, who had just published a well-received book on *Kant's Critique of Pure Reason,* Dewey states:

> I find his lectures on Kant thus far rather elementary thanks to my introduction under your auspices to Kant at the beginning of my studies. I think that I have had a much better introduction into philosophy than I could have had any other way. Kant shows so clearly the nature of the problems of philosophy and gives each a standard and criterion by means of the critical method for judging the nature and results of other investigations, that I think a good knowledge of him saves almost years of work in approaching philosophy. It certainly introduced a revolution into all my thoughts, and at the same time gave me a basis for my other reading and thinking.[86]

Torrey himself had intensively studied Kant early in his own philosophical training and he started Dewey off in a similar fashion.[87] "Everybody studied Kant in those days,"[88] recalls Dewey, and his own words in 1883 point to the thought of Kant as the major influence at work in his general philosophical development before graduate school.

In the area of the philosophy of religion and morals the ideas in Kant's *Critique of Practical Reason* (1788) were very important to young Dewey, but the primary influence on him in this matter was not first and foremost the writings of Kant himself. The James Marsh tradition did not accept Kant uncritically, and it took its primary inspiration not just from Kant, but also from the transcendentalist revision of Kant in the writings of Samuel Taylor Coleridge and

James Marsh. Dewey read both Marsh's edition of Coleridge's *Aids to Reflection* (1825) and *The Remains of the Rev. James Marsh* (1843) during his college years, and the transcendentalist revision of Kant's theory of practical reason in these books had both a liberating influence on his religious outlook at the time and an enduring impact on the development of his philosophy of religion over the years. Marsh himself never had much sympathy with some of the more radical currents of New England Transcendentalism, and he remained loyal to the Congregational Church and the major social institutions of Vermont. However, he was an educational reformer as well as an innovative philosophical thinker, and he radically revised the curriculum of the University of Vermont so that it culminated in the senior year in a program of philosophy designed to provide the student with a sense of the organic unity of all knowledge.[89] As a result of his influence, the university became a stronghold of Transcendentalist philosophical thinking with a primary emphasis on Kant and Coleridge. Marsh was succeeded in the chair of philosophy in 1842 by one of his colleagues and followers, Joseph Torrey, who edited Marsh's *Remains* with a memoir. Joseph Torrey was the uncle, teacher, and father-in-law of Henry A.P. Torrey.[90]

As a young man Henry had been much influenced by Vermont Transcendentalism. He joined the Congregational Church during his sophomore year at the University of Vermont, and some time thereafter, like many Transcendentalists, he had his moment of "illumination." "To him walking in the woods in spring alone and brooding, there came, suddenly and definitely, a clear shining, in light of which the things of the spirit came into harmonious and vital relation, and that light grew and did not pass."[91] At the age of twenty-seven after attending Union Theological Seminary in New York City, Torrey was ordained as a Congregational minister in Vergennes, Vermont, and throughout his life the Christian faith remained his most vital concern. Even though he had no doctor's degree and no formal philosophical training beyond his basic theological education for the ministry, he was called in 1868 from his pastorate in Vergennes to replace his uncle as Marsh Professor of Intellectual and Moral Philosophy. In an effort to further prepare himself for this position, Torrey over the next few years systematically worked his way through Kant's three Critiques in the original German and prepared his own exposition of Kant's thought in the form of questions and answers.[92]

Torrey continued in a significant way the James Marsh tradition in his philosophy courses, which were part of the senior year program introduced originally by Marsh in the 1830s. He guided his students through Plato's *Republic,* lectured on Kant, Coleridge, and Marsh in courses on psychology, moral science, and metaphysics, and assigned readings in Joseph Torrey's edition of Marsh's *Remains* in the course on psychology and Joseph Torrey's *A Theory of Fine Art* in the course on aesthetics. However, despite the strong influence of Kant and Coleridge at the University of Vermont, both Joseph and H.A.P. Torrey continued over the years to assign and recommend to their students the writings of Locke, Reid, Stewart, and William Hamilton. These authors were not required reading in Dewey's senior year, but in the courses on metaphysics and morals Torrey did use texts by Noah Porter, the president of Yale, and Henry Calderwood, who had both been trained initially in the Scottish School. In these courses, then, the influence of Scottish realism was present, but it is significant that both Calderwood's *Handbook of Moral Philosophy* (1872) and Noah Porter's *The Elements of Intellectual Science* (1871)—the books Torrey assigned—evidence the attempt to use Kant to revise Scottish epistemology and morals and also show the influence of post-Kantian German and British idealism. In his course on evidences of religion (philosophy of religion), Torrey used an old standby in American colleges from the days well before Marsh, Bishop Joseph Butler's *Analogy of Religion, Natural and Revealed, To the Constitution of Nature* (1736), which is a dry compendium of logical arguments against skepticism and deism in support of revealed religion.[93]

Dewey has described the philosophy which he learned from Torrey as intuitionalism. Intuitionalism or intuitionism was a term often applied in the nineteenth century to the Scottish School of commonsense realism. However, Torrey was more influenced by Kant and German idealism than by the Scottish philosophers. If the term intuitionalism is taken to mean the general theory that the first principles of being, the existence of God, moral values, freedom, and immortality are known by some power of direct spiritual insight involving, for example, feeling, conscience, or pure reason, but distinct from sense experience and discursive reason, then it is correct to call Torrey an intuitionalist.[94] In Kant, Coleridge, Marsh, Calderwood, Porter, and the Scottish philosophers as well as Plato, he found different brands of intuitionalism in this general sense. These modern thinkers all shared a common opposition to Hume's theory of knowledge, skepticism, atheism, and materialism. Dewey recalls that at the University of Vermont "somehow the cause of all holy and valuable things was supposed to stand or fall with the validity of intuitionalism; the only vital issue was that between intuitionalism and a sensational empiricism that explained away the reality of all higher objects."[95] Intuitionalism in the broad sense was "the Burlington philosophy."[96]

After he left Vermont, Dewey was very critical of the dualisms that he encountered in the philosophy he studied in Burlington, but late in his career he expressed deep appreciation for other aspects of the James Marsh tradition, especially for the way in which it related philosophy and religion. Regarding his criticisms, in "From Absolutism to Experimentalism" (1930), he writes: "I learned the terminology of an intuitional philosophy, but it did not go deep, and in no way did it satisfy what I was dimly looking for."[97] What Dewey was searching for, of course, was a philosophical vision of organic unity which would free him from the divisions and separations he experienced as a youth in Burlington, and it could hardly be expected that under the direction of a Vermont Congregational minister like Torrey, he would be able to arrive at such a vision. In fact, much of the philosophy Dewey studied with Torrey was full of dualisms. Scottish realism was content with a separation of God and the world, subject and object, mind and matter, and the moral sense and empirical knowledge. Attacking the outlook of the *New Princeton Review* in 1886, Dewey calls Scottish realism "commonsense dualism" and describes it as the "dreary, highly sensible and highly meaningless compound of metaphysics and psychology, with a dose of the morals of propriety for flavoring which has been taught in American colleges for several generations."[98]

In Kant, Dewey encountered a profound clarification of philosophical problems, an exciting epistemology which emphasized the activity rather than the passivity of the mind, and an ethical theory which internalized the moral law by identifying it with the law of human reason. Of most importance for Dewey's philosophy of religion, he found a theory of human nature that made will and practical reason the vital center of the moral and religious life. However, he also encountered in Kant the dualism of phenomena and noumena, a radical separation of the realm of empirical fact from the realm of moral values, a division of scientific knowledge and religious faith, and a sharp distinction between natural desire and the sense of duty. At Johns Hopkins, Professor G.S. Morris would teach Dewey how to overcome Kant's dualisms by reconstructing Kant in the light of Hegel, and Dewey recalls: "I was glad to get away from Kant's dualisms—I made a very thorough study of Kant."[99]

Even though the dualisms in Kant and Burlington intuitionalism left Dewey dissatisfied, he did discover certain liberating ideas in the philosophy of religion associated with the James Marsh tradition. During his later years as a professor at Columbia, Dewey's colleagues in the department of philosophy had a birthday party for him at which time he was presented with a copy of Marsh's edition of *Aids to Reflection,* and Professor Herbert Schneider recalls Dewey saying in response: "Yes, I remember very well that this was our spiritual emancipation in Vermont. Coleridge's idea of the spirit came to us as a real relief, because we could be both liberal and pious; and this *Aids to Reflection* book, especially Marsh's edition, was my first Bible."[100] Not long after this occasion on November 26, 1929, Dewey returned to Burlington to give the James Marsh lecture in commemoration of the centenary of the publication of Marsh's introduction to Coleridge's *Aids to Reflection.*[101] The lecture was titled "Coleridge, Marsh and the Spiritual Philosophy." In it Dewey presented a sympathetic exposition of the philosophy of Marsh, calling attention to the influence of Aristotle as well as Kant and Coleridge, and indicating his own appreciation of what Marsh had stood for as a philosopher and educator in his time in America. Schneider also reports that on another occasion after the publication of *A Common Faith* in 1934, Dewey commented: "All I can do on religion is to say again what I learned from Coleridge way back in my childhood, and this *A Common Faith* is, as far as I am concerned, just a restatement of my early faith that I got at the University of Vermont through Marsh and Coleridge."[102] Dewey went on to say he was not any longer interested in institutional religion, "but religion as a dimension of human experience does interest me and I've taken it for granted ever since my early introduction to Coleridge."[103]

Neither Joseph nor H.A.P. Torrey made Coleridge assigned reading. However, Marsh's edition of *Aids to Reflection* at the University of Vermont in Dewey's student days was like Emerson's essays in New England generally, that is, it was something thinking men and women read for their edification. Dewey read it, and as his comments indicate the spirit of Marsh's and Coleridge's teaching was a profoundly liberating influence in his intellectual and moral development. Further, unlike Butler's *Analogy of Religion,* which had no positive influence on Dewey's religious outlook,[104] the Marsh edition of *Aids to Reflection* provided Dewey during a time of considerable doubt with a religious faith and philosophy of religion that had a life long influence. It is, therefore, useful to consider more carefully Marsh's "Preliminary Essay," *Aids to Reflection,* and Marsh's *Remains,* which Dewey has also described as "very important" to him as a young man.[105]

"Were I to select a single passage that might serve as an illuminating test of what he thought and taught," writes Dewey of Marsh, "it would be, I think, the following: The thinking man has and can have but one system in which his philosophy becomes religious and his religion philosophical."[106] It is this idea that most appealed to young Dewey in Marsh's edition of *Aids to Reflection.* It encouraged his faith in intelligence and philosophical quest. It assured him that he could be "both liberal and pious," holding out the promise of a complete reconciliation between reason and Christianity. *Aids to Reflection,* explains Coleridge, is written for "all who . . . do in good earnest desire to form their religious creed in the light of their own convictions, and to have a reason for the faith which they profess."[107] Moreover, Coleridge not only insists that the Christian faith is entirely consistent with right reason, but that "the Christian Faith is the perfection of human intelligence."[108] Expounding Coleridge's ideas Marsh asserts that it is "our prerogative, as rational beings, and our duty as Christians, to think, as well as to act, *rationally,* — to see that our convictions of truth rest on the ground of right reason. . . . "[109]

Quoting a seventeenth-century Cambridge Platonist, *Aids to Reflection* cautions: "He that speaks against his own reason, speaks against his own conscience: and therefore it is certain, no man serves God with a good conscience, who serves him against his reason."[110] Coleridge argues that to contradict one's reason for the sake of some religious belief results in moral corruption of the personality: "He, who begins by loving Christianity better than truth, will proceed by loving his own sect or church better than Christianity, and end in loving himself better than all."[111] There can be no stronger moral claim in defense of the life of reason. The words of Coleridge and Marsh found a ready response in young Dewey.

These convictions about the value of reason in the religious life led Coleridge and Marsh to defend the need for philosophy—what they called the art of reflection. Marsh explains Coleridge's view: "For to determine what *are* the grounds of right reason, what are those ultimate truths, and those universal laws of thought, which we cannot rationally contradict, and by reflection to compare with these whatever is proposed for our belief, is in fact to philosophize." Such philosophizing is a necessity, "for what is not rational in theology, is, of course, irrational, and cannot be of the household of faith."[112] The art of reflection as Coleridge and Marsh conceive it is the art of self-knowledge. It is basically an introspective undertaking which challenges persons "to reflect . . . upon their own inward being, upon the constituent laws of their own understanding, upon the mysterious powers and agencies of reason, and conscience, and will."[113] In other words, *Aids to Reflection* urges its readers to discover for themselves in their own minds and wills the governing principles of human nature that have been articulated by philosophers such as Plato and Kant. In the light of such self-knowledge, which culminates in a knowledge of spirit and the spiritual world, a person is then in a position to become an authentic and original philosopher and to form his or her own moral and religious convictions. Coleridge and Marsh were also confident that the art of reflection would lead a person to recognize the inherent rationality and ultimate truth of Christianity.

The view that there can be no real conflict between philosophy and religion and that a thinking person can have but one system of beliefs, a system formed by the method of reason or intelligence, became for Dewey a lifelong conviction. In 1886 , for example, he asserts: "All religious and philosophical systems must possess perfect rationality, must be tested by reason and conform to it."[114] Guided first by Coleridge and Marsh, and then by G.S. Morris and the neo-Hegelians, Dewey came to believe that he could use reason to unite Christianity, philosophy, and science in one coherent system that would perfectly manifest the rational structure of reality. In pursuing this objective, Coleridge's idea of the art of reflection had an important influence on Dewey. The discipline of seeking in one's own being and experience for the grounds of right reason, so that one might have what Plato called knowledge instead of mere opinion, became for young Dewey the primary method of liberation as it had been for Marsh, Emerson, and other New England Transcendentalists. Furthermore, from Coleridge and Marsh he acquired the conviction that the art of reflection is in itself an important aspect of the religious life, for God is the truth itself. Philosophy became for Dewey the practice of reflection, and his first book, *Psychology* (1887), is an expression of his own search for self-knowledge, for what Marsh calls "the great and constituent principles of our permanent being and proper humanity."[115]

In their rationalizing of religion, Coleridge and Marsh did not go so far as to argue that revelation is unnecessary or that the Kantian discursive understanding and theoretical speculation by itself can arrive at the full truth of human nature. Coleridge was a devout Anglican and Marsh had deep roots in New England Calvinism. In rationalizing Christianity they meant only to show that Christian revelation properly understood does not contradict reason and that the truth which philosophy seeks is found in a Christian view of reality, human nature, and God. In other words, for Coleridge and Marsh just as an authentic understanding of Christian revelation must be rational, so also philosophy must become religious and find its completion in the moral and religious intuitions of a faith that goes beyond the discursive understanding. They try to preserve the coherence of their position by maintaining that these spiritual intuitions are themselves the operations of reason or intelligence, and that, therefore, there is actually only one system of truth even though there are higher and lower methods of knowing. In order to understand this approach it is necessary to explore how Coleridge drew upon Kant's idea of practical reason in developing his idea of spirit, an idea that had a lasting influence on Dewey.

Spirit is the essence of human nature according to Coleridge, and he defines spirit as rational will. He contrasts the spiritual with the natural, which is by definition what is causally determined by some antecedent reality. Spirit is a power of "absolute self-determination" coupled with the power to know the true and the good.[116] Following Kant, Coleridge distinguishes between the understanding, which is dependent on sense and can only know the natural world, and reason, which includes practical reason and is able to know the spiritual world. Reason is the spirit's distinctive rational power. Attributing to reason a power of real knowledge that Kant did not allow, Coleridge defines the rational faculty of the spirit as "the power of universal and necessary convictions, the source and substance of truths above sense, and having their evidence in themselves." He puts special emphasis on practical reason arguing that the universal and necessary truth apprehended by the spirit is most importantly the moral ideal, that is, the principles according to which the will should act. In addition to being "the light of the conscience," practical reason is also according to Coleridge a power of direct inward knowledge of God, the self and the freedom of the will.[117]

Kant's ethical rationalism had excluded from the functioning of practical reason all emotion except for a feeling of reverence for the law. Coleridge gives to the heart and the emotions a much greater role in the life of the spirit. The workings of practical reason, as Coleridge understands it, involve a synthesis of mind, conscience, heart, and will.[118] The spirit does not just know moral and religious truths in a detached, purely intellectual fashion. A spiritual faith in a great moral ideal or in God as Spirit is the result of being grasped in the depths of one's subjectivity or personal being by the supreme worth of this idea. Coleridge describes this experience as "the oblivion and swallowing up of self in an object dearer than self or in an idea more vivid" or "the enlargement and elevation of the soul above its mere self."[119] Coleridge condemns the doctrine of literal inspiration as a superstition, explains Dewey, but "he urged the acceptance of the teachings of Scripture on the ground that they 'find' one in the deepest and most spiritual part of one's nature."[120] Further, for Coleridge spiritual truth has to be adopted by the will in action— has to be lived—in order to be truly known. He emphasizes what he calls "experimental religion." "Christianity is not a *theory* or a *speculation,* but a *life.* Not a philosophy of life, but a life and a living process," states Coleridge. Marsh adds that Christianity is "not, therefore, so properly a species of knowledge, as a form of being."[121] For Coleridge "faith was a state of the will and the affections, not merely intellectual assent to doctrinal and historical perspectives," explains Dewey, who remembered this teaching of Coleridge when he came to write his own philosophy of religion at the end of his career.[122]

Marsh, who vigorously attacked Locke's empiricism and Scottish realism as incompatible with a genuinely spiritual view of human nature and reality, developed in his own fashion Coleridge's ideas in a series of essays on psychology, ethics, and religion, which are contained in *The Remains.* The spiritual principle in human nature is "that free intelligence and will by which we become capable of responsible action and of moral good and evil," asserts Marsh. Strong emphasis is placed on the role of conscience, which he identifies closely with the working of practical reason. The idea of the will as a responsible will "is inseparable from the idea of conscience, or the self-conscious recognition of a *law* by which it ought to be governed, as prescribing its *true* and *rightful end.*" The law of conscience is identical with the will of God. It is universal law, one and the same for all persons and directing all to the same ultimate end. It is "the perfection of reason," "the ultimate good of all rational beings," the first principle of all truths for which no reason can be given but which is the reason of all else. The human conscience apprehends this highest truth directly or intuitively, and it recognizes it immediately as the absolute truth and highest good. For Marsh it is through the conscience that "the higher spiritual consciousness in man finds itself in immediate intercourse with the spiritual world; rather in the immediate presence of God." "The light and law of conscience" is "the necessary form in which God manifests himself to the spiritual intuition of his rational creatures." Marsh goes on to argue that one finds the light and law of conscience and God manifest supremely in the New Testament account of Jesus Christ."[123]

In the final analysis, Coleridge and Marsh insist on the need for Christian revelation because they accept the classical Christian doctrine of original sin and the Fall. Here lies the major difference between Vermont Transcendentalism and the thought of Emerson. Coleridge and Marsh argue that the controlling principle of action in every unredeemed human will is inevitably a principle contrary to the Law of God, the universal law of right reason, and all human beings share the burden of responsibility for this sinful condition of the will. Coleridge acknowledges that the fact of original sin is a mystery, "a problem, of which any other solution than the statement of the fact itself was demonstratively impossible."[124] However, he argues that acknowledgement of the fact "follows necessarily from the postulate of a responsible will," for no person after honest self-scrutiny can answer positively the following question: "Am I at one with God, and is my will concentric with that holy power, which is at once the constitutive will and the supreme reason of the universe?"[125] As Marsh puts it: "we have the evidence in ourselves that we are fallen beings."[126] The fundamental problem is that the will has adopted as its ultimate end one or more of the many ends proposed by the powers, appetites, and affections of humanity's natural being as distinct from its spiritual being.[127] In this fallen condition, the human spirit is held in bondage to nature and is but a potentiality until awakened through repentance and faith by God's act of redemption in Christ. In and through the personal experience of being found and grasped by the person of Christ the spirit awakens once again to "the true light" which is the divine reason. Coleridge writes: "Whenever by self-subjection to this universal light, the will of the individual, the particular will, has become a will of reason, the man is regenerate: the reason is then the spirit of the regenerate man, whereby the person is capable of a quickening intercommunion with the Divine Spirit. And herein consists the mystery of Redemption, that this has been rendered possible for us."[128]

It is clear why Coleridge and Marsh were able to bolster Dewey's religious faith at the University of Vermont. With their doctrine of the spirit and interpretation of religious experience they succeeded in convincing him that properly understood, the Christian religion is not pious sentimentality coupled with an externally imposed arbitrary moral law, which a person obeys out of fear and a servile hope of reward, and it is not just a matter of dry intellectual belief in historical propositions and doctrines, for which reason can find no justification and of which there is no direct personal experience. They gave Dewey a sense that there is in Christianity profound personal truth, which is at once universal truth, because it involves real insight into the nature and destiny of the human being understood as a rational will. They convinced him that this "living truth" can be verified by the spirit, the reason and will, of every person. By rationalizing the divine nature of Christ they also enabled Dewey to preserve a faith in what in 1886 he called "the perfect and matchless character of Christ." [129]

The notion that practical reason and will constitute the heart of human personality was an inspiring idea to young Dewey in the midst of his own quest for freedom and self-realization. The influence of Coleridge and Marsh in this matter fell in with the subsequent influence of the neo-Hegelians and Dewey became at the outset of his career a voluntarist. In 1885 he writes: "The will has taken its place as the basal and central conception of the best of modern psychological inquiry." [130] The essence of will he explains is "freedom or determination by ends" and "at bottom a man's activities spring from and are rooted in the fundamental moral freedom—the choice of the end of man's life." Coleridge and Marsh both teach that the highest expression of this freedom is found in guidance by enlightened practical reason culminating in faith in the supreme moral end or ideal. By faith they mean an act of the spirit involving the mind, heart, and will—a kind of knowing and being known by the ideal which expresses itself in action, a way of living. Such wholehearted moral faith lies at the heart of the religious life, and in and through such faith a person is related to God, the absolute good. These were ideas that reinforced Dewey's youthful moral idealism and stayed with him over the years as he wrestled with the problem of the religious life and the unification of the ideal and the actual first as a neo-Hegelian and then as a naturalist.

Coleridge and the James Marsh tradition introduced Dewey to German philosophy and the kind of rationalized religion and ethical idealism that he eventually developed for himself in his own early

writings after entering Johns Hopkins. However, the thought of
Coleridge and Marsh by itself was not entirely satisfactory to young
Dewey. He was not interested in the details and subtleties of Coleridge's Anglican theology or Marsh's Calvinism. He did not take up
the study of Coleridge beyond *Aids to Reflection* until the mid 1880s.[131]
During the early 1880s before graduate school, he was more interested in reading the philosophical classics including Plato, Aristotle,
Descartes, Spinoza, Kant, and Hegel.[132] Dewey found Marsh's psychology as well as his philosophy of religion instructive, but Marsh
died at the age of forty-eight before he had fully developed his
thinking in the areas of logic, epistemology, and metaphysics, which
especially interested Dewey. There were also some substantive problems for young Dewey in the religious thought of Coleridge and
Marsh. It involves a number of dualisms including sharp distinctions
between the natural and the spiritual, desire and the law of conscience, and God and fallen humanity. These are among the ideas in
Vermont Trancendentalism that contributed to Dewey's sense of
isolation and separation. Influenced by philosophers of science like
Comte and Huxley and "reacting against the too moralistic morals"
in which he had been brought up, Dewey also began pondering
whether Kant, Coleridge, and Marsh had posited an unnecessary and
problematic split between the understanding and natural science on
the one hand and pure reason and the moral good on the other.[133]

Rejecting the idea of original sin was not an easy task for young
Dewey. His opposition to the idea of the sinful nature of humanity
stems, in the first place, from his very early experience. The idea of
sin had been misused during his childhood and was closely associated
with painful memories of guilt feelings that were the products of an
oppressive religious training rather than any inborn corruption of his
own will. In addition, the idea of what Marsh calls "a deep and
radical evil," which in the final analysis is a mystery to the understanding, offended Dewey's sense of the intelligibility of the world,
and it did not fit well into the vision of the organic unity of all things
to which he aspired as a young philosopher.[134] However, even though
he certainly did not like the idea as a young man, it was too intimately connected with sacred Vermont traditions and it had too great
an emotional hold for him to be able to free his mind completely of

the notion as long as he was living in Burlington and had strong ties to that community.

In a talk before the Students' Christian Association at the University of Michigan in 1884, Dewey referred to "the sins ... of actual human nature" and explained that "to sin morally" is a "moral defect" in a person stemming from an "attitude of his will and desires" which are under his control.[135] These comments indicate that he was still under the influence of the Christian notion of sin in the early 1880s, but they do not necessarily indicate a belief in the idea of original sin, of a universal corruption of the human will. In a letter to Alice Chipman in 1886, Dewey indicated that he was still puzzled by the origin of moral evil in the motives of the will but did not want to fall back on the doctrine of original sin as an answer.[136] He writes that it is beyond his understanding how anyone could knowingly do what is evil—evil in the Socratic sense of what is contrary to the highest good of the person concerned—unless the person is ignorant of the good. However, if an individual is ignorant, he or she is not morally responsible, and Dewey could not accept the latter notion. He found himself being pushed back to "the total depravity theory," the doctrine of the Fall and the bondage of the will, but he did not want to take that position either. Dewey never did return to the idea of original sin, and he explicitly rejected the notion in his later writings.

Wordsworth, Mystical Feeling, and Pantheism

Pursuing their aesthetic intuitions, the poets and philosophers of the Romantic movement frequently imagined the totality of being to be an organic unity manifesting the infinite life of one great Spirit, and they put special emphasis on the feeling of oneness with nature and the larger whole.[137] For English and American Transcendentalists, one of the most moving expressions of this theme was found in Wordsworth's poetry, especially in "Ode: Intimations of Immortality from Recollections of Early Childhood," and "Tintern Abbey." In these poems Wordsworth turns to the feelings of the heart and to childhood memories of a world "apparelled in celestial light" in search of a "faith that looks through death," and he sets forth a pantheistic vision of spirit pervading the world and expresses his joy and trust in nature.[138] Such poetry was destined to have an important impact on young Dewey in the course of his quest to overcome the dualisms of self and world, and self and God. As noted at the outset of this essay, one of the three ways in which Dewey came to believe that the world may be idealized is in and through "moments of intense emotional appreciation when . . . the beauty and harmony of existence is disclosed."[139] Under the influence of Wordsworth, he came to experience such moments as a young man with the result that an element of romantic intuitionalism remains a permanent aspect of his outlook.

Dewey's attraction to Wordsworth is undoubtedly closely related to his boyhood experience with nature. He enjoyed life on his grandfather Rich's farm, and he came to know well the great wilderness areas that surrounded his home. Jane Dewey writes:

> The unusual natural beauties of the surroundings were not consciously appreciated but were somehow absorbed. John and Davis tramped through the Adirondacks and to Mt. Mansfield. They outfitted Lake Champlain rowboats with a tent, blankets, and cooking utensils and explored the lake from end to end. On similar trips they rowed into Lake George or, with the help of a lumber wagon hired to carry the rowboat, descended the river and canal that connects Lake Champlain with the St. Lawrence and rowed up another river in French Canada to a beautiful inland lake.[140]

In the midst of these adventures the unpleasant pressures of home life and the dualisms of Vermont culture must have seemed far away. In the wilderness he was free to be himself and could feel himself to be a part of an awesome and wonderful vast whole. Lake Champlain, the Green Mountains and the Adirondacks became to him "old friends," and the sight of them as an older man brought back warm memories of good times.[141]

It was these early experiences with nature coupled with his craving for unity that led Dewey to read Wordsworth carefully in the early 1880s, if not before. In 1886 he indicated what appealed to him most in the poet's romantic vision:

The art which deals with nature is perfect and enduring just in the degree in which it reveals the fundamental unities which exist between man and nature. In Wordsworth's poetry of nature, for example, we do not find ourselves in a strange, unfamiliar land; we find Wordsworth penetrating into those revelations of spirit, of meaning in nature, of which we ourselves had already some dumb feeling, and this the poetry makes articulate. All products of the creative imagination are unconscious testimonies to the unity of spirit which binds man to man and man to nature in one organic whole.[142]

In Wordsworth, then, Dewey found confirmation of his own intimations of the organic unity of the world, which had been brought to life by reading Huxley.

One early experience in particular goes far in explaining Dewey's appreciation of Wordsworth and the lasting influence of the poet's natural piety. Following graduation from the University of Vermont in 1879, Dewey sought a high school teaching position. He was invited by Affia Wilson, his cousin and the principal of a small school in Oil City, Pennsylvania, to join her staff.[143] The two years he spent in Oil City (1879–1881) were among the loneliest and most uncertain times of his early life. During this period Dewey recounts that he found himself questioning whether he really meant what he said when he prayed in church and at the opening of school sessions. At times the practice of prayer seemed to be a purely external performance and his heart was not in it. In the poetry of Wordsworth, however, he did find expression of the real prayer that was in his heart. One evening at a time when he was reading Wordsworth he had what many years later he described to Max Eastman as "a mystic experience," which seemed to come in answer to that prayer. It was a blissful experience in which his worries and fears seemed to fall away and he was filled with a sense of deep trust and oneness with the universe.[144]

Dewey explained to Eastman that his experience was a purely emotional one, and he called it "mystic" because it could not be conveyed fully in words. There were no visions or voices, just a supremely blissful feeling. He compared it to Wordsworth's "poetic pantheism" and "Walt Whitman's sense of oneness with the uni-

verse." It seems that Dewey's experience was of the kind Wordsworth endeavors to describe in "Tintern Abbey" when he writes:

> And I have felt
> A presence that disturbs me with joy
> Of elevated thoughts; a sense sublime
> Of something far more deeply interfused,
> Whose dwelling is the light of setting suns,
> And the round ocean and the living air,
> And the blue sky, and in the mind of man:
> A motion and a spirit, that impels
> All thinking things, all objects of all thought,
> And rolls through all things.[145]

When Dewey was pressed by Eastman to explain further what his
experience meant to him he put its significance this way: "What the
hell are you worrying about anyway? Everything that's here is here,
and you can just lie back on it. . . . I've never had any doubts since
then,—nor any beliefs. To me faith means not worrying. . . . I claim
I've got religion, and that I got it that night in Oil City." [146]

The immediate impact of the Oil City experience is exaggerated
in the Eastman account. Dewey attributed much greater significance
to this kind of experience in 1930 than he did in his psychology of
religious experience in the 1880s. Further, until well into the 1890s
Dewey continued to hold some explicitly Christian theological beliefs,
and he remained an active member of the Congregational Church.
His emotional sense of separation persisted with at least some degree
of intensity until he had achieved a philosophical unification of the
ideal and the actual and worked out a satisfying social adjustment in
both his private and professional life. Nevertheless, for a few blissful
moments, which he never forgot, Wordsworth's poetry freed Dewey
of the anxieties and doubts under which he was laboring in Oil City
during long evenings of introspection and study, and it awakened a
sense of wholeness and of belonging to the larger universe. He had a
taste emotionally of that unity of the ideal and the actual that he
craved. This experience undoubtedly strengthened Dewey's will to
believe what he most wanted to believe at the time, which is that the
deeper truth of human nature and the universe is organic unity, not
separation and isolation. By giving support to this faith it contributed

significantly to the emotional resources he had for dealing with the problems that lay ahead.

As the Eastman account indicates, the Oil City experience was one influence—there were a number of others as well—which led Dewey eventually to abandon his traditional Christian theological beliefs and to move away from reliance on the institutional church. Dewey certainly knew well the words of Jesus: "Come unto me, ye who labor and are heavy laden, and I will give you rest" (Matt. 11:28). However, it was not through a confession of sin, repentance, and faith in Christ as the divine-human mediator and redeemer that he found rest and peace. He found it in the case of the Oil City experience under the inspiration of Wordsworth's pantheistic poetry. Since throughout the 1880s Dewey preserved a faith in God as the organic unity of the world in whom the ideal and the real are one, he would have interpreted this experience at the time as an intuition of God. Nevertheless, it is not surprising that such an immediate appreciation of harmony with the universe as possessed the heart of young Dewey would become a rival to an orthodox Christian piety that relied on a transcendent God and the historical Jesus as the divine-human mediator.

A Decision for Philosophy

In the summer of 1881 Dewey returned to Burlington and spent much of the following year reading the classics in the history of philosophy and studying philosophic German under Professor Torrey's guidance. He also taught during the winter semester at the Lake View Seminary, a secondary school in the small village of Charlotte, sixteen miles south of Burlington. One of his students remembered "how terribly the boys behaved, and how long and fervent was the prayer with which he opened each school day."[147] It was a trying experience for Dewey, who had too gentle and scholarly a disposition to be effective in this situation, and he did not want to continue high school teaching. Encouraged by Torrey he was now seriously considering a career in philosophy. By this time he was avidly reading *The Journal of Speculative Philosophy*.[148] Here he discovered neo-Hegelian idealism and the movement of midwestern American transcendentalism. In the pages of *The Journal of Speculative Philosophy* he found translations of Kant, Fichte, and Hegel and articles by William Torrey Harris, Denton J. Snider, Henry C. Brokmeyer, John Watson, Edward Caird, and George Sylvester Morris. In the writings of these men he encountered a vitality and depth of thought which awakened him to the possibility of a philosophical idealism that could complete the critical reconstruction in philosophy begun by Kant and that could take him beyond the dualisms that remained in Burlington intuitionalism.

Inspired by what he read, he tried his hand at writing two philosophical essays which he sent off to W.T. Harris, the St. Louis Hegelian who edited *The Journal of Speculative Philosophy* and directed the Concord Summer School of Philosophy. The first essay, entitled "The Metaphysical Assumptions of Materialism," was an attempt to show that a metaphysical materialism involves unresolvable contradictions.[149] It reveals young Dewey's concern to demonstrate the need for a spiritual philosophy—a metaphysical idealism. The second essay was a study of pantheism and Spinoza. Under the influence of the idea of organic unity and Wordsworth, Dewey began pondering the possibilities of a pantheistic metaphysics. Coleridge and Marsh knew the attraction of Wordsworth's poetic pantheism, but they both warned against it as inconsistent with a sound Christian theology.[150] In the same spirit, Torrey advised Dewey that "undoubtedly pantheism is the most satisfactory form of metaphysics intellectually, but it goes counter to religious faith."[151] With this caution in mind, Dewey read Spinoza's *Ethics* and wrote up his findings.

Dewey's essay, "The Pantheism of Spinoza," begins with a statement of what he understands the task of philosophy to be: "The problem of philosophy is to determine the meaning of things as we find them, or of the actual. Since these things may be gathered under three heads, the problem becomes: to determine the meaning of Thought, Nature, and God, and the relation of one to another." The attraction of pantheism, reasons Dewey, is that it seems to achieve a real reconciliation of God, self, and nature. "God becomes the Absolute, and Nature and Self are but his manifestations. This is Pantheism, and the view of Spinoza. Thought and being become one; the order of thought is the order of existence. Now a final unity seems obtained, and real knowledge possible." However, he finds that Spinoza's pantheistic system, which identifies God and the world, fails in the final analysis, for it leaves a major problem unresolved: "If . . . all things are divine, how, then, do they appear to us otherwise?"[152] This problem of the relation of appearance and reality, which is created by any philosophy that identifies the real with the ideal, became for Dewey the heart of the problem of evil in its metaphysical aspect.[153] It would continue to trouble him as long as he remained a philosophical idealist.

Dewey's two essays were published by *The Journal of Speculative Philosophy* in 1882, and Harris' enthusiasm for his work was an important factor in Dewey's decision to pursue graduate study in philosophy at Johns Hopkins University in the fall of that year.[154] Given his own state of mind at the time and the strength of "the philosophic instinct" he did not have the will to do anything else. "By some sort of instinct, and by the impossibility of my doing anything in particular, I was led into philosophy and idealism," explained Dewey to William James in 1891.[155] This was a critical moment in his own intellectual and religious development. His decision to become a professional philosopher and to go to Johns Hopkins was more than just a surrender to a craving for an intellectual vision of order and harmony. It was also a final resolution to commit himself to become an independent critical thinker regardless of the financial, social, and religious consequences. Dewey's decision did involve potential problems. He would have to borrow money to go to graduate school, and even with a Ph.D. in philosophy he might well have trouble finding employment.[156] Even though the situation was beginning to change, with few exceptions the teachers of philosophy in American colleges were, like Torrey, clergymen, and the task of philosophy was traditionally thought to be properly defined by the requirements of theology. However, Dewey had no interest in being ordained and his primary commitment was from the beginning to philosophy as distinct from any particular theological tradition even though he still had certain theological beliefs and ties to the Congregational Church.

Had Dewey at this time been deeply convinced that unification with God and the ideal could only come in and through repentance and faith in the historical Jesus, understood quite literally as the mediator between humanity and God, he would almost certainly have chosen to go to a theological seminary in the process of preparing himself for a career as a college or university professor of philosophy. However, Dewey's decision for philosophy and for Johns Hopkins, which placed special emphasis on the sciences, indicates that what he really believed in as the mediator between the divine and the human, the ideal and the actual, was reason, intelligence. In short, from the beginning of his career as a philosopher, Dewey put his faith first and foremost in intelligence rather than in the Christ understood as a supernatural savior. His choice of a career as a philosopher meant that, from here on out, he would trust only a liberated critical intelligence in matters of intellectual belief, for his instincts told him that only in this way could he find his freedom as an individual and the integration of ideas leading to the unity within himself and with his world that he craved. This is not to deny that for over a decade he endeavored to hold a faith in intelligence together with a faith in God and in Christ by rationalizing Christianity and trying to show that the moral ideals manifest in Christ are one with the ideals of practical reason. His early faith in intelligence was one with a faith in cosmic organic unity, in God, in the harmony of the ideal and the real. He would endeavor to preserve this uneasy union between philosophy and theology as long as he considered it necessary to believe in some traditional concept of God in order to guarantee the reality of the ideal and the unity of the ideal and the actual.

By 1882, then, Dewey's religious quest for unity was to a large extent channeled by his faith in intelligence into a philosophical quest for certain knowledge regarding nature, the self, and God. However, philosophy and religion were not identical in young Dewey's mind. They did overlap for him. Philosophy had a religious dimension for it was concerned with God, and it was young Dewey's principle guide in his effort to understand the ideal and the relation of the ideal to the self and the world. Furthermore, insofar as the practice of philosophy itself contributed to the experience of actual unification it had a religious function or effect. Nevertheless, young Dewey did not imagine that the religious life could be reduced to a search for philosophical knowledge.

It would be more correct to assert that Dewey's philosophical quest was founded upon a religious faith. This faith was a faith in intelligence in the broad sense indicated, that is, a faith not only in human reason but also a faith in God as the Divine Reason and the ground of organic unity, of the intelligibility and meaningfulness of all existence. This faith led Dewey into philosophy; it precedes his philosophical quest in the sense that it provides a basis for his quest. It also transcends philosophical knowledge, which can be explained with reference to the influence of Coleridge and Wordsworth.

As his religious thought matured, two themes emerge as especially prominent in his understanding of the religious life, and both of these strands of thought reflect his early religious experience and thinking. First and foremost, there is the idea of the religious life as involving a unifying moral faith arising out of the experience of being possessed by a supreme spiritual ideal that harmonizes the self and self and world. Here the emphasis falls on the will, practical reason, and moral action, and it reflects the influence of Kant, Coleridge, Marsh, and Vermont Transcendentalism generally. For Dewey philosophical speculation is no substitute for wholehearted trust in and practical devotion to the ideal, even if the former is a necessary instrument in clarifying the object of faith.

Second, in his mature thought Dewey also associates religious experience with an attitude of piety toward nature and with mystical intuitions of oneness with the larger whole which is the universe. In this connection one encounters an enduring element of romanticism in his thought, which shows the influence of Wordsworth. Given his scientific bent of mind and concern with moral autonomy and self-realization, Dewey was not attracted to a Neoplatonic mysticism in which discursive reason and the individual are absorbed into an undifferentiated One. The unity he sought is an organic unity, in which the freedom and significance of the individual are preserved, but he maintained in his mature thought an important place for mystical feelings of unity, for emotional intimations of belonging to the larger community of being. In short, a religious moral faith in a unifying ideal and the mystical sense of belonging are from very early major themes in Dewey's religious outlook, and they remained central. There is here for Dewey, then, a realm of religious experience which is to be distinguished from intellectual experience even though it may influence, and be positively influenced by, the latter.

In conclusion, as Dewey prepared to leave Vermont for graduate school certain ideas, interests and aspirations had already begun to take form which would have a lasting influence on the development of his philosophical and religious thinking. His central concern was a quest for unity and liberation from dualism. He longed to know for certain and to realize in his own life experience the truth that reality is an organic unity in which the actual world is thoroughly organized by a liberating ideal. The ideal unity that he was seeking involved both psychological integration and social adjustment. It was also for him a matter of a religious adjustment, for he continued to believe beyond all his doubts that an eternal God is the ultimate source and necessary foundation of all true ideals and enduring unity. His search for the ideal self and community was all one with a search for God. He would eventually abandon the God of the Congregational theologians, but he would never cease his battle against dualisms and he would always consider to be divine whatever unified the ideal and the actual and created organic unity. He would always be deeply concerned as a philosopher with unifying experience, and he would view the profoundly unifying as religious in quality. The unification of self, of society, and of self and world became for him vitally important religious values.

Under the influence of Coleridge, Wordsworth, and his early experience with philosophy in the 1880s, Dewey gradually came to the realization, then, that most fundamental to a vital religious life are personal experiences of unification whether they be predominantly moral, aesthetic, and mystical, or intellectual in nature. This concern with direct religious experience when coupled with his early trust in intelligence in matters of intellectual belief, which had been encouraged by Coleridge and Marsh, brought Dewey to a further conviction of great importance for the long term evolution of his own religious thinking. Reflecting in 1930 on his early years, Dewey recalls that there emerged in him "a feeling that any genuinely sound religious experience could and should adapt itself to whatever beliefs one found oneself intellectually entitled to hold—a half-conscious sense at first, but one which ensuing years have deepened into a fundamental conviction."[157] In other words, in the light of his own intellectual, moral, and mystical experience, he did not doubt the existence or importance of the religious dimension of experience, but given his faith in intelligence he was not willing to let traditional theological ideas control his own philosophical inquiries and eventual interpretation of religious experience. "I have enough faith in the depth of the religious tendencies of men to believe that they will adapt themselves to any required intellectual change," remarks Dewey.[158] The development of Dewey's religious thought involves, then, the evolution of his interpretation of religious experience under the impact of a changing philosophical perspective and the deepening in his own life of what he came to call the religious quality of experience.

Neo-Hegelian Idealism and the New Psychology

WHEN DEWEY ARRIVED at Johns Hopkins in 1882, American philosophy was on the threshold of a new era. Johns Hopkins was itself a new institution that had been founded in 1876 with a special emphasis on the sciences, graduate study, and original research. It had a young philosophy department that was keenly aware of the vital currents of thought in Europe and was alive with fresh ideas that anticipated the future. The department offered courses in the history of philosophy, logic, psychology, and pedagogy. It was something of a disappointment to Dewey that courses were not offered also in social and political philosophy.[1] However, the three professors with whom Dewey worked in philosophy, G. Stanley Hall, George Sylvester Morris, and Charles Sanders Peirce, were each in different ways destined to exercise a profound influence on his development.

Peirce was a mathematician and physicist as well as a philosopher. During the 1870s he had already developed the outlines of a new theory for making clear the meaning of ideas and beliefs, which would lead him in time to be recognized as the founder of the doctrine of philosophical pragmatism. Dewey attended Peirce's lectures on logic in Baltimore, but he was not able at this early stage to appreciate Peirce's thinking, which seemed to him too much concerned with mathematics and the methodology of science. In the 1890s Dewey would rediscover Peirce's thinking and eventually base his own theory of logic on Peirce's work.[2] Dewey's relationship to Hall and Morris was quite different. He responded enthusiastically to Hall's lectures on the new psychology and Morris' exposition of neo-Hegelian idealism. As a result, during the 1880s he devoted himself as a philosopher largely to developing and integrating the ideas to which they had introduced him. This chapter is primarily concerned with the approach to philosophy, the ideas of nature and God, and the theory of moral and religious experience to which this endeavor led him.

The religious situation into which Dewey entered at Johns Hopkins was somewhat freer and more relaxed than what he had known at the University of Vermont. Hall comments that "rather extreme conservatism in religion focusing in Presbyterianism was characteristic of Baltimore ... and the difference in the attitude of believers in such creeds and the standpoint of nearly every member of the faculty was immense."[3] Johns Hopkins himself had been a Quaker and the board of the University was made up predominantly of Quakers. "Fortunately, however, this faith stressed dogma but little," writes Hall, "although it revered the scriptures and the inner light and was friendly and sympathetic to the psychological study of both Old and New Testament, and not unduly appalled by the higher criticism."[4] President Gilman and his Board of Trustees were, nevertheless, concerned about the religious views of the faculty and the charges of pantheism, materialism, and mechanical evolutionism that were from time to time levelled against the university by the community. Gilman encouraged his faculty as well as students to attend a local church of their choice, and Hall and Morris both did so.[5]

Morris and Hall at Johns Hopkins

Morris had received a Puritan Congregationalist upbringing in Vermont, attended Dartmouth College, served in the Union Army, and then enrolled at Union Theological Seminary in 1864 with the intention of entering the ministry. Led into doubt by British empiricism, he was encouraged by Professor Henry Boynton Smith and by Professor W.G.T. Shedd, who had edited the American edition of Coleridge's collected works, to go to Germany to study with Ulrici and Trendelenburg.[6] His studies with Trendelenburg left him with the lasting conviction that philosophy must be grounded in scientific methods of truth, but Trendelenburg guided him away from British empiricism to an Aristotelian idealism. His exposure to German philosophy led him to discover Fichte, Hegel, and the British neo-Hegelian movement, especially the work of T.H. Green and John and Edward Caird. In the writings of these philosophers he found a philosophical and religious worldview that he could embrace wholeheartedly.[7] By the time Dewey met him at Johns Hopkins in 1882 he had joined the Episcopal Church and had taught philosophy at the University of Michigan and the Concord Summer School of Philosophy. He had also published a widely acclaimed translation of Friedrich Ueberweg's *History of Philosophy,* a critique of British empiricism, and a volume on Kant. The Kant book was the first in a series he was editing on "German Philosophical Classics For English Readers and Students."[8] Morris had also just given a series of lectures at Union Theological Seminary, which would shortly be published as *Philosophy and Christianity.* In his writings Morris sought to achieve his own neo-Hegelian synthesis of Plato, Aristotle, Kant, Hegel, Fichte, Trendelenburg, and Christian theism. G. Stanley Hall, who was awed by Morris's scholarship as a graduate student, described him years later as "by far the most scholarly man in the history of philosophy that America has even yet produced."[9]

Dewey has written that the Hegelian philosophy to which Morris introduced him "supplied a demand for unification that was doubtless an intense emotional craving. . . . My earlier philosophic study had been an intellectual gymnastic. Hegel's synthesis of subject and object, matter and spirit, the divine and the human, was, however, no mere intellectual formula; it operated as an immense release, a liberation."[10] In short, in Morris' teaching and Hegel, Dewey found the vision of organic unity for which he had searched ever since his encounter with the image of organic unity in Huxley's physiology textbook. However, it was not just what Morris wrote and said that inspired Dewey. It was also Morris the man. Dewey found Morris' philosophy "fused with his personal character."[11] He appeared to be the living embodiment of the wholeness, the integration of the ideal and the actual, to which Dewey aspired. Thought, feeling, and action seemed to be beautifully integrated in Morris' personality. In 1889, following Morris' early death, Dewey wrote: "To those who do not know him, no use of adjectives would convey an idea of the beauty, the sweetness, the wholeness of his character."[12] Forty years later this impression of Morris had not changed, and he states: "I have never known a more singlehearted and whole-souled man—a man of a single piece all the way through."[13] Dewey was fascinated by the Hegelian organicism that Morris taught, and for Morris the person he developed great love and admiration. Morris had a lasting influence as well as an immediate dramatic impact, and it is, therefore, important to consider his character and thought further.

First of all, Dewey found in Morris a man whose passion for ideas was equal to his own.

> My chief impression of Professor Morris as a teacher, vivid after the lapse of years, is one of intellectual ardour, or an ardour for ideas which amounted to spiritual fervor. His very manner as he lectured on a theme dear to him was like an exemplification of his own attachment to the Aristotelian doctrine, that the soul is the form, the entelechy, of the body. His spare and tense frame seemed but an organ for the realization of thought. The image as it stands forth in my mind today is accentuated by the fact that his energy was never vehemence. His emphasis always seemed moral rather than physical. ... As his eye lit up and his face shone, there was fire without heat, energy without violence—an exhibition of the life of thought.[14]

Dewey also recalls Morris's displeasure at having to test and grade students. In part this was due to his kindly disposition, but, more importantly, he considered it a contradiction to the way a free mind functions.

> Freedom, inspiration drawn from itself, joy in its own realization, were the very breath of the nostrils of intelligence. To deal with a student, even the average undergraduate, as anything but a potential intelligence was an aversion to him. ... [15]

The spirit of his work was that which he declared should be the spirit of all truly university work—a free teacher face to face with a free student. He once defined idealism as faith in the human spirit; this faith he had. . . . [16]

In Morris Dewey encountered a teacher with a deep respect for the freedom and integrity of a person's mind, values which young Dewey from an early age had prized.

Regarding the task of philosophy Morris taught that properly understood philosophy is "in the highest and most preeminent degree experimental science." Its objective is "the scientific examination of experience." It "claims to do nothing but comprehend experience." Its arguments must follow "the logic of fact." The difference between philosophy and the other sciences is that philosophy is "the science of experience as such," that is, it investigates the absolute nature of experience and of reality insofar as it is given in experience. Morris calls philosophy absolute intelligence explaining that "intelligence is nothing but the full, self-manifesting and self-recognizing light of experience." [17] Dewey adopted this general view of philosophy in graduate school, and he devoted his life to working out the implications of this position. Not all of Morris' colleagues at Johns Hopkins, of course, believed that his philosophy of absolute idealism was actually consistent with a scientific experimentalism, and the ideal of an experimental philosophy would eventually lead Dewey in the 1890s to empirical naturalism causing him to abandon much that Morris tried to defend as an absolute idealist.

Fundamental to Morris' Hegelian thinking is the distinction that he makes between a mechanical and an organic relation. A mechanical relation is a purely external and accidental relation involving things that are wholly independent and separated in space or time. Objects that are mechanically related merely coexist as a loose aggregate or follow each other, and if they are held together it is by an external power, a mechanical force.[18] Morris contrasts an aggregate of mechanically related parts with an organic whole in which all the parts are spiritually interrelated. In an organic unity, each and every member of the whole is animated by a common principle of activity making them into a community of beings "sharing in a·common life." Morris gives this description of an organic whole.

A whole organism is something more than any of its particular members, or than the mere mechanical aggregate of all its members. It is, or represents, the common life or animating and uniting principle of all its parts.... As it, the unifying and vivifying principle, permeates them all, so it presupposes them all, as the condition of its own reality and perfection. The life and reality of the whole are in and through the life and reality of its parts or members.[19]

An organic unity is not, then, an undifferentiated one or a dead conglomerate of mechanically related parts, but rather it is a living unity of distinct individuals, a whole which exists in and through diversity.

Dewey writes that Morris' "adherence to Hegel was because Hegel had demonstrated to him in a great variety of fields of experience, the supreme reality of this principle of a living unity maintaining itself through the medium of differences and distinctions."[20] In his own philosophy Morris repeatedly contrasts the mechanical and the organic, and cites the concept of the organic as the key to a proper understanding of the relationship of intelligence and the world, God and nature, the divine spirit and the human spirit, and the individual and society. It was with this Hegelian concept of organic unity that Dewey at the outset of his professional career began the process of systematically breaking down dualisms, which was one of his chief concerns as a philosopher throughout his life. Long after Dewey had rejected the Hegelian notion of a cosmic organic unity, he continued to believe in organic unity as a social ideal and to search for a unifying moral faith.

For Morris the most fundamental and critical problem in modern philosophy has to do with epistemology and the relation between intelligence and the external world or subject and object. British empiricism, Scottish realism, and Kant all assumed that intelligence and the world are separate entities and are only mechanically related creating insoluble intellectual puzzles. Hegel and the neo-Hegelians showed Morris how to overcome this problem.[21] While it may seem a matter of common sense to assume that intelligence and the world are separate realities related only accidentally and mechanically through sense experience, a close examination of experience reveals that this view is false. In actual experience the primary fact is that subject and object are originally given together. Only later are they distinguished by the intellect. The idea of a knowing subject distinct from an object is actually an abstraction from primary experience.[22] Subject and object, intelligence and the world are discovered in fact to be organically related. Dewey, who learned this solution to the most vexing problem in modern philosophy from Morris, never questioned the general soundness of the main point of this Hegelian argument. He rested satisfied throughout his career that there is continuity rather than dualism between subject and object, or experience and nature as he would later put it, and therefore, real knowledge of the external world is possible.

Following Hegel, Morris proceeds from recognition of the continuity of subject and object to acceptance of the idealist theory that the organic unity embracing both intelligence and the world is an ideal activity or "a *power* and life of spirit," which is to be identified with a universal or cosmic self-consciousness.[23] In the light of experience and intelligence, subject and object only exist in relationship to each other runs the argument. The objective world only exists in and for intelligence, and intelligence can only realize itself in relation to an objective world. Kant correctly described intelligence as a synthesizing and unifying activity but failed to recognize that self-consciousness actually embraces and transcends the distinction between phenomena and noumena. There is a real correlation between the intelligible structure with which the mind organizes experience and the very nature of reality. In short, being as such is an energy of mind, that is, a spiritual or ideal activity as opposed to dead matter.[24]

Since human self-consciousness is fragmentary, incomplete, and dependent, Morris introduces the notion of an absolute and eternal self-consciousness as the "omnipresent ground and creative source" of individual human consciousness. This "Universal and Absolute Self" is identified with God. It constitutes the organic unity of the world comprehending the unity of subject and object, spirit and matter, divine and human, ideal and real, universal and particular. "The Spiritualistic Idealist holds," writes Morris, ". . . that the universe is an organism of Mind, of activities whose ultimate origin is in Will, of purposes whose explanation is Intelligence, of laws and of orders whose reason is the Good. . . . It is the Catholic doctrine of philosophy."[25] At least initially, Morris convinced Dewey that this idealist doctrine may be scientifically defended, and Dewey embraced it with enthusiasm.

Dewey recalls that Morris had a deep appreciation of the beautiful, especially as manifested in music and poetry, and that his philosophy was expressive of his aesthetic feelings. Plato's writings had strong appeal to Morris in this regard, and Dewey comments that Morris' delight in "the beauty of spirit, the beauty of the eternal idea manifesting itself in outward form ... made his idealism poetic as well as philosophic."[26] Young Dewey was looking for an inspiring vision of reality that fused *eros* and intellect—that integrated his deeper longings and aesthetic intuitions with his philosophic understanding. Working with Morris he found it.

In the neo-Hegelian vision of the nature and destiny of humanity there is no dualism of God and human nature. Indeed, the theme of the unity of God and humanity lies at the core of neo-Hegelian ethical and religious teaching. The development of individual human consciousness is viewed as a process whereby the individual participates in and reproduces the universal and absolute mind of God, which "consists in an eternal and ever-complete process of self-actualization."[27] The ethical life according to Morris is concerned with a process of growth in and through which a person realizes the ideal or universal self by identifying his or her will with the will of God. The challenge of the ethical life is to rise above what is purely individual, finite, and transitory and to identify one's self with the common good, the essential life of the whole—what is universal and absolute.

In explaining the process of ethical self-realization, a strong existentialist theme emerges in Morris' ethics, and it found a permanent place in Dewey's thought. Like Coleridge and Marsh, Morris conceives the essence of human nature to be spirit, that is, self-conscious intelligence and free will. Human nature is perfected only in and through the exercise of the power of self-determination. Morris writes: "A spirit is not made; it is self-made. It realizes itself. Self-determination is the universal form of all spiritual activity." "In other words, the true and perfect being of man is dependent on his *doing* .... By his own self-conscious, self-determining, purposeful activity, he must redeem and realize the divine possibility that resides in him. In order to be himself, he must create himself."[28]

For Morris knowledge is essential to virtue. In order to choose and to do the good that leads to self-realization and perfection, a spiritual being must first know it. More specifically, self-realization requires a knowledge of the Absolute and of the organic relation of the human spirit and divine spirit and also an appreciation of the material and mechanical as the "instrumental or necessary means" of the realization of spirit. However, Morris asserts that the "truths of *life*—the truths of man's perfect being—can only be, in any proper and adequate sense, known, as they are actually lived." A sound spiritual knowledge of God and the law of perfection must be "founded in and must be confirmed by experience—taking this latter term in its truest and original sense, as denoting, not a mere passive reception of impressions, but an active 'testing,' 'trying,' or 'finding out,' ..."[29] The best guidance in this process of knowing by doing is found in the Biblical account of the life and teachings of Jesus and also in the ethical writings of Plato and Aristotle. Morris's teachings on the experimental nature of ethical understanding contributed to Dewey's efforts to overcome the Kantian dualism between scientific methods of knowledge and practical reason.

Morris, who teaches that "the body is the necessary mechanical basis and instrumental condition of man's spiritual self-realization," rejects otherworldliness and a "mystic quietism and asceticism." "The 'universal self' of man is not an abstraction, but, like all true universals, a power to realize itself in and through the materials of particular circumstances and opportunities," asserts Morris. "Far from being privileged to withdraw himself from the world's work, the 'perfect man' realizes that it is only through him that the world's work can be truly done." The task of the universal man or woman is to make "heaven and the will of God to reign on earth." Those who approach their responsibilities in this spirit turn "the world's life and work into a sacrament."[30] In this very practical Hegelian way, Morris showed Dewey how to overcome the dualism of God and the world, the spiritual and the material, the sacred and the secular.

Dewey believed that Morris lived the ethics that he taught. He was a man who sought to find and realize himself in and through his social relations with others.

> At one with himself, having no conflicts of his own nature to absorb him, he found the substance of his being in his vital connections with others; in the home, in his friendships, in the political organization of society, in his church relations. It was his thorough realization in himself of the meaning of these relationships that gave substance and body to his theory of the organic unity of man with nature and with God.[31]

In this same vein Dewey spoke of Morris' "gentle courtesy in which respect for others and for himself were so exquisitely blended." "He was kindness itself in all human relations. He was gentleness in person—a gentleness which never suggested weakness."[32] In 1889 he closed his tribute to Morris with the words of another unidentified admirer of Morris, words that reflected the completeness and depth of spiritual maturity Dewey sensed in his teacher: "There was nothing which he held as his own; he had made the great renunciation."[33] In a statement issued by the Philosophical Society of the University of Michigan at the time of Morris' death and signed by a student and three faculty members (including Dewey, who probably wrote it), it is stated: "To us he seemed near his own ideal of manhood—to be 'living truth.' In him the intellect and the moral character were at one.... Philosophy called out the services of his intellect and the devotion of his heart, because he saw in it a means of rising from self to that other Self who is God, of whom all knowledge, all experience, all history, were the revelations."[34]

It is Morris' view that philosophy and religion—especially the Christian religion—are closely interrelated. Following Hegel, he argues that all religions and philosophies are expressions of different stages of development in humanity's attempt to attain full self-consciousness and to achieve a knowledge of God, the world, and human nature and their interrelationship. Philosophy and religion have the same object, and "true religion and true philosophy agree." Morris summarizes the difference between religion and philosophy as follows: "Religion involves the living and practicing of that which philosophy, as such, only contemplates and endeavors, with cool and unbiased judgment, to understand." Religion is "a practical expression of the truth in one's whole, and actual, and living being." "Religion is organic unity with God—in heart, in will, in conscious thought, and in life." However, following Hegel, Morris asserts that religious faith is only "inexplicit" or "abbreviated knowledge," and philosophy "comprehends" and makes explicit that which religion only "apprehends" and presupposes. In short, philosophy is a scientific demonstration and justificatioñ of the ideas or beliefs which are involved in religious faith and symbolically expressed in religious creeds, rites, and ceremonies. For example, Morris finds the Christian doctrine of the Trinity to be a symbolic rendering of the dialectical process of the divine life which involves separation and reunion, opposition and synthesis. Both a philosophical or theoretical understanding of the truth and a religious or practical living of the truth are "functions" necessary to the perfect life of the whole person.[35]

In his rationalizing of Christianity in neo-Hegelian fashion, Morris goes beyond Coleridge and Marsh. He identifies the essence of Christianity with a philosophical knowledge of the unity of God and humanity rather than with an historical event in and through which the disunity of God and humanity is overcome. In short, he abandons the Augustinian and Reformation doctrines of original sin and of Christ as a supernatural savior. For Morris there is nothing inherently evil about the realm of the flesh, and spirit requires the material and mechanical in order to realize its divine possibilities. Nevertheless, there can be a wrong relation between spirit and nature. Like Marsh, he understands domination of the spirit by natural impulses and desires to be a state of bondage and sin. However, unlike the Vermont Transcendentalists Morris believes that human beings have the capacity to free themselves from this state of affairs apart from a miraculous divine intervention and atonement. Jesus' life and death possess saving power because his words and example awaken men and women to their essential unity with God and to their true destiny as spiritual beings, which if they would but recognize they can realize with God's ever-present aid through the power of self-determination.[36]

Dewey summarizes Morris's reconciliation of religion and philosophy as follows:

> It was characteristic of Professor Morris that the two writings from which he most often quoted were the Dialogues of Plato and the Gospel of St. John. In the fundamental principle of Christianity, he found manifested the truth which he was convinced of as the fundamental truth in philosophy—the unity of God and man so that the spirit which is in man, rather which is man, is the spirit of God. "The very sense of philosophical idealism," he says in one of his works, "is to put and represent man in direct relation with the Absolute Mind so that its light is his light and its strength is made his." The firmness with which he held this truth is the key to all his thinking.

What made Morris "so complete a man and his life so integral" to Dewey was that he seemed to have perfectly harmonized profound thought and deepest faith, philosophy and Christianity, intelligence and moral and religious will.

> He was preeminently a man in whom those internal divisions, which eat into the heart of so much of contemporary spiritual life, and which rob the intellect of its faith in truth, and the will of its belief in the value of life, had been overcome. In the philosophical and religious conviction of the unity of man's spirit with the divine he had that rest which is energy. This wholeness of intelligence and will was the source of the power, the inspiring power of his life.

Dewey further notes that this quality of Morris' character made his students "instinctively realize that there was something real called truth, and this truth was not only capable of being known by man but was the very life of man."[37]

At an especially critical moment in young Dewey's spiritual development, Morris became for him, mentor, and idealized father. Dewey's admiration and devotion were well placed. By all accounts Morris was an exceptional teacher and human being. He showed Dewey genuine affection, and recognizing his student's intellectual gifts, he arranged for Dewey to have a teaching assistantship at Johns Hopkins. In 1884 Morris left Baltimore to become chairman of the

Department of Philosophy at the University of Michigan, and he secured for Dewey there a full-time appointment as an instructor.

Dewey modeled his own early ethical idealism after his teacher's and many important themes in Morris' philosophy had an enduring influence on his thinking. For example, over the years Dewey developed the following ideas prominent in Morris' thought: the method of philosophy should be scientific or experimental; the task of philosophy is to explore the meaning of experience; there is continuity between subject and object; the mind is an active organ; knowing, especially in the area of moral truth, involves doing; hard and fast intellectual dualisms involve misinterpretations of experience and reality; there is no basic dualism of the spiritual and the material; the divine is to be associated with the organic unity of the ideal and the real; the essence of human nature is intelligence and the power of self-determination; a vital philosophy must include expression of the role of aesthetic feeling; the ethical life is as much a matter of self-realization as social responsibility; the religious life concerns wholehearted commitment to the living truth; the supreme moral and religious task is to idealize the world making the material and mechanical instrumental to the spiritual and ideal. During the 1880s Dewey set about developing these ideas in his own way within a neo-Hegelian framework. Morris' teaching on the subject of religion fell in with what Dewey had found most congenial in the thought of Coleridge and Marsh, but it also encouraged Dewey in his efforts to free himself from their idea of original sin.

The first essay in which Dewey's indebtedness to Morris is evident appears in 1884 in the *Journal of Speculative Philosophy* under the title "Kant and Philosophical Method." Like Dewey's Ph.D. thesis, "The Psychology of Kant," it is an attempt to come to terms with Kant's thought, which Dewey regards as "the *crisis,* the separating, dividing, turning point of modern philosophy." In brief, the essay is an endeavor to establish a philosophic method "for discovering Absolute Truth," and the key to such a method Dewey finds in Kant's theory of the categories of human understanding as reconstructed by Hegel in his theory of experience as an organic unity. He seeks to overcome Kant's dualism and subjectivism by introducing the Hegelian notion of reason as unity in difference, the idea of organic unity. "In short, the relation of subject and object is not a 'transcendent' one, but an 'immanent,' and is but the first form in which Reason manifests that it ... separates itself from itself, that it may thereby reach higher unity with itself.... The material which was supposed to confront Reason as foreign to it is but the manifestation of Reason itself." "Whether we consider the relations of subject and object, or the nature of the categories," argues Dewey, "the only conception adequate to experience as a whole is organism." In Hegel's logic he concludes, is found "the completed Method of Philosophy," because "it is an account of the conceptions or categories of Reason which constitute experience, internal and external, subjective and objective, and an account of them as a system, an organic unity in which each has its own place fixed." The completed system of the categories in its organic wholeness is "*the* Truth," for it gives us the form of experience to which all the facts of experience as organic members must conform."[38] Dewey's further philosophical development cannot be fully appreciated without first considering his studies with G. Stanley Hall.

Hall's upbringing and early intellectual development were quite similar to that of Morris, but by the mid-1870s graduate work in philosophy at Harvard with William James, who was far more impressed with Darwin and the new experimental psychology than Hegel, had led him into new intellectual fields unfamiliar to Morris. As a young man Hall had struggled to free himself from the harsher aspects of New England Congregationalism by studying Emerson, Coleridge, Tennyson, Schleiermacher, and Hegel. However, after completing graduate work in Germany and theological training at Union Theological Seminary, his interest in Hegelian idealism as well as the ministry waned. After receiving his Ph.D. from Harvard, he returned to Germany to pursue studies with Helmholtz and Wundt in the new field of physiological psychology and the related areas of child development and education. As a result of this experience Hall finally found a field of research to which he could commit himself.[39]

Hall returned from Germany to America in 1880 with the conviction that philosophy should be thoroughly reconstructed in the light of the new psychology, physiology, and evolutionary biology. He devoted his major efforts, however, to the application of the new psychology to educational theory. Hall had been interested in socialism, but his interests in social change were now channeled into a concern with educational reform. His work in the 1880s established pedagogy as a legitimate field for university instruction, and he was one of the very first Americans to call for the scientific study of child development as the necessary foundation for a sound theory of education. In 1882 Hall's writings and extensive lecturing finally won him an appointment as a lecturer in psychology and pedagogy in the philosophy department at Johns Hopkins. Two years later, in 1884, President Gilman appointed Hall rather than Morris to the one available full professorship in philosophy. Gilman felt Hall was a stronger personality, and he preferred Hall's scientific research and grounding to Morris's concern with the history of philosophy and absolute idealism. It was at this point that Morris returned to the University of Michigan.[40]

Dewey took several courses from Hall, including some experimental laboratory work in physiological psychology, and Hall led him to consider more seriously the significance for philosophy of evolutionary biology as well as functional psychology and to recognize the social importance of pedagogy, the theory of education. Hall warned that Hegel could lead "young men to make a premature 'surrender to the ideal' so unconditionally that the logical faculties will be divorced from reality, that consistency will be more thought of than objective truth" with the result that they will "reason their way up and down the universe ... without acquiring their hard earned experience."[41] From his studies with Hall and such admonitions, Dewey became more conscious of his "inclination toward the schematic and formally logical" and his tendency "to give way to the dialectical development of a theme." Hall helped him to recognize the need to balance this "formal, theoretic interest" with careful attention to "the concrete, empirical and 'practical.' "[42]

By the time Dewey came to study with Hall the latter's religious beliefs had departed in a radical way from the Congregational faith of his youth. He was also very skeptical of any philosophy like absolute idealism that claimed to be a science of sciences and to have comprehended the universe in a final and fixed system of thought.

However, Hall retained a genuine religious interest and sought to reconcile religious experience with natural science. It was Hall's position that there are in human nature certain natural religious "instincts" or "sentiments" such as "reverence, dependence, adoration," and "the desire for purpose and moral order in the cosmos."[43] Consequently, there is naturally a religious aspect of human life and culture. At different stages in the development of the individual and the race the religious instincts express themselves in different ways involving a development from immature to more mature religious beliefs. The crisis of modern religious faith caused by modern scientific discoveries is due to a narrow-minded Biblical literalism and the inability of people to develop mature religious beliefs. If the religious instincts of Americans are to attain maturity and to find adequate expression in a scientific age, it is necessary, according to Hall, first of all "to rescue the higher mythopoeic faculties from the present degradation to which prejudice and crass theories have brought them."[44] Hall finds in religious myths, creeds, and rituals, and especially those of Christianity, important psychological insights into human nature rather than historical accounts which are to be taken as literally true. A mature religious belief recognizes in creeds and rituals symbols of moral and social values.[45] Hall rationalized Christianity by psychologizing it. In all of this he was much influenced by what he described as "the wonderful *Essence of Christianity* by Feuerbach."[46]

Dewey's early enthusiasm for what he was learning from Hall found expression in an essay on "The New Psychology," which he published in the *Andover Review* in 1884. It begins with reference to the intellectual dangers involved in the tendency of the human mind to seek unity, simplicity, fixity, and finality and to ignore complexity and diversity.[47] Dewey finds that earlier English psychology has vastly oversimplified the facts of man's psychical life and has been dominated by mechanical conceptions, the method of subjective introspection, and a purely formal logic. The new psychology in contrast has learned to supplement and correct subjective introspection with the methods of experiment developed by physiology and the methods of observation in the social sciences. In the place of a formal logic it seeks to form all its ideas in the light of "the living, concrete facts of experience." It employs as criterion of the truth "the logic of fact," "the logic of concrete experience, of growth and development." Further, concrete experience discloses that the most appropriate concept for understanding mental life is the biological concept of organism. Dewey also notes that "the idea of environment is a necessity to the idea of organism," and he asserts "the impossibility of considering psychical life as an individual, isolated thing developing in a vacuum."[48]

Dewey finds the new psychology "intensely ethical in its tendencies" because it "emphasizes the teleological element ... regarding life as an organism in which immanent ideas or purposes are realizing themselves through the development of experience." He further argues that ethical ideals are themselves to be formulated in the light of the concrete possibilities and needs of life as revealed in experience. The movement of modern experimental science has caused in some quarters "the perishing of ideals," "decay of enthusiasm," and "a cynical pessimism," but it "was a necessity to bring the Antaeus of humanity back to the mother soil of experience, whence it derives its strength and very life, and to prevent it from losing itself in a substanceless vapor where its ideals and purposes become as thin and watery as the clouds towards which it aspires." In these words Dewey sees the ideal as intimately interrelated with, or rooted in, the concrete, the actual, rather than as something purely formal or otherworldly which is externally and arbitrarily imposed on the actual.[49] Over time he developed this into a major theme in his theory of the origin and nature of authentic moral ideals.

Following Hall, Dewey also writes that the new psychology makes "possible for the first time an adequate psychology of man's religious nature and experience." As it "goes into the depths of man's religious nature it finds, as stone of its foundation, blood of its life, the instinctive tendencies of devotion, sacrifice, faith, and idealism which are the eternal substructure of all the struggles of the nations upon the altar stairs which slope up to God."[50] Dewey's reference to "the altar stairs which slope up to God" is borrowed from Hall's favorite poem, Tennyson's "In Memoriam," and this statement by Dewey shows the influence of Hall's theory of the religious instincts and faith.[51] In 1930, Dewey is found declaring a "faith in the depth of the religious tendencies of men."[52] Jane Dewey has commented that he acquired "the belief that a religious attitude was indigenous in natural experience" from Alice Chipman.[53] Alice may have encouraged this belief in Dewey, but as early as 1883 Hall was teaching him that even the evolutionary naturalist and experimental psychologist has to recognize that there is an instinctive religious tendency in all human beings. It was also Hall's conviction that the religious tendencies of modern men and women could best be freed and developed toward maturity if they would adopt the habits of thinking involved in the new science and would abandon religious beliefs that explicitly conflict with the conclusions of this science. This fit in with what Dewey had learned about the reconciliation of faith and reason from Coleridge, Marsh, and Morris, and he adopted this approach as a graduate student. However, it would be at least another fifteen years before he had settled in his own mind just what a philosophy consistent with science should teach about the nature and reality of God. It would take Dewey much longer to clarify fully his own naturalistic theory of the religious dimension of experience. It is, nevertheless, noteworthy that Dewey began the task of trying to develop an empirical and naturalistic theory of religious experience at the outset of his career.

In time Hall's biological, psychological, and sociological interpretations of experience would lead Dewey to William James and cause him to question Hegelian metaphysics. However, at Johns Hopkins, Hall's concept of experience was sufficiently organic and his theory of religion and his personal idealism were both positive enough and vague enough to permit Dewey to speculate and believe that there was no real conflict between Hall's experimentalism and new psychology and Morris's "experimental" philosophical idealism. Between the years 1883 and 1887 when Dewey published his first book, entitled *Psychology*, the intellectual task that most excited and challenged him was the fusion of the new psychology and philosophical idealism.

The Fusion of Philosophy and Psychology

In much of his very early writing Dewey is primarily concerned with a method with which philosophy can discover absolute truth and show that the absolute truth is an organic system. Following Morris, he argues that philosophy must be experimental and scientific, that is, start with the facts of experience and have as its sole goal a knowledge or science of the nature and meaning of experience. In short, Dewey aspires to establish a science of the absolute truth and organic unity of experience, which as an absolute idealist he believes is also the absolute truth of objective reality. Thereby he intends to achieve a perfect reconciliation of science and philosophy and also science and religion. In two essays published in the English journal *Mind* and entitled "The Psychological Standpoint" (1885) and "Psychology as Philosophic Method" (1886), Dewey adds a new dimension to his thinking on this subject. He argues that the key to perfecting the neo-Hegelian theory of the science of absolute truth is to be found in the recognition that the task and method of a sound philosophy are identical with the task and method of the science of psychology. The relation of philosophy and psychology was a matter of considerable discussion in the early 1880s among the British neo-Hegelians, and Dewey's arguments in defense of this position are his first attempt at original philosophical thinking. In arguing in favor of completely identifying philosophy with psychology, Dewey went beyond anything he had learned from Morris and took issue with the British neo-Hegelians, and in trying to make psychology into a method of absolute truth which confirms the Hegelian concept of experience, Dewey adopted a position opposed by Hall as well as William James.

In his attempt to fuse the new psychology and absolute idealism, Dewey follows Morris in arguing that despite all the inadequacies of British empiricism, Locke after all does start with the right approach when he takes the position, as Dewey puts it, that "nothing shall be admitted into philosophy which does not show itself in experience." This approach Dewey calls "the *psychological* standpoint"—a phrase used by T.H. Green with reference to the approach of British empiricism. The psychological standpoint as originally formulated by Locke keeps philosophy on "positive scientific ground" argues Dewey. It means simply that the task of philosophy is nothing more nor less than to give an account of the nature and meaning of experience as a whole and of its parts and their relations.[54]

Conscious experience, self-consciousness, is "the ultimate fact," "the whole fact" with which a scientific philosophy is or ever can be concerned. Philosophy cannot explain how or why experience comes to be, because it is "the fact for which no reason can be given except precisely just that it is what it is." "How experience became we shall never find out, for the reason that experience always is. We shall never account for it by referring it to something else, for 'something else' always is only for and in experience. *Why* it is, we shall never discover, for it is a whole." Conscious experience is, then, the absolute, the unconditioned whole, in and for which all things are. Philosophy's task is to explain how and why the various elements of experience beginning with subject and object come to be by explaining them with reference to each other and to the whole. This understanding of the task of philosophy is correctly called the psychological standpoint, reasons Dewey, because psychology is itself the science of conscious experience. The problem with Locke and his followers is that they quickly abandon the psychological standpoint by arbitrarily making the unwarranted ontological assumption that there is some thing-in-itself outside of and opposed to conscious experience. As a result they have given psychology as philosophy a bad name. T.H. Green and the neo-Hegelians are correct in rejecting British psychology as philosophy even though wrong in rejecting a true psychology as philosophy.[55]

In the endeavor to defend a rigid adherence to the psychological standpoint, Dewey is led to posit a universal consciousness. He does not deny that individual consciousness is a transitory event that is dependent upon and conditioned by other existences prior to and outside itself such as the nervous system of the human being, objects which affect this nervous system, and a whole series of past events described by evolutionary theory. Like Morris he goes on to argue, however, that all the things with which a thinker accounts for the origin and functioning of individual consciousness are things known, that is, things existing in and for consciousness. He then proceeds to draw the very debatable conclusion that consciousness as such is thereby revealed to be something in and for which all things exist and that it, therefore, can never itself have come to be or pass away. The consciousness of particular individuals is relative and its origin can be explained, but consciousness as such is eternal and absolute. In this manner Dewey asserts the existence of a universal consciousness, and argues that "individual consciousness is but the process of realization of the universal consciousness through itself." It is "the universal nature of individual consciousness" which English empiricism overlooks, according to Dewey, leading inevitably to the abandonment of the psychological standpoint.[56]

Dewey also rejects Edward Caird's distinction between psychology as the science of the modes by which the absolute is realized in human experience, and philosophy as the science of the absolute itself. The absolute cannot be conceived as existing complete in itself totally separate from its "realization and manifestation in a being like man," argues Dewey, because if it is in fact complete in itself there would be no reason for it to go beyond itself to manifest itself in a temporal process of becoming in humanity. "The absolute self-consciousness must involve within itself, as organic member of its very being and activity, this manifestation and revelation. Its being must be this realization and manifestation." Dewey's point is that the universal is only realized in and by an individual. "The universe except as realized in an individual, has no existence. . . . Self-consciousness means simply an individualized universe." In short, Dewey identifies the reality of God with God's realization "in a being like man" and rejects any notion that God is an eternal static being existing wholly apart from the world of time, process, and becoming. However, Dewey is careful to avoid asserting that the realization and manifestation of God occurs *in* time, as a time-conditioned product. Time is a form within the absolute itself, "one of its organic functions by which it organically constitutes its own being."[57]

It is also noteworthy that Dewey does not completely identify the reality of God with the manifestation of the universal in individual human beings. God himself remains for Dewey in some undefined sense an individual center of self-consciousness distinct from all other individuals in whom his being is realized and revealed. He asserts that in humanity the universal consciousness "is partially realized, and man has a partial science; in the absolute it is completely realized, and God has a complete science." The eternal absolute consciousness is to be conceived as "for ever realized, yet as for ever having time as one of its functions," states Dewey. He does not explain exactly in what sense God is "eternally completed," "for ever realized." There is a tension here between theism and pantheism in Dewey's thought that is evident in all his idealist theology.[58]

However, despite the lack of clarity on the question of the individuality of God, Dewey rests satisfied that he has justified his identification of philosophy and psychology: "If the material of philosophy be the absolute self-consciousness, and this absolute self-consciousness is the realization and manifestation of itself, and as material for philosophy exists only insofar as it has realized and manifested itself in man's conscious experience, and if psychology be the science of this realization in man, what else can philosophy in its fullness be but psychology, and psychology but philosophy?"[59] Since philosophy as psychology is an account of the unconditioned unity of experience which constitutes the absolute, Dewey argues that it constitutes not just one among the many sciences but "Science." Philosophy in other words seeks to apprehend the whole of which each of the special sciences is an organic member. Philosophical truth is "the organic living unity of the sciences."[60] At least one philosopher, Shadworth Hodgson, in England, challenged Dewey in his attempt to identify philosophy and psychology, but despite the criticism and the lack of support from Hall Dewey persisted.[61]

The effort to fuse philosophy and the new psychology reveals an important characteristic of young Dewey. From the beginning of his career as a philosopher the "experimentalist," in the general sense of one who trusts experience as the best guide of intelligence in its search for the true and the good, is present in his personality alongside the "absolutist," who craves intellectual certainty, eternal truth, finality, and all-embracing organic unity. Encouraged and instructed by Hall, Dewey took Morris's rhetoric about scientific experimentalism in philosophy more seriously than Morris himself. The result was that an uneasy tension develops in his thought between a respect for the findings of the new observational and experimental methods of scientific investigation and his absolutism and rationalism. However, during the 1880s the absolutist is stronger in him than the experimentalist, and young Dewey trusts experience in the firm conviction that intelligence reflecting on experience will discover beyond all dualisms the organic unity of reason and reality, the divine and the human, the ideal and the actual. Morris and the British neo-Hegelians, especially T.H. Green, for whom Dewey expressed in 1886 a "deep, almost reverential gratitude,"[62] remain the dominant philosophical influence until well after Morris's death in 1889.

The Psychology

Until 1889, when Dewey became chairman of the Department of Philosophy, his teaching at the University of Michigan was divided about evenly between courses that emphasize various aspects of psychology and courses in philosophical subject matters like formal logic, Plato's *Republic,* Aristotle, Kant's *Critique of Pure Reason,* Kant's ethics, and Herbert Spencer.[63] Given his beliefs about the identity of the method of philosophy and the method of psychology, Dewey, of course, viewed his courses in philosophy and psychology as intimately related. Indeed, much of his energy during the years 1885 and 1886 was devoted to writing a psychology text book which has the dual purpose of presenting the findings of the new scientific psychology and of providing an introduction to philosophy that will "above all ...develop the philosophic spirit."[64] Dewey tries to achieve this twofold objective by organizing his scientific data with "the greatest possible unity of principle."[65] Toward this end the *Psychology* incorporates the research of the new psychology into a neo-Hegelian theory of self-realization, that is, a theory of how human personality develops and is perfected in and through identification with the absolute or perfect personality of God.

Just prior to writing the *Psychology,* Dewey prepared an essay entitled "Soul and Body" (1886), in which he employs certain findings of the new psychology to support philosophical arguments against any radical dualism of the spiritual and material in human personality. It is Dewey's argument in "Soul and Body" that the concept of a soul that is both immanent in and transcendent to the body is a necessary principle of intelligibility for interpreting the activities of the human mind and certain teleological activities of the human nervous system. Even though certain mental events occur only on the occasion of a physical event, human consciousness cannot be explained in mechanical and physical terms. Where there is evidence of purpose, action for an end, there is at work a factor transcending the purely physical and material, argues Dewey. "The soul," he explains, "is a living acting force which has formed and is constantly forming the body as its mechanism," and the body is "the outward form and living manifestation of the soul." In conclusion Dewey cites passages from Aristotle's *De Anima,* the Gospel of John, the Pauline Epistles, and the Apostles' Creed in an attempt to show that they all agree with the new psychology in asserting an intimate relationship between soul and body, spiritual and material.[66]

Dewey's *Psychology* endeavors to set forth the latest findings of "the Science of the Facts or Phenomena of Self." Since the fundamental characteristic of the self is consciousness, psychology may also be called the science of consciousness. The way Dewey sets out to investigate, classify, and explain the facts of self or consciousness, however, is based on a particular idealist assumption as to what constitutes the essential nature of the self. It is his conviction that the self or consciousness is essentially a self-determining teleological activity. Understood as activity directed toward the attainment of an end—a purposeful activity—the essence of the self may be called will. The goal of the will, or the end of the activity which constitutes the self, is the perfection of itself. The self, in short, is a process of self-realization. Personality is another term Dewey uses to refer to the essence of the self so understood. The human being is a person, a self, a center of self-determining will—what Coleridge, Marsh, and Morris call a spirit.

At birth the human self is "a bare form, an empty ideal without content" and its life is a process of giving this form a definite content, that is, of actualizing or realizing itself. In Aristotelian language the ideal self is the formal and final cause of the natural human organism. The process of realizing the self, which in "Soul and Body" Dewey describes in Pauline language as a transformation of a natural body into a spiritual body, he in the *Psychology* calls a process of idealization. Insofar as the self does actualize its ideal self, it attains happiness or fulfillment. All the activities which go to make up consciousness are to be understood then, in terms of a process whereby the actual self identifies itself with, realizes and finds itself in the ideal self.[67]

The task of the *Psychology* is to explain the nature of this process of self-realization and unification of ideal and actual by studying the various aspects of developing human consciousness. Dewey begins by observing that every state of consciousness involves knowledge, feeling, and will. It provides awareness of and information about some object; it expresses in and through feeling the quality of value that this awareness has for the self; and it is the expression of a volition, a purposeful activity. He also points out that within all states of consciousness a distinction can be made between subject and object and between an individual element and a universal element, which he associates closely with feeling and knowledge. The will, which is the essence of the self, he contends, is a principle of organic unity which perfects itself by interrelating subject and object, the individual and the universal. With these considerations in mind Dewey divides the *Psychology* into three major parts on knowledge, feeling, and will in that order. He explores the process of self-realization by studying the way in which each of these aspects of consciousness contributes to the unification of the actual self with the ideal self and to an overcoming of the separation of subject and object, individual and universal.

In the section on knowledge he analyzes the various stages of the process in and through which the mind of the individual knowing subject relates itself to the world of objective reality and reproduces in itself the absolute truth which constitutes the universal mind. He then analyzes the role of feeling in the process of idealization and unification with special emphasis on the love of knowledge, beauty, persons, and the absolute ideal. In the section on will he studies the way in which knowledge and feeling are interrelated by will as it develops the power of self-determination in the areas of moral and religious experience culminating in the perfection of the self through identification with what is absolute in truth, beauty, goodness, and being. Following Plato's *Republic,* Dewey conceives the ideal self, then, as an absolute reality that embraces the true, the good, and the beautiful. In the spirit of Morris's theism he further identifies this absolute with God and conceives of the unification of the actual self with the ideal self as an identification of the individual person with the perfect personality of God and as a reproduction of the divine in the human. In other words, the *Psychology* is a study of the way in which the self finds its true self and union with the divine in and through science, philosophy, art, social relations, and religion.

Such is the general structure of the *Psychology*. Its 360 pages contain an extraordinary mass of detailed information derived from the findings of German, British, and American psychologists and philosophers including Wilhelm Wundt, Hermann Lotze, Hermann von Helmholtz, Johann Herbart, Alexander Bain, Herbert Spencer, James Sully, William James, and G. Stanley Hall as well as many others. However, all this material is organized in the light of Dewey's basic philosophical convictions as an ethical idealist, and it clearly manifests the religious concern of the author. Indeed, the book is young Dewey's major defense of the world view of ethical idealism, which he learned from Coleridge, Marsh, Morris, and T.H. Green.

Shortly after finishing his *Psychology,* Dewey argues that "it is not what comes before the formulation of a theory which proves it, it is not the facts which suggest it, or the processes which lead up to it: it is what comes from the formation of the theory,—the uses it can be put to; the facts which it will render significant." Applying this experimental and pragmatic approach to the basic hypothesis of spiritualistic idealism, Dewey further contends that "the truest witness to the spiritual character of reality is found in the capacity of this principle to comprehend and explain the facts of experience. With this conception, the reason of things can be ascertained, and light introduced into what were otherwise a confused obscurity."[68] For Dewey, then, the justification of his method of using neo-Hegelian categories to organize the material of the new psychology is to be found in the success a thinker has in comprehending the phenomena of consciousness by use of them. As he asserts in the *Psychology,* "there is no such thing as pure observation in the sense of a fact being known without assimilation and interpretation through ideas already in mind."[69]

Some psychologists and philosophers were impressed by Dewey's attempt to fuse idealism and the new psychology, but others were very skeptical. Morris warmly praised the book stating: "More than any other book of the kind in English that I have ever read it is a real contribution to self-knowledge."[70] Dewey must also have been pleased by the fact that eight major colleges and universities adopted the book as a course text.[71] However, Hall and James were very critical of the way Dewey had imposed his neo-Hegelian categories on the findings of the new psychology.[72] They were not convinced that idealism does provide the best explanation of the facts. Reading the book is tough going and in some of the sections where he discusses the deeper relationship between the Absolute and the individual human psyche his meaning is obscure. One can imagine the difficulties students had with it. Nevertheless, the *Psychology* contains an impressive intellectual vision, which it is necessary to appreciate if one wishes to understand the origins of Dewey's psychological, moral, and religious thought.

Moral and Religious Will

Dewey's neo-Hegelian theory of self-realization in the *Psychology* culminates with a theory of moral and religious will that endeavors to explain how the self completes the process of unifying the ideal and the actual, the divine and the human. This discussion takes one to the heart of Dewey's early philosophy of religion, which includes a theory of religious feeling. Preceding his consideration of moral and religious experience, he also sets forth a theory of the knowledge of God, which he distinguishes from the final unification of the self with God achieved by religious will, or faith. It is helpful to begin this further exploration of Dewey's idealist theory of self-realization with a few comments regarding his understanding of the way in which the process of knowing contributes to the growth of the self and union with the divine.

Dewey explains how, through the processes of sensation, perception, memory, imagination, conception, judgment, and reasoning (culminating in science and philosophy), a knowledge of the objective world as a universe, an organic unity, is realized. He is careful to point out, however, that "all knowledge is . . . of an individual" and that the goal of science and philosophy is "to reach an individual object of knowledge which is at the same time thoroughly universal." Dewey is not a Platonist who believes that universals exist in an ideal world of pure being separate from the world of particulars and concrete fact. He is an Aristotelian and an Hegelian for whom the real world is the world of particular things and for whom the significance of universals is that they constitute the relations and intelligible meaning of particulars, of facts. Assuming that the world is an organic unity, and every fact is interrelated with every other, the goal of knowledge is not just to contemplate an abstract system of relations, but "to see exemplified in any fact the relations of the whole system." "A completely universalized or related individual, which is at the same time perfectly definite or distinct in all its relations, is, therefore, the end of knowledge."[73] Dewey's notion of a universalized individual is very similar to Leibniz's idea of a monad, and after finishing the *Psychology,* Dewey went to work on a book that tries to show that Leibniz's philosophy anticipates much that is best in the German philosophical movement from Kant to Hegel.

In and through the process of developing a knowledge of the objective world, the self as the knowing subject develops its own intellectual or idealizing powers leading to a knowledge of itself as a universal idealizing activity. Dewey explains that "when we perceive the world as an interdependent whole, every part of which is in orderly connection with every other, we are perceiving objectified intelligence." Furthermore, the self is manifestly a universal permanent activity, that is, a universal mind, reasons Dewey, because knowledge involves construction by the mind of a universe common to all minds, a permanent objective reality.[74]

This knowledge of the world as an organic unity, and of the self as a universal idealizing activity, leads to a knowledge of the interrelationship of intelligence and the world, which is a knowledge of God, asserts Dewey. God is the reality of the organic interconnection between intelligence and the world. The apprehension of the organic unity of self and world, ideal and real, involves knowing God. Dewey calls the knowledge of God an intuition, but he does not mean by intuition in this context either an emotional realization or a direct intellectual perception. He reserves the word intuition in the *Psychology* for acts of knowledge of ultimate wholes, explaining that "in the act of intuition we grasp that which is self-related" by apprehending the relations which constitute the being of such entities. It is his argument that "the true self-related must be the organic unity of the self and the world, of the ideal and the real, and this is what we know as God."[75]

The idea of God as the organic unity of the ideal and the real is the foundation upon which all science and philosophy ultimately rest in Dewey's idealist system. It asserts the ultimate intelligibility and rationality of the world. It justifies a faith in intelligence. It guarantees the meaningfulness of all meanings. As Dewey explains it: "Since reality is, and is what it is, through intelligence, whatever relations intelligence rightly perceives are not 'extraneous' to reality, but are its essence."[76] The idea of God provides Dewey's objective idealism its epistemological defense against Hume's skepticism and Kant's subjectivism. The Absolute is the universal mind engaged in an eternal process of self-objectification, an organic unity of intelligence and the world.

Since God is the principle of the unity of the ideal and the real, every act of knowledge involves at least some intuition of God, for it identifies the ideal and the real. To realize fully all that is implied in the intuition of God as the unity of the ideal and the real is the beginning and the end of all knowledge. All scientific and philosophical knowledge acquires for young Dewey, then, a religious meaning and value. It has the function of "enriching the primal and the ultimate intuition" in and through which the individual reproduces the universal intelligence of God.[77] It is with this in mind that Dewey told a University of Michigan audience in 1889 that "the Spirit of God ... is the intelligence in all men's science."[78] In the same vein, several years later he is found asserting that the divine revelation of the nature of God about which the Bible speaks continues today in the research and discoveries of modern science.[79] In the conclusion of the *Psychology,* however, he notes that due to the limitations of finitude no human being will ever attain a complete knowledge of the Absolute or God.[80]

The endeavor to know God as a scientist or philosopher does not by itself lead to the perfection of the self according to the *Psychology.* The self must also develop itself in and through the realms of art, morality, and religion. Dewey's theory is based on the idea that the process of self-realization always involves the active relation of subject and object, an individual and a universal element. In brief, the self in and through its activities objectifies itself and identifies itself with its object; it projects itself into and finds itself in the object. Dewey states "that without relation to things and to persons the self would not be realized ... realization takes the form of these relations."[81] He divides the realm of things into intellectual and aesthetic objects and the realm of persons into human beings and God. As the self widens its intellectual, aesthetic, social, and religious experience, it progressively identifies itself ever more completely with its true and universal self.

Dewey's theory that the self realizes itself in and through relationship involves a very significant idea of the nature and role of feeling, the emotions, which it is useful to note at this conjuncture before going on to his interpretation of moral and religious experience. In the active process of interrelating subject and object, feeling is the internal subjective aspect of consciousness. Each object has a special significance and value—positive or negative—for experience. It gives experience a certain quality which is expressed in and through feeling. The "qualitative feelings" are the subjective manifestations of the meaning of these different activities and relationships which constitute the life of the self. Dewey divides the qualitative feelings into intellectual, aesthetic, moral, and religious.

In this connection he argues in the *Psychology* that "all natural, healthy feeling" is absorbed in some object or in the end of some activity. Speaking to what he views as a widespread tendency of the time, he warned that it is an unhealthy and dangerous practice to cultivate feelings for their own sake and to use one's relationships simply as a means to the stimulation of the emotions.

> Emotion turned inward eats up itself; and the result is either the assumption of cynicism and the *nil admirari* spirit, or the restless searching for some new thing, the latest sensation, which may stimulate the jaded and worn-out emotional nature. If any one violates the law of his being by living upon his feelings, rather than upon the objects to which those feelings normally belong, his power of feeling becomes gradually exhausted, and he defeats his own end. He commits emotional suicide. There has probably never been a time when this unhealthy employment of feeling was so prevalent as it is now.

> The sole remedy is for the man to get outside of himself by devoting himself to some object, not for the feelings which such devotion will bring him, nor for the sake of getting outside of himself, but for the sake of the object. True feelings, as true knowledge, must be thoroughly objective and universal. There is no contradiction between this statement and the one that feeling is the internal, the subjective side of self, for the true self finds its existence in objects in the universe, not in its own private states. Although it does and must have these private states, it pays attention to them only for the sake of their universal worth. They exist not for their own sake, but as the medium through which the universe makes its significance and value apparent.[82]

It is important to note that in this last sentence Dewey makes it clear that the values registered in and by healthy feeling are not merely subjective phenomena but rather are a realization of values that inhere in the nature of the things that make up the world of objective reality.

About the same time that Dewey was writing the *Psychology,* he delivered a talk before the Students' Christian Association at the University of Michigan on the proper function of religious emotion. He warns against the kind of religious sentimentalism that he had found troublesome in his mother's religion and against any attempt to use religion primarily as a means for stimulating various private states of feeling.

> How many of us are making religion an occasion for the production and observation of spiritual weather in ourselves, and even of regarding God more as a means for affording us certain religious emotions than as a person to whom the reverence and service of our lives is most humbly due? So far as feeling is regarded simply as a state of our own selves, and is interesting to us simply as an experience, as an occasion for remorse on our deadness or for self-gratulation on our quickness, it does more than fail in being religious: it is irreligious; for it keeps us shut up in our poor and paltry being, while the essence of religion is humble self-surrender of our wills to the Divine will. . . . Healthy emotion, whether religious or otherwise, is that which finds no time nor opportunity to dwell upon itself and see how it is getting along; which loses itself in pushing on to the work of the prize of the high calling.[83]

These two quotations demonstrate how Dewey in Ann Arbor would have interpreted the New Testament theme of losing oneself in order to find one's true self. It is also noteworthy that Dewey's emphasis on relations and on the object-oriented nature of healthy feeling form the major reason for his early rejection of hedonist ethical theories which identify the good with pleasure.[84] These concerns are also fundamental to his later preference for a social psychology as opposed to an introspective and individualistic psychology.

It is possible now to turn directly to Dewey's concept of moral and religious will. He states that "volition is impulse consciously directed towards the attainment of a recognized end which is felt as desireable." In short, a volition involves knowledge and feeling. It also frequently requires deliberation and choice, for human beings face conflicting desires and competing ends of action. They must constantly choose between the desires of the private self and the aspirations of an expanding ideal self.[85]

In explaining the relation between the supreme end, full self-realization, and the many particular desires and ends involved in the progressive development of the self toward this final end, Dewey is careful to reject any dualism of means and ends. Stating a position that becomes fundamental to his ethical thinking, he argues that, properly understood, true means are the end analyzed into its constituent factors, rather than elements which are only externally and mechanically related to the desired end. Those desires, objectives, and acts which contribute to the positive growth of the self are the means to full self-realization: "this self-realization is not a last term over and beyond the means, but is only the organized harmonious system of the means. It is the means taken in their wholeness."[86] The goal of the will is to harmonize all the various intellectual, aesthetic, moral, and religious ends of action forming an integrated personality, that realizes the authentic ideal. The ideal self, or God, is a principle of organic unity, and the activities of the will are the process in and through which this harmony is imaginatively set up as the ideal and then actualized.

In order to achieve this goal, the will must achieve self-control culminating in the power of self-determination. The will first develops control over the physical impulses and the body. It next learns how to direct its desires and activities so that the results of its actions are advantageous or beneficial to the self. The will becomes worldly-wise in its behavior. It learns how to acquire knowledge, protect itself, enjoy itself, and create beauty. It is, however, only when the will enters the sphere of moral awareness and action that it is finally able to realize the power of full self-determination. A moral action is one that directly affects the inner core of a person's being, the will itself, what a person is as distinct from what a person has. Further, the only matter which affects the inner being of a person is the intention of the person, the motive of the action as distinct from the result, which is a matter external to the self. Since the motive of any action performed by a person is under the control of the will, human beings have the power of self-determination in matters affecting their being. Dewey concedes that the content of what different persons consider good and bad will vary according to their education and surroundings, but only the will of each individual determines whether the form of their moral choices is the good or the bad. He writes that "we reach here an ultimate fact in the psychological constitution of man. *He has the power of determining himself.* He has the power of setting up an ideal of what he would have himself be, and this ideal in form depends only upon himself. . . . In moral matters a man *is* what he would have himself be. The will to be good is the being good."[87]

In Dewey's theory of will, the spring to action is the impulsive force of desire or love, and in his moral theory he puts special emphasis on the role of love of persons or sympathy. Sympathy takes the self beyond the intellectual realm of meanings (relations between objects) and aesthetic enjoyment of ideal values into a larger universe —the social world of personal relations. Sympathy involves identification with and active interest in other persons, and it develops naturally in human beings due to "the essential unity of human nature." Through identification with and interest in others the self deepens its own consciousness of its own nature. In its active relations with the human community the self finds its real self, "a self more comprehensive, more permanent" than its "private and particular being." Dewey is careful to point out that the practice of sympathy properly understood does not mean the loss of distinct individuality.

On the contrary, "growth in individuality is a necessary accompaniment of growth in universality." The universal person is the complete individual.[88]

As a neo-Hegelian, Dewey sees social institutions as an objective manifestation of the universal self, of moral reason, of intelligence guided by sympathy: "Personal feeling can find its goal only in relations to persons, which are permanent and universal; and all that we call society, state, and humanity are the realization of these permanent and universal relations of persons which are based upon active sympathy." Love in the form of sympathy is the real bond holding society together rather than law or physical force.

> Psychologically, the bond of union in society and the state is not law in a legal or judicial sense; much less force. It is love. Sympathy is the bond of union between men; it is to the social sphere what gravitation is to the physical. It is the expression of the spiritual unity of mankind. While it may, in its undeveloped condition, be confined, it is always widening to reach more men, and deepening to include more fundamental relations between men. It constitutes society an organic whole, a whole permeated by a common life, where each individual still lives his own distinct life unabsorbed in that of the community.[89]

Furthermore, insofar as a society is an authentic community held together by love or sympathy, it is a manifestation of the life of God who is the universal self. The very being of God is expressed in the social order.

Along with the experience of sympathy there develops what Dewey calls the moral feelings: the sense of rightness, the feeling of reverence for the moral ideal, the feeling of unconditional obligation to do what is right, and the feeling of remorse or guilt for failing to actualize the ideal. The feeling of the rightness of an act is "the feeling of the harmony existing between an act of a person and the ideal personality." "Reverence is the feeling that the object towards which it [the self] is directed is completely universal, realizing in itself the wills of all men, and hence is entirely 'right' or perfect, combined with the feeling that this personality is not foreign to our nature, but is its true being, and hence is an absolute obligation." The ground of absolute obligation in this idealist system is the eternal and infinite value of human personality, that is, the identity of the divine and the human.

Building on his theory of moral feeling Dewey sets forth an intuition-alist theory of conscience and practical reason. Conscience is the feeling of rightness and of obligation made explicit in consciousness in the form of moral judgments. A person's "moral sense" develops as his or her personality grows and matures. Formulations of the moral law are developed by rational reflection on the principles underlying "the spontaneous and intuitive declarations of feeling."[90]

Following Kant, Hegel, and the American Transcendentalists, Dewey's ethics rejects any notion that the moral law is arbitrarily imposed on human beings by an external deity. The moral law is derived from intuitions of the essential nature of humanity. He adds that "the moral individual does not live to realize moral laws, but to realize himself, and what are termed moral laws are those modes of action which are observed to be harmoniously related to such reali-zation."[91] Thus did Dewey reconcile for himself the demands of his own personality for realization and the demands of the moral law. Furthermore, as an idealist who subscribes to the ultimate identity of the divine and the human, he believes that the law of individual self-realization is also the law of social well-being. The end of self-realization is the full development of personality, and to become a person means treating all other persons as persons, or in the language of Kant's categorical imperative treating other persons as ends in themselves and never as a means only. In other words, self-realization involves becoming a person in a community of persons in which development of personality is the supreme value. As the universal self and the perfect personality, God is the principle of harmony in society.

The discussion of moral feeling and the moral law concludes with these words: "The heart of the moral life lies in the free personal determination of right and wrong. No set of rules can take the place of this personal determination without destroying the vital springs of morals."[92] In other words, what concerns Dewey is not just that the moral law be intelligently derived from a sound understanding of human nature, and all persons be made to conform to it, but, more importantly, that each individual be given the freedom and responsi-bility to find the true law for himself or herself. It is Dewey's conviction that in no other way can a person attain self-realization and actualize the divine possibilities in human nature. This, not external conformity to law, is the true ethical ideal. Dewey thus ends with an emphasis shared by the early Platonic dialogues—in the final analysis one must look to the attractive power of the ideal and love and to intelligent choice to make human beings good. As he put it in 1888: "The ideal is already at work in every personality, and must be trusted to care for itself."[93] To do otherwise is to stifle the natural and spontaneous growth of a person and thus to show disrespect for personality, which is "the one thing of permanent and abiding worth."[94] Furthermore, "love is the only motive which can be relied upon for efficient and sure action."[95] This trust in the passion for growth and for the ideal and this concern for individual self-determination and responsibility became for Dewey fundamental guiding principles in his general approach to education as well as social philosophy.

Dewey points out that moral will and the moral life are not able to overcome completely the dualism between the ideal and the actual in either the self or in the world. First of all, the moral will cannot of its own efforts perfect the self. In making this point he does not introduce a Pauline Augustinian notion of the bondage of the will to a power of evil. Rather he defines moral experience as necessarily partial and incomplete. The activity of the moral will does not establish the unity of the ideal and the actual in a permanent and final fashion. It does establish the will as one with the ideal in each case when a good choice is made. However, even though repeated sound moral behavior builds strong character, it cannot guarantee the perfection of the will in the future. Some conflict between good and bad desires, the private self and the universal self, will continue, and deliberation and choice remain necessary.[96] Second, the moral will can only establish that the ideal ought to be real in the world, but moral striving is not able to idealize the world perfectly. Given this twofold problem, the moral life is inevitably accompanied with anxiety and a certain sense of "hopeless struggle."[97] The recognition that moral action by definition cannot achieve perfect self-realization leads Dewey to introduce the concept of religious will. Dewey's thinking on this matter of the relation of moral and religious will follows closely the argument in John Caird's *Introduction to the Philosophy of Religion,* which appeared in 1880.[98]

Dewey defines the general nature of religious experience as follows:

> Our nature can be completely objectified or realized only when the chasm between what is and what ought to be, between the actual and the ideal self, is overcome. Religious experience is the sphere in which this identification of one's self with the completely realized personality, or God, occurs.[99]

Religious experience, as Dewey conceives it, involves intellectual and emotional aspects, but it is most importantly related to the activity of will. The essence of the religious consciousness is perfect identification of the actual with the ideal, and this is in the final analysis only achieved by an act of the whole self, an act of will. "It is religious will which performs the act of identification once for all. The will as religious declares that the perfect ideal will is the only reality; it declares that it is the only reality in the universe, and that it is the only reality in the individual life." Religious will affirms the ultimate identity of God and the self and of God and the world. Dewey adds that "this will that the real and the perfect will or personality are one constitutes the essence of the religious act known as *faith.*"[100] "Faith," Dewey explained to the Students' Christian Association in 1891, "means the practical belief and trust that God is in all our life, and in all around us and about us."[101]

The moral consciousness by itself only recognizes that the ideal ought to be real, and without a religious faith that the ideal is real men and women would lose heart in the moral struggle and fall into hopelessness and pessimism. If people think that ideals are merely a product of human imagination and wish, they will lose their moral convictions and determination, believed young Dewey. A vital moral life presupposes a religious faith in the ideal. "The moral ideal is not a mere fact in the world; it is truly an ideal, that which ought to be actual, but is not seen to be so. . . . The moral life is one of faith, for it constantly asserts that the final reality for man is that which cannot be made out actually to exist."

> The religious life only brings this element to conscious recognition. It says that that of which alone the individual can be sure as a matter of fact, namely his private self, is unreal, and that the sole reality is the

perfect and universal personality, God, who cannot be immediately felt to be. It asserts that this Personality is not only ideal, and an ideal which *ought* to be real, as moral feeling asserts of its object, but that it *is* perfectly real.[102]

In short, a religious faith in the ideal provides the moral life with a sense of ultimate meaning, which is essential to sustained moral effort.

The *Psychology* further explains that religious faith actually transforms the quality of the moral life, and as a result moral action becomes "religious action," which is the consummation of the moral and religious life. "The religious will declares that God, as the perfect Personality or Will, is the only Reality, and the Source of all activity." The religious will, therefore, makes the perfect Will of God "a motive, once for all, of action; and not of this or that action, but of life, and of life generically and absolutely." The religious person "has renounced his own particular life as an unreality, and asserted that the sole reality is the Universal Will, and in that reality all his actions take place." Action performed in the light of this religious consciousness, which firmly believes that the ideal and the real are one, is religious action as distinct from moral action, which is based on the belief that the ideal and the real ought to be one. "In short, while moral action is action directed to render the actual conformable to the ideal, religious action is action directed to the embodiment of the ideal in the actual." Dewey also explains that, in and through religious will and religious action, the self realizes complete freedom, because it affirms and lives the unity of the finite and infinite personality. The discussion of religious will concludes with Dewey's assertion that in the light of the act of faith human life "may be indifferently described as the progressive realization by the will of its ideal self, or as the progressive idealization of the actual through the ultimate, absolute reality."[103]

In order to clarify further Dewey's concept of faith and religious experience, it is necessary to consider his views on the relationship of faith and knowledge and faith and feeling. Since philosophy is concerned with the knowledge of God, it is related to the religious quest and may contribute to the growth of religious experience. However, Dewey asserts that faith "transcends knowledge" and that the human

quest for knowledge is based on faith in rather than actual knowledge of the reality of God, that is, the absolute truth and the unity of
the ideal and the real. His point is that no human being ever perfectly
achieves the intellectual intuition of God. However, the love of
knowledge and the will to seek it are founded upon the *"belief* that
there is truth, and that every act of intellect, legitimately performed,
leads to truth." In science and philosophical knowledge there is no
absolutely certain justification for this belief. In the final analysis this
trust in intelligence and the intelligibility of the world is a matter of
religious faith. "It finds its validity and the revelation of its meaning
only in the will that the real and the ideal of truth are one in a perfect
personality—God." Religious will or faith is the ultimate foundation
of the intellectual life as well as the moral life.[104]

In two brief popular essays written while he was completing the
Psychology, Dewey makes it very clear that neither scientific knowledge nor philosophical knowledge can ever be a substitute for religious faith. He explains that the religious life is not essentially a
matter of intellectual belief regarding matters of fact either with or
without evidence. It is a matter of will. "The specifically religious
life" concerns "the attitude which the *will* takes towards the facts, the
vital personal setting of the soul."[105] It involves a commitment of the
whole feeling, thinking, willing self to the truth and reality of the
ideal. Regarding the religious life, he writes:

> Its root is not, I know that the soul and its eternal destiny exist, for I
> have been a member of a society for psychical research, and have seen
> with my eyes, and heard with my ears; but, I *will* that they be real,
> for without their reality I myself am not real. It is ... upon this
> staking of the whole being, though this utterance of entire devotion
> be amid things not yet known, that the religious life consists.[106]

Dewey does not identify faith primarily with a feeling as some
Romantic poets and intuitionalists had done. "The act of faith ...
precedes and transcends feeling." The religious feelings are the internal side of the objective unification of the ideal and the actual realized
by will. Regarding the religious quality of experience expressed in
and through feeling Dewey writes: "the emotion which accompanies
the religious life is that which accompanies the completed activity of

ourselves; the self is realized and finds its true life in God," who is "a completely realized personality, which unites in itself truth, or the complete unity of the relations of all objects; beauty, or the complete unity of all ideal values; and rightness, or the complete unity of all persons." In religious emotion, "we feel our self identified, one in life, with the ultimate, universal reality." Dewey in one instance refers to this religious quality acquired by feeling as "the feeling of faith." [107]

He distinguishes various aspects or elements of religious emotion, including feelings of dependence, peace, and joy. Since religious faith recognizes that "whatever we have and are is not of our particular selves, but from God," it involves the feeling of dependence. "In religious feeling we recognize the worthlessness, the *nullity*, of this private separate self, and surrender ourselves wholly to the perfect personality, God," writes Dewey, and as a result we feel total dependence on God. In contrast to Schleiermacher, the feeling of absolute dependence is interpreted here as an aspect rather than the very essence of religious experience. Another element of religious feeling is the feeling of peace—of complete reconciliation, of perfect harmony, of rest—which is experienced "so far as one gives up wholly his own particular self (and except as he does this, there is no religious life), and takes the life of the completely harmonious Personality for his own." The *Psychology* also states that the religious life brings with it the feeling of joy. It asserts that joy is experienced when a conflict is ended by an adjustment involving a harmonizing of the different elements involved in such a way that none is totally repressed and all are included in some comprehensive activity. Identification with the ideal self is union with the perfectly integrated personality, and, therefore, it involves a "complete adjustment" that brings with it "the feeling of reconciliation, which may become joy." [108]

According to the *Psychology*, aesthetic experience and religious feeling are closely related. His explanation of aesthetic experience is difficult to follow, but he seems to suggest that the essence of aesthetic experience is the feeling of harmony, of unity in variety. More specifically, the feeling of beauty is the feeling of accord existing between our inmost nature, the ideal self, and some painting, poem, piece of music, or nature. It is a sense of an indwelling ideal. He distinguishes aesthetic and religious feeling by asserting that aesthetic experience involves "the feeling of the ideal as such," while religious experience concerns realization of the identity of the ideal and the real. In short, aesthetic experience may contribute to religious feelings of harmony; religious experience includes aesthetic experience and goes beyond it.[109]

In 1889 Dewey addressed himself directly to the relation of religious faith and the problem of meaninglessness. He had read Paul Bourget's *Essais de psychologie contemporaine,* which concludes from an analysis of the works of Baudelaire, Renan, Flaubert, Taine, and Stendhal that the French spirit is afflicted with a sense of the utter meaninglessness of existence leading to pessimism, the decay of hope, courage, and endeavor, and nausea at the emptiness of life. In an essay entitled "The Lesson of French Literature," Dewey argues that neither a dilettante love of culture, nor romanticism in the sense of "the attempt to find satisfaction of life in the enjoyment of intense emotion," nor the methods of physical science can overcome the sense that life is at bottom meaningless, that it has no unifying purpose, that in the final analysis the universe is indifferent to all ideals. The only antidote to the sense of meaninglessness is a religious faith in some ideal. Only in and through an act of free moral choice in which one ideal is declared to be of absolute value is life given unity and purpose. In addition, adds Dewey, "back of this choice must lie faith in the supreme reality of such an ideal." In other words, the ideal must be identified with God, and moral action must become an expression of devotion to God. "Given faith, the pessimism which results from the conclusions of natural science becomes a buoyant faith that the very natural processes are the tributary mechanisms of an end, a purpose, an ideal which does not manifest itself to the eye of sense." In and through the act of moral self-determination coupled with religious faith, modern men and women will find the key to the realization of personality and they will discover "peace, hope, and courage." "The problem of the nineteenth century," concludes Dewey, "reduces itself to a choice between faith and pessimism."[110]

At the outset of this study, mention was made of Dewey's assertion as a mature thinker that there are three ways in which the world may be idealized involving thought, feeling, and practical action. It has also been noted that, as a young philosopher, Dewey was especially interested in metaphysical speculations and in trying to idealize the world in and through the exercise of thought. While there is truth in this point, study of the *Psychology* reveals an important qualification. Even though Dewey was heavily influenced by Hegel's philosophy of religion, he did not follow Hegel in asserting that the religious quest for the unification of the divine and the human culminates with philosophical theology. Dewey, like Morris, accepted Hegel's position that philosophy does apprehend on the level of pure thought the truth which religion and theology apprehend in lower cognitive forms involving myth and representational thinking. However, Dewey does not in the final analysis, like Hegel, identify the highest manifestation of religion with the knowledge of God achieved by philosophy. The heart of religion for Dewey is an attitude of the will, faith, and ethical action. Hegel gave feeling and ethical action important roles in the religious life, but the emphasis falls on knowing. Dewey accepts the importance of knowing but puts the emphasis on the volitional and practical following Marsh, Morris, and T.H. Green. He is in this sense an ethical idealist.

Many of the ideas in the *Psychology* involve early formulations of concepts that are developed or reconstructed in his later thought. The idea that human life is a process of growth concerned with realizing freedom and unifying the ideal and the actual remains basic to his thinking. The attack on an atomistic individualism and the emphasis on relationship as fundamental to self-realization becomes characteristic of Dewey's outlook. He remains convinced that the quality of a person's feelings reflect the quality of their relations and activities, and that preoccupation with one's feelings as opposed to one's relationships is unhealthy. The continuity of means and ends becomes a recurrent theme. In his moral thought Dewey never doubts the fundamental importance of sympathy, or compassion. He continues to emphasize the role of will, choice, and to view moral choice as determinative of the quality of a person's inner being. On the religious side, the *Psychology* contains a number of ideas which reappear in a revised form many decades later including: the association of religious experience with will and a commitment of the whole self to the ideal; the distinction between religious faith and the moral will; the intimate connection between the religious life and moral action;

the attack on religious sentimentalism; the rejection of any radical dualism of the spiritual and the material, spirit and body; the association of religious life with complete adjustment and unification; the notion that religious experience involves certain distinctive qualitative feelings; the idea that philosophic knowledge and aesthetic experience may contribute to religious experience; the identification of God and religious experience with unification of the ideal and the actual.

God and Dynamic Idealism

On request from Morris, Dewey contributed a volume on Leibniz to the series Morris was editing on German philosophy. Consideration of this study provides an opportunity to further clarify and summarize the major themes in Dewey's neo-Hegelian vision of the nature of reality and God.

Dewey finds "the very conception and birth of the modern interpretation of the world" in the philosophy of Leibniz, whom he describes as "the greatest intellectual genius since Aristotle." Generalizing from the new science of mechanics which endeavored to explain all events in terms of motion, Leibniz arrived at his initial great discovery: "Reality is activity. *Substance c'est l'action.* . . . Motion is that by which being expresses its nature, fulfills its purpose, reveals its idea." In other words, "the universe is radically dynamic." Generalizing from the fact that the laws of motion which govern nature may be expressed mathematically Leibniz further concluded that "the universe is one of order, of continuity, of unity." This means that the universe is a rationally ordered whole, an interconnected system in which there is unity in the midst of diversity. In other words, mind and will govern the universe. "Activity is seen to mean Intelligence." Leibniz's vision of the universe as a dynamic, rationally ordered whole leads him to adopt the biological conception of life as a basic metaphysical conception. The universe is an organic unity, a living whole in the process of organic growth. Dewey emphasizes that the principle of intelligence—of life, continuity, organic unity—is not a principle of undifferentiated unity but rather a principle of unity in and through diversity. In short, "distinct individuality as well as ultimate unity is the law of reality." At the heart of reality is a principle of individuation as well as unity.[111]

With these principles in mind, Leibniz develops his monadology involving the notion of the universe as constituted by an infinite number of unique independent entities, each of which is "self-determined to show forth the order, the harmony, of the universe." Since the universe is governed by Intelligence or Spirit, it is teleological both as a whole and in its parts. Further, there is no dualism of spiritual and material, teleological and mechanical, supernatural and natural. "Nature is instrumental in that it performs a function, realizes a purpose, and instrumental in the sense that without it spirit, the organic, is an empty dream. The spiritual, on the other hand, is the meaning, the *idea* of nature. It perfects it, in that it makes it instrumental to itself." Dewey found certain problems with Leibniz's philosophy stemming in large part from his use of "the scholastic formal logic," but as regards these general ideas, which constitute what might be called the basic principles of dynamic idealism, Dewey was in wholehearted agreement.[112]

God is the first principle of the dynamic process of organic growth which is the universe according to Dewey. Developing this idea in his book on Leibniz, he rejects several conceptions of God, and in all of this he is following Hegel's general position. First, he rejects what he calls Cartesian theism, which would include deism and any doctrine that imagines God to be a particular being who dwells outside the universe and imposes a harmony on the beings in the universe, a harmony which is foreign to the intrinsic nature of these beings. In this view, the unity of the universe is nothing more than the mechanical togetherness of externally related atomic parts, and God is just one among many atomic beings who are only externally related. Second, Dewey rejects any pantheistic doctrine which understands God to be one comprehensive substance from which all things emanate and of which all things are but transitory and nonessential modifications. This position, which Dewey identifies with Spinoza, and which Hegel also attributed to Hinduism and Buddhism, explains the unity of God and the world and the presence of an immanent harmony among all things but at an unacceptable price.

Spinoza's pantheism cannot explain "how, on the basis of the unlimited, self-identical substance, to account for even the appearance of finitude, plurality and individuality." All differentiation becomes purely phenomenal and unreal. Particularity and individuality have no ultimate meaning and value. Dewey finds much of Leibniz's theological writing wavering between Cartesian theism and pantheism, but he also identifies a third idea of God in Leibniz, which he views as the true implication of dynamic idealism. "It is the doctrine that God is the harmony of the monads,—neither one among them nor one made up of them, but their organic unity." God is not a being among other beings; nor is he the sum total of all beings; he is the organic unity of all beings, that is, the unity of the ideal and the world.[113]

In his Hegelian doctrine of God, Dewey is not asserting something primarily about a being called God and secondarily about the world which happens to stand in an external relationship to this being called God. He is first and foremost affirming that nature, the universe, is an organic unity. This means that the world as a whole and in its parts is governed by an immanent harmony, and such a harmony implies the presence of mind, intelligence. It means that the world is one with intelligence. If this be the case the first principle of intelligibility with respect to the world is the unity of intelligence and the world, of the spiritual and the natural. Furthermore, intelligence, argues Dewey, is a principle of unity in diversity, of dynamic process, of plurality in continuity, and therefore, the idea of God as the unity of the ideal and the real makes real individuality and differentiation possible and necessary. In other words, in order for God to realize himself as the harmony of the world, he must generate out of himself independent centers of intelligence and will. These independent existences realize themselves in the final analysis by identifying themselves with the divine mind and will, but in this reconciliation of individual and universal the individual is not absorbed back into an undifferentiated unity.

As noted earlier, Dewey's dynamic idealism is also an ethical idealism. Following Fichte in revision of Kant, the natural world exists for a moral and spiritual purpose, which is the realization of spirit, rational will, personality. The dynamic processes of growth and development that make up the interrelated worlds of nature and spirit have a final end of absolute value, and this supreme good is the realization of personality. Personality emerges as the highest value in Dewey's vision of the universe. Dewey's idealism expresses this idea of the absolute value of personality in the doctrine that God, who is the meaning and purpose of the world, is the perfect personality.

When Dewey asserts that God is the perfect personality as he does in the *Psychology,* he does not mean that God is a particular person among other persons. Only once did Dewey refer to God as "a person" and that was in an 1886 talk before the Students' Christian Association at the University of Michigan.[114] In the *Psychology,* he nowhere states unambiguously that God is a self or a person. When he uses the term "a perfect personality" with reference to God, it is in the context of asserting that the self finds and realizes itself in a perfect personality, that is, in God. Dewey at one point refers to God as "the ground of the actual self," and the implication of his general position is that God is not a particular person but rather the ground of personality. In line with this, Dewey points out that God or the ideal self is not one particular good or end of action utterly distinct from all others, but rather the ideal harmony of all the ends of the self.[115] God, then, is the principle of organic unity which is manifest in the integration of a perfect personality. Since this spiritual principle is identical with ultimate reality and with the true self or essential nature of every person, God may be said to be the ground of personality wherever it manifests itself.

There was general agreement among Christian theologians in the nineteenth century that pantheism was a dangerous and unchristian doctrine. There was also much debate as to whether Hegel was guilty of pantheism. Hegel and his defenders claimed that he was not. Many of the more orthodox theologians charged that he was. Dewey entered the debate trying to maintain that his Hegelian conception of the divine immanence was consistent with Biblical theism, which, of course, he distinguishes from Cartesian theism. Despite his denials there is actually a strong tendency towards pantheism in Dewey's thinking, and it is debatable as to whether his theology can legitimately be called a form of theism. Theism clearly distinguishes between God and the world, and it accordingly has a well-developed doctrine of the transcendence of God even though it also often recognizes the importance of a doctrine of divine immanence. In Dewey's doctrine of God it is not entirely clear how God is distinguished from the world, the doctrine of divine transcendence is rather vague, and all the emphasis is on the immanence of God as the organic unity of the world and on the identity of the human spirit and the divine spirit. Dewey does assert that, as the organic unity of the world, God is not to be identified with any one being or the sum total of all beings, and he also argues that the universal mind is an infinite and eternal reality which in some sense transcends all particular finite beings. However, these aspects of his theology are not fully developed and clarified.[116]

Even though there are pantheistic leanings in Dewey's theology, it is more to the point to recognize that at the heart of Hegel's and Dewey's doctrine of organic unity lies a paradox — real difference in the midst of identity. Given the fact of this paradox the best term for their theology is panentheism. The panentheist is opposed to all radical dualisms between God and the world but also resists a monism in which the ultimate meaning of individuality is denied and the being of God is exhausted by the existing universe. Panentheism with its emphasis on the divine immanence is one of the major ways in which nineteenth-century religious thought tried to reaffirm the reality of God and to reawaken a sense of the sacred at a time when supernaturalism seemed to have become untenable and mechanistic materialism threatened to deny God. It has continued to be an important alternative for religious thinkers in the twentieth century down to the present day.[117]

Labelling Dewey's neo-Hegelian theology panentheism rather than pantheism is not meant to deny that there may be in this theology a problematical identification of God and the world, or more specifically, as will be shown, of God and human society. Hegel brought Christian theology to the brink of a thoroughgoing humanism. This is actually the most important theological issue related to the problem of Hegelianism and pantheism. It is not so much a question of whether the individual is absorbed into the universe but of whether

God in the final analysis disappears in the human. This became a critical issue in the course of the development of Dewey's thinking on the relation between God and society and the religious and the ethical.

Along with the absolutism and rationalism that characterize Dewey's early thought, one also finds themes and ideas that reveal tendencies toward empirical naturalism that would in time transform his philosophy including his religious thinking. From the start, in his quest for unity, he adopted a one-world hypothesis that recognized no dualism of the material and the spiritual and that anticipates his naturalistic world view. His emphasis on experience and science in his epistemology disclosed an early appreciation of empiricism and experimentalism. He viewed the mind as an active creative organ intimately related to the body, and he experiments with Darwinian categories of organism, environment, and adjustment in his efforts to conceptualize the function of the mind and will. There are also the beginnings of pragmatist modes of thought according to which the truth of an idea is revealed in its consequences.

In noting that there were tendencies in Dewey's dynamic idealism that would move him toward empirical naturalism, it is equally important to remember another point. Dewey's empiricism, which took clear form in the twentieth century, would be a new brand of empiricism distinct from classical British empiricism precisely because it was developed as a reconstruction of his earlier neo-Hegelian ethical idealism. Any number of ideas with which Dewey worked as a neo-Hegelian remained with him as a naturalist in reconstructed form giving his naturalism its distinctive character. A number of these ideas in the area of his religious thinking have been identified including the close association of God and the religious life with unification of the ideal and the actual. One further example is worth noting. According to Dewey's idealism, which knows no dualism of subject and object, self and world, the qualitative feelings awakened in the self by objects and activities are "the medium through which the universe makes its significance and value apparent."[118] Here one finds the origins of Dewey's later naturalistic theory of immediate experience as a medium in and through which real values in nature are disclosed. With the aid of such ideas derived from neo-Hegelian idealism Dewey the naturalistic empiricist endeavored to avoid the subjectivism and mechanistic materialism which came to be associated with earlier forms of empiricism.

THREE

Christian Liberalism and Social Action

D EWEY BEGAN his first full-time teaching job as a professor of
philosophy during a period when the Christian faith in America found itself facing a major challenge. Vast forces of intellectual,
economic, and political change were transforming society. Thoughtful men and women in the church could not escape the questions
these changes raised for religious belief and practice. This was particularly true of young Dewey, who as both a philosopher and a
member of the Congregational Church recognized that an individual
could not achieve the unification of self that he longed for apart from
thinking through the meaning of democracy and the new science for
traditional moral and religious values. He understood that the religious dimension of experience is not an isolated sphere but one facet
of a dynamic life process and is developed in a healthy fashion only
when it is understood in relation to the whole.

The problems with which the nineteenth century confronted the
church and theology were many. Traditional beliefs regarding creation, the authority of the Bible, the nature of humanity, the historical
Jesus, and the finality of Christianity as a religion were being thrown
into question by Darwinian biology, the new psychology, historical

research, studies in comparative religion, and the higher criticism. The new knowledge was causing some to leave the churches in the name of materialism, skepticism, and agnosticism, but others, who took the new knowledge no less seriously, tried to remain in the churches as theological liberals. These church liberals were those who respected reason and scientific modes of inquiry. Accordingly, they sought what one called "a full adjustment between reason and Christianity."[1] Abandoning Biblical literalism and strict adherence to dogmatic statements of the truth of Christianity, they struggled, as another put it, to restate the essentials of the Christian faith anew "in forms more rational and more consistent with modern habits of thought."[2]

During the 1880s and 1890s Christian liberals were also faced with the task of adjusting their institutions and thinking to a rapidly developing and often turbulent social environment. The history of American society in the last quarter of the nineteenth century is a story of both extraordinary progress and the development of serious social ills. On the one hand, great advances were made in technology, transportation, and industry. The telegraph and telephone became important parts of American life. The railroad spanned the continent. The oil, iron, and steel industries grew rapidly, taking full advantage of the rich natural resources of the country, and the great modern corporation made its appearance. On the other hand, wealth and economic power tended to concentrate in the hands of the few, government was often corrupted by special interests, and severe social problems confronted farmers, laborers, small businessmen, Native Americans, blacks, and unskilled immigrants, who were pouring by the thousands into rapidly growing urban slum areas. America's technological and economic successes coupled with the continued vitality of her democratic social institutions promoted the rapid development of an energetic middle class and led the majority of Americans to be optimistic about the future and to put great faith in progress. At the same time, the mounting social, economic, and political problems of this era produced unrest and outrage in many quarters, and there developed an urgent demand for social change that led to a wide variety of reform efforts.

Led by the Knights of Labor and the American Federation of

Labor, the labor union movement became a force to be reckoned with. In pursuit of fair wages and reasonable working hours, laborers conducted thousands of strikes, some of which ended in riots and pitched battles. An extensive literature written by humanitarians, visionaries, and muckrakers appeared, including such widely read volumes as Henry George's *Progress and Poverty* (1879), Edward Bellamy's *Looking Backward* (1888), Jacob Riis' *How The Other Half Lives* (1890), and Henry Demarest Lloyd's *Wealth Against Commonwealth* (1894). Inspired by the English example, Jane Addams in Chicago and Lillian Wald in New York emerged as leaders of the settlement house movement. Their objective was to bring education and opportunity to the growing number of those trapped in America's city slums, which had become breeding grounds of crime, vice, and disease. The short lived Populist Party gave political expression in the early nineties to the protests and aspirations of farmers, laborers, socialists, and reformers.

The response to this situation among some of the religious liberals was the Social Gospel movement. It endeavored to transform the church into an instrument of social betterment in the belief that any program to save individuals must involve social reform. The Social Gospel theologians attacked the extreme individualism of much evangelical religion, arguing that individuals do not exist as isolated entities but as members of a social order that profoundly shapes their habits and character. They generally rejected the doctrine of original sin and maintained faith in the perfectibility of human nature, believing that the power of moral evil can be subdued in and through the reform of social conditions. They shared in a widespread social belief in progress. For them realization of the kingdom of God on earth was a real hope and inspiration. In all of this the liberals were expressing the major shift in cultural mood that marked the emergence of modern urban industrial society out of the medieval world: a shift of controlling interest from otherworldly salvation of the soul to a this-worldly realization of well-being and fulfillment. Among the earliest champions of Social Gospel theology were the midwestern Congregational ministers Josiah Strong, who published in 1885 a widely read volume on *Our Country: Its Possible Future and Its Present Crisis,* and Washington Gladden, who authored many books on the theme including *Applied Christianity* in 1886. Lyman Abbott was not as radical a spokesman of the Social Gospel as Gladden and Strong, but his editorials on social reform during the 1880s in *The Christian Union* stimulated much debate. Central to his reform strategy was a call for "industrial democracy," by which he meant a partnership between labor and capital involving shared ownership and control of industry.[3]

Coleridge, Marsh, and Morris had convinced Dewey that a person could be both liberal and genuinely religious, and by the time he began teaching at the University of Michigan there was considerable support for this position within his own denomination, the Congregational Church. Men like James Marsh and Horace Bushnell had shown the way. During the 1880s a number of liberal Congregational preachers began to embrace Darwin and to promote "the New Theology."[4] In 1884 the faculty of the Congregationalists' Andover Theological Seminary launched the publication of a new liberal theological journal, the *Andover Review,* with a series of editorials seeking to define what they called "Progressive Orthodoxy."[5] When Dewey arrived at the University of Michigan that same year, his primary allegiance was to the discipline of philosophy, but he was also one of these liberal Congregationalists who were trying to adjust the Christian faith to new methods and ideas. He was much concerned to demonstrate that a person could be both liberal and genuinely religious. To this end he early became involved in the religious life of Ann Arbor as a speaker, teacher, and active church member.

Between 1884 and 1894 Dewey gave twelve addresses before the University's Students' Christian Association, taught five courses on the Bible and the history of Christianity, spoke at a number of other church-related meetings or conferences, and actively involved himself in the life of the Congregational Church. Much of what Dewey said and taught on these various occasions was printed in the S.C.A. publication, *The Monthly Bulletin.* During his years in Michigan Dewey also wrote book reviews and essays dealing with contemporary religious issues for a variety of journals concerned with liberal theological thinking. Among these publications were the *Andover Review* and several weekly journals including the *Index, The University,* and *The Christian Union (The Outlook* after 1893), which was edited by the outspoken preacher, evolutionary theologian, and social critic Lyman Abbott. Dewey's writings in these journals and *The Monthly Bulletin,* together with several of his other essays from this period, provide a good idea of what he thought and taught as a liberal about such critical contemporary issues as the method of theology, the essence of Christianity, the historical Jesus, evolution, the higher criticism, the role of the church, and the approach of the Social Gospel.

In the course of his second year at the University of Michigan (1885–1886), the issue of the social meaning of the Christian faith in the context of American society emerged as the chief focus of his concern as a liberal Congregationalist. He had become increasingly aware as a young man of the serious social ills that accompanied the dramatic economic growth in America. He shared the optimism and hope of his time, but he was also profoundly influenced by the cry for social reform. Even as a college and graduate student, he had shown a genuine interest in social philosophy. As the decade of the 1880s progressed, this interest deepened and the sensitive moral conscience that had been fostered in him by Vermont Congregationalism was transmuted into the demanding social conscience of a liberal reformer. As a result, his religious thought became centered on the task of demonstrating with the aid of neo-Hegelian theology and social thought that Christianity in contemporary America is to be identified with the developing life of the democratic social organism. In other words, Dewey's theological liberalism evolved into a radical version of the Social Gospel or what a later generation would call a form of liberation theology.

From the point of view of the history of American Protestant thought, it is possible to regard Dewey's early philosophy as a radical variation on some of the novel themes in the New Theology and Andover's Progressive Orthodoxy. However, even though Dewey was an active Congregationalist and was concerned to further the development of a new progressive Protestant Christianity, it would be incorrect to think of him during the 1880s as being a church theologian in the sense of one whose thought is ultimately controlled by a faith in an historical revelation and a concern for correct church doctrine. When Dewey was asked late in his life whether he had been interested in the problems of theology including the issues discussed in the *Andover Review,* to which he contributed four essays, his brief reply was: "Never had much interest in theology as such."[6] In short, Dewey was from the beginning of his professional career first and foremost a philosopher with a faith in experience and intelligence. He also was a religious liberal who took certain aspects of the Christian faith very seriously and consequently tried to integrate them into his philosophy. In the course of sorting out the meaning of Christianity for himself as a philosopher, he remained active in the church and shared his views in various church related contexts.

It is also to be emphasized that Dewey's struggle to discover the meaning of Christianity for contemporary American society was of fundamental importance to his growth as a philosopher. It had a profound and lasting influence on his thought. Moreover, Dewey viewed his own mature philosophy in part as a radical reconstruction of the liberal Protestant Christian tradition. An understanding of how he went about this process of reconstruction throws considerable light on the deeper spiritual significance of his mature thought.

In what follows, this chapter will explore the forces shaping the development of Dewey's social and religious thought and the way that he as a neo-Hegelian ethical idealist and a Congregational liberal sought to reconcile the Christian faith with reason and the cause of democratic social reform. It is useful to begin with a fuller inquiry into his religious activities in Ann Arbor.

Religious Activities in Ann Arbor

The Christian faith had wide and substantial support at the University of Michigan in the 1880s and 1890s, even though the University gave no formal official recognition to any particular sect or creed and all attendance at religious services was purely voluntary. President James Angell, who had been President of the University of Vermont and a friend of Dewey's family during Dewey's boyhood, remained loyal to the church and usually was the leader of a daily prayer service on campus.[7] A survey conducted by the Students' Christian Association in 1887 concluded that of the ninety-two faculty members 84 percent were church goers and 65 percent were members of Evangelical churches.[8] A survey of student religious attitudes in 1886 revealed that out of 1,331 students, 55 percent were found to be professing Christians and 44 percent were members of some church.[9] Twenty-four percent (316) were members of the Students' Christian Association, which was "the most active and potent religious influence in the University."[10] As the enrollment in the University increased steadily over the next eight years to over 2,600 students, the S.C.A. membership rose also, but less dramatically, to 474.[11] The University's philosophy department had been under the control of clergymen with little if any professional training in the discipline until 1881, when Morris became the chairman of the two-person department.[12] Morris and Dewey established philosophy as an independent discipline, but Dewey noted that there remained in the University community some restraint when it came to freethinking on religious matters.[13]

In October 1884, soon after Dewey had gotten his fall courses under way, he addressed the University's Students' Christian Association at their Sunday morning worship service for the first of many times. He was particularly anxious on this occasion to assure his audience that his philosophical interests and liberalism had not been developed at the expense of an authentic religious concern. Dewey chose for the subject of his brief and rather intense talk "The Obligation to Knowledge of God," which is a recurrent theme in Hegel's philosophy of religion.[14] According to Hegel, the Bible and Christianity teach that humanity's highest duty is not only to love but also to know God. Dewey seems to have been inspired by passages in Hegel such as this: "In the Christian religion God has revealed Himself, which means he has given man to understand what He is, and thus is no longer concealed and secret. With this *possibility* of knowing God the *obligation* to know Him is imposed upon us."[15] Even if the details of Dewey's thinking this Sunday morning were hard to understand, his main point was clear enough: the Holy Scriptures assert that to be without knowledge of God is a "sin"; skepticism in theological matters is morally reprehensible. "Many skeptics declare that their greatest sorrow is that they live as orphans in an orphaned world, without the Divine Father," asserts Dewey. However, knowledge of God depends solely upon the attitude of a person's will and desires, which are under his control. "God is everlastingly about us," and "if the desires and will of man are for God, he will find God in all his knowledge." For the Christian, knowledge of God is a duty, but Dewey avoids saying with Hegel that it is the highest duty. This is a stern doctrine, but at least it involves the consolation in an age of widespread skepticism and agnosticism that God is knowable. Dewey also makes the point in the course of his talk that science and philosophy are "worthless" until their significance in relation to the ultimate end of all human activity, which is realization of God's will, has been apprehended and acted upon by the will. In summary, knowledge properly understood, is intimately related to the will and moral action, and the will finds its final end in desiring, knowing, and doing God's will.

This first appearance before the S.C.A. of the new young philosophy instructor left no doubts with his audience that he was a morally earnest man with a sincere religious concern even if it was expressed in a somewhat obscure philosophical language. The students were impressed and interested enough to invite him back the next month, and perhaps for the purpose of clarification he spoke on "The Search for God."[16] This same fall Dewey formally joined the Ann Arbor Congregational Church and announced that he would teach an S.C.A. Bible class.[17] Dewey's course description was clearly aimed at students with liberal religious interests. It stated that the course was designed especially "for the accommodation of those persons who, not members of the Association, desire to pursue a critical study of the Bible and of Christian doctrine." Its subject was listed as "the life of Christ, with special reference to its importance as an historical event."[18] Thus did Dewey begin a decade of active involvement as a theological liberal in the institutional religious life of Ann Arbor.

Dewey gave the S.C.A. considerable support during most of his years at the University of Michigan. He addressed the organization's Sunday morning meeting, which was attended by 150 to 500 students, on the average of at least once every academic year, taught five S.C.A.-sponsored religious education courses, and served for four years on the Board of Trustees, beginning in 1889 when he became

Chairman of the philosophy department.[19] The S.C.A. stated its general purpose to be "to unite the Christian students of the University in order to strengthen their own Christian life and extend the cause of Christ among their classmates."[20] On Sundays the S.C.A. sponsored a morning worship service, Bible study classes, and prayer meetings in the afternoon at two hospitals.[21] They also published *The Monthly Bulletin* and a *Students' Handbook*. In 1870 the S.C.A. had admitted women; and in 1885 (after a fight within the organization) they gave up their membership in the state and national Y.M.C.A. rather than comply with the latter's demand that the S.C.A. divide into separate men's and women's organizations. Dewey gave his active support to those in the S.C.A. who sought to keep it coeducational.[22]

One student officer of the S.C.A., Jessie Phelps, who worked with Dewey during these years, later recalled the nature of Dewey's influence: "I knew him personally in S.C.A. board meetings. How gently he helped us.... He never offended any one in any way, but was able to help us think through certain problems." Miss Phelps adds: "I was doing some questioning of religion myself. He evidently claimed to be a Christian, but he was certainly the most liberal one I had ever met.... His influence helped me to rid myself of my religious superstitions, and made me tolerant of all whom I met."[23]

The texts of only six of the twelve known S.C.A. addresses by Dewey have been preserved, but with only one exception the titles of these talks were published. They include: "The Obligation to Knowledge of God" (October 1884), "The Search for God" (November 1884), "Faith and Doubt" (January 1886),[24] "The Place of Religious Emotion" (Fall 1886),[25] "The Social Nature of Christianity" (January 1887),[26] "The Motive of the Christian Life" (Spring 1888),[27] "Christ and Life" (June 1888),[28] "The Value of Historical Christianity" (October 1889),[29] "Relation of Morality and Religion" (February 1891),[30] untitled talk (October 1891),[31] "Christianity and Democracy" (March 1892),[32] and "Reconstruction" (May 1894).[33] Judging from what is known of these talks, they were in general constructed as popular lectures dealing with the Christian life, the historical development of Christianity, and the meaning of Christianity in the modern world.

At times Dewey did some preaching citing Scripture in support of a point, employing moral exhortation, and challenging his audience in the style of a Biblical prophet.

As a neo-Hegelian ethical idealist Dewey defended the church as a necessary social institution. For example in 1885, he writes:

> All society is based on the development of the universal side of the individual, and has as its function the redemption of this universal element. The church lays this subordination of the individual to the ultimate universal, God, upon each as an obligation, and thus merely consciously proclaims what is unconsciously involved in the very substance of all society.... The function of the church is precisely to see that men are bound together by truly universal or social relations. This is the establishment of the Kingdom of God.[34]

In the *Psychology* Dewey reiterates these views, explaining that the church understands and proclaims the supreme importance of love, or sympathy, for both individual self-realization and society. It "brings into explicit consciousness the elements involved in all social organizations. It *requires* love as the supreme obligation, and it brings to light the relation of this love to the perfect and universal personality, God." In the light of these considerations, Dewey declares in 1887 that "the highest product of the interest of man in man is the Church."[35] He did not delete this statement in his revision of the *Psychology* for reprinting in 1889 and 1891. In line with this thinking, Dewey probably regularly attended Sunday morning worship services at the Congregational Church throughout his years in Ann Arbor. On at least two occasions he presided at the business meetings of the church.[36]

The Congregational Church was the location for a number of Dewey's religious education courses for university students. He followed his first course on "The Life of Christ" with a second on "Church History" in 1887. *The Monthly Bulletin* commented that "the name of its teacher is all the guarantee of profitableness the class needs."[37] During the Spring semester of the year 1889–1890 he offered "a course of lectures" at the Congregational Sunday school on "Ancient Life and Thought in Relation to Christianity."[38] Dewey divided his lectures into three parts: "The Greek Preparation for Christianity," "Christianity in Contact with Greek Culture," and "Roman Life and Christianity." The course emphasized the relation of philosophy and religion, the development of Christian theology, and the formation of the Church up through the time of St. Augustine. Readings involved extensive assignments in Plato, Aristotle, Hellenistic Greek philosophy, the Church fathers, and a variety of secondary sources.

In the spring of 1893 Dewey offered another course at the Congregational Church entitled "Philosophic Study of Paul's Epistles."[39] In the *Students' Handbook* (1892–1893) it was noted that religious education courses such as Dewey's met once a week and required the same amount of work as a regular college course.[40] Dewey's last contribution to this program of Christian education was a "largely attended" series of ten lectures during the year 1893–1894 on "The Early Development of Christian Doctrine."[41] In the fall of 1892 Dewey's interest in early Christian thought found its way into his university course offerings in the form of a seminar on "The Development of Christian Philosophy in the First Four Centuries after Christ."[42] About this course Dewey comments: "I have this year a small class of graduate students engaged upon the study of early Christian theology, the object being to trace the continuity of Greek thought over into Christian formulations."[43]

The Monthly Bulletin reported that on two occasions in the early 1890s Dewey spoke before "the Ministerial Band," a group of student members of the S.C.A. with an interest in the Christian ministry. In March 1891 he invited this group, which then had twenty-five members, to his home and gave them a sobering talk on the theme from I Corinthians 14:18–19, "I had rather speak five words with my understanding than ten thousand words in an unknown tongue."[44] The following Spring, Dewey addressed the Ministerial Band on "The Relation of Philosophy to Theology."[45] A record of both these talks remains. In June 1891 Dewey spoke before a Congregational Church Convention in Ann Arbor on the topic of "The Relation of the Present Philosophic Movement in Religious Thought," which probably was a discussion of neo-Hegelian idealism and Christianity.[46] The following year he addressed a three-day Bible Institute sponsored by the S.C.A. and chose for his subject "The Significance of the Parables."[47] Early in 1894 he gave a lecture on "The Economic Evolution of Religious Ideas" before the Ann Arbor Unity Club, a local citizens' organization.[48]

In 1893 he resigned his position as a trustee of the S.C.A., because the organization voted to require that student members of the Board of Trustees must subscribe to the principles of evangelical Christianity.[49] Dewey himself could not personally subscribe to such principles, and this conflict with the S.C.A. was symptomatic of major changes going on in his whole philosophical and religious outlook at this time. Some students in the S.C.A. still regarded Dewey as "one of our strongest supporters,"[50] but one commented to the philosophy department in 1894 that he hoped Dewey's successor would be a person whose "active, moral and religious influence would be felt more than [Dewey's], more openly and heartily on the side of the Church."[51] Dewey's interest in the Church was rapidly declining at this point in his career. However, the record of Dewey's activities and lectures at the University of Michigan give evidence of a substantive involvement over a period of almost ten years in the religious life of the University community and of some serious study of Biblical theology, early Christian philosophy, church history, and the relation of Christianity and the church to contemporary culture.

The Teachings of a Liberal Congregationalist

In expounding his own religious position as a Congregationalist liberal, Dewey relied upon Hegel for his approach to the question of a method of truth in matters of religious belief. It is Hegel's argument that philosophical theology is the purest form of theology as well as the highest expression of religion. Hegel taught that the history of the religious consciousness of humanity as manifested in the history of the different religions involves various stages in the development of a genuine apprehension of the nature of the absolute and of the relation between God and humanity. This process culminates with Christianity. Hegel viewed Christianity as the absolute religion, because in the Biblical myths and stories and in the principle doctrines of Christian theology the absolute truth is fully revealed with one important qualification. Traditional Christianity expresses the absolute truth in a representational mode or figurative form of thinking, which is inferior to the pure rational form of philosophy. For Hegel philosophical theology, therefore, supersedes all previous theology, and theology loses its status as a unique intellectual discipline distinct from philosophy. Underlying this whole approach is the assumption that religious truth is essentially rational truth, universal truth, even though it may be first revealed in history in a particular concrete form such as the life of Jesus. Therefore, it may be clearly apprehended by intelligence, by philosophical inquiry into the nature of experience and reality.[52]

As an idealist Dewey adopted the Hegelian position that the best theological method is identical with the method of philosophy. He asserts that "theology is philosophy" and that "it is the business of philosophy to go on till it has got to the radical living unity which it calls God."[53] The philosophy of religion, argues Dewey, is "the only final Apologetics for Christianity." The task of the philosophy of religion is "to show forth religion as a necessary and genuine factor in the conscious life of man, to show forth Christianity as the fruition of religion."[54] Neo-Hegelian philosophy successfully does this, contends Dewey, thereby demonstrating the rationality and truth of Christianity. As a neo-Hegelian, he asserts that "the fundamental principle of Christianity" is identical with "the fundamental truth in philosophy—the unity of God and man so that the spirit which is in man is the spirit of God."[55]

During Dewey's years at the University of Michigan there was heated debate in theological circles over the question of evolution. Dewey, who had been taught Darwin's theory at the University of Vermont, early on accepted the theory. He found the writings of the British scientists and philosophers such as Huxley, Tyndall, Lewes, and especially Herbert Spencer persuasive.[56] He studied Spencer's synthetic philosophy thoroughly and offered courses on Spencer and evolution at the university. Using the idea of evolution as his first principle of intelligibility and claiming to employ a scientific methodology, Spencer endeavored to construct a great philosophical system that incorporates and integrates all knowledge. What Dewey found in Spencer, and what appealed to him as a young man, was a compound of the ideals of eighteenth-century liberalism, nineteenth-century organicism, and evolutionary theory. He writes: "It was the individualism of the French Encyclopedist, with its unwavering faith in progress, in the ultimate perfection of humanity, and in 'nature' as everywhere beneficently working out this destiny, if only it can be freed from trammels of Church and State, which in Spencer mingles with the generalizations of science, and is thereby reawakened to new life." Dewey did not accept Spencer's system in the final analysis because it was too materialistic, and it preserved a Kantian dualism between experience and reality leading to agnosticism. Furthermore, he found in the tradition of German idealism "ideas which in the long run are more luminous, more fruitful, possessed of more organizing power." However, Dewey remained impressed with the way in which Spencer was able "to employ the mass of scientific material, the received code of scientific formulation, to give weight and substance to philosophical ideas" thereby furnishing "the common consciousness of his day" with a language and imagery for appropriating for ordinary use the fundamental ideas of both science and philosophy.[57]

As a neo-Hegelian idealist Dewey had no special problem in reconciling Darwinian evolution and religion. Hegelian philosophy conceived the universe as a dynamic process of growth, and long before Darwin it had harmonized Christianity with a theory of cosmic development and historical evolution. The Hegelians had elaborate philosophical arguments available to defend the doctrine of design and teleology in the universe. The challenge to the authority of the Bible posed by Darwin was not a serious problem, because the Hegelians did not take the Bible literally anyway. Hegel had tried to demonstrate that Biblical doctrine properly understood is nothing more nor less than a mythical and representational apprehension of the truths of his absolute idealism. The complete naturalization of humanity by Darwin presented no special difficulty because idealism with its doctrine of the divine immanence and the organic unity of the ideal and the real had thoroughly spiritualized nature as well as humanity. Philosophical idealism was able to reconcile the new science and religion with such seeming success that during the 1890s it became the philosophical tradition to which most American theologians turned in search of philosophical support.

Dewey entered the theological debate over evolution in 1885 with a scathing review of *Evolution and Christianity*, a book which attacks evolutionary theory as being contrary to the teachings of Christianity.[58] Dewey charged its author, a clergyman named Benjamin Tefft, with being scientifically and philosophically uninformed and intellectually dishonest. Not long thereafter Dewey became "a regular contributor to the editorial columns of *The Christian Union*," which was headed by Lyman Abbott, one of the first prominent evangelical preachers to embrace evolution and the New Theology.[59] Abbott published his attempt to reconcile evolutionary thinking and Christianity in a volume entitled *The Evolution of Christianity* (1892). Dewey undertook his own further inquiry into the significance of Darwin for theology in an essay entitled "Ethics and Physical Science" that he wrote in 1887 for the *Andover Review*.

In "Ethics and Physical Science," Dewey makes two major points. First, he continues his attack on a mechanistic and materialistic philosophy arguing that it is not able to attribute to human life any final end or ultimate meaning, and consequently it cannot speak about moral ideals or human beings as moral beings. The material as such acts exclusively "according to the principles of physical causation, and not of final causation, because it is determined by its antecedent, not by an end working itself out in it," explains Dewey.[60] Therefore, attempts by evolutionary philosophers like G.H. Lewes to construct a new theory of cosmic teleology and ethics on the basis of a scientific materialism are doomed to failure. Dewey concludes that if philosophy is to affirm the idea of teleology in nature and defend a theory of the moral ideal, it must go beyond materialism to a spiritual interpretation of reality, the idea of the world as "the embodiment of reason and a manifestation of intelligent purpose." In other words, philosophy must embrace the idea of God in Christian theology and neo-Hegelian idealism. "We believe that the cause of theology and morals are one," states young Dewey.[61]

Second, Dewey asks in "Ethics and Physical Science" if it is possible to harmonize Darwinian theory with a spiritual interpretation of the world. Darwin completed the scientific view of the universe by including human nature wholly within the sphere of the mechanical and the material. Consequently, Darwin leaves philosophy and theology asking: "Is man the last outcome of a series of physical changes following mechanical laws, or is he the spiritual end which nature in all her processes has been aiming towards? Is ... his origin from God, that in his very life in nature he may yet find a way to make life divine and God-like?" In pursuing this issue, Dewey does not wish to question the truth of Darwinian naturalism insofar as it asserts that human beings are creatures of nature whose being and destiny is intimately tied up with the evolution of the natural and material cosmos. In this sense he accepts the perspective and findings of physical science and evolutionary naturalism. Furthermore, since physical science entirely rejects any reference to the supernatural in its interpretation of reality, a philosophy that involves a dualism of the natural and the supernatural, or a God-in-the-gaps type of theology must be rejected. Dewey, therefore, concludes that if the evolutionary perspective on nature and human life is to be given a spiritual interpretation, it is necessary for philosophy to demonstrate "the divine and spiritual character of *all* reality."[62]

One way in which Dewey tries to demonstrate the presence of a spiritual principle in and through all things is to identify evidence of teleology in the natural world and then to argue that purposive activity necessarily means the operation of a spiritual principle immanent in the natural. In "Ethics and Physical Science," Dewey uses Darwinian biology as evidence that nature is "teleological all the way through" just as he had done earlier in "Soul and Body." He understood Darwinism in the 1880s, then, as simply confirming the truth of the worldview of his dynamic and ethical idealism. However, during the 1890s Dewey would come to understand the significance of Darwinism in far more radical terms. This new understanding would raise serious doubts in his mind about absolute idealism and lead him to reconstruct his understanding of teleology in nature.

Darwinian ideas were but one cause of the crisis of faith and theological controversy that went on in the churches and seminaries of America during the last quarter of the nineteenth century. The eighteenth and early nineteenth centuries had witnessed a growing interest in the study of history leading to a new awareness that everything, including religious personalities, texts, creeds, and institutions, were part of history and consequently should be understood in this light. Beginning in Germany during the first half of the nineteenth century, scholars such as D.F. Strauss and F.C. Bauer endeavored to apply these attitudes and the new methods of historical research to such subjects as the history of the ancient Hebrews, the life of Jesus, the emergence of the early church, and the development of Christian doctrine, treating this material in the same fashion as they would any natural or secular historical occurrence. The approach of these scholars raised difficult questions about supernaturalism and miracles, and it forced Christians to ask in what sense their religion was a relative, historically conditioned phenomenon, and in what sense it was absolute and final. The growing study of comparative religion in the nineteenth century added to the complexity of this latter problem. In addition, new critical-historical methods of textual analysis, which became known as the higher criticism, were applied to the sacred books of the Bible leading to major discoveries regarding their origin and composition. For example, the research of J. Wellhausen led to the conclusion that the Pentateuch was not written by Moses and was actually a compilation of various documents from different historical periods. Such discoveries challenged the theory of the Holy Scriptures as the infallible Word of God and threw into question the authority of the Bible.[63]

Dewey was well aware of the findings of the higher criticism and of the new historical approaches in religious studies. Where sound intellectual methods of truth were employed he accepted the results, and he found it "astounding that large bodies of men should think themselves at liberty to ignore or defy the established results of physical and historical science."[64] On certain occasions in S.C.A. talks and in some of his more popular writings he addressed himself to issues being raised by the new scholarship. For example, he wrote an article for the *Christian Union* in 1889 dealing with the "higher criticism" and the personality of Jesus, and the titles of his S.C.A. addresses and courses indicate a concern with the critical-historical issues raised by nineteenth-century scholarship. As noted, there is no record of much of what Dewey said on these subjects, but some of his liberal Christian views were published.

"We would not impugn in the least the great value of this Higher Criticism as manifested in the facts it has made known," writes Dewey in an unsigned article in the *Christian Union* entitled "The Higher Criticism and the Highest" (1889). As a result of this new knowledge "the present generation knows more about Jesus of Nazareth than any except his own and perhaps the one immediately following." However, something is missing in the way the higher criticism treats Jesus, asserts Dewey. The problem is that it "investigates everything excepting that which is of highest importance—Personality." It is the living spirit of a person, the organizing spiritual principle behind all that he thinks, says, and does that is supremely important, and it is this living spirit, the force of personality, that actually influences others. This living spirit is not the end product of a series of events or historical influences, and it cannot be apprehended simply by analyzing the ideas of a person and records of his deeds. The mistake of the Higher Criticism is that it takes "knowledge *about* Jesus for knowledge *of* Jesus." Exactly how a person acquires knowledge of Jesus Dewey does not say, but he asserts that this knowledge is the key to "the Highest Criticism." "There can be no hesitation in asserting that a personal life which has come into contact, say rather union, with the personal life of Jesus is a better judge of the highest and chief point of criticism, the Being of Jesus himself, than any criticism, however learned in historical, linguistic, and philosophical analysis, which has no organ for discriminating and laying hold of this Personality."[65]

Even though Dewey did not view Jesus as a supernatural savior who redeems humanity from bondage to original sin, he did consider Jesus to be a uniquely great religious figure. In 1886 he spoke of "the perfect and matchless character of Christ."[66] His account in 1889 of T.H. Green's view of Jesus well expresses his own.

> Green undoubtedly held that in Jesus Christ this communication of God, which in us, at best, is partial and hindered by seeking of the private self, was perfect and pure. Christ was to Green, in actuality, what every man is in capacity; He was in reality what we are in idea. Undoubtedly he held that Christ was subject to the same physical conditions and possessed of the same physical powers as all men; he would allow neither a miraculous birth nor miraculous, that is, super-

natural power; but morally and spiritually, he held Christ to have embodied in his personality perfect union with the Spirit of God.[67]

Describing the unique significance of Jesus, Dewey writes in 1892: "As far as we have evidence, he was the first character in history to bring man to realization of his unity with God and do it consciously. And he did it the best any man ever did."[68] According to Hegel, Jesus' consciousness of the unity of God and humanity and his perfect realization of it is a critically important moment in the evolution of human consciousness, world religion, and world history generally. From this point onwards God stands revealed as the unity of the universal and the individual, of the ideal and the actual, and the meaning of human history is disclosed as being the realization or incarnation of that unity. In other words, with Jesus humanity begins to become conscious that God is truly immanent in the world and that God is actually realizing his own being in and through the history of humanity's evolving social and cultural life. Dewey seems to be in general agreement with Hegel on these issues.

Dewey summarized the teaching of Jesus in 1886 as follows:

> The teaching of Jesus is that the kingdom of God is within ... that the kingdom of God is a spiritual kingdom, and its life one of the spirit. The sole requirement of Christianity is faith in the supreme reality of spirit, and complete devotion to it. That there is no dualism between spirit and nature, the soul and flesh, follows from this; for reality is one, not two. That the spirit will manifest itself in and through the workings of nature and of the flesh, follows also.[69]

In his published writings Dewey had little to say on the crucifixion, resurrection, and eternal life, but he was probably in agreement with the views he attributes to T.H. Green in 1889:

> We share in the death of Christ when we share in his spirit of absolute sacrifice of all self-seeking and selfish interest and will; we share in his resurrection when we share in the unity of his Spirit and Will with God's. For the resurrection is the other side of the Crucifixion; it is the life of the Spirit, as the Crucifixion is the death of the flesh....
> We are saved, to use the theological formula, so far as there really is in us interrupted, imperfect, partial though it be, union with that death and resurrection which in Christ was eternal, perfect and entire.[70]

Shortly after writing the essay on Green in which the above words appear, Dewey received the news that G.S. Morris had died of exposure during a fishing trip. In a "Memorial of Professor Morris," which he signed along with three other members of the University of Michigan Philosophical Society, there is this reference to eternal life: "In common sadness, the Society desires to make some record of the broad and accurate scholar, of the inspiring teacher, and of the sweet complete man, who now walks, in fullness of life with Him who is Life Eternal."[71] *The Monthly Bulletin* reports that in 1892 when asked by a student what philosophy has to say about the future life, Dewey replied that "insofar as future life has nothing to do with experience, philosophy can have nothing to do with it." However, Dewey did not reject the notion entirely, preferring to take an agnostic position: "The man who denies what cannot be proved, goes by faith as much as the one who accepts it." When asked about immortality he went further and suggested that the idealist concept of the universal consciousness, which is reproduced in the individual consciousness, provides some grounds for a notion of personal immortality.

> In one sense no man ever fully lives while he is alive. He is hemmed in by local bearings. Death is the condition of the removal of local and temporal bearings. After death any man's thought has its full force. This is what Jesus meant in saying that it was better that he should go away. So as the truth for which a man stands becomes more strong and true after death, why should it not also be purer and truer to him? Any consciousness that is not self-consciousness, is not true consciousness. Self-consciousness cannot become, for all becoming is in terms of it.[72]

This statement confirms other evidence that in 1892 Dewey was still an absolute idealist, and in idealism he seemed to find grounds for belief in immortality.

It is reported that early in the year 1887 Dewey delivered an S.C.A. talk on "The Social Nature of Christianity." By this time he, like a growing number of other liberals, had become convinced that the key to an understanding of the real meaning and value of Christianity is to be found in the idea of its social purpose. Therefore, in order to give a further account of the evolution of Dewey's liberal religious thinking, it is necessary to consider the varied social, political, economic and philosophical factors involved in his endeavor to relate religious life and social life.

Romance, Reformers, and Radicalization

The first evidence of a practical turn in Dewey's writings appears in connection with two articles he wrote during the fall and winter of his second year in Ann Arbor (1885–1886) dealing with the effects of college life on the health of women and calling for further scientific study of ways in which to improve women's education.[73] At about the same time he is also found stating in *The University* ("the pioneer of scholarly journalism in the west") that "the question of capital and labor ... is the question of the age." He further comments: "Modern Christianity is getting itself alive to the fact that there is an industrial problem, and that the church has a duty in the matter.... For the church not to interest itself actively in such questions as the industrial one, means not only a loss to society, but death to religion."[74]

It was in the Spring of 1886 that Dewey first began to do some serious research and to speak out on contemporary economic and industrial problems in America. The occasion was an invitation to address the university's Political Science Association on "The Rise of the Great Industries."[75] Dewey's research in preparation for the address had a real impact on him as he explained in a letter to a young woman who was urging him to get more involved in concrete social issues: "My forenoons now are spent in the library reading up on machinery and wages.... It has opened up a new field to me. I almost wish sometimes I was in political science, it is so thoroughly human."[76] In another letter Dewey comments: "Things are bad enough now, but what they were before government began to interfere in the factories about 1830 makes the present state seem nothing. To read some of those things makes one want to indulge in a little *ex post facto* dynamiting."[77] Dewey was no anarchist or advocate of bomb throwing; he was only trying to tell his friend that he shared her passion for economic justice. In fact his social conscience had been aroused.

Dewey's speech came at a critical moment in the history of the conflict between labor and capital—shortly after the huge strike for an eight-hour workday which erupted into the Haymarket Riot in Chicago, leading to the death of over a dozen people and causing a widespread reaction against the union movement. In his address he traced the development of industry from ancient domestic systems through its various changes to the great corporations and explored some of the economic, social, and moral problems created by the latter. He then attacked the philosophy of laissez-faire, called for government regulation of the modern corporation, and defended the rights of workers to form unions as a means of insuring for themselves some measure of control over working conditions. The following winter Dewey is found urging another university audience that the educated person and the scholar must keep in sympathy with "the people" and use their learning in support of social reform.[78] This was but the beginning of a lifetime of involvement in the cause of liberal social change.

The person who had the greatest single influence on Dewey's social experience and thought at the University of Michigan was a third-year college student who happened to be residing in the same boardinghouse where he settled upon his arrival in Ann Arbor. This student was also enrolled in his first psychology course during the Fall semester of 1884. Her name was Harriet Alice Chipman. It was she to whom he had been writing while doing research on the process of industrialization.

Alice Chipman, who was the same age as Dewey, had grown up in the small industrial town of Fenton, located in farm country forty miles northwest of Ann Arbor. Having lost both of her parents at age five, she and her younger sister were taken in and raised by their grandparents, Fred and Evaline Riggs. Fred Riggs was a colorful, rough-cut, independent spirit who had spent much of his life on the American frontier managing Native American trading posts, farming in the wilderness, mining for gold, and exploring. He learned the Chippewa language, was initiated into the tribe, and became a defender of Native American rights. He contributed to various churches but identified himself with none and had the reputation of being a religious free-thinker. His wife, who had shared his life on the farm before they moved to Fenton, also had an independent mind, and individualism was encouraged in the home.

After Chipman finished high school, she attended the Fenton Baptist Seminary where she studied music. She served for a time as the organist in the Presbyterian church and taught in the local schools. However, a desire for further education and a growing interest in the women's rights movement led her to leave Fenton and to enroll at the University of Michigan in 1882. The young woman Dewey met in his boardinghouse in 1884 was not especially beautiful, but he soon discovered in her something of Fred Riggs' freedom of spirit combined with an unusually strong inquiring mind that readily cut through sham and pretense to the essence of a situation. On top of all that she was attracted to him. Dewey had never met a young woman like this. Before long the shy rather solitary metaphysician and psychologist from Vermont and this strong-minded young woman raised by a midwestern pioneer family were falling in love.[79]

In 1885 Dewey was still a young man struggling to outgrow feelings of isolation and separation. His passion for the absolute — his "search for God" — remained intense. In his mystical experience at Oil City he had enjoyed a momentary feeling of unity with the larger whole. The completion of his doctoral studies and his appointment to a university teaching position had strengthened his sense of self. In Hegel's philosophy he was finding a profoundly satisfying intellectual vision of organic unity. However, his romance with Alice Chipman probably did as much, if not more, to liberate Dewey from his sense of estrangement than any other single factor. This is certainly the impression created by his love letters to her, which reveal that he was ecstatically happy in the passionate love that possessed them both. Reflecting on the experience toward the end of his life, Dewey could still comment: "No two people were ever more in love."[80]

During a brief separation in December 1885, the depth and intensity of feeling awakened in John by his relationship with Alice, or "Chippie" as he called her, was expressed like this:

Sweetest when are you coming back to bless me with the beloved joy beyond joy of your love? Loved one of my soul, myself, my own true self, my awakener of life and desire, my fulness of life and satisfaction of want, my source of all that I can be, and giver of all that I am — do I say that I love you? ... I can only give back to you that of which you have given me, for without the blessed finding of me by your love, I would be nothing. . . . Oh, my lover darling, it is the thought that I can give you love which thrills me through and through with the joy of life. . . . How should I not be proud of all I am or can be, when that all is to love you?[81]

Alice's love for him completely engulfed him and seemed to fill the universe:

My love, how your love fills everything. Darling, it is me and everything about me. I am it and I am in it, my own love, and it is the sweetness of the world. Darling, how can I but love you with my life, with my being, with my all, which yet is not mine, but yours sweet one.[82]

As he expressed it to Alice on another occasion: "You are all and my life in the All."[83] Her love for him seemed to be "the explanation for everything" and "the source of all love."[84] It seemed to be something "eternally new, because it unchangeably is," and on New Year's Eve, 1885, there seemed to be no coming and going of the years but only the eternal life of their love.[85] In Alice's presence he felt a "joyous peace" and in her love he found himself "perfectly happy."[86] To Alice, John was "the joy of all the world," and she promised, "I love you eternally and am forever yours."[87] In July 1886, after Alice Chipman had graduated and Dewey had received a much-needed raise in salary, they were married in the home of Fred and Evaline Riggs.

Dewey had been learning from the Hegelians that the divine is realized in human relations, and if in 1885 he had any doubts that the divine is immanent in the human, his love affair with Alice Chipman convinced him. As the love they shared overwhelmed him, he seemed to find the wholeness and happiness his heart had been seeking. It was as if the All, the absolute, was immanent in their relationship. A Freudian might wish to point out that Dewey's love letters reveal that his quest for the Absolute was from the beginning a sublimation of sexual desire. There is undoubtedly some truth in this, which Dewey himself did not deny.[88] However, it is more important to recognize that Dewey's relationship to Alice Chipman —first the love affair and then the children and family experience— was one of those formative experiences in his life which convinced him that what is really good, true, and divine is to be found and realized in the relations between persons.

Life with Alice Chipman radically changed Dewey's existence. Three children were born during Dewey's Michigan years, Frederick Archibald in 1887, Evelyn Riggs in 1889, and in 1893 Morris, who was named after G.S. Morris. Having established a family household, Dewey and his wife accepted responsibility for the care of his aging parents, who came from Burlington to live with them in 1889. Archibald was saddened by his son's defection from the Republican Party, and Lucina was hurt at his abandonment of her brand of evangelical Christianity. However, Dewey was sure enough of himself at this stage in his life, and there was sufficient understanding and affection within the family, so that these differences did not cause serious problems.[89] Dewey very much enjoyed his children, whose development he carefully observed with the aid of his latest psychological and educational theories, and he derived great satisfaction from family life in general. At the age of seventy, reflecting on the conditions of human happiness, he found the "deepest source of happiness in life" to be in "one's own family relations."[90] Among the happiest times in the Dewey family history were those early years in Ann Arbor.

With Alice Chipman's encouragement and assistance Dewey also began to get out and meet people and to expand his interests. In the language of his own *Psychology,* he began to broaden his sympathies and to identify himself more fully with the concerns of the larger community. During his years in Michigan he became involved in a wide variety of educational, literary, religious, journalistic, political, and social activities in and around the university and Ann Arbor. Together with his wife, he also frequently entertained students, faculty, and others in their home.[91] By the end of his ten years in Ann Arbor the lonely, bookish, and self-conscious graduate student of the early 1880s had become a well-adjusted, well-liked, and highly respected (if controversial), professor, active citizen, and family man. In the eyes of students, Dewey was among their "true and helpful friends" and "his easy, earnest and unconscious manner before the class, the utter lack of any spirit of pedantry, and the attitude, as far as desirable, of equality with his students" made him "one of the most popular, most satisfying classroom lecturers in the University."[92] One of Dewey's colleagues described him as "simple, modest, utterly devoid of any affectation or self-consciousness" and "a delightful man to work with."[93]

Dewey would always be a modest person with a simple, unassuming manner, and he would always be first and foremost a thinker with a strong inclination to dwell in an intellectual world governed by the logical connection of ideas. However, during the Michigan years he began to realize the truth in his own philosophical and psychological theory that a person finds himself and real happiness in and through his social relationships. He found that his life gained in wholeness and integration and was greatly enriched by opening himself up to involvement in romance, the family, and the larger social world around him with all its diverse interests and problems. Dewey's passion for ideas continued unabated, but he also found out that he really liked people—all sorts of people—and sharing in their lives and problems. As he put it years later, he found "the broadening of intellectual curiosity and sympathy in all the concerns of life . . . an ever growing source of satisfaction in life."[94] Hegel, G.S. Morris, and T. H. Green gave Dewey the theory, but it was his relationship with Alice Chipman that initially enabled him to begin the practice. Their daughter describes this influence:

> Awakened by her grandparents to a critical attitude towards social conditions, she was undoubtedly largely responsible for the early widening of Dewey's philosophic interests from the commentative and classical to the field of contemporary life. Above all, things which had previously been matters of theory acquired through his contact with her a vital and direct human significance.[95]

After getting involved with Alice Chipman, philosophizing became much more difficult. Dewey from this time onwards was faced with the task of integrating his natural interest in the formally logical and systematic with "the material of a maturing experience of contacts with realities."[96]

The Jane Dewey biography also notes the direct influence of Alice Chipman on her husband's religious thinking: "She had a deeply religious nature but had never accepted any church dogma. Her husband acquired from her the belief that a religious attitude is indigenous to natural experience, and that theology and ecclesiastical institutions had benumbed rather than promoted it."[97] While Alice Chipman was not the only source of such ideas, Dewey's relationship with her was a major influence leading him to pursue a full integration of the spiritual and the natural, the religious and the secular.

There are a number of other important influences which shaped and intensified Dewey's social conscience during the period 1885 to 1895. One of them was T.H. Green. In 1889 Dewey describes Green as "the prophet of our times" who has "articulated the best political desire and conduct of today."[98] About Green's political thinking Dewey comments:

> Green and his followers remained faithful, as the romantic school did not, to the ideals of liberalism; the conception of a common good as the measure of political organization and policy, of liberty as the most precious trait and very seal of individuality, of the claim of every individual to the full development of his capacities.

Dewey goes on to outline the way Green and his followers went beyond the old liberalism.

> They served to break down the idea that freedom is something that individuals have as a ready made possession and to instill the idea that it is something to be achieved, while the possibility of the achievement was shown to be conditioned by the institutional medium in which an individual lives. These new liberals fostered the idea that the state has the responsibility for creating institutions under which individuals can effectively realize the potentialities that are theirs.[99]

It is under the influence of thinking such as this that Dewey began working out his own social philosophy. Further, Dewey writes that it was Green's conviction that "now interest in the problem of social deliverance, in the development of the 'mass of men whom we call brethren, and whom we declare to be meant with us for eternal destinies,' forbids a surrender to enjoyments, however innocent, however valuable in themselves, which do not aid in this social deliverance."[100] By the late eighties, Dewey, too, had come to believe that "the problem of social deliverance" is the central issue for both Christianity and philosophy.

Inspired by Hegel a tradition of idealist democratic social philosophy had developed in America. Hegel himself had formulated an
elaborate social and political philosophy, which G.S. Morris expounded in a new book, *Hegel's Philosophy of the State and of History*
(1887). Furthermore, Hegel had predicted in his *Lectures on the
Philosophy of History* that "America is ... the land of the future,
where in the ages that lie before us, the burden of the World's
History shall reveal itself." [101] Among the American Hegelian social
thinkers were the St. Louis Hegelians, Elijah Mulford, and Walt
Whitman, all of whom Dewey read. Mulford's books, *The Nation*
(1870) and *The Republic of God* (1881), were among the most influential political and theological writings of the times and lent support
to the Social Gospel movement. They emphasized the religious values
embodied in democratic social institutions and taught that the nation
is a moral organism with a divine mission, which is "to enter the
battle for righteousness and freedom ... with faith in the redemption
of humanity." Such faith entails for Mulford the belief that "the
Kingdom of heaven has come, it is coming, it is to come" in and
through "the realization of righteousness in the life of humanity." [102]
Mulford argues in *The Republic of God* that Jesus had no interest in
establishing a cult and creed and put all the emphasis on "realization
strictly of an ethical principle and an ethical spirit in the life of
humanity." [103] Mulford's writing had a direct influence on Dewey's
thought in "Christianity and Democracy" (1892) and possibly on
earlier essays.

In April 1887 Dewey wrote to Alice: "I have been reading Walt
Whitman more and find that he has a pretty definite philosophy. His
philosophy of democracy and its relation to religion strikes me as
about the thing." [104] Whitman found in Hegel's vision of unity in the
midst of diversity "an essential and crowning justification of New
World democracy." [105] In America Whitman saw a new social order
of world historical significance coming to birth inspired by faith in
the common people, an Emersonian individualism, confidence in
science, and a religious sense of a unifying moral purpose at work in
and through all things. "The genius of the United States is ... always
most in the common people," he taught. [106] His best known collection
of poems, *Leaves of Grass,* was in part a great summons to the average man and woman to affirm their own unique individuality, to rec-

ognize the divinity of their own being, and to embrace life wholeheartedly in all its diversity and concreteness. "Hurrah for positive
science," he shouts, confident that science will be a source of "encouragement and support" for New World democracy.[107] Indeed "modern science and democracy" together present to the poet of the New
Age the real challenge of the times, which is "to give ultimate
vivification to facts, to science, and to common lives, endowing them
with glow and glories and final illustriousness which belong to every
real thing, and to real things only."[108]

Whitman's naturalism, humanism, and individualism are coupled
with a very real moral and religious concern. In *Democratic Vistas* he
calls for "a sublime and serious Religious Democracy."[109] Religious
life is not dependent upon churches or related to creeds. It is rooted
in an individual awareness that "there is a moral purpose, a visible or
invisible intention certainly underlying all" and a "belief in the
wisdom, health, mystery, beauty of every process, every concrete
object, every human or other existence, not only considered from the
point of view of all, but of each."[110] Whitman finds a religious
element at the core of democracy, because it is an endeavor to realize
the "moral purpose ... underlying all." It is in this connection that
he argues that if the United States is to fulfill its "spiritual and
heroic" destiny, it needs most of all "more moral identity," a greater
sense of common purpose. To achieve this he calls for the emergence
of "a cluster of poets, artists, teachers fit for us, national expressers,
comprehending and effusing for men and women of the States, what
is universal, native, common to all...."[111] Young Dewey came to
aspire to be among these teachers. Whitman goes on, describing well
in all of this an important aspect of what in time would become
Dewey's endeavor to articulate "a common faith."

> For, I say, the true nationality of the States, the genuine union, when
> we come to a mortal crisis, is, and is to be, after all neither the written
> law, nor (as is generally supposed) either self-interest, or common
> pecuniary or material objects—but the fervid and tremendous Idea,
> melting everything else with resistless heat, and solving all lesser and
> definite distinctions in vast, and indefinite, spiritual, emotional power.[112]

Under the impact of his social concerns Dewey's religious thinking
became increasingly a quest for such "a fervid and tremendous Idea,"

a great moral ideal, rooted in what is "universal, native, common to all" and hence capable of awakening widespread wholehearted devotion and unifying all people.

The Ethics of Democracy and the Kingdom of God

Under the influence of Alice Chipman, the New Theology, and Hegelian social thought, Dewey turned his attention to social philosophy, and in 1888 he delivered an address on the subject before the university's Philosophical Society. It was published as *The Ethics of Democracy*. Here one finds Dewey beginning to make the identification of Christianity and the democratic life, and in the process he articulated liberal social values that became lifelong convictions fundamental to his democratic humanism.

The metaphysical assumptions underlying Dewey's social thinking at this time are set forth in his book on Leibniz. There he points out that a universe constructed along the lines of Leibniz's monadology, which asserts the existence of real individuality in the midst of a preestablished harmony, is "a true democracy, in which each citizen has sovereignty" and "each is an embodiment in its own way of the harmony, the order, of the whole...."[113] Dewey's neo-Hegelian idea of the universe as an organic unity is just such a democratic order. Since the fully developed individuals in this universe are persons, the sphere where this democratic order, this harmony in the midst of diversity, is to be most perfectly realized and made manifest is human society. Dewey's early democratic social theory is basically an elaboration of his neo-Hegelian ethical theory of self-realization, in which the autonomous individual identifies himself or herself, each in his or her own unique way, with the universal self, and the shared life of the social organism.

In *The Ethics of Democracy* Dewey endeavors to outline "the tremendous Idea" that lies at the heart of American democratic life. The democratic ideal, he argues, is much more than a form of government. Quoting James Russell Lowell, Dewey asserts that democracy is first and foremost " 'a sentiment, a spirit, and not a form of government, for this is but the outgrowth of the latter and not its cause.' " Dewey's major point is that democracy is a supreme ethical ideal, "a form of moral and spiritual association," that should govern all human relationships. "Democracy and the one, ultimate, ethical ideal of humanity are to my mind synonyms," he declares.[114] This means for Dewey in 1888 that Christian ethics are identical with the ethics of democracy.

The ideal of democracy is summed up for Dewey in the values of "liberty, equality, and fraternity." In order to appreciate his understanding of these values, it is necessary to view them in relation to his neo-Hegelian theory of the supreme value of personality and self-realization. In Dewey's universe God as the cosmic principle of organic unity is the ideal personality or ground of personality, and accordingly, the final end of the universe is the realization of personality. Personality is sacred and divine. This is the supreme value at the heart of his Christian ethics and social liberalism. In putting this emphasis on realization of personality, he adopted a position that became characteristic of Christian liberal thinking in the late nineteenth and early twentieth centuries. The great ethical significance of democracy according to Dewey is that it is the social embodiment of the values included in the idea of personality: "In one word, democracy means that *personality* is the first and final reality." "Democracy is an ethical idea, the idea of a personality, with truly infinite capacities, incorporate with every man." [115]

The ethical ideal of equality means guaranteeing to every man and woman the opportunity "to become a person" and to realize his or her unique capacities. "In every individual there lives an infinite and universal possibility; that of being a king and priest," writes Dewey. The mention of king and priest here refers to the political theory that "every citizen is a sovereign" and the Reformation doctrine that "every man is a priest of God," which for Dewey involves recognition that God is incarnate in all persons as their true self. Equality means providing all persons with the chance to become self-governing citizens who have a direct relation with the ideal, the divine.[116]

Freedom, too, is essential to the realization of personality, because personality is self-determining will, and if personality is to be perfected, "the choice to develop it must proceed from the individual." Dewey notes that both democratic and aristocratic theories of the ethical ideal assert that the individual person finds perfection in and through harmonizing his or her will with the common will, or common good, but he emphasizes that in a truly democratic society as opposed to an aristocratic one, force is not used to attain this end. He criticizes aristocratic theories such as that in Plato's *Republic* because they lack the faith that every human being is capable of forming a true idea of the ideal and striving to reach it. He rejects any method for creating social harmony that places absolute control in the hands of the enlightened few for two reasons. First, power has a tendency to corrupt the best of people. Why this is so Dewey does not try to explain. Second, Dewey argues that a democratic approach recognizes that self-realization necessarily involves "an individualism of freedom, of responsibility, of initiative to and for the ethical ideal." If it is asked what will motivate the common people, Dewey appeals to the Hegelian doctrines of the immanence of God in human nature and the working of the ideal within every personality.[117] When he praised Emerson in 1903 as "the Philosopher of Democracy," it was in part because Emerson had "reverence for the instincts and impulses of our common nature" and championed self-reliance and self-determination.[118]

In his *Outlines of a Critical Theory of Ethics* (1891) Dewey further explains how he harmonizes a philosophy of freedom and individual self-realization with a concern for the common good and social harmony. He states his position in what he calls the "ethical postulate," that is, the fundamental assumption upon which all ethical theory rests: "In the realization of individuality there is found also the needed realization of some community of persons of which the individual is a member; and conversely, the agent who duly satisfies the community in which he shares, by that same conduct satisfies himself." A person, explains Dewey, commits himself or herself to the common good most effectively by "devotion to the capacity which was given one," and by developing and employing that capacity in response to the needs of the social environment. "The basis of moral strength is *limitation,* the resolve to be one's self only, and to be loyal to the actual powers and surroundings of that self.... All fruitful and sound human endeavor roots in the conviction that there is something absolutely worthwhile, something 'divine' in the demands imposed by one's actual situation and powers."[119] Underlying Dewey's faith in the ethical postulate are his psychological, social, and religious convictions regarding the organic unity of the individual, society, and God.

Before leaving this discussion of the values of freedom and equality, it is important to note the first appearance in Dewey's writings of an interest in "industrial equality" and his statement "that democracy is not in reality what it is in name until it is industrial, as well as civil and political." By industrial democracy Dewey does not mean "socialism in the sense which that mode of life destroys that individual responsibility and activity which are at the very heart of modern life." Fundamental to his idea of industrial democracy is the notion "that all industrial relations are to be regarded as subordinate to human relations, to the law of personality," that is, they are "to become the material of an ethical realization." In other words, Dewey wanted American industrial life thoroughly humanized, so that it functions as an instrument for the realization of personality.[120]

Dewey made no specific proposals for realizing the goal of industrial democracy in *The Ethics of Democracy* except to argue that as a first step it is necessary to uproot the old habit of thought traceable back to Plato and Aristotle which divides life into two distinct spheres: the material, which includes within it everything related to the acquiring and distributing of wealth, and the spiritual, which embraces the ethical life of humanity. As a result of this dualism, the work and relations associated with the material and industrial are regarded as only a mere means to the realization of an ethical community and as in themselves existing wholly outside the ethical. The problem here is that all radical dualisms of means and ends, of industrial and spiritual, have the effect of degrading the material by stripping it of inherent moral meaning and hence of dehumanizing the life of the common people whose existence is largely bound up with industrial concerns. With the church and the Social Gospel movement much in mind, Dewey notes that it is often claimed that ethical rules should be applied to the industrial sphere. However, "that economic and industrial life is *in itself* ethical, that it is to be made contributory to the realization of personality through the formation of a higher and more complete unity among men, that is what we do not recognize."[121]

This notion that the material is in itself ethical gave Dewey's religious and moral thinking a distinctive emphasis. The idea was, of course, derived from his idealist world view in which the material and spiritual are organically related in such a way that the ideal is only realized and made manifest in and through the material. In other words, ends are constituted by means and cannot exist without them so that means, when properly understood, have the meaning and value attributed to ends. Returning to Dewey's main point, the economic and industrial aspect of society should be so organized that it becomes truly an organ of the life of the whole, an expression of the unifying purpose of society, and a means to realization of personality. When this occurs the principles of freedom and equality will have been embodied in the industrial sphere. These ideas about means and ends, the spiritual and the material, and industrial democracy become recurrent themes in Dewey's later writings on social philosophy.

The democratic ideal, which includes devotion to the values of individual freedom, equal opportunity, and authentic community, expresses what is divine and sacred in Dewey's vision of the universe. In a democracy, realization of personality is made the governing principle of the life of the social organism, which is understood to incorporate the material and industrial as an organic part of itself. So conceived, the idea of democracy represents the perfection of the social organism. Furthermore, since in a democracy all of experience is made functional to the divine life of the whole, a democracy is "a society in which the distinction between the spiritual and the secular has ceased, and as in Greek theory, as in the Christian theory of the kingdom of God, the church and the state, the divine and the human organization of society are one." [122] The ideal of democracy is, then, for Dewey a modern version of the idea of the kingdom of God. The implication of this notion is that the democratic life is identical with the life of religious action. Having explored this idea of the identity of religion and social life from the side of social theory in *The Ethics of Democracy,* Dewey approached the question from the side of the theory of religion in his 1889 S.C.A. address on "The Value of Historical Christianity."

A Gospel of Freedom and Social Action

In 1888 Dewey accepted an offer to become head of the Philosophy Department at the University of Minnesota, which is an early indication of a desire to assert his independence in his relation with G.S. Morris. However, he had been there less than a year when Morris died and President Angell persuaded him to return to the University of Michigan to take Morris's position. Shortly after moving back to Ann Arbor as the newly appointed chairman of the Philosophy Department, he joined the Board of the Students' Christian Association, and on an October Sunday he addressed that organization on the subject of "The Value of Historical Christianity." In this talk, Dewey outlined a neo-Hegelian theory of the unique nature and superiority of the Christian religion, and in the process he closely identified God and Christianity with the developing ethical life of western society.

Dewey began his S.C.A. address with some comments about the nature of religion at large. "Religion, generally, has had for its aim," states Dewey, "the uniting of man to some force greater, more permanent, more real, than himself, to some power which underlies nature." In the language of his *Psychology,* the goal of all religion is unification of the individual self with God, the universal self. In the development of all vital religion there is both an external and an internal aspect in this process of unification. The religious life involves outward forms and various acts, which constitute the objective social and historical side of religion. In and through participation in these external expressions, unity with God is lived, and celebrated. Regarding the subjective and personal side of religion, Dewey explains that in a healthy religious situation these outward manifestations are spontaneous expressions of individual feelings of devotion and aspiration, and the experience of living in harmony with God brings with it "a sense of reconciliation and peace."[123]

Whenever unity with God is sought by emphasizing one of these aspects of religion to the exclusion of the other, religion degenerates into something unhealthy and oppressive. On the one hand, religion may turn into a body of external practices that have no vital connection with the individual. It can become solely a matter of blindly believing what some external authority declares about matters not experienced by the self and of dutifully performing in mechanical fashion prescribed rites and actions. When this occurs religion alienates men and women from themselves and God.

> Teaching once incarnate with personal zeal and inspiration tends to harden into formal dogma. Deeds, once the spontaneous and necessary because the unforced expression of sympathy and devotion, become ceremonial rites without meaning. A community once bound together by common interests and love tends to become an outward ecclesiastical organization. When zeal and inspiration depart and give place to rites the life of the religion has departed. There remains but a skeleton —a source of fear and of bondage. The unity that was to unite man to God has somehow grown into an institution which with its dogmas, rites, sacred events, and sacred books keeps man from coming nearest to his God. The individual who thinks finds these forms all outside of himself. They touch him nowhere. It is either a burden he must bear or a bondage he must shake off. It is a dream imposed on him in his sleep: if he should awake, the dream, and with it his religious faith will vanish.[124]

This kind of dead and oppressive religion, into which Christianity has repeatedly relapsed, suffers from a lack of subjective meaning and real religious value, because vital connection with the current social situation and the living experience of the individual has been lost.

On the other hand, the religious quest for unity with God may be focused on the inner self, and people may become absorbed in trying to realize the "final peace" in their hearts. Frequently the religious life is then identified primarily with the cultivation and possession of certain feelings. Dewey describes the problem:

> Religion is reduced to internal experiences of morbid and health destroying introspection. The individual must watch his every thought and feeling to see if it please God or not. His life is one vast query. Have I the evidences of salvation? Religious activity becomes sentimentalism. Let the individual now awake to self-consciousness, and he is convinced that the realm of religion is a realm of cant; that there is no reality in it. ... If the merely outward form of religion is a

skeleton, the merely inward form is a fibreless and sinewless pulp, equally lifeless.[125]

Dewey's thinking here is probably influenced by Hegel's critique of romantic subjectivism and Schleiermacher, but Dewey has directed his attack specifically at the kind of emotionalism and subjectivism which characterized much revivalism in America and to which he had been subjected as a boy.

Even though Christianity has often degenerated into an oppressive ecclesiasticism or an empty sentimentalism, its value as an "historical force," argues Dewey, is found in its unique capacity to overcome these false expressions. Authentic Christianity maintains a balanced connection between the subjective and objective sides of the religious life, developing forms that express living shared values and that make possible the active unification of God and humanity. In explaining his theory, Dewey turns attention to the doctrine of the incarnation. His reflections lead to some radical conclusions regarding the interrelation of the psychological, social, and religious dimensions of experience.

In line with Hegelian thinking, Dewey interprets the New Testament statements regarding the identity of the divine and the human in Jesus as a metaphor for the immanence of God in the life of humanity in general.

> Surely Christ did not mean that the man who had looked on him with bodily eye had seen the Divine Spirit. Surely St. John did not mean that he had actually seen and touched and heard, physically, the Eternal One—The Spirit of Life that was from the beginning. Both these are tremendous metaphors, the most tremendous and magnificent that have fallen from men's lips. They express in the only language which man can command that God is no remote Being away from the world, that He is no Force which works in physical Nature alone, but that He is an ever present fact in life, in history, and in our social relations. They express the fact that the Divine Spirit has touched our actual life so immediately, so directly and so certainly, that men have seen Him and touched Him. Surely only the vast meaning and reality that lies within the words save them from blasphemy. No, God is neither a far-away Being, nor a mere philosophic conception by which to explain the world. He is the reality of our

ordinary relations with one another in life. He is the bond of the family, the bond of society. He is love, the source of all growth, all sacrifice, and all unity. He has touched history, not from without but has made Himself subject to all the limitations and sufferings of history; identified Himself absolutely with humanity, so that the life of humanity is henceforward not for some term of years, but forever, the Life of God.[126]

This idea that "the Spirit of God has entered into history" and that God "is Himself working in and through humanity to realize its highest good" as "the reality of our ordinary relations with one another in life" is the heart of Dewey's version of the Christian Gospel. Historical Christianity comprehends all that is involved from the time of Jesus onwards in the coming to consciousness and out-working in society of the divine immanence. It includes the history of the church, but it also comprehends the growth of human society in general insofar as it has been a realization of the moral and religious ideal.

In Dewey's view, the incarnation of God in humanity is not, then, a unique supernatural event limited first to the man Jesus and subsequently to those of his followers who receive the supernatural or miraculous gift of the Holy Spirit, which has been the dominant traditional Christian view. On the contrary, from the beginning God is immanent in the world and implicitly incarnate in all persons. Jesus is unique only in that he became fully conscious of what is true about every human life, and he perfectly lived this truth. Living this truth means, of course, understanding that God is not incarnate in persons as isolated individuals but as members of the human community. In other words, the divine in humanity is actualized just insofar as persons realize themselves in and through their relationships as members of the social organism. The Christian Gospel is the proclamation of the unity of God and every person understood as a social being, that is, the unity of God and society. It is the message that God is, always has been, and always will be the essential nature of humanity and one with the life of real human community.

Faith in the truth of this Gospel will, according to Dewey, bring a person freedom from the oppressive feeling of being separated from God. However, having faith in the Gospel and finding freedom and religious peace involves more than just entertaining philosophical ideas about God and humanity, and it is not just a matter of having private feelings in relation to God. The person who truly believes that God is "no far away being" but has "identified Himself absolutely with humanity, so that the life of humanity is ... the Life of God," will wholeheartedly seek "union with humanity and humanity's interests, and surrender individual desires." It is in this act of faith, self-surrender, and moral commitment that the individual is reconciled with God and freed from feelings of sin and guilt.

> Consciousness that the purpose of one's life is to be like God gives no help in the attainment of that likeness so long as it shuts the individual within his own interests. Such consciousness but weighs man down with the feeling of his utter impotency and the entire hopelessness of his case. But man is not thus isolated, and hence he does not have to deal with God face to face, but through the mediator of that corporate humanity of which he is a member, and Jesus the head.... The individual has but to surrender himself to the common interests of humanity in order to be freed from the claim upon him as an individual. He stands no longer isolated, but a member of that humanity whose living spirit is God himself.[127]

For Dewey, the Body of Christ is not just the church but human society at large, and it is humanity, not exclusively the man Jesus, which is the mediator between the individual and God. By identifying with the shared life of the community, the common good, the individual finds liberation from sin and guilt and unity with God, for the life of the social organism is God. Dewey declares that this is the central meaning of the teaching of Jesus, John, and Paul.

Dewey concludes "The Value of Historical Christianity" by pointing out that if God is "the reality of our ordinary relations with one another in life," then there is properly no separation of the religious aspect of life and the everyday affairs of people, of the sacred and the secular.

> The chief danger after all, in our practical religious life, is the tendency for the religious life to become a sphere by itself, apart from the interests of life and humanity. The healthy religious life knows no separation of the religious from the secular, which has no Sunday or week-day divisions in it, which finds in every daily duty, whether in

> study or business, or recreation an approach to God as surely and truly as in the retirement of the closet. This frame of mind can never be attained unless we realize that God is in history, is in the social state of life, reconciling men unto Him. He who finds in every true and pure relationship in life a bond of union with God, has his religious life built upon a rock which cannot be shaken by the storms of life, nor undermined by the subtleties of temptation.[128]

Dewey not only wished to help those burdened with sin and guilt to find reconciliation with God and peace. He also, and perhaps more importantly, wished to reconcile all people—including the conventionally religious people—to their everyday existence. Dewey employed his concept of the immanent God as a tool to point to and assert the divine meaning and value inherent in the ordinary and practical life of humanity.

The full social and religious implications of Dewey's thinking become clear when "The Value of Historical Christianity" is read together with his essay on *The Ethics of Democracy*. He himself makes these radical implications explicit in a statement before the S.C.A.'s Ministerial Band in 1892.

> The next religious prophet who will have a permanent and real influence on men's lives will be the man who succeeds in pointing out the religious meaning of democracy, the ultimate religious value to be found in the normal flow of life itself. It is the question of doing what Jesus did for his time. "The Kingdom of God is among you," was a protest against Judaism.

For Dewey, the identification of Christianity and democracy, of religious life and everyday life, was a protest both against forms of institutional and personal religion that were empty of vital meaning and against forms of social and economic life that were unjust and dehumanizing. With the aid of his Hegelian social psychology and doctrine of the divine immanence, he recognized that the deepest social, psychological, and religious problems facing Americans could only be dealt with by reconstructing both religious life and social life and, in addition, by fully integrating them.

In concluding this discussion of Dewey's Christian liberalism, a few summary comments and further reflections are in order. Under the influence of the new psychology, T.H. Green, the American Hegelians, the New Theology, the Social Gospel movement, and Alice Chipman, Dewey during the 1880s became increasingly convinced that the fundamental concern of philosophy should be the dynamics of human growth, the ethical quality of human relations, and the practical problems of society. The task of the philosopher is in the final analysis to develop the intellectual tools and practical wisdom needed for the guidance of life in the contemporary world. In this view the primary significance of metaphysics and theology is found in the intellectual foundation that it provides for humanity's social ideals and the ethical life. Metaphysics and theology clarify the ultimate meaning and religious values inherent in humanity's everyday existence. The final goal is to create a society in which all aspects of life including the mechanical, industrial, and financial are made functional or instrumental to the liberation, integration, and moral perfection of personality. In line with this thinking Dewey as a liberal Congregationalist developed a socialized version of Christianity, in which he endeavors to harmonize thoroughly theology and philosophy, the religious and the secular, Christianity and democracy. The democratic ideal is identified with the Christian ideal of a kingdom of God.

Developing and refining his thinking in the *Psychology,* Dewey contends that the supreme religious value, which is unification with God, is in the final analysis identical with the supreme social value and the end of all individual self-realization, which is the perfection of personality. This divine and sacred value is achieved in and through social relationships, participation in the shared life of the community. In short, God is immanent in the world as the life of humanity, or the life of the social organism. In opposition to the dominant currents of traditional Christianity, Dewey's neo-Hegelian philosophy of religion agrees with the great mystical traditions of Hinduism, Buddhism, and Neoplatonism that the essential nature of humanity in general, and not just of Jesus the Christ, is identical with God and that the goal of the religious life is an ever more perfect realization of this identity of the divine and the human in and through a process of dying to what is purely private and ego-centered. However, Dewey's philosophy of religion is closer to the mainstream

Hebrew-Christian tradition than these mystical traditions when it comes to formulating the nature of the way of liberation and unification.

An introvertive mystical tradition like Neoplatonism, of which there is, of course, a Christian version, stresses the presence of God within the secret depths of each individual person. Accordingly, the major emphasis in this theory of the way of liberation is on turning inward, withdrawing attention from all sense images, detaching the mind from all worldly passions, silencing the processes of discursive thinking, and emptying the mind of all multiplicity and duality. A mind thus detached, quieted, emptied, and concentrated, may then be unified with its essence, the eternal One, which is the power of being in all that is. To Hegel and his followers this type of introvertive mysticism seems to swallow up individuality in undifferentiated unity, and it fails to apprehend the ultimate significance of time-history, social life, and the individual. In contrast to the approach of introvertive mysticism Dewey's neo-Hegelian philosophy puts stress on the presence of God in society and asserts that the goal of liberation from ego-centeredness and of unification with God is to be sought primarily through a life of ethical action grounded in an act of faith in which the private self freely surrenders itself to the ideal, the common good, the organizing purpose of the world, which is its true being. The religious life means a life of faith and ethical action in which the self dies to what is exclusively individual, subjective, and private, and lives in what is universal, objective, and shared. In this way the unity of God and humanity is realized, the social order is idealized, and the personality of the individual is harmonized and perfected.

Rejecting the orthodox doctrines of original sin and the absolute transcendence of God and adopting a neo-Hegelian panentheism, Dewey, then, interprets Christianity as a kind of world-affirming ethical mysticism. The major significance for nineteenth-century religious thought of Dewey's brand of philosophy of religion is to be found here in the way in which religion and ethics are closely interrelated. The religious aspiration for unity with God is channeled into an active social and ethical life. It is important to keep in mind, however, that Dewey has not simply reduced religion to morality. The heart of the religious experience remains for Dewey in the eighties and early nineties an act of faith in God, in the ideal, which act involves the identification of the ideal with ultimate reality. Faith manifests and develops itself in and through ethical action, but it involves an act of will distinct from morality.

What made Dewey's neo-Hegelian interpretation of Christianity more radical than most versions of the Social Gospel is the way in which he interrelates the material and the spiritual, the secular and the divine, so completely. His point is not that the everyday social affairs of people and the material world are originally and normally lacking in spiritual meaning and value and that Christians should import spiritual values into this sphere. On the contrary, as a neo-Hegelian idealist he contends that the spiritual is inherent in the ordinary life of humanity and the natural world. It is just waiting to be actualized. Again, there is no fundamental dualism of the ideal and the real. For Dewey the kingdom of God is being realized in and through the development of machinery, economic organizations, and the democratic community of persons in general. The great significance of American democracy with its commitment to the values of freedom, equal opportunity, and the common good is that it has created a social situation where the promise of the spiritual possibilities of existence can be widely realized for the first time in human history. The implication of this line of thinking is, of course, that the idea of the church as a distinct sacred institution separate from the secular world is no longer a relevant notion. He had little to say about the church in "The Value of Historical Christianity," but in 1892 the direction in which his thought was moving became explicit. "The function of the church," declared Dewey, "is to universalize itself and pass out of existence." [129]

In and through this philosophy of religion and social action, Dewey was striving to bring to full consciousness for his society the highest creative possibilities—the supreme ideals—that he sensed were inherent in the middle-class Christian democratic culture in which he was rooted. More than that, he was searching for a vision of wholeness, integration, union with the divine, a unity of the ideal and the real, that could satisfy his spiritual quest and sustain the common person in democratic America with a sense of ultimate meaning. During his remaining years at the University of Michigan he continued to work on his idea of the Christian democratic life developing the more radical implications of his outlook.

FOUR

"The Truth Shall Make You Free"

I N 1939 Dewey noted that many of his writings on the subject of religion during the latter part of his career had been "devoted to making explicit the religious values implicit in the spirit of science as undogmatic reverence for truth in whatever form it presents itself, and the religious values implicit in our common life, especially in the moral significance of democracy as a way of living together."[1] By the end of the eighties Dewey had gone far in integrating Christianity and the process of democratic social reconstruction. It was during the last four years in Ann Arbor (1890–1894) that the idea of the social and religious meaning of science, the experimental search for truth, first emerged as a central theme in his writings.

In the early 1890s, Dewey began to focus attention on the role that experimental science could play in the process of democratic social reconstruction. He came to believe that the most critical problem facing American society is achievement of a better integration of thought and social action. At the same time he adopted the belief that the scientific method should govern the quest for truth in the moral sphere as well as in the areas explored by the physical sciences. A democratic society should use the experimental method to determine what ought to be as well as what is. Having identified God and the life of the social organism—Christianity and democracy—Dewey was led to attribute high religious value to the scientific method of truth once he had concluded that it should be used in directing the social and ethical life. In short, Dewey closely linked the ethics of democracy and experimentalism and endowed both with deep religious significance.

Dewey's concern with the problem of the relation between the ideal and the real, then, came to focus increasingly on the relation between the experimental method and moral action; his faith in intelligence, which had earlier found prominent expression in his neo-Hegelian metaphysical speculations, became largely a faith in the method of experimental science as *the* instrument of moral guidance and democratic social reconstruction. It is also to be noted that it was in wrestling with the problems of the relation of thought and social action and of science and morals that Dewey was led slowly but surely to give up trying to use Kantian and Hegelian categories of thought and to develop the new pragmatist or instrumentalist theory of knowledge and logic with which he became identified as a mature thinker.

Charles Frankel has commented that "Dewey's trust in science gives a bit of the feeling of listening to a Strauss waltz, a melody from the time when the world was young."[2] From the perspective of the late twentieth century, America in the 1890s was relatively young at heart. In many quarters there was an optimistic idealism that after two world wars it is hard to appreciate. The problems generated by the new technology were not nearly as threatening and omnipresent as they have become. More importantly Dewey's early career coincides with the rise of the social sciences. In general the leaders of these new disciplines adopted an evolutionary perspective on social institutions, and they focused much of their attention on the way society shapes the behavior of individuals. In intellectual circles the social sciences were enthusiastically supported as enlightened instruments of social planning. The problems of poorly designed industrialization and urbanization would be corrected by fresh scientific analysis and reconstruction. The social sciences also promised to be effective tools of social criticism providing objective criteria with which to expose outmoded conventions and dogmas that deny freedom and equal opportunity to all. The prophets of the new science perceived society to be on the brink of an era of unlimited progress.

In many quarters this enthusiasm for the social sciences was fused with religious aspirations. For example, the Social Gospel movement had the support of social theorists like Henry George, whom Dewey came to regard as "one of the world's great social philosophers."[3] It was endorsed by economists and political scientists such as Richard J. Ely of Johns Hopkins and Henry Carter Adams of the University of Michigan. Ely, who had been an important influence in the education of Dewey's brother Davis at Johns Hopkins, published a volume on *The Social Aspects of Christianity* in 1889. His Christian social values were incorporated in the goals of the American Economic Association, which he led in founding in 1885. The AEA included Washington Gladden and Lyman Abbott and twenty-one other ministers among its original members.[4] In 1892 Ely founded the American Institute of Christian Sociology which had as its purpose: "To study in common how to apply the principles of Christianity to the social and economic difficulties of the present time."[5] Henry Carter Adams, who developed a liberal democratic social philosophy and had frequent discussions with Dewey in Ann Arbor, joined Dewey in 1892 in an S.C.A. program dealing with "Social Aspects of Christianity." He spoke on "Christianity as a Social Force" calling for the reform of American business through the application of the Golden Rule in new legislation and standards of conduct.[6]

Dewey was part of this movement which saw in the social sciences liberating instruments of Christian social reform. In addition, his fascination with the possibilities of social science and his concern to integrate experimental intelligence and social action caused him to get seriously interested in the role of the communications industry and public education in the shaping of American society. As a result, his faith in intelligence was gradually coupled with a faith in education as a fundamental instrument of social change. Dewey's interest in the schools emerges as of critical significance for him as a philosopher and reformer after his move to Chicago in 1894, but during the early 1890s one can see at work the intellectual and social currents that would take him eventually in this direction. There is a mounting concern with education of the public as essential to democratic social reconstruction. This, of course, was not a new idea in America. The role of a free press in maintaining an informed electorate was fundamental to the vision of the nation's founders, and from the 1830s onwards Americans increasingly viewed popular education as fundamental to the health of their society and to constructive social change.[7] Dewey was destined to develop and apply these characteristic American ideas in novel ways in the new social and intellectual context of his time.

Dewey's writings up through 1892 continue to show the strong influence of the absolute idealism and panentheism he embraced in the 1880s, even though much of this thinking is undergoing constant change. However, after 1892 his enthusiasm for neo-Hegelian idealism clearly begins to wane and references to God become increasingly scarce. In exploring Dewey's final years in Ann Arbor it is useful, therefore, to consider first his views on science, democracy, and Christianity during the years 1890–1892 when the categories of absolute idealism are still much in evidence and then to discuss the years 1893–1894. The earlier period also coincides with the time of Dewey's association with a flamboyant social activist who fired his imagination with dramatic visions of a new social order and impressed upon him the urgent need to reform American journalism. The story of this relationship provides the framework for understanding Dewey's intellectual and religious development in the early nineties.

Socializing Intelligence and the "Thought News" Affair

During the spring of 1888 an eccentric, utopian visionary and socialist reformer named Franklin Ford arrived at the University of Michigan looking for some social scientist or philosopher whom he could convert to his scheme for saving America, and, as he put it: "I got to John Dewey."[8] Ford was a former editor of a commercial paper in New York City, and he had become convinced that the key to the cure of the country's economic and social ills was a revolution in the newspaper business. It was Ford's thesis that the nation was an organism made up of diverse parts with different functions and in order for all of the parts to function well as a whole there was needed a centralized intelligence system. A reorganization of the American newspaper could answer this need, argued Ford. He dreamed of creating a centralized national news organization with subdivisions corresponding to the various divisions of labor in society. His idea was to liberate the newspaper from control by advertisers and special interests so that it would genuinely serve the public interest. He wanted to transform the newspaper into the primary vehicle for scientifically and systematically inquiring into, organizing and distributing the information essential to the successful functioning of the economic, political, and social life of the nation. The modern inventions of the locomotive and telegraph made this possible for the first time, he contended. What would preserve the integrity of this new organization of journalists is that it would be in the business of selling truth, facts, intelligence, and it would be successful as a business just insofar as it did this well. Self-interest and public interest would thus be harmonized.[9]

There was much to Ford's criticisms of American journalism, and even though his overall scheme was so idealistic as to be impractical, some of his ideas had merit. However, Ford was an intense, aggressive man whose personality undoubtedly set people against him. He expressed his visions in dramatic metaphors and sought followers willing to give him complete loyalty. When he arrived in Ann Arbor his only convert had been his brother Corydon, a physician among the copper miners in northern Michigan, who was a nonconformist and a volatile political radical. Together the Ford brothers managed to win over Dewey to their cause. As Corydon described the situation in his autobiography, *The Child of Democracy* (1894), Dewey "welcomed the proposition of a new economy in the State through the organization of intelligence—he was searching for the State when my brother and I found him, and his consciousness seized upon the division of labor as the key to the organic."[10]

Throughout his adult life Dewey was attracted to and unusually tolerant of eccentric, flamboyant, and forceful personalities who had some pet idea or project which interested him. In part, he was probably fascinated by something in these people that was repressed in himself as a result of his New England upbringing, but more to the point they enabled him to expand his interests and sympathies in novel ways that he could not accomplish alone, especially given his own reserved personality. What drew him in the case of Franklin Ford was Ford's firsthand knowledge of the newspaper business and the possibility of using Ford's project to apply his philosophical theories about the relation of intelligence and the world to the problems of society. As a neo-Hegelian, Dewey was, of course, familiar enough with the idea of society as an organism, the parts of which are coordinated by a principle of intelligence, and he especially liked the idea of setting up "the inquiry business in a systematic, centralized fashion." Ever since reading Auguste Comte as an undergraduate, Dewey had been interested in "his idea of a synthesis of science that should be a regulative method of an organized social life."[11] As early as 1886 Dewey was calling on the schools to "follow the example of the special sciences" and to organize cooperative research into their problems and to apply methods of solution in a systematic way.[12] In short, from very early Dewey was impressed by the promise of the social sciences. In Ford's scheme, Dewey thought he saw the possibility of creating a vast intelligence communications network that would greatly aid the organization of research in many fields and assist in the unification and direction of the life of the nation, the social organism.

Dewey's relationship with Ford was destined to last four years. From 1888 to 1892 the two men spent many hours together discussing politics, education, and philosophy and working on Ford's idea. In June of 1891 Dewey wrote to William James of the "wonderful personal experience" he had had collaborating with Ford.[13] In his *Outlines of a Critical Theory of Ethics* (1891), he mentions in the preface his indebtedness to Ford for helping him to understand "the social bearings of science and art."[14] Indeed, his work with Ford was one of the more critical factors that brought his thought to a focus around the idea of the experimental method of science as *the* method for discovering practical truth, including moral truth. With reference to his *Outlines,* he told James that "whatever freedom of sight and treatment there is in my ethics ... I got it from Franklin Ford."[15] Ford also succeeded in persuading Dewey in 1891 to become the director of a novel and ambitious newspaper venture called *Thought*

News, which was designed to put Ford's theories into practice. Dewey's decision to take on this vast project involved a moral commitment with a religious meaning, for the project was conceived as a strategy for idealizing the world in and through social science and journalism. With this commitment, a faith in education as a fundamental instrument of democratic reform begins to emerge as a force in Dewey's life and to take definite shape.

During the period of his association with Ford, Dewey became especially interested in logic, that is, the theory of the method to be employed by intelligence in the search for truth. At Johns Hopkins, Dewey had acquired a high respect for the scientific method, and he sought to harmonize his philosophic method with a scientific approach. In 1890 he stated clearly his conviction that since the scientific method of inquiry is *the* method for dealing with concrete fact, it alone is worthy of being called the method of truth.[16] Following Lotze, Sigwart, Bradley, and Bosanquet, he therefore contended that the new logic must be the theory of the method of intelligence employed by science. He persistently attacked what he called the old, scholastic, formal logic, because the latter has no aim except noncontradiction of original premises, that is, self-consistency. In "The Present Position of Logical Theory" (1891), he describes the purpose of the new logic as follows: "Its sole attempt is to get hold of and report the presupposition and rationale of science; its practical aim is to lay bare and exhibit the method of science so that the only seat of authority—that is, the authority, the *backing,* of truth—shall be forever manifest."[17] In the new age the method of science will be regarded as the sole intellectual authority on matters of truth, and the task of the logician, to which Dewey devoted his best efforts as a technical philosopher, is to clarify this method.

In an essay on "Poetry and Philosophy" (1891), Dewey expresses his continuing respect for poetic feeling and imagination as legitimate and important modes of apprehending and expressing truth. Poetry worthy of the name great is so precisely because it is "the genuine revelation of the ordinary day-by-day life of man," that is, it "flashes home to us some of the gold which is at the very heart and core of our everyday existence." However, states Dewey, the neo-Hegelian idealist: "I do not understand how that can be true for the imagination, for the emotions, which is not also true for intelligence." Furthermore, "without the basis of fact, of fact verifiable by science," poetic vision is "dainty foolery." In short, only if science and philosophy can justify to intelligence "in the cold, reflective way of critical system" the moral and metaphysical truth expressed in poetry, will poetry retain and expand its capacity to sustain and guide life, which is its vitally important social function. In the final analysis, the seat of intellectual authority is occupied by the method of intelligence, of science, alone.[18]

In developing his theory of logic, Dewey argues that the scientific method presupposes "some sort of fruitful and intrinsic connection of fact and thought," and the central problem of logic is to explain this relation of reality and ideas to each other. The whole Hegelian system had been an attempt to explain this interrelationship, asserts young Dewey, and during the early nineties he is still bent on showing that Hegel's conception of "the rationality of fact" and his logic are an expression of "the quintessence of the scientific spirit." "What Hegel means by objective thought," explains Dewey, "is the meaning, the significance of fact itself; and by methods of thought he understands simply the processes in which this meaning of fact is evolved." Thus Dewey tries initially to develop an experimental logic using Kantian and Hegelian categories.

He goes so far as to envision a triumphant union of the scientific spirit and philosophical idealism that would give the modern world the authoritative guidance, organization, and inspiration which he believes it so much needs. One major problem of the times, he argues, is that despite the tremendous developments in the sciences, "we have apparently the greatest disorganization of authority as to intellectual matters that the world has ever seen," and "the prevalent attitude and creed of scientific men is philosophic agnosticism, or disbelief in their own method when it comes to fundamental matters." By fundamental matters Dewey means moral value questions. Articulating a theme that becomes characteristic of his mature thought, he explains "that the contradiction is due to the fact that science has got far enough along to make its negative attitude towards previous codes of life evident, while its own positive principle of reconstruction is not yet evident." In other words, social science is still in its infancy, and a true science of moral values, which can give men and women the guidance they need in the modern world, has yet to be developed. One reason why young Dewey is so optimistic about scientific methodology is that he is an idealist who is convinced that the world, the whole fact, is rational through and through. Therefore, a method of truth proven in its ability to acquire a knowledge of facts should, if properly refined for philosophic use, be able to get at the full truth of the whole fact.[19]

Scientists resist discussion of an interrelationship of fact and thought such as is found in philosophical idealism because they fear moving "from the certainty of science into the cloudland of metaphysics" where "someone will spring upon them the old scholastic scheme of external, supernatural unrealities," observes Dewey. However, he is hopeful that this fear of metaphysics and idealism will soon dissolve for two reasons. First, the agnosticism which is so widespread is indicative that "the whole set of external, or non-immanent entities, is now on the point of falling away, of dissolving. We have got just so far, popularly, as holding that they are unknowable. In other words, they are crowded to the extreme verge. One more push and off they go. The popular consciousness will hold them not only to be unknowable, but not to be." The God of supernaturalism is almost dead. Secondly, the development of science is reaching the stage where the truth of the neo-Hegelian view of reality as an interconnected system is being demonstrated by scientific discovery and technological invention. Science is justifying the faith that the ideal and the real, intelligence and the world, are one. Human consciousness will soon know the true God who is immanent in the world as the meaning and organic unity of the world, and science will be recognized as the method by which this meaning or truth is being disclosed.[20]

Inspired by the Hegelians and encouraged by Ford, Dewey began to speak and write prophetically in grand historical terms. World history had arrived at a critical moment in the course of its onward progress. For several centuries a great spiritual movement had been underway "bringing man and man, man and nature, into wider and closer unity."[21] It had found expression in the poetry of Wordsworth, Shelley, Browning, and Whitman and in philosophical idealism. Now it was becoming apparent that science, which had seemed to be primarily destructive of spiritual values, was itself part of this movement with a critically important role to play as a synthesizing force in the future. In addition, democracy was giving these historical forces a vehicle of social expression. "The secret of this movement" is that there is "a single, comprehensive, and organizing unity," a principle of intelligence, underlying nature, society, and history. "Physical science in its advance has got to the thought of a continuous unity embodied in all natural process," and "social organization has gone far enough in the direction of democracy that the principle of movement towards unity comes to consciousness in that direction." Indeed, "in every direction there is coming to consciousness the power of an organizing activity underlying and rendering tributary to itself the apparent rigid dualisms holding over from the medieval structure." [22]

In 1890 Dewey told audiences at Smith College and the University of Vermont that it is the task of philosophy to apprehend the way in which this principle of intelligence, this unifying spiritual power is at work in nature and the varied aspects of modern culture, and then "to tell it in straightforward, simple syllables to the common consciousness." Dewey was convinced that this could be done. Paraphrasing the prophet Joel as quoted by Peter on the day of Pentecost (Acts 2:17), Dewey further asserts that when science and philosophy have accomplished this task, it will hasten "the day in which our sons and our daughters shall prophesy, and our young men shall see visions, and our old men dream dreams." [23] The spirit of a new world is about to possess the minds and hearts of men and women, and in this new world there will be a great synthesis of art, religion, science, philosophy, and democracy. The integration of scientific, poetic, and religious truth will stimulate a flowering of art and religion, and this new world will make possible liberation and self-realization for the common people. In all of this Dewey was further developing the rather abstract vision in the *Psychology* and trying to connect it to the American situation.

The general outline of much that he was urging about the constructive role of science in relation to art, religion, and society is close to the views of Ernest Renan as expressed in *The Future of Science*

(1850), which was one of Dewey's favorite books during this period.[24] In 1892 he published two essays on Renan's thought in the *Open Court,* an American journal founded in 1887 by Paul Carus, which had a special interest in both the science of religion and the religion of science.[25] In *The Future of Science,* Renan predicts that a religious faith in science will become the new unifying social faith replacing the dying faith of Christianity. However, toward the end of his life Renan became skeptical, and he lost his early faith in the common people, democracy, and the capacity of science to become a humane and moral influence. Criticizing Renan for his loss of faith, Dewey argues that unless "science itself advances to that comprehensive synthesis which will allow it to become a guide of conduct, a social motor" the result will be to leave dogmatic authority—the kind of authority Renan himself rejected in leaving the Roman Catholic Church—in control over the practical affairs of humanity.[26]

If the new social order is to be actualized the most critical problem, contends Dewey, is to relate thought and action, to bring human conduct into harmony with the organizing principle of intelligence at work in the world. As Dewey explained it in 1891 to his students in a course on "Movements of Thought in the Nineteenth Century," the eighteenth century, typified by Voltaire, had worked to free the individual by freeing thought from all external restrictions. However, the result was moral, social, and intellectual anarchy, because no positive meaning was developed for freedom. The nineteenth century witnessed the search for this positive meaning.

> The problem of nineteenth century thought has been to find the end or function of the individual, the freedom of the individual in social action, and not simply as a self-sufficing end in itself. If we take it on the side of intelligence, the problem of nineteenth century thought has been to find the conditions under which intelligence can pass into action, and thus become the controlling social force. The attempt to socialize intelligence, i.e., the attempt to make TRUTH the basis of social order and freedom, is the key to the nineteenth century.[27]

There are two grand Hegelian assumptions in this program to make intelligence the controlling social force and thereby the basis of social order and freedom. First, there is the conviction that the human being is essentially a rational and social being, and, second, there is the presupposition that truth is ultimately one and will consequently lead to unity of action and social harmony. This last idea is expressed in Dewey's *Outlines of a Critical Theory of Ethics* (1891).

> The intellectual movements of the last four or five centuries have resulted in an infinite specialization in methods and in an immense accumulation of fact. It is quite true, since the diversity of fact and of method has not yet been brought to an organic unity, that their social bearing is not yet realized. But when the unity is attained (as attained it must be if there is unity in the object of knowledge), it will pass into a corresponding unity of practice.[28]

Given the existing "divorce of knowledge from practice," Dewey contends that *"the* duty of the present is the socializing of intelligence —the realizing of its bearing upon social practice."

This interest in the relation of intelligence and social action and his speculations about the promise of social science led Dewey at this point in his career to undertake the task of trying to work out a scientific theory of ethics that would abolish the dualism of science and moral values once and for all. Reflecting on his career as a philosopher Dewey writes:

> I became more and more troubled by the intellectual scandal that seemed to me involved in the current (and traditional) dualism in logical standpoint and method between something called "science" on the one hand and something called "morals" on the other. I have long felt that the construction of a logic, that is, a method of effective inquiry, which would apply without abrupt breach of continuity to the fields designated by both these words, is at once our needed theoretical solvent and the supply of our greatest practical want.[29]

In the early 1890s his ethical thinking remained under the heavy influence of the philosophical idealism of T.H. Green, F.H. Bradley, and Edward Caird. Using the neo-Hegelian concept of organic unity to harmonize the individual and society, he continues to argue that ethics is the theory of human growth, self-realization, and freedom, and that there is no radical Kantian dualism between human desire and the moral good. However, he now begins to develop lengthy arguments in defense of the theory that there is no dualism between what is and what ought to be. His main point is that "moral insight, and therefore moral theory, consist simply in the everyday workings of the same ordinary intelligence that measures dry-goods, drives nails, sells wheat, and invents the telephone."[30] "The intelligence that is capable of declaring truth, or what is, is capable also of making known obligation. For obligation is only *practical* truth, the 'is' of doing."[31] "I should say that the 'right' always rises from and falls back into the 'is,' and that the 'right' is itself an 'is,'—the 'is' of action."

In other words, a knowledge of the moral good and of what a person should do in any situation may be arrived at simply on the basis of a rational analysis of the relations involved without reference to any transcendental realities or moral laws which are external to the situation.

> A man's duty is never to obey certain rules; his duty is always to respond to the nature of the actual demands which he finds made upon him,—demands which do not proceed from abstract rules, nor from ideals, however awe-inspiring and exalted, but from the concrete relations to men and things in which he finds himself.[32]

Dewey concedes that a moral guide like the Golden Rule may be useful as a tool of analysis, that is, as "an aid in discriminating what the nature of these relations and demands is." He also points out that the nature of the demands created by a situation will vary according to the individuality, the special capacities, of the person involved. A person's moral obligation is only to perform his or her "specific function" as Dewey puts it, and by function he means an activity in which the unique capabilities of an individual are exercised in response to the opportunities and needs created by the environment, "which when taken in its fullness is a community of persons."[33]

Dewey goes on to argue that the way to awaken moral aspiration on the part of people is to use intelligence to clarify what the moral good is. He is satisfied that "hortatory preaching" is useless; the "deadest of all dead things" is "a preacher's mere exhortation."

> People are somewhat tired of hearing, "You ought to do thus and so." ...This condition of fatigue may be due to the depravity of human nature; but I think it is rather due to its goodness; human nature

refuses to be moved except in the one truly human way—through intelligence. Get the fresher, more open outlook, the refined and clarified intelligence, and the emotions will take care of themselves. They *are* there, and all they need is freeing. And it is, in power and not in word, the truth that makes free.[34]

This is good Platonic psychology. All persons desire the good; evil is the result of ignorance; and virtue is knowledge. In an essay on "The Chaos in Moral Training" published in 1894, Dewey extends this thinking to apply to children urging that in their moral education, "the ideal is to appeal to the child's own intelligence and interest *as much as possible.*"[35]

Thomas Davidson, the Scottish-American philosopher, raised what is perhaps the most problematic aspect of Dewey's attempt to turn moral theory and conduct into behavior guided solely by the workings of intelligence. In a letter, he argued that Dewey had not explained the ground of obligation, that is, "Why I am bound." Dewey the existentialist replies:

Why, what am *I? I am* nothing but this binding; it is my bindings which make me what I am. "Why am I bound to do good?" Because that is what *I am.* And I have yet to see any other theory which can tell why I am bound to do good. I confess I have no meaning to remorse but failure. Failure of a man to be himself. I can imagine no deeper ruin.[36]

Dewey's point is that a person who has used intelligence to analyze the problematic situation in the human community will feel obligated to act in a responsible fashion from the perspective of the community, "because he *is* only as a member sharing in its needs, constituted by its relations and formed by its institutions."[37] In addition, the emphasis in Dewey's ethics falls on the critical importance for self-realization of will, decision, choice. One is reminded of Morris's statement: "A spirit is not made; it is self-made." Dewey seems to be saying that a person is bound to do the good in the final analysis simply because he or she chooses to be this kind of person and chooses the moral good for its own sake. It is noteworthy that in response to Davidson, Dewey does not appeal to the relationship of the human self to God, the perfect self, as the ultimate ground of moral obligation. In the light of this fact, Davidson might have pressed Dewey and asked: Does a person have the right to neglect his potential and to waste himself? Is the self ultimately constrained and bound in any sense from beyond itself?

Dewey's *Outlines of Ethics* (1891) was not very well received by most reviewers, but William James liked it and so did many of Dewey's students. A letter of support from James very much pleased Dewey, who was just discovering James' *Principles of Psychology* (1890). He wrote back to James contrasting his critics with his students.

> Unless a man is already living in the gospel and not under the law, as you express it, words thrown at him are idle wind. He doesn't understand what you mean, and he wouldn't believe you meant it, if he did understand. The hope seems to be with the rising generation.... Many of my students, I find, are fairly hungering. They almost jump at any opportunity to get out from under the load and to believe in their own lives. Pardon the somewhat confessional character of this note, but the man who has seen the point arouses the confessional attitude.[38]

The "load" to which Dewey refers here is the experience of being oppressed by an idea of the will of God that involves an arbitrary ideal external to the needs and possibilities of the actual situation. It concerns the feeling of a fundamental separation between everyday life and what is truly good and ultimately meaningful. Dewey's new theory of ethics and his elevation of experimental intelligence into the position of supreme intellectual authority grows out of his own search for wholeness, self-affirmation, and autonomy in the face of supernaturalism and a repressive brand of morals. It is part of his endeavor to demonstrate to himself and to others that liberating truth and the good are inherent in and may be found in the concreteness of everyday life as individuals interact compassionately and intelligently with the larger world around them. A person can and should believe in his or her own life, because it is full of divine possibilities which may be realized by relying on the light of one's own experience and intelligence.

It was Dewey's work in logic, ethics, and social philosophy all centering around the nature and function of the scientific method of intelligence that made him consider ever more seriously devoting his time and energy to Ford's scheme as a practical solution to the problem of relating intelligence and social action. On June 3, 1891, he wrote to William James urging him to take an interest in Ford's work, commenting: "I believe that a tremendous movement is impending, when intellectual forces which have been gathering since the Renaissance and Reformation, shall demand complete free movement, and by getting their physical leverage in the telegraph and printing press, shall, through free inquiry in a centralized way, demand the authority of all other so-called authorities."[39]

Two days later, on June 5, Ford told Dewey the time for action had come. The meeting at which this occurred is described by Dewey in a letter to Alice Dewey:

> Ford says he has done more thinking in the last two weeks than he ever did before in the same time. I never saw anything like his mind at work except the Corliss engine. I can fairly hear and feel it work when he is in the house. . . . He meant what he said about you being the bravest man and meant it for *me*. He told me last night that you were more ready for action than I was. He has got this thing figured out now and gave it to me last night in about two hours straight.

After giving an account of Ford's vision of the task ahead, which Ford likened to putting an immense revolving "spiritual belt about the earth's pulley," Dewey described the challenge with which Ford confronted him. Ford, writes Dewey, spoke as follows:

> Now it is your turn. You have helped me work out the thought— that's done. Our relationship on that basis is ended tonight. The question is whether you are going to have it go on on the basis of action—the thought has ended and the scheme has begun. You haven't taken the latter on your will yet and I'm not free until you do. There are two ways in which I can draw up the prospectus and go to Chicago. One is to say that the *idea* is organized and men in sight— the other is to say that a movement is already organized, which I represent. For me to say the latter would be a lie. You haven't given yourself enough to the scheme as action for me to say that. When I can get the burden off me and on to other men the thing is done.[40]

In short, Ford wanted Dewey to become the chief organizer of the "tremendous movement" about which Dewey had written James and been speculating in his writings. Ford addressed Dewey with the single-mindedness and intensity of the religious missionary or political revolutionary. The appeal was primarily directed to Dewey's social conscience, but Ford used their personal friendship to put added pressure on Dewey threatening to terminate their relationship if Dewey did not agree.

At first Dewey was hesitant, but Ford continued to work on both him and Alice Dewey. Then in August Dewey wrote to his wife that he had committed himself.

> Ford and I have been down the river a couple of miles twice this week and been swimming. The point about the "situation and the relationship" is that I have told Ford I stood beside him and my relationship to the University would have to take care of itself as subordinated to the primary relationship.[41]

Working with Ford had intensified Dewey's social conscience and brought his concern with social and political reform to a focus around the ideal of a centralized intelligence system. Now Dewey had committed himself to act for the sake of social change guided by this ideal regardless of what the university's attitude might be. As Dewey explained it to William James, Ford had led him to understand "the true or practical bearing of idealism," that is, he had made Dewey recognize that the philosophical idealist who knows that in theory there is a unity of intelligence and the external world "must finally secure the conditions of its objective expression."[42]

However, Dewey was not entirely convinced that he and Ford really knew exactly what they were doing. His anxiety was revealed in a brief essay entitled "The Scholastic and the Speculator," which he wrote up for a student journal during the fall. The essay is full of complex metaphors and bombastic assertions revealing the influence of Ford's own literary style. It attacks scholars who do not employ their learning as "a means of understanding and facilitating human action." The responsible thinker must at some point take his fund of intelligence and "jump into the flood of moving fact" contends Dewey. Then, undoubtedly describing his feeling about his own situation with Ford, he writes: "This jump into the unknown ocean off the springboard of the known ... always is and always must remain the individual venture: the stake of self or some part of self against the ongoing stream of life. Every judgment a man passes on life is perforce, his 'I bet,' his speculation."[43]

Dewey knew there was a risk in what he had agreed to do with Ford, and he did not go so far as to give up his university responsibilities during the academic year 1891–1892. Nevertheless, having committed himself he worked hard planning what was to be the first step in actualizing Ford's idea: publication of "A Journal of Inquiry and a Record of Fact" to be entitled *Thought News.*[44] Dewey was to be the director of the project. On March 16, 1892, Dewey issued a press release announcing that publication of the new journal would commence in April.

Democracy as the Revelation and Incarnation of Truth

Just three days prior to this announcement, Professor Fred Newton Scott, who had collaborated with Dewey and Ford on this project, delivered a lengthy Students' Christian Association address entitled "Christianity and the Newspaper." It was carefully designed to point out to the university community the great moral and religious significance of the newspaper and of the kind of undertaking that was shortly to be unveiled.[45] Scott's address was part of a larger S.C.A. program created to obtain the views of university faculty on religion. Nineteen faculty members in all participated delivering Sunday morning talks in four general areas: "Historical Aspects of Christianity," "Social Aspects of Christianity," "Science and Religion," and "The Christian Life."[46] Scott, Dewey, and Henry Carter Adams spoke on the social aspects, and Dewey's lecture, "Christianity and Democracy," came just a week after Scott's. The lecture by Scott is a revealing document. It sets forth with great clarity a view of Christianity very similar to Dewey's position, and undoubtedly Scott was heavily influenced by Dewey, who had been his teacher. Furthermore, Scott's address discloses the kind of moral interest and religious enthusiasm which was attached to the *Thought News* undertaking and which accounts for much of the excitement and sense of high purpose that marked Dewey's own involvement in it.

Scott was himself an expert telegrapher and had had considerable experience in the newspaper business before finally committing himself to university teaching in the areas of literature and rhetoric. Dewey came to recognize Scott's superior intellectual gifts when the latter was one of his graduate students, and after Scott joined the faculty of the English department in 1889, he and Dewey cooperated in teaching a course on aesthetics in the philosophy department. Scott's "theory of the social character of literary expression," a theory "which sees in the style and matter of literature phases of the movement of intelligence toward complete social expression," especially interested Dewey.[47] The two men also worked together during the early nineties as faculty advisers to the *Inlander,* a student literary monthly. His interests in journalism led Scott to introduce in 1891 the first course on that subject offered by an American university and to assist Dewey and Ford with *Thought News.*[48] Another colleague of Dewey's, young George Herbert Mead, who had joined the Philosophy Department in the fall of 1891, had also played with the idea of using the newspaper as an educational tool of social reform, and he, too, became enthusiastic when he learned about the Ford scheme.[49]

Scott began his lecture on "Christianity and the Newspaper" by asserting that Christianity is not to be viewed as a particular religion among other religions, but rather as the culmination of the evolution of world religion and the realization of the very essence of all religion. This essence Scott identified with a social reality. Christianity is the vital principle in the advance of civilization, and it is embodied in the material works of humanity as well as in its laws and institutions.

> Christianity exists today, not in creeds, but in the lives of men, and not in individual men, but in men as parts of the social organism. It is embodied in their institutions, in their tools, in all their instruments of progress, in all their means of communication, in their laws, their prisons, their asylums, their schools, their places of business. It has found its way into material substances. Wherever iron and steel and copper have been so shaped as to serve as an instrument for bringing men closer together, there Christianity is embodied; and whosoever uses that instrument rightly is inevitably furthering the spread of Christianity. In the same way, whoever is voting for laws which

embody Christian principle is working for Christ. He is making more efficient that organism in which society is working out its own salvation.[50]

Insofar as they do not realize the underlying unity of the spiritual and the material, God and the world, Christian people suffer conflict and division in their lives. Scott's answer is to tell people the truth regarding the meaning of their secular activities in relation to God and the life of the whole. "Show to the business man, the farmer, the lawyer, the real meaning of the work in which he is engaged, and he will be set free, the chasm between his working life and his religious life will be bridged. . . . His integrity in the true sense, his oneness and wholeness of mind and purpose, will be restored." This is the heart of the gospel preached by Scott. To wake up to the religious meaning, the ultimate meaning, of one's everyday secular life is nothing less than a truly liberating religious experience: "It amounts to a conversion: It is the recovery of one's birthright. It is the conviction that life, insofar as it is real is Christian—Christian to the very core."[51] Dewey could only have said "amen" when he heard these words, because his life at this time was determined by just such a conversion and he was preaching the same gospel.

The critical task for those concerned with social liberation and progress is, then, to make people conscious in specific and concrete terms of the interconnection between what they do in their everyday activities and the life of the social organism as a whole. For Scott this is the real significance and purpose of "all investigation in science, in philosophy, in economics, in the whole range of human knowledge —it is simply a huge searching after Christianity, an attempt to bring home to men the meaning of their lives." According to Scott this meaning is the truth of which Christ spoke when he said, "Ye shall know the truth and the truth shall make you free" (John 8:32). At this juncture Scott introduced the novel idea in his talk. "The newspaper is the most powerful ally that Christianity has ever had," for by means of the newspaper men and women may be educated and enlightened. Following Ford he called for reform of the newspaper business. All newspapers should "band together into one great organism bent upon conveying the truth of life to the minds of men." In a vague reference to Dewey's project Scott commented that a movement in this direction has already begun. Scott further asserted that the newspaper, which meets the requirements of the times as he has outlined them, "is for us today, the voice of the real, the living Christ." In short, in a reformed and centralized newspaper lies the hope of the world.[52]

This is Christianity transformed into social ethics and a faith in the liberating power of intelligence, truth, and education. Underlying Scott's whole argument is the assumption that if you can persuade people to give up otherworldliness and supernaturalism and to believe in the unity of the religious and the secular, the only further thing they need in order to liberate themselves and to regenerate society is intelligence, education. Communicate to people, who are essentially rational and social beings, the truth, the facts about what is happening in and to society, the social organism, and they will all cooperate for the common good. This is the core of the optimism that possessed Scott and many other late nineteenth-century liberals. Dewey basically shared this view, but his own position as set forth in "Christianity and Democracy" is more subtle and complex.

Dewey's press release announcing plans to publish *Thought News*, came shortly after Scott's S.C.A. address. According to the release the new paper would "report new investigations and discoveries in their net outcome instead of in their overloaded gross bulk," and "note new contributions to thought, whether by book or by magazine." However, the central idea of the new publication was to "treat questions of science, letters, state, school and church as parts of the one moving life of man ... and not relegate them to separate documents of merely technical interest."[53] "Thought News," continued the announcement, would "not discuss philosophic ideas *per se* but use them as tools in interpreting the movements of thought." Dewey elaborated on the intended relations between philosophy and his new paper in a press interview.

> There is some fact to which philosophic ideas refer. That fact is the social organism. When philosophic ideas are not inculcated by themselves but used as tools to point out the meaning of phases of social life they begin to have some life and value.... Where it can be seen for example, that Walt Whitman's poetry, the great development of short stories at present, the centralizing tendency in the railroads and

the introduction of business methods into charity organizations are all parts of one organic social movement, then the philosophic ideas about organism begin to look like something definite. The facts themselves get more meaning, too, when viewed with relation to one principle than when treated separately as a jumble.[54]

Thought News using philosophic ideas as tools of interpretation would try to bring people to a greater awareness of the moving life of American civilization and would further the growth of society by supplying critical information to "people around the country who are scientifically interested in the study of social questions."[55]

Dewey's S.C.A. address, "Christianity and Democracy," did not directly discuss the newspaper. It was hardly necessary after Scott's address. Nevertheless, "Christianity and Democracy" was written in part with the intention of indicating the moral and religious signifi-cance of a project like *Thought News*, which was now a major topic of conversation in the university. The general theme of the address was a recurrent one in Dewey's religious thought: the identity of the religious and the social, Christianity and democracy. Like Scott, Dewey closely identifies Christianity with the disclosure of practical truth to humanity in the course of the advance of civilization. What is novel in his address is the way he develops this idea. Citing Elijah Mulford's *The Republic of God* as an authority, he argues that the essence of Christianity is the revelation of truth. He closely links the revelation of truth to the process of divine incarnation, which had been a prominent theme in some of his earlier religious writings. He then asserts that the essence of democracy is freedom—the freedom to discover, to communicate, and to embody truth leading to the progressive liberation and unification of humanity. Consequently, authentic Christianity today is practiced and experienced by those who participate in the liberating processes of revelation and incarna-tion that constitute democratic community life.

Dewey begins with a sociological interpretation of the origin and nature of religion, to which he continued to adhere throughout his life. Clarifying views expressed earlier on this subject, he argues that modern research demonstrates that "every religion has its source in the social and intellectual life of a community or race." Religious symbols, rites, and doctrines are expressions both of "the sacred and divine significance" of the values embodied in the social relations of a community and of "the mental attitude and habit of a people," their aesthetic and intellectual values. As long as religious cults and creeds express the existing social, aesthetic, and intellectual values the religion remains vital, but when these change the old religion with its symbols and rites becomes separated from life and begins to die. The mistake commonly made is to identify the essence of religion with these external manifestations. The problem of religious readjustment in a time of social and intellectual change is to find new forms adequate to the new values.[56]

Turning to Christianity, Dewey asserts that of all religions Christianity should be the last to be identified with "a religion," that is, a fixed set of doctrines and rites, because the essence of Christianity is the ongoing process whereby truth is disclosed and realized in practice. Following closely Elijah Mulford's exegesis of certain passages in the Gospel of John, Dewey explains his point:

> Jesus had no cult or rite to impose; no specific forms of worship, no specific acts named religion. He was clear to the other side. He proclaimed that this very setting up of special acts and institutions as part of the imperfections of life.... "The hour cometh and now is when true worshippers shall worship the Father in spirit and in truth" —the hour when worship shall be simply the free and truthful expression of man in his action. Jesus had no special doctrine to impose—no special set of truths labeled religious. "If *any* man will *do* his *will,* he shall know the doctrine." "Ye shall know the truth and the truth shall make you free." The only truth Jesus knew of as religious was Truth. There were no special religious truths which he came to teach; on the contrary, his doctrine was that Truth, however named and however divided by man, is one as God is one; that getting hold of truth and living by it is religion.

Seeking and acting according to truth and coming to understand truth by living it is the heart of Jesus' teaching. The essence of Christianity is, then, a process of ongoing revelation. We live in a "moving world," and Christianity is not to be restricted to some fixed historical revelation. "The revelation of truth must continue as long as life has new meanings to unfold, new action to propose." "Christianity if universal, if revelation, must be the continuously unfolding, never ceasing discovery of the meaning of life." Wherever this is going on, there is to be found "the real Christianity."[57] Dewey has come very close here to associating Christianity with what he later identifies as the process of education in the broadest sense.

Dewey tries to drive his point home by criticizing the church for its "faithlessness" insofar as it has opposed the rise of science. Failing to understand the plain direct sense of Jesus' teaching, the church identified Christianity with a limited historically conditioned set of ideas about the relations of God and the world and humanity and nature.

> But it turned out then as ever — truth exists not in word, but in power. As in the parable of the two sons, the one who boasted of his readiness to serve in the vineyard went not, while the younger son who said he would not go, went out into the vineyard of nature and by obedience to the truth revealed the deeper truth of unity of law, the presence of one continuous living force, the conspiring and vital unity of all the world.[58]

In the modern world, the revelation which is Christianity is being extended and deepened by science and philosophy.

Dewey fuses his earlier emphasis on the theme of incarnation in "The Value of Historical Christianity" with his idea of Christianity as revelation. In 1892 he still had an Hegelian version of the Gospel to preach. Jesus, John, and Paul did become fully conscious for the first time in human history of the liberating truth that "man was an incarnation of God and in virtue of this incarnation redeemed from evil."[59] In other words, "the individual is free in his life because the individual is the organ of the absolute Truth of the universe."[60] Dewey explains more fully this fundamental Christian idea:

> The one claim that Christianity makes is that God is truth; that as truth He is love and reveals Himself fully to man, keeping back nothing of Himself; that man is so one with the truth thus revealed that it is not so much revealed to him as *in* him; he is its incarnation; that by the appropriation of truth, by identification with it, man is free; free negatively, free from sin, free positively, free to live his own life, free to express himself, free to play without let or limitation upon the instrument given him — the environment of natural wants and forces.[61]

There is no essential or unbridgeable dualism between human nature and saving truth. Human beings in their everyday existence are free to discover this truth and to realize themselves and to create social well-being. Their progressive appropriation and realization of the living truth in and through their daily social life is the revelation of the divine in the human, the incarnation of God in human nature. It is with this understanding of the central truth of Christianity in mind that Dewey could tell a student group in the spring of 1892 that "what Jesus taught and the fourth Gospel and Paul interpreted him to mean was that man *is* saved, not to add another burden to seek his salvation."[62] In the latter part of his address Dewey endeavors to identify the ongoing process of revelation and incarnation of truth, which is Christianity, with democracy.

> Democracy ... appears as the means by which the revelation of truth is carried on. It is in democracy ... that the incarnation of God in man (man, that is to say, as organ of universal truth) becomes a living, present thing, having its ordinary and natural sense. This truth is brought down to life; its segregation removed; it is made a common truth enacted in all departments of action, not in one isolated sphere called religious.

Democracy is the means of the revelation and incarnation of truth because it means freedom.

> Democracy is, as freedom, the freeing of truth. Democracy ... means the loosening of bonds, the wearing away of restrictions, the breaking down of barriers. . . . Through this doing away with restrictions, whatever truth, whatever reality there is in man's life is freed to express itself. . . . Truth makes free, but it has been the work of history to free truth—to break down walls of isolation and of class interest, which hold it in and under.

As the barriers to the discovery and communication of truth are broken down by democracy, the truth is shared widely and "becomes the Common-wealth, the Republic, the public affair." A "community of truth" develops leading to "the spiritual unification of humanity, the realization of the brotherhood of man, all that Christ called the Kingdom of God." Such is Dewey's vision of the way in which democracy is the realization of the essence of Christianity.[63]

Dewey recognizes that his identification of Christianity with experimental inquiry and democracy, which involves free communication and education of the public, contradicts traditional interpretations of Christianity. In this connection he points out that in earlier historical periods, it was not possible for people to appreciate the "direct, natural sense" of Jesus' teaching about freedom or to understand the true essence of Christianity as an ongoing unfolding revelation and incarnation of truth. In explaining why this has been so, he returns to the idea of experimental religion that he learned from Coleridge, Marsh, and Morris. He points out that a person is able to appreciate and understand liberating practical truth only by doing it, embodying it, which involves participating in a community where this truth is concretely expressed in habits and institutions. He writes:

> Had Jesus Christ made an absolute detailed and explicit statement upon all the facts of life, that statement would not have had meaning —it would not have been revelation—until men began to realize in their own action the truth he declared—until they themselves began to *live* it. In the final analysis, man's own action, his own life movement, is the only organ he has for receiving and appropriating truth. Man's action is found in his social relationships—the way in which he connects with his fellows. It is man's social organization, the state in which he is expressing himself, which always has and always must set the form and sound the key-note to the understanding of Christianity.

In earlier historical epochs people were not free and were not treated as organs of universal truth. Class divisions prevented free communication. Access to the truth was restricted. Consequently Jesus' teachings were understood in an "unnatural and sentimental sense." It was thought that an individual could receive saving truth only through external and supernatural agencies accessible in a special religious sphere isolated from ordinary life. The emergence of the democratic organization of society has dramatically altered the situation making it possible for people to understand the plain meaning of Jesus' teaching and the real meaning of Christianity.[64]

His idea that real learning and understanding come about in and through working and living with other persons became a basic principle of Dewey's later theory of education. For example, in *The School and Society* (1899) Dewey writes about his model elementary school: "Learning? certainly, but living primarily, and learning through and in relation to this living."[65] The formulation of social values by moral teachers and the social sciences is vitally important in the direction of society, but just telling children or people *about* the truth is not by itself enough to lead them to a real understanding of these values. The truth must be encountered experimentally, that is, it must be practiced and institutionalized, directly experienced, in order to be appropriated personally.[66] Pursuing a line of thought consistent with new sociological ways of thinking, Dewey has here arrived at an important distinction between a purely theoretical knowledge, which by itself does not change character and foster growth, and the kind of experiential understanding that does alter habits and attitudes and leads to growth.

Dewey ends his address with a prophetic challenge and warning to the church. Unwillingness on the part of the church to devote itself to the cause of social democracy, he declares, is evidence of "practical unbelief in the presence of God in the world." The question before the church, then, is this:

> Is the partial revelation ready to die as partial in order to live in the fuller? Can we surrender—not simply the bad *per se*—but the possessed good in order to lay hold of a larger good? Shall we welcome the revelation of truth now going on in democracy as a wider realization of the truth formerly asserted in more or less limited channels and with a more or less unnatural meaning?

In short, will the church with its rites and creeds recognize in democracy and experimental science "the fuller expression of its own ideal and purpose?" Dewey concludes:

> Surely to fuse into one the social and the religious motive, to break down the barriers of Pharisaism and self-assertion which isolate religious thought and conduct from the common life of men, to realize the state as the one commonwealth of truth—surely this is a cause worth battling for.
>
> Remember Lot's wife, who looked back, and who, looking back, was fixed into a motionless pillar.[67]

In summary, the Christian moral and religious life finds its fulfillment in the democratic way of life coupled with the experimental search for truth, for this way promises the liberation and unification of humanity.

The end of the *Thought News* affair itself actually turned out to be a great anticlimax. The project received considerable publicity in the press, and before long exaggerated accounts of what Dewey had planned were circulating and editorials were poking fun at him. Dewey himself began playing down the novelty and radical nature of the undertaking asserting early in April that "its object is not to introduce a new idea into journalism at large, but to show that philosophy has some use."[68] Before long he had to face the harsh and embarrassing truth that the whole project was too much for him to handle. The first issue of *Thought News* never went to press. "No issue was made," explained Dewey many years later. "It was an over enthusiastic project which we had not the means nor the time to carry through. . . . The *idea* was advanced for those days, but it was too advanced for the maturity of those who had the idea in mind."[69] Admitting this to himself, Scott, and Ford must have been painful. It brought his association with Ford to an abrupt and no doubt stormy end. Some years later Dewey commented that the man with whom he had so much enjoyed working had eventually revealed himself to be a "scoundrel."[70] Nevertheless Dewey's collaboration with Ford between 1888 and 1892 and the *Thought News* affair did a great deal to bring his social and religious thought to a focus around the democratic and scientific methods of discovering, communicating, and realizing practical truth. Much of Dewey's future work in logic, education, moral theory, and social philosophy would be an endeavor to clarify the exact nature of these methods and values. During the Chicago years (1894–1904) Dewey's identification of Christianity with democracy and the revelation of truth would enable him to make the school and the process of public education his central interest as a religiously concerned progressive philosopher.

Even though the school rather than the newspaper was destined to become the chief focus of his interests as a reformer, it is noteworthy that Dewey did not abandon the ideas involved in the *Thought News* project itself. The idea of communication would emerge as a major concept in his later philosophy. He continued to call for a union of the daily press with up-to-date social science as essential to the creation of an authentic democratic community having "an organized, articulate Public." For example, in his essay "Search for the Great Community" (1927), he writes:

> The highest and most difficult kind of inquiry and a subtle, delicate, vivid and responsive art of communication must take possession of the physical machinery of transmission and circulation and breathe life into it. When the machine age has thus perfected its machinery, it will be means of life and not its despotic master. Democracy will come into its own, for democracy is a name for a life of free and enriching communion. It had its seer in Walt Whitman. It will have its consummation when free social inquiry is indissolubly wedded to the art of full and moving communication.[71]

Dewey himself would never again try to edit or manage a newspaper, but he would continue to write for a variety of popular journals in an effort to relate his philosophical understanding to contemporary social issues.

Something of the faith and enthusiasm that radiated from Dewey during the years under consideration is expressed in several letters written during the summer of 1892 by George Herbert Mead, Dewey's brilliant young colleague in the Philosophy Department.[72] In time Mead's work on the idea of the human being as a social being would exercise an important influence on Dewey and American social psychology at large. As a youth he had seriously considered the ministry as a profession but had abandoned orthodox religion and Scotch intuitionalism during his college years in the early eighties. As a result he was plunged into a prolonged spiritual crisis. He became an agnostic but was haunted by the idea of a universe without meaning and purpose. While at Harvard, Josiah Royce restored his faith for a brief time, and as a graduate student in Germany he tried to give life meaning by identifying himself with the cause of social liberation. However, it was not until he came to Ann Arbor in 1891 and began working with Dewey that he really found the philosophical perspective and sense of meaning he was searching for. Mead writes: "Mr. Dewey is a man of not only great originality and profound thought, but the most appreciative thinker I ever met—I have gained more from him than from any one man I ever met."[73]

Besides technical help with his physiological psychology, which was Mead's special field, Mead gained from Dewey a profoundly satisfying philosophical vision, which he explains as follows:

> I have seen ... that all matter, especially the human organism, becomes spiritual when one sees in it the processes of life and thought, that the body and the soul are but two sides of one thing, and that the gulf between them is only the expression of the fact that our life does not realize the ideal of what our social life will be when our functions and acts shall be not simply ours but the processes of the great body politic which is God as revealed in the universe.[74]

Working with Dewey, Mead developed "an unshakeable faith in a single reality to which all paths lead," a "faith in the unity and meaning of life," and he was able to affirm that "what I am at work on has all the meaning of social and religious life in it."[75] For men like Scott and Mead, and undoubtedly for many students as well, Dewey, with his mix of philosophical idealism, Christianity, democracy and science had himself become something of a social and religious prophet, and they became supportive colleagues as he continued to explore the more radical implications of his thought.

The Ethics of Democracy and Experimentalism

In 1891 Dewey issued a revised edition of his *Psychology* for the last time. Publications such as "Self-Realization as the Moral Ideal" (1893) and *The Study of Ethics: A Syllabus* (1894) indicate why he did not attempt another revision. He no longer could accept T.H. Green's theory of the ideal self and his own theory in *Psychology* that self-realization is a process of reproducing in the individual some presupposed ideal personality and universal self. In short, largely under the influence of James' *Principles of Psychology,* which was rapidly winning recognition as the most important contribution to psychology of the century, Dewey by 1893 was rethinking his psychology and ethics and cutting them loose from neo-Hegelian metaphysics and theology. As he put it in 1911, James' "biological conception" of the psyche "was perhaps the fundamental thing" in causing the major shift in his thought.[76] According to this Darwinian approach the capacities of the mind have been developed in and through the struggle of the human organism to achieve a satisfactory adjustment with its environment. Thought is organically related to conduct. The original and primary function of thought is the direction of practical action, solving problems, selecting means for the achievement of desired ends. In this view ideas and beliefs are understood to have an essentially instrumental function in guiding human activity through problematic situations to realization of chosen purposes. Dewey writes that James' biological interpretation "worked its way more and more into all my ideas and acted as a ferment to transform old beliefs."[77] The end result would be pragmatism and a new humanistic naturalism.

In 1893 Dewey continued to identify the self with will and the ethical ideal remained for him self-realization, but he now found serious problems with the neo-Hegelian concept of the ideal self, that is, the idea of God as he conceived it in the *Psychology:*

> The difficulty ... bound up with the question why a completely realized self should think it worth while to duplicate itself in an unrealized, or relatively empty, self, how it could possibly do this even if it were thought worth while, and why, after the complete self had produced the incomplete self, it should do so under conditions rendering impossible (seemingly eternally so) any adequate approach of the incomplete self to its own completeness—this difficulty, I say, should make us wary of the conception.[78]

What most bothered Dewey was that the concept of some eternal perfect self or absolute ideal is of little use in giving practical guidance in concrete situations, and "it makes a dualism, practically unbridgeable, between the moral and scientific phases of our experience."[79] Dewey was finally having to concede that neo-Hegelian metaphysical categories could not be so easily fused with experimental science.

Dewey's ethical studies during his last years in Ann Arbor are especially concerned with employing the categories of biological science and functional psychology in an effort to develop a scientific theory for making moral value judgments. Sounding very much like an ethical naturalist even though he calls his position "experimental idealism," Dewey asserts that the science of ethics is continuous with and "completes the analysis of reality—experience—begun by physical and biological science" and "does not introduce a new and opposed set of ideas."[80] In the course of his new psychological and ethical studies he reformulates his definition of the self and the general nature of ideals. He also refines his idea of the criterion for judging the moral value of an act. In all of this Dewey is concerned to formulate ideas which are experimentally verifiable, of practical use, and consistent with the ethics of democracy. Finally, his work in ethics includes an experimentalist's reinterpretation of the nature and meaning of Christian love.

The self, explains Dewey, is to be conceived as "always a concrete specific activity."[81] The self is to be identified with concrete processes of feeling, thinking, and willing going on in this particular person at this particular time and place. The ideal or moral end, that is, the self which is the end of the process of realization, is not something outside and beyond this concrete specific activity. Ideals are specific possibilities. They express the full meaning and value of the present activity. They are apprehended in and through a reflective analysis of the relations involved in the situation at hand and of the consequences of current activity. "True ideals are the *working hypothesis* of action; they are the best comprehension we can get of the value of our acts; their use is that they mark our consciousness of what we are doing, not that they set up remote goals. Ideals are like stars; we steer by them, not towards them."[82] To be guided in action by an ideal means to seek to realize the full objective meaning and value of this present specific activity, which here and now constitutes one's real and true self. So conceived, ideals must necessarily change with the special circumstances of different situations and vary according to the unique capacities of different persons. Dewey has arrived here at the kind of "situation ethics" approach that characterizes his mature thought.

What is the criterion Dewey would have a person use in judging or determining what constitutes the ideal in a particular situation? Moving toward the concept of growth that plays a major role in his later thought, Dewey writes: "The basis for discriminating between 'right' and 'wrong' in the judgement is found in the fact that some acts tend to narrow the self, to introduce friction into it, to weaken its power, and in various ways to disintegrate it, while other acts tend to expand, invigorate, harmonize, and in general organize the self."[83]

In other words, the ideal in general is the growth and integration of the self, and, therefore, the specific ideal in a concrete situation will always be to act so as to harmonize the impulses seeking expression in the present activity with the life of the whole self. The good deed is always organically related to, and, therefore, supportive and expressive of the whole self rather than the assertion of some particular aspect of the self at the expense of the whole. Again, Dewey does not conceive of the whole self as necessarily conforming to some fixed idea, and in introducing the idea of the whole self into the process of judging right actions Dewey is only urging that the consequences of present activity for the future growth and harmony of the self be taken into consideration in the process of valuation.

Since a good act so conceived realizes the full positive value of present activity in the sense that it is "the organ through which the whole self finds outlet," Dewey argues that the act is an end in itself worthy of being performed for its own sake and the whole self is, therefore, free to devote itself with undivided attention to the act. "The good man, in a word, is his whole self in each of his acts," and "his whole self being in the act, the deed is solid and substantial, no matter how trivial the outer occasion."[84] This complete identification of self with a concrete specific action characterizes all truly moral conduct. "To find the self in the highest and fullest activity possible at the time, and to perform the act in the consciousness of its complete identification with self (which means, I take it, with complete interest) is morality, and is realization."[85] Dewey further points out that, if the ideal is some fixed self or absolute ideal outside the concrete activity, then the act is not done for its own sake but as a means to, or partial preparation for, attaining some remote ideal outside the situation. This is not true moral action and self-realization as he defines them. "Acts are to be done as good, not for the sake of goodness."[86]

In *The Study of Ethics* Dewey retained his faith in what he had earlier termed the "ethical postulate," which seeks to harmonize the individual concern for self-realization with the need of the community for morality and social responsibility. A right action, argues Dewey, contributes both to the organizing of the self and the organizing of the situation. "The postulate is verified by being acted upon.

The proof is experimental."[87] No longer did Dewey invoke some neo-Hegelian cosmic principle of organic unity to justify the postulate. However, he continued to adhere to a social psychology that rejects an atomistic individualism and any fundamental dualism of self and world. With this social psychology, he had the theoretical framework with which to make intelligible his reconciliation of the individual and society, self-realization and the common good.

Even though *The Study of Ethics* does not discuss the idea of God and religious faith, it does argue that the consciousness of a truly liberated moral agent may acquire a religious quality.

> The very aim of the good man is itself a unification in thought, as the deed is in act, of the realties of the situation.... In doing the deed, then, the universe of Reality moves through him as its conscious organ. Hence the sense of the dignity and validity of the act—the essence of the religious consciousness. Hence the joy, the feeling of full life, and the peace, the feeling of harmonized force, which accompany the good act.[88]

In this statement Dewey has identified the religious consciousness— or what in the 1930s he would designate "the religious quality of experience"—with a sense of being in active harmony with the larger universe growing out of an experience of unifying the ideal and the real.

In line with his earlier teachings on the nature of healthy religious emotion, Dewey emphasizes that the experience of joy and peace, which constitute the religious quality of the moral consciousness, is not realized by doing certain deeds as a means of achieving these feelings. It comes about spontaneously when the self identifies itself completely with the moral action to be performed. The feelings of joy and peace appear as unsought fruits of the action. The moral and religious consciousness "is not a distinct thing, apart from the act: *it is the act realized in its full meaning.*"[89]

The Study of Ethics shows that Dewey's religious thinking was undergoing important changes, but in 1894 he is still anxious to demonstrate that his new thinking is in keeping with the true spirit of historical Christianity. For example, in *The Study of Ethics* when he is defending his notion that the task of a theory of ethics is not to prescribe moral rules but to develop experimental insight into the nature and meaning of moral action, he appeals to the authority of Jesus asking: "Did he [Jesus] lay down rules for life, or did he give insight into [the] nature of life? That is, is 'salvation' conformity to some scheme laid down, or is it the freeing of life reached through knowledge of its real nature and relations?"[90] Again, he cannot resist offering a naturalistic explanation of the Pauline doctrine of repentance and "salvation by grace." Guilt arises, asserts Dewey, when the self in retrospect realizes that some past action was bad in the sense of not being an organic expression of the whole personality. However, the fact that a person recognizes what was bad as bad and feels guilt means that he or she is already becoming a better person. Consequently, one should not dwell on bad acts and cultivate guilt feelings. A person should use the experience of guilt simply as a stimulus to learn from past experience, and then the past should be put behind one trusting that there is at work in the self already a good capable of overcoming past evil. In Paul's writings there appears, states Dewey, "the first historical consciousness, on the part of humanity, that sin, when it becomes a *consciousness* of sin organically referred back to character, means also a consciousness of a good which can take that evil up into itself and so conquer it, which in fact, has already begun so to do."[91]

Finally, *The Study of Ethics* concludes with a paragraph in praise of the supreme value and comprehensive nature of the virtue of love, which Dewey may well have written with the intention of offering a contemporary experimentalist's version of a hymn in praise of love such as Paul sets forth in I Corinthians 13.

> Psychologically, then, love ... is the fulfilling of the law—the law of self. Love is the complete identification of subject and object, of agent and function.... It is complete interest in, full attention to, the objects, the aims of life, and thus insures responsibility. It provides the channel which gives the fullest outlet to self, which stirs up the powers and keeps them at their fullest tension, and thus guarantees, or *is,* freedom, adequate self-expression.

Having noted that "in many respects the discussions of virtue by Plato and Aristotle are still unequalled," Dewey goes on to argue that love as he has defined it comprehends the chief virtues of the classical Greek tradition.

> It alone is wisdom, for anything but love fails to penetrate to the reality, the individuality of self, in every act, and thus comes short in its estimate of values. It alone is courage, for, in its complete identification with its object, obstacles exist only as stimuli to renewed action. It alone is temperance, for it alone provides an object of devotion adequate to keep the agent in balance and power. It alone is justice, dealing with every object, aim and circumstance according to its rights as a constituent, a member, an organ of self—the sole ultimate and absolute.[92]

In short, Dewey's ethics in the mid 1890s is an experimentalist's attempt to reconstruct the ideals of Greek wisdom and Christian love.

The Study of Ethics reveals that in 1894 Dewey believed that in the new democratic scientific age the moral and religious life of the individual is best understood as a process of self-realization guided by love and experimental intelligence. In his new ethics Dewey tried to overcome every trace of dualism between the moral ideal and the everyday world of practical events as well as between self and activity. The effort led him to reject all supernaturalism and transcendentalism and to adopt a form of situation ethics. This outlook involved a strong element of relativism, but with his scientific approach, he endeavored to avoid moral subjectivism and to preserve a basis for objectively valid moral judgments. Dewey's attempt to identify his new idea of the moral life with the real meaning of Christian love departs from much traditional Christian interpretation insofar as the latter is tied to a theory of moral absolutism and divine grace. However, it is worth noting that religious teachers as diverse as St. Francis of Assisi, Zen Master Dōgen, and Martin Buber all assert that authentic religious practice involves "the complete identification of subject and object, agent and function" in a person's everyday life.[93] They emphasize the spiritual significance of being able to respond to a situation with the energy and attention of the whole self. Dewey is working here to formulate what could be called a secular democratic conception of spiritual practice. He continues to develop his thinking on these matters in his later ethical and educational thought, which persistently seeks to overturn every moral, religious, and philosophical notion that would prevent a person from giving wholehearted attention to the possibilities of the present and from finding fullness of life and inherent meaning in the concrete activities of everyday existence.

Making Peace with the Tradition

As his philosophical and religious thought was moving rapidly in new directions Dewey found encouragement and support in several new associations with intellectual leaders and social reformers in America. Having enjoyed a summer vacation in the early 1890s at Thomas Davidson's Summer School of the Cultured Sciences in Keene Valley in the Adirondack Mountains, Dewey and his family built a cottage nearby and regularly returned during the 1890s.[94] Davidson was a Scotsman, a private philosopher, and fine scholar. He had a strong interest in morals and religion, especially Christian community life, which led him during the 1880s to found the Fellowship of the New Life with branches in England and America. The religion of the Fellowship was defined as "a determined endeavor to know well, to love well and to do well," and Davidson sought help in this endeavor from art, science, and philosophy as well as from traditional religion.[95] Davidson's Summer School was designed along lines similar to the Concord Summer School of Philosophy. Dewey sought guidance from Davidson in the areas of New Testament studies and early Christian philosophy, and he found the ethical and humanistic quality of Davidson's religious attitude congenial.[96] However, he was not in full sympathy with Davidson's attempts to foster moral self-discipline in those who attended his school.[97] Periodically Dewey gave lectures in Davidson's program of courses, and some of them dealt with religious themes. For example, one year in a course on T.H. Green he gave a lecture on "Green's Religious Philosophy" and in a course dealing with "The Relations of Church and State" he spoke on "The Politico-Philosophical View."[98] What made the Summer School of the Cultured Sciences especially attractive to Dewey is that it provided him with the opportunity to become personally acquainted with figures like W.T. Harris, William James, Josiah

Royce, and Felix Adler, the founder of the Society for Ethical Culture.

The example of Felix Adler's career could only have convinced Dewey that his religious and social thought was on the right track. Adler had emerged as a controversial religious and social leader in the 1870s. His father had left Orthodox Judaism to become a Reformed Rabbi, and young Adler was raised in the Reform tradition with the expectation that he would succeed his father as Rabbi in Temple Emanu-El in New York City. However, graduate study in philosophy, science, and comparative religion in Germany led Adler to reject the basic tenants of Reform Judaism involving monotheism, supernaturalism, and the idea that the Jews had been called to fulfill a special divine mission. He also found himself unable to justify intellectually the continued existence of the Jews as a separate religious community.[99] In an action that jarred the American Jewish community, he broke his ties with Judaism and set out to start a new universalistic humanitarian religion grounded in a neo-Kantian brand of ethical idealism and dedicated to ethical growth and social reform. The result was formation in 1876 of the Ethical Culture Society, which over the years attracted a small but dedicated following of former Jews and Protestants who had become disillusioned with theological liberalism. Dewey and Adler were destined to become colleagues at Columbia University in the early 1900s. While they did not have a major influence on each other in the technical areas of philosophy, they did come to share a number of interests as social and educational reformers and cooperated in a variety of projects.

Inspired by Felix Adler and the example of Toynbee Hall in London, Stanton Coit in 1886 opened on the Lower East Side of New York City the first settlement house in America. In the course of the next three decades, the settlement house would emerge in dozens of American cities as a major vehicle in and through which progressive religious leaders, intellectuals, and reformers endeavored to respond to the problems of urban poverty and to overcome the divisions created by class, religion, and national origin. Many of the most talented members of a new generation of college educated women became prominent as leaders in the settlement house movement. The best example was Jane Addams, who together with Ellen Gates Starr founded Hull House in Chicago in 1889.[100]

Early in 1892 while still engaged in the *Thought News* project, Dewey met Jane Addams at Hull House where he stayed for several days during a trip to Chicago. He was much impressed, and in a letter to Addams following his visit, he noted especially the religious and moral significance of Hull House for the American churches.

> Every day I stayed there only added to my conviction that you had taken the right way. I am confident that twenty-five years from now the forces now turned in upon themselves in various church organizations will be finding outlet very largely through just such channels as you have opened.[101]

Dewey and Addams were destined to become fast friends and to collaborate on many projects. In her life and thought Dewey would continue to find confirmation of much that he was coming to believe about Christianity and democracy.

Born in 1860 and raised in Illinois, well educated and widely traveled, Jane Addams found herself in the 1880s dissatisfied with the usual women's role in American society and with traditional forms of religion. She hungered for some vital moral and religious meaning in her life. In search of this meaning and influenced by Auguste Comte's religion of humanity, Leo Tolstoy's religious writings, the Fabian Essays, and a brief stay at Toynbee Hall in 1888, she resolved to settle and work among the poor and immigrant peoples in Chicago.[102] The result was the opening of Hull House, which soon won an international reputation as a center of some of the most advanced social research and educational thinking in America.

As Addams explains it in a widely read essay, "The Subjective Necessity for Social Settlements" (1892), three interrelated interests prompted her action.[103] First, there was the desire "to share the life of the race," that is, to identify with the lot of the common people and to aid in their progress. Second, Addams mentions her faith in the ideal of democracy and "the desire to make the entire social organism democratic, to extend democracy beyond its political expression." This meant making Hull House into a place where people of all backgrounds and persuasions—men and women, rich and poor, immigrant and native American, laborer and employer, socialist and capitalist, Jew and Christian—could meet to share experiences, educate each other, and work together solving problems. Personal growth and social liberation through mutual education and cooperation was the objective. Third, Addams asserts that the settlement house movement is part of "a certain renaissance of Christianity, a movement towards its early humanitarian aspects."[104] In expounding on the nature of this movement she may have drawn on Dewey's thinking in "Christianity and Democracy," for she argues that Christianity is to be identified with the ongoing process of revelation of truth, and she concludes that the new Christianity "shall seek a simple and natural expression in the social organism."[105] Addams shared Dewey's belief that practical religion and the democratic life are synonymous.

In the fall of 1894 Dewey wrote Alice Dewey that he had just heard a lecture by Addams in which she asserted that "the great awakening of social consciousness in the labor movement was one of the most deeply religious things in modern times—if not the most so. To come in contact with that alone meant an awakening into new life." Dewey describes Addams' lecture and subsequent discussion with him as "the most magnificent exhibition of intellect and moral faith I ever saw."[106] Later Dewey writes: "Leaders, whether political or intellectual, were to her trustees for the interests of the common people. Theirs was the duty and the task of giving articulate and effective form to the common impulses she summed up in the word 'Fellowship.' "[107] The sense of religious peace and enduring meaning Addams found in the democratic life is suggested in the closing paragraph of *Democracy and Social Ethics* (1902): "As the acceptance of democracy brings a certain lifegiving power, so it has its own sanctions and comforts. Perhaps the most obvious one is the curious sense which comes to us from time to time, that we belong to the whole, that a certain basic well being can never be taken away from us whatever the turn of fortune."[108] This too was Dewey's sentiment. In Jane Addams, Dewey found a kindred spirit. During the Chicago years he became actively involved at Hull House, gaining fresh insight into America's social ills and their remedy.

It was in March 1894 that Dewey formally accepted President William Rainey Harper's offer of the chairmanship of the Philosophy Department at the newly founded University of Chicago.[109] As a result of a large endowment from John D. Rockefeller and a brilliant recruiting effort by Harper, the University of Chicago, which was only four years old, had already won recognition as one of the leading centers of graduate education in America. Before departing from Ann Arbor, Dewey gave a farewell address before the S.C.A. on May 27, 1894, entitled "Reconstruction." It was in many ways a summation of the major conclusions of a decade of reflection on religious issues, which had involved metaphysical and psychological inquiries, Biblical studies, historical research into the origins of Christian doctrine, and an exploration of the moral and religious significance of science and democracy.

The general theme of Dewey's talk is the idea that periodically a reconstruction of human ideas and values is a necessity in the realm of religion as well as in all other areas of human experience and that the present is such a time. Humanity finds itself in an evolving world. Ideals are not fixed and static entities. They, too, must evolve and be redefined so as to meet the demands of changing situations. What occasions the need for reconstruction in religion today, he argues, is the success the original Christian ideals have had in embodying themselves in the habits and institutions of western society. The realization of these ideals demands a further development and redefinition of Christian aims and values. Dewey goes on to develop this point with reference to what he identifies as the three major original Christian ideals: the absolute value of the individual self, the kingdom of God, and the revelation and incarnation of absolute truth in the individual and society. In presenting his argument he elaborates on the distinction he made in "Christianity and Democracy" (1892) between the direct natural meaning of Christian teaching and a sentimental supernatural interpretation.

The idea of "the absolute, immeasurable value of the self ... formed the very heart of the Christian consciousness," explains Dewey. However, in actuality the individual in the ancient world was not treated as "a free self-possessed end in himself," that is, as a person. People were politically and industrially everywhere in bondage and treated as a mere means to things external to themselves. As a result the idea of the absolute value of the individual became an ideal that "was held to be true only in emotion, or at some remote time, or by some supernatural means." Nevertheless, the ideal inspired a gradual transformation of society, and "democracy as a social fact was born." As a result of the growth of democracy individuals are now free to realize the infinite value of their personalities and able to enjoy the feeling of this freedom in common everyday acts. Revealing an overly optimistic view of the advance of democracy in America, he cites "the emancipation of the Negroes in the South" as an example.[110]

Regarding the ideal of the kingdom of God, Dewey argues that the social and political facts of ancient life were a contradiction to the concept. As a result "the idea lost its original, normal significance, the true relationship between man and man in all forms whatsoever, and assumed the form of the special organization of the church." However, the ideal gradually found expression outside the church. By interpreting the ideal of the kingdom of God as no more and no less than a community of free persons bound together in their practical activities by common interests and shared values, Dewey argues that what Christians have hoped for is actually being realized in modern secular society in and through the forces of commerce, the new technology, and democracy. The church must come to realize that "the organism of grace, the means of lifting up the individual and binding men together in harmony are now found working in all forms of life; ... political, domestic and industrial institutions have become in fact an organized Kingdom of God on earth, making for the welfare of the individual and the unity of the whole." The duty of the church, he advises, is "to take its place as one among the various forces of social life, and to cooperate with them on an equal basis for the furtherance of the common end."[111]

Finally, taking up again the theme of Christianity as revelation, Dewey asserts that Christianity brought to consciousness the idea of "the revelation of absolute truth to man—absolute, that is, in the sense of being sufficient and supreme for the guidance of life." Again, in the ancient world this idea was only an ideal, since "the access of the individual to truth, the methods for realizing and testing it were feeble and inadequate." As a result the natural meaning of this teaching—"that the individual in and through the very process of living had access to truth as such"—was obscured. With the development of the experimental method of science this meaning has finally become clear. Dewey does not again explicitly discuss the idea of democracy as revelation as he had in "Christianity and Democracy." All emphasis is placed on the revelatory power of science, but his remarks imply that democracy provides an ideal social structure for the pursuit of the social sciences, the communication of practical truth, and the achievement of universal education.

With regard to science he abandons all caution and expresses an unqualified enthusiasm for and faith in the scientific method of intelligence.

> Science as a method of inquiry, as an organized, comprehensive, progressive, self-verifying system of investigation has come into existence. The result has been an almost boundless confidence in the possibility of the human mind to reach truth. We feel that our instruments are so ample and so mighty that, given time, nothing can resist them. . . . All truth which promises to be of practical avail in the direction of man's life, may be gotten at by scientific method.[112]

It is important to note that in "Reconstruction" Dewey carefully qualifies his use of the term "absolute truth" and his claims for the scientific method by asserting that what he is speaking about is the knowledge necessary for the guidance of life. Using the scientific method, intelligence can arrive at practical wisdom.

In his final words Dewey spoke to those who felt "a conflict between loyalty to the past and faithfulness to new truth," a conflict which Dewey himself had struggled to resolve in his own life. They must ask themselves: "What is the meaning, the idea which has animated the past, and what attitude, what change of outward form does that spirit demand of me in order that I may remain true to it?"[113] Dewey had answered that question for himself to his own satisfaction this Sunday morning in May of 1894. It was an essential task he had to complete. Christianity, which he had been taught from the cradle to revere as being identical with all that is sacred and most dear in life, still had a certain authority for him, and he could not depart the church, abandon theology, and turn his attention wholeheartedly to the experimental method of truth, democracy, and education until he had extracted the blessing of the Christian tradition on this new adventure. Now he had it. In his closing words he looks ahead.

> The responsibility now upon us is to form our faith in the light of the most searching methods and known facts; it is to form that faith so that it shall be an efficient and present help to us in action, in the cooperative union with all men who are sincerely striving to help on the Kingdom of God on earth.[114]

Dewey is talking here about a moral faith that is so wholehearted as to be religious in nature, and in the most general terms he has in mind a faith in the the democratic way of life and the experimental method. Dewey says nothing about faith in God, and he actually only mentions God when he speaks about "the Kingdom of God." In "Reconstruction" only a very thin veneer of Christian theological language is used to present a position that is basically a form of ethical naturalism and democratic humanism.

"A Sure Way To Regain the Lost Treasure and More"

With his departure from the University of Michigan at the age of thirty-five, the formative period in the development of Dewey's religious thought comes to a close. The shift of his general philosophical position from absolute idealism to empirical naturalism, which began during his last years in Ann Arbor, would involve some further major reconstructions. Dewey's later philosophy of religion involves working out the full implications of the convictions and ideas formed in this early period and harmonizing them with his maturing philosophical outlook.

The Michigan years had been a period during which Dewey had gone far in achieving a well-integrated personality and a satisfying social adjustment. It had been a time for clarifying his basic commitments and values. Now this had been achieved, and it is no accident that the end of the formative period in the development of his religious thought coincides with this accomplishment. From the beginning Dewey's religious interests and quest for God had been intimately bound up with a search for his own identity and for a sense of belonging, of being a member of the larger whole. From very early, his search for God, self-realization, and community had been a search for the truth of experience. By 1894 Dewey firmly believed that he had found the key to the discovery and realization of this truth in the experimental method and the democratic life. Dewey's religious quest for God, integration of personality, and community finds its end in faith in experimental moral science and social science pursued in a community governed by the democratic values of freedom, equal opportunity, and open communication. This faith brought Dewey a deep personal sense of well-being, and he was satisfied that to live guided by such a faith is the essence of a genuinely religious life in the modern world.

The record suggests that apart from one important essay on the psychology of childhood religious experience Dewey did little new thinking in the area of religion during his ten years at the University of Chicago. He did continue teaching some courses on idealist metaphysics, but before long he had entirely given up on trying to use Hegelian metaphysics in his own philosophizing. In July 1894 Dewey visited the university's Baptist Divinity School, which was destined to become an important center of liberal Protestant thought in America. However, he was not very impressed with what he found there as he reported to Alice Dewey: "The students in the Theological Seminary are afraid of their teachers, don't know what is coming or where they are going; some of the faculty (theology) also think Harper is ruining the University and are in a blue funk...."[115] In August, Dewey made an attempt to give these confused students his radical view of what was happening and where they ought to be going. Writing again to Alice he commented: "Sunday evening I'm going to speak to the University Christian Union on 'Psychology and Religion.' It seemed as well to make known my heterodoxy first as last—if it isn't already known."[116] What Dewey actually said was not recorded. At any rate this address, which was given before he actually started teaching, was his first and last talk before the Christian Union. With only two exceptions, he did not address any other church related group in Chicago during his ten years there. What seems to have happened is that Dewey's views on religion in 1894 were too liberal for the members of the Christian Union and the Divinity school, and the religious question had been worked out and settled in his own mind. His interests became largely absorbed in other matters, that is, such secular and moral concerns as he believed should occupy the attention of a contemporary religious person.

Dewey used his move to Chicago as an opportunity to quietly terminate his membership in the institutional church. He, Alice, and their children did not join a church in Chicago. Then in 1898 Dewey decided to withdraw his membership in the Ann Arbor Congregational Church.[117] Lucina Dewey was unhappy that her grandchildren were not being sent to Sunday school. When queried about this, Dewey is reported to have replied that as a child he had gone enough for all of his children.[118]

At the end of this exploration of the formative period in the development of Dewey's religious outlook, it is useful by way of summary and clarification to address a basic question raised by Dewey's interpretation of Christianity in such addresses as "The Value of Historical Christianity," "Christianity and Democracy" and "Reconstruction." Did Dewey really understand the idea at the core of traditional Christianity and give it a legitimate modern formulation, as he claims, or is his position in fact a rejection of Christianity? In trying to answer this question it is helpful first to review briefly the way Dewey tries to rationalize and naturalize Christian doctrine, translating various theological concepts into what he calls their direct natural meaning. He does this by asserting that God is the immanent organizing life and truth of nature, personality, and society, making possible a complete reconciliation of the sacred and secular; the divine spirit is intelligence and the power of self-determination; divine revelation is the disclosure of truth in general, especially practical truth, to intelligence and will; the Incarnation is the presence of God in all persons and society; Jesus is a great moral teacher and an example of a universal man; the Mediator is humanity; the Body of Christ is the human community at large; the Crucifixion and Resurrection involve dying to life as an isolated self and to all that is narrow and partial, and entrance upon life in the larger whole, the human community at large; the law of love is identical with the law of self-realization; Christian love is wholehearted responsiveness to the needs and ideal possibilities of the present situation; the true church and kingdom of God are to be identified with the democratic community; practical religion is truth seeking in the experimental spirit and ethical action, including the task of communicating the truth and educating the populace; the true eschatology is a realized eschatology coupled with a faith in progress; theology is philosophy, which is the scientific investigation of experience in its totality.

In this liberal, or modernist, rendering of Christian teaching, Dewey has abandoned theism, supernaturalism, original sin, and a substitutionary theory of the atonement. He does not take the doctrine of special historical revelation seriously and his thought is not Christocentric. He does not rely upon the church or the sacraments as channels of grace. In short, Dewey has rejected most of those aspects of Christianity associated with the institutional church and church related theology. Practically everything in Christianity that is an offense to the rationality and confidence of a modern secular person has been removed.

What remains in Dewey's position that is Christian in spirit is the conviction that God and humanity are reconciled, the profound ethical concern, and an element of ethical mysticism. However, Dewey's interpretation of the meaning of the Christian doctrine of the unity of the divine and human is not a distinctly Christian religious teaching, and it would be declared a false interpretation by anyone who takes original sin and classical theism seriously. Also, it is not possible to maintain that a profound ethical concern or ethical mysticism is exclusively Christian. In summary, by 1894 Dewey had rejected all those religious teachings which are unique to the Christian tradition, but he does preserve much of the Christian ethical and religious spirit.

However, by 1894 the problem is actually more complicated than this because not only had Dewey's interest in the church faded, but he was beginning to lose his belief in the God of absolutism as well as theism. It is rather difficult to separate Christianity from some such belief in God. There is inextricably bound up with the fundamental ideas of historical Christianity a faith in God in the sense of a source and power of being, goodness, and truth, which is eternal and absolute, and which in some real sense transcends nature and the flux of time-history even while active within it. From the traditional Christian perspective human existence shares in and realizes ultimate meaning and value just insofar as it is united to or related to this eternal and unconditional source of all being and meaning. As long as Dewey remained an absolute idealist he continued to adhere to one of many various forms of this idea, which is so fundamental to Christianity. However, by 1892 Dewey had stopped speaking about God as the perfect personality and ideal self. He simply identifies God with the absolute truth and organic unity of the world. By 1894 he seems to be questioning this idea. There is no explicit affirmation of belief in the God of absolute idealism in *The Study of Ethics* (1894) or Dewey's other published writings thereafter. Dewey was not yet done with the idea of God, as we will see, but he had rejected all the traditional metaphysical conceptions of God.

It is actually a short, even if critically important, step from Dewey's neo-Hegelian panentheism and social mysticism to a thoroughgoing humanism and naturalism. The immanent God need only be finally understood as basically a projection of human values, and the absolute need only be interpreted quite simply as the human community and those aspects of nature that support it. Working out of the Hegelian tradition, Feuerbach had taken this step half-a-century earlier, and had gone on to argue that the true essence of Christianity is actually atheism and humanism. During his last years in Ann Arbor, Dewey was traveling in this general direction, identifying religious values with social values, arguing that imaginative projections of unrealized ideals created the religious notion of the "other world," and gradually abandoning references to God.[119] In some ways Dewey is an American Feuerbach. Like the author of *The Essence of Christianity* he left the church in the name of human community, abandoned the idea of special revelation in the name of truth and morality, and eventually rejected the God of the church theologians in order to overcome humanity's alienation from its own essential goodness and in order to realize the spiritual meaning inherent in ordinary human relations.

Neither Feuerbach nor young Dewey believed that they had rejected the true essence of Christianity—what Feuerbach liked to call the true anthropological essence as distinct from the false theological essence. Both of them argue that their new humanism and ethical naturalism preserves the most important religious values in the Western tradition. As Dewey put it: "men do not throw away their belief in the most valuable things in life unless they feel themselves possessed of a sure way to regain the lost treasure and more." [120] He was convinced and determined to show that modern humanity could not only respect science as the sole intellectual authority and preserve morality, but that it could also embrace humanism and naturalism and continue to find profound religious meaning and value in life. Some of his critics in both the church and the community of scientific agnostics undoubtedly felt this was a case of a man trying to have his cake and eat it at one and the same time, but Dewey was not dissuaded. If in 1894 he was losing his Hegelian faith in the ultimate identity of the ideal and the real, he was not losing his faith that life is in the final analysis worthwhile and full of ideal meaning. He was also not surrendering his conviction that there need be no radical split between the understanding of the intellect on the one hand and the desires of the heart and aspirations of the will for enduring moral meaning and purpose on the other. How Dewey in the twentieth century tried to develop a philosophy of democratic humanism and naturalism that justifies this faith, and how he sought to develop a naturalistic theory of religious experience and values is the subject of the remaining chapters of this book.

PART II

The Way of Freedom and Community

FIVE

Democracy, Education, and Religious Experience

D URING THE 1890s the American nation struggled with a crisis of identity and direction. A simpler, hallowed way of life associated with the frontier and rural America was being lost under the impact of industrialization and urbanization, and there was no way to return to the lost Eden. In addition, even though the machine, the factory, and the city brought prosperity to some, it was difficult for the average citizen to believe that these new forces could be harnessed so as to serve the common good and equitably distribute America's abundance. These issues were very much on the minds of Dewey and his new colleagues at the University of Chicago.

Some Americans, like the midwestern historian Frederick Jackson Turner, who had a romantic vision of virgin wilderness as a well spring of spiritual rejuvenation, saw the vanishing of the frontier as a tragic loss for the nation. The forces of urbanization and industrialization were generating a civilization alienated from nature, believed Turner, and the end result would inevitably be decline and decadence. At Yale University, Professor William Graham Sumner saw the problem quite differently. Appealing to Herbert Spencer's optimistic evolutionary world view, he combined a tough-minded social

Darwinism with a faith in social progress. Sumner argued that an economic policy of laissez-faire and survival of the fittest was the true meaning of American democratic freedom and life in harmony with nature as well as the necessary condition of economic growth. Sumner's vision evoked an enthusiastic response among the leaders of American finance and industry, but laissez-faire in the 1890s clearly meant an end to any hope of realizing the Jeffersonian ideal of a republic of free and equal citizens cooperatively engaged in self-government. At the end of a long career of reflection on the American experiment, Mark Twain concluded that neither a life close to nature nor scientific-technological progress could solve the problems facing America, because the basic problem was "the limitations and infirmities of our human nature." In Twain's view the source of evil resides within human nature itself.[1]

It was the emergence of the Progressive movement as a political force at the turn of the century that lifted the nation out of its confusion and gave it a new sense of confidence and direction. The Progressives were made up largely of energetic, optimistic, bright younger middle-class Americans like Jane Addams and John Dewey, who during the 1880s and 1890s had gradually been moving toward a new way of thinking about the American situation. They saw no sense in trying to preserve a past that was gone. They looked to the future. They believed that the urban-industrial environment itself provided America with a new challenging frontier with great possibilities. American democracy would find fulfillment in industrial democracy. They enthusiastically embraced Darwin, but they rejected social Darwinism and laissez-faire for a brand of reform Darwinism that put faith in the social sciences and social planning. In their view no idea, law, or institution is a fixed absolute above criticism and beyond alteration. Human beings in an evolving historical process may and should change the social environment as well as adjust to it.

The progressives had no use for the older ideas of the self-made, self-sufficient individual. They believed that individuals are by nature social beings who find meaning and freedom in community working together cooperatively rather than in a brutal competitive struggle. Furthermore, the new American frontier involved social and economic forces which no person could manage as a lone individual.

What was needed was government regulation of the economy and a major reconstruction of social institutions that would eliminate injustice and encourage people in their natural tendency to cooperate. Evil existed but it could be overcome by transforming the social environment and by universal education. Given seemingly unlimited natural resources and an industrial system capable of producing abundance for all, the progressives reaffirmed the American faith in progress. They dreamed of finally fulfilling the New World's highest ideal of a truly democratic society completely free of the oppression and corruption flowing from the feudal and authoritarian traditions of the Old World. To accomplish their task, they needed new tools of social criticism and new methods of social change. Intelligence, science, and education coupled with moral faith and cooperative effort could solve the problem.

Dewey already had the mind of a progressive when he settled in Chicago, and he was bent on further developing his progressive answers to the needs of the times. By 1894 his psychological, ethical, social, and religious thought had come to a focus around the problems of individual self-realization and freedom, democratic social reconstruction, and the scientific search for practical truth including moral values. These three issues were closely interconnected in his mind. The general problem comprehending the whole situation Dewey continued to conceptualize as the problem of the relation between the ideal and the actual. He was also beginning to view education as the field where society could most effectively deal with all these matters. In working with these problems during a decade at the University of Chicago and on into his years at Columbia University, his attention became concentrated first and foremost in two related areas: the theory of inquiry, or logic, and the philosophy of education. In the early 1900s he emerged in both of these fields as a leading progressive intellectual and a national figure.

This chapter is concerned primarily with the relationship between Dewey's faith in democracy and his theory of education including his idea of its social function. In short, during the Chicago and early Columbia years (1894–1918) education became for Dewey the progressive reformer the focus of his concern with individual liberation and social reconstruction. In other words, education emerged as the most fundamental method for realizing the democratic ideal for the individual and society. As a consequence, pedagogy acquired in Dewey's mind great philosophical significance as the chief practical issue with which philosophy should be ultimately concerned. Education also acquired a distinct moral and religious meaning.

During the Chicago and Columbia years Dewey's general religious attitude did not undergo major changes. However, he did further develop the meaning of his own liberal religious faith in democracy and the experimental method, and he integrated it with a faith in education. In addition, over the years Dewey gradually worked out the implications of his new naturalistic philosophy for a general theory of the religious dimension of life. In this connection, his work in social theory, psychology, and education led him to set forth the outlines of a naturalistic theory of religious as well as moral development, and he refined his theory of the relation of religion and society.

The Triumphs and Trials of the Chicago Years

Dewey assumed the responsibilities of chairman of the Department of Philosophy at the University of Chicago in July 1894. Before long he had assembled an unusually gifted group of young philosophers as his colleagues in the department. They were all committed to exploring the implications of evolutionary biology, functional psychology, and the new social sciences for philosophy, and they were united by shared progressive social concerns. The core of this staff was made up of James H. Tufts who had been a colleague of Dewey's in Ann Arbor and who specialized in ethics and aesthetics; George H. Mead, the social psychologist, who was one of Dewey's closest friends and most influential colleagues; Addison W. Moore, who taught theory of knowledge and logic; James Angell, whose field was experimental psychology; and Edward Scribner Ames, who after 1900 taught the psychology and philosophy of religion. Dewey's own course offerings at Chicago ranged widely over the fields of psychology, philosophy, and education, and his many publications during this period covered all these areas.[2]

Under Dewey's leadership the Chicago philosophers worked cooperatively in a fashion rare in American academic departments to develop the new revolutionary school of thought known as pragmatism. Pragmatism as a philosophical movement had been started by Charles Sanders Peirce in the 1870s and had been advanced by the work of William James in the 1890s. The pragmatists were concerned with the nature of the mind, the role of ideas in living, the standard of truth, and the logic of scientific inquiry and problem-solving. They rejected the classical spectator theory of knowledge and radically reconstructed earlier British and German theories of experience and mind. In Dewey's view, pragmatism, or instrumentalism as he preferred to call it, provides the key to a sound method of moral valuation for a rapidly changing world—a method that harnesses the scientific method to serve humanity's ethical and social life. In other words, Dewey conceived his instrumentalism as an experimental method for guiding and transforming the interactions of human beings with their world. With the publication of *Studies in Logical Theory* (1903), the contribution of Dewey and his colleagues began to win wide recognition.

Tufts had a personal interest in the church, but Ames was the only one of Dewey's Chicago colleagues who taught and wrote extensively in the area of religion.[3] Ames, who completed his doctoral studies in the Department of Philosophy in 1895, served as pastor of a liberal religious organization, the University Church of Disciples of Christ, from 1900 to 1940. His efforts to develop a theory of religion in harmony with evolutionary biology, functional psychology, and philosophical pragmatism, culminated in two important books, *The Psychology of Religious Experience* (1910) and *Religion* (1929). These volumes may well have had a noteworthy influence on Dewey that will be considered at a later point in this study.

Not only did Dewey have an outstanding group of colleagues in the philosophy department; he and his department also had the advantage of working closely with a distinguished group of social scientists at the university, including Edward W. Bemis, Frederick Starr, Albion Small, W. I. Thomas, and Thorstein Veblen. These men shared Dewey's liberal social interests, and he benefitted much from the exchange of ideas with them. They in turn, like many other progressive social scientists in America, found Dewey's pragmatist philosophy of problem-solving and social action very helpful in providing an intellectual foundation for and clarification of their own critical perspective and social values. As the economist J. Allen Smith commented: "We were all Deweyites before we read Dewey, and we were all the more effective reformers after we read him."[4]

One of the factors that had prompted Dewey to accept the position offered him at the University of Chicago was an arrangement whereby, as chairman of the philosophy department, he would also be responsible for directing the university's work in education. At Johns Hopkins, G. Stanley Hall had introduced Dewey to developmental psychology and some of the problems related to early education. During his years in Michigan his interest in psychology led him to study the learning process and to begin exploring the problems of the elementary and secondary schools. In the course of the *Thought News* affair, he came to identify Christianity with the disclosure and communication of truth made possible by modern democracy and science, and as a social reformer he was led to recognize the critical importance of a free press and enlightened popular education. After his unsuccessful attempt to enter the world of journalism, Dewey's interests in social reform and education came to focus on the school. By putting his trust and hope as a reformer in a reconstructed school system, Dewey was developing an attitude toward education that was characteristic of much nineteenth-century American social thinking. In this connection, one historian comments that the American commitment to popular education, which emerged in the 1830s and 1840s, "held that certain long term reforms in society were better achieved through education than through politics, indeed, that education was a form of politics insofar as it altered traditional relationships among individuals and groups."[5]

By the mid-1890s the times were ripe for fresh visions and new initiatives. In 1893 Joseph Mayer Rice published his comprehensive study of *The Public-School System of the United States* (1893), which focused national attention on the very poor condition of many American schools and issued a call to action. The traditional method of instruction in American elementary and secondary schools, which Rice termed the "mechanical" approach, tended to be teacher- and curriculum-centered, to rely on acquisition of skills by drill, to be oriented toward preparation for the future, to undertake socialization by imposing external discipline in an authoritarian fashion, and to encourage docility and conformity in the child. In a large number of school systems Rice found this kind of approach combined with administrative incompetence and uninspired classroom teaching that showed practically no understanding of child psychology. Furthermore, many urban schools were under the control of corrupt political machines, and school appointments were often used as a form of political patronage. However, Rice also reports that in a number of cities a new progressive spirit among teachers was beginning to have beneficial effects.[6] In various innovative centers of learning the influence of European educational reformers such as Rousseau, Pestalozzi, Herbart, and Froebel was leading to reforms. New departures were being tried in such places as Jane Addams' Hull House and the Cook County Normal School managed by Colonel Francis Wayland Parker. As a result of such developments and studies like that of Rice, the progressive education movement was beginning to take form and to challenge traditional educational theory and practice.

The progressives set out to alter the American school system by developing a science of education based on the findings of the new psychology and the social sciences. They argued in defense of more child-centered and active methods of teaching and gentler approaches to discipline. Confident in their faith in human nature, the objective of the progressives was to free and stimulate the inner springs of intellectual interest, moral goodness, and creativity that are fundamental to real learning and harmonious social progress. The progressives also became much concerned to introduce industrial education and vocational instruction into the schools and to employ the schools as instruments for building up the social and economic life of the community. Finally, the reformers battled with the political bosses in an effort to establish the schools as an independent system managed by scientifically trained professionals. With his move to Chicago, Dewey joined the vanguard of this movement.[7]

Encouraged by President Harper to develop a strong university program in the science and philosophy of education, Dewey created a new independent Department of Pedagogy, of which he was named the head, and established an experimental elementary school, which came to be known as "the Laboratory School" or "the Dewey School."

By the turn of the century he was administering a major graduate school program in education and directing one of the most advanced experimental programs in the psychology of children's education in the country. The work of Dewey and his colleagues in philosophy informed his work in education, and his experimental work in education became a testing-ground for his philosophical principles. His little book of lectures, *The School and Society,* which appeared in 1899, was soon on its way to becoming a classic in the American literature on education and to being translated into twelve foreign languages.

Dewey's new activities in education also provided Alice Dewey with an opportunity to become involved in her husband's professional work in a way that had not been possible before. From 1901 to 1904 she served as the principal of "the Dewey School," and her passion for social action and reform, with which she had often inspired her husband, found a channel of direct expression that was deeply satisfying to her.[8] During the Chicago years Dewey also worked closely with Ella Flagg Young, who was the first woman to become superintendent of schools in Chicago and president of the National Education Association. Jane Dewey writes that her father found Young to be "the wisest person in school matters with whom he has come in contact," and his collaboration with her had the effect of "crystallizing his ideas of democracy in the school and by extension, in life."[9]

Shortly after his move to Chicago, Dewey joined the Board of Trustees of Hull House, and Jane Addams provided the educator with an education. For example, one evening in September of 1894 she arranged for him to be taken on a tour of Chicago night life. He described the adventure in a letter to Alice Dewey.

> Mr. Miller and a man about town he knew, took us around. We went to a salvation meeting out of doors, a 'Happy Gospel' meeting in doors, part of the show at the Park Theater, the worst one in town, four or five wine rooms where some of the street women hang around, a ten cent lodging house, then two gambling places but they were all shut up for the first time in a year and three houses of prostitution. We were out from about 8–12, and I think I saw typical specimens of everything except the gambling.[10]

At Hull House Dewey was thrust into dialogue with leading social critics such as Henry Demarest Lloyd, and tough-minded, practical reformers like Florence Kelly. In the Working People's Social Science Club and in the Plato Club, he listened to laborers, shopkeepers, union organizers, anarchists, Marxists, and disciples of Henry George argue the latest educational, economic, and political theories and debate the pros and cons of proposals for new legislation. When Dewey lectured he was forced to defend his own ideas before "the people."[11] Dewey later commented about Jane Addams that "one of the things that I have learned from her is the enormous value of mental non-resistance, of tearing away the armor plate of prejudice, of convention, isolation that keeps one from sharing to the full in the larger and even more unfamiliar and alien ranges of the possibilities of human life and experience." Hull House revealed to Dewey the deep sense of satisfaction to be "found simply in this broadening of intellectual curiosity and sympathy in all the concerns of life."[12]

Dewey's decade at the University of Chicago (1894–1904) may well have been his most creative period, but these years were not without great sorrow and painful conflicts. The Chicago years began with the death of a child, and they ended with the loss of the Dewey School and the death of another child. Perhaps the greatest personal loss Dewey suffered in the course of his long life was the death of his second son, Morris, who had been named after his beloved teacher George Sylvester Morris. Dewey thoroughly enjoyed his children, who in the spirit of domestic democracy often called him John or Papa John. His powers of concentration were such that he had no difficulty working while his children scampered and played about the house. Morris, who was born in 1892, especially delighted his father. In May 1894, Alice Dewey journeyed to Europe with the two older children, Frederick and Evelyn, and left Morris with his father and grandmother, Lucina Dewey. In July, Dewey wrote to his wife that Morris "is the most perfect work of art in his attitude toward the world I have ever seen."[13] When Alice Dewey wrote to suggest that Morris be sent to Europe, if he was too much trouble, Dewey replied:

> As for Morris himself, he is the joy of my life and the delight of my eyes and all other things which all lovers have ever said of their beloveds. I think he looks more and more like the infant Jesus in the Sistine [?] picture and perhaps it is on that account, I am just begin-ning to appreciate the marvel of that picture. I suppose I saw it so

early and so long as a "religious" picture that I never saw anything but the label till recently. Now it seems to have all the promise of all future free humanity in it.[14]

After Dewey completed his fall semester teaching, he and Morris took a steamer across the Atlantic to join the family in Europe. Dewey later recalled a passenger, who had been observing his two-and-a-half-year-old son, commenting: "If that boy grows up what he is now there will be a new religion in the world." In Italy Morris became sick with diphtheria and died. Jane Dewey writes that Morris's death was "a blow from which neither of his parents ever fully recovered," and Max Eastman comments that fifty years after the event Dewey still remembered Morris as "a kind of saintly genius" whom he "could not mention without a catch in his throat."[15]

During Dewey's years in Chicago three more children were born into the family: Gordon in 1895, Lucy Alice in 1897, and Jane Mary (who was named after Jane Addams) in 1900. Shortly after Dewey's resignation from the University of Chicago in the spring of 1904, the entire family again travelled to Europe and another child was lost. Gordon died of typhoid fever in Ireland at the age of eight. Jane Addams conducted a service in his memory at Hull House.[16] Dewey had lost a second son whom he as well as others believed was extraordinarily gifted. Before returning home from Europe, the Deweys while in Italy adopted Sabino, an orphan boy about Gordon's age.

The full impact of Gordon's death on John and Alice Dewey can only be appreciated when it is understood in the context of the circumstances surrounding Dewey's resignation from the University of Chicago. The situation that precipitated the resignation developed following the addition to the University in 1901 of the Chicago Institute, which had been founded by Colonel Parker. The Institute had its own progressive elementary school that had been established for the purpose of training teachers. As a consequence of this addition there came to be substantive disagreements as well as misunderstandings between Dewey and President Harper and between Dewey and the Chicago Institute. Dewey also found himself saddled with administrative and personnel problems that he did not have the time to manage properly, given his many other responsibilities. Further, when the university merged the "Dewey School" with the "Parker School" in 1903, the staff of the latter objected to Mrs. Dewey's appointment as principal. As a result, Harper asked for her resignation after one year as head of the combined schools. Frustrated and angered with the entire situation, and especially with what he perceived as Harper's deviousness and lack of support, Dewey finally resigned his position in philosophy and psychology as well as education to the dismay of his colleagues. The separation under these circumstances from all that they had labored so long and hard to build at the University of Chicago was a profoundly disheartening experience for the Deweys. They left Chicago for Europe in June and in September they were faced with Gordon's death.[17]

Some time the following year Dewey wrote a poem about the way he and Alice Dewey experienced the deaths of Gordon and Morris.

> To us you came from out of dark
> To take the place of him who went—
> Quenched that glimmering joyous spark—
> Not ours you were, but lent.
>
> To us you came from out of light
> Brightest of lights that ever shone
> To make dark life sweet and white;
> Not ours you were, but God's own loan.
>
> With us a little while, our light, you dwelt—
> And did we fail to care or did we care too much?
> Again we saw a dying light to darkness melt
> While our aching arms vainly strove to touch
> And hold our own
> God's blessed loan.[18]

By 1905 Dewey had ceased all references to the God of Hegelian idealism in expositions of his own thought, but this poem reveals that when confronted with the mystery of death he could still return to the theological language of his Congregational heritage. In fact, as will become clear in later portions of this study, he never did entirely abandon the idea of God.

Dewey easily found another position. Columbia University quickly appointed him Professor of Philosophy with the understanding that he would also be a member of the faculty of Teachers College.

However, his new appointment involved no administrative responsibilities, and for the most part, he avoided university administrative work for the remainder of his academic career. The loss of Morris, Gordon, and "the Dewey School" was never forgotten, but it did not break his spirit. His gentle kindly disposition and fundamentally positive attitude toward life remained intact. He continued to find a sustaining sense of meaning in his life and work, which was carried on in a prodigiously productive way at Columbia.

The lasting impact of these sad events on Alice Dewey, however, seems to have been more negative. She was a gifted woman who performed the role of wife and mother that society expected of her, but she was at heart an activist aspiring to a professional career on the forefront of social change. She not only cared for her husband and managed their home, but she was instrumental in bringing John Dewey's brilliant mind to focus on the problems of people. Then after her sixth child was born she finally found a position at the Dewey School that was a real challenge to her own abilities. When after four years of dedicated and productive labor she was defeated in this venture, in part by circumstances beyond her control, and she and John felt compelled to abandon all they had worked to build at Chicago, it was more than she could manage. The death of Gordon could only have compounded the sense of injustice and irreparable loss. In New York City, Alice remained active in the women's suffrage movement, but with the loss of her salary and a reduction in her husband's salary given the absence of administrative responsibilities in his new position, she found most of her energies absorbed in housekeeping and caring for her large family. Max Eastman asserts that these events combined to leave Alice angry and depressed, resulting in "habits of perpetual objection" and "ironical nagging" that gave "a bitter flavor to her witty charm."[19] The Dewey children have rejected this image of their mother as very unfair.[20] However, there may well be some truth in Eastman's account; Alice had reason to feel aggrieved and deeply frustrated. There is some evidence that in the course of the next decade some of the light went out in the relationship between Alice and John, and it is possible that the changes in Alice described by Eastman contributed to this further problem.

Philosophy and A Social Faith in Education

Dewey's moral faith in education is rooted in his deep conviction regarding its profound social and philosophical significance. The meaning of this faith is most fully expressed by Dewey in *Democracy and Education* (1916), which was the culmination of over two decades of study in the interrelated fields of philosophy, education, and social reform. Regarding this book Dewey comments that it "was for many years that in which my philosophy, such as it is, was most fully expounded." Further, it was written with the conviction that "philosophy should focus about education as the supreme human interest in which moreover, other problems, cosmological, moral, logical, come to a head." [21]

Dewey takes this position regarding education and philosophy because, first of all, he views philosophy as being in both origin and purpose intimately connected with social problems. He argues that the problems with which philosophy wrestles—even the most technical issues—have their origin in fundamental social conflicts over the moral and intellectual values that should govern conduct and regulate community life. The proper function of philosophy is to bring society to a clear consciousness of the nature and meaning of these conflicts and then to seek "some more comprehensive point of view from which the divergencies may be brought together." [22] In undertaking this task, philosophers are led into cosmological, epistemological, and logical as well as moral issues, but the true meaning of philosophy is always its bearing on the social problems which first generated reflection. Some professional philosophers seem not to know this, acknowledges Dewey, but their blindness to the practical meaning of their work does not alter the fact. Dewey's unmasking of the social origins of philosophical problems, most notably epistemological, moral, and metaphysical dualisms, and his effort to preserve the social relevance of philosophy are among the major contributions of his thought.

With his theory of the social origins and function of philosophy in mind, Dewey contends that philosophy should be conceived as the general theory of education, because education—especially in a democratic society—"is the fundamental method of social progress and reform." "By law and punishment, by social agitation and discussion, society can regulate and form itself in a more or less haphazard and chance way," explains Dewey in 1897. "But through education society can ... shape itself with definiteness and economy in the direction in which it wishes to move."[23] Employing language reminiscent of the Platonic dialogues, he describes education as an "art based on scientific knowledge," "the most perfect and intimate union of science and art conceivable."[24] He defines the art of education as "the supreme art," "the art of ... giving shape to human powers and adapting them to social service." In other words, education is "an intelligent art of guiding formation of intelligence and affections"—that is, of beliefs and desires.[25] It is this art that should be the final concern of philosophy. As he puts it in *Democracy and Education,* in its efforts to resolve social problems a philosophy urges upon a society certain basic attitudes, a "fundamental disposition towards the world," and he regards "education as the process of forming fundamental dispositions, intellectual and moral, toward nature and fellow-man."[26] Reflecting on the special moral qualities essential to a democracy and on the democratic principle of equal opportunity, Dewey comments that "democracy has to be born anew every generation, and education is its midwife."[27] For Dewey the democratic social reformer, then, the inquiries and reflections of the philosopher come to a focus in the theory and practice of education.

It is these convictions about society and education that led Dewey to make education an object of moral and religious faith. For example, in 1897 Dewey concludes a concise summary of his philosophy of education entitled, "My Pedagogic Creed" with this statement:

> I believe that every teacher should realize the dignity of his calling; that he is a social servant set apart for the maintaining of proper social order and the securing of the right social growth.
> I believe that in this way the teacher always is the prophet of the true God and the usherer in of the true kingdom of God.[28]

This is the last time that Dewey would employ the word God in a positive fashion in his own philosophical vocabulary for almost forty years, that is, until publication of *A Common Faith* in 1934. By "the kingdom of God" Dewey meant in 1897 the shared life of the authentic democratic community. His use of this phrase in "My Pedagogic Creed" underscores the high moral and religious meaning that he attached to both education and democracy.

In 1922 Dewey reaffirmed his faith in education and his idea of its religious import in an essay for the *New Republic* entitled "Education as Religion." With the content of society's moral faith in mind, he states: "If we have any ground to be religious about anything, we may take education religiously." In explaining his understanding of the meaning of this faith in 1922, Dewey focuses on the progressive view of teaching as an "art based on scientific knowledge."

> Faith in education signifies nothing less than belief in the possibility of deliberate direction of the formation of human disposition and intelligence. It signifies a belief that it is possible to know definitely just what specific conditions and forces operate to bring about just such and such specific results in character, intellectual attitude and capacity.[29]

He adds that "this particular form of faith testifies to a generous conception of human nature and to a deep belief in the possibilities of human achievement in spite of all its past failures and errors." Here lies the root of Dewey's hope for humankind.

Dewey cautions, however: "Worship of education as symbol of unattained possibilities of realization of humanity is one thing; our obstinate devotion to existing forms—to our existing schools and their studies and methods of instruction and administration or to suggested specific programs of improvement—as if they embodied the object of worship—is quite another." In other words, "the first act evoked by a genuine faith in education is a conviction of sin and act of repentance as to the institutions and methods which we now call education." Genuine repentance, asserts Dewey, will lead to a devotion to scientific research into human nature and conduct: "However much or little other religions may conflict with science, here we have a religion which can realize itself only through science: only, that is, through ways of understanding human nature in its concrete actuality and of discovering how its various factors are modified by interaction with the variety of conditions under which they operate." He calls upon teachers to undertake the hard work of developing this new science and art of education by combining with their faith in education a "creatively courageous disposition" that is not afraid to try imaginative experiments. In a civilization where there is no dualism of the religious and the secular, the "rites and cults" of the new religion of education will be, then, the experimental inquiry necessary to reform existing school systems and the activities required to maintain the practice of the true art of education.[30]

Democracy, experimentalism, and education are, then, interrelated ideal values that lie at the heart of Dewey's mature philosophy and personal unifying moral faith. It is important, therefore, to explore further Dewey's idea of democracy and theory of education and their interrelationship. Such an inquiry also has the special advantage of being the best way of beginning a study of Dewey's mature philosophical writings. Nowhere is the moral vision and the spirit of liberation that animates his humanism and naturalism better expressed than in his writings on democracy and education.

Education and the Democratic Ideal

In his philosophy of education Dewey undertakes a radical revision of his earlier neo-Hegelian view of human nature and self-realization. Continuing to develop ideas derived from evolutionary biology and functional psychology, he effects a naturalistic reconstruction of his earlier neo-Hegelian concept of the organic unity of the individual and the universal and the related theory of the way in which the individual reproduces the universal mind and realizes the ideal self. In the following autobiographical statement pertaining to the enduring influence of Hegel, Dewey indicates the way this developed.

> Hegel's idea of cultural institutions as an 'objective mind' upon which individuals were dependent in the formation of their mental life fell in with the influence of Comte and of Condorcet and Bacon. The metaphysical idea that an absolute mind is manifest in social institutions dropped out; the idea, upon an empirical basis, of the power exercised by cultural environment in shaping ideas, beliefs, and intellectual attitudes of individuals remained. It was a factor in producing my belief that the not uncommon assumption in both psychology and

philosophy of a ready-made mind over against a physical world as an object has no empirical support. It was a factor in producing my belief that the only possible psychology, as distinct from a biological account of behavior, is a social psychology.[31]

As this statement indicates, Dewey's educational theory and psychology are founded upon the idea that there is an organic connection between the individual and society and that the mind of the individual is developed in and through the interaction of the two. As Dewey expresses it in *The School and Society,* the new psychology has come "to conceive individual mind as a function of social life—as not capable of operating or developing by itself, but as requiring continued stimulus from social agencies, and finding its nutrition in social supplies."[32] He further explains that evolutionary biology leads philosophy to the conclusion that "the equipment of the individual mental as well as physical, is an inheritance from the race: a capital inherited by the individual from the past and held in trust by him for the future."

In short, "the individual to be educated is a social being" and finds and realizes his or her humanity in and through social interactions that lead to the recapitulation in the individual of the moral and intellectual achievements of centuries of human evolution and progress. Dewey writes in "My Pedagogic Creed":

> I believe that all education proceeds by the participation of the individual in the social consciousness of the race. This process begins unconsciously almost at birth, and is continually shaping the individual's powers, saturating his consciousness, forming his habits, training his ideas, and arousing his feelings and emotions.... The most formal and technical education in the world cannot safely depart from this general process. It can only organize it or differentiate it in some particular direction.[33]

The school emerges in modern civilization as the social institution which is primarily responsible for ensuring that this essential process of transmission and growth is carried on.

According to Dewey the specific nature of education will vary according to the nature of society and the moral and intellectual values that govern it. As an American philosopher, he, therefore, asks: what kind of education is most appropriate for a democracy in an urban, industrial, and technological society which is constantly being changed under the impact of experimental science? He also asks: what is the meaning of democracy? In *Democracy and Education* Dewey sets out to answer these questions. This volume is one of Dewey's most important philosophical treatises, but it is also a prime example of the kind of writing that has caused him to be criticized for not defining his terms precisely and for employing a difficult prose style. However, if one keeps in mind Dewey's general approach to an understanding of the democratic ideal as set forth both before and after the writing of *Democracy and Education,* his general theory in this book becomes fairly clear.

Dewey's conceptualization of the democratic ideal in his later thought builds upon the ideas set forth in *The Ethics of Democracy* (1888) and "Christianity and Democracy" (1892). In *Democracy and Education,* he continues to view the idea of democracy as involving much more than a theory of political organization. It is more fundamentally a great moral ideal—a "form of moral and spiritual association"—that comprehends human relations in the family, the school, the church, business, and industry as well as in political life. In other words, Dewey is more interested in what might be called social democracy and moral, or spiritual, democracy than political democracy. He once defined the latter as follows:

> Politically, democracy means a form of government which does not esteem the well-being of one individual or class above that of another; a system of laws and administration which ranks the happiness and interests of all as upon the same plane, and before whose law and administration all individuals are alike, or equal. But experience has shown that such a state of affairs is not realizable save where all interests have an opportunity to be heard, to make themselves felt, to take a hand in shaping policies. Consequently, universal suffrage, direct participation in choice of rulers, is an essential part of political democracy.[34]

Dewey goes on to point out that a political democracy can be effectively maintained only in a society that is characterized by "social democracy." A social democracy, he explains, is the expression of "a moral democracy," certain fundamental attitudes and values that constitute the core of the democratic way of life. In other words, for Dewey the democratic ideal embraces both a general social philosophy, including an experimental method of social reconstruction, and a philosophy of "a personal way of individual life."[35]

Dewey describes a social democracy as a society shaped throughout by the ideals of freedom and equal opportunity, and he identifies the key to its successful workings with free communication and the sharing of experience. He offers this account:

> A social democracy signifies, most obviously, a state of social life where there is a wide and varied distribution of opportunities; where there is social mobility or scope for change of position and station; where there is free circulation of experiences and ideas, making for a wide recognition of common interests and purposes.... Without ease in change, society gets stratified into classes, and these classes prevent anything like fair and even distribution of opportunity for all.... Since democracies forbid, by their very nature, highly centralized governments working by coercion, they depend upon shared interests and experience for their unity, and upon personal appreciation of the value of institutions for stability and defense.[36]

In Dewey's view, "free and open communication ... is the heart and the strength of the American democratic way of living." The sharing of ideas and experience is an educative and liberating process. It makes possible cooperation and creates social unity. "Men live in a community in virtue of the things which they have in common; and communication is the way in which they come to possess things in common. What they must have in common in order to form a community or society are aims, beliefs, aspirations, knowledge—a common understanding—like mindedness as the sociologists say." All barriers to communication and sharing of experience are antithetical to the democratic way. "Prejudices of economic status, of race, of religion, imperil democracy because they set up barriers to communication, or deflect and distort its operation." The democratic way of life commits us," declares Dewey, "to increasing effort to break down the walls of class, of unequal opportunity, of color, race, sect, and nationality, which estrange human beings from one another."[37]

Dewey contends that a group, organization, or nation with the democratic spirit cultivates communication in its external as well as internal relations. In some societies groups are organized as exclusive entities simply for the purpose of protecting what they have, but a democratic association seeks a free give and take with other groups with a mind to progressively reorganizing and readjusting itself in response to the novel situations created by new and expanded relationships. Dewey's democratic community would, then, keep expanding itself through communication and shared experience until its shared interests and values embrace all humanity. Every barrier to free and full communication must be lowered to satisfy Dewey's democratic principle as stated in *Democracy and Education*. For example, insofar as nationalism and patriotism are obstacles to those common interests such as art, commerce and science, which can unite people irrespective of national boundaries and racial or religious distinctions, they must be abandoned. Social democracy means that "the secondary and provisional character of national sovereignty in respect to the fuller, freer, and more fruitful association and intercourse of all human beings with one another must be instilled as a working disposition of mind." [38] In short, Dewey continues to adhere to the view he expressed in the early 1890s that the democratic life is a strategy for dissolving all social divisions and for creating a worldwide human community. The experience of the two world wars only deepened Dewey's convictions on this matter.

As these comments suggest, Dewey did not believe that it was productive in the twentieth century to regard the nation-state as the fundamental social unit. "Groupings for promoting the diversity of goods that men share have become the real social units." [39] These communities or societies are as numerous as the ways in which human beings associate together to share their experience and pursue common aims. They may be local, some national, or some international. Where the spirit of democracy is at work they are voluntary in nature, and Dewey would have them all organized and functioning according to his democratic principles. The function of the nation-state in a world in which the creative and dynamic social unit is a plurality of voluntary democratic associations is to promote, protect, and regulate these associations.

Communication is the vital center of social living, believes Dewey. In addition to its instrumental value, it is for him a supremely important good in its own right. "Of all affairs, communication is the most wonderful. That things should be able to pass from the plane of external pushing and pulling to that of revealing themselves to man, and thereby to themselves; and that the fruit of communication should be participation, sharing is a wonder by the side of which transubstantiation pales." "Shared experience is the greatest of human goods," states Dewey in *Experience and Nature* (1925). He has in mind that "Communication is ... an immediate enhancement of life, enjoyed for its own sake." "There is no mode of action as fulfilling and as rewarding as is concerted consensus of action," argues Dewey, for "it brings with it the sense of sharing and merging in a whole."[40] Thus communication is not only a means of pursuing common ends, but it is also the realization of a sense of communion, of belonging to a community, which is for Dewey the deepest of human joys.

Social democracy also means to Dewey what in 1888 he called industrial democracy. Throughout his career he argued that all social institutions should exist first and foremost, not as means of producing things, but as "means of *creating* individuals," as agencies for developing responsible, self-motivated, resourceful and creative persons.[41] In other words, all social organizations have an educational task to perform, as he explains in *Reconstruction in Philosophy* (1920):

> The test of all the institutions of adult life is their effect in furthering continued education. Government, business, art, religion, all social institutions have a meaning, a purpose. That purpose is to set free and to develop the capacities of human individuals without respect to race, sex, class or economic status. And this is all one with saying that the test of their value is the extent to which they educate every individual into the full stature of his possibility. Democracy has many meanings, but if it has a moral meaning, it is found in resolving that the supreme test of all political institutions and industrial arrangements shall be the contribution they make to the all-around growth of every member of society.[42]

Dewey further explains what this means: "Full education comes only when there is a responsible share on the part of each person, in proportion to capacity, in shaping the aims and policies of the social groups to which he belongs."[43] He regards the ideal of industrial democracy as the chief meaning for modern society of the Christian imperative to love your neighbor and of the classical Roman definition of justice as "rendering to another that which is his due." It gives concrete expression to the British utilitarian ideal of a society committed to achieving "the greatest good of the greatest number." [44]

In *Democracy and Education* Dewey writes: "If democracy has a moral and ideal meaning, it is that a social return be demanded from all and that opportunity for development of distinctive capacities be afforded to all." [45] This statement emphasizes Dewey's belief that a social democracy is characterized by a high sense of individual social responsibility, a commitment to the common good, as well as by equal opportunity. Every member of the democratic community should be both a "sustaining and a sustained" member of the social whole. [46] His objective as a social reformer was to create a society in which the need for social responsibility and social efficiency is fully harmonized with the ideal of individual self-development and the pursuit of culture. He envisions a society in which "making a living economically speaking, will be at one with making a life that is worth living." [47] Democracy means breaking down feudal class divisions that permit a privileged elite to live in leisure with opportunity to pursue culture while the masses are committed to the production of material goods at the expense of their development as persons. Not only is such a social system unjust; it also fails to perceive the dynamic interconnection between development of personality and socially productive work. It is Dewey's firm conviction as a social psychologist that a person develops his or her capacities fully only by exercising them in and through responding to the needs of the community, and the community's best interests are served by providing all its members with the educational and occupational opportunities to realize their capacities. "The best guarantee of collective efficiency and power," writes Dewey, "is liberation and use of the diversity of individual capacities in initiative, planning, foresight, vigor, and endurance." [48]

Dewey also explains that political and social democracy cannot be effectively sustained unless democracy also becomes "a *personal* way of individual life" signifying "the possession and continued use of certain attitudes, forming personal character and determining desire and purpose in all the relations of life." [49] Developing a theme that first appeared in the *Psychology* (1886), Dewey states in *Democracy and Education* that one essential democratic virtue is "intelligent sympathy." "Sympathy as a desireable quality is something more than feeling; it is a cultivated imagination for what men have in common and a rebellion at whatever unnecessarily divides them." It involves the will "to join freely and fully in shared or common activities."[50] It is sensitive responsiveness to the interests, sufferings, and rights of others. Dewey finds sympathy "the animating mold of moral judgment . . . because it furnishes the most efficacious intellectual standpoint." "Sympathy . . . carries thought out beyond the self," "renders vivid the interests of others," and "humbles . . . our own pretensions" encouraging the development of impartial moral judgments. Sympathy, asserts Dewey, "is the tool, par excellence, for resolving complex situations."[51] Dewey, however, did not believe that feelings of compassion by themselves are an adequate guide in the moral life. He urged development of what he calls "intelligent sympathy," that is, a union of benevolent impulses with experimental intelligence. The way Dewey interrelates democracy, sympathy, and experimentalism will be further explored in subsequent chapters.

In "Creative Democracy—The Task Before Us," (1939), Dewey described several other fundamental democratic attitudes clarifying convictions he had held throughout his long career. First of all, the democratic way of life is guided by "a working faith in the possibilities of human nature," a "faith in the potentialities of human nature as that nature is exhibited in every human being irrespective of race, color, sex, birth and family, of material or cultural wealth." Dewey adds "that this faith may be enacted in statutes, but it is only on paper unless it is put in force in the attitudes which human beings display to one another in all the incidents and relations of daily life." He further explains the meaning of a democratic faith in human nature: "The democratic belief in the principle of leadership is a generous one. It is universal. It is belief in the capacity of every person to lead his own life free from coercion and imposition by others provided right conditions are supplied." The important concluding qualification regarding "right conditions" refers to "the objective conditions of personal growth and achievement." Unless there is willingness to provide these conditions, the belief in equal opportunity and freedom is little more than sentimentalism, asserts Dewey.[52]

Dewey has often been criticized for maintaining a faith in human nature that is naive or unduly optimistic. His response is as follows:

Democracy is a way of personal life controlled not merely by faith in human nature in general but by faith in the capacity of human beings for intelligent judgement and action if proper conditions are furnished. I have been accused more than once and from opposed quarters of an undue, a utopian, faith in the possibilities of intelligence and in education as a correlate of intelligence. At all events, I did not invent this faith. I acquired it from my surroundings as far as those surroundings were animated by the democratic spirit. For what is the faith of democracy in the role of consultation, of conference, of persuasion, of discussion, in formation of public opinion, which in the long run is self-corrective, except faith in the capacity of the intelligence of the common man to respond with common sense to the free play of facts and ideas which are secured by effective guarantees of free inquiry, free assembly, and free communication? I am willing to leave to upholders of totalitarian states of the right and the left the view that faith in the capacities of intelligence is utopian.[53]

The Protestant theologian Reinhold Niebuhr, who in the 1930s was a harsh critic of Dewey's liberal optimism, conceded in 1944 that democracy presupposes faith in the possibilities of human nature and that a consistent pessimism regarding human nature leads invariably to "tyrannical political strategies." Niebuhr concluded: "Men's capacity for justice makes democracy possible; but men's inclination to injustice makes democracy necessary."[54] Dewey, who appreciated the democratic system of checks and balances as necessary to prevent the abuse of power, was in accord with this statement, but he did not accept Niebuhr's attempt to use the classical Christian doctrine of sin to explain "men's inclination to injustice."

In "Creative Democracy" Dewey also argues that the democratic way of life involves an attitude of cooperation and peace that includes a commitment to non-violent methods of resolving conflicts whenever possible.

Democracy as a way of life is controlled by personal faith in personal day-by-day working together with others. Democracy is the belief that even when needs and ends or consequences are different for each individual, the habit of amicable co-operation—which may include, as in sport, rivalry and competition—is itself a priceless addition to life. To take as far as possible every conflict which arises—and they are bound to arise—out of the atmosphere and medium of force, of violence as a means of settlement, into that of discussion and of intelligence, is to treat those who disagree—even profoundly—with us as those from whom we may learn, and in so far, as friends. A genuinely democratic faith in peace is faith in the possibility of conducting disputes, controversies, and conflicts as co-operative undertakings in which both parties learn by giving the other a chance to express itself, instead of having one party conquer by forceful suppression of the other—a suppression which is none the less one of violence when it takes place by psychological means of ridicule, abuse, intimidation, instead of by overt imprisonment or in concentration camps. To co-operate by giving differences a chance to show themselves because of the belief that the expression of difference is not only a right of the other person but is a means of enriching one's own life-experience, is inherent in the democratic personal way of life.[55]

This statement reveals the depth of "intelligent sympathy and good will" demanded by Dewey's idea of creative democracy. The evidence is that in his own personal life he practiced what he preached in these matters to a remarkable degree.[56] Regarding Dewey's attitude toward nonviolence, he was led to support World War I, but deeply disillusioned by the consequences of the war, he worked tirelessly during the 1920s and 1930s in support of the international movement to outlaw war.

Dewey's philosophy of creative democracy takes one to the heart of his democratic humanism. Here one finds the sense of union with God associated with his early Christian and idealist ethical mysticism reinterpreted but not lost. His deep, even mystical, feeling about communication and shared experience is well expressed in the concluding pages of *Reconstruction in Philosophy* where he uses imagery borrowed from Wordsworth's "Elegiac Stanzas" and writes: "When the emotional force, the mystic force one might say, of communication, of the miracle of shared life and shared experience is spontaneously felt, the hardness and crudeness of contemporary life will be bathed in the light that never was on land or sea."[57] In short, the democratic way of life has the capacity to transform experience and the world. Communication and shared experience are values of a certain religious reverence for Dewey: "Communication and its congenial objects are objects ultimately worthy of awe, admiration, and loyal appreciation."[58] Passages such as these led John Herman Randall, Jr., to refer to Dewey's humanistic "religion of shared experience," and the phrase is well chosen.[59] In short, a unifying moral commitment to the democratic way and the sense of belonging with which it enhances experience remain important religious values in Dewey's mature philosophy.

Dewey's convictions about the supreme value of communication and shared experience reflect the dynamics of American social life. The America in which Dewey lived and wrote was an increasingly pluralistic culture made up of diverse peoples for whom creating community was often an especially challenging undertaking. However, this task brought its own distinctive spiritual rewards to those who persevered in building bridges of communication across the dividing lines presented by class, race, religion, and national origin. In this sense Dewey's religion of shared experience is characteristically American.[60] Regarding the influence of his own personal experience, Dewey found that by constantly expanding his own interests and widening his relationships his life gained in meaning and worth. He learned this and had it confirmed through marriage, family life, teaching, professional work, Hull House, and countless other encounters and experiences with diverse individuals and groups, including the people of Japan and China with whom he lived for two and a half years right after World War I. Dewey's point is not that all associated life automatically provides one with a sense of communion, as some critics seem to suppose, but simply that insofar as a person adopts democratic attitudes and genuinely opens his or her mind and heart to the experience and needs of diverse individuals and groups the sense of belonging, of community, which sustains life is deepened.

A Theory of Education and Moral Development

In 1897 Dewey returned to the University of Michigan to give an address before the Philosophical Club, and he used the occasion to reflect on the critical social issue that was his fundamental concern as a philosopher of education. The forces of the Renaissance, Reformation, and Enlightenment, observed Dewey, have caused a decline in the authority of church and state and freed individuals to think for themselves, to discover truth on their own, and to act autonomously. As a consequence: "The cause of modern civilization stands and falls with the ability of the individual to serve as its agent and bearer." In other words, "the practical problem of modern life is the maintenance of the moral values of civilization through the medium of the insight and decision of the individual."[61] For Dewey, the spiritual meaning of modern democratic culture is intimately bound up with the liberation of the mind and will of the individual, and the great challenge of the age is the problem of the responsible use of individual freedom. The problem of individualism and freedom has been central to the concerns of modern thinkers as diverse as Emerson, Dostoevski, Kierkegaard, Nietzsche, and Sartre. What is distinctive about Dewey's thinking on this matter is his insistence that the psychological, social, and religious crisis generated by the "burden and stress" of dealing with the new freedom can only be effectively addressed by a thoroughgoing democratic reconstruction of society that begins with reform of the schools and commitment to the ongoing education of every citizen in what it means to be a free and responsible individual.

The task of the school in a free society, Dewey asserts, is twofold: the socialization of children and the development of their individual capacities, including especially the ability to think clearly and to make intelligent choices. The child and the curriculum constitute two sides of the educational process. Neither side can be subordinated to the other or neglected without adverse consequences. "The child's own instincts and powers furnish the material and give the starting point for all education," states Dewey. Traditional methods that treat the child in a mechanical fashion employing external pressure to conform to a preestablished inflexible curriculum are to be rejected. All education must be child-centered in the sense that it begins with the impulses, interests, and initiative of the particular individual. "Unless impulse and desire are enlisted, one has no heart for a course of conduct; one is indifferent, averse, not interested;" and without the motivation of personal interest learning does not occur and attempts to force learning by external pressure "result in friction, or disintegration, or arrest of the child's nature."[62]

Dewey's emphasis on a child-centered approach has led to criticisms that he did not properly appreciate the structure and direction supplied by a well-developed curriculum. While this is a legitimate criticism of some teachers in the progressive education movement, it reflects a misunderstanding of Dewey himself. He insists on a carefully planned but flexible curriculum. He points out that there need not be an unbridgeable gulf between the child's experience and interests and the subject matter of study as is often imagined. In *The Child and the Curriculum* (1902), Dewey explains how the teacher should understand the two to be organically related.

> From the side of the child, it is a question of seeing how his experience already contains within itself elements—facts and truths—of just the same sort as those entering into the formulated study; and, what is of more importance, of how it contains within itself the attitudes, the motives, and the interests which have operated in developing and organizing the subject matter to the plane which it now occupies. From the side of the studies, it is a question of interpreting them as outgrowths of forces operating in the child's life, and of discovering the steps that intervene between the child's present experience and their richer maturity.[63]

Dewey's emphasis here falls on learning and teaching as a single process of interaction. The teacher is called upon to appreciate the full meaning and value of the child's present and developing instincts, powers, interests and activities by translating them "into terms of their social equivalents—into the terms of what they are capable of in the way of social service."

The teacher, then, must be a wise psychologist who understands the processes of growth in and through which the social meaning of the child's capacities may be realized. With this knowledge the teacher can intelligently direct the activities of a child by applying the curriculum as appropriate given the situation. As Dewey puts it, the achievements and expressions of humanity embodied in the curriculum say in effect to the teacher:

> Such and such are the capacities, the fulfillments, in truth and beauty and behavior, open to these children. Now see to it that day by day the conditions are such that *their own activities* move inevitably in this

direction, toward such culmination of themselves. Let the child's nature fulfill its own destiny, revealed to you in whatever of science and art and industry the world now holds as its own.[64]

Dewey is endeavoring here to combine the radical individualism and respect for natural capacity found in Rousseau and Emerson with the Hegelian concern for socialization. To achieve a reconciliation of these values is the goal of social progress.

Socialization does not mean programming children to accept the values associated with the status quo. Quite to the contrary, children imbued with the democratic spirit will be persons who have learned how to think for themselves and to make fresh intelligent value judgements when confronting changed circumstances and new possibilities. Dewey is most critical of Hegelian moral and educational theory on just this point. In reacting to the excesses of eighteenth-century individualism, the Hegelians too readily identified the good of the individual with conformity to existing institutions and social values. However, in a rapidly evolving social environment, it is neither desirable nor possible to prepare a child for any fixed set of social conditions. The schools must be concerned instead with providing students with "the instruments of effective self-direction."[65] For Dewey this boils down in the final analysis to teaching children how to think. Thinking, in Dewey's biological view, is basically a problem-solving art, which enables a person to deliberate, make value judgements, choose, and act intelligently, and thereby work out a satisfactory adjustment with the environment. Autonomous individuality develops with the ability to think, which requires initiative, inventiveness, and resourcefulness.

By generalizing on the method of experimental science Dewey believed that modern society had the key to all productive thinking, including the process of moral valuation. The task of both the social philosopher and the school is "to humanize science" and to teach it "as furnishing in its method the pattern for all effective intelligent conduct."[66] It is the method of science understood as the method of thinking, and not any particular body of scientific information, that Dewey views as of the highest social and educational significance: "Were all instructors to realize that the quality of mental process, not the production of correct answers, is the measure of educative growth something hardly less than a revolution in teaching would be worked."[67] Dewey sets forth his conclusions about the general nature of the method of thinking in chapter 6 of *How We Think* (1912) and in two chapters of *Democracy and Education*. He further clarifies his views on this matter in *Experience and Nature* (1925), *The Quest for Certainty* (1929), and *Logic: The Theory of Inquiry* (1938). His instrumentalist theory of ideas, problem solving, and moral valuation are discussed more fully in chapters 8 and 9.

As a pragmatist who believed that the essential function of the mind and ideas is the direction of action, Dewey put special emphasis on teaching children to think by challenging them to solve practical problems arising out of their daily experience. When ideas are presented without a connection to practical problems that are real in the life experience of the child, they appear to the child as "a mass of meaningless and arbitrary ideas imposed from without" and the result is almost inevitably a deadening of interest. The goal of education is not to generate in the child information about things as an end in itself, but rather to develop "understanding." "Understanding has to be in terms of how things work and how to do things. Understanding, by its very nature, is related to action."[68]

For Dewey all education is a social process: "the only true education comes through the stimulation of the child's powers by the demands of the social situation in which he finds himself."[69] In other words, education is a product of communication and shared experience. He, therefore, adopts Francis Parker's view that the school should be set up and directed as a simplified version of existing social life—as "a miniature community, an embryonic society," in which the child has an inherently worthwhile and challenging life. The child can best learn by participating in the cooperative activities and problem-solving that make up this simplified democratic community, which "should take up and continue the activities with which the child is already familiar in the home."[70] Dewey explains that "by doing his share in the associated activity, the individual appropriates the purpose which actuates it, becomes familiar with its methods and subject matters, acquires needed skill, and is saturated with its emotional spirit."[71] Authentic learning grows out of living and doing. In critical moments, states Dewey, we all realize the profound truth in the common saying that "we learn from experience, and from the books or sayings of others *only* as they are related to experience." He also notes that the kind of living experience in and through which real learning occurs is that which is inherently meaningful to the child and not that which is understood as a mere preparation for some distant future living. Accordingly, "the school should be a place in which the child should really live, and get a life-experience in which he should really delight and find meaning for its own sake."[72]

"The subject matter of the school curriculum should make a gradual differentiation out of the primitive unconscious unity of social life," writes Dewey.[73] The sciences, literature, history, and geography are all of human interest and value because they are each related to varying aspects of the one life of the community. In order to prevent the fragmentation of knowledge and the curriculum, they should be presented to the child in this light. He further explains "that to become integral parts of the child's conduct and character, they must be assimilated, not as mere items of information, but as organic parts of his present needs and aims—which in turn are social." In order to achieve this, Dewey proposes that the school involve the child in a wide range of practical activities which require "natural divisions of labor, selection of leaders and followers, mutual cooperation and emulation."[74] These activities are to be designed so as to direct the interests of the child to discover the relevance and value of the curriculum. Dewey writes that "the problem is to unify, to organize education, to bring all its various factors together, through putting it as a whole into organic union with everyday life," and "the aim, then, is not for the child to go to school as a place apart, but rather in the school so to recapitulate typical phases of his experience outside of school, as to enlarge, enrich, and gradually formulate it."[75] Thus does Dewey, using the idea of organic connection, endeavor in his philosophy of education to overcome the dualisms of the individual and the universal (society), the child and the curriculum, the school and society, theory and practice, liberal education and practical training.

Given these views, Dewey supported the development of industrial arts and vocational education programs in the public schools in the early decades of the twentieth century, a time when the issue was hotly debated. Many children need such programs so as to prepare them to find jobs, asserts Dewey. They also need to be trained so that they are able "to counteract the endless monotony of machine industry" and "are equipped to reconstruct the system" so as to realize the possibilities for a true industrial democracy. Industrial and vocational education programs also can instill "a genuine respect for useful work" and a "contempt for social parasites" and idlers. Furthermore, Dewey believed that manual, industrial, and vocational programs could be used to great advantage in the traditional school as instruments for learning in and through doing. He strongly opposed separating the vocational programs from the regular schools for the reason just cited and also because such a separation would promote social divisions.[76]

Dewey's concern with the practical and instrumental aspects of education did not lead him to neglect the aesthetic and more contemplative aspects of experience. A careful reading of his major works on education reveals that he was concerned with the education of the whole feeling, thinking, and willing person. Repeatedly he refers to the effect of education on the formation of character, attitude, and emotion as well as intelligence. In *Democracy and Education* he provides this summary of his own view of the educational objectives of the school.

> We may say that the kind of experience to which the work of the schools should contribute is one marked by executive competency in the management of resources and obstacles encountered (efficiency); by sociability, or interest in the direct companionship of others; by aesthetic taste or capacity to appreciate artistic excellence in at least some of its classic forms; by trained intellectual method, or interest in some mode of scientific achievement; and by sensitiveness to the rights and claims of others—conscientiousness.[77]

Dewey sums up his approach with the assertion that "the main effect of education" should be "the achieving of a life of rich significance" by broadening and intensifying direct appreciation and enjoyment of intrinsic values.[78] This statement needs explication.

In *Democracy and Education* one finds Dewey beginning to develop the theory of immediate experience, intrinsic values, and aesthetic experience that he sets forth more fully in *Experience and Nature* and *Art as Experience*. An immediate experience involves "a personal, vitally direct experience" of some thing or person in contrast with merely reading or thinking about the subject. Immediate experiences engage feeling as well as intellect and include a felt realization of the nature of the reality experienced. Dewey further points out that what makes life worthwhile are immediate experiences of intrinsic values, that is, direct appreciations of things enjoyed as inherently good, as ends in themselves. There are many such goods and they vary with the situation, explains Dewey.

> We may imagine a man who at one time thoroughly enjoys converse with his friends, at another the hearing of a symphony; at another the eating of his meals; at another the reading of a book; at another the earning of money, and so on. As an appreciative realization, each of these is an intrinsic value. It occupies a particular place in life; it serves its own end, which cannot be supplied by a substitute.[79]

Each of these intrinsic values is the ultimate good in the situation in which it functions as an end in itself and as something irreplaceable.

Intrinsic values may be contrasted with instrumental values. The latter are goods which are valued because they serve as a means to realization of some intrinsic good. Dewey's philosophy as a whole is centrally concerned with the interrelationship between instrumental goods and intrinsic or final goods, because a clear understanding of this interrelationship is the key to addressing the most fundamental human problem, unifying the ideal and the actual. He often emphasizes the instrumental, and especially the instrumental function of sound experimental thinking, because he believes that the experimental method is the only sure guide in the effort to identify what is really good and to make intrinsic goods more readily available and secure.

Dewey stresses the value of literature and the fine arts in the curriculum because "they select and focus the elements of enjoyable worth which make any experience directly enjoyable." Dewey views the fine arts as "the chief agencies of an intensified, enhanced appreciation," for "in their fullness they represent the concentration and consummation of elements of good which are otherwise scattered and incomplete." In addition they form tastes and set the standards with which people evaluate the qualities of their experience. This brief discussion indicates the way in which Dewey's mature thought asserts an intimate connection between aesthetic experience and the ideal values in which human beings find fulfillment. In his vision of the school in an industrial democracy, then, the arts "are not luxuries of education, but emphatic expressions of that which makes any education worthwhile." [80]

It has been noted that in Dewey's view education is the intelligent art of shaping the beliefs and desires of children. This raises the question as to how the school may effectively form in children good standards of value judgment—what Dewey calls good tastes. He makes it clear that good taste is as important in intellectual and moral matters as in aesthetic spheres. By tastes Dewey means "habitual modes of preference and esteem, an effective sense of excellence." Tastes are habits that fix the attitude of a person toward various values. He makes an important distinction between, on the one hand, attitudes toward values that have been acquired in a purely intellectual fashion by mechanically learning about certain conventional standards, and on the other hand, attitudes that are effectively integrated into a person's character as a result of direct appreciative realization of certain values. The former are superficial and do not effectively determine personal preferences while the latter are what actually fix the quality of a person's tastes. Frequently persons experience a conflict between what they have learned about standards of values and what they personally appreciate and enjoy, between professed standards and actual standards, in which case education has failed to be genuinely effective.

If standards of taste cannot be transmitted directly by teaching and preaching, how are they to be formed? Dewey's answer goes to the heart of the matter: "Working as distinct from professed standards depend upon what an individual has himself specifically appreciated to be deeply significant in concrete situations." Therefore, good tastes can only be formed by providing persons with direct experiences of those intrinsic values which most effectively broaden and enhance the quality of experience. "If the eye is constantly greeted by harmonious objects, having elegance of form and color, a standard of taste naturally grows up."[81] As far as formation of a healthy emotional life in students is concerned, Dewey explains that "the emotions are the reflex of actions," and "if we can only secure right habits of action and thought, with reference to the good, the true, and the beautiful, emotions will for the most part take care of themselves."[82] In all of this Dewey again applies the principle of learning by doing. Exhortations, external discipline, examinations, and rewards are ineffective by themselves. Life situations and direct appreciative realizations are the foundations of a sound education.

All that has just been asserted about the formation of habits applies to Dewey's view of the way to teach morals and specifically the ethics of democracy. Dewey rejects a pedagogical approach that relies primarily upon external authority and fear of punishment as undemocratic in spirit. His objective is to create autonomous citizens capable of enlightened independent moral judgment and voluntary cooperation. If the school is managed as a miniature social community where the quality of interpersonal relations is governed by democratic principles, Dewey believes that moral education will take care of itself. He writes: "the best and deepest moral training is precisely that which one gets through having to enter proper relations with others in a unity of work and thought."[83] He explains that "a youth who has had repeated experience of the full meaning of the value of kindliness toward others built into his disposition has a measure of the worth of generous treatment of others," and that "without this vital appreciation, the duty and virtue of unselfishness impressed upon him by others as a standard remains purely a matter of symbols which he cannot adequately translate into realities."[84]

Dewey adopts a thoroughly democratic approach to creating and maintaining the kind of moral community in the school that provides the child with a genuinely educative moral experience. A method of moral education that relies exclusively on the authority of the teacher is abandoned in favor of a means of social control that does not violate the freedom of the individual child. In Dewey's ideal classroom "control of individual actions is affected by the whole situation in which individuals are involved, in which they share and of which they are co-operative or interacting parts."[85] The teacher, then, should not function as a boss, external to the child's situation but as a leader of the group process. "It is not the will or desire of any one person which establishes order but the moving spirit of the whole group. The control is social, but individuals are parts of a community, not outside of it."[86] To work and think in a community governed by this kind of democratic moral life is for Dewey the only sound approach to moral education in a democracy, which must rely to a large extent on a voluntary spirit of cooperation growing out of a multitude of common interests to maintain social order.

Consistent with his democratic spirit of free communication, Dewey was a strong defender of coeducation. For example, in an essay that appeared in the *Ladies' Home Journal* in 1911, he describes coeducation in high schools and colleges as morally and intellectually beneficial to both sexes and as "an intellectual and moral necessity in a democracy."

> Co-education fosters the temper and capacity for freer and fuller sociability; segregation tends to restrict and hamper. It works against the free play of instinctive sympathy and understanding; it makes for the creation of deep-seated unconscious attitudes of aloofness, distrust and even antagonism. Steady, frank effective cooperation in the main interests men and women have in common, upon whose successful realization all social advances depend, cannot be achieved without a sympathetic and practically instinctive understanding by each of the point of view and method of the other. And this is simply impossible of attainment if the sexes have in all the most plastic years of life been kept in a state of artificial isolation.[87]

Dewey also attacks as "sheer mythology" and "dogmatic assertion" most of the attempts to characterize the male and the female mind as distinct and different. He notes that "it is scientifically demonstrable that the average difference between men and women is much less than the range of *individual* differences among either men or women by themselves." How are men and women to be adequate parents to the opposite sex, asks Dewey, if they have no experience of the needs, capacities, and reactions of the opposite sex during their years of formal education? In the early decades of this century, ninety-five percent of the students in public schools in America were in coeducational institutions and most women attending colleges and universities were in coeducational institutions. However, it would be over half a century before the vast majority of private secondary schools and colleges in America would embrace a philosophy of full coeducation with equal opportunity for both sexes.

Much of Dewey's philosophy of education won wide acceptance in the United States during the late forties and fifties.[88] However, at times progressive educators have carried the child-centered approach to extremes that he did not support, and his methods have been applied unevenly in most cases. Furthermore, the nation has never been willing to make the commitment to education necessary to attract and train on a broad scale the cadre of gifted schoolteachers required to apply his philosophy successfully in the public schools at large. Even though many of Dewey's ideas may have become commonplace assumptions among educators, he has had and continues to have his stern critics from the left and the right.

During the 1930s, Marxists such as Theodore Brameld and Zalmen Slesinger joined those who attacked Dewey for overstating the role the school could play in social reconstruction. They found Dewey's faith in education unrealistic, for it failed to understand the rigidity of the class structure in American society and the need for revolutionary force.[89] From Robert M. Hutchins' *The Higher Learning in America* (1936) to Allan Bloom's *The Closing of the American Mind* (1987), Dewey's progressive theory of education has been attacked from the right. The issue for educators like Hutchins, who was president of the University of Chicago, centered on the progressives' attempt to adapt the schools and the university to the special needs of the times emphasizing vocationalism and particular social agendas. Stressing what is unchanging in human nature and the universal nature of truth, Hutchins advocated that the schools return to a classical core curriculum of basic subjects and the colleges adopt a curriculum centered on the great books of the western tradition.[90]

Dewey attacked Hutchins' program as an attempt to return American education to an authoritarian kind of rationalism that assumes the existence of fixed first principles and a preestablished hierarchy of truths. Hutchins was criticized for having contempt for the experimental method of science and for ignoring the role of the school in a democracy. Dewey had no objection to the study of the history of ideas including readings in Plato, Aristotle, and St. Thomas, which

Hutchins especially recommended, but he would have students learn from them something quite different than a respect for permanent truths.

> Their work is significant precisely because it does not represent with-drawal from the science and social affairs of their own times. On the contrary, each of them represents a genuine and profound attempt to discover and present in organized form the meaning of the science and the institutions that existed in their historic periods. The real conclusion to be drawn is that the task of higher learning at present is to accomplish a similar work for the confused and disordered conditions of our own day.[91]

Hutchins with some justice protested that Dewey in order to make a point had confused his position with that of nineteenth-century German philosophy. However, the emphasis in their approaches is clearly different, and the debate has continued to the present day.[92]

Dewey was one of the first Americans to explore the question of moral training from the perspective of the social scientist. Today there is wide agreement among social scientists with Dewey's view that children learn moral values in and through experience, that is, by interacting with others in a community.[93] It is also recognized that children's moral development is nurtured most effectively by discussing moral dilemmas with them as conflicts and difficulties arise. Only in this way do they develop the ability to think clearly about moral problems and to express their feelings on these subjects. Even though social scientists today, by and large, agree with Dewey's general approach, there continues to be a vocal group of Americans who call for a return to traditional methods of moral instruction. Critics from the religious and educational right charge that the progressive ap-proach has failed, and they point to the widespread moral chaos in American society in connection with alcohol, drugs, pregnancy, vio-lence, and white-collar crime. The problem is undeniable. It is also true that Dewey's method cannot work in schools with major disci-pline problems. These disciplinary problems, of course, are not just school problems; they are intimately tied up with massive social problems that Dewey hoped to head off with creation of genuine industrial democracy in the society at large. Given the current social situation, Dewey would appreciate the need for tough disciplinary measures in many Americans schools today. He would also correctly point out that America will have failed to educate its children in the meaning of freedom and democracy as long as it finds it necessary to resort to authoritarian and mechanical methods as its main means of moral education. "The cause of modern civilization" is at stake.

Religious Development in the Sunday School and Public School

Between 1894 and World War I, Dewey wrote very little directly about religion, but he did find time to prepare two brief but important papers on the theme of religious experience and development in the Sunday schools and the public schools. These two essays indicate clearly the direction in which his religious thinking was moving during this period.

By the turn of the century an increasing number of social liberals were proclaiming the school and the teacher as the answer to the ills of society, and soon the churches were examining their methods and agencies of religious education. The most extensive effort on the part of the Protestant churches to respond to this concern was the formation in 1903 of the Religious Education Association, a national nondenominational organization largely under the leadership of liberal churchmen. President William Rainey Harper, who was an Old Testament scholar and champion of religious liberalism, was among the principal early organizers. Dewey was persuaded to join the REA, and together with four hundred others, including thirty-three university, college, and seminary presidents, he signed the call for a national convention of educators and religious leaders. The convention was a three-day affair, and during the second day Dewey and Henry Churchill King, President of Oberlin College and author of *Reconstruction in Theology* (1901), gave the addresses in the session on "Religious Education as Conditioned by the Principles of Modern Psychology and Pedagogy."[94]

Dewey's address, which was entitled, "The Relation of Modern Psychology to Religious Education," is a clear persuasive summons to

apply the basic principles of developmental psychology to programs
of religious education for children.[95] In the early 1900s an American
movement for the scientific study of religious experience was beginning to take form under the leadership of William James, who had
just published *The Varieties of Religious Experience,* G. Stanley Hall,
Edwin D. Starbuck, and James H. Leuba. By focusing on the issue of
developmental psychology and the religious experience of children,
an area in which very little research had been done, Dewey identified
for the REA the most fundamental problem facing progressive religious educators.

Dewey's main point is that the various stages in the development
of human personality involve qualitatively different mental and emotional standpoints, and all education of children should be carefully
geared to specific stages in the growth process. He notes, however,
that in most religious as well as secular education programs, the child
is treated as "an abbreviated adult, a little man or a little woman,"
the difference between child and adult being conceived only as one
of degree or quantity of capacity. This problem commonly arises in
Christian religious instruction because it is assumed "that the spiritual
and emotional experiences of the adult are the proper measures of all
religious life; so that, if the child is to have any religious life at all, he
must have it in terms of the same consciousness of sin, repentance,
redemption, etc., which are familiar to the adult." It is a mistake,
contends Dewey, to "make the child familiar with the forms of the
soul's great experiences of sin and reconciliation and peace, of discord
and harmony of the individual with the deepest forces of the universe, before there is anything in his own needs or relationship in life
which makes it possible for him to interpret or to realize them."
Dewey summarizes the issue as follows: "In a word, it is a question
of bringing the child to appreciate the truly religious aspect of his
own growing life, not one of inoculating him externally with beliefs
and emotions which adults happen to have found serviceable to
themselves."

Dewey does not try to identify "the truly religious aspects" of the
experience of children at the various stages in their development,
which would have been helpful, and he does not believe in 1903 that
the science of child psychology had accumulated the facts necessary

in order to formulate inductively the general principles of a sound theory of religious education. However, he is quite specific about the nature of the problems that arise when the principles of developmental psychology are ignored. At a minimum, "something of the bloom of later experience is rubbed off; something of its richness is missed because the individual has been introduced to its form before he can possibly grasp its deeper significance." The religious experience of such people may become so conventionalized that "it becomes a matter of conformation rather than transformation." When some people came to realize that their religious life has been largely a matter of passively accepting ideas and reproducing feelings that are not a vital part of their own being, they are thrown into a crisis of doubt regarding the reality of spiritual truth and "the very worth of life itself." For others such a realization may lead to a long-lasting distaste, or even contempt, for the forms of religion.

In concluding his address, Dewey made his usual call for a movement to organize systematic cooperative scientific research into the problem at hand. He urged his audience to recognize "that it is possible to approach the subject of religious instruction in the reverent spirit of science, making the same sort of study of this problem that is made of any other educational problem." With all the progress being made in the various branches of secular education by scientific research, Dewey asked: "How can those interested in religion—and who is not?—justify neglect of the most fundamental of all educational questions, the moral and religious?"

Dewey did not again appear before the REA, and he did not carry out the important line of research in child psychology that he had advocated. However, his philosophy of education and democracy influenced the work of REA leaders like George A. Coe of Union Theological Seminary.[96] Among other related works, Coe authored *A Social Theory of Religious Education* (1917), and his theology, which emphasized the divine immanence, personality, and democracy, remained faithful to the kind of religious philosophy that Dewey had espoused in the early 1890s. It is also noteworthy that G. Stanley Hall, who had a lifetime interest in the scientific study of religion and who sensed the dawning of a "new Universal religion," launched in 1904 the short-lived *American Journal of Religious Psychology and*

Education.[97] Dewey's colleague at the University of Chicago, Edward Scribner Ames, devoted his energies as a follower of Dewey to the writing of *The Psychology of Religious Experience* (1910), which included chapters on "Religion and Childhood" and "Religion and Adolescence." While considerable work has been done in recent decades in the way of scientific research on the moral development of children, relatively little has been accomplished in the area of their religious development. It is not surprising, then, that the journal *Religious Education* saw fit to reprint Dewey's address on this subject as late as 1974.

In 1908, a controversy over whether the public schools should be offering religious instruction led Dewey to write an essay entitled "Religion and Our Schools" for the *Hibbert Journal,* a liberal quarterly review of religion and philosophy edited at Oxford University.[98] Dewey's objective was to explain some fundamental American attitudes on this subject and to set forth some of his own thinking on religion and its relationship to democracy, science, the public schools, and the problem of social unification. He concluded that the public schools should not attempt to offer any special program of religious instruction for the foreseeable future. A major part of his argument in defense of this view is based on a theory about the social nature and function of the religious aspect of life, which forms a recurrent theme in his religious writings, appearing first in essays like "The Value of Historical Christianity" (1889), "Poetry and Philosophy" (1891), and "Christianity and Democracy" (1892) and finding full expression in the concluding pages of *Reconstruction in Philosophy* (1920). It is useful to summarize this theory at this juncture.

As a student of Hegelian philosophy, Dewey was taught that God is immanent in the world as the Spirit of a people, and long after he had rejected the Hegelian metaphysical system, he retained the Hegelian view that the religious consciousness has its origins in the social consciousness of a people. Consequently it evolves as an expression of the intellectual, moral, and aesthetic values that lie at the heart of a people's life together. Edward Scribner Ames states the point very clearly in his *The Psychology of Religious Experience:*

> Religion arises naturally, being an inherent and intimate phase of the social consciousness. . . . The religion of a people is a reflex, the most inward and revealing reflex, of the civilization and spirit of that

people. The process by which the individual comes to share in the religion of his people—or of another people—is just the process by which he enters into and becomes dominated by the civilization, the art, the science, the social ideals of that people.[99]

For Ames the core of religious consciousness is faith in those ideals —especially the moral ideals—which are valued by a people most highly. This too, of course, is Dewey's view. Ames and Dewey believed that much evidence in support of the idea of a dynamic intimate connection between religion and society can be found in the research of the new psychology of religion and also in the work of anthropologists and sociologists such as E.B. Tyler, W. Robertson Smith, and W.I. Thomas.

The emphasis on the social origins and meaning of religious life also links Dewey with the kind of sociological interpretation of the meaning of religion found in Emile Durkheim's *The Elementary Forms of Religious Life* (1912). The sociological approach may be contrasted with the orientation of James in *The Varieties of Religious Experience,* which focuses on the psychological and individualistic aspects of religious experience. Dewey was especially interested in the social aspect of religious experience, because he identified the religious with the unifying, shared experience, the sense of belonging and moral faith. However, he was also interested in the psychological and more individualistic aspects of religious experience, and he learned from James as well as Hegel and the social scientists.

Dewey's theory regarding the future of religion in American culture is as follows. The scientific and democratic revolutions are transforming the intellectual, moral, and social values of society, and consequently, they are affecting traditional forms of religious expression. Since the beliefs and practices of traditional religion are intimately connected with ideas about the supernatural, and since modern science "has made supra-nature incredible, or at least difficult of belief," it is science that is having the most unsettling effect on traditional religion. Dewey concedes that the loss of belief in the supernatural and the emergence of new social values has created for many a real spiritual crisis: "There is undoubted loss of joy, of consolation, of some type of strength, and of some sources of inspiration in the change. There is a manifest increase of uncertainty; there is some paralysis of energy, and much excessive application of energy in materialistic directions."[100] However, in spite of these problems, and even though traditional forms of institutional religion will eventually die (being products of the social consciousness of earlier historical periods), there is no reason to be pessimistic about the future of religion itself. Dewey rejects the idea that vital religious experience is necessarily bound up with belief in supernaturalism and related rites, symbols, and emotions.

What is needed, he believes, is a reconceptualization along naturalistic lines of what actually constitutes the nature and meaning of religious experience. In this regard he notes that anthropology, psychology, and comparative religion all supply evidence that supports the view that religion is "a universal tendency of human nature," "a universal function of life." Religion, asserts Dewey, is "a natural expression of human experience." He defines it in 1908 as "the consciousness of the spiritual import of experience."[101] The religious tendencies of human nature will adapt themselves and find fresh expression as the intellectual and social situation evolves.[102] In short, Dewey is confident that the values connected with democracy and experimentalism will in due season cause the new culture taking form to put forth spontaneously its own distinctive religious and artistic expressions.

However, the time is not yet. The reconstruction of social life called for by the democratic ideal and the experimental method of truth has not progressed far enough. Dewey explains the dynamics of the social process that will generate a new religious orientation:

> As the new ideas find adequate expression in social life, they will be absorbed into a moral background, and the ideas and beliefs themselves will be deepened and be unconsciously transmitted and sustained. They will color the imagination and temper the desires and affections. They will not form a set of ideas to be expounded, reasoned out and argumentatively supported, but will be a spontaneous way of envisaging life. Then they will take on religious value. The religious spirit will be revivified because it will be in harmony with men's unquestioned scientific beliefs and their ordinary day-by-day social activities. [103]

When the values of social democracy and the experimental method are fully integrated into everyday experience and are spontaneously affirmed in imagination and feeling as the way to social progress and meaningful existence, they will give rise naturally to fresh religious expressions.

In the closing words of *Reconstruction in Philosophy* Dewey offers this advice to those who would foster the natural development of the religious spirit in the new age:

> Poetry, art, religion are precious things. They cannot be maintained by lingering in the past and futilely wishing to restore what the movement of events in science, industry and politics has destroyed. They are an out-flowering of thought and desires that unconsciously converge into a disposition of imagination as a result of thousands and thousands of daily episodes and contact. They cannot be willed into existence or coerced into being. The wind of the spirit bloweth where it listeth and the kingdom of God in such things does not come with observation. But while it is impossible to retain and recover by deliberate volition old sources of religion and art that have been discredited, it is possible to expedite the development of the vital sources of a religion and art that are yet to be. Not indeed by action directly aimed at their production, but by substituting faith in the active tendencies of the day for dread and dislike of them, and by the courage of intelligence to follow wither social and scientific changes direct us. We are weak today in ideal matters because intelligence is divorced from aspiration. The bare force of circumstance compels us onwards in the daily detail of our beliefs and acts, but our deeper thoughts and desires turn backwards. When philosophy shall have co-operated with the course of events and made clear and coherent the meaning of the daily detail, science and emotion will interpenetrate, practice and imagination will embrace. Poetry and religious feeling will be the unforced flowers of life. To further this articulation and revelation of the meanings of the current course of events is the task and problem of philosophy in days of transition.[104]

As Dewey expressed it in "Religion and Our Schools," a vital new religious spirit will be to a large degree the product of "unconscious, organic, collective forces." When it appears, it will come as an "unforced" flower of a reconstructed society.

Regarding the question as to whether the public schools should be used as a vehicle for teaching and instilling religion, Dewey in 1908 contended that "the church and the school must ... be thoroughly reconstructed before they can be fit organs for nurturing types of religious feeling and thought which are consistent with modern democracy and modern science." They should not try to teach traditional religion, because this means using formal dogmatic methods out of harmony with experimental methods of inquiry. "Nothing is gained," declares Dewey, "by deliberate effort to return to ideas which have become incredible, and to symbols which have been emptied of their content of obvious meaning." He gives this advice: "Bearing the losses and inconveniences of our time as best we may, it is the part of men to labour persistently and patiently for the clarification and development of the positive creed of life implicit in democracy and in science, and to work for the transformation of all practical instrumentalities of education till they are in harmony with these ideas." This is the course of action dictated by "honesty, courage, sobriety, and faith." [105]

Dewey opposed proposals that public schools adopt a released time program whereby students who elect to do so are released from school at certain hours to attend religious education classes at a religious institution of their choice. Underlying his rejection of this idea lies his conviction about the high spiritual value of what he calls "the state consciousness," which he explains as follows:

> The United States became a nation late enough in the history of the world to profit by the growth of that modern (although Greek) thing —the state consciousness. This notion was born under conditions which enabled it to share in and to appropriate the idea that the state life, the vitality of the social whole, is of more importance than the flourishing of any segment or class. [106]

The doctrine of separation of state and church involves for Dewey recognition of this idea, and he asserts that it really means "the subordination of churches to the state." In Dewey's view, there is nothing antireligious about the subordination of particular ecclesiastical institutions to the state. Coming out of the Hegelian tradition where God is the principle of the organic unity of the world and of society as a whole, he argues that the public school system has great religious significance simply by virtue of the fact that it is an institution that promotes "the state consciousness," that is, social unity.

Dewey objects to the released-time proposal because it would weaken the effectiveness of the schools in performing this important religious function.

In a forceful statement that reveals his deep passion for social unification upon a sound moral basis and his identification of religious life with unifying experience, Dewey sets forth his criticisms of institutional religion and the released time proposal:

> The alternative plan of parcelling out pupils among religious teachers drawn from their respective churches and denominations brings us up against exactly the matter which has done most to discredit the churches, and to discredit the cause, not perhaps of religion, but of organised and institutional religion: the multiplication of rival and competing religious bodies, each with its private inspiration and outlook. Our schools, in bringing together those of different nationalities, languages, traditions, and creeds, in assimilating them together upon the basis of what is common and public in endeavour and achievement, are performing an infinitely significant religious work. They are promoting the social unity out of which in the end genuine religious unity must grow. Shall we interfere with this work? Shall we run the risk of undoing it by introducing into education a subject which can be taught only by segregating pupils and turning them over at special hours to separate representatives of rival faiths? This would be deliberately to adopt a scheme which is predicated upon the maintenance of social divisions in just the matter, religion, which is empty and futile save as it expresses the basic unities of life.[107]

Dewey's basic criticism is that the traditional institutional religions do not provide an intellectual and moral basis for local, national, and international community in a pluralistic world. Moreover, this is a fundamental reason why the traditional religions cannot meet the deepest needs of the individual for unification of self and of self and world in modern culture. Dewey goes on to assert that, without ever having clearly formulated the principle:

> The American people is conscious that its schools serve best the cause of religion in serving the cause of social unification; and that under certain conditions schools are more religious in substance and in promise without any of the conventional badges and machinery of

religious instruction than they could be in cultivating these forms at the expense of a state-consciousness.

Dewey partially misjudged the American attitude in this matter. Released time programs have been established in many schools. However, Dewey's position did not change over the years. In 1940 he testified against a released time program before the Board of Education in New York City, and in 1947 he opposed the efforts to provide public financial support to Roman Catholic schools and the schools of any other religious sect.[108]

In concluding his 1908 essay, Dewey suggests that the modern age may not actually be such an irreligious time as many people think. He finds "the integrity of mind" involved in "the scientific attitude of undogmatic reverence for truth," which is leading men and women to abandon the rites, symbols, and emotions associated with dogmatic supernatural beliefs, "potentially much more religious than all it is displacing." The new scientific knowledge of nature seems to many an irreligious influence, observes Dewey, but "possibly if we measured it from the standpoint of the natural piety it is fostering, the sense of the permanent and inevitable implication of nature and man in a common career and destiny, it would appear as the growth of religion." This comment reveals that even though Dewey had given up the idealist belief in a unifying purpose at work in the cosmos as a whole, he did not find it necessary to accept the idea of a radical separation between nature and humanity. The latter notion had been one of the chilling ideas young Dewey had found associated with mechanistic materialism and against which he, following the Romantic poets and transcendentalists, had rebelled. In order to emphasize that modern science and the new naturalism affirm a positive relationship between humanity and nature, Dewey, like the Harvard philosopher George Santayana, borrows a phrase from the Romantic poetry of Wordsworth, "natural piety." His idea of natural piety was to become an important theme in his mature philosophy of religion. Finally, Dewey mentions again the religious value to be found in the way democracy and science foster social unity. He speculates that "it may be that the symptoms of religious ebb as conventionally interpreted are symptoms of the coming of a fuller and deeper religion."

As Dewey worked out his philosophy of social democracy and joined it with a progressive theory of education, he also harmonized both with a sociological theory of the origin of religious consciousness and a developmental theory of individual moral and religious growth. Dewey did not write extensively on the question of the religious experience of children. However, "Religion and Our Schools" makes clear the approach he took with regard to fostering the religious development of children as "a natural expression of human experience." He was content to trust that involvement in the process of progressive education would awaken in children a unifying moral faith in democracy and the experimental method of truth and generate intimations of "the miracle of shared life and shared experience" and a sense of the interdependence of humanity and nature. Dewey believed that these values joined with a faith in education itself together constitute a natural liberating religious orientation in the context of modern American society.

Pragmatism, Progressivism, and the War

IN THE SPRING of 1915, shortly after he had finished *Democracy and Education,* Dewey wrote to a friend: "Not till the present year have I felt that things have fairly come together in my own mind so that I could venture on anything 'systematic' . . ."[1] By 1915 he was well established as a leading progressive intellectual in America, and he was ready to start constructing a more complete account of his new naturalistic vision of the relation between the ideal and the real. However, it would be at least four years before he could begin giving his attention to the task. In the interim, he would be forced to deal with one of the most difficult personal and philosophical challenges of his entire career, and his life would be affected in ways he could not imagine. The challenge was entirely unexpected and Dewey was not prepared for it. It came as a consequence of the outbreak of World War I in 1914.

Suddenly Dewey found himself as a philosophical pragmatist and naturalist plunged into the politics of war and peace. He was forced to respond to problems that he had not contemplated. Friendships were strained and disrupted. Some of his former supporters became his critics, and his philosophy was attacked as a moral failure when put to the test in a time of social turbulence. The crisis the war precipitated for Dewey personally was but one episode in the larger crisis into which the war plunged the entire Progressive movement in America. It is useful, therefore, to begin the account of Dewey's experience with a further discussion of this movement and his place in it as a reformer.

The forces of Progressivism were at high tide during the period that spanned the presidencies of Theodore Roosevelt (1901–1908) and Woodrow Wilson (1912–1920) until the World War divided the reformers and shattered many of their greatest hopes. During the early years of the twentieth century muckraking journalism emerged for the first time as a national force focusing attention on a whole host of serious national ills. A torrent of books and articles informed the public about widespread poverty, the misery of life in city tenements, the cruelty of child labor, the widespread problem of alcoholism, the evils of prostitution, the exploitation of factory workers, and the abuses of power by political bosses and giant corporations. The idea was widely shared that people were basically good, and if they knew the truth about the injustice and suffering in their society, they would take cooperative action to right the wrongs. In fact, middle-class America, which was the dominant force at the polling booth, by and large got into a reform-minded mood. In a general atmosphere of idealism and optimism, many things were changed. City and state governments were cleaned up, business practices were regulated, wages were raised, prisons reformed, playgrounds built, prohibition laws were passed, and women's rights became a national concern.

Within American Protestantism in the North and West during the period 1900 to 1914, the movement of religious liberalism, with which Dewey had been associated in the 1880s, established itself as the most influential theological orientation, especially among Baptists, Congregationalists, Disciples of Christ, Episcopalians, Methodists, Quakers, and Unitarians. The University of Chicago Divinity School, Harvard Divinity School, and Union Theological Seminary in New York City became strongholds of liberal thinking, and their faculties exercised a widespread influence in religious circles. The most popular and dynamic form of liberalism during the Progressive Era was the Social Gospel. Between 1880 and 1915, an increasingly large majority of liberal Protestant preachers embraced the new social theology. A number of Reform Rabbis and a few Catholic priests also offered variations on this theme. The most widely read and persuasive theological defense of the Social Gospel appeared in Walter Rauschenbush's *Christianity and the Social Crisis* (1907). Rauschenbush, whose views were shaped by his years as a pastor in Hell's Kitchen in New York City, presented his vision with apocalyptic warnings. Given the poverty and injustice in the industrial world, Christians must act to reconstruct society or face doom and destruction. Emphasizing a social psychology and the supreme religious importance of ethics, the German Baptist minister called on Christians to rediscover the original social Christianity of Jesus' teaching and to unite in working to realize a democratic kingdom of God on earth. In the final analysis, his crisis theology is a vision of hope. Progress and social salvation are not inevitable, but they are possibilities for humanity with the aid of Christian faith and right effort. Despite the differences in their philosophies and styles, Roosevelt and Wilson agreed in supporting the dominant moral and religious attitudes of the day, which included a basic faith in human nature and social progress, a confidence in the eternal truth of moral right, and an idealistic determination to reform society in the face of political corruption, ruthless power, and inequality.[2]

A few anarchists and Marxists talked about social revolution during the Progressive Era, but for the vast majority of progressives violence and war seemed an outmoded and unnecessary means of social change, especially in America. The need for new economic markets was causing Americans to shed some of their isolationist attitudes and to begin thinking seriously about a role for the United States in the international arena, but when the nation elected Woodrow Wilson President in 1912, the possibility of a major war involving the European powers and the United States did not seem to be even a remote possibility. Many arguments had been put forth to demonstrate the impossibility of war. The development of modern commerce had rendered people so interdependent that war seemed out of the question. Modern warfare would be too difficult to finance. The new technology made warfare so destructive that it rendered war impossible as a practical matter.[3] The nation had vexing social problems certainly, but the majority of Americans were quite confidently going about their business with a trust that science, industry, technology, and peaceful methods of reform would ensure ongoing progress at home and abroad.

There were limitations to the visions of equal justice that one finds among the progressives. The leaders of the Social Gospel movement, for example, were not willing to support the battle for women's suffrage and were slow in giving assistance to organized labor. Some progressives clung to theories of the superiority of the Anglo-Saxon race.[4] The progressives generally failed to incorporate black America into its program of liberation and justice. Some black leaders—most notably, W.E.B. Du Bois—were led by the progressive spirit of the times to become cautiously optimistic about America confronting the problem of racism. However, their hopes turned to disillusionment, for white America was not ready for this kind of change. This was, however, the age that saw whites and blacks join together to form the NAACP and the Urban League.[5]

During the early decades of the twentieth century there were also strong currents of thought that ran counter to the dominant progressive outlook. Large numbers of farmers held to conservative ideas that made them wary of the progressives' trust in the eventual benefits of industrialization and urbanization. Even though many wealthy men and women did support numerous progressive causes, businessmen generally opposed the progressive movement's support of a strong federal government with the power to control corporations. While the spirit of religious liberalism, or what is often called modernism, tended to be dominant in American Protestantism during this period, it provoked conservative reactions that were destined to become major forces in American religion for the remainder of the century. This development confounded the liberals and prevented the ecumenical fellowship and social unity that they had rather naively imagined would be the outcome of their labors. The clash between the modernists and conservatives merits further comment.

Both the modernists and the conservatives believed in a personal God, a universal moral order, some form of personal immortality, and the importance of the Bible as a source of revelation, but whatever agreement they had in these matters was only superficial. They were deeply divided over radically different views of the authority of the Bible, the authority of science, the meaning of history, the meaning of secularism, the nature of God, the nature of divine revelation, the makeup of human nature, the purpose of religion, and the way of salvation. For example, in the face of the modernists' respect for the scientific method and their consequent rejection of Biblical supernaturalism, the conservatives denied the authority of scientific and historical-critical methods of inquiry in the area of religious belief, affirmed supernaturalism, and tried to defend the literal truth of the Scriptures. Whereas the modernists searched for the cause of evil in the strength of the natural impulses, the weakness of the will, the structures of society, or miseducation, the conservatives generally adhered to some form of the classical Christian doctrine of original sin involving the bondage of the will. The modernists believed in a God immanent in the evolving processes of nature and history and in an ongoing progressive revelation of divine truth in and through culture; the conservatives emphasized the transcendence of God and the final authority of Biblical revelations and historical creeds. The modernist impulse was, then, to be oriented primarily toward the future with a faith in enlightened reason, Christian love, and social progress; the conservative inclination was to be pessimistic about modern society and to look to the past with a faith in unchanging values, external authorities, and a supernatural savior. The modernists closely identified the purposes of religion and God with the secular humanistic goals of development of personality and construction of a just peaceful world with the aid of science and democracy; the conservatives fought to preserve a clear distinction between the religious life and secular life and stressed that the purpose of religion is first and foremost worship of a transcendent God and salvation of the individual soul by powers of divine grace working through the church.

In the Protestant community, antimodernism found its chief scholarly defense in the tracts of the Princeton Seminary faculty. The most popular form of American religious conservatism found expression in the rise of the Protestant fundamentalist movement. The fundamentalists presented their supernaturalistic brand of evangelical Christianity in twelve volumes of essays entitled *The Fundamentals: A*

Testimony to the Truth, which were published between 1910 and 1915.[6] Fundamentalism is a religion fueled by a nostalgia for older, passing ways of life and a fear of urban industrial change, and it is built upon a fixed belief in the inerrancy and literal truth of the Scriptures. Consequently it was driven to battle doggedly any modern idea such as the Darwinian theory of evolution that contradicts this basic belief. Within the Jewish community, Orthodox congregations and the emerging American Conservative movement resisted the modernizing tendencies of Reform Jews and radicals like Felix Adler. In 1908, Pope Pius X condemned and repressed the small modernist movement that had briefly flowered in the Roman Catholic community under the leadership of Alfred F. Loisy and George Tyrrell.[7] In the mind of all these diverse conservative religious groups, a popular philosopher like Dewey, who had moved to the extreme left wing of religious liberalism, could only be viewed as a dangerous rival and enemy of true religion. From their point of view, the evolution of his thought toward humanistic naturalism revealed the hidden tendencies and perils of all theological modernism.

Teacher and Reformer in New York

By the time of Wilson's election Dewey was fifty-three years old and well established at Columbia University in a philosophy department which was widely recognized as exceptionally strong. The department included Wendell Bush, William P. Montague, Frederick J.E. Woodbridge, and Felix Adler, who taught graduate students on a part-time basis. Unlike the Chicago Department of Philosophy, which constituted a school of philosophy, Dewey's Columbia colleagues represented a variety of viewpoints, and he benefitted from the give-and-take. Bush, who had been trained at Harvard by James and Santayana, combined a strong interest in the aesthetic and religious aspects of culture with Dewey's experimentalism. Montague, who was the author of *Belief Unbound: A Promethean Religion for the Modern World* and *Great Visions of Philosophy,* was "a speculative thinker of brilliant imaginative power" and "an unconventional anticlerical theist." He was also an epistemological realist who rejected Dewey's pragmatist approach to knowledge. Divided on technical philosophical issues, they held much in common on questions of social reform. Woodbridge's intellectual odyssey is a familiar American story. He had studied at Union Theological Seminary and had intended to enter the ministry, but after two years of graduate work in Germany, his interests shifted from theology to philosophy. He shared Dewey's general orientation as an empirical naturalist, and even though the two men had their epistemological differences, it was partly as a result of Woodbridge's influence that Dewey came to recognize the possibilities of a naturalistic metaphysics. Bush and Woodbridge edited the *Journal of Philosophy* and Dewey's writings regularly appeared in its pages. In time the approach of Dewey and Woodbridge came to dominate the philosophical orientation of the department, and the work of the next generation of Columbia philosophers made up of Herbert W. Schneider, John H. Randall, Jr., Irwin Edman, Horace L. Freiss, and Ernest Nagel showed their strong influence.[8]

Felix Adler, who headed the Ethical Culture Society, was well respected as a thinker and social critic, but his own philosophy involved a neo-Kantian orientation with which his Columbia colleagues did not agree. In spite of their divergent methods of philosophy, Adler and Dewey had a number of shared interests as social and educational reformers, and they cooperated in a variety of practical endeavors. Dewey's respect for Adler's work as an educator was such that, for a number of years, he enrolled several of his children in the Ethical Culture School in New York City. Dewey also fully supported Adler's efforts to channel people's religious interests in moral and social directions. Dewey and Adler disagreed, however, on how best to teach ethics in the school. Adler favored special classes on the subject. Dewey was concerned that such an approach would make the children too self-conscious about ethics. He recommended focusing attention on ethical considerations as they emerge naturally in connection with the problems and conflicts of school life.[9]

Dewey's course offerings at Columbia reflected for the most part his major philosophical interests. He did not have the reputation of being an exciting lecturer. "He was naturally shy, reticent and undemonstrative in manner."[10] In lectures he used only a few notes on sheets of paper that were crumpled up as the class proceeded. He spoke thoughtfully and "slowly with little emphasis and long pauses" often looking out the window or up toward the ceiling.[11] As one student put it: "He hardly seemed aware of the presence of the class."[12] Dewey readily admitted that his thought process tended to be quite abstract, because "he had difficulty in thinking of concrete dramatic illustrations to drive home general principles."[13] However, the attentive student could perceive behind Dewey's rather impersonal and abstract style an uncommon demonstration of experimental philosophical thinking, and those who took notes came to realize that what Dewey said was well organized and full of "acute analyses and original insights."[14] Following his first meeting with Dewey in 1914, Bertrand Russell observed: "He has a large slowly-moving mind, very empirical and candid, with something of the impassivity and impartiality of a natural force."[15] Sidney Hook, who studied with Dewey at Columbia prior to World War I and worked closely with him over the years, writes: "what stands out most vividly in my mind about Dewey's intellectual habits is the freshness of his thinking, the variety of starts he would make, and his own sense of the adventure of thinking."[16]

Max Eastman, another student of Dewey's in the early Columbia years, recalls Dewey's "luminous eyes" as his most striking characteristic: "Dewey's eyes were wells of dark, almost black, tenderly intelligent light such as would shine more appropriately out of a Saint Francis than a professor of logic." Dewey was at his best in the classroom when responding to questions and entering dialogue with his students. When a question was asked, "those glowing eyes would come down from the ceiling and shine into that pupil, and draw out of him and his innocent question intellectual wonders such as the student never imagined had their seeds in his brain or bosom."[17] Irwin Edman, who studied during the war years with Dewey, asserts that Dewey's greatest gift as a teacher was "that of initiating inquiry rather than that of disseminating a doctrine."[18] A number of Dewey's associates have commented about the way he embodied a democratic attitude in his dealings with students and people in general. Eastman, for example, notes "Dewey's instinctive and active deference, and unqualified giving of attention to whatever anybody, no matter how dumb or humble, might have had to say."[19] Hook writes: "Dewey was a man of no pride—no pride of dress, literary style, social origins, or intellectual achievement. He was prepared to learn from anyone.... There were no hidden ambitions, no vain regrets, no sense of being anything more than a citizen, a neighbor, a teacher, a friend—and a philosopher."[20]

As in the case of the Universities of Chicago and Michigan, there was at Columbia a small but very talented group of progressive-thinking faculty members who played important roles in advancing the progressive cause in America. Of special significance were Franz Boas in anthropology and Charles Beard and James Harvey Robinson in history. The writings of Boas emphasized the relativity of all cultural traditions in a way that was very useful to the reformers who were bent on changing so much from America's past. Beard and Robinson were the leaders of the "new history" movement, which emphasized ongoing evolutionary change. Beard insisted on the relativity of even such a sacred tradition as the American constitution. He conceived of history as progress, teaching that the American promise would be realized in the industrial democracy that was in process of being created.[21] Dewey's outlook was reinforced by what he learned from these scholars. The significance of what Dewey's philosophy meant to progressive intellectuals is suggested by a comment of Beard: "He's the quiet one, my friend who looks like your milquetoast uncle and who is undermining the whole world of the nineteenth century with his pragmatism."[22]

By the time of the publication of *Democracy and Education,* Dewey was well established as the foremost philosopher of the progressive movement. His influence extended from Columbia not only through his writings and frequent speaking engagements, but also through his students, some of whom became leaders among the younger intellectuals on the left wing of the progressive movement. Among this group were Max Eastman and Randolph Bourne, both of whom became enthusiastic proponents of Deweyan pragmatism. Eastman, who also had an interest in Marx and socialist art, found an outlet for his talents as the editor of the *Masses* in 1912. Bourne, who adopted Dewey's hope for reform through progressive education, became a prophet of social, aesthetic, and spiritual regeneration in the late progressive era and wrote regularly after 1916 for the avant-garde publication, *Seven Arts.*[23]

Perhaps the best brief introduction to Dewey's general philosophical orientation as a humanistic naturalist and progressive reformer during the early Columbia years is found in a dialogue—the only dialogue he wrote—that was published by the *Hibbert Journal* in 1909 under the title "Is Nature Good? A Conversation." The dialogue, which was reprinted in a collection of Dewey's essays entitled *The Influence of Darwin on Philosophy* (1910), presents five different current approaches to the problem that he viewed as the fundamental issue for philosophy: the relation between the ideal and the real. The discussion starts off with the nineteenth-century formulation of the problem involving the notion that "modern science ... has stripped the universe bare not only of all moral values which it wore alike to antique pagan and to our medieval ancestors, but also of any regard, any preference, for such values."[24] The five voices in the dialogue represent the perspectives of absolute idealism, speculative evolutionary theory, mysticism, Marxism, and pragmatism. In this conversation Dewey is found once again arguing that one cannot idealize the world by thought or feeling alone. The answer lies in will and a mode of practical action that integrates feeling and intelligence.

The absolute idealist (Moore) is concerned to demonstrate with the aid of logic and metaphysics that the values of truth, beauty, and goodness are not just illusions, mere appearances, subjective realities existing only in the human mind and subject to the ravages of time and death. He argues that a close critical examination of scientific knowledge itself reveals the activity of an unchanging all-embracing absolute mind that guarantees the ultimate reality of humanity's treasured values. The speculative evolutionary philosopher (Arthur) does not feel the necessity for a belief in a transcendental realm of spiritual values or God, but he agrees with the absolute idealist that the idea of a purposeless universe is oppressive to the human spirit. Espousing a view Dewey had held in the 1880s, he tries to show that Darwinian theory may be used to correct Newtonian physics and to support the idea of cosmic teleology, the notion that nature is moved by regard for values.

The mystic (Stair) argues that feeling, immediate appreciation, rather than reason is "the ultimate organ" for apprehending the truth of things and for realizing the supremacy of ideal values in the universe. In accord with Henri Bergson, the influential French philosopher and author of *Introduction to Metaphysics* (1903) and *Creative Evolution* (1907), he contends that "reason, intellect, is the principle of analysis, of division, of discord" and cannot apprehend unity and the deeper truth of things.[25] Appealing to "direct vision" and "mysticism" as "the heart of all positive empiricism," he explains that "the sole possible proof" of "the supremacy of ideal values in the universe" is "the direct unhindered realization of those values" for "each value brings with it of necessity its own depth of being." Mystical feelings occur frequently, awakening in the common people a sustaining faith in an unseen supreme good, or God. "Let pride of intellect and the pride of will cease their clamor," the mystic declares, "and in the silences Being speaks its own final word, not an argument or external ground of belief, but the self-impartation of itself to the soul."[26]

The dialogue includes a tough-minded radical reformer (Grimes), who presents a Marxist analysis of the problem. He attacks all metaphysical speculations about a transcendental realm of ideal values as concern for artificial problems generated by the boredom and sentimentalism of a leisured class. Furthermore, ideas about God and the other world are employed by monopolists and tyrants as opiates to pacify the oppressed. The only real problem of the relation of Nature to human good is an economic problem: "The genuine question is why social arrangements will not permit the amply sufficient body of natural resources to sustain all men and women in security and decent comfort, with a margin for the cultivation of their human instincts of sociability, love of knowledge and of art."[27] He rejects the approach of the mystic, because mysticism pursues a vision of the good that is unrelated to economic and social change leading to quietism.

The final participant (Eaton) is a naturalistic humanist and a philosophical pragmatist, or experimentalist, who articulates Dewey's position. He agrees that the real problem concerning the relation of value and nature is a practical and social problem. His major criticism of the speculative metaphysical arguments of the idealists regarding

God, the universal mind, is that in addition to being unconvincing they are for the most part of no practical significance.

> Is any value more concretely and securely in life than it was before? Does this perfect intelligence enable us to correct one single mis-step, one paltry error, here and now? Does this perfect all-inclusive good-ness serve to heal one disease? Does it rectify one transgression? Does it even give the slightest inkling of how to go to work on any of these things? No; it just tells you: Never mind, for they are already eternally corrected, eternally healed in the eternal consciousness which alone is really Real. Stop: there is one evil, one pain, which the doctrine mitigates—the hysteric sentimentalism which is troubled because the universe as a whole does not sustain good as a whole. But that is the only thing it alters. The "pathetic fallacy" of Ruskin magnified to the *n*th power is the *motif* of modern idealism.[28]

In short, the only practical value of absolute idealism is the consola-tion it offers to the tender-minded, but in the view of Dewey's pragmatist, to be preoccupied with the need for such consolation is childish.

The problem as to whether humanity's ideals are merely passing illusions or ultimate realities, which troubles the idealists, is, then, an artificial problem that fails to formulate the real issue. Showing some agreement with the mystic, who appeals to the direct realization of values as ground for trusting in their reality, the pragmatist en-deavors to clarify the critical problem.

> My point is precisely that it is only as long as you take the position that some Reality beyond—some metaphysical or transcendental real-ity—is necessary to substantiate empirical values that you can even discuss whether the latter are genuine or illusions. Drop the presup-position that you read into everything I say, the idea that the reality of things as they are is dependent upon something beyond and behind, and the facts of the case just stare you in the eyes: Goods *are,* a multitude of them—but unfortunately, evils also *are;* and all grades, pretty much, of both.... The trouble and the joy, the good and the evil, is *that* they are—the hope is that they may be regulated, guided, increased in one direction and minimized in another.[29]

This leads the pragmatist to his major point, which adheres to William James' biological conception of the nature and function of intelligence: "We say that intelligent discrimination of means and ends is the sole final resource in this problem of all problems, the control of the factors of good and ill in life. We say, indeed, not merely that that is what intelligence *does,* but rather what it *is.*" In the experimental method of intelligence lies the key to dealing with the problem of nature and good, or the ideal and the real.

Responding to the evolutionary philosopher's quest for cosmic teleology, the pragmatist states: "Nature, till it produces a being who strives and who thinks in order that he may strive more effectively, does not know whether it cares more for justice or for cruelty ... Literally it has no mind of its own." He does not deny that experiences of a mystical quality occur and are important, but such experiences, in and of themselves, are not an adequate answer to the problem of good and evil.

> To invite us, ceasing struggle and effort, to commune with Being through the moments of insight and joy that life provides, is to bid us to self-indulgence—to enjoyment at the expense of those upon whom the burden of conducting life's affairs falls. For even the mystics still need to eat and drink, be clothed and housed, and somebody must do these unmystic things. And to ignore others in the interest of our own perfection is not conducive to genuine unity of Being.[30]

The concern here is for genuine democratic community. The criticism is again that mysticism leads to quietism. The pragmatist remains unconvinced by the mystic's contention that it is the mystical vision of unity and justice that inspires the morally concerned social activist, an idea that Bergson fully developed in *The Two Sources of Morality and Religion* (1932).[31] The only criticism the pragmatist has of the Marxist reformer is that in reacting to the overvaluation of contemplative knowledge and abstract philosophy in the past, he fails to appreciate fully the need for a method of intelligence in the direction of practical action and for philosophical analysis of social conflicts and their resolution.

"Philosophy recovers itself when it ceases to be a device for dealing with the problems of philosophers and becomes a method, cultivated by philosophers for dealing with the problems of men."[32] This often quoted statement of Dewey's appears in "The Need for a Recovery of Philosophy," which was the lead essay in a collection of papers by eight American philosophers on the pragmatic attitude entitled *Creative Intelligence* (1917). Emphasizing one of his major themes, Dewey goes on to explain that with respect to addressing the problems of men, "the central need of any program at the present day is an adequate conception of the nature of intelligence and its place in action."[33] "Faith in the power of intelligence to imagine a future which is the projection of the desirable in the present, and to invent the instrumentalities of its realization, is our salvation."[34] This faith in experimental intelligence was Dewey's conception of the heart of the pragmatic attitude. In a steady stream of books, journal articles, and popular essays, he urged his fellow citizens to adopt this pragmatic attitude and to address the problems of the common people.

Having spent much of his life in the great urban industrial centers of North America, Dewey recognized clearly enough that the new science and technology had created a host of new problems for the human race and that these problems together constitute the crisis of the age. However, he argues "that while the evils resulting at present from the entrance of 'science' into our common ways of living are undeniable, they are due to the fact that no systematic efforts have as yet been made to subject the 'morals' underlying old institutional customs to scientific inquiry and criticism."[35] In other words, the new science and technology often have destructive consequences for human life because they are employed by institutions and persons who are governed by attitudes, habits and customs from a prescientific age. These prescientific values do not provide the guidance needed for dealing with the inventions and innovations of the new science. The result is that modern civilization is adrift without effective moral direction.

> The science that has so far found its way deeply and widely into the actual affairs of human life is partial and incomplete science: competent in respect to physical, and now increasingly to physiological, conditions (as is seen in the recent developments in medicine and public sanitation), but non-existent with respect to matters of supreme significance to man—those which are distinctively of, for, and by, man.[36]

It is one of Dewey's deepest convictions that only when the experimental method is humanized and applied to the values that govern human relations will the destructive consequences of the new technology be overcome. This, in Dewey's mind, is the real problem of science and moral values. The nineteenth-century problem of how in the face of Newtonian physics one is to go on believing that ultimate reality is identical with the ideals of truth, beauty, and goodness fails to formulate the problem in a way that it can be productively resolved leading to democratic social progress.

Perhaps the most radical teaching of intellectuals like Boas, Beard, and Dewey was their evolutionary moral relativism. For Dewey moral relativism was a direct consequence of Darwinian evolutionary theory. As he interpreted it, Darwinian thought rejects all ideas of fixed first and final causes and emphasizes the pervasive presence of change. There are no absolute fixities in nature. Even species come to be and pass away. By implication, reasons Dewey, moral and religious values also change.[37] Instead of seeking for absolute ideals and offering ready-made solutions to moral problems, pragmatism adopts a genetic and experimental approach to moral values and focuses on developing a method for dealing with specific moral difficulties as they arise in concrete situations. It directs a person facing a moral dilemma to carefully clarify the nature of the problem and then to give attention to specific alternative values or ideals that might guide conduct in the situation, noting especially the conditions that are necessary to actualize them, that is, the means to their realization. With the aid of this knowledge of conditions or means, it studies the actual consequences that flow from acting under guidance of the alternative values in question. In the light of a knowledge of consequences, it then evaluates these ideals, taking into consideration the specific needs of the moral problem at hand. This is the process of pragmatic moral evaluation. Charles S. Peirce "took the term 'pragmatic' from Kant, in order to denote empirical consequences," explains Dewey, and he adds:

> I again affirm that the term "pragmatic" means only the role of referring all thinking, all reflective considerations, to consequences for final meaning and test. Nothing is said about the nature of the consequences; they may be aesthetic, or moral, or political, or religious in quality—anything you please. All that the theory requires is that they be in some way consequences of thinking; not indeed, of it alone, but of it acted upon in connection with other things.[38]

Pragmatism, then, evaluates moral values or ideals with reference to specific problematic situations and in the light of the means involved in their realization and the consequences that necessarily follow. Given its interest in the means-ends continuum, pragmatism is also concerned to point out the contradictions that arise when people embrace certain moral ideals but fail to inquire into or tend the actual conditions of their realization.

In summary, from the point of view of pragmatism, no moral value stands above critical evaluation and reconstruction, especially in times of social transition. The vital moral issue is to use experimental intelligence and a knowledge of conditions and consequences to guide this process wisely. Dewey's moral relativism and pragmatic method of moral valuation was a potent weapon in the fight against conservative interests whether they be economic, class, racial, or religious. However, the idea of moral relativism was also a notion that could be used to foster moral subjectivism, cynicism, and crass materialism. Dewey had no use for these orientations, and in the years ahead he would work hard to defend his brand of pragmatism and experimentalism from the charge that it fosters these attitudes.

In the spirit of his experimentalism, Dewey directly engaged himself in a great number of reform efforts and social causes during his early years in New York City. His major contributions came in and through his extensive work on behalf of progressive children's education, but he also found occasion for many other involvements as well. He participated from time to time in the life of New York City's radical intellectuals, many of whom congregated in Greenwich Village. His acquaintances included socialists and feminists like Charlotte Perkins Gilman and Emma Goldman, as well as advocates of the new arts and radical politics like Max Eastman and Randolph Bourne. Shortly after his arrival at Columbia he became an adviser to Helicon Hall, which was organized by the socialist critic Upton Sinclair as an experiment in cooperative living. At about this same time, American society turned its back on the visiting Russian revolutionary writer, Maxim Gorky, because he was travelling with a woman companion of many years to whom he was not married; in response, John and Alice Dewey publicly invited the ostracized couple to stay in their home. Dewey taught at the Rand School, a small but lively institution set up near Greenwich Village by the socialist

Carrie Rand in an effort to benefit young immigrants. He also served as chairman of the education committee at Lillian Wald's Henry Street Settlement and involved himself in Mary Simkhovitch's Greenwich House.[39]

During the years 1912 and 1913, Dewey was a leader in forming the Teachers' League of New York, which eventually became the New York Teachers' Union. Between 1913 and 1915, he helped to found the American Association of University Professors and served as its first president.[40] The AAUP was designed to foster cooperation among university professors in improving higher education, to protect the academic freedom of faculty members, and to support greater participation by faculties in the governance of colleges and universities.[41] In helping to create teachers' unions and the AAUP, Dewey was concerned to free the intellectual life in the nation's schools and universities from all "alien and sinister influences." Teachers may be appointed by school boards and boards of trustees, but teachers are first and foremost responsible to "their moral employer," the public. They are "the servants of the community, of the whole community, and not of any particular class interest within it." Their "primary loyalty is to an idea, to a function and calling," which is "the pursuit and expression of truth," and they have a responsibility and right to organize to insure that they and their institutions carry out this social function. Dewey in his writings repeatedly attacks the notion that school boards and university trustees have the moral right to use their legal powers of appointment to fire teachers arbitrarily without respecting their academic freedom and right to due process, as if they were employees subject to the absolute and arbitrary authority of management in some factory or business corporation.[42]

Dewey's "knowledge of the character and intelligence" of Ella Flagg Young, Jane Addams, and his wife led him to become a feminist, that is, to accept fully the idea of women's equality and to commit himself to the social and political action necessary to making the ideal real.[43] It has already been noted that Dewey strongly endorsed the principle of coeducation as fundamental to his idea of moral democracy. Working with Alice Dewey, he also marched and spoke out in support of the women's suffrage movement, which after seventy years of protest finally won the right to vote for women in 1920.[44] Speaking to a packed audience at Columbia University in

1912, Dewey is quoted as stating: "You can't have a real democracy where there is caste and cliques or sets. Women are shut out from the culmination and seal for full citizenship, the outward and visible sign of the inward and spiritual grace which is liberty."[45] The enfranchisement of women is necessary to the completion of the democratic ideal, argues Dewey. Participating in a symposium on women's suffrage, he opposed any property or educational qualifications being attached to the right to vote for either men or women, arguing that "it is the masses—the poor—that most need the protection of the ballot. If by an educational qualification is meant a certain degree of literacy, it is a piece of academic foolishness to suppose that ability to read or write is an adequate test of social and political intelligence." Dewey did not support use of "militant methods" by the women's movement in the United States unless such pressure was necessary, as (in his opinion) it had been in England. In 1911 he did not think it would be necessary.[46]

Jo Ann Boydston and Mary Dearborn have pointed out that Dewey had the kind of "political awakening that is essential to feminism."[47] The most striking evidence of this is found in his personal correspondence. In 1915, for example, Dewey writes to an unconverted philosopher, Scudder Klyce, that he knows four or five women "superior in concrete intelligence to almost any man I know." He confesses: "Only women have ever given [me] really intellectual surprises; I'll be damned if I can see how they do it—but they do. Their observations ... are more honest than men's. They are much less easily imposed upon; and they are more willing to face the unpleasant side of facts. I am not generalizing; I am only reporting what I have seen."[48] Dewey points out to Klyce that the notion that men are more courageous is "purely conventional, based on comparing men with ladies, an artificial social product of men. Women, not 'ladies,' have more courage than men, in the sense of willingness to face and bear the disagreeable. Women bear children—bear the race. If you think they could do that without more courage than men, guess again."[49]

In a statement that anticipates the feminist viewpoint of the 1960s and 1970s, Dewey in 1915 explains to Klyce:

If you ever have the fortune to hear some clear-headed and honest women, not professional feminists—women who have used their experience—express their opinions about men as a "class" you will find that they agree that men are essentially hogs—and that the worst of it is they haven't the slightest idea of the fact, since what they hog are intangible things; in other words, they assume that *their* work is the really important thing in the world. Till my attention was called to it, I am bound to say I had always assumed that, and I don't think I have ever met a man who didn't practically say to himself, "Why, of course it is. How funny that anybody should question it." If that is not being a hog, I don't know what it is.[50]

Dewey acknowledges that it is necessary for there to be a division of labor between men and women, but he observes that the present division is just a matter of convention which upon the whole reflects the judgment of men. "The only way to find the real balance of division of labor is by experimenting," states Dewey, "and the world has never had the experiments which make the facts perceptible." Dewey concludes: "It is truistic that if there is a division of labor then women must have a reciprocal chance in discovering what it is ... that chance they have never had. It has been settled by man's opinion of anatomy. That statement is the woman question in a nutshell."[51]

Even though Dewey did not attempt a substantive analysis of the problems faced by the black community in America, he did participate in the founding of the NAACP and consistently spoke out clearly against racism. Concerned about the denial to blacks of basic civil and political rights, a rise in lynchings and race riots, and the inferior educational facilities provided blacks, fifty black and white social leaders, including W.E.B. Du Bois, Oswald Garrison Villard, William E. Walling, and William Lloyd Garrison, Jr., met together at a National Negro Conference in 1909 to demand equal rights and equal opportunity for all blacks.[52] Dewey also participated, and in his address he argues that from a scientific standpoint there is no basis to the notion of the inferiority of the Negro race. All blacks, he reasons, should be provided with the same opportunities as whites to develop their capacities and interests in the school and society at large. He concludes:

> For if these race differences are, as has been pointed out, comparatively slight, individual differences are very great. All points of skill are represented in every race, from the inferior individual to the

superior individual, and a society that does not furnish the environment and education and opportunity of all kinds which will bring out
and make effective the superior ability wherever it is born, is not
merely doing an injustice to that particular race and to those particular
individuals, but it is doing an injustice to itself for it is depriving itself
of just that much of social capital.[53]

The deliberations of the National Negro Conference led to the founding
of the NAACP in 1910.

The racial discrimination directed at blacks was particularly severe, but they were not the only group to suffer the consequences of
racism in America during the early 1900s. As new waves of immigrants flowed into the United States, they too encountered the ugly
face of American racism and religious and ethnic prejudice. In response to this situation, Dewey persistently emphasized that racism
in any form is contrary to the fundamental idea of American democracy. For example, in an address before the National Education
Association in 1916, he states:

> No matter how loudly any one proclaims his Americanism, if he
> assumes that any one racial strain, any one component culture, no
> matter how early settled it was in our territory, or how effective it has
> proved in its own land, is to furnish a pattern to which all other
> strains and cultures are to conform, he is a traitor to an American
> nationalism. Our unity cannot be a homogeneous thing like that of
> the separate states of Europe from which our population is drawn; it
> must be a unity created by drawing out and composing into a harmo-
> nious whole the best, the most characteristic which each contributing
> race and people has to offer.[54]

He goes on to encourage the public school teacher to become "an
active agent in furthering the common struggle of native born, Afri-
can, Jew, Italian and . . . a score of other peoples to attain emancipation and enlightenment." "The peculiarity of *our* nationalism," argues Dewey, "is its internationalism," and he laments the effect the
war spirit is having on American attitudes toward the immigrant and
the oppressed as well as foreign peoples overseas. "Our democracy
means amity and good will to all humanity (including those beyond
our border)." Teachers should "remember that they above all others
are the consecrated servants of the democratic ideas in which alone

this country is truly a distinctive nation—ideas of friendly and helpful intercourse between all and the equipment of every individual to serve the community by his own best powers in his own best way."[55] The war experience and his travels in Japan and China led Dewey in the early nineteen-twenties to study the psychological, social, political, and economic causes of racism, which he described as a "social disease," and to explore ways of overcoming it.[56]

In 1914 Herbert Croly, whose *The Promise of American Life* (1909) served as a brilliant diagnosis of the national situation and a provocative reconstruction of eastern progressive ideals, gathered together a gifted staff of writers, including Walter Lippmann and Walter Weyle, to edit a weekly journal of liberal opinion. It was named the *New Republic*, and it fast became the major popular voice of the progressives in the East. Croly did not believe that the powerful forces unleashed in urban industrial America would fulfill the social, economic, and moral promise of American life if American society was left in the hands of leaders who believed in unchecked Jeffersonian individualism and a social Darwinism that supports economic laissez-faire.[57] He fully agreed with Dewey's central thesis that if the ideals of American democracy are to be realized, the pressing, critical issue is a clear idea of the role of social intelligence. He called for a fresh vision of the national purpose and effective socioeconomic planning guided by a strong central government. He also endorsed Dewey's goal of a reconstructed educational system which would produce liberated individuals with a high sense of democratic moral purpose.[58] Having been initiated into Comte's religion of humanity as a boy, Croly envisioned the democratic ideal fulfilled in a "religion of human brotherhood" founded on "loving-kindness." Early on, Croly involved Dewey in the *New Republic* as a regular contributor, and between 1915 and 1935 Dewey wrote over 150 articles for the journal on a wide range of national and international issues.

War and Peace

The *New Republic* was founded by liberal intellectuals with a primary interest in issues of domestic policy, but they soon found themselves wrestling with issues of international war and peace that eventually disorganized the liberal reform movement. Dewey had a vivid memory of the Civil War as a terrible conflict with far-reaching destructive consequences for the nation's social and economic life, and he believed that it could and should have been avoided.[59] His philosophy up to 1914 had advocated peaceful methods of social transformation. In response to the outbreak of war in Europe, he initially joined the vast majority of progressives who vigorously opposed entry into the war on the grounds that the war was basically a clash between competing economic interests in Europe and that entry would brutalize American society, sidetrack the progressive movement, and benefit only industrialists and bankers. Dewey also consistently opposed the introduction of military training into schools and colleges during the war years. He found the authoritarianism and rigid discipline of military training to be utterly inconsistent with the democratic progressive values, which in his view should govern the education of the young.[60]

Some progressives like Jane Addams, who founded a Women's Peace Party, embraced pacifism and assiduously studied Leo Tolstoy's later writings. Dewey did not go this route. Given the threat to democracy posed by German militarism and imperialism, he kept his mind open to the possibility that entry into the war might eventually be necessary. The war situation led many progressives, who had been isolationists with respect to foreign policy, to consider the possibility that the struggle for democratic social progress could require international involvement. Dewey's thinking was aligned with this approach, and the war years mark the beginning of a strong interest in international affairs that persisted throughout the remainder of his life. Using his pragmatic perspective, he in characteristic fashion tried to find a commonsense middle way between the extreme pacifists who oppose all use of force as evil and those who glorify the use of brute force in war or economic competition without regard to the actual consequences.[61] Both groups fail, according to Dewey, to analyze carefully the relation between means and ends and to recognize that the use of force in any situation is a specific means to be evaluated with respect to its concrete results.

In four essays published in the *New Republic* and the *International Journal of Ethics,* "Force, Violence and Law" (1916), "Force and

Coercion" (1916), "Conscience and Compulsion" (1917), and "The Future of Pacifism" (1917), Dewey spelled out his criticism of the pacifists in some detail while trying to chart a middle way on the issue of war and peace. These essays are a clear expression of Dewey's pragmatic approach to moral issues and are also a prime example of the way the war experience divided the progressives. Many of the pacifists were, of course, liberal Protestants, and Dewey's criticisms anticipate the kind of attack on Protestant liberalism that became widespread during the 1930s. As a pragmatist with faith in social intelligence, his objections to the pacifist position involve two inter-related issues. He found that the pacifists had an irrational "emotional animosity to the very idea of force" and they mistakenly emphasized the emotions rather than intelligence and social reconstruction in seeking the moral improvement of society. Each of these criticisms deserves closer scrutiny.[62]

The pacifists whom Dewey attacked were followers of Leo Tolstoy, who argued that the heart of Jesus' ethical teaching and of all moral wisdom is the injunction "Resist not evil." Proceeding from this fixed abstract principle Tolstoy developed a radical philosophy of nonresistance and nonviolence, opposing as intrinsically immoral any use of coercive force by individuals or governments. He not only opposed war but also coercion and constraint by the police and prison systems. Dewey knew Tolstoy's position. He read his *Confessions* and studied his philosophy, and he participated in discussions concerning Tolstoy's theory of nonresistance in Chicago and New York.[63] He admired the Russian mystic and social reformer as "a figure that the thought of today must absolutely reckon with." However, Dewey was left unsatisfied by Tolstoy's religious and moral philosophy because his "solutions . . . are too much on the All or Nothing basis; they make too absolute a separation between sense and reason, between the physical and the moral, between the individual self and humanity."[64] What especially bothered Dewey as a pragmatist about the Tolstoyan pacifists was their passionate adherence to an inflexible abstract moral principle, the idea that all force is violence and evil, which led them to be content to oppose American involvement in the war without carefully examining the actual situation or trying to do anything about it. Dewey believed that their position involved flawed unrealistic ("moonstruck") moral thinking.

Dewey's attack on the pacifists involved a complex stinging critique which demonstrates the power of his pragmatic perspective as a tool of criticism. However, in an attempt to discredit the pacifist position, Dewey interwove with his pragmatist critique a very questionable redefinition of the term "force" that resulted in an unfortunate distortion of the pacifist position adding confusion to his argument.[65] Dewey was often upset by philosophers like Bertrand Russell who seemed willfully to distort the pragmatist position, and it was out of character for him to do this to the pacifists, especially since some of them were his friends and supporters.[66] The explanation is probably to be found in the tension created by the war situation, and Dewey was obviously irritated by the pacifists' moral absolutism and sentimentalism.

In political forums, the term "force" is usually equated with methods of physical coercion and constraint, and it is often equated with violence. It was with this understanding that the pacifists employed the term. However, Dewey, in an effort to make the pacifists' blanket opposition to force look utterly foolish, tried to give the term a much wider meaning. He identifies force with energy and power in the broadest sense and asserts that no social problem can be resolved without the possession and exertion of force. We live in a pluralistic world of competing forces and "no ends are accomplished without the use of force." Dewey cites as examples of the use of force persuasion by argument and publishing books as well as building bridges and manufacturing goods. When force is so defined, it is obviously absurd for even a pacifist to oppose all use of force. Dewey goes on to explain that force is called energy or power when it is used effectively as a means to a desired end. When force runs wild with wasteful and destructive consequences, it may be called violence. Violence is obviously bad. Dewey argues that coercive force is not to be called violence when coercion or constraint is the necessary means to a good end. In some situations coercive force may be necessary.[67] The confusing implication of Dewey's distinction between violence and coercive force is, of course, that the use of machine guns and bombs is not to be called violence if and when intelligence has determined that it is the only effective—and, therefore, moral—means to a worthy end.[68]

Ends are only realized by means, and means to ends always involve use of some form of force, that is, power or energy. Playing on the double meaning of the term "force" (the pacifists' meaning and his own), Dewey contends that since the pacifists oppose the use of force, they do not take seriously the problem of the means necessary to realize the ends—such as peace—which they claim to embrace. He cites as proof of this their lack of interest in projects like the League of Nations. "To be interested in ends and to have contempt for the means which alone secure them is the last stage of intellectual demoralization," asserts Dewey.[69] The pacifists agonize over whether the use of force is moral, but Dewey (using his own definition of force) argues that the question must be reformulated in order to focus attention on the real issue: "The only question which can be raised about the justification of force is that of comparative efficiency and economy in its use."[70] What is "the most effective use of force in gaining ends in specific situations?"[71] "What is justly objected to as violence or undue coercion is a reliance upon wasteful and destructful means of accomplishing results." "An immoral use of force is a stupid use." As a pragmatist Dewey is also insistent that fixed antecedent abstract rules like "resist not evil" are not adequate guides in moral matters. In our pluralistic, evolving world, it is not wise to rule out the use of any form of power including coercion in an absolute fashion. "The criterion of value lies in the relative efficiency and economy of the expenditure of force as a means to an end." In other words, moral guidance comes from intelligence as it focuses on "a specific means to a specific end" and considers the relative effectiveness of particular uses of force or energy in a concrete situation. This is pragmatic moral relativism. The use of coercive force and war can only be discussed productively in the light of a specific situation and as a specific means to a specific end.[72]

Dewey's very practical approach to the use of power, including coercive force, appeals to common sense. However, his argument is weakened by his confusing attempt to discredit the pacifists by a trick of language regarding the meaning of the term "force." He himself later returned to using the term as equivalent to coercion and violence.[73] Also, his emphasis on economy and efficiency in the adaptation of means to ends is an example of the kind of terminology that created the false impression that his pragmatism was more concerned about efficient means than high moral ends. Dewey emphasized means because he perceived so many others talking at length about ends in rather vague abstract terms and as separated from the means necessary to their realization. The pacifists long for the ideal of peace but do not try to understand how to realize it. Opposing them, others call for war in the name of the abstract ideals of justice, honor, and law, but they fail to think through how war as a means will further these ends.[74]

Dewey had another major objection to the pacifist position. Being guided by a philosophy of nonresistance and lacking a pragmatic concern with appropriate means to world peace, he found that the pacifists were led into a naive sentimental idealism. He writes:

> It is hostility to force as force, to force intrinsically, which has rendered the peace movement so largely an anti-movement, with all the weaknesses which appertain to everything that is primarily anti-anything. Unable to conceive the task of organizing the existing forces so they may achieve their greatest efficiency, pacifists have had little recourse save to decry evil emotions and evil-minded men as the causes of war. Belief that war springs from the emotions of hate, pugnacity, and greed rather than from the objective causes which call these emotions into play reduces the peace movement to the futile plane of hortatory preaching. The avarice of munition-makers, the love of some newspapers for exciting news, and the depravity of the anonymous human heart doubtless play a part in the generation of war. But they take a hand in bringing on war only because there are specific defects in the organization of the energies of men in society which give them occasion and stimulation.
>
> Until pacifism puts its faith in constructive, inventive intelligence instead of in appeal to emotions and in exhortation, the disparate unorganized forces of the world will continue to develop outbreaks of violence.[75]

Dewey's concern with reorganizing social and political forces in the world led him to support formation of a League of Nations.[76] However, he cautioned that an international police force is not an adequate answer to the problems of world peace. "Force is efficient socially not when imposed upon a scene from without, but when it is an organization of the forces in the scene.... And no league to enforce peace will fare prosperously save as it is the natural accompaniment of a constructive adjustment of the concrete interests which are already at work."[77] As noted, he faulted the pacifists for not aggressively pursuing such a practical solution to the problem of war. Jane Addams protested this criticism in a public address. In response, Dewey acknowledged her interest in creating new international agencies and praised her position as "intelligent pacifism."[78]

Dewey traced the misguided sentimentalism of the pacifists to a tendency in the evangelical Protestant tradition "to locate morals in the personal feelings instead of in the control of social situations" and to be preoccupied with "the nurture of personal motives rather than the creation of social agencies." Evangelical Protestantism also has left many religious liberals and pacifists with "a somewhat mushy belief in the existence of disembodied moral forces which require only an atmosphere of feelings to operate so as to bring about what is right."[79] Conversely, evil emotions of greed and hatred are viewed as the chief cause of injustice and war. Dewey's rejection of this outlook stands as a criticism not only of much nineteenth-century American Protestantism, but also of much religion the world over which tends to view cultivation of emotions like compassion and the love of peace as the key to social progress. Anticipating a theme in Reinhold Niebuhr's *The Children of Light and the Children of Darkness* (1944), he states: "Let us perfect ourselves within, and in due season changes in society will come of themselves is the teaching. And while saints are engaged in introspection, burly sinners run the world."[80]

Dewey explained his own theory of the relation of the emotions to moral progress in society in an essay on "Progress" in 1917:

> My purpose is in lesser part to suggest the futility of trying to secure progress by immediate or direct appeal to even the best feelings in our make-up. In the main, there is an adequate fund of such feelings. What is lacking is adequate social stimulation for their exercise as compared with the social occasions which evoke less desirable emotions. In greater part my purpose is to indicate that since the variable

factor, the factor which may be altered indefinitely, is the social conditions which call out and direct the impulses and sentiments, the positive means of progress lie in the application of intelligence to the construction of proper social devices. Theoretically, it is possible to have social arrangements which will favor the friendly tendencies of human nature at the expense of the bellicose and predatory ones, and which will direct the latter into channels where they will do the least harm or even become means of good. Practically, this is a matter of the persistent use of reflection in the study of social conditions and the devising of social contrivances.[81]

"We must work on the environment, not merely on the hearts of men," contends Dewey the social psychologist.[82]

A classic example of the approach recommended by Dewey may be found in Aeschylus's *Oresteia,* where the goddess Athena breaks the cycle of vengeance in ancient Athenian society by creating for the first time a public court of law to deal with cases of murder and violence. The result is that the Furies become the Eumenides or Kindly Ones.[83] Feelings of anger and hatred find expression in controlled orderly channels. The energies saved from chaotic acts of private vengeance are released into constructive social undertakings and there are fresh opportunities for feelings of goodwill and kindliness. Such an approach is Dewey's general answer to what Christian theologians call the problem of sin. Preaching about sin, calling on people to repent, and appealing to kindly emotions has little effect from his point of view, unless there is an actual change in the social situation that calls forth the desired positive feelings. The one approach focuses on what is subjective; the other is concerned with objective conditions. Writing in the early 1930s, Dewey stated his point forcefully in his *Ethics:*

> As we have had occasion to observe, each community tends to approve that which is in line with what it prizes in practice. Theoretical approvals that run counter to strong social tendencies tend to become purely nominal. In theory and in verbal instruction our present society is the heir of a great idealistic tradition. Through religion and from other sources, love of neighbor, exact equity, kindliness of action and judgment, are taught and in theory accepted. The structure of society, however, puts emphasis upon other qualities. "Business" absorbs a

large part of the life of most persons and business is conducted upon the basis of ruthless competition for private gain. National life is organized on the basis of exclusiveness and tends to generate suspicion, fear, often hatred, of other peoples. The world is divided into classes and races, and, in spite of acceptance of an opposed theory, the standards of valuation are based on the class, race, color, with which one identifies oneself. The convictions that obtain in personal morality are negated on a large scale in collective conduct, and for this reason are weakened even in their strictly personal application. They cannot be made good in practice except as they are extended to include the remaking of the social environment, economic, political, international.[84]

Moral idealism must be coupled with social intelligence to be effective.

In 1917, after President Wilson had declared war on Germany, Dewey's critique of the pacifists focused specifically on the situation and attitudes of conscientious objectors. On the one hand, Dewey deplored the harsh criticism leveled against the conscientious objectors by many newspapers, and he supported a proposal to give drafted conscientious objectors work "which will put the least heavy load possible upon their consciences." On the other hand, he found these young men examples of the muddled moral thinking of their culture. An emphasis on the emotions as opposed to intelligence caused this group to be preoccupied with inner purity of conscience and issues of personal motivation rather than with controlling social situations. As a result, they were led to believe "that by not doing something, by keeping out of a declaration of war, our responsibilities could be met." The conscientious objectors bemoan the wickedness of those who control the direction of events, but since they refuse to get actively involved, Dewey finds their protest to be "largely self-conceit" as well as an exercise in "moral futility."[85]

Dewey also returned to the issue of adherence to fixed moral rules: "our legal tradition has bred the habit of attaching feelings to fixed rules and injunctions instead of to social conditions and consequences of action as these are revealed to the scrutiny of intelligence." As a result, many conscientious objectors tend "to dispose of war by bringing it under the commandment against murder"—Thou shalt not kill. From the point of view of pragmatism, antecedent abstract moral principles like the Ten Commandments may be useful in focusing attention on important aspects of a moral problem, but, in the final analysis, effective moral guidance comes from experimental intelligence as it explores specific means for effectively solving specific problems. Dewey's advice to the conscientious objector is to lift moral problems "out of the emotional urgencies and inhibitions of inner consciousness into the light of objective facts," which the pragmatic approach makes possible.

> The more one loves peace (of course I do not mean by peace the mere absence of military war) the more one is bound to ask himself how the machinery, the specific, concrete social arrangements, exactly comparable to physical engineering devices, for maintaining peace, are to be brought about. Conscience proceeding on this basis would operate very differently from that whose main concern is to maintain itself unspotted within, or from that whose search is for a fixed antecedent rule of justification.

Dewey recognized the genuine distress of "a perplexed and resentful overridden conscience," but he was impatient with those who are "merely conscientious."[86]

Dewey, who was a man full of humanitarian feeling, did not mean to deny the importance of positive emotions like sympathy or compassion. Interestingly, he found in Tolstoy a shining example of the ideal integration of such feelings with intelligence.

> There are many striking likenesses, as well as equally marked differences between Tolstoy and Rousseau. Among the likenesses is an extraordinary sensitiveness to the feelings, the joys and sufferings of all sentient creatures. If in some sense Rousseau is the discoverer of democracy as a social idea, not merely as a governmental arrangement, it is because Rousseau had such a vivid perception that whatever the differences of men in social rank, political power and in culture, they are alike in their power to feel, in their sensitiveness to misery and happiness, and that by the side of this fundamental likeness all differences are trivial and superficial. Capacity for sympathy with the pain and pleasure of others is, fortunately, among the commonest of human endowments; capacity for abstract reflection is not infrequent; but capacity to reflect widely and deeply on the basis of and in terms of

this sympathetic sensitiveness to the weal and woe of others is perhaps the rarest of gifts: so rare that its occurrence is as good a definition of genius as any we are likely to find. And this gift Tolstoy, like Rousseau, had in extraordinary measure.[87]

It is with these issues in mind that Dewey commented in 1915 that what the world needs is a leader with "Bismarck's brains and Lincoln's emotions."[88] This important aspect of Dewey's moral theory is often neglected. It is briefly mentioned in his *Ethics* in 1908 and more fully explained in a new section on "Sensitivity and Thoughtfulness" in the revised edition of the *Ethics* published in 1932.[89] Keeping this appreciation of the role of sympathy in mind helps to put in perspective what often appears as a one-sided emphasis on intelligence in Dewey's thought. He emphasized intelligence because he perceived it as a neglected but essential factor in a realistic plan for social and moral progress.

In 1915 Dewey tried to throw light on the emergence of militarism and imperialistic nationalism in Germany by publishing a small book entitled *German Philosophy and Politics,* which grew out of three lectures at the University of Virginia. He advanced the controversial thesis that, above all others, it was Kant, rather than Hegel or Nietzsche, whose thought had "intensified and deepened" the dangerous characteristics of German civilization.[90] Even though the initial published reviews of the book by Tufts and Santayana were favorable, a number of Dewey's younger intellectual followers who were opposed to United States involvement in the war were dismayed by it.[91] Especially in the light of Dewey's attacks on the pacifists, it seemed to them to be "a contribution to the war propaganda rather than to the history of thought."[92] This criticism is unjust. What Dewey identified as the heart of Kant's philosophy and then attacked is Kant's classic formulation of the dualism of science and morals.[93] Throughout his career Dewey had battled the dualism of science and morals. He regarded it as the chief obstacle to integrating intelligence and action and to providing contemporary industrial society with the kind of scientifically based moral guidance that it desperately needs. It was natural, therefore, that he would look to find this dualism as the root problem underlying contemporary German militarism and imperialism.

It is Dewey's thesis that, without intending it, Kant's dualism of the world of facts and the world of moral ideals encouraged the Germans to pursue science and technology vigorously divorced from reference to moral values and to develop a style of mechanical authority and obedience in the workaday world. At the same time, Kant's philosophy led to cultivation of a high sense of moral duty coupled with a very abstract definition of the moral ideal. Empty of specific content, the German sense of moral duty was easily channeled into a nationalistic moral idealism without reference to its social and international consequences. *German Philosophy and Politics* ends with a defense of American experimentalism, as involving the needed corrective to the Kantian separation of science and morals. Critics have continued to argue that the book fails to prove Dewey's thesis pertaining to Kant's influence; nevertheless, he reissued the book unaltered in 1942, with a new introduction dealing with Hitler's rise to power.[94]

As relations worsened between the United States and Germany and entry into the war seemed increasingly inevitable, Dewey prepared an essay early in 1917 for *Seven Arts* expressing the inner conflict and sadness he felt in relation to the whole situation. It was entitled "In a Time of National Hesitation." In it he explained that the war has made it very clear that the New World is not the Old World: "We are a new body and a new spirit in the world." The full meaning of the American democratic experiment is not yet clear, but it is clear "that the gallant fight for democracy and civilization fought on the soil of France is not our fight"—"for better or for worse, we are committed to a fight for another democracy and another civilization." Therefore, even though it may be necessary to join the war against Germany in order to prevent the triumph of German militarism and imperialism, the American cannot "join with full heart and soul even though we join with unreserved energy."[95]

In April 1917, President Wilson declared war on Germany, arguing that it was necessary to prevent the triumph of German militarism and to make the world safe for democracy. It was Wilson's contention that those who were concerned with progressive reform at home had to embrace a new internationalism to ensure the success of their goals. Convinced by the President's idealism, Dewey "with unreserved energy" but with divided heart joined Herbert Croly, Charles Beard, and the vast majority of progressives in the universities and the churches in giving their support to the move. They also insisted on a just peace that would not leave Germany humiliated and bent on revenge. In addition, they promoted the idea of a League of Nations, "a democratically ordered international government," that would be founded on a just postwar settlement and would be the "beginning of the end of war."[96]

Direct entry into the war generated many of the social problems that the progressives feared. Conservative business interests became more powerful and influential. Repressive measures were often adopted by government agencies, schools, and other institutions in the name of patriotism and the national interest. Persons suspected of pacifism, socialism, and pro-German sympathies were harassed, censored, fired, and sometimes imprisoned. "Respect for the individual has almost vanished," declared the liberal social critic Harold Stearns, and he identified the most evil effect of the war as "the contemporary strident harshness of temper, the almost fanatical intolerance of opposing leadership and doctrine."[97] The abridgement of civil rights struck close to home with Dewey when Professor James M. Cattell, who had been instrumental in bringing him to Columbia University, was dismissed by the University's Board of Trustees in 1917 for lobbying for a bill that would have protected the rights of conscientious objectors. Shortly thereafter, two other Columbia professors, Henry Dana and Leon Fraser, were dismissed for alleged unpatriotic antiwar activities. Charles Beard resigned in protest. There were similar scenarios at other schools, colleges, and universities across the country.[98]

Early in 1917, Dewey had protested in the *New York Times* the action of one of his colleagues who had denied Leo Tolstoy's son, the Count Ilya Tolstoy, the right to speak at Columbia University out of concern that Tolstoy would deliver an unpatriotic address.[99] Shortly after the declaration of war, Dewey cautioned in the *New Republic* against conscription of thought as ineffective and undemocratic. However, he confessed that "I am not specially concerned lest liberty of thought and speech seriously suffer among us, certainly not in any lasting way."[100] On another occasion, even though he expressed alarm over the rapid rise of intolerance and repression in the nation, he seemed to excuse it insofar as it was the result of an inexperienced nation trying to fulfill its war duties quickly and effectively. He even expressed some amusement over the spectacle. He concluded his observations, however, with a warning: "Let the liberal who for expediency's sake would passively tolerate invasions of free speech and action take counsel lest he be also preparing the way for a later victory of domestic Toryism."[101]

Incidents like the dismissal of Cattell, Dana, and Fraser shocked Dewey and evoked a strong protest from him at Columbia, and he worked through the AAUP to protect academic freedom.[102] During the war years, he also joined with Jane Addams, Felix Frankfurter, Clarence Darrow, Helen Keller, and Norman Thomas in developing the institution that in 1920 became the American Civil Liberties Union. In addition, he worked with Herbert Croly, Charles Beard, Thorstein Veblen, and others to found in New York City the New School for Social Research where adult education in the social sciences could be pursued in an atmosphere of complete academic freedom.[103]

The Bitter Consequences

The disenchantment with Dewey's intellectual leadership as a result of his support of the war was considerable in certain quarters. The most searching criticism came from the pen of his former student, Randolph Bourne, in a widely read essay, "Twilight of Idols," which appeared in *Seven Arts* late in 1917. Bourne expressed dismay that Dewey "is so much more concerned over the excesses of the pacifists than over the excesses of military policy, ... can feel only amusement at the idea that anyone should try to conscript thought," and "assumes that the war-technique can be used without trailing along with it the mob fanaticisms, the injustices and hatreds, that are organically bound up with it." Bourne's essay, however, was much more than a criticism of Dewey's stand on the war and pacifism. It was also the first major attack against pragmatism as a philosophy of life by a respected American liberal intellectual, and it raised fundamental questions about the adequacy of Dewey's whole approach.[104]

"In this difficult time the light that has been in liberals and radicals has become darkness," laments Bourne. "We suffer from a real shortage of spiritual values." Bourne traced the cause of this spiritual crisis to problems inherent in the most influential philosophy of the day, Dewey's pragmatism. "Dewey's philosophy is inspiring enough for a society at peace, prosperous and with a fund of progressive good will. It is a philosophy of hope, of clear-sighted comprehension of materials and means. Where institutions are at all malleable, it is the only clue for improvement. It is scientific method applied to 'uplift.' " However, when confronted with war it proved inadequate. Bourne observed that American colleges had trained a whole generation of young men in Dewey's instrumentalist way of thinking. What disturbed him was that these intelligent and energetic young men had been content to become "efficient instruments of the war-technique accepting with little question the ends as announced from above." In a poignant passage Bourne tried to identify the core of the problem.

> To those of us who have taken Dewey's philosophy almost as our American religion, it never occurred that values could be subordinated to technique. We were instrumentalist, but we had our private utopias so clearly before our minds that the means fell always into place as contributory. And Dewey, of course, always meant his philosophy, when taken as a philosophy of life, to start with values. But there was always that unhappy ambiguity in his doctrine as to just how values were created, and it became easier and easier to assume that just any growth was justified and almost any activity valuable so long as it achieved ends.... It is now becoming plain that unless you start with the widest kind of poetic vision, your instrumentation is likely to land you just where it has landed this younger intelligentsia which is so happily and busily engaged in the enterprise of war.... The working out of this American philosophy in our intellectual life then has meant an exaggerated emphasis on the mechanics of life at the expense of the quality of living.... Our intellectuals have failed us as value-creators, even as value-emphasizers.[105]

Bourne recognized full well that Dewey, with his background in the Christian faith and ethical idealism, was himself a man of deep moral concern. However, his essay raised an urgent question: what happens to those trained in Dewey's philosophy who never had a Christian idealist philosophical upbringing? Where does pragmatism cut loose from such moorings lead?

The financial backers of *Seven Arts* withdrew their support from the journal because of the editor's attitude toward the war, and late in 1917 publication was suspended. Bourne, who had been born seriously crippled, died an early death a year later.[106] Shortly thereafter, the *New Republic* published a review written by Bourne criticizing the philosophy of F. Matthias Alexander as presented in a book for which Dewey had written a very favorable introduction. Alexander, with Dewey's enthusiastic support, prophesied a new age of conscious self-control by humanity, and Bourne asked: "Is an era of world war, in which statesmen are proving as blind and helpless as the manipulated masses, quite the most convincing time for so far-flung a philosophy of conscious control?"[107] On many occasions during his life Dewey went out of his way even with his opponents to defend their right of free speech. However, so on edge was he over the war issue and so stung was he by Bourne's attacks that he advised the *New Republic* that he would no longer write for them if they continued to publish material by Bourne.[108] At this point in time Dewey's liberalism and good will had its limits.

Despite the efforts to silence him, Bourne remained a prophet and hero to many of the younger radical intellectuals, and his criticisms of Dewey's philosophy marked a disillusionment with pragmatism among those in this group that persisted into the nineteen twenties. Bourne's attack was followed by Harold Stearns' *Liberalism in America: Its Origin, Its Temporary Collapse, Its Future* (1919). In a chapter on "The Débâcle of Pragmatism," Stearns blamed the philosophy of pragmatism for the liberals' support of a misguided war effort that compromised the values of liberalism. He was especially critical of pragmatism's moral relativism and emphasis on utility, which left most liberals without a strong emotional commitment to basic values such as truth, respect for the individual, freedom of conscience, and tolerance. The result was that the liberals "lost sight of genuine ends" and were too easily influenced by the drift of events and war propaganda. About pragmatism Stearns concluded: ". . . it failed miserably during the war. Instead of controlling events, it found itself subservient to them."[109] As Morton White has observed, the criticisms of

Dewey's philosophy and wartime politics dramatically altered his image in the minds of many liberals: "Dewey had served as a symbol of intelligent humanitarianism, of a desire to mold society in the interests of peace, economic security and freedom. His support of the war, therefore, came as a shock to those who saw it as a direct contradiction of all these values. Dewey ceased to be the gentle, sage spokesman of creative liberalism in certain quarters."[110] Max Eastman has written that the crisis in the progressive movement created by the rift between Dewey and men like Bourne and Stearns "was momentous in Dewey's history as well as theirs. He was not only alienated from them, but somewhat from himself, I think, by his support of the war against Germany."[111]

As he journeyed to the Versailles peace negotiations in 1919 following the armistice in late 1918, Woodrow Wilson was hailed as a world hero by democratic and peace-loving people everywhere, but when the peace settlement was announced, severe disillusionment swept through the ranks of his liberal supporters in the United States. Out-maneuvered at the peace table by European diplomats driven by national self-interest and vengeance against Germany, Wilson returned home with a treaty that did not conform to the ideals he himself had identified in his Fourteen Points as the goals of American involvement in the war. Writing for the *New Republic,* Dewey along with many other liberals denounced the Versailles Peace Treaty. Instead of laying a secure foundation for world peace and economic recovery, the Peace Treaty, which imposed crippling economic penalties on Germany, seemed to guarantee that Germany would seek revenge and that international disorder would continue. Dewey had written extensively in support of the League of Nations prior to the Versailles settlement, but the terms of the Treaty were such that by late 1919 he withdrew his support. The League in Dewey's view promised to be nothing more than an instrument of the governments and diplomacy that had prevented a sound peace settlement. He distrusted European international politics. The "hesitation" he had felt in early 1917 about the Old World surfaced again, and this time he wanted no part in its doings.

The whole war experience led Dewey to reexamine a number of liberal assumptions and attitudes. As early as 1916 he confessed in the first person plural that in the light of the world war, the liberals' optimistic faith in progress must be seen as sentimental, naive, and irresponsible. This was to attack one of the sacred assumptions of nineteenth-century America. For many, faith in progress had become either identical with or a substitute for faith in God. Dewey did not, however, question the validity of belief in the possibility of progress, and he sought to understand the conditions necessary for it. The world war, asserted Dewey, demonstrated that there is no cosmic law of evolution guaranteeing automatic human progress in history. The development of industry and commerce, the production of wealth, and the advance of the sciences do not of themselves insure moral growth and material well-being for society as a whole. They may lead to exploitation, poverty, and war. The great social changes that have characterized the nineteenth century do, however, create opportunity for progress. The critical factor is human foresight, choice, and planning. Human beings should no longer trust in Providence, natural evolution, or manifest destiny, but must themselves assume active responsibility for the moral and material improvement of society. "If we want it, we can have it, if we are willing to pay the price in effort, especially in the effort of intelligence." [112] Even after the Depression and World War II, Dewey did not abandon this revised version of his liberal faith and hope.

The sad outcome of the Versailles Conference left Dewey pondering the correctness of his criticism of the pacifists, his own idealistic support for the war, and his hopes for the aftermath. He had to confess that those whom he had criticized for opposing the war could find much in retrospect to justify their opposition. What lessons could the liberals learn from Versailles? In an essay written in China and published in the *New Republic* with the title "The Discrediting of Idealism," he set out to answer that question. The chief cause of the defeat of the ideals and hopes of the liberals is to be found in a failure of intelligence on their part, asserted Dewey, or more specifically, a failure to use power intelligently in pursuit of their ideals. Returning to a recurrent theme in his wartime commentary, Dewey traced the problem to a certain naive sentimental optimism in much nineteenth-century American Protestant culture.

> It may fairly be argued that the real cause of the defeat is the failure to use force adequately and intelligently. The ideals of the United States have been defeated in the settlement because we took into the

war our sentimentalism, our attachment to moral sentiments as efficacious powers, our pious optimism as to the inevitable victory of the
"right," our childish belief that physical energy can do the work that
only intelligence can do, our evangelical hypocrisy that morals and
"ideals" have a self-propelling and self-executing capacity.... Imma-
turity and inexperience in international affairs consequent upon our
isolation mitigate the blame. But they would not have taken the form
they took were it not for our traditional evangelical trust in morals
apart from intelligence, and in ideals apart from executive and engineering force. Our Christianity has become identified with vague
feeling and with an optimism which we think is a sign of a pious faith
in Providence but which in reality is a trust in luck, a deification of
the feeling of success regardless of any intelligent discrimination of
the nature of success.[113]

Prior to the war some religious liberals such as Rauschenbusch and
William Wallace Fenn, the dean of Harvard Divinity School, had
challenged the more sentimental brands of liberal optimism regarding the inevitability of historical progress, but Dewey's comments in
1916 raised an issue that most religious liberals and many other
progressives had not fully faced. The war and its aftermath would
make the issue inescapable, and this would in time have a profound
impact on liberal social and religious thought.[114]

Reflecting on the war experience and the problem of sentimental
idealism, Dewey in 1919 criticized traditional philosophy as well as
liberal Christianity for maintaining a false notion of the ideal, for
imagining that ideals exist "independent of the possibilities of the
material and the physical." The lesson of World War I is "the
impotency and harmfulness of any and every ideal that is proclaimed
wholesale and in the abstract, that is, as something in itself apart
from the detailed concrete existences whose moving possibilities it
embodies." Perhaps with criticisms like that of Bourne in mind,
Dewey argued:

It is false that the evils of the situation arise from absence of ideals;
they spring from wrong ideals. And these wrong ideals have in turn
their foundation in the absence in social matters of that methodic,
systematic, impartial, critical, searching inquiry into "real" and operative conditions which we call science and which has brought man in
the technical realm to the command of physical energies.

Philosophy can help to correct this "by making it clear that a sympathetic and integral intelligence brought to bear upon the observation and understanding of concrete social events and forces, can form ideals, that is aims, which shall not be either illusions or mere emotional compensations."[115]

The war years were a disheartening time of painful tension for Dewey. The ultimate objective of his philosophical and social activism was the overcoming of dualism and the unification of the ideal and the actual. However, when confronted by this international crisis, his attempt to use his pragmatic method to find a just middle way between the sentimental pacifist and intolerant militant and thereby to further the goals of progressive democracy had not succeeded. He was by nature a reformer, not a revolutionary, a man who enjoyed the clash of ideas but not of arms. Through extraordinary effort he had established himself as the leading philosopher of a reform movement that many believed meant final realization of the promise of the New World. His supporters and friends were many. Then came the war. Political circumstances, a sense of international responsibility, a philosophy of intelligent idealism, and some wishful thinking led him to support the war. Consistent with his liberal ideals, Dewey had fought the militarizing of the schools, had defended academic freedom and civil rights, and had spoken out in support of a new spirit of international cooperation. Faced with the international crisis precipitated by the war, he tried to develop a realistic and intelligent approach to the use of power. Many of his criticisms of the pacifists made a valid point. However, he was unnecessarily hard on the pacifists and used dubious tactics in arguing his case with them. On a few occasions, denial and resentment seem to have overwhelmed his better critical judgment as a liberal. All of this suggests that he was not entirely convinced by what he was asserting about the war. Making the arguments that he did and the way he did alienated him from many liberals and deepened the split within the progressive movement. Self-doubt and the criticism of others began to plague him. When the war ended, he watched his hopes for a new era of international peace and democracy perish. Given his own liberal ideals and objectives, and in the light of the consequences, his position regarding American involvement in the war seemed to have been grievously misguided.

In response to this situation, Dewey was not moved to question his faith in intelligence or to alter his pragmatic approach to social problems. He renewed his efforts to clarify his thinking and to present his philosophy in a more systematic form. However, so disillusioned was Dewey by the impact of World War I on American society and international affairs that he never again called upon his fellow citizens to take up arms. He became convinced that war in the modern age is not a means that can be used to idealize the world and to achieve freedom and peace. The cause of democracy and world peace are best served by using intelligence to develop nonviolent methods of conflict resolution and by educating the people to give impassioned support to such approaches thereby pressuring governments and diplomats to cooperate.[116] After 1918 Dewey the pragmatist and liberal activist became an antiwar activist and crusader for world peace.

Dewey's opposition to war and to the influence of the military on society led him to fight the Department of the Army's efforts to establish a Reserve Officer Training Corps on college campuses following passage of the National Defense Act in 1920. Throughout the 1920s he served as the chief intellectual spokesman for Salmon O. Levinson's crusade to outlaw war and to create a new code of international law and a world court of justice to buttress the outlawry of war. In this endeavor, Dewey worked closely for a decade with Levinson, Senator William E. Borah of Idaho, Charles Clayton Morrison (who edited the *Christian Century*), and a host of other liberals and pacifists. The outlawry of war movement culminated in the Kellogg-Briand Pact in August 1928. Dewey viewed the pact—which did outlaw war—as only a partial victory, for it recognized the right of nations to undertake war in self-defense. His concern was that legalization of any form of war clouds the issue and makes it too easy for nations to rationalize and justify military action.[117]

The depth of Dewey's distrust of war as a constructive means of action in the modern world is seen finally in his resistance to America's entry into World War II prior to Pearl Harbor. In 1939, he stated: "If there is one conclusion to which human experience unmistakably points, it is that democratic ends demand democratic methods for their realization."[118] Military force, he argued, is inconsistent with the democratic way, and modern war undermines the foundations of democracy in the nations that engage in it.

> There is no single force so completely destructive of personal freedom as is modern war. Not merely the life and property of individuals are subjected by war to external control, but also their very thought and their power to give them expression. War is a kind of wholesale moral enslavement of entire populations. Peace is a necessary and urgent condition of attainment of the goal of freedom.[119]

In a statement entitled "No Matter What Happens—Stay Out," Dewey in 1939 recalled the dire effects of World War I and expressed his fear that entry into the developing war in Europe could have far more severe and long-lasting consequences, leading to the emergence in America of a government that was fascist in effect if not in name.[120]

The preceding account of Dewey's life during the war years has concentrated primarily on his activities and the public debates in which he engaged. There is a further story to be told about the impact of these turbulent times on his personal life. It is a story that emerges largely from poems and letters, and it contributes in a significant way to an understanding of his moral and religious development. To this story we will now turn.

SEVEN

Poems, Letters, and Lessons

THE WAR YEARS not only challenged and tested Dewey's thought in a radical way; they also tried and tested the man. As the poetry that Dewey wrote during this period reveals, the problems which he faced were personal as well as political. For example, the warmth and closeness seems to have gone out of his relationship with Alice Dewey. The need which this generated is expressed in two lines of verse in which Dewey describes himself as "Longing like dumb and winter chilled ground/For touch of life, warm, palpitant, flow'r crown'd."[1] Further, the evidence is that after years of hard work and strife on the forefront of social reform, Dewey was simply exhausted emotionally and physically. His poems are filled with expressions of a craving for rest, sunlit gardens, or a time to enjoy "sweet soft things alluring," and on occasion he discloses a desire for the peace and forgetfulness of death.[2] Closely related to Dewey's sense of exhaustion and the experience of his life as "winter chilled," is the fact that he was still overburdened with the stern conscience and hard driving sense of moral responsibility instilled in him by Vermont Congregationalism. In a poem entitled "To Conscience," he pleads for freedom from his conscience which relentlessly commands:

"Arouse! Fight on! Combat and conquer;/Evil are the forces!" In protest Dewey complains, "Others work and take their joy;/Now stern comrade so shall I,/Sick, sick of thy endless employ/... Give me rest for I am tired."[3] In short, in spite of all his progressive arguments about a new Darwinian moral relativism, Dewey was still struggling with a conscience formed by a church that believed in moral absolutism and a fearful God. Problems that he had worked through intellectually in his philosophy had not yet been fully resolved emotionally.

The war, the problems in his relation with Alice, his burdensome sense of duty, and his sense of burnout all created a crisis in Dewey's life that seems to have been most severe during the years 1915 to 1918 when he was in his late fifties. Dewey managed to get through this unsettling period with the aid of a diverse set of resources and the support of four extraordinary relationships. In 1909 the Deweys had purchased a farm in Huntington, Long Island, and Dewey found much quiet pleasure over the years working and strolling in his garden of flowers and vegetables. Shortly after acquiring this retreat, the philosopher who loved the arid pathways of logical theory developed a habit of writing poetry, and this poetry became a satisfying vehicle of emotional self-expression. In 1915 he started corresponding with an eccentric private philosopher, Scudder Klyce, whom he never met. The correspondence quickly took on a very personal quality, and Dewey was confessing things about himself that he had not shared with others. The following year fatigue, eye trouble, and depression led him to seek out F. Matthias Alexander, an Australian practitioner of a novel method of psychophysical therapy. His "lessons" with Alexander brought him considerable relief, and the experience deepened his insights into the relation of the body and mind, the possibilities of control by intelligence, and the dynamics of human growth. During the fall of 1917 he entered into a romantic relationship with a much younger woman, Anzia Yezierska, who was a Jewish immigrant from Eastern Europe and an aspiring novelist. This same year he began a long-lasting productive friendship with an irascible but brilliant inventor and art collector, Albert Barnes, who opened up to Dewey the world of painting and aesthetic experience in a new way.

In and through these various resources and relationships involving nature, poetry, painting, physical therapy, self-disclosure, and romance, Dewey the gentle reserved intellectual and philosopher of creative intelligence was struggling to respond to personal problems and to emotional needs which had been to some degree suppressed in the process of many intense years of thinking, writing, and organizing. His poetry and letters illuminate the nature of these problems and needs, and they provide insights into some of the personal issues related to certain aspects of his philosophical thinking. Dewey's poems and letters are also especially helpful in clarifying the development of his personal religious feelings and thoughts on the subjects of faith, natural piety, mysticism, and God. What is especially remarkable about Dewey's response to this time of crisis is the way in which he was able to transform it into an occasion for personal growth, both intellectually and emotionally.

Poems of Paradise Lost and Renewal

As a boy Dewey acquired a taste for poetry from his father, and during his forties and fifties he began writing his own verse. A few poems were written for his children and others close to him, but most were composed for his personal satisfaction, and he did not intend them for publication. Among the ninety-five poems that have survived, there are children's poems, love poems, poems that celebrate nature, and poems on a wide range of personal, social, moral, philosophical, and religious themes. The evidence indicates that most of this verse was written between 1911 and 1918. A few poems were probably written before this period, and some may have been written in the course of the following decade. With only a few exceptions, Dewey discarded his poetry. Some of it he put in an office wastebasket at Columbia University, and a number of poems were left behind in his desk when he moved out of his office at the end of his career. Unbeknownst to him, this material was retrieved by a librarian at Columbia and preserved in the University's Columbiana collection.[4] The quality of the poems varies a great deal. Their general value for a study of the evolution of Dewey's attitudes and values lies in the fact that in and through them Dewey gives expression to a wide range of emotions encompassing in his words, "fresh joys, and woes of fresh made hells."[5]

In exploring the Dewey poetry, it is useful at the outset to note the images and themes that give evidence of his "woes" and disclose the nature of the more negative experiences and feelings with which he struggled. The poetry demonstrates that the battle against dualism and the quest to unite the ideal and the actual continued to be a critical issue in Dewey's private experience as well as in his political life. It reveals how he wrestled with some of the darker sides of life; the positive attitudes that were controlling in his philosophical writings did not go unquestioned in the inner man. However, in spite of the problems that Dewey faced, he never lost his faith, hope, and sense of direction.

In relation to Dewey's religious experience and thought, it is striking that in a number of poems he developed variations on a theme common to much western religious literature—the theme of paradise lost. He recalls an earlier time of harmony, innocence, and joy, which contrasts with his current experience of being caught in a cold harsh wilderness where life is strife and pain, and he craves a return to the lost unity and peace. In "The Child's Garden," for example, Dewey yearns to find the Eden he once knew.

> Would God my feet might lead
> To that enclosèd garden
> That had innocence for warden
> And hopes and dreams for seed.
>
> But freezing years did harden
> And shut me in this barren field
> —Docks and thistle its only yield—
> And I cannot find that closèd garden.[6]

Other poems describe his world as "a wilderness" that is "thorny, hard to bear" and picture his life as "this road embriared" or "this path of rocks with no drug for bruise save its stain."[7]

In "Two Births," Dewey describes being nourished for nine months in his mother's womb, that "dark hutch of warm and precious solitude," where he was "sweetly bedded" in a "soft haven" and fed on "wonder food/More miraculous than that the raven/Brought Elijah, God's nested brood." In his youth he was filled with "life's fire of kindled rage divine," and he set out to seek "the golden fleece." However, these fires had "long since burnt low" and his life became "an unadventurous trudge."[8] In other poems he refers to his life as a "weary way," and he writes that "joyless, griefless, begins the round/ Of day's unillumined duties," by which he feels "bound" and "smothered."[9]

A sense of frustration and failure is communicated by several poems. He laments, for example, that: "I have fought and got no gain;/Toiled and been passed by/By all save wound and pain."[10] On occasion Dewey feels that all life's striving is futility. He writes in "But——" of "lives launched to fail/Mid weeds and slimy grass," and with a note of bitterness as well as dejection in his voice, he asserts: "Nor is it life nor is it death/This dying life of ours/But idle blowing of a breath/That fills and sucks the hours."[11] In "Two Weeks," a very personal poem written to a woman friend, he speaks of "the harsh divisions of my mind" and confesses the truth of himself to be "the broken parts of an ineffectual whole." He concludes: "Then take me as I am,/Partly true and partly sham . . . If I have not wholly stood/Neither have I wholly bent./ Just th' usual mixed up mess of bad and good/I bring to you as it was sent."[12]

Two poems speak of "the doom of separation" experienced by all human beings as a consequence of the development of human consciousness and thought, which he finds symbolized in "the fierce divisive sun" with its "sund'ring rays of harsh light."[13] Caught in this condition of separation, men and women experience life as struggle and strife, and eventually wearied by "the shock and strain" of it all, they crave rest and unity. In short, many of the poems reveal that the craving to overcome dualism and to achieve unity, which was strong in Dewey as a young man, lived on as a felt need in the older man. The intensity of the passion was gone and often it was marked by world-weariness, but the aspiration persisted. In spite of the unifying power of his own moral faith and his many professional achievements, he continued to have his moments of doubt and to wrestle with the unification of the ideal and the actual in his self and in the relation of self and world.

The pain of separation, the "harsh divisions" of his mind, and weariness with life's battles led Dewey to seek release and peace in a variety of ways. On the one hand, at certain times he desired simply to escape life's trials by passing into some mode of unconsciousness. For example, in some poems he seeks peace in forgetfulness, night, sleep, or death. On the other hand, in other poems he aspires to find peace in some altered form of consciousness. He writes of the beauty and harmony to be found in contemplative intellectual and mystical experiences, and he celebrates the rest and joy experienced in nature, flower gardens, and a woman's love. In most cases these various realities, in which he seeks rest and harmony, are either explicitly identified as feminine or they are described as possessing qualities closely associated with the feminine. He introduces images of the womb or bosom of the Great Mother where he would like to lose himself forgetting the world and shedding the burden of individual consciousness and responsibility. In poems such as "The Child's Garden," he expresses a craving to recover the spontaneity, innocence, and happiness of childhood and of a world that is made warm and secure by an all-embracing unconditional mother's love. In other instances his poems are simply expressions of his wish for "pleasured ease" and for what is gentle, warm, and delightful, especially a woman's love, and they reveal Dewey's effort to integrate this aspect of experience more effectively into his personality.

Some more specific illustrations from Dewey's poems on forgetfulness, night, death, and nature will clarify the quality of his feeling in these matters. In one he describes how "all embracing night,"—"Mystic mother" and "womb of God"—merges "the struggling spirits of severed men" into the "oneness of the first creation" overcoming the suffering of "day's wedge-like doom of separation." He likens the experience of night and deep sleep to what happens "within death's majestic solitude."[14] In another poem, he speaks of night coming "from some God's forgiving source," mercifully stilling thought and strife, and bringing peace to human beings through the "oblivion" of "the shapeless dark."[15] "Forgetfulness" is a poem that praises forgetfulness as the "Mother" of sleep and death. It is "Thought's peaceful sepulchre" where hope and grief, desire and hate are finally vanquished.[16] A poem entitled "To Death" seems to describe a desire for the "pale gold silence" of death where he will pass to "more than rest, at one with thee."[17] In "Two Births" he looks forward to death as leading to a "second secret womb" and a second birth in and through which "mother" nature will transform him into "wondrous food for the mysterious life/With which the world, our God, is rife." He seems to delight in the thought that "brother worm and sister flower" will consume him, and his being will "feed the tender sprouting plants/Till in their mingled life I share/And in new measures tread creation's dance."[18] Here one encounters a kind of nature mysticism where God and nature are identified and the thought of an unconscious union with the mysterious life of the natural world brings a sense of relief and joy.

To some degree Dewey's desire for forgetfulness and the unconscious oneness of night and death is a consequence of his being world weary, but his feelings in this matter are complex. In "Forgetfulness," for example, he indicates that he finds it better with respect to certain memories to suppress rather than recall them. Noting the pain associated with remembering, he writes dejectedly of there remaining in him after fifty-eight years of experience, "But stored up memories in detachment/From the things that might have been, and stains/Of things that should not have been and are—/The choked fountain and th'uneffacèd scar."[19] These lines speak of sadness over missed opportunities and denied passion and guilt over some bad decisions. In 1927 he confided to a friend: "Being too introspective by nature, I have had to learn to control the direction it takes." More specifically he explains that he does not allow himself to indulge frequently in "autobiographical introspection ... as it is not good for me."[20]

One of Dewey's poems about night culminates in a mystical experience of unity transcending the dualisms of night and day, self and world, and life and death. In this poem Dewey describes how, standing upon a hill overlooking a city and a bay, he watched the night fall with a growing sense of peace. As the darkness settled over the landscape his "pleasures and woes" were forgotten and "tho't was lost in the endless reaches of night."

> ... Then rose the swelling moon
> And gently sought its magic way
> Across the waters. In a tune
> Of silver'd silence merged the day

With night, earth with sky, the world and me.
Through the moonlight's softly shining grey
Merged rigid land and fluent sea;
By the magic of inaction beguiled
Life and death slept close reconciled.[21]

This poem gives evidence of a mystical experience comparable to the
one he had as a young man when reading Wordsworth (see chapter
1). Another poem, "A Moment and a Time," also seems to indicate a
moment of mystical loss of self in the stillness and beauty of twilight,
which Dewey describes as "an eternal moment's self-contempla-
tion."[22]

The sense of a lost harmony, the craving for peace of mind, and
mystical intuitions of non-dualism are experiences that have led many
sensitive men and women to seek solace in traditional religious ideas
and in various forms of meditation. His poems show that Dewey
could well understand what prompts such people, because even as an
older man he experienced these emotional needs at least on certain
occasions with some degree of intensity, and he had his mystical
moments. These personal feelings and experiences probably explain
why he responded so positively to a Buddhist chanting service which
he attended in Nanking, China, in 1919. Afterwards he wrote his
family: "At first the music sounded to my ears much like Negro
chanting; it's more hypnotic than Catholic mass, more soothing to
the nerves; if I were near, I would go in every day."[23] After abandoning absolute idealism, however, Dewey did not allow longings for
rest and peace in the arms of the Great Mother or contemplative
moments of mystical experience to influence the main thrust of his
ethical activist philosophy. Nevertheless, he does set forth in his major
later works his own naturalistic perspective on the human need for
peace and for a sense of being one with the larger universe. This
perspective involves Dewey's theories of religious faith, natural piety,
and aesthetic experience, which will be considered further in a subsequent chapter. Mystical experiences such as are described in the
poem just mentioned contribute to the sense of trust involved in his
developing idea of natural piety.

Dewey's desire to escape the severe demands of his conscience and
his need for rest and affectionate companionship find moving expres-

sion in a poem that shows the strong influence of the Twenty-third Psalm.

> Not now thy scourging rod—
> Thy staff, instead, oh God;—
> Something to support and stay,
> A guide along the ling'ring way.
> Thy wrathful rod withhold
> E'en tho my sins be infinite, untold.
> Since to punish thou hast eternity,
> Now for a little space let be, let be.
> Spare thy just avenging wrath;
> Walk with me a grassy path
> Beside still waters for a little hour—
> —Eternity thou hast to show thy power—
> Lean with me upon thy staff
> And, pacing the cool earth, laugh
> To hear the foolish crickets sing
> And see the pent in worms take wing
> —Butterflies—unmindful of thee on high—
> E'en as thou art for a little while—and I.
>
> 'Tis already known that thou art strong and I am weak
> In all the long eternity thou canst thy justice wreak.
> Then for a little while, come God and play—
> Yet all too long shall be thy eternal day.[24]

This rather delightful poem expresses Dewey's yearning for the rest and tranquility that the author of the Twenty-third Psalm found in God, but which Dewey has not been able to achieve fully because his God—that is, the God of his youth, who lives on in him in his hard-driving conscience—will not allow it. The God of traditional theology no longer had a place in the thought of Dewey the philosopher, but the image of God that Dewey had acquired as a boy was still a presence in the psyche of Dewey the private man and poet.

In three other poems Dewey also employs the traditional image of God as the object of a prayerful entreaty concerned with rest and enjoyment of simple natural pleasures.[25] In none of these poems is God identified as wrathful even though, in several, monarchical imagery is used to depict God. The idea of God also appears in other kinds of poems. In "A Peripatetic's Prayer," Dewey celebrates Aristotle's contemplative ideal and concept of God as the unmoved mover. It concludes: "By Love of learning let me find/ My own last essence, Mind,/So for a little while to share/Immortality, divine, eternal,/ Forgetting city, deed and things diurnal."[26] Aristotle's contemplative orientation, which is quite contrary to the dominant spirit of pragmatism, seems to fascinate Dewey in this poem because it, too, promises rest and peace above the battle.

There are four poems where Dewey either rejects the traditional theological idea of God or speaks of "a new created God."[27] These poems hint at new ideas of God consistent with Dewey's new naturalistic worldview. In one of these poems, God and the world are identified, even though the unqualified identification of God and nature is not an idea that Dewey develops as a naturalist in his published philosophical writings.[28] In "Unfaith" he writes to "you who do not now believe/The things you learned in childhood days" and "live forlorn" over the fact that "truth should follow changing ways." Dewey does not deny that periods of change and adjustment may be trying, but he is optimistic that people will in due course find their way to an appropriate new faith. He writes:

> For if the things you claim to greet
> Were known by you from light of inner soul
> —Light flowing from your own life's self-mined coal—
> You would also know that others too with feet
> Unbound, springing like flowers from unfrozen sod,
> Would make their own way to their soul's own God.[29]

In summary, then, Dewey's poetry reveals that during his fifties the symbolic image of God was still active in the inner dialogue that went on in his imagination and that he was reflecting on new ways of thinking about God.

The love of nature is a recurrent theme in Dewey's verse, and he often found renewal and great satisfaction in his garden.

> Fair flowers grow in my garden ground,
> They grow in rows, some short, some tall
> In beds that gravelled paths surround;
> Without, a grey and ivied wall.

And there each day I take a stroll
And see the winged creatures dart
And quick bees suck their honied toll
From out the flow'r's empassioned heart.
The warm air hangs in a lazy swoon
Drunk with perfumes that lang'rous time
Distilled from magic of its daughter June.

Come to this slow and gracious peace.
Let striving be; let conquest go.
Abide Thou too where noises cease
To stir, where quiet roses blow
In careless beauty, without thought
Of yesterday or morrow. How
Shall we not rest, by nature taught![30]

Dewey's delight in nature was a factor that strengthened his natural piety. This is well illustrated in a poem that begins with the lines: "Because the plan of the world is dim and blurred/Not some wise God's clear utter'd word,/Shall I resentful stand in scorn/Or crushed live dumb in mood forlorn?" The poem concludes:

Wag if you wish your gloomy head
Because some man hath solemn said
"The world just happ'd by accident,
Whose good and beauty were never meant"—
But ask not me to join your wail
Till loving friendships pass and fail;
Till wintry winds do lose their glee
And singing birds no more are free.[31]

The affirmative attitude expressed in this verse is one aspect of the doctrine of natural piety which is set forth in *A Common Faith* (1934).

As in the case of the poem just cited, much of Dewey's poetry celebrates the attitudes, values, and outlook of his mature philosophy and published writings. He had times of sadness and depression. There were in his personality introspective and contemplative impulses. On occasion he felt a need for withdrawal and escape. However, he never allowed those feelings to alter the social faith and philosophy of democratic humanism he had been developing over the years. He was sustained by a sense of an illuminated pathway as is expressed in "My Road."

> Adown the mottled slopes of night
> With smile that lit the dark,
> Ran a little lane of light
> That none but I could mark.[32]

In "The New World" he likens a courageous adventuresome soul exploring a new world of thought and life to "a blazing star" crossing untravelled space in a lonely but meaningful journey, and he admires "the strong stars,/ Strong to seek and find each its own."[33] Several poems present the choice between dwelling in "the incense laden space within" or life "on the stony peak ... in a world that is open, free."[34] It is clear that Dewey prefers the latter. "Let souls dispirited and craven/Whine for some rewarding haven," but "For us the salty sea, th'untamed wind."[35]

As a naturalistic humanist Dewey celebrates in his verse the sacredness of human love and friendship. "Love's light tether/Holds all together," he writes in "Ties."[36] In another poem he finds "the world set free" and made meaningful by the relationship of "a me and thee."[37] In a love poem, the joy and wonder of a personal relationship are described as holy communion—"communion with the wine and bread."[38] "My Body and My Soul" rejects the dualism of body and soul, physical love and spiritual love, associated with traditional church theology, and asserts that only an authentic love that grows "from flesh and blood" has the power to transform hell into heaven.[39]

The sacredness of the human mind is another theme that is recurrent in Dewey's verse.

> My mind is but a gutt'ring candle dip
> With flick'ring beams the wind doth blow around;
> Yet the scant space thus lit is holier ground
> Than that where prophet did his sandal slip
> In token of the presence of his Lord.[40]

In a poem that seems to reveal a contemplative's appreciation of the serene bright clarity of the mind, he writes of the awesome beauty of the mysterious sources of the mind, using imagery that reminds one of his early connections with the Romantic movement.

> A pool of clear waters thy mind,
> Sunlit, unrippled by any wind;
> Transparent mirror of lovely things,
> With depths that feed from secret springs,
> Flowing from some snow capped mountain peak
> Which ling'ring sun rays loving seek.

> Thy faithful mind reflecting clear
> All charming forms, or far or near,
> Draws from that high peak its dignity,
> And from those depths strange mystery.[41]

The awakening of the mind to the joy and excitement of learning is compared in another poem to the descent of "the holy spirit's dove."[42]

"Paradise Lost and Regained" is a pragmatist's poem on John Milton's theme. It rejects the idea of a fixed definition of good and bad and a dualism of heaven and fallen earth. The world is constituted by "mingled flowing good and ill." Progress is possible in and through intelligent choice of "the better from the worse," and humanity's "sole bliss" is to be found in the "growth of better."[43] In a carefully constructed but rather abstract philosophical poem entitled "Creation," Dewey describes the evolutionary process that begins with "virgin time" dwelling "In world that one with itself, unconscious/Moved on, unforgetting, unremembering ..." until Life appeared with his "large lusts" and "love of change." From the union of Time and Life evolves the human race, the clash of armies, and the search for wisdom. Time guides Life's love of change wisely and manifests a "love of feeble things that die" and "tender care of all that grows." In this way, Time "Recovered, conscious now, eternal peace/And Eternity knew Death and Care her own."[44] This conclusion seems again to be an expression of Dewey's natural piety and to suggest that "eternal peace" can be found in our evolving natural world by giving "tender care" to all that grows and by using experimental intelligence to direct change wisely while accepting that we are "feeble things that die."[45]

Dewey's poetry describes the way he on a personal level encountered and interpreted in his fifties the universal human experience of paradise lost. It also identifies a number of those resources and values in which he found hope and renewal. His ability to write poetry must be counted among these resources. In his poetry as distinct from his philosophy, Dewey employs language for the most part simply to express feelings and needs rather than to solve problems. This act of expression itself undoubtedly had a certain healing effect, helping him to achieve a better integration in his personality of thought and feeling, work and play, duty and pleasure, moral striving and aesthetic enjoyment. In addition to the poetry, Dewey also found opportunity to vent his feelings in and through his private correspondence. This is especially true of his letters to one man in particular with whom he had an unusual relationship.

"I Am Something of a John the Baptist"

On April 4, 1915, Dewey received a letter from an unknown private philosopher, Scudder Klyce, who wrote to solicit Dewey's assistance in publishing a manuscript that proposed a method for unifying science, philosophy, and religion.[46] In characteristic fashion, Dewey was supportive and encouraging. Sidney Hook comments that "Dewey encouraged and overencouraged many who showed a glint of promise. Whatever the quality of their work, they achieved more because of his apparent faith in them."[47] He read Klyce's manuscript, made some suggestions, and, believing that Klyce had a contribution to make in the area of logic, he wrote some lines of endorsement for him to use with publishers.[48] Thus began a correspondence between Klyce and Dewey that lasted for twelve years.

Very quickly the exchange between the two men became intense and personal. Dewey wrote on May 13, 1915: "I have written myself out to you, even if briefly and too carelessly, more than I have put myself on record anywhere."[49] Early in the correspondence, Klyce's letters revealed that he was emotionally unstable, and he confesses that "I have always been called 'crazy' " and "I have been looking for years for someone with sense enough to control me."[50] In spite of this Dewey persisted, patiently advising Klyce on philosophical matters and allowing himself to be drawn into a very personal exchange of views. Klyce's inquisitive style and persistent attempts to interpret Dewey's character as well as his thought provided Dewey with the opportunity to share with Klyce feelings about himself and reflections on his life and thought that for the most part he was not prepared to share with others or publish. Klyce became something of a private confessor for Dewey, and he in turn tried to use Dewey to get help with his personal problems and to advance his career. There is no evidence that Dewey and Klyce ever met, and Dewey preferred it that way. From the beginning Klyce's letters are very flattering. He declares Dewey to be the most competent living philosopher and compares him to Christ, Buddha, Confucius, Newton, and Darwin.[51] About his significance as a philosopher, Dewey writes in response: "I am no Jesus; I am something of a John the Baptist or forerunner."[52] Early on religion became a topic of discussion in the correspondence, and Klyce urged Dewey to "become . . . a religious guide, in replacement of the mess the theologians and others have made of the job."[53] In response to Klyce's suggestions and observations pertaining to religion, Dewey writes:

> My endeavor has been to reach professional philosophers and teachers of philosophy, not the public as [William] James for example reached it. This job I shall have to stick to; twenty years ago or more, the job of general or religious teacher you suggest as a possibility would probably have appealed to [me]. But I guess I have died on that side; I have got enough religion for my own working equilibrium but not enough to go at things the way you suggest. . . .[54]

In another letter Dewey observes that "James was a much more all around human being than I am, and consequently went directly to religion."[55] He clarifies this in a subsequent letter.

> I did not say I think that James was a man of greater ability—that is a technical matter. In some respects I have greater ability, in others he had. And the respects in which he had greater ability are just the things in which he was more of an all around man or personality. What is called his artistic or literary style is just a greater, a much greater, more vivid and more persistent realization of other people than I have. . . . James I think was in no sense a mystic in his personal

experience; he wasn't religious in *that* sense, the sense he wrote about. But he had a great sympathy with human nature even in its pathological phases.[56]

In this same letter Dewey criticizes James' essay on the need for a moral equivalent of war as an idea which was influenced by James' aristocratic upbringing and which showed that "even his sympathies were limited by his experience." "I think he had no real intimation," writes Dewey, "that the 'labor problem' has always been for the great mass of people a much harder fight than any war; in fact one reason people are so ready to fight is the fact that it [is] so much easier than their ordinary existence."

In this comparison of his own personality with that of James, Dewey acknowledged a lack of sympathetic interest when it came to the subject of the varieties of religious experience and behavior. His own painful experience with certain forms of religion and the scars it left go far in explaining his lack of feeling for this subject as an area of intellectual inquiry. However, Dewey does confess: "I have got enough religion for my own working equilibrium." Moreover, he would eventually develop a significant naturalistic theory of religious experience. In fact, his correspondence with Klyce reveals that he already had worked out for himself by 1915 several ideas which are basic to the philosophy of religion that he finally published in *The Quest for Certainty* (1929) and *A Common Faith* (1934).

Dewey's comments on his personal religious outlook appear in the context of an extended discussion about monism and pluralism. Klyce pushes Dewey to accept a form of monism and Dewey resists. In the process, however, he explains in what sense he does believe that the universe is one. "I have become a confirmed infinite pluralist," asserts Dewey. "I simply can't get monism with any reality. What you say sometimes about the beauty and so forth of the monistic experience leaves me cold. As I said before, twenty years ago it would have met me."[57] In these passages on monism, Dewey is rejecting any notion that the universe has a fixed preestablished harmony or fixed final end as is asserted by absolute idealism. However, he explains that as an infinite pluralist he views reality, the universe, as one in the sense that it is a process marked by continuity and involving "a continuous reorganization of unity."[58] "Briefly stated again, and with an attempt to make language do what it won't do, the 'one' is always pluralizing and recovering its diversities before they escape (or become plural) and thereby keeping itself going." Dewey goes on to explain as a pragmatist that: "Knowledge is the effort of man to give direction to the process; or it *is* the process self-conscious in man and thereby giving preferentialness to its ongoing; guessing at its own pluralizing tendencies in terms of their outcomes ... and liking some of them better than others."[59]

Given his view of reality as a process of the one pluralizing and reorganizing itself, Dewey explains his personal religious orientation. "I am [an] infinite pluralist—and my religion has to do not with the realized but with the future—an attitude toward possibilities."[60] In other words, Dewey puts his religious faith in ideal possibilities, trusting that the process which is the universe is full of possibilities for the good and the process can be directed by intelligence to realize these possibilities. With this in mind, he affirms to Klyce his basic optimism: "I am very skeptical about things in particular but have an enormous faith in things in general."[61]

Even though Dewey had this "faith in things in general," which implies a trust in the universe at large, he chose not to call the universe God. He does identify God and the world in one of his poems, but this is not the direction his philosophical reflections take him. He explains why.

> I prefer to use such terms as God, truth, etc. as preferential or distinctive terms—i.e., pluralistically. I don't like to call anything true that mightn't be false, so I don't like to call the universe or the whole Truth. In other words, I would use both true and false as quantitative terms—better or worse statements under the given conditions. (That again is 'pragmatism' or 'science' as I see them). So I would use God to denote *those* forces which at a given time and place are actually working for the better.[62]

This statement indicates that the idea of God that Dewey endorsed publicly for the first time in *A Common Faith* in 1934 had taken form in his mind as early as 1915. His reflection on the idea of God in his letter to Klyce concludes with a further significant observation: "I admit that any (relative) falsity acted upon tends, in time, to correct itself—to expose itself and discover the truth. In that sense the whole might be called true or good, but even here it is the pluralistic interaction rather than the whole which works." Again, this reveals the ground of Dewey's optimism and "faith in things in general." Further, if the universe as a whole is not to be called good or God, it is certainly worthy of natural piety, because it includes the good or God, that is, a process making for progress. This is the way Dewey increasingly came to think.

Klyce's unpublished manuscript and his correspondence with Dewey about the one, the universe as a whole, and monism led Dewey to clarify further his view of mysticism and related philosophical issues. He publicly acknowledged his indebtedness to Klyce in these matters in a long footnote in *Essays in Experimental Logic* (1916) and more fully explained what Klyce had helped him to understand in an introduction that he wrote in 1920 to Klyce's proposed book.[63] He approached the matter from the perspective of his logic and theory of language. Dewey argues that any intelligible statement from pointing to or naming something to a sophisticated scientific discourse involves explicit references to a number of specific things related together and also an implicit reference to the larger situation within which the specific related things are distinguished and with which the distinguished things are continuous. "The *situation* as such ... is taken for granted. *It* is not stated or expressed. It is implicit, not explicit. Yet it supplies meaning to all that is stated, pointed at, named. Its presence makes the difference between sanity and insanity." Dewey further argues that the encompassing situation which is implied in any statement "shades off from the explicit, indefinitely and continuously" so that it must be understood to involve "everything," the universe as a whole. In short, the implied presence of the universe as the setting for every explicit statement provides such statements with intelligibility or "meaning-giving force."[64]

The presence of "the vast and vague continuum," which is the universe, can never be stated in words. It must remain an implication which is "strictly ineffable." However, it is useful to have words that "remind us that whatever we explicitly state has this implied, unstateable, ineffable implication." Klyce calls such words "One words."

Terms like the "Absolute," the "All," or "God" are examples of terms that may function as "One words." When so used they do not refer to a specific object of thought and they have no definite meaning; they just point to the reality and presence of the vast continuum which is the all-encompassing whole. However, Dewey does assert that a person may have an emotional intimation of the meaning of these terms.

> An experimental realization of this meaning is had only emotionally, and the emotion may be poetic, aesthetic or in some cases mystic. Speaking in philosophical terminology we have here revealed the truth and falsity of the whole brood of absolutist, transcendental philosophers. They had a genuine experience of the *All* which is required for the meaning of any consistent statement. But they assert that these *One* terms themselves have a meaning; that they are terms *of* statement. Or if they were professional mystics, the ineffable character was recognized, but the experience was regarded as a special and separated, not to say unique, experience, instead of as what is implicit, in some degree of intensity, in every experience.[65]

For Dewey, then, the presence of the All, which is a dimension of every experience, may become an intensely felt presence in the form of poetic intuitions, aesthetic intimations, and mystical experiences. Dewey later clarifies his thinking on these matters, which shows the influence of the romantic poets, in *Human Nature and Conduct* (1922) and *Art as Experience* (1934).

In his exchange with Klyce, he also indicates that emotional realizations of the All may lead to a sense of "eternity, perfect peace or rest, complete salvation."[66] Dewey's poetry indicates that he had experiences involving an intense poetic and mystical realization of the presence of the All. As a philosopher Dewey relates such experiences to his doctrine of natural piety, which concerns his general attitude toward the universe as a whole. However, as noted earlier, he makes it clear to Klyce that he personally prefers not to use the term God to refer to the All, because he wishes to use it as a "preferential or distinctive" term. This raises an interesting question as to how Dewey as a naturalist understands the interconnection between the All, inner peace, and God. If an experience of the larger whole generates a sense of "perfect peace," does not the All possess qualities that are properly called divine? We will return to this issue in a later chapter.

Dewey explains to Klyce that he has avoided writing out his thinking about the All. "I am content just to take it for granted and let it go. I am interested in the question of social control—a method which will do practically for our human associations what physical science has done for control of nature or 'matter.' "[67] Dewey further explains that "I have long taught—to my classes, I have never been ready to publish much but offshoots—that the meaning of everything stated lies in what is 'understood'—that is taken for granted without statement, tacit or otherwise and that what is understood is —just the whole damn business—the 'universe' if one clings to that phrase."[68] Again, Dewey explains: "I do teach that every experience is of the whole, with just the emphasis or focus varying, even then I keep from attaching any eulogistic predicates to the 'whole' or else they, the students (and readers are the same), will lapse into the morass."[69] The "morass" is supernaturalism and the absolute idealism from which Dewey confesses that "I... had the devil of a time freeing myself."[70] An emotional experience of the All has for Dewey very positive religious meaning, but he prefers to let people discover that for themselves.

The difficulty according to Dewey is that there is an "unconscious hypocrisy that prevails: people must learn to think pluralistically; they come to their thinking with conventional monistic preferences which they think are thoughts and which aren't even genuine emotions—mere protective masks; it is dangerous to use with students words having ordinary religious associations; they jump at them, and pass over the whole thinking part."[71] Dewey goes on to assert that if people adopt the correct method of thinking, then the religious issue will in due course take care of itself.

> I have a great faith in the rectitude of other persons' responses, including religious; when they see things, they will respond. On the other hand, the fact that I have mainly taught and dealt with persons of conventional religious training, who largely have factitious and institutionalized not genuine religious responses, has shown me the great danger of using an old and for many outworn phraseology; the words call up a semblance of emotional response and become a substi-

tute, or even a screen which effectively prevents their seeing the things which would actually call out the genuine emotions.[72]

As Dewey puts it in one of his poems cited earlier: people guided by "light flowing from" their own "life's self-mined coal" will "make their way to their soul's own God."

About the figure of Jesus Dewey had these comments in 1915. "I have given up trying to make anything very certain out about Jesus. I don't believe we have the documents for it. Certainly more or less that is attributed to him was made up afterwards; the gospels, I am pretty sure, are largely party writings." Dewey goes on to explain:

> I prefer not to think of him as a reformer and sorehead. He was I think a man of tremendous intensity and simplicity and consequently when others said things he thought the words meant the same as they would have meant if he had said them. So he naturally was too hard on people and also gave them too much credit when they happened on a good thing. For instance the higher critics think, I believe, that his conversation with Peter where he tells Peter that flesh and blood hadn't revealed it to him that he, the Son of Man, was the Son of God, was made up after the rise of theological controversy and dogma. I prefer to think it really happened and meant simply that he thought Peter had really got on to the fact that he, an ordinary peasant, and hence every other man equally, was a son of God. But if Peter ever said it, it is more likely he never got the point at all, but was clinging to some superstitious notion.[73]

These views are consistent with the outlook Dewey adopted in the 1890s when he attempted to identify what he called the plain natural meaning in Jesus' teachings. When Klyce questioned Dewey further on his view of the significance of the great religious teachers, his reply was curt: "I confess I don't care how great Christ or Buddha [is] anyway—especially as we don't know anything about them."[74]

In the course of their exchange Dewey made a number of observations about his own weaknesses, difficulties, and accomplishments. For example, he did not like administrative duties, and he confessed to Klyce: "My weakness as a man" is that "I dislike taking responsibility. I tend to get out of it and to let George do it."[75] "I'm deeply aware of my lack of art in writing. But in the main I think I am headed right and it will all come out in the wash that needs to," states Dewey. "Perhaps this is conceit; perhaps it is faith in the one, no less faith because it isn't heralded."[76] Regarding his writing, he adds: "It is too balanced in thought to have a grip on the reader, or to have its meaning very perceptible. But when it gets a man it sticks —so much may be said."[77]

In November 1915 Klyce began complaining that he was miserably unhappy in his marriage and wanted to divorce his wife. If he could not get a divorce, he would commit suicide. Dewey tried to dissuade him from considering suicide and then stopped writing. In February 1917, Klyce's wife died of cancer. He remarried in 1919. The correspondence picked up again, and in 1920 Dewey wrote an introduction to Klyce's book, *Universe,* which Klyce eventually published himself a year later. In 1927 Klyce showed signs of increasing mental instability. He also wanted to cooperate with Dewey on a book on logic, and he proposed publishing their correspondence. When Dewey refused, Klyce became increasingly angry and abusive. Dewey patiently tried to reason with him and to preserve their association. Finally recognizing the situation as hopeless, Dewey terminated the relationship.

Klyce's persistent questioning may have helped Dewey as a philosopher refine his philosophical understanding in certain ways. However, Dewey seems to have continued in his correspondence with Klyce largely because, like the composing of poems, it met a need for the expression of some strong feelings on a wide range of issues on which he had strong personal feelings. However, by 1916 Dewey found himself trying to cope with problems that he could not work through by writing poems and letters or retreating to his garden. As a consequence he began taking lessons in the art of the Alexander technique.

The Alexander Technique and the Body-Mind

F. Matthias Alexander was born in Sydney, Australia in 1869, and after beginning a career there as a Shakespearean actor, periodic loss of voice forced him to give it up. In an effort to discover the cause of his difficulty he began to study carefully the way he used his muscles when he spoke. Over time this led him to discover what has come to be known as "the Alexander Principle," which is the idea that "there are certain ways of using your body which are better than certain other ways; that when you reject these better ways of using your body, your functioning will begin to suffer in some important respects; that it is useful to assess other people by the way they use themselves."[78] In short, "use affects functioning," that is, the way the muscles and body as a whole are used affects a person's physical and psychological well-being. Alexander focused special attention on the alignment of the head, neck, and back and on such simple activities as standing, sitting down, getting up, lying, and breathing. He discovered that in performing these activities most people exhibit harmful muscular tension habits and their head, neck, and back are not in correct relationship. The consequence is the creation of frustrating problems in demanding situations such as competitive sports, public speaking, interpersonal communications, and sexual relations. His technique was as one commentator described it, "a kind of reversed psycho-analysis, unwinding the psychic knots by getting control of the physical end-organs."[79] "Body use *is* the 'unconscious' for most people," asserts a follower of Alexander. "As use becomes more conscious, the unconscious habit can lose its grip."[80] In 1904 Alexander settled in England and by the 1930s his work had attracted considerable attention even though, by and large, the medical profession remained skeptical. Among his pupils were George Bernard Shaw, Aldous Huxley, and Archbishop William Temple.

In 1914 Alexander journeyed to New York City to introduce his technique to Americans. After hearing about Alexander's work and reading his first book, *Man's Supreme Inheritance* (1910), Professor Wendell Bush of the Columbia Philosophy Department hosted a dinner for Alexander in 1916 and invited a number of his Columbia colleagues including Dewey. Following that dinner James Harvey Robinson and Dewey began taking lessons from Alexander.[81] Dewey soon became a lifelong convert to the Alexander technique and philosophy. Professor Horace Kallen reports that "Dewey told me that at one time he'd suffered from a stiff neck and that he'd had difficulty with his eyes ... he said that Alexander had completely cured him, that he was able to read, to see, to move his neck freely."[82] There is evidence, however, that it was more than a stiff neck and eye trouble that brought Dewey to Alexander. In 1923 Alexander published *Constructive Conscious Control of the Individual,* and it includes a description of an unnamed patient who may well have been Dewey in 1916.

> A pupil of mine, an author, had been in a serious state of health for some time, and had at last reached the point where he was unable to carry on his literary work. After finishing his latest book he passed through a crisis described as a "breakdown," with the result that even a few hours of work caused him great fatigue and brought on a state of painful depression.[83]

By 1916 Dewey's rigorous work habits and the conflicts of the war years were taking their toll in the form of nervous tension, fatigue, and depression.[84]

At a time when a number of intellectuals were turning to Sigmund Freud and psychoanalysis as the new scientific cure for nervous and emotional disorders, Dewey turned to F.M. Alexander. Alexander's physiological approach to the psychological and his method of therapy and learning, which involved empirical verification by sense observations, appealed to Dewey's intellectual predilections. "Each lesson was a laboratory experimental demonstration," writes Dewey approvingly.[85] So enthusiastic about Alexander was Dewey that he wrote introductions to three of Alexander's books between 1919 and 1932. Even though these introductions are written in very abstract language, they reveal what Dewey found to be the great significance of Alexander's thought and technique. First, it is Alexander's thesis that as human civilization has developed and the human brain and nervous system have rapidly evolved in complex ways, the bodily functions of digestion, circulation, and respiration and the muscular system have remained relatively unchanged. The result has been all sorts of maladjustments in the form of nervous tension, emotional disturbance, and exhaustion. Dewey accepts these ideas and asserts that Alexander's method modifies a person's bodily habits and activities so that the body is effectively coordinated with and supports the activities of the brain and nervous system. Mental and physical health follow.[86]

Second, the key concept for Dewey in estimating the value of Alexander's discovery is the idea of the art of "central and conscious ... control of our use of ourselves."[87] Dewey understood this major

theme as involving the idea of "control by intelligence," and as such
he viewed the Australian's philosophy and method as a welcome vital
addition to his own philosophy of creative intelligence and education.
He believed that Alexander had scientifically demonstrated "the existence of a central control in the organism," which may be consciously directed by intelligence.[88]

> The school of Pavlov has made current the idea of conditional reflexes.
> Mr. Alexander's work extends and corrects the idea. It proves that
> there are certain basic, central organic habits and attitudes which
> condition *every* act we perform, every use we make of ourselves. . . .
> The discovery of a central control which conditions all other reactions
> brings the conditioning factor under conscious direction and enables
> the individual through his own coordinated activities to take posses-
> sion of his own potentialities. It converts the fact of conditional
> reflexes from a principle of external enslavement into a means of vital
> freedom.[89]

The central control of the personality involves "certain basic . . .
habits and attitudes," and Dewey asserts that these basic "habits and
ways of doing things" constitute the self.[90] According to Alexander,
who insisted on the fundamental unity of the physical and psychical,
these "psycho-physical habits" are expressed in and through posture
and the use of the body. By educating people in his science of the
right use of their bodies, "a new sensory consciousness" involving
new habits and attitudes is generated, replacing the old "perverted
consciousness" which afflicts most people.[91] The result is not only
physical health but "a changed emotional condition and a different
outlook on life."[92] Alexander has discovered, claims Dewey, "the
principle for developing human well-being." "The technique of Mr.
Alexander gives to the educator a standard of psycho-physical health
—in which what we call morality is included. It supplies also the
'means whereby' this standard may be progressively and endlessly
achieved. . . . It provides therefore the conditions for the central direction of all special educational processes."[93]

Just what Dewey means by these assertions regarding the Alexander method is difficult to understand. He explains himself more fully
in a chapter on "Habit and Will" in *Human Nature and Conduct*
(1922), which grew out of a series of lectures delivered at the Univer-

sity of California at Berkeley in 1918. In this chapter Dewey offers his own theory of how human nature, including moral character, may be changed and controlled. The chapter is a blend of Dewey's social psychology and theory of knowing by doing with what he learned from taking lessons from Alexander, and he explicitly mentions his indebtedness to the latter. This material further clarifies Dewey's theory of pursuing social progress by using intelligence to reconstruct objective conditions.

Fundamental to Dewey's psychology and theory of how to control human nature is his idea of habit. He gives the term "habit" a broader meaning than is usual: "The essence of habit is an acquired predisposition to ways or modes of response." Habits are acquired in the sense that they are built up by prior activity. They are also "projective, dynamic in quality" and guide behavior. They are affections and aversions that are "demands for certain kinds of activity." Habits are not just a matter of subjective predispositions. They involve the organized interaction of an organism with its environment. "They are working adaptations of personal capacities with environing forces" or, in other words, "the joint adaptation to each other of human powers and physical conditions." As such, habits constitute the working capacities and the actual means available to a person seeking to realize an end of action (including moral ends). Dewey further explains that a habit influences a person's ways of thinking and acting even when it is not overtly manifest. Habits interact with each other. "Character is the name given to the working interaction of habits." In short, the habits of a person in their interconnectedness "constitute the self." "In any intelligible sense of the word will, they [habits] *are* will. They form our effective desires and they furnish us with our working capacities. They rule our thoughts. . . ." To change a person's behavior and character, then, involves the reconstruction of habits.[94]

It is often thought that character and behavior can be changed simply by awakening a desire and wish to change, by deliberate efforts of Victorian willpower, by setting up rules and laws, or by generating psychical insight as with Freudian psychoanalysis. Dewey rejects all of these approaches as inadequate by themselves. These notions are based on a faulty psychology and theory of how people learn, change, and grow. Using his experience with Alexander as an example, Dewey explains that a person who does not know how to stand up straight cannot achieve this result simply by having this idea in mind and wishing to do it. The problem is twofold. First of all, a person cannot have a correct idea of how to stand straight who does not actually do it. "Only when a man can already perform an act of standing straight does he know what it is like to have a right posture and only then can he summon the idea required for proper execution. The act must come before the thought. . . ." In other words, the way a person stands is controlled by existing habits involving the body, and these habits and the sensory consciousness involved influence how we think. If the habits are bad, then thinking will be distorted. "Only the man whose habits are already good can know what the good is. Immediate, seemingly instinctive, feeling of the direction and end of various lines of behavior is in reality the feeling of habits working below direct consciousness." In other words, a person's intuitions in matters of physical well-being, morals, and aesthetic taste are only as good as the person's habits or acquired predispositions.[95]

Second, a person in the grip of bad habits is not capable of achieving an end contrary to these habits, even if by some circumstance he or she acquires a correct idea of it. Dewey notes that this experience has traditionally been viewed as a conflict of the flesh and the spirit, but in actuality it is a conflict between conscious purpose and old acquired habit. An idea, a desire, and a fiat of will are not themselves capable of achieving an end of action. They do not constitute the effective means necessary—"the means whereby"—to achieve the result. The actual means needed are reconstructed habits. The ways in which a person tries to do something affects what is actually accomplished. In summary, only good habits can generate good ideas of the ends of action and only good habits can actualize these ends.[96]

How can a person or society reconstruct human habits and character for the better? Dewey asserts that we can change the character and the effective will of a person only by changing the objective conditions which enter into the person's habits. We cannot change a habit directly by wish and order of will, "but we can change it indirectly by modifying conditions, by an intelligent selecting and weighting of the objects which engage attention and which influence the fulfillment of desires."[97] To accomplish this it is necessary to take habits apart, recognizing that they involve a continuum of means and ends. A bad habit involves a series of acts or conditions, each of which serves as the means to another, with a negative end-result such as bad posture or drunkenness. To alter a bad habit one must use intelligence to break and inhibit the chain of conditions leading to the negative end and initiate another series with a positive end result. Such an experience repeated will gradually have the effect of changing the old habit, creating a new consciousness, and forming a correct idea of the new desired end.

Citing again the problem of standing straight and his experience with the Alexander technique, Dewey explains how this can be accomplished involving what he calls an indirect approach or "a flank movement."

> We must stop even thinking of standing up straight. To think of it is fatal, for it commits us to the operation of an established habit of standing wrong. We must find an act within our power which is disconnected from any thought about standing. We must start to do another thing which on one side inhibits our falling into the customary bad position and on the other side is the beginning of a series of acts which may lead into the correct posture. The hard-drinker who keeps thinking of not drinking is doing what he can to initiate the acts which lead to drinking. He is starting with the stimulus to his habit. To succeed he must find some positive interest or line of action which will inhibit the drinking series and which by instituting another course of action will bring him to his desired end. In short, the man's true aim is to discover some course of action, having nothing to do with the habit of drink or standing erect, which will take him where he wants to go. The discovery of this other series is at once his means and his end. Until one takes intermediate acts seriously enough to treat them as ends, one wastes one's time in any effort at change of habits. Of the intermediate acts, the most important is the *next* one. The first or earliest means is the most important *end* to discover.[98]

This line of thought was consistent with the way Dewey's psychology had been developing for over two decades, and his work with Alexander crystalized his thinking on these matters.

Along with the discovery of a specific method for the reconstruction of habits and character, Dewey believed that his experience with Alexander had given him a fresh appreciation of the human body and of the unity of the body and the mind. It deepened his convictions that knowing involves doing and the operations of the mind are shaped by the activities of the body and the related sensory consciousness. In his 1919 introduction to Alexander's book *Man's Supreme Inheritance,* he writes that the body is "the most wonderful of all the structures of the vast universe," and he finds that working with Alexander instills "a religious attitude toward the body," that is, "reverence for this wonderful instrument of our life, life mental and moral as well as that life which somewhat meaninglessly we call bodily."[99] Summarizing the influence of Alexander in 1939, Dewey writes: "My theories of mind-body, of the coordination of the active elements of the self and of the place of ideas in inhibition and control of overt action required contact with the work of F.M. Alexander and in later years his brother A.R., to transform them into realities."[100] In *Human Nature and Conduct* and other books written after his discovery of the Alexander technique, Dewey does not endorse Alexander's theory of "a central control" which conditions all other reactions. Even though his introductions to Alexander's books make it clear that he accepts this idea, he did not support it beyond these introductions because the data had not yet been assembled for a full public demonstration of its scientific basis. Dewey believed that he had personally experienced an empirical verification of the idea and that a full-scale scientific justification was possible. He urged Alexander to undertake the necessary work and became frustrated with Alexander's reluctance to do it. Some of Alexander's disciples have pursued the task.[101]

Believing as he actually did in the scientific soundness of Alexander's theory of a central control as well as in his method for reconstructing habit and character, Dewey asserted in his introduction to Alexander's second book, *Constructive Conscious Control of the Individual* (1923), that Alexander's discoveries are directly relevant to the overcoming of the international social crisis created by modern science and the new technology:

Mr. Alexander has demonstrated a new scientific principle with respect to the control of human behavior, as important as any principle which has ever been discovered in the domain of external nature. Not only this, but his discovery is necessary to complete the discoveries that have been made about non-human nature, if these discoveries and inventions are not to end by making us their servants and helpless tools. . . .

Through modern science we have mastered to a wonderful extent the use of things as tools for accomplishing results upon and through other things. The result is all but a universal state of confusion, discontent, and strife. The one factor which is the primary tool in the use of all these other tools—namely, ourselves—in other words, our own psycho-physical disposition, as the basic condition of our employment of all agencies and energies, has not even been studied as the central instrumentality. Is it not highly probable that this failure gives the explanation of why it is that in mastering physical forces we have ourselves been so largely mastered by them, until we find ourselves incompetent to direct the history and destiny of man?

Never before, I think, has there been such an acute consciousness of the failure of all external remedies as exists today, of the failure of all remedies and forces external to the individual man. It is, however, one thing to teach the need of a return to the individual man as the ultimate agency in whatever mankind and society collectively can accomplish, to point out the necessity of straightening out this ultimate condition of whatever humanity in mass can attain. It is another thing to discover the concrete procedure by which this greatest of all tasks can be executed. And this indispensable thing is exactly what Mr. Alexander has accomplished.[102]

In the wake of the war Dewey was searching for a new ground for progressive optimism in a disillusioned world, and he here latches onto the Alexander technique as the answer. Governments, diplomats, scientists, philosophers, and reformers had failed to prevent world war, and Dewey knew that it could happen again. The Alexander principle now offers the hope of changing that. The claims made for Alexander's work by Dewey in 1919 and 1923 are extraordinary. It is almost as if Dewey has found the method of personal liberation and growth that religions and philosophers have long been seeking, except that Dewey does not promise eternal life. Some may regard these claims as a temporary lapse of judgment reflecting both an intense need to fight off pessimism and the enthusiasm which often accompanies conversion to a new beneficial mode of healing and growth. However, it is important to recognize that in 1932 Dewey repeated his claims for the Alexander method, stating: "I do so fully aware of their sweeping nature."[103]

Dewey's training with Alexander in conscious control led him to be especially appreciative of certain aspects of the martial arts that he observed during his visit to Japan in the spring of 1919. Following his visit to a women's school in Tokyo he writes:

> We went to the gymnasium and saw the old Samurai women's sword and spear exercises, etc. The teacher was an old woman of seventy-five and as lithe and nimble as a cat—more graceful than any of the girls. I have an enormous respect now for the old etiquette and ceremonies regarded as physical culture. Every movement has to be made perfectly, and it cannot be done without conscious control. The modernized gym exercises by the children were simply pitiful compared with these ceremonies.

After observing a Judo demonstration Dewey comments:

> It is an art.... I think a study ought to be made here from the standpoint of conscious control. Tell Mr. Alexander to get a book by Harrison—a compatriot of his—out of the library, called *The Fighting Spirit of Japan*.... I noticed at the Judo ... they breathe always from the abdomen.... I have yet to see a Japanese throw his head back when he rises. In the army they have an indirect method of getting deep breathing which really goes back to the Buddhist Zen teaching of the old Samurai.

In the course of a visit to Kamakura, Dewey had a two-hour meeting with Soyen Shaku, the Abbot of the Zen monasteries Engaku-ji and Kencho-ji, who had visited the United States and Europe in 1905 and 1906. However, they did not apparently discuss actual Zen training and meditation practice. Dewey reports that Shaku's "talk was largely moral but with a high metaphysical flavor, somewhat elusive and reminding one of Royce." Dewey, however, adds that "he was more modern than Royce in one respect; he said God is the moral ideal in man and as man develops the divine principle does also."[104] Dewey apparently did not pursue with Alexander the idea of studying traditional oriental methods of physical training.

Dewey clearly found his work with Alexander enormously helpful both physically and emotionally. It brought him relief and healing and a fresh sense of life and growth. Even if Alexander was not destined to lead the entire human race to conscious self-control, it did help Dewey get better control of himself at an especially difficult time when certain aspects of his own life, as well as much in the world outside him, were out of control. Dewey's words about Alexander and his technique have the ring of one who is intensely grateful. Dewey took lessons from Alexander and his brother for many years, and they developed a warm friendship. He confessed to being "an inept, awkward, and slow pupil," but he delighted in learning and pursuing what he viewed as Alexander's highly scientific method of self-education. "I used to shuffle and sag," said Dewey. "Now I hold myself up."[105] At the age of eighty-seven Dewey commented that "my confidence in Alexander's work is unabated. He has made one of the most important discoveries that has been made in practical application of the unity of the mind-body principle. If it hadn't been for their treatment, I'd hardly be here today—as a personal matter. I don't talk about it very much because unless one has had personal experience it sounds to others just like another of those enthusiasms for some pet panacea."[106]

Some of Dewey's colleagues refused to take his firm belief in the Alexander principle and technique seriously. Aware of such skepticism, Dewey sought to clarify the difference between a practice like Alexander's and other schemes which are of lesser value or fraudulent. He drew up a list of criteria to be used in evaluating the rapidly growing number of mind cures, therapies, and religions that promised Americans liberation and happiness. These sensible criteria are as relevant today as in the 1920s.

> Is a system primarily remedial, curative, aiming at relief of sufferings that already exist; or is it fundamentally preventive in nature? . . . Does it deal with the "mind" and the "body" as things separated from each other, or does it deal with the unity of man's individuality? Does it deal with some portion or aspect of "mind" and "body" or with the

re-education of the whole being? Does it aim at securing results directly, by treatment of symptoms, or does it deal with the causes of malconditions present in such a way that any beneficial results secured come as a natural consequence, almost, it might be said, as by-products of a fundamental change in such conditioning causes? Is the scheme educational or non-educational in character? If the principle underlying it claims to be preventive and constructive, does it operate from without by setting up some automatic safety-device, or does it operate from within? Is it cheap and easy, or does it make demands on the intellectual and moral energies of the individual concerned? ...

Any sound plan must prove its soundness in reference both to concrete consequences and to general principles. What we too often forget is that these principles and facts must not be judged separately, but in connexion with each other. Further, whilst any theory or principle must ultimately be judged by its consequences in operation, whilst it must be verified experimentally by observation of how it works, yet in order to justify a claim to be scientific, it must provide a method for making evident and observable what the consequences are; and this method must be such as to afford a guarantee that the observed consequences actually flow from the principle.[107]

Dewey, of course, believed that Alexander's teaching was scientifically based, focused on the body-mind as a unity, concerned with the whole person, preventive as well as remedial, aimed at dealing with underlying causal conditions, morally and intellectually challenging, educational, and directed at self-control. Even though Alexander's followers in the late twentieth century make more modest claims than their teacher and Dewey, the technique is still taught and many people continue to believe that they are benefitted by it. Alexander's work involves an important contribution to the growing fields of body-mind research and kinesthetics.

French Painting and Natural Magic

Reflecting on his first lecture course with Dewey in 1915, Irwin Edman recalls that it "was well attended; there were even some fashionably dressed society ladies, for Dewey had become a vogue."[108] Outside visitors in Dewey's classes were not uncommon, and two such visitors in 1917 were destined to have a major impact on his life. One was the inventor, businessman, and collector of modern French paintings, Albert C. Barnes, who helped to guide Dewey into an intense study of art and aesthetic experience. The other was a vivacious and talented writer, Anzia Yezierska, who led Dewey to rediscover the "natural magic" of romantic love.

Albert Barnes began his career as a doctor in the 1890s, but he turned to chemistry and succeeded in making a fortune by inventing argyrol. Settling in Philadelphia, he used his wealth to create an outstanding collection of modern French painting, which was eventually installed in a museum under the care of a foundation that he controlled. An interest in art and education led Barnes to read *Democracy and Education* in 1917. He was so impressed that he decided to study philosophy with the author. Each week throughout the academic year 1917–1918 he would journey with his secretary from Philadelphia to New York to attend Dewey's lectures.[109] According to one observer, he would frequently fall asleep during the hour, but he and Dewey formed a lasting friendship built around their common interests in art, education, and philosophy. Dewey, who had long enjoyed poetry and who had no ear for music, set out at this time to deepen his appreciation of painting, and he found Barnes immensely helpful.[110]

Barnes had a reputation for being an extraordinarily difficult personality who frequently became angry, arbitrary, and abusive in his dealings with people. However, he had great respect for Dewey, who seemed to be the only person who could restrain him and bring him to reason.[111] Dewey enjoyed studying the art in Barnes' collection, and in 1926 they travelled to Madrid, Paris, and Vienna together visiting museums and artists.[112] Some of Dewey's colleagues were critical of him for being so indulgent toward his wealthy cantankerous friend. However, he found Barnes to be possessed of good critical judgment in matters of art and to be a stimulating influence as he worked to clarify the nature of aesthetic experience and to give it a central place in his philosophic vision. Dewey's studies in aesthetics culminated in *Art as Experience* (1934), which was dedicated "to Albert Barnes in Gratitude." In the Preface he states that "the great educational work carried on in the Barnes Foundation ... is of a pioneer quality comparable to the best that has been done in any field during the present generation, that of science not excepted."[113]

As Dewey began studying the romantic images in Barnes' collection of paintings by Renoir, Monet, and Matisse, he had more on his mind than art theory. Among his poems written prior to 1919, when he departed for Japan and China, are a number of love poems. Many of them were written to or about Anzia Yezierska, a Russian Jewish immigrant and novelist from the Lower East Side in New York City. Battle-scarred, tired, and lonely, Dewey met and fell in love with Yezierska during the summer or fall of 1917, and their romantic relationship lasted for a year.

When Dewey met Yezierska she was a woman in her mid-thirties whose life had been a valiant struggle to escape from oppression and poverty, and she was filled with an intense longing for freedom, self-expression, and understanding. Born in a Russian-Polish village near Warsaw, her childhood memories were of a warm Jewish community life frustrated by want and disrupted by frightening persecution. With fresh hope and brave dreams Yezierska at the age of twelve journeyed with her large family to America in the early 1890s like thousands of other Eastern European Jews. However, life in New York City's Lower East Side, which contained America's largest Jewish immigrant community, was harsh and confining in its own way and offered no easy route to the opportunities that were the promise of America. Acquainted with the value of learning through the example of her father, who was a Talmudic scholar, and driven by a desire to escape the cruel fate of so many poor women in the ghetto, she set out to get an education. With the assistance of an East Side settlement house, she eventually managed to attend Teachers College at Columbia University, and she went on to become a domestic science teacher. She also married. However, she soon found marriage as well as the domestic science curriculum limiting. By 1917 Yezierska had rejected the orthodox faith of her father and had left two husbands and a small daughter. Her new life involved friendships with many of New York's radical intellectuals including feminist and socialist reformers. Intent upon telling the story of the suffering and hopes of her people, two million of whom had immigrated from Eastern Europe to America between 1881 and 1914, she aspired to a career as a writer. She was a woman midway between two worlds—the old world of her Russian-Polish ancestry and the new world of Anglo-Saxon America, to which she looked for acceptance and support.[114]

Yezierska was a striking woman with blue-green eyes, white velvety skin, and thick auburn hair. She had a vibrant excitable personality and a determined will. Her daughter, Louise Levitas Henriksen, gives this account of her first meeting with Dewey in 1917 following a stay in California.

> When she did return to New York and tried to get a teacher's job, she was told that she lacked credentials. In characteristic, angry contempt for authority, she stormed without knocking into the Columbia University office of the leading authority on education in the country, John Dewey. He listened to her. She said she had been denied a teaching certificate by ignorant bureaucrats and asked him to watch her teach a class. In such dramas she was a star performer. Dewey actually went downtown to watch her teach, and he read her stories, which she had flung on his desk as evidence of her value.[115]

Dewey advised Yezierska to give up teaching and to develop her talent as a writer. He also gave her, as well as Albert Barnes, permission to audit his seminar in social and political philosophy, and she attended the class throughout the academic year.[116]

Dewey was quickly attracted by Yezierska's youthful passion, warmth, and directness. Her quest to free herself from an oppressive past was something with which he could readily identify. He admired her courage and determination to tell the story of the Jewish immigrants, and she provided him with another way of linking himself with the struggle of the poor and oppressed peoples in urban America. Yezierska was attracted to Dewey initially by his reputation and influence, but it was his understanding, kindness, and encouragement that drew her irresistibly to him. In a novel that is based on her experience with Dewey, she writes: "I tasted the bread and wine of equality." He became a Christ-like father to her: "I thought if ever God was visible in a human face it was here in him."[117] Dewey's philosophy seemed to express the compassion and liberating spirit she found in the man, and she believed that if *Democracy and Education* were to be written in a simpler language, it would become the "new Bible of America."[118] In the words of Louise Henriksen: "An intense relationship, never consummated, developed rapidly between the seemingly austere Yankee Puritan and Anzia, the passionate rebel."[119]

Early in their relationship Dewey sent to Yezierska a poem that expressed in a poignant fashion his compassion, encouragement, and faith in her as a writer and person.

> Generations of stifled worlds reaching out
> Through you,
> Aching for utt'rance, dying on lips
> That have died of hunger,
> Hunger not to have, but to be.
>
> Generations as yet unuttered, dumb, smothered,
> Inchoate, unutterable by me and mine,
> In you I see them coming to be,
> Luminous, slow revolving, ordered in rhythm.
> You shall not utter them; you shall be them,
> And from out the pain
> A great song shall fill the world.[120]

Yezierska perceived Dewey's capacity to identify with her as a Jew and her attraction to him as an Anglo-Saxon Gentile as part of the special power of their relationship. Again in a story of a relationship similar to the one she had shared with Dewey, she explains: "It's because he and I are of a different race that we can understand one another so profoundly, touch the innermost reaches of the soul, beyond the reach of those who think they know us. . . ."[121]

The nature of Dewey's feelings for Anzia Yezierska are sensitively described in a long letter that he wrote to her in the form of a poem. After explaining that given his existing commitments, he was not free to enter a long-term relationship with her, he writes:

> Yet would I have you know
> How utterly my thoughts go
> With you to and fro
> In a ceaseless quest,
> Half annoy
> And all a blessed joy.
> Does she now think or write or rest?

What happens at this minute—it's just eight—
Has she written or shall I wait
In sweet trouble of expectancy
For some fresh wonder yet to be?
Whate'er, howe'er you move or rest
I see your body's breathing
The curving of your breast
And hear the warm thoughts seething.
I watch the lovely eyes that visions hold
Even in the tortured tangles of the tenement
Of a life that's free and bold.
I feel the hand that for a brief moment
Has been in mine, and dream that you are near
To talk with, and that I can hear
Your crystalled speech
As we converse, each to each.
While I am within this wonder
I am overcome as by thunder
Of my blood that surges
From my cold heart to my clear head—
So at least she said—
Till my body sinks and merges
In communion with the wine and bread.[122]

In this poem Dewey the naturalistic humanist finds divine communion in human communion.

Dewey celebrates Anzia's beauty and the wonder of their love in a poem entitled "Autumn," the time of her birthday and the time in the cycle of his life when he discovered her.

Fair is my love in body's grace
And fair and white in soul is she
Like the white wonder that lights up space
When sudden blooms th'apple tree
   That yields itself acquist.

Yet not spring's perilous daughter she
But child of fall, dear time of year
When earth's fair fruits perfectèd be;—
Gold of grain and grapes' purpling tear
   Of pendant amethyst.

Had not rich fall her ripe fruit brought
As proof of time's fulfillèd good
Life's inner speech I had not caught.
For how should I have understood
   Its final meaning missed?[123]

In another love poem, "Natural Magic," he writes that, "For ere the world began, thy soul was wed/By nature's mystic marriage pledge" to all the delightful, changing beauties of nature "So that as you swiftly pass/Full hearts upleaping glad rejoice/As at holy incense from an altar's urn...."[124]

At this time in Dewey's life when many others were distant and critical, Yezierska's admiration and affection must have been a source of welcome comfort as well as the gift of a new sense of life. However, their relationship was not without its complications and pain. He worried about the twenty-five years in age that separated them.[125] He resisted the impulse to surrender himself to her out of a sense of responsibility to those "with whom I've loved, and fought,/ Till within me has been wrought/My power to reach, to see and understand...."[126] He experienced these obligations as something of an "iron band," but he also feared the consequences of acting on "untamed desire."[127] At times he experienced his desire as a painful craving, and he also discovered that it could bring an aftermath of disappointment, frustration, and emptiness.[128] In addition, Anzia was herself a very complex, insecure, and demanding person, who was burdened with a number of painful unresolved problems from her past. Feelings of uprootedness and alienation, ambivalent feelings about sexual intimacy, and a tendency to impose utterly unrealistic expectations on a relationship may well have introduced complications into Dewey's interactions with her.[129]

At the instigation of Albert Barnes, Dewey in the spring of 1918 organized a group of Columbia University graduate students to undertake a study during the summer months of the social conditions and values in the Polish immigrant community in Philadelphia. Barnes was particularly concerned to know why the Polish immigrants were not being assimilated into American democratic culture.[130] Yezierska was made a translator for the team and given the responsibility of investigating conditions affecting family life and women.[131] The study was conducted out of a house in the Polish district. After returning from a lecture tour in San Francisco in June, Dewey regularly travelled to Philadelphia to supervise the project, which provided him with an opportunity to see Yezierska frequently during July and August. However, their relationship was not to last.

Between the war and romance, Dewey's public and private life was in a good bit of turmoil by the summer of 1918. Gardening, poetry, letters, and the Alexander technique had helped him to get through the war years, but he needed to get away, tend his wounds, and collect himself. The opportunity came when the University of California at Berkeley invited him to give a series of lectures during the fall semester, and Barnes suggested that he go on to Japan to study the political situation there and offered financial assistance with the trip.[132] Dewey was granted a year's leave from Columbia, and before his departure he brought his relationship with Yezierska to an end. He had advised her as their relationship developed that "What I am to anyone is but a loan/From those who made, and own."[133] For a short time it had been a joy to know Anzia, to be able to help her, and to experience her love and admiration. However, continuing their relationship involved difficulties for his family and himself that he did not want, and he may also have believed that he had given Yezierska all that he could.[134]

The sadness Dewey felt when he parted from Anzia Yezierska may well be expressed in the following poem that becomes a prayer, moving in the simple humanity of its sentiment.

> Is this the end?
> A past with a closing door
> Thru which I hardly grasp
> From out of time's jealous clasp
> A scant fleeting store
> Of memories retreating:
> A future all hope defeating
> Closing in with tight shut door.
> Twixt the two the present penned.
>
> Great God, I thee implore
> A little help to lend: —

> I do not ask for much,
> A little space in which to move,
> To reach, perchance to touch;
> A little time in which to love;
> A little hope that things which were
> Again may living stir—
> A future with an op'ning door:
> Dear God, I ask no more
> Than that these bonds may rend,
> And leave me free as before.[135]

The memory of the intensity and beauty in his relationship with Anzia—a relationship that for at least a brief time bridged many social divisions—was in all likelihood one important source of the poetic vision of the ideal possibilities of new world democracy that led Dewey to write in 1919: "And when the emotional force, the mystic force one might say, of communication, of the miracle of shared life and shared experience is spontaneously felt, the hardness and crudeness of contemporary life will be bathed in the light that never was on land or sea."[136]

Yezierska went on to win fame as a writer in America during the 1920s, and two of her novels were made into films by Hollywood. However, she never succeeded in creating a lasting relationship with a man, and she "never got over the crushing disappointment" of losing her close tie with Dewey. Blending fact and fantasy, she periodically reconstructed the story of their relationship in her novels and short stories, using it as her primary metaphor for the possibilities and impossibilities of bridging the gulf between the old world immigrant and modern America.[137]

In September 1918, Dewey traveled again to the West Coast where he joined Alice, who had spent the summer in California. During his stay in Berkeley, he was invited to lecture in Japan. In February 1919, he and Alice began the voyage across the Pacific for what would soon turn into a two-and-a-half-year stay in the Far East. Thus ended a momentous period in his life.

In the course of their relationship, Yezierska raised with Dewey an issue that is of importance with respect to much that was happening to him in his personal life and also of significance in connection with the development of his philosophy. She perceived Dewey as the cool, reasonable Anglo-Saxon suffering from an overdose of New England Puritan culture. She often chided him for being "cold in the heart, clear in the head." [138] In a review of *Democracy and Education,* Yezierska observed: "Unfortunately, Professor Dewey's style lacks ... that warm personal touch that could enable his readers to get close to him," and "he thinks so high up in the head that only the intellectual few can follow the spiraling point of his argument." [139] Assessing the strengths and weaknesses of pragmatism in 1922, Harold Chapman Brown, a pragmatist who had taught with Dewey at Columbia, also raised a related issue. He found the greatest weakness in Dewey's philosophy to be a lack of appreciation of the role of "emotionality" in human nature, and he called on Dewey to develop a philosophy of art and religion.[140]

Dewey had given emotion a significant place in his philosophy of education and he also recognized that it played an important role in the moral and religious life. However, given his Vermont religious upbringing, it had never been easy for Dewey to express his emotions, and he did describe himself to Yezierska as "the choked fountain." He was a man of strong feeling, but his passions to a large extent had been channeled into a rarefied form of philosophical discourse and social idealism. His temperament led him to be especially attracted to abstract theoretical reflections and he had a keen interest in logic. He emphasized the role of intelligence in morals and social reconstruction and often came down hard on people who relied primarily on emotional inspiration to get things done in the world. Concentrating his attention on logic, epistemology, and the science of morals, he had not fully developed a theory of aesthetic experience. His early experience with institutional religion had had a damaging effect on his own emotional growth and saddled him with an excessively demanding conscience. He also had had a very difficult time breaking free of the church and its influence. As a result, Dewey developed a lifelong bias against institutional religion. Furthermore, even when he had broken with traditional religion intellectually, the effects of the old injuries were such that he had little enthusiasm for anything that seemed to be associated with it. His interest in writing about religion had faded, and he deliberately avoided using a vocabulary that might stir up the emotions of people with traditional religious interests. In the light of all these factors it is not surprising that Dewey's writing style tended to be dry, and his books and essays left many readers feeling that something to do with the emotions, the heart, and values was missing. The criticisms of Brown and Yezierska were another way of raising the kind of questions about Dewey's philosophy discussed by Randolph Bourne.

It is true that Dewey's pragmatism and naturalistic humanism as it had been developed up through the war years does not give a complete account of the function of emotion in human life and has not fully worked out a way for the modern person to integrate the head and the heart. However, it is also true that during the war years he was wrestling with this problem as a person and was better preparing himself to address the issue as a philosopher. He is found trying to relieve the tension and tiredness in his body. In a variety of ways he seeks to free himself from the oppressive effects of his overdeveloped conscience and to express his emotional need for rest, pleasure, and affection. He is driven to find a practical method of individual well-being. He learns to listen to the needs of his body and develops a fresh appreciation of the interrelationship of body and mind. His personal writings manifest a high degree of self-awareness. At times self-doubt, regrets, sadness, guilt, loneliness, and exhaustion tempt him to seek relief or release in forgetfulness and death. However, his passion for creative life persists. His poems and letters reveal him to be a man of many passions—romantic, aesthetic, and religious as well as moral and philosophical. The affirmation of life in his heart constantly overcomes the forces of darkness and negation.

Even though he does not concentrate attention as a philosopher on the subject of religion, he is found quietly nurturing his own private religious experience and faith. As a naturalistic humanist he celebrates the sacredness of the human mind and of human relationships, and he writes of a religious attitude toward the body. He rejoices in the beauty of nature. Central to his personal religion is a moral faith in the ideal possibilities of the future, which includes a faith in democracy, experimentalism, and education. His religious attitude also includes "a faith in things in general"—a sort of cosmic trust or natural piety—that is fed by emotional experiences of a poetic, aesthetic, and mystical nature. The word "God" still had a certain symbolic power in his poetic imagination, and he was pondering a new way of conceiving of the reality of God consistent with a naturalistic worldview. Unlike many other Americans who had turned away from traditional religion, Dewey had not given up on the idea of being religious—but being religious in a new way consistent with democracy and naturalism. A love of nature, delight in poetry, romantic feelings, and a fresh discovery of the world of painting were also leading him to inquire with fresh intensity into the nature and meaning of aesthetic experience.

By the time Dewey set sail on the Pacific in 1919 he could certainly testify to the truth in Henry F. May's assertion many years later that the war years marked "the end of American innocence."[141] It was true of his society and of his own experience. Nothing would ever appear as simple again—building a democratic society, creating international peace, marriage, human friendship, moral decision-making, and doing philosophy. Many Americans were undone by the conflicts and confusion of the war years, and they sought to escape the harsher realities of life in the twentieth century in diverse ways. Large numbers abandoned themselves to hedonism and materialism. Some became angry Marxists or retreated in despair to the Left Bank in Paris. Others embraced a new religious individualism or explored a world-denying mysticism. Dewey went to Japan and China. While this was for him a retreat involving a needed change of environment, it was also a challenging new adventure from which he returned revitalized. He had been shaken by the war experience. He had dreamed of controlling world history with enlightened intelligence and then found that Americans did not have control over their own history and he did not even have control over important aspects of his own life. However, he never lost his faith and courage. In part this was because his mind and heart were so profoundly shaped by the confident spirit of late nineteenth-century American progressivism. It was also because Dewey was a man of enormous creativity, courage, moral energy, and stamina. The war years left him with some painful new regrets. However, he also learned from it all, and when he sat down after the war to write his big books, he was a wiser man for having lived through those turbulent times. His vision of the interrelationship of the ideal and the actual was becoming more comprehensive, and he would in time endeavor to integrate into his philosophy of experimental intelligence a more sensitive and complete understanding of moral feeling and of aesthetic and religious experience.

EIGHT

Nature, Science, and Values

I F T H E W A R experience shook Dewey's confidence or faith in any way, the China experience restored it. About his two years in China, Jane Dewey writes:

> China remains the country nearest his heart after his own. The change from the United States to an environment of the oldest culture in the world struggling to adjust itself to new conditions was so great as to act as a rebirth of intellectual enthusiasms. It provided a living proof of the value of social education as a means of progress.[1]

Dewey's stay in China coincided with a period of social and political upheaval. Only days after he arrived in Shanghai on May 1, 1919, student riots in Peking led to formation of the New Culture movement, which brought new focus and energy to the forces for change. The objective of the movement was to free China from both its feudal past and from exploitation by the Western powers and Japan. It sought to accomplish this in and through the adoption of western ideas and methods in industry, politics, and education. Buddhism and Confucianism were under attack as part of the old order that had to be replaced. The leadership of the New Culture movement was largely in the hands of Chinese intellectuals who had been trained in the West. Many of them were educators, and a significant number had studied with Dewey at Columbia University. They included Chiang Monlin, the Chancellor of National Peking University, who invited Dewey to come to China, P.W. Kuo and Li Chien-hsun, who were presidents of teachers colleges in Peking and Nanking, and Hu Shih, who was a professor of philosophy and literature and a chief architect of the New Culture movement.[2]

Dewey came to China as the first major western scholar to visit at the invitation of the Chinese. He was based during his two years in Peking and Nanking and gave lectures in eleven different provinces. His ideas were widely disseminated through newspapers, pamphlets, journals, and books. The Chinese warmly received Dewey as a champion of a liberating western philosophy. He soon found himself enjoying the kind of popularity and acclaim in progressive circles that he had experienced in the United States before the wartime controversies disrupted the situation. The Chinese were little concerned about his support of the war and pleased with his condemnation of the imperialism of Japan and the western powers. He advocated creation of a new culture in China that would integrate the best in old Chinese traditions with what the Chinese found to be best in modern Western culture. He attacked both laissez-faire individualism and the centralized state socialism of the Communists and defended liberal democracy, progressive education, and experimentalism. In China, Dewey was once more the untarnished kindly progressive hero leading the forces of light into a new world of great promise. His major influence was in the area of education, and as Hu Shih has testified, this influence was far-reaching and persisted until the Communist takeover in 1949.[3]

Dewey returned from China rested and revitalized. The western world to which he came home in the 1920s was not from his perspective in a happy state. Encumbered with an outdated nationalism and afflicted with an unjust ineffective peace settlement, the European powers were struggling to recover from the devastation of war. In America the old progressives, who now increasingly preferred to be called liberals, were disillusioned and disorganized. A reaction to the progressive era had set in and a conservative temper was spreading through the land. American politics witnessed a swing to the right. Big business was entering a period of great prosperity and fought successfully during the presidencies of Harding, Coolidge, and Hoover for control of government. However, the prosperity of the majority stood in sharp contrast to the economic injustice and poverty experienced by large numbers of farmers and laborers. The economic and social pressures of the times led to growth of a narrow-minded factionalism among competing interest groups and a rise in racial and religious prejudice. Shaken by the war, the capture of government by big business, and the general reactionary mood of the nation, the liberals tried to reassert themselves by embracing pacifism, working for peace, and championing economic reforms of a socialist nature.[4]

Dewey's own perspective on the world in the early twenties was a very sober one. Reflecting in 1923 on the current state of things in the light of the historical struggle to overcome human suffering, he wrote an essay entitled "A Sick World," in which he observed:

> The world has always been more or less a sick world. The isles of harmony and health with which we dot the map of human history are largely constructions of the imagination, cities of refuge against present ills, resorts for solace in troubles now endured. But it may be doubted if the consciousness of sickness was ever so widespread as it is today.[5]

Beneath the glitter and bravado of American life, he sensed "the pervasive and overhanging consciousness of disease." What immediately prompted Dewey to make these observations was the great fascination of the American public with a touring French hypnotist named Coué, who claimed to cure individuals of various disorders by auto-suggestion. However, the sickness of the world in Dewey's view involved far more than the nervous and emotional problems of individuals. It was related to the massive social disorders of the age, which threatened, economic breakdown and renewed war, and from the perspective of Dewey's psychology there can be no lasting cure for the problems of individuals apart from dealing with the problems of society. Therefore, Dewey contended that the fundamental need was scientific inquiry into the conditions of social well-being coupled with education pertaining to these conditions.

When Dewey made these observations he was a man in his mid-sixties with a distinguished career behind him, and he might well have retired from the public scene to find in private life the peace that was not in the world about him. However, there is no evidence he considered retirement as an alternative. In actuality he was now a fully matured thinker at the peak of his intellectual powers. Revitalized by the China years, he plunged again into the world of American education, philosophy, and politics with new vigor and continued to expand his international interests and activities. During his sixties he wrote ten to fifteen journal articles, popular essays, and reviews each year on a wide range of academic, national, and international issues, and he published seven books. He engaged in local and national politics and served as an active member of the League for Industrial Democracy, which fought for socialist economic reforms. Two of his books, *The Public and Its Problems* (1926) and *Individualism, Old and New* (1929) were attempts to redefine the meaning of political and social liberalism for the times. As noted earlier, disarmament and the outlawry of war movement were major concerns of Dewey's during the twenties, and in this connection he entered heated public debates with Walter Lippmann, Arthur O. Lovejoy, and James T. Shotwell.[6] Widely regarded as the foremost authority on education in the world, he accepted invitations to study and report on the schools in Turkey in 1924, Mexico in 1926, and the Soviet Union in 1928. Dewey practiced the internationalism that he preached. In spirit and in deed he was a citizen of the world working to make it whole, and he became a figure of world renown.

During Dewey's trip to Mexico in the summer of 1926, Alice developed a heart condition which forced her to return home. Her condition worsened as the year progressed. In order to tend his failing wife, Dewey took a leave from his teaching responsibilities at Columbia during the spring semester of 1927. On July 14 of that year Alice died.[7] They had been married forty years. Two years later Dewey remarked that the "deepest source of happiness in life comes to one, I suppose, from one's own family relations; and there too, though I have experienced great sorrows, I can truly say that in my life companion, in my children, and in my grandchildren, I have been blessed by the circumstances and fortunes of life."[8] Following Alice's death, Dewey's children shared the responsibility of assisting their father with domestic matters, and one of them lived with him until his remarriage in 1946.

During the late summer of 1927, Dewey's son Frederick and his wife Elizabeth took him to Hubbards, Nova Scotia, for some rest. While staying there Dewey wrote the following letter to Professor E.A. Burtt, and it expresses well the way Dewey as a humanist and naturalist found the divine in shared experience and grace in nature.

> Thank you deeply for your kind message of sympathy. Our friends have been very kind and have brought the sense of the abiding Good very close. I have been very fortunate in having five children and as many grandchildren and I realize as I never did before how fortunate I am compared with those who are really left alone. I am spending some weeks here with the family of my oldest son. It is a charming, simple and peaceful spot—just the place for rest.[9]

Shortly after his stay in Nova Scotia, Dewey purchased a small cottage on a freshwater lake in Hubbards, and it became his favorite vacation place for the remainder of his life.[10]

Perhaps the most enduring of Dewey's many contributions in the 1920s are to be found in the publication of several major books in which he endeavors to present a more systematic and comprehensive statement of his philosophy. In his lectures in Japan he had attempted a straightforward overview of his thought, and these lectures were published in 1920 in a clearly written volume entitled *Reconstruction in Philosophy*. In 1922 he revised and published the lectures on *Human Nature and Conduct* which he had delivered in Berkeley in 1918. These two volumes, however, did not fully develop the metaphysical assumptions involved in his humanistic naturalism, and his epistemology needed clarification. He was also concerned to respond to those critics who doubted the value of his experimentalism as an effective instrument of moral guidance for the modern world. Dewey took an invitation from the Paul Carus Foundation to deliver a series of lectures as an opportunity to address these issues, and his lectures were published in 1925 as *Experience and Nature*. He further refined his thinking in the course of delivering the Gifford lectures in Edinburgh, Scotland, which were published in 1929 under the title *The*

Quest for Certainty. These two works contain Dewey's most complete statements on his understanding of the nature of the universe, the human situation, and the relation between the ideal and the real. They also contain his general theory of moral valuation. An appreciation of this philosophic vision is essential to an understanding of Dewey's mature thought and to his theory of the nature and function of religious experience. The remainder of this chapter and the next chapter are concerned with elaborating this philosophic vision and related matters.

At the outset it is useful to consider the empirical method of knowledge that Dewey employed as a naturalist in trying to understand the general nature of things and the human situation. Then attention is turned to Dewey's criticisms of supernaturalism and transcendentalism from the perspective of his empirical naturalism. This is followed by a discussion of his naturalistic metaphysics, that is, his view of the general nature of reality or the world in which human beings find themselves wrestling with the problem of good and evil and the ideal and the real. When Dewey abandoned absolute idealism he at first lost interest in the subject of metaphysics, which he viewed as a speculative undertaking dealing with artificial problems, and he concentrated his attention on education, logic, morals, and social theory. However, as a result of the influence of his colleague Frederick Woodbridge and a rediscovery of Aristotle's naturalistic approach to metaphysics, Dewey set out in *Experience and Nature* to clarify the general idea of the universe, or nature, implicit in his new instrumentalism and democratic humanism. "Nature" emerges in Dewey's naturalism as the all-comprehensive term replacing the idea of the absolute, which comprehends the all in his earlier idealist system.

Experience and the Empirical Method

In 1930 Dewey explained that his intention as a philosopher over the years had been to develop "a new, coherent view of nature and man based upon facts consonant with science and actual social conditions."[11] A trust in experience is for Dewey central to the scientific attitude, or experimental temper of mind, and a philosophy that intends to develop a view of the world consistent with science must accordingly employ an empirical method of knowledge. All concepts and theories must be derived from and verified by directly experienced subject matters. In line with this Dewey labeled his approach in *Experience and Nature* "empirical naturalism" and asserted that his purpose is to offer a defense of a "faith in experience when intelligently used as a means of disclosing the realities of nature."[12] In a later essay entitled "What I Believe," he explained that his whole naturalistic philosophy including his theory of nature and theory of moral valuation is based on the conviction that "experience itself is the sole ultimate authority" in matters of knowledge and belief.[13] This is one of Dewey's deepest convictions, which was firmly established in his mind early in his career.

In general, modern men and women are inclined to trust experience as the criteria for judging the truth and reality of an idea. People want the facts, public hard evidence, that is, something which can be directly experienced when the truth of an idea is in question. Dewey expressed the nature of the modern respect for experience succinctly as a young man when he wrote in 1884: "Experience is realistic, not abstract."[14] Direct experience gives access to reality. Reason divorced from experience, theoretical arguments unsupported by empirical data, carry little weight. This characteristically modern attitude is the direct result of the scientific revolution and the success of the experimental approach to knowledge. Science has taught modern culture that the knowledge which is power is knowledge tested and verified by experience. Dewey's philosophy throughout his career breathes this modern spirit, and it is a major reason for the wide appeal which it has had.

In such early essays as "The Psychological Standpoint" (1886), he had as an idealist defended Locke's empiricist approach, which maintains that philosophy must derive its knowledge from experience, and he had noted that this keeps philosophy on "positive scientific ground." Dewey's idealism purported to be nothing more nor less than a thorough philosophical analysis of the nature and meaning of experience. Indeed, his entire career as a philosopher is devoted to this enterprise. The changes and developments in his thought all derive from either refinements in his understanding of the nature of an empirical method of knowledge or new insights generated in and through use of this method by others as well as himself.

Dewey's idea of the main characteristics of a sound empirical method is quite simple. The empirical investigator starts with a problematic situation which is directly encountered in ordinary experience. The investigator in seeking a solution to the problem may well use imagination, reason, and calculation extensively. The critical point, however, is that all such imaginative and theoretical reflection must in the final analysis be referred back to directly experienced subject-matters for testing and verification. Verification involves determining if a solution to the original problem has been in fact achieved. An empirical inquiry, then, starts and terminates in concrete experience. As a consequence an empirical investigation and the knowledge it generates increase understanding of the things of concrete experience and function as a means of control making possible an increase in the beneficial use and enjoyment of these things.

When philosophy fails to use an empirical method, Dewey contends that there are three negative consequences.

> First, there is no verification, no effort even to test and check. What is even worse, secondly, is that the things of ordinary experience do not get enlargement and enrichment of meaning as they do when approached through the medium of scientific principles and reasonings. This lack of function reacts, in the third place, back upon the philosophic subject-matter in itself. Not tested by being employed to see what it leads to in ordinary experience and what new meanings it contributes, this subject-matter becomes arbitrary, aloof—what is called "abstract" when that word is used in a bad sense to designate something which exclusively occupies a realm of its own without contact with the things of ordinary experience. [15]

Dewey concludes that the value of any philosophy is measured by question: "Does it end in conclusions which, when they are referred back to ordinary life experiences and their predicaments, render them more significant, more luminous to us, and make our dealings with them more fruitful?" [16]

So described, Dewey's empirical approach may sound uncomplicated and straightforward, but modern philosophy raises a whole host of problems surrounding the appeal to experience as a method of knowledge. For example, the British empiricist tradition from Hobbes to Hume employed an appeal to experience as an effective tool of social criticism for attacking superstition, prejudice, class interests, and outdated institutions, but it involved problematic dualistic assumptions about the relation of subject and object and ended in subjectivism and skepticism. An empirical method was also widely used in the eighteenth and nineteenth centuries to defend a mechanistic and materialistic idea of nature. Dewey from the beginning of his career had no taste for dualistic theories which presuppose a gulf between experience and reality leading to subjectivist interpretations of knowledge and skepticism, and, having joined the widespread nineteenth-century reaction against mechanistic materialism as a neo-Hegelian, he had no intention of returning to this interpretation of nature. His purpose was to develop a new, reconstructed idea of the nature of experience that overcomes the vexing problems associated with British empiricism and to develop a new view of nature.

Beginning early in his neo-Hegelian period, Dewey recognized that the earlier British empiricist view of experience involved a faulty psychology. It presupposed a separation of mind and matter, experience and nature, and interpreted experience as a mechanical affair involving the impressing of disconnected atomic sensations on a passive mind by a material world. Using neo-Hegelian theories of experience, which he in time reconstructed in the light of the Darwinian psychology of James and Mead, Dewey developed a new biological and social view of experience. This approach replaced the dualistic, mechanical, atomic, and passive emphasis in British sensationalism with a stress on experience as a fundamentally active affair involving interactions—or transactions, as he preferred to call them late in his career—between an organism and its environment with which it is intimately related. A further discussion of the various aspects of this approach helps to clarify Dewey's view of the human situation and human nature as well as his way of dealing with certain technical philosophical issues.

The most fundamental idea in Dewey's critique of British empiricism and in his new idea of experience is his rejection of any radical dualism of subject and object, mind and matter, experience and nature. By this step Dewey found a way through the most difficult epistemological problems that have faced modern philosophy since Descartes, and he was able to develop a theory of knowledge that could support a new naturalistic vision of the dynamic interrelation of nature and values, the real and the ideal. It was G.S. Morris and the neo-Hegelians who taught Dewey in graduate school how to overcome the dualism of subject and object, and in his early essays, he stated the basic position he adhered to on this issue throughout his life (see chapter 2). The most complete restatement and refinement of his position in his mature works is found in the opening chapter of *Experience and Nature* (1925). Here he makes a distinction between primary and secondary experience. Primary experience is identified with our ordinary direct experience of things and events. The point is that experience "recognizes in its primary integrity no division between act and material, subject and object, but contains them both in an unanalyzed totality."[17] In other words, experience is not to be conceived as something exclusively mental and subjective but as originally and primarily an inclusive unity of both subject and object. Dewey notes, for example, that "when a man is eating, he is eating *food*. He does not divide his act into eating and *food*." Likewise, "in well-formed, smooth-running functions of any sort,—skating, conversing, hearing music, enjoying a landscape,—there is no consciousness of separation of the method of the person and of the subject matter. In whole-hearted play and work there is the same phenomenon."[18] Such is primary or direct experience.

However, the undifferentiated unity of subject and object, which is primary experience, may be transformed by the process of intellectual reflection into conceptual objects including the distinction between subject and object, that is, the various processes of experiencing and what is experienced. If instead of just having an experience we reflect upon it—for example, if a scientific investigation is conducted into the act of eating—we inevitably distinguish between subject and object. The process of reflection leads to development of what Dewey calls secondary experience. He terms it reflective, cognitive, or intellectual experience because it is experience which is dominated by the objects of intellectual activity.

A consistent empiricist philosophy must start its inquiry into experience with the "inclusive integrity of 'experience' " as its primary datum and not with the refined products of secondary or reflective experience. If it proceeds in this fashion, it faces no fundamental problem of how subject and object are related and how real knowledge of nature is possible. As Dewey puts it, "experience is *of* as well as *in* nature." When Dewey first made this argument as a naturalist, he was accused of identifying everything with experience as if experience were in some sense the all-comprehensive absolute. This idea Dewey as a naturalist does reject, noting that "there is no evidence that experience occurs everywhere and everywhen." Parts of nature exist outside of experience at any given time. Dewey's point is only "that when experience does occur, no matter at what limited portion of time and space, it enters into possession of some portion of nature and in such a manner as to render other of its precincts accessible."[19] For Dewey significant evidence in support of this theory of the interrelation of subject (the processes of experiencing) and object (what is experienced), experience and nature, mind and physical world, is the success of the scientific search for knowledge of nature. Experimental inquiry has led to a knowledge of prehistorical events, the ability to predict future events, and control over large spheres of nature. In the face of the scientific and industrial revolutions, the assumption of a radical dualism between nature and experience is seen to be unwarranted and to create an artificial problem. Dewey's way of dealing with the problem of knowledge in modern philosophy is typical of his approach to many other modern philosophical puzzles. He argues that the problem of knowledge as it has been formulated in recent centuries is an insoluble problem, and philosophy can get beyond it only by abandoning the faulty dualistic assumptions that have created it.

The neo-Hegelians also led Dewey to think of experience as involving an active, as opposed to a purely passive, mind, and under their influence he conceived of experience as the reproduction of a universal mind in an individual mind, in and through the interaction of the self and society. As a naturalist Dewey abandoned all references to a universal mind. He did, however, retain the active and social view of experience, reconstructing and deepening these ideas in the light of biological findings and concepts. His approach rejects the theological vision of the human being as a special creation which has been put into nature and is not fully a part of nature. It starts with the Darwinian view of the human being as a creature which is an evolutionary product of nature. Again, there is no dualism between nature and human nature. In this view, experience is identified with the basic life-process of development in human beings, which is conceived as a process of interaction between the human organism and its environment, importantly including society as well as air, earth, water, and growing things. From a biological perspective the human being does not exist and grow in isolation; like every other life-form it comes into being and develops in and through its inter-actions with other things and persons. These interactions are prompted by the need of the organism to achieve an adaptive adjustment.

When experience is so defined as a process of interaction, it is conceived as an affair of doing or acting, but it also has a passive aspect. On the one hand, the human being acts upon or does some-thing with and to other things and persons. Such activity is character-istic of the relation of all organisms to their environment, and the higher the life form the more extensive and important is such activity. Even a child is not a passive recipient of sense impressions, but rather his or her experience involves reaching, touching, pushing, hitting, etc. in response to sensory stimulation. On the other hand, experience involves undergoing—suffering or enjoying—the consequences of such active responses to things and persons. In reaction to the child's activities, things and people do something to him or her, furthering in a cooperative fashion some activities and resisting and blocking others.[20] This twofold process of interaction or transaction is experi-ence. Dewey writes: "the brain and nervous system are primarily organs of action-undergoing; biologically, it can be asserted without contravention that primary experience is of a corresponding type."[21]

Conceived as action-undergoing, primary experience is not cogni-tive or intellectual in quality. Dewey emphasizes this point noting that there is a widespread misguided tendency among philosophers to identify all experiencing as a mode of knowing. Experience itself reveals on the contrary that the subject matters of experience are things directly enjoyed, suffered, and used before they are things cognized.[22] However, Dewey does argue that there is at least implicit in all experience in the vital sense of that term a certain cognitive element. This he explains by noting that experience involves the combination and conscious connection of action and undergoing. "It is not experience when a child merely sticks his finger into a flame; it is experience when the movement is connected with the pain which he undergoes in consequence. Henceforth the sticking of the finger into flame *means* a burn. Being burned is a mere physical change, like the burning of a stick of wood, if it is not perceived as a consequence of some other action."[23] Experience as Dewey uses this term refers to a process of interaction in which there is a perception of the connections between what we do and what we suffer and enjoy as a consequence. To become aware of connections, interrelations between things, is to awaken to the meaning of things. Experience by definition has, then, a certain educative quality. Even in its primary phase ongoing experience is a cumulative learning-process facilitating adaptation. Dewey's definition of experience is consistent with the common usage of this term in such statements as "he is very young and lacks experience" or "her travels have been a source of valuable experience." Here experience is associated with a kind of practical learning.

Primary experience, which is not predominantly cognitive, is transformed into secondary experience becoming cognitive in quality when the search for knowledge becomes pronounced. Conceiving of primary experience as a process of action-undergoing in an organism that must adjust to and reconstruct its environment in order to survive, it is understandable why discrimination is made in experience between subject and object and the origin and function of secondary experience becomes clear. Experience alternates between settled situations, in which there is harmony with the environment and a sense of well-being, and problematic situations which generate dissatisfaction, anxiety, and desire. Reflection and the quest for knowledge arise when the self in the course of the action-undergoing that constitutes primary experience encounters disharmony with its environment or suffers certain problems. The basic function of thinking is increased power of prediction and control, making it possible to expand and better the subject matters of experience. The brain is first and foremost an organ of adaptive response. Dewey argues that this Darwinian outlook is confirmed by the findings of cultural anthropology.[24] He further explains that the understanding of connections developed in everyday experience is limited. The method of trial and error may lead to recognition that a connection exists between certain actions and certain consequences, but it does not understand how they are connected.[25] Reflection, or thinking, is a method of experience by which regulated inquiry is conducted into conditions and consequences, causes and effects, and the cognitive element in primary experience is made explicit. According to Dewey, this process is perfected in the method of the experimental sciences. Experimental science is a highly refined version of the action-undergoing that constitutes all experience. Likewise, authentic education is identical with the process of experience, especially experience that has become genuinely experimental.

It remains in this discussion to clarify the relation of reason and experience. Dewey's Darwinian approach has no use for a philosophical rationalism that understands reason as a faculty which operates outside and beyond the reach of experience and which is a power of direct insight into self-evident truths. Reason is to be identified with experimental intelligence, and Dewey prefers to use the term intelligence rather than reason in order to differentiate his position from that of the rationalists. Reason or intelligence is developed within the human being as a natural power with the function of guiding and improving the quality of the process of action-undergoing which is life-experience.

It is also noteworthy that Dewey, having rejected the mechanistic psychology of British empiricism, finds no need for a set of super-empirical epistemological categories to connect and synthesize the elements of experience such as one finds in Kantian rationalism. First, experience is not made up of unconnected atomic elements. Second, experience includes within itself biological and social principles of connection and organization. Experience is synthesized by natural factors governing the relations of the human organism to nature and society. These factors, which include language and the beliefs and values of society, are developed in and through the process of action-undergoing. As a naturalist Dewey rejects the neo-Hegelian notion that experience as a whole is governed by a preestablished organic unity, but he does affirm that the organizing factors in experience may periodically lead to moments of deep harmony between the self and its world satisfying the human longing for truth, beauty, and goodness.[26]

In Dewey's naturalistic philosophy, experience is, then, a biological and social process of interaction or action-undergoing between the self and its world. It is *of* as well as *in* nature. It knows no radical dualism of subject and object. In its original and primary form, it is not cognitive in quality, but it may become reflective and intelligent. So defined, experience is inclusive of all that is involved in human culture including the realization of and quest for values, ideals. It is with this idea of experience that Dewey approached the task of an empirical investigation of the generic traits of nature and developed his empirical theory of moral valuation.

The Attack on Transcendentalism

During the Chicago years Dewey became convinced that supernaturalism and transcendentalism, which include classical and modern forms of philosophical idealism and all traditional theology, are inconsistent with the spirit and substance of the new naturalistic worldview toward which he was moving, guided by his own faith in experience and the empirical method of inquiry. Throughout his years at Columbia University he, therefore, kept up a sustained attack against the ideas of the supernatural and transcendental. It is useful to consider his criticisms of these ideas before going on to the idea of reality that he proposed as an alternative to these conceptions.

Dewey rejects the idea of the supernatural because he finds it inconsistent with the scientific attitude. He adopts the view of the scientific investigator whose experimental inquiries are conducted on the assumptions that there is one world, the world of nature explored by scientific observation and reason, and that all observable events are interrelated with other events in this one world and can be explained accordingly by use of an empirical method. The idea of the supernatural is untenable in this outlook because "the supernatural signifies precisely that which lies beyond experience"—and nature.[27] Neither science nor philosophy, of course, can conclusively prove that there is no supernatural realm. Science and an empirical philosophy can only try to demonstrate that all events in nature can be fully explained naturalistically. Of this Dewey is convinced in the light of the success of scientific inquiry, and he contends that there is nothing in experience—whether it be a supposed miracle or some kind of personal intellectual, moral, religious, or mystical experience—which provides intellectual justification for belief in a supernatural world. Whatever is experienced has a naturalistic explanation even though it may not yet have been discovered. Dewey's extensive readings in the rapidly developing science of anthropology led him to draw the conclusion that the idea of supernatural forces and beings is a projection of the human imagination which has its origins in ignorance, fear, and the need for security and assurance.[28]

The transcendental realm of the philosophers is in Dewey's judgment originally and basically just a rationalized version of the supernatural realm of religion. He finds it to be conceived as a realm lying beyond experience and nature which is apprehended by pure thought alone. He rejects it as an illusion created by the philosophical imagination under the influence of anxiety and a desire for a metaphysical support for social values. Beyond the charge that the idea of a transcendental realm is unempirical, he presents a variety of arguments in opposition to it. These arguments are primarily directed against the classical philosophical tradition and nineteenth-century idealism, and they tend to focus on the idea of the inherent unity of the ideal and the real, which Dewey views as the central notion involved in philosophic conceptions of God, the absolute, the universal mind, and a transcendental realm of values.[29]

For example, in his later works he frequently points out certain dialectical contradictions involved in the idea of the absolute or the universal mind of the idealists, and his comments are reminiscent of his critique of Spinoza in 1884 and of T.H. Green in the 1890s. For example, regarding the philosopher's absolute, he writes in *Experience and Nature:*

> Although absolute, eternal, all-comprehensive, and pervasively integrated into a whole so logically perfect that no separate patterns, to say nothing of seams and holes, can exist in it, it proceeds to play a tragic joke upon itself—for there is nothing else to be fooled—by

appearing in a queer combination of rags and glittering gew-gaws, in the garb of the temporal, partial and conflicting things, mental as well as physical, of ordinary experience.[30]

Dewey elaborates on his point in *The Quest for Certainty* with direct reference to the idea of the unity of the ideal and the actual:

> The assumption of the antecedent inherent identity of actual and ideal has generated problems which have not been solved. It is the source of the problem of evil; of evil not merely in the moral sense, but in that of the existence of defect and aberration, of uncertainty and error, of all deviation from the perfect. If the universe is in itself ideal, why is there so much in our experience of it which is so thoroughly unideal? Attempts to answer this question have always been compelled to introduce lapse from perfect Being:—some kind of fall to which is due the distinction between noumena and phenomena, things as they really are and as they seem to be. There are many versions of this doctrine. The simplest, though not the one which has most commended itself to many philosophers, is the idea of the "fall of man," a fall which, in the words of Cardinal Newman, has implicated all creation in an aboriginal catastrophe. I am not concerned to discuss them and their respective weaknesses and strengths. It is enough to note that the philosophies which go by the name of Idealism are attempts to prove by one method or another, cosmological, ontological or epistemological, that the Real and the Ideal are one, while at the same time they introduce qualifying additions to explain why after all they are not one.[31]

Here is another example of Dewey trying to resolve a traditional philosophical problem by altering the assumptions which create the problem. In this case Dewey's objections reveal his discomfort with the kind of paradoxes that are characteristic of traditional religious belief.

Another mode of attack involves the subjection of transcendental philosophies and theologies to a genetic method of analysis. Dewey tries to show that the ideas of a transcendent, eternal, immutable, perfectly good realm of absolute truth and pure being do not arise out of some insight of pure thought, but rather these ideas are imaginative creations generated under the pressure of various social interests and emotional needs. All the ideas pertaining to the supernatural and transcendental developed by religion and philosophy may be traced back to factors at work in experience and nature, argues Dewey: "The most fantastic views ever entertained by superstitious people had some basis in experienced fact; they can be explained by one who knows enough about them and about the conditions under which they were formed." In *Reconstruction in Philosophy* (1920), Dewey points out that a genetic analysis of the great metaphysical systems in the West discloses that they basically attempt to give support and justification to various social values even though their authors have not been fully conscious of this fact. "Instead of the disputes of rivals about the nature of reality, we have the scene of human clash of social purpose and aspiration. Instead of impossible attempts to transcend experience, we have the significant record of the efforts of men to formulate the things of experience to which they are most deeply and passionately attached."[32] For example, philosophic theories about the relations of the individual and the universal are in the final analysis attempts to justify some theory of the relation of the individual and society, and in a feudal society, God is depicted as a monarch, and reality is conceived to have a hierarchical structure.

In *The Quest for Certainty,* Dewey explains that the philosophers in the classical tradition, anxious about the transitoriness of all goods enjoyed in experience and about the uncertainties involved in all practical attempts to make cherished values secure in existence, have been involved in "a quest for a certainty which shall be absolute and unshakeable." "The quest for certainty is a quest for a peace which is assured, an object which is unqualified by risk and the shadow of fear which action casts."[33] In other words, philosophers have sought a safe haven for prized social values free from the instabilities and hazards of temporal existence. Inspired by the discovery of mathematics, which suggests the idea of a realm of eternal truth that may be entered by pure thought, the philosophers have tried to use reason to demonstrate that there is a realm of pure being, permanence, absolute unity, and perfect goodness beyond the change, instability, disharmony, and evils of the world, and that this eternal realm is identical with the highest values of their society. Absolute certainty about the identity of the ideal and the real is, then, to be acquired by pure knowing alone, as distinct from social action, and this has been the goal of most western philosophy. For "deliverance by means of rites and cults," which primitive men and women used to secure the favor of the supernatural powers that they imagined control their destiny, the philosopher substitutes "deliverance through reason."[34] Philosophy thus tries to idealize the world through pure reason, and has transformed the supernatural world of the gods into a transcendent realm of pure being and absolute truth toward this end. In making these arguments against supernaturalism and transcendentalism, Dewey is quite aware that a knowledge of the origins of an idea does not settle the question of its truth, but it is his hope that his genetic analysis will weaken interest in transcendentalism and encourage interest in a new humanistic naturalism.

Dewey offers yet another argument which takes us to the major reasons why he personally lost interest in and rejected transcendentalism as he developed the conscience and concerns of a democratic social reformer. The gist of the argument, which is a pragmatic one introduced in his 1910 dialogue "Is Nature Good?," is as follows. The philosophy and worldview of a society should provide it with a view of the nature of things and with the guidance necessary to make progress in solving the most fundamental and urgent human problem, which is the reconstruction of social conditions so that the values of health, love, friendship, productive employment, communication between peoples, art, science, and recreation can be shared and enjoyed by all. The quest for assurance and certainty regarding the reality of God and the identity of the ideal and the real, which is the heart of the transcendentalists' agenda, is of no practical value in solving this problem and often serves as an obstacle. Therefore, transcendentalism should be abandoned and replaced with a new naturalistic humanism which develops and supports the attitudes and instrumentalities necessary to social progress.

Dewey describes transcendentalism as a philosophy that seeks "wholesale justification" of life in all its aspects, evil as well as good. "It turns thought to the business of finding a wholesale transcendent remedy for the one and guarantee for the other." As a result, it gets absorbed in questions about the absolute origin of things—some inclusive first cause—and about some absolute final goal of the universe. It assumes that life and the values that are encountered in and through common experience are ultimately meaningless unless the task of wholesale justification can be accomplished. Dewey's objection is that this entire enterprise is misguided, for it does nothing to improve actual social conditions. "Were it a thousand times dialectically demonstrated that life as a whole is regulated by a transcendent principle to a final inclusive goal, nonetheless truth and error, health and disease, good and evil, hope and fear in the concrete, would remain just what and where they now are. To improve our education, to ameliorate our manners, to advance our politics, we must have recourse to specific conditions of generation."[35]

Moreover, transcendentalism is not only irrelevant to the problems of social reconstruction, it actually frustrates efforts in this direction by encouraging otherworldliness, laziness, and social irresponsibility, the feeling of being on what James calls a "moral holiday."[36] Transcendental theories about the moral good, God, and the absolute become for theologians and philosophers "a refuge, an asylum for contemplation or a theme for dialectical elaboration, instead of an ideal to inspire and guide conduct."[37] Thus transcendentalism and supernaturalism have had the effect of "distracting attention and diverting energy" from important social problems and tasks. Dewey argues: "History is testimony to this fact. Men have never fully used the powers they possess to advance the good in life, because they have waited upon some power external to themselves and to nature to do the work they are responsible for doing. Dependence upon an external power is the counterpart of surrender of human endeavor."[38] In the light of the hazardous nature of existence, the preoccupation of religion and philosophy in earlier ages with a transcendent God or metaphysical absolute is understandable, but given the rapid modern development of science and technology Dewey finds it no longer justified.[39] Through applications of the experimental method the possibilities for the amelioration of social ills have greatly increased. However, supernaturalism and transcendentalism have relied upon "means and methods that lie outside the natural and social world" rather than upon the scientific method for which they have little respect when it comes to moral and social affairs. As a consequence they have "operated to prevent the application of scientific methods

in the whole field of human and social subject matter," and have
"thereby prevented science from completing its career and fulfilling
its constructive potentialities...."[40]

Speaking from his humanistic perspective Dewey further explains
his objection to the attitude fostered by supernaturalism and transcendentalism:

> Natural relations, of husband and wife, of parent and child, friend
> and friend, neighbor and neighbor, of fellow workers in industry,
> science and art, are neglected, passed over, not developed for all that
> is in them. They are, moreover, not merely depreciated. They have
> been regarded as dangerous rivals of higher values; as offering temp-
> tations to be resisted; as usurpations by flesh of the authority of the
> spirit; as revolts of the human against the divine.[41]

Pursuing this theme Dewey summarizes his major criticisms as
follows.

> The most serious indictment to be brought against non-empirical phi-
> losophies is that they have cast a cloud over the things of ordinary ex-
> perience.... They have discredited them at large. In casting aspersion
> upon the things of everyday experience, things of action and affection
> and social intercourse, they have done something worse than fail to
> give these affairs the intelligent direction they so much need.... The
> serious matter is that philosophies have denied that common experi-
> ence is capable of developing from within itself methods which will
> secure direction for itself and will create inherent standards of judg-
> ment and value. No one knows how many of the evils and deficiencies
> that are pointed to as reasons for flight from experience are themselves
> due to the disregard of experience shown by those peculiarly reflective.
> ... The transcendental philosopher has probably done more than the
> professed sensualist and materialist to obscure the potentialities of
> daily experience for joy and for self-regulation.[42]

This harsh criticism reflects Dewey's strong belief in the possibility of
using the experimental method to develop a sound empirical method
of moral valuation and guidance, which would meet the greatest
need of contemporary western society.

The high point of the liberal faith in science and social progress
was the Progressive Era prior to World War I. The war, and then

the Great Depression, shook this faith and a reaction began to set in. With the advent of World War II, the loss of liberal optimism became pronounced, and democratic liberalism, faith in science, and naturalism came under heavy attack, especially from neo-orthodox theologians like Reinhold Niebuhr. In response, Dewey defended his values in essays like "Anti-Naturalism in Extremis" (1942) with renewed and aggressive attacks on supernaturalism and transcendentalism. For example, he argues that supernaturalism and transcendentalism have historically identified themselves with belief in ultimate and immutable truths, which are viewed as the only sure foundation for the moral life and social order, and insofar as they have been characterized by such moral absolutism they have involved an undemocratic tendency toward dogmatism, authoritarianism, and fanaticism. Dewey finds this tendency especially manifest in the case of religious supernaturalism. He notes "that conflict between truths claiming ultimate and complete authority is the most fundamental kind of discord that can exist," and that "religions in the degree in which they have depended upon the supernatural have been, as history demonstrates, the source of violent conflict, and destructive of basic human values...."[43] Dewey concedes that, in spite of their belief in ultimate and final truths, modern philosophical transcendentalism has as a result of liberal influences not displayed the kind of fanaticism evidenced by theological supernaturalism, "but from the standpoint of logic, it must be said that their failure to do so is more creditable to their hearts than to their heads."[44] In other words, Dewey agrees with Feuerbach's assertion that there is a malignant principle at work in traditional theism and supernaturalism. He sees progress toward democracy and amicable cooperation between the peoples of the world as requiring the abandonment of moral absolutism and the supernaturalism and transcendentalism that have nurtured it.

In short, transcendentalism offers no real solution to the problem of the ideal and the real. It does not even put the problem correctly. As noted, Dewey acknowledges that one qualification must be made. A philosophy of wholesale justification offers the tender-minded the consolation that they crave. However, Dewey finds such a craving a childish need that should be outgrown. When this, together with the futility of transcendentalism in contrast with the efficacy of other approaches, is recognized, Dewey believes that interest in this kind of philosophy and the problems it makes central will fade. "In fact," writes Dewey, "intellectual progress usually occurs through sheer abandonment of questions together with both the alternatives they assume—an abandonment that results from their decreasing vitality and a change of urgent interest. We do not solve them: we get over them."[45]

Dewey's attack on transcendentalism is carried out in an effort to clear away the beliefs and attitudes from the past that obstruct and frustrate development of respect for and reliance upon experience, practical intelligence, and the possibilities for good that are resident in this world. It is part of his lifelong hostility to dualisms. The supernatural and transcendental, in Dewey's view, are inherently dualistic notions which by definition involve the idea of something that exists beyond nature and the reach of experience and which involve the setting up, over against experience, of other authorities and methods in matters of belief such as special historical revelations, dogmas, and pure reason. Dewey's genetic analysis (which points up the social origins and significance of past metaphysical systems) is illuminating, and like Marx he has identified a real tension that exists between a transcendental worldview and the interests of social reform. With Feuerbach, he has correctly identified a contradiction that often exists between moral absolutism and supernaturalism on the one hand, and an ethic of universal love and toleration on the other.

Dewey's views on supernaturalism and transcendentalism were not universally accepted by other leading American philosophical pragmatists. For example, William James embraced a form of radical empiricism and emphasized the central importance of practical action and the moral life, but he did not believe that empiricism and transcendentalism were irreconcilably opposed. James argued that certain mystical experiences supply empirical evidence that points to the possibility of a supernatural spiritual dimension of reality, and he allowed for the possibility of a pragmatic philosophical defense of the idea.[46] In other words, James and Dewey disagreed on the way in which certain experiences may be interpreted and the way certain religious ideas function in experience. C.S. Peirce also affirmed a belief in the supernatural, but he did not think that his pragmatic logic or science could demonstrate the reality of the supernatural. Rather, on this question he appealed to the sentiments of the heart in the tradition of American Transcendentalism.[47] Dewey often wrote as if no educated twentieth-century man or woman who understood the scientific method and trusted in experience could responsibly give credence to the idea of the transcendental, but the examples of James and Peirce indicate that the case is not so simple as Dewey liked to imagine. Dewey was not unaware of these questions, and in a later chapter we will return to this issue.

The chief argument Dewey offers in defense of his naturalistic outlook is not a negative critique of transcendentalism, but the good sense of his own alternative vision. To his constructive thought as an empirical naturalist attention must now be turned.

The Metaphysics of a New Evolutionary Naturalism

Dewey's career as a philosopher roughly spans the period of the great post-Darwinian evolutionary philosophies, and his own naturalistic metaphysics and theory of nature should be viewed in this context. It is worth recalling the historical situation. The single most influential idea affecting philosophy and its view of the universe in the nineteenth and early twentieth centuries was the idea of evolution. Decades before the idea was adopted by biologists, it was advanced by historians and social thinkers like Condorcet and Comte and by cosmic philosophers like Schelling and Hegel, and then finally by scientists beginning with Darwin. After Darwin, the dominant tendency among nineteenth-century philosophers was to use evolutionary theory as the key to an explanation of the universe which they set forth in some new up-to-date cosmic evolutionary philosophy. There were many variations on this theme. Some, like the neo-Hegelians, used evolution to defend traditional religious values, while others rejected the theological tradition. However, more often than not, those who rejected traditional religious values in the name of the new science ended up using evolution to justify a new faith in historical progress as in the case of Marx or Herbert Spencer. At first, cosmic evolution was interpreted in either mechanistic terms or along idealistic lines such as one finds in the thought of young Dewey. The mechanistic theory was abandoned in the face of new discoveries in the area of mutations and genetics, leading in the early twentieth century to the development of Henri Bergson's theory of "creative evolution" and William James' evolutionary speculations. This approach in turn suffered criticism at the hands of the philosophers of mathematical physics, who were led by Bertrand Russell, with the result that a new group of evolutionary philosophies appeared on the scene. Even though these philosophies were quite different in many respects, each in one form or another put emphasis on the idea of emergent evolution, that is, the notion that the evolutionary process involves genuine novelties, qualitative changes, and creativity. The thinking of the emergent evolution philosophers matured in the 1920s, finding expression in Samuel Alexander's *Space, Time and Deity* (1920), Roy Wood Sellars' *Evolutionary Naturalism* (1921), Conway Lloyd Morgan's *Emergent Evolution* (1923), and Alfred North Whitehead's *Process and Reality* (1929). Dewey's *Experience and Nature* (1925) is to be seen as part of this wider intellectual movement which centered in England and America.[48]

Before describing the evolutionary view of nature contained in Dewey's empirical and naturalistic metaphysics, it is important to clarify his understanding of the proper task of metaphysics. As an empirical enterprise it is not concerned with any matter beyond experience and nature. It is also not concerned with questions about the origin and causation of things, which are properly the business of the various sciences. Adopting the approach to metaphysics of an Aristotelian naturalism, he argued that the task of metaphysics is continuous with and complementary to the empirical inquiries of the different sciences, but it goes beyond the work done by any one specific science. In short, its task is to reflect on the diverse subject matters investigated by all the various sciences and to identify those characteristics of things which are universal and irreducible.[49] Metaphysics is concerned solely with the "detection and description of the generic traits of existence," that is, "the generic traits of existences of all kinds."[50] As an empirical undertaking metaphysics asks what experience discloses about the general or common features of the great diversity of experienced things. All of human experience, which is in as well as of nature, is relevant to understanding the metaphysical character of nature, argues Dewey: "This is the extent and method of my 'metaphysics':—the large and constant features of human sufferings, enjoyments, trials, failures and successes together with the institutions of art, science, technology, politics, and religion which mark them, communicate genuine features of the world within which man lives."[51] In short, Dewey's empirical naturalism is a humanistic naturalism. From Dewey's point of view, the practical value of such an empirical and naturalistic metaphysics is that it describes the general nature of the world in which human beings exist, and it can be used to clarify the general character of the problems human beings confront when they seek to idealize the world.

The conception of the world that Dewey arrived at in his naturalistic metaphysics is a radical departure from classical, medieval, Newtonian, and idealist views. It involves the complete rejection of supernaturalism, transcendentalism, and "block universe" monism, but it is equally opposed to a thoroughgoing mechanistic materialism and an extreme atomistic pluralism. Indeed, Dewey seems much concerned to find a middle way between the extremes of materialism and spiritualism, or what James called a tough-minded and tender-minded view of reality. In seeking to formulate a modern idea of nature that avoids these extremes, Dewey emphasized the ideas of the universality of change, infinite pluralism, the intermixture of contingency and necessity, interaction, continuity, qualitative individuality, and the immanence of values and ideals in nature.

The most fundamental idea in Dewey's naturalistic metaphysics is the notion that each and every thing in the universe is characterized by process, change. This for him is the most basic meaning of the idea of evolution. Dewey is a process philosopher who, like Bergson, James, and Whitehead, identifies the real with becoming rather than with being (i.e., something static or fixed). He repeatedly notes that in traditional Western philosophy and religion, right up into the nineteenth and twentieth centuries, the dominant tendency has been to exalt the fixed and permanent and to depreciate the changing. The modern scientific revolution gradually altered this attitude. First, during the sixteenth, seventeenth, and eighteenth centuries astronomy, physics, and chemistry shifted their attention from fixed final causes and essences to efficient causes and processes of change and in time doubt was thrown on the very existence of final causes. Darwin firmly established this approach in biology and opened the door to its adoption by the other life sciences, including sociology, politics, and morals by demonstrating that biological species come to be and pass away.[52] Evolutionary theory in its various forms pointed to the universality of change in the universe, and twentieth-century physics has confirmed the idea, banishing the remnants of the older ways of thinking that were associated with Newtonian physics.

With these developments in mind Dewey writes that "the outstanding fact in all branches of natural science is that to exist is to be in process, in change."[53] Dewey might more correctly have said that to exist is to *be* process or a process of change. The point is that there are no unchanging entities in the universe. There are no Platonic essences or Aristotelian final causes, and there are no immutable substances underlying the processes of change observed by the sciences. Natural science has been "forced by its own development to abandon the assumption of fixity and to recognize that what for it is actually 'universal' is *process*."[54] Dewey notes that even "the fixed and unchanging being of the Democritean atom is now reported by inquirers to possess some of the traits of his non-being, and to embody a temporary equilibrium in the economy of nature's compromises and adjustments." He sums up his position with the assertion that "every existence is an event." For him nature is a "complex of events."[55]

Dewey does not deny that the rate of change at work in some existences is so slow or rhythmic as to function relative to other existences as something permanent and stable. However, this is only a relative and functional distinction. He further points out:

> The laws in which the modern man of science is interested are laws of motion, of generation and consequence. He speaks of law where the ancients spoke of kind and essence, because what he wants is a correlation of changes, an ability to detect one change occurring in correspondence with another. He does not try to define and delimit something remaining constant in change. He tries to describe a constant order of change.[56]

All things are processes changing at varying rates, and the slower and more regular processes of change constitute the structures found in nature.

As a follower of Hegel and a dynamic idealist, Dewey had embraced a philosophy that tries to overcome a radical dualism of natural and supernatural, and that identifies reality with process. However, Dewey argues that the emphasis on change in Hegel and other evolutionary philosophers such as Herbert Spencer and Henri Bergson is not sufficiently radical. In the final analysis they subordinate change to what is fixed and finished.

> They have deified change by making it universal, regular, sure.... Flux is made something to revere, something profoundly akin to what is best within ourselves, will and creative energy. It is not, as it is in experience, a call to effort, a challenge to investigation, a potential doom of disaster and death.[57]

As a naturalist Dewey abandons any idea of a cosmic purpose, a preestablished harmony, or absolute mind governing all things.

> A thoroughgoing evolution must by the nature of the case abolish all fixed limits, beginnings, origins, forces, laws, gods. If there is evolution, all these also evolve, and are what they are as points of origin and of distinction relative to some special portion of evolution. They are to be defined in terms of the process, the process that now and always is, not the process in terms of them.[58]

Such comments make Dewey one of the most thoroughgoing and radical twentieth-century process philosophers.

The universality of change, the absence of fixed essences, and the open-ended nature of the processes of change in the world lead Dewey to an idea of the world that James had suggested in the title of his 1908 Hibbert Lectures at Oxford, *A Pluralistic Universe.* "The further I go the more I see that I have become a confirmed infinite pluralist. I simply can't get monism with any reality," writes Dewey in 1915 to a correspondent.[59] The world of classical, medieval, and much modern philosophy has been "a closed world, a world consisting internally of a limited number of fixed forms, and having definite boundaries externally." In contrast to this finite universe, the world opening up before modern scientific investigation is infinite in space, time, complexity, and internal variety of forms:

> Instead of a closed universe, science now presents us with one infinite in space and time, having no limits here or there, at this end, so to

speak or at that, and as infinitely complex in internal structure as it is infinite in extent. Hence it is also an open world, an infinitely variegated one, a world which in the old sense can hardly be called a universe at all; so multiplex and far-reaching that it cannot be summed up and grasped in any one formula.[60]

"No matter what idealists and optimists say, the energy of the world, the number of forces at disposal, is plural, not unified. There are different centers of force and they go their ways independently. They come into conflict; they clash."[61] In short, we live in a radically open universe in which infinite plurality is a characteristic of existences in nature.

Implicit in Dewey's idea of an open changing world is the idea that the processes of nature are genuinely creative. In the prescientific western idea of nature, the number of changes going on in nature is understood to be limited and to operate within fixed limits governed by a set number of final causes. Darwinian evolution alters this view with its assertion that mutations from existing species issue in the emergence of new species. Nature is pregnant with "the possibility of novelty, of invention, of radical deviation."[62] The emergence of novelties in nature is one of many reasons why Dewey rejects a doctrine of complete determinism and insists that there is contingency in nature. Indeed, he lists contingency among the generic traits of existence.

Dewey's discussion of contingency in the second chapter of *Experience and Nature* fails to produce an entirely clear understanding of just what he means by the idea.[63] However, it seems that a key to the central thrust of his thinking on this subject may be found in *The Quest for Certainty* where he contrasts the contingent with the necessary and explains that a world without contingency would be "only a block universe, either something ended and admitting of no change, or else a predestined march of events."[64] It follows that a world characterized by contingency as well as necessity is a changing world in which the processes of change are not entirely predetermined as to their outcomes. Such is our world according to Dewey:

We live in a world which is an impressive and irresistible mixture of sufficiencies, tight completeness, order, recurrences which make possible prediction and control, and singularities, ambiguities, uncertain possibilities, processes going on to consequences as yet indeterminate.[65]

In making such statements Dewey has at least two ideas of contingency in mind. First, he takes the position that there is that in nature which is inherently unpredictable and uncontrollable. He has in mind here the biological phenomenon of mutations which advance evolution, and he also finds support for this idea in Heisenberg's principle of indeterminacy which contradicts Newtonian mathematical and mechanistic determinism.[66] In line with this, modern physics conceives of its laws as statistical averages rather than exact descriptions of the structure and behavior of individual things, and hence scientific predictions possess a high degree of probability but not absolute certainty. "No mechanically exact science of an individual is possible. An individual is a history unique in character," writes Dewey.[67]

Second, the idea of contingency means to Dewey something less dramatic but yet of great significance, which is that we live in a world which is incomplete, unfinished, open and in which human knowledge and choice can and do make a difference in the outcome of various situations. This view of contingency does not necessarily contradict the idea that all occurrences in nature are causally determined. It merely asserts that situations contain various alternative possibilities within them depending upon the nature of their interactions with other factors, and human choice can determine these interactions. The work of the experimental scientist is a prime example. When Dewey asserts that we live in "a world which is not finished and which has not consistently made up its mind where it is going and what it is going to do," he is pointing to the fact that the future is open and by the exercise of the power of decision human beings can determine the outcome of processes "as yet indeterminate."[68] In short, a world in which contingency in this sense is a generic trait of existence is a world in which human beings have the freedom to shape the future, and no idea is more fundamental to Dewey's instrumentalist attitude toward the world than this. Freedom, in his mind, means precisely the power to choose between alternative possibilities and to realize chosen objectives. "Contingency is a necessary although not, in a mathematical phrase, a sufficient condition of freedom," contends Dewey.[69] By pursuing this point it is possible to further clarify his understanding of the role of contingency in nature and its significance for the human adventure.

A world in which there are "singularities, ambiguities, uncertain possibilities" is a world in which existence is problematic, hazardous, perilous. Therefore, Dewey asserts that "we are free in the degree in which we act knowing what we are about."[70] Knowing, thinking, is itself a natural event which arises in response to the hazardous and problematic nature of the world. It seeks to apprehend what is necessary, ordered, and recurrent in nature so as to overcome the dangers and difficulties generated by the factor of contingency. Through an experimental knowledge of "the recurrent and stable, of facts and laws," it is possible for human intelligence to minimize the negative effect of the unpredictable and uncontrollable in nature and to regulate and direct the consequences of processes as yet indeterminate."[71] With such knowledge, choice becomes intelligence and real freedom is achieved. In summary, experience discloses that neither contingency nor necessity are exclusive characteristics of nature. Nature is neither a scene of complete chaos and disorder nor "a block universe." In the things of nature, contingency and necessity are intermixed. For human beings this fundamental characteristic of existence threatens trouble, provokes reflection, provides opportunity for freedom of choice, and demands the intelligent administration of the unfinished processes of nature which it makes possible.

Both individuality and interaction (interconnection) are also generic traits of natural existences in Dewey's metaphysics. Every existence exhibits a certain "irreducible uniqueness," "ultimate singularity," and "centeredness," and it sets up "qualitative and intrinsic boundaries" demarcating itself from its environment. This trait of singularity will be further discussed shortly in connection with Dewey's idea of qualitative immediacy. In addition to its singularity "every existence ... has affinities and active outreachings for connection and intimate union. It is an energy of attraction, expansion and supplementation." Dewey further comments: "Everything that exists in as far as it is known and knowable is in interaction with other things. It is associated, as well as solitary, single. The catching up of human individuals into association is thus no new and unprecedented fact; it is a manifestation of a commonplace of existence."[72] Every existence "includes within itself a continuum of relations or interactions brought to a focus." It is involved in "a continuity of interactions and changes" that extends from the past and stretches into the future.[73] This aspect of things is explored by scientific knowledge, which seeks to formulate the relations and causal mechanisms that are the conditions of the appearance of things and provide nature with its stability and regularities. While Dewey's naturalistic doctrine of interaction involves rejection of an extreme atomistic pluralism, it does not mean acceptance of the neo-Hegelian idea of the world as an organic unity. He notes that "while there is no isolated occurrence in nature, yet interaction and connection are not wholesale and homogeneous," and he speaks of "the miscellaneous and uncoordinated plurals of our actual world."[74] Here again one encounters the notion that there is something unfinished, incomplete, and problematic about the universe.

Dewey employs the ideas of interaction and continuity to deny any radical dualism between the kinds of existences that emerge in nature such as material entities and minds. Each of the events in nature is in interaction with other events, and they form what Dewey calls "fields of interaction." According to the complexity of the interactions involved, these fields of interaction have different general properties and consequences. Matter and mind properly understood are not radically distinct, fixed substances but terms referring to the traits of differing fields of interaction. Dewey argues that in general, three plateaus of such fields may be discriminated: matter, life, and mind. "The distinction between physical, psycho-physical and mental is . . . one of levels of increasing complexity and intimacy of interaction among natural events." Matter, or the physical, refers to that field of interactions which is described by physics in mathematical and mechanical terms. Life, or the psychophysical, refers to a more complex organization and interaction of the same energies at work on the level of matter, and biology gives an account of its characteristics. About the third level of interaction, mind, Dewey writes: "As life is a character of events in a peculiar condition of organization, and 'feeling' is a quality of life-forms marked by complexly mobile and discriminating responses, so 'mind' is an added property assumed by a feeling creature, when it reaches that organized interaction with other living creatures which is language, communication." There are significant differences between matter, life, and mind, but there is also continuity and no gulf or radical break between them. Dewey rejects any form of reductionism whether it be that of materialists or spiritualists, which conceives one level of interaction as more real than another. His naturalism is not, therefore, properly characterized as a form of materialism any more than it is a form of spiritualistic idealism. It is also noteworthy that Dewey avoids any radical dualism of body and mind. He often speaks of "the body-mind," emphasizing that as far as the empirical evidence is concerned intelligence and mind do not exist apart from the body. The appearance of the kind of activity that one finds in human life is simply due to a more complex organization of the same energies at work in animal life, and it has a naturalistic explanation.[75]

The Ideal and the Real

The most important aspect of Dewey's naturalistic metaphysics centers on the question of the status of purposes and values in nature. Dewey states the problem succinctly: "How is science to be accepted and yet the realm of values to be conserved?" The difficulty arises with the notion that the new science requires rejection of the classical and medieval doctrine of teleology and conceives the objectively real world of nature as a conglomerate of colorless, soundless, scentless, tasteless particles of dead matter moving about mechanically according to mathematical law without purpose or meaning. It is further concluded that this view confines to human consciousness all purposes, values, and the directly perceived qualities of events that make the world pleasurable, beautiful, and generally worthwhile. So conceived, a great gulf separates human consciousness and nature, which becomes an alien world, and the appearance of consciousness itself becomes inexplicable. The result of this interpretation of the meaning of the new science is that modern philosophy has been "dominated by the problem of reconciling the conclusions of natural science with the objective validity of the values by which men live and regulate their conduct." This problem has constituted "the philosophic version of the popular conflict of science and religion."[76] Systems as diverse as Spinoza's pantheism, Kant's dualistic philosophy of moral theism, and Hegel's absolute idealism have all been attempts to resolve the problem in a positive fashion. Dewey finds none of these answers satisfactory, and he traces the source of the difficulty to a misunderstanding of the problem presented by science, that is, a misinterpretation of the nature and significance of scientific knowledge. He seeks to reconcile science and a theory of the objective validity of human values by using his empirical method to construct a doctrine of teleology in nature that occupies a middle ground between classical doctrines and mechanistic materialism.

It is Dewey's contention that the root of the problem of the conflict between science and values lies "in the prior uncritical acceptance of the traditional notion that knowledge has a monopolistic claim to access to reality." Beginning with classical Greek thought, philosophers have assumed that there is a complete correspondence between what is known and what is real. "The doctrine was thus formed that all experience of worth is inherently cognitive; that other modes of experienced objects are to be tested ... universally by reduction to the terms of known objects."[77] Given this assumption it is clear why the new science is conceived to be in conflict with a worldview that asserts the objective reality and enduring meaning of aesthetic, moral, and religious values. If the real is identified with the known, and science is accepted as the prime source of authoritative knowledge, the result is "the denial to nature of the characters which make things lovable and contemptible, beautiful and ugly, adorable and awful"; nature is pictured as "an indifferent, dead mechanism," and human values and ideals become purely subjective phenomena, that is, illusions, appearances, but not realities.[78] Dewey, however, maintains that the assumption of the identity of the known and the real manifests an "arbitrary 'intellectualism' " that is utterly unempirical—he calls it "the great intellectualistic fallacy"—and its acceptance has created what a sound empirical philosophy must regard as an artificial problem.[79] A sound empiricism starts with "no presuppositions save that what is experienced, since it is a manifestation of nature, may and indeed, must be used as testimony of the characteristics of natural events."[80] In the light of this method of analysis, Dewey finds human values to be just as real as the objects of scientific knowledge.

His argument begins with the observation that there are two distinct phases in our experience of things, which correspond to what was earlier described as primary and secondary experience, and these two phases disclose two distinct characteristics of things. In short, empirically all existences have a twofold character. On the one hand every object in experience is characterized by possession of immediately perceived qualities, qualities which are directly suffered and enjoyed. Included among them are the qualities apprehended by the five senses, such as colors, sounds, tastes, etc., and also the qualities of things apprehended by the emotions or feelings, the qualities that render them beautiful, humorous, annoying, fearful, etc. Empirically, argues Dewey, things possess these qualities "immediately and in their own right and behalf."[81] These qualities are not to be viewed, then, as merely subjective impressions mysteriously produced by but unrelated to the true nature of the real object and the natural world. As Dewey explains it:

> Interactions of things with the organism eventuate in objects perceived to be colored and sonorous. They also result in qualities that make the object hateful or delightful. All these qualities, taken as directly perceived or enjoyed, are terminal effects of natural interactions.[82]

In brief, natural objects really possess secondary and emotional qualities in the context of the situation created by the interaction. These qualities are "products of the doings of nature," and as such they should be "for the philosopher what they are for the common man: —real qualities of natural objects." Dewey further points out that each object possesses its own unique individuality or distinctive immediate qualities. "Everything directly experienced is qualitatively unique; it has its own focus about which subject matter is arranged, and this focus never exactly recurs." In this sense nature is characterized by the presence of "qualitatively diverse individualities."[83]

On the other hand, as noted, every qualitatively unique individual is also characterized by interconnection, and it is part of a continuity of interactions with other existences which extends from the past and into the future. In other words, every existence is the consequence of past causal conditions and in turn will function in the future itself as the cause of further occurrences. This aspect of things is not directly and immediately perceived. It is apprehended through reflection, and such reflection is perfected in scientific methods of inquiry. Thus existences become objects of knowledge as well as of direct experience. Dewey actually restricts use of the term "knowledge" to the apprehension of the interrelations of things and causal mechanisms, which he understands to be the substance of scientific knowledge. Knowledge is strictly concerned with how things come to be and with the use or instrumental function of things as causes in their relations with other things.

In further clarifying the nature and significance of the realm of immediate qualities Dewey draws a contrast between what is fundamentally ineffable (unknowable), final, consummatory, and aesthetic in nature with what is knowable and instrumental. Immediate quality, asserts Dewey, is "a direct ineffable presence." "Things in their immediacy are unknown and unknowable. . . . Immediate things may be *pointed to* by words, but not described or defined." Dewey's point is simply that immediate qualities such as the green in the grass or the beauty of a sunset just are what they are directly perceived to be and there is nothing to say about them as such. When reflection enters into the experience of a thing, it is concerned with relations and causal connections. Dewey goes on to point out that when existences are suffered and enjoyed as direct ineffable presences, they possess "a certain ultimacy and finality." Each directly experienced thing is a unique individual, a whole complete in itself, just what it is and nothing else. Describing this character of finality Dewey writes: "In every event there is something obdurate, self-sufficient, wholly immediate, neither a relation nor an element in a relational whole, but terminal and exclusive." This quality of finality is the special mark of aesthetic experience. An object normally termed aesthetic in quality is one which is valued for its immediate quality as an end in itself rather than for its instrumental quality, that is, as a means to some other experience. An object termed aesthetic is viewed as a consummation or fulfillment complete in itself. Stretching the normal use of the term "aesthetic," Dewey argues that all immediately experienced objects have an element of aesthetic quality, for in experience they all possess to some degree this character of finality.[84]

The significance of the realm of immediate quality in Dewey's view is that it contains everything that makes life worthwhile. All that human beings value in things and persons are immediate qualities. "They alone ... are of interest, and they are the cause of our taking interest in other things."[85] Dewey's point is not, of course, that all things possessed of immediate quality are of positive value to humans, but only that all positive values—beauty, compassion, truthfulness, etc.—are to be found among the immediate qualities of things and persons. Anything without valued immediate quality is of interest to human beings only insofar as it functions as an obstacle to or a means to a direct experience of something with positive immediate qualities, that is, insofar as it has a positive or negative instrumental function relative to something final and consummatory in the full sense.

With these ideas in mind Dewey tries to put scientific knowledge in its proper perspective. Things function in experience in a twofold fashion: both as finalities, that is, as sources of immediate enjoyment and suffering, and as instrumentalities to other direct experiences. Science is concerned primarily with the instrumental function of things, which is not to deny that scientific inquiry and knowledge may involve its own immediate satisfaction. Employing his biological perspective, which finds thinking and knowing originally developed by the human race in response to problematic situations, and emphasizing the instrumental function of knowledge, Dewey writes:

> If we start from primary experience, occurring as it does chiefly in modes of action and undergoing, it is easy to see what knowledge contributes—namely, the possibility of intelligent administration of the elements of doing and suffering. We are about something, and it is well to know what we are about, as the common phrase has it ... when there is possibility of control, knowledge is the sole agency of its realization.[86]

Control is possible only to the degree that the causal mechanisms of nature are apprehended, and it is just this aspect of things upon which science focuses. From the point of view of empirical naturalism, then, there is no necessary conflict between science and values.

The office of physical science is to discover those properties and relations of things in virtue of which they are capable of being used as instrumentalities; physical science makes no claim to disclose the inner nature of things but only those connections of things with one another that determine outcomes and hence can be used as means. The intrinsic nature of events is revealed in experience as the immediately felt qualities of things.[87]

Both direct experience and reflective experience disclose real characteristics of things, and, properly understood, scientific knowledge should be viewed as providing the means for making the valued immediate qualities of things enjoyed in direct experience more secure in existence.[88]

The position that Dewey's empirical naturalism adopts on the question of the reality of immediate qualities and science is in line with a commonsense outlook. It is based, however, on the belief that the identification of the real exclusively with the known is empirically unjustified, which is not a matter of common sense. Dewey's rejection of this assumption in the light of the evidence of primary experience has force, but it leaves one wondering in what sense it is possible to know that things have immediate qualities. Dewey's discussion of immediate qualities can also create the impression that he believes that immediate experience is always a sound judge of what is really true, good, and beautiful. This is decidedly not his meaning. Sound judgments in such matters require experimental inquiry, and we will return to this issue.

Dewey's doctrine of natural teleology finds support in his theory of immediate quality. When nature is described as a complex of events, it is understood to be "a scene of incessant beginnings and endings." In this simple, direct sense of the term "end" there are ends, termini, closings of temporal episodes in nature. Dewey further argues that the character of finality in all immediate qualities gives empirical evidence that there are endings, termini, arrests in nature as well as interactions and relations.[89] The very existence of directly perceived qualities in nature points to the fact that the processes of change explored by science have outcomes, conclusions, results. Immediate qualities are the "terminal effects of natural interactions."[90]

In short, there are natural endings in nature, and each such ending is characterized by its own unique immediate quality.

It should be clear at this juncture that Dewey's theory of natural teleology, unlike the classical doctrine, does not suggest that nature is pervaded by purposes or that natural endings necessarily possess positive meaning and value from a human point of view. Dewey accepts the outlook associated with physical science "that nature has no preference for good things over bad; its mills turn out any kind of grist indifferently." In his open universe there is no God or universal mind guiding all processes to fixed ends and ultimately to some supreme good. Intelligent purpose and conscious awareness of good and evil appear in nature only with the emergence of individualized intelligences, and the empirical evidence is that this has occurred only in the human race. Further, in Dewey's natural teleology "being an end may be indifferently an ecstatic culmination, a matter-of-fact consummation, or a deplorable tragedy. Which of these things a closing or terminal object is, has nothing to do with the property of being an end."[91]

At first glance this idea of natural teleology may seem to be of little consequence, but its significance becomes apparent as Dewey uses it to develop a naturalistic theory of the relation of value and nature, of the ideal and the real. All human values are natural ends with immediate qualities. Nature is a scene of many ends in the sense of termini of natural events. Among these many ends some satisfy human needs, become the objects of desire and effort, and are prized as fulfillments. Such are human values and ideals.

In further explaining his theory of the relation of nature and the ideal, Dewey calls attention to the difference between a natural end that is just an ending and a natural end that has become an end-in-view. When an object with a certain immediate quality has been discovered accidentally and spontaneously, as all such objects initially are, and is judged to be a good worthy of planned effort and attainment, it becomes an end-in-view. Ends-in-view are chosen purposes, that is, "aims, things viewed after deliberation as worthy of attainment and as evocative of effort."[92] Only when human intelligences form such ends-in-view is it correct to assert that there are ends in the sense of purposes in nature. Human ideals are ends-in-view, purposes.

These observations lead Dewey to conclude that ideals do exist in nature. There is no gulf separating the ideal and the real, nature and human values. However, he emphasizes that ideals exist in nature as possibilities rather than as actualities. Ideals are possibilities resident in natural events. Such possibilities become ideals when they are apprehended by human intelligence and projected by the human imagination as desired objectives and guides to action. In short, nature is full of ideal possibilities.[93] To apprehend the ideal possibilities of the here and now is to awaken to and enjoy the deeper meaning of the present. Dewey terms the actual realization of an end-in-view or ideal a consummatory experience which is truly a fulfillment. Such consummatory experiences are what make life worthwhile.

The occurrence of consummatory experience leads Dewey to assert that, even though nature is not characterized by the identity or unity of the ideal and the real, there is continuity between the ideal and the actual and "nature ... is idealizable." Unifications of the ideal and the real may be achieved.

> Nature ... lends itself to operations by which it is perfected. The process is not a passive one. Rather nature gives, not always freely but in response to search, means and material by which the values we judge to have supreme quality may be embodied in existence. It depends upon the choice of man whether he employs what nature provides and for what ends he uses it.

The conviction growing out of his empirical theory of nature that the world is idealizable is the ground of the hope and the faith in progress that continued to pervade Dewey's philosophical thinking. Even though he abandoned the metaphysics of philosophical idealism, this conviction enabled him to continue speaking confidently of "an idealism of action."[94]

The way of idealizing the world and the dynamics of consummatory (aesthetic) experience constitute the deepest concern of his instrumentalism, ethics, and democratic humanism, and are also explored in his theory of art. The unifying of the ideal and the real in experience through the work of creative intelligence and imaginative vision is art, argues Dewey. The fine arts are but one outstanding example of art in this general sense. He defines art as any "mode of activity that is charged with meanings capable of immediately enjoyed possession." He further asserts that " 'science' is properly a handmaiden that conducts natural events to this happy issue." In other words, art is intelligent practice that is "inherently and immediately enjoyable." In this fashion Dewey seeks to reconcile art and science, the aesthetic and the practical. "Thought, intelligence, science is the intentional direction of natural events to meanings capable of immediate possession and enjoyment; this direction—which is operative art—is itself a natural event in which nature otherwise partial and incomplete comes fully to itself." "Experience as art" is "the complete culmination of nature."[95] The integration in everyday life of the active and the contemplative, the practical and the aesthetic, the material and the spiritual, the real and the ideal, is the art of the good life and the general objective of Dewey's philosophical explorations.

In summary, Dewey relies upon an empirical method of knowledge that begins with problematical situations in experience and ends with a return to experience for experimental verification. The problem with nonempirical methods from his point of view is that they do not develop ideas which illuminate the meaning of ordinary life and its predicaments, and consequently, they fail to realize "the potentialities of daily experience for joy and self-regulation." Employing an expanded idea of experience and an empirical method of inquiry, Dewey inquires into the metaphysical or generic traits of nature. The result is a radical form of process philosophy that explores a middle way between a despairing atheistic materialism and a sentimental absolute idealism. Dewey's universe is one "which is not finished and which has not consistently made up its mind where it is going," but it is a universe rich in ideal and aesthetic possibilities. It is also a universe in which human beings can claim the freedom to actualize these possibilities, provided they have the courage and make the intellectual and moral effort required. According to Dewey, the deepest consummations enjoyed in experience involve realizations of the beauty and harmony of existence that include a religious quality, and his theory of the continuity of the ideal and the actual provides a foundation for his naturalistic theory of religious experience. His theory of the art of moral valuation and growth and his philosophy of religion are the subject of the following three chapters.

NINE

The Moral Life in an Evolving World

DEWEY'S naturalistic metaphysics lays the groundwork for understanding and appreciating the significance of his theory of moral valuation, which lies at the center of his interests as a philosophical pragmatist or instrumentalist. According to Dewey, human beings live in a changing and open but problematic world, full of possibilities for good and for ill. In such a world human knowledge and choice can make a critical difference. Knowledge, which apprehends the causal connection between things, has an instrumental function and may be used to control the changing world of nature and to guide the interactions that constitute human experience to immediate experiences that are realizations of the ideal possibilities of nature—consummatory experiences in which life finds fulfillment. However, knowledge is incomplete without wisdom—a knowledge of true and false ideals, of what is good and bad. The search for knowledge culminates, therefore, in a search for a method of valuation that can empower human beings to make wise choices and decisions in their efforts to idealize their evolving world.

Dewey endeavored to address this fundamental problem by developing a method of moral valuation consistent with science and democracy and with a process philosophy perspective on nature and the self. Having shown in his metaphysics that there is continuity between the ideal and the real in nature, Dewey's concern to reconcile human values and science culminated with his efforts to formulate an empirical and experimental procedure for making value judgments. Dewey's defense of experimental empiricism in morals is the highest expression of his faith in experience and intelligence. As has been noted, Dewey began work on an experimental method of moral valuation in the early 1890s, and the main outlines of this theory have already been indicated. It remains to spell out the nature and significance of this method in greater detail.

The significance of experimental empiricism in morals is not only that it overcomes the split between science and values; it is also, argues Dewey, an expression of the meaning of democracy understood as an ethical way of life. In "Creative Democracy—The Task Before Us" (1939) Dewey offers the following statement of "the democratic faith in the formal terms of a philosophic position."

> So stated, democracy is belief in the ability of human experience to generate the aims and methods by which further experience will grow in ordered richness. Every other form of moral and social faith rests upon the idea that experience must be subjected at some point or other to some form of external control; to some "authority" alleged to exist outside the processes of experience. . . .[1]

Democracy means a confidence in the capacity of experience to develop its own regulative standards. By giving authority in matters of knowledge, including moral values, to experimental intelligence rather than something external to experience, Dewey contends that it is possible to develop a method of objective moral valuation consistent with the democratic values of individual freedom, public education, open debate, and collective participation. In the method of experimental intelligence he believed that he had found for the democratic moral life a constructive middle way between the extremes of authoritarianism and absolutism on the one hand and subjectivism on the other. Democracy as a way of social life is the expression of a humanized experimentalism. In other words, the ethics of creative democracy are an expression of wide sympathy and a heartfelt concern for the common good guided by experimental empiricism.

Throughout the early decades of the twentieth century Dewey published numerous essays that explore the relation between the logic of experimentalism and the process of making moral value judgments. Essays such as "Logical Conditions of a Scientific Treatment of Morals" (1903) and "Intelligence and Morals" (1908) reveal the directions in which his thought was moving. Dewey's mature reflections on his instrumentalist theory of moral valuation, however, are contained in *Experience and Nature* (1925), *The Quest for Certainty* (1929), and a long essay prepared for the *International Encyclopedia of Unified Science* (1939) entitled "Theory of Valuation." In part due to the nature of these writings, Dewey's empirical theory of moral valuation is often considered apart from his larger moral philosophy, leading to certain misunderstandings about his conception of the moral life and the process of moral deliberation itself. His interpretation of the moral life as a whole is set forth in *Human Nature and Conduct* (1922) and *Theory of the Moral Life,* which is his contribution to a book on *Ethics* (1908, 1932) that he and James H. Tufts published together. There he offers a naturalistic view of the origin, nature, and function of moral ideas, feelings, and practices. He argues that the moral life develops naturally out of social life, and he rejects supernaturalistic and transcendentalist accounts of the origin of moral ideals, moral laws, conscience, and the sense of obligation. In an effort to put Dewey's theory of valuation in its proper perspective within the framework of this larger moral philosophy, particular attention will be given in due course to Dewey's understanding of the role of emotion in the process of moral deliberation and also to his idea of growth as the inclusive human good.

In an open pluralistic universe with no fixed ends, growth is the inclusive human end or good, Dewey argues. His concept of growth is one of the big unifying ideas in his evolutionary philosophy of human nature and society. It ties his theory of the moral life together with his psychology, theory of education, and social thought. It is Dewey's view that psychology is centrally concerned with the dynamics of growth; education is to be identified with the process of growth; the inclusive moral end is growth; and democratic social reconstruction means making all institutions instruments of human growth. Further, when there is growth there is the experience of freedom, and life is felt to be inherently meaningful and worthwhile. Dewey's experimental method of valuation is designed to guide the self and society in the way of freedom and growth in the evolving world of nature.

Instrumentalism and an Idealism of Action

At this conjuncture, it is instructive to return to Dewey's idea that there are three ways in which human beings may seek to idealize the world. The first way involves the quest for certainty and relies on reason and philosophical speculation. It may provide consolation, but it does not resolve the practical problems that face human beings in their everyday life. The second way finds an answer in "moments of intense emotional appreciation when ... the beauty and harmony of existence is disclosed in experiences which are the immediate consummation of all for which we long." Dewey concedes that this way is "the most engaging," and it generates in the human imagination the vision of the ideal possibilities of human existence. However, in a world made up of interacting events and characterized by change, the values or goods that accidentally occur in human experience are insecure, transitory, and elusive. Furthermore, in a world where events have consequences as well as antecedent causes, the meaning of immediate enjoyments is uncertain.

> First and immature experience is content simply to enjoy. But a brief course in experience enforces reflection; it requires but brief time to teach that some things sweet in the having are bitter in after-taste and in what they lead to. Primitive innocence does not last. Enjoyment ceases to be a datum and becomes a problem.[2]

The problematic nature of existence leads Dewey to a third way: "idealization through actions that are directed by thought."[3] This constitutes what he calls "an idealism of action." Nature is idealizable, but only action directed by intelligence can realize nature's ideal possibilities leading to individual growth and social progress.

The problem is not just to exercise control over the processes of nature. Scientific knowledge provides this power of control, but there is a deeper problem. For the sake of what ends should control be exercised? This is "the supreme problem of practical life."[4] More specifically the urgent need is for what Dewey calls a method of criticism. He means by criticism valuation, that is, discriminating judgment concerning the goods, values, ends, desires, and purposes that direct human activities. In short, an idealism of action requires a method of making value-judgments leading to what the Greeks called wisdom. He emphasizes that the need is for a theory of valuation rather than for a theory of values: "Of immediate values as such, values which occur and which are possessed and enjoyed, there is no theory at all; they just occur, are enjoyed, possessed; and that is all." Criticism or valuation starts with the immediate values which are given in and by life experience. This includes all the likings, affections, preferences, and purposes operative in the lives of individuals and society, and among these goods are moral ideals and aesthetic tastes. The task of criticism is to discriminate between the real and the apparent good and thereby to offer the individual and society guidance in the diagnosis and resolution of their major problems. A socially responsible philosophy in Dewey's view has no more important task than furthering the process of criticism, which first and foremost means criticizing the methods of criticism.[5]

Since Dewey finds the key to a sound method of criticism or valuation in the experimental method of inquiry, it is necessary to return again to his understanding of this method beginning with his instrumentalist theory of the nature and function of the mind. Regarding the role of thinking or knowing Dewey writes:

> The intellectual phase of mental action is identical with an *indirect* mode of response, one whose purpose is to locate the nature of the trouble and form an idea of how it may be dealt with—so that operations may be directed in view of an intended solution.... Anything that may be called knowledge, or a known object, marks a question answered, a difficulty disposed of, a confusion cleared up, an inconsistency reduced to coherence, a perplexity mastered ... thinking is that actual transition from the problematic to the secure, as far as that is intentionally guided.[6]

Knowing is literally intermediate and instrumental—"intermediate between a need in experience and its satisfaction" and "instrumental to reconstruction of situations."[7] Accordingly Dewey rejects classical and modern theories that conceive of the mind as a spectator beholding the world from without or that view contemplation of truth as the supreme end of intellectual activity. He recognizes that thinking and knowledge do provide certain persons with aesthetic satisfaction, and he does not deny the value of such aesthetic enjoyment. His point is that "the mind is within the world as a part of the latter's own on-going process" and that its most fundamental purpose is a practical one.[8]

Dewey's instrumentalism involves a redefinition of traditional conceptions of the nature of ideas. Traditional empiricism correctly finds the source of ideas in concrete experience but mistakenly identifies ideas with sensations and representations of things. Philosophical idealists correctly attribute to ideas creative and productive power. However, idealists and rationalists mistakenly imagine ideas to be innate properties of reason separate from nature and corresponding to traits of ultimate reality, or they wrongly think of ideas as a priori categories imposed on sense experience so as to provide it with structure and continuity. Reflecting on the role of ideas in experimental inquiry, Dewey proposes that ideas are guides to action in concrete problematic situations, that is, "plans of operations to be performed or already performed."[9] They arise as a mode of response to a problem and they guide action so as to resolve the problem. Ideas are not correctly conceived as reproductions of what already exists, but as plans of something to be done and anticipations of some result to follow. They are tools, instrumentalities.

The validity or truth of an idea can only be determined empirically by putting the idea to use and observing the consequences of the actions to which the idea leads. This notion that the meaning of ideas is established and their truth verified with reference to their consequences rather than with reference to some antecedent existence of which they supposedly are reproductions, is one of the central and most revolutionary tenets of the philosophical pragmatism of Peirce, James, and Dewey, and Dewey developed the pragmatist approach in a more thoroughgoing fashion than either Peirce or James.[10] Dewey offers this summary of his version of the pragmatic conception of truth.

If ideas, meanings, conceptions, notions, theories, systems are instrumental to an active reorganization of the given environment, to a removal of some specific trouble and perplexity, then the test of their validity and value lies in accomplishing this work. If they succeed in their office, they are reliable, sound, valid, good, true.... Confirmation, corroboration, verification lie in works, consequences.... By their fruits shall ye know them. That which guides us truly is true—demonstrated capacity for such guidance is precisely what is meant by truth.[11]

Dewey's position, for example, is that the test of the assertion that a certain object will satisfy a need for something sweet is "to predict that when it is tasted—that is, subjected to a specified operation—a certain consequence will ensue." The meaning of the assertion that a certain object is sweet is the prediction that it will have a certain consequence. In line with these views, Dewey identifies the object of knowledge with the consequences of directed operations rather than with something which exists prior to or apart from the operations involved in an act of knowing.[12]

Dewey's view of ideas as plans of action also leads him to reject any notion that ideas are finalities, fixities, unchangeable principles. All ideas and theories are to be regarded as they are in science, that is, as hypotheses.

Notions, theories, systems, no matter how elaborate and self-consistent they are, must be regarded as hypotheses. They are to be accepted as bases of actions which test them, not as finalities. To perceive this fact is to abolish rigid dogmas from the world. It is to recognize that conceptions, theories and systems of thought are always open to development through use. There is no infallible source of ideas and ideas themselves are tools to be rejected, accepted or remade in the light of the consequences of their use.[13]

Dewey defines his logic as a theory of inquiry, that is, a theory of the way in which intellectual inquiry achieves knowledge and reconstructs problematic situations. All thinking originates in response to problems, but not all thinking is successful in resolving problems. Thinking easily gets sidetracked into daydreaming, fantasizing, and unproductive patterns of reasoning. The task of the philosopher is not to develop some purely formal theory of rules of correct reasoning apprehended by intuition or pure reason, but to examine the various ways in which human beings actually have gone about thinking and in the light of this empirical evidence to clarify and systematize the procedures of thinking that have been efficacious. Reflecting on the history of human thinking, Dewey concludes that the experimental method of inquiry constitutes the most fruitful way of thinking whether a person is dealing with an everyday problem or a complex issue in scientific research.

The experimental method involves at least five phases. First, a problem is encountered in a concrete situation. Second, careful observations of the facts of the situation are made toward the end of clearly defining the nature of the problem. Third, reflecting on the problem at hand, imagination is used in developing ideas which might possibly serve as solutions to the problem. Developing these hypotheses may lead to the making of additional observations in an effort to further clarify the problem. Fourth, a selection of the most promising hypotheses is made. It is then carefully refined by use of deductions and calculations until it can be experimentally tested. Fifth, experimental testing of the hypothesis is undertaken by using it as a guide in action. If the hypothesis is validated and the problem is solved, inquiry comes to an end and knowledge has been acquired.[14]

The kind of action involved in experimentation will vary according to the problem, but Dewey insists that all knowing and inquiry involves some kind of doing that involves physical modifications, and he denounces all traditional theories that separate knowing and doing, theory and practice. Likewise, just what constitutes verification of an idea and the solution of a problem will vary according to the kind of problem at hand. In all cases, experimentation and verification take place in a fashion that is open to public observation. "A public and manifest series of definite operations, all capable of public notice and report, distinguishes scientific knowing from the knowing carried on by inner 'mental' processes accessible only to introspection, or inferred by dialectic from assumed premises."[15]

Dewey's attempt to comprehend all knowing within his problem-solving theory has provoked considerable debate. A misunderstanding easily results from failure to keep in mind his distinction between immediate experience and knowledge. Simply to hold an object in direct perception or to have feelings about it is not to know it. To know an object is to apprehend its interrelations with other things. "The more connections and interactions we ascertain, the more we know the object in question. Thinking is search for these interconnections," asserts Dewey.[16] In other words, knowing is concerned with causes and effects. To know a thing is to know how it is made, what interactions are the conditions of its appearance, what it will do, and how it will respond to various other things. To know that a certain foodstuff is sweet is to ascertain what it is made of and how it will affect the human sense of taste. "When there is anything beyond bare immediate enjoyment and suffering, it is the means-consequence relation that is considered. Thought goes beyond immediate existence to its relationships, the conditions which mediate it and the things to which it is in turn mediatory."[17] Dewey's theory of inquiry and the five stages of a fruitful thinking process are his account of the way in which such knowledge of things is acquired.

Dewey's instrumentalist theory of inquiry and knowledge provides the foundation of his theory of valuation. It is his position that the same logical method may be used in making moral judgments or aesthetic criticisms as is used in scientific inquiry. Indeed, he argues that the scientific method is used by scientists themselves as a method of valuation, for it is a method of criticizing the satisfactoriness of beliefs: "Science is inherently an instrument of determining what is good and bad in the way of acceptance and rejection." The heart of his argument is quite simple. The basic problem of valuation in matters of intellectual belief, interpersonal relations, and aesthetic appreciation is judging whether what is good in immediate experience has consequences for later experience that warrant accepting the immediate good as a true good. In short, all sound criticism requires "a method of discriminating among goods on the basis of the conditions of their appearance and of their consequences."[18] Criticism as distinct from immediate enjoyment of goods—valuation, appraisal, as distinct from valuing, prizing—requires intellectual inquiry into causes and effects, a search for knowledge or the meaning of things. It is Dewey's argument that the only sound method for seeking such knowledge and making the necessary appraisal of the good in question is the five-phased experimental method of problem-solving. He asserts that the only alternative to this approach to value judgments is reliance upon impulse, accident, blind habit, arbitrary authority, class-interest, or self-interest.

Writing in 1929, Dewey finds philosophers divided between two unsatisfactory approaches to a theory of morals. On the one hand, theologians and philosophical idealists, who desire to preserve the objective nature of value judgments, defend various forms of absolutism. Distrusting the capacity of experience to develop its own regulative ideals, they appeal to transcendent and immutable values, which are conceived as either divinely revealed or known by nonempirical rational methods. On the other hand, the empiricists, including the logical positivists, embrace subjectivism and an uncritical relativism in morals. They identify moral values with goods revealed by experience, but they make no distinction between immediate goods and goods approved by critical reflection. Consequently they argue that beliefs about value are purely subjective in character. Dewey seeks a middle ground in his moral theory between absolutism and subjectivism. His aim is to formulate an empirical theory of moral valuation that justifies belief in the objective character of moral value judgments. Toward this end he points out that current empirical theories are correct in connecting values with concrete experiences involving desires and satisfactions. However, they fail to appreciate that experience can be directed and regulated by an experimental method that makes possible the testing of immediate values leading to objective judgments about what are real as opposed to apparent goods. "Experimental empiricism" in the field of moral values is what is needed.[19]

Dewey's experimental empiricism approaches moral problems in a fashion quite similar to that found in classical Greek philosophy in the sense that he emphasizes the central significance of need, desire, and satisfaction in human behavior. However, his biological and social orientation gives his treatment of these factors a distinctive character. He views the human being as a creature of needs and wants interacting with a problematic world. In response to needs, conflicts and difficulties, desires arise. Desires involve projections of ends-in-view and function as the main spring of human actions including moral actions. The resolution of a problem and the fulfillment of desire brings satisfaction. That which overcomes problems and satisfies desire is good. It is the part of moral wisdom to discriminate between desires (ends-in-view, goods) and to judge which contribute to enduring satisfaction or well-being and are, therefore, truly good and worthy of our desire.

In line with this approach, Dewey asserts that the basic distinction which must be made by an empirical theory of objective moral value judgment is that between the desired and the desirable, or the satisfying and the satisfactory.

> To say that something satisfies is to report something as an isolated finality. To assert that it is satis*factory* is to define it in its connections and interactions. The fact that it pleases or is immediately congenial poses a problem to judgment. How shall the satisfaction be rated? Is it a value or is it not? Is it something to be prized and cherished, *to be* enjoyed? Not stern moralists alone but everyday experience informs us that finding satisfaction in a thing may be a warning, a summons to be on the lookout for consequences. To declare something satis*factory* is to assert that it meets specifiable conditions. It is, in effect, a judgment that the thing "will do." It involves a prediction; it contemplates a future in which the thing will continue to serve; it *will* do. It asserts a consequence the thing will actively institute; it will *do*. That it is satisfying is the content of a proposition of fact; that it is satisfactory is a judgment, an estimate, an appraisal.[20]

Dewey's idea of the satisfying refers to what is as a matter of fact. The notion of the satisfactory refers to what ought to be.

Again, basic to Dewey's theory of valuation is the idea that "judgments about values are judgments about conditions and the results of experienced objects."[21] Ends are constituted by the means necessary to their realization. A desired end is evaluated by inquiring into the means or conditions of its appearance and all the consequences involved in actually working to realize it. Dewey writes: "For what is deliberation except weighing of various alternative desires (and hence end-values) in terms of the conditions that are the means of their execution, and which, as means, determine the consequences actually arrived at?"[22] These matters may be known by open and public methods of inquiry, and consequently Dewey argues that moral value propositions or judgments about what is desirable, good, and right possess objective verifiable meaning. Dewey is a relativist in the sense that he believes that the moral good is to be defined in the light of the needs of the situation at hand. He is not a relativist, if by that is meant one who believes that moral values are merely a matter of subjective liking and have no relation to objective criteria of goodness.

It is Dewey's hope as a democratic social philosopher that the spirit and practice of his experimental empiricism in morals will gradually become the guiding authority in all social institutions leading to cooperative inquiry into the causes of social problems and their solutions. Throughout his career he continued to emphasize the necessity for widespread cooperation in the application of the method of intelligence. To socialize experimental intelligence in this fashion is Dewey's approach to a progressive reconstruction of society and the moral life. He is careful to point out that significant advances in the use of his proposed empirical method of valuation, which requires a knowledge of conditions and consequences, are intimately tied to progress in the development of the sciences of biology, psychology, sociology, and cultural anthropology.[23] In this approach to moral issues the emphasis falls on identifying the causes of moral and social problems in concrete situations and on framing ideals with reference to the available means for overcoming such problems. Ideals that are framed apart from the study of the problems and possibilities of concrete situations are dreams, wish-fantasies, and useless as instrumentalities in directing practical affairs.[24] Further, adoption of experimental empiricism in morals means that all moral principles and social purposes are to be taken as hypotheses, that is, as guides to action in a problematic world to be tested, confirmed, and reconstructed in the light of their consequences. Dewey believes that this approach to all moral, religious, and political tenets and creeds "would do away with the intolerance and fanaticism that attend the notion that beliefs and judgments are capable of inherent truth and authority; inherent in the sense of being independent of what they lead to when used as directive principles."[25] In this view loyalty to moral laws and ideals is not by itself a virtue unless such loyalty arises out of critical appraisal. The reconstruction of moral values and social policies is an ongoing task. Such is Dewey's democratic idealism of action.

The Role of the Heart in the Moral Life

Some of Dewey's writings on moral deliberations can create the impression that for him it is all a process of cool scientific calculation in which emotion plays almost no role. However, this is a misunderstanding of his position as his *Theory of the Moral Life* (1932) makes clear. In this regard it is useful to remember that Dewey's early training in moral philosophy was heavily influenced by Vermont Transcendentalism and by intuitionalism, and from the beginning of his career he was dissatisfied with the Kantian dualism of moral reason and emotion. As a naturalist he does reject the intuitionalist theory that there exists some special nonnatural faculty of moral insight capable of moral knowledge apart from social influences and education. However, he never lost an appreciation of the role in moral affairs of intuition—the heart and the emotions, what he terms "immediate sensitive responsiveness."[26] The emphasis in his moral theory is on the role of intelligence, but these other factors are not denied an important function. For example, his well-known essay in the *International Encyclopedia of Unified Science* (1939) on the "Theory of Valuation," which summarizes his mature thinking on the subject, concludes with this observation:

> In fact and in net outcome, the previous discussion does not point in the least to supersession of the emotive by the intellectual. Its only and complete import is the need for their integration in behavior—behavior in which, according to common speech, the head and the heart work together, in which, to use more technical language, prizing and appraising unite in direction of action. [27]

"The permanent element of value in the intuitional theory," writes Dewey, "lies in its implicit emphasis upon the importance of direct responsiveness to the qualities of situations and acts."[28]

It has already been noted that Dewey views desire, passion, or affection as the primary spring to action in human life, and this is one reason why immediate responsiveness is a necessity in moral matters. Reason divorced from emotional involvement has no moving power. Therefore, even though Dewey writes critically that "the glorification of affection and aspiration at the expense of thought is a survival of romantic optimism," he also asserts that "the separation of warm emotion and cool intelligence is the great moral tragedy."[29] Passion separated from reason is unstable, undisciplined, and without trustworthy guidance, but reason divorced from passion is without energy. " 'Cold blooded' thought may reach a correct conclusion, but if a person remains anti-pathetic or indifferent to the considerations presented to him in a rational way, they will not stir him to act in accord with them." Real moral understanding actually involves the heart and the gut as well as the head according to Dewey:

> Resentment, ranging from fierce abhorrence through disgust to mild repugnance, is a necessary ingredient of knowledge of evil which is genuine knowledge. Affection, from intense love to mild favor, is an ingredient in all operative knowledge, all full apprehension, of the good.[30]

In short, if moral reflection is to influence behavior, it must engage the whole feeling, thinking, and willing person.

Dewey also points out that since moral deliberation is fundamentally concerned with being rather than having (i.e., with what kind of a person one wishes to be), it is more like a dramatic process that engages personal feeling than an impersonal process comparable to a mathematical calculation. He often lauds the British utilitarians for their efforts to develop a scientific method of moral valuation and for emphasizing objective consequences in making moral judgments. However, he also criticizes them, especially Jeremy Bentham, for identifying moral reflection with a quantitative calculation of future pleasures and pains, as if moral affairs were analogous to a business calculation of profit and loss. In this regard he argues that whereas the quantitative calculations involved in economic matters are concerned with what the self will get and possess, moral deliberation is concerned with "what kind of a person one is to become, what sort of self is in the making."[31] A desire, an object, or an act acquires moral significance "when it is thought of as making a difference in the *self*, as determining what one will *be*, instead of merely what one will *have*. . . . The choice at stake in a moral deliberation or valuation is the worth of this and that kind of character and disposition." The objective meaning of a desire or act is defined by its consequences, but in choosing certain consequences as morally better than others a person is making an existential decision about what kind of a person he or she wishes to be.

With this in mind, Dewey points out that moral deliberation is "a dramatic rehearsal (in imagination) of various competing lines of action," and as such it is an intensely personal process that stirs into life a person's likes and dislikes, desires and aversions. In this connection he notes that "*emotional* reactions form the chief materials of our knowledge of ourselves and of others. Just as ideas of physical objects are constituted out of sensory material, so those of persons are framed out of emotional and affectional material. The latter are as direct, as immediate as the former, and more interesting, with a greater hold on attention." Dewey adds: "Unless there is a direct, mainly unreflective appreciation of persons and deeds, the data for subsequent thought will be lacking or distorted. A person must *feel* the qualities of acts as one feels with the hands the qualities of roughness and smoothness in objects, before he has an inducement to deliberate or material with which to deliberate."[32] In the process of moral deliberation, then, as the consequences of different courses of action are considered imaginatively by the mind, there is developed a running commentary of direct emotional responses which stamps the various actions as good or bad. "It is this direct sense of value, not the consciousness of general rules or ultimate goals, which finally determines the worth of the act to the agent. Here is an unexpungeable element of truth in the intuitional theory."[33]

This view of moral reflection as a dramatic process involving the intuitive factor, immediate responsiveness, leads Dewey to emphasize that the only guarantee that moral deliberation will be conducted impartially and that a wise and just choice will be made is the quality of a person's moral character.

> It is true, on the one hand, that the ultimate standard for judgment of acts is their objective consequences; the outcome constitutes the meaning of an act. But it is equally true that the warrant for correctness of judgment and for power of judgment to operate as an influence in conduct lies in the intrinsic make-up of character; it would be safer to trust a man of a kind and honest disposition without much ability in

calculation than it would a man having great power of foresight of the future who was malicious and insincere.

As Aristotle pointed out, only the good man is a good judge of what is truly good; it takes a fine and well-grounded character to react immediately with the right approvals and condemnations.[34]

Dewey concedes that since a person's moral intuitions reflect dispositions and habits acquired from past education and social influences and since all social environments involve some "limiting and distorting influences," even the intuitions of a relatively good person may involve certain biases and prejudices.[35]

In describing a person of good moral character, who will be trustworthy in matters requiring moral deliberation, Dewey throughout his career singled out sympathy as an especially important trait. He does not regard sympathetic impulses by themselves as adequate guides to direct action, but he does find sympathy "morally invaluable" as a principle of sound moral thinking. The argument is that "sympathy widens and deepens concern for consequences."

> It is sympathy which carries thought out beyond the self and which extends its scope till it approaches the universal as its limit. It is sympathy which saves consideration of consequences from degenerating into mere calculation, by rendering vivid the interests of others and urging us to give them the same weight as those which touch our own honor, purse, and power. To put ourselves in the place of others, to see things from the standpoint of their purposes and values, to humble, contrariwise, our own pretensions and claims till they reach the level they would assume in the eye of an impartial sympathetic observer, is the surest way to attain objectivity of moral knowledge.[36]

In short the person with a sympathetic attitude is most likely to be the most reasonable and trustworthy person in moral affairs. "Our moral failures go back to some weakness of disposition, some absence of sympathy, some one sided bias that makes us perform the judgment of the concrete case carelessly or perversely," explains Dewey.[37]

Thus Dewey as a naturalist would find much of value in the traditional Christian emphasis on *agape* in the sense of a deep active concern for the well-being of the other, or the Buddhist emphasis on *karuṇā,* compassion. His criticism would be that too often *agape* and *karuṇā,* are taken as in themselves sufficient principles of action rather than as guiding principles of reflection on the consequences of alternate possible courses of action. Dewey writes: "To give way without thought to a kindly feeling is easy; to suppress it is easy for many persons; the difficult but needed thing is to retain it in all its pristine intensity while directing it, as a precondition of action, into channels of thought. A union of benevolent impulse and intelligent reflection is the interest most likely to result in conduct that is good."[38]

In this regard Dewey put special emphasis on the role of the imagination and the arts in the moral life. "Imagination is the chief instrument of the good," asserts Dewey, noting that "a person's ideas and treatment of his fellows are dependent upon his power to put himself imaginatively in their place." He also points out that "a sense of possibilities that are unrealized and that might be realized are when they are put in contrast with actual conditions, the most penetrating 'criticism' of the latter that can be made," making us "aware of constrictions that hem us in and of burdens that oppress." The "moral potency of art" resides in its imaginative vision of new possibilities transcending existing customs and moral traditions. "Art has been the means of keeping alive the sense of purposes that outrun evidence and of meanings that transcend indurated habit." Dewey approvingly quotes the English poet Shelley: "A man to be greatly good must imagine intensely and comprehensively."[39]

Finally, when defining the general nature of moral virtue in the 1932 edition of *Ethics,* Dewey returns to a theme from his *Study of Ethics* (1894). He identifies virtue with love and offers an experimentalist's definition of love. "In its ethical sense, love signifies completeness of devotion to the objects esteemed good." It is wholehearted persistent active interest in the ideal ends or values approved by imaginative critical evaluation. In other words, love is the self responding with "complete interest" and intelligent sympathy to the needs of the situation, and it involves the union of subject and object, self and activity, in pursuit of the ideal possibilities of the situation. Dewey goes on to point out that such wholehearted concern is moral virtue in a comprehensive sense. He rejects the idea that there are many independent moral virtues; rather, what are often listed as the different moral virtues are actually interrelated traits or qualities characteristic of love. As in the *Study of Ethics,* he argues, for example, that the classical Greek virtues of temperance, courage, justice, and wisdom are all included in the virtue of love. Dewey describes sympathy as an especially important quality of love and as fundamental to the workings of wisdom.[40]

These observations are sufficient to indicate that, in his theory of moral deliberation, Dewey is seeking an alternative to all radical dualisms of the head and the heart, reason and desire, intellectual analysis and emotionalized intuition. In his experimental ethics he endeavors to find a middle way between sentimentalism and rationalism, between an uncritical intuitionalism and an exclusive reliance on intellectual technique. Sound moral thinking and choice require the integration of intelligence and sensitive responsiveness, of experimental method and sympathy. This outlook prompts the basic question: how is virtuous character developed? Dewey's most frequent answer is that sympathy, for example, is a natural human emotion and to a large extent its development is determined by the social environment and education. Character is shaped by the quality of the social interactions that constitute a person's experience. Therefore, Dewey stressed the need to create social conditions in the family, the school, work place, and the world of international affairs that foster the essential moral qualities. Building on his early neo-Hegelian emphasis on moral and religious will, he also gave increasing attention as a mature philosopher to the critical role of moral decision and religious faith in the formation of character. These issues will be explored further in this and the succeeding chapter.

The Nature of the Moral Good

An objection frequently raised against Dewey's experimental method of valuation is that it does not provide a person with a definition of the final good or the ultimate end of action, which in the final analysis is the criterion that must be used in judging good and bad consequences. How is a person to determine if the consequences of an act are good unless he or she has some prior understanding of what constitutes the final good? The problem can be stated more concretely. If I choose to be healthy, Dewey's method (which explores conditions and consequences) will enable me to make a value judgment about a mushroom salad. If I seek the full realization of my child's capacities, an exploration of the consequences of various courses of action will help me decide what to do as a parent about the child's education. If equal justice is my objective, experimental empiricism will be a useful guide. The experimental method when applied to moral situations is, then, of great value. The question is: how does a person, who has adopted an experimental approach in morals, decide that health, responsible parenthood, and concern for equal justice are ends to which he or she should be loyal? Dewey's theory of the role of sympathy in moral deliberation provides part of the answer to this question, but as a radical process philosopher he would make a number of additional points in clarifying his outlook.

First of all, Dewey notes that "ethical theory ... has been singularly hypnotized by the notion that its business is to discover some final end or good or some ultimate and supreme law," but as a radical evolutionary naturalist and democratic social thinker he abandons this approach. [41]

> A philosophy of experience will accept at its full value the fact that social and moral existences are, like physical existences, in a state of continuous if obscure change.... In the futile effort to achieve security and anchorage in something fixed, it will substitute the effort to determine the character of changes that are going on and to give them in the affairs that concern us most some measure of intelligent direction. [42]

It is the notion of a static good or fixed hierarchy of goods to which Dewey especially objects. He views such notions as products of feudal and aristocratic social structures and argues that they have no place in a democratic society which rejects rigid social divisions and is open to genuine change and novelty.

Second, Dewey reasons that the primary task of the moral philosopher is not to seek and define some absolute final good, but rather to develop a method for criticizing and reconstructing those desires, goods, and values which have been spontaneously discovered and adopted in the course of experience. Moral theory does not propose ready-made solutions to moral problems but rather a method of inquiry for identifying ills and discovering solutions to dilemmas as they arise in experience.[43] The work of the moral philosopher may also, of course, extend to applying the method to specific problems.

Third, regarding the criteria for making moral decisions, Dewey points out that deliberation and criticism are called into play when a problematical situation arises and the criteria for evaluating alternative courses of action and consequences are supplied by the situation itself. The end of action is judged good which overcomes the original problem and reestablishes a harmonious situation.[44] He emphasizes "a plurality of changing, moving, individualized goods and ends."[45] His point is that the good will vary according to individual need and capacity and the situation. Each situation is unique having "its own irreplaceable good." It is the task of intelligence using the method of experimental empiricism to determine just what the good is in any particular situation. The supreme value at any one time varies with the situation, which is a further reason for rejecting the idea of a fixed hierarchy of goods. "Every case where moral action is required becomes of equal importance and urgency with every other. If the need and deficiencies of a specific situation indicate improvement of health as the end and good, then for that situation health is the ultimate and supreme good." It is "a final and intrinsic value" and "the whole personality should be concerned with it."[46] One finds Dewey here broadening the idea of what constitutes moral action and again seeking to break down the dualism of the spiritual and the material. He is endeavoring to liberate people to live wholeheartedly in the present, realizing the inherent meaning and value of even the most ordinary everyday tasks which are necessary parts of living.

Fourth, just as Dewey opposes fixed ideas of the good, so he rejects the notion that laws and standards are to be taken as absolute unchanging rules. Moral laws and standards are products of human social experience, and they inevitably require reconstruction as social conditions change. They do not proceed from some absolute authority that transcends human social life (whether it be conceived as a divine will, a secular ruler, pure reason, or conscience), and the moral life is not to be thought of as obedience to some such higher authority and to an unchanging set of rules. To conceive it in this fashion, Dewey believes, inevitably leads to authoritarianism, striving to conform to external commands, and an emphasis on punishments and rewards. Such an approach is oppressive. It often leaves people feeling alienated from their moral life and deprives the moral life of freedom and spontaneity. Dewey wishes to shift the emphasis in morals from conformity to the letter of the law and rewards and punishments to the exploration and discovery of the special possibilities for good inherent in each concrete and unique situation. This puts the center of moral attention inside the concrete process of living. It is the difference Dewey tells us between what Paul called living under the law and living in the spirit.[47]

Dewey does not deny the value of general moral laws and standards. However, he argues that such laws and standards should be regarded as principles rather than rules. Rules prescribe definite courses of action; they tell a person what to do and how to do it. Principles, on the contrary, are "aides and instruments in judging" possible courses of action. They provide standpoints for surveying a situation and analyzing the moral significance of the various aspects of it. In other words, principles do not tell us specifically what to do but rather what to think about in deciding what to do. Dewey cites the Golden Rule as an example of a useful guide in moral deliberations when it is taken as a principle in the sense just defined.

> The "Golden Rule" does furnish *us a point of view from which to consider acts;* it suggests the necessity of considering how our acts affect the interests of others as well as our own; it tends to prevent partiality of regard; it warns against setting an undue estimate upon a particular consequence of pain or pleasure, simply because it happens to affect us. In short, the Golden Rule does not issue special orders or commands—but it does clarify and illuminate the situations requiring intelligent deliberations.

In other words, the Golden Rule calls attention to the values Dewey associates with the attitude of sympathy. Moral injunctions such as "Love your neighbor" or "Love your enemy" and standards such as the common good have a certain "binding force" in Dewey's theory of the moral life, but exactly what they mean for action is relative to the needs and possibilities of the concrete situation. Dewey emphasizes the importance of an open-minded flexible attitude of inquiry.

When confronting new problematic situations, he urges the development of fresh insights into the meaning of general moral values like compassion, justice, and the general welfare.[48]

Fifth, in response to the questions about some ultimate criterion for use in deciding a moral issue, as noted earlier, Dewey in moral matters is an existentialist who emphasizes autonomy, individual decision, and personal responsibility. Each person must decide for himself or herself what kind of a person he or she wishes to be. Moral problems provide the self with the opportunity for such decisions. Dewey does not wish to provide the self with any external authority upon which it can rely and thereby escape the freedom and responsibility for making these existential choices. In Dewey's view, to be a self is to make real moral choices and thereby to become an individual self. In other words, the ultimate good in any situation is something a person must choose at his or her own risk. This is not, of course, for Dewey a matter of arbitrary decision. His empirical method of moral valuation is designed to clarify the alternatives so that moral decisions have objective validity. However, the method does not remove the burden of responsibility for decision from the self. For Dewey as a naturalist, the final ground of moral obligation is the realization that I am bound to do what is consistent with the self I choose to be, because to fail to do so means that I lose that self and become another self.

Sixth, Dewey opposes any idea of a fixed final good, but as an evolutionary naturalist and democratic social thinker, he was not without his own general definition of the moral good and a comprehensive end of moral action, and it is this idea that he uses as a general criterion or guide in evaluating moral ideals and their consequences. He argues in *Experience and Nature,* for example, that to common sense "the better is that which will do more in the way of security, liberation and fecundity for other likings and values," because "the best, the richest and fullest experience possible" is "the common purpose of men."[49] Dewey assumes, then, that there is a commonsense common purpose generated by experience, which is growth toward the richest and fullest experience possible. However, having abandoned the idea of some preestablished notion of the universal self and every other idea of a fixed end, Dewey's thought shifts the emphasis from achievement of a set distinct goal to a concern with the process of growing itself, emphasizing the intrinsic value of the process as lived each day and its ongoing open-ended nature. "Not perfection as a final goal, but the ever-enduring process of perfecting, maturing, refining is the aim in living," states Dewey.[50] Resolution of the problem at hand, the values associated with intelligent sympathy, the quality of one's own being, and ongoing growth are, then, the general criteria at work in the process of intelligent evaluation as Dewey conceives it.

Growth as the Inclusive Moral End

The concept of growth is a connecting theme running through Dewey's psychology, theory of education, theory of the moral life, and social philosophy. Further exploration of the way that he employs this concept will clarify his understanding of the critical function of experimental moral valuation, the idea of freedom, and the deeper meaning of the democratic way of life. His reflections on the idea of growth include some of the most radical thinking in his philosophy and illuminate the spiritual meaning and power of his humanistic and naturalistic vision. It is useful to begin this examination of the idea of growth as the inclusive human end with a further discussion of Dewey's idea of the self and his view of education as a process of growth.

Students of Dewey's philosophy are often left puzzled by just what he means by the self in his mature thought. In this regard, first of all, it is helpful to keep in mind that even though he rejected the neo-Hegelian idea of the universal self, he retained as a mature thinker the voluntarism and much of the broad vision regarding the development of the self that is associated with his early psychology. Second, in seeking an understanding of Dewey's idea of the self as it is reconstructed in his naturalistic process philosophy, it is instructive to begin with the assertions about individuality that one finds in his metaphysics. The relevant issue is addressed in an exchange that he had with George Santayana. In a review of *Experience and Nature,* Santayana criticized Dewey for failing to appreciate the full significance of human individuality: "In Dewey . . . as in current science and ethics, there is a pervasive quasi-Hegelian tendency to dissolve the individual into his social functions, as well as everything substantial or actual into something relative or transitional. For him events, situations, and histories hold all facts and all persons in solution."[51] In response Dewey clarified his meaning:

> Since I find in human life, from its biological roots to its ideal flowers and fruits, things both individual and associational—each word being adjectival—I hold that nature has both an irreducible brute unique "itselfness" in everything which exists and also a connection of each thing (which is just what *it* is) with other things such that without them it "can neither be nor be conceived." And as far as I can follow the findings of physics, that conclusion is confirmed by the results of the examination of physical existence itself.[52]

In every self there is, then, "an irreducible brute unique 'itselfness' " or unique qualitative individuality. For Dewey this is true of all things in the universe. Individuality as well as interconnection is a given. He did not seek to probe the mystery that lies behind this characteristic of nature. He was content to accept and affirm it, but as a psychologist he tried to describe the emergence and development of selfhood or individuality in persons. If he tended to emphasize "the associational aspects of experience" in much of his work, it was because he was concerned to counteract the subjectivism in traditional theories of experience and the atomistic individualism that pervaded much psychology. However, as in all his thinking, his objective was to find a middle way—in this case a middle way between the extremes of atomistic individualism and political collectivism.

Regarding the unique individuality of the self, Dewey writes: "Individuality is inexpungeable because it is a manner of distinctive sensitivity, selection, choice, response and utilization of conditions." It is a creative potentiality resident in each person.

> Individuality is at first spontaneous and unshaped; it is a potentiality, a capacity of development. Even so, it is a unique manner of acting in and with a world of objects and persons. It is not something complete in itself, like a closet in a house or a secret drawer in a desk, filled with treasures that are waiting to be bestowed on the world. Since individuality is a distinctive way of feeling the impacts of the world

and of showing a preferential bias in response to these impacts, it develops into shape and form only through interaction with actual conditions; it is no more complete in itself than is a painter's tube of paint without relation to a canvas. The work of art is the truly individual thing; and it is the result of the interaction of paint and canvas through the medium of the artist's distinctive vision and power.[53]

Like David Hume, Dewey could find no empirical evidence to support the idea that there is a ready-made fixed unified self at work behind the activities of a person, and he, therefore, chose to think of the self as a creative process of becoming.

"Selfhood . . . is in process of making," states Dewey. This is "an ongoing process" unless the self has been entrapped in mechanical routine. The self of the infant involves a multitude of instinctive tendencies and impulsive activities, which are originally blind and often conflicting, and which are only gradually coordinated and developed so as to enable the child to adapt to its environment. In this fashion the self or character of a child comes into being. The process of becoming or growth continues. Even in adults, human personality does not give evidence of a finished and fixed self. "Inconsistencies and shiftings in character are the commonest thing in experience." For Dewey, then, the self is a process, and he further argues that psychology cannot identify any fixed end toward which the process is evolving, which is not to deny that the self can and does develop ends and goals.[54]

The capacity of the self for growth is viewed by Dewey as the ability of both young and old "to learn from experience; the power to retain from one experience something which is of avail in coping with the difficulties of a later situation."[55] Learning is made possible by what Dewey describes as "the continuity of experience," that is, the idea "that every experience both takes up something from those which have gone before and modifies in some way the quality of those that come after."[56] In other words, "our actions not only lead up to other actions which follow as their effects, but they also leave an enduring impress on the one who performs them, strengthening and weakening permanent tendencies to act."[57] This notion of continuity in the midst of change is one of the significant lessons of Darwinian evolution, argues Dewey, who writes that "the ethical import of the doctrine of evolution is . . . a gospel of present growth."[58] Continuity means that growth in the sense of learning is possible. By learning Dewey means more than gaining additional information or acquiring new skills that increase ease and efficiency of action even though that is included. More fundamentally, learning means an increased perception of the meaning of things that leads to a modification of character (i.e., of basic dispositions and attitudes). In short, growing and learning involve the reconstruction and transformation of the self leading to an improved capacity of the self to adjust to its environment and to control and direct subsequent experience.

The concept of habit is the fundamental idea in Dewey's psychology of the development of the self or character. Dewey insists that the self is essentially identical with its active interests, purposes, and choices. There is no self apart from these activities. The core of the self is formed and defined by the concrete things about which it cares and by the choices which it makes in pursuit of these things.[59] He writes that "*interest* defines the self" and "the self reveals its nature in what it chooses."[60] Dewey uses the term "habit" to comprehend these fundamental activities which constitute the self. The active interests and preferences of the self are conceived by Dewey to be certain formed dispositions or habits.

He explains the comprehensive meaning he gives to the term "habit" as follows:

> We are given to thinking of a habit as simply a recurrent external mode of action, like smoking or swearing, being neat or negligent in clothes and person, taking exercise, or playing games. But habit reaches even more significantly down into the very structure of the self; it signifies a building up and solidifying of certain desires; an increased sensitiveness and responsiveness to certain stimuli, a confirmed or an impaired capacity to attend to and think about certain things. Habit covers in other words the very makeup of desire, intent, choice, disposition which gives an act its voluntary quality. And this aspect of habit is much more important than that which is suggested merely by the tendency to repeated outer action, for the significance of the latter lies in the permanence of the personal disposition which is the real cause of the outer acts and of their resemblance to one another.[61]

Habits are inclusive, then, of patterns of physical behavior including skills and techniques and also of emotional and intellectual attitudes such as ways of thinking, ways of approaching problem situations, aesthetic tastes, and active interests including moral and social concerns. "The self or character as the abiding unity in which different acts have their lasting traces" is made up of various habits.

Dewey's idea of continuity of experience means that habits can be formed and reformed and that all acts have the effect of strengthening or weakening habits. Growth means reinforcing those habits that contribute to human well-being and reconstructing those habits that do not. Children with their curiosity, responsiveness, and openness of mind are well disposed to grow. They do develop, if their social environment is one that encourages growth. Certain habits work to obstruct or arrest growth in adults. This occurs when habits are not formed intelligently, that is, when they are merely routine ways of acting uninformed by real understanding and there is not developed the habit of continued learning, involving retention of a certain childlike openness and responsiveness to life.[62]

As the preceding comments have suggested, it is Dewey's position that authentic education is all one with the process of growth. For example, he writes: "The educative process is a continuous process of growth, having as its aim at every stage an added capacity for growth."[63] His position is more fully stated as follows:

> Getting from the present the degree and kind of growth there is in it is education. This is a constant function, independent of age. The best thing that can be said about any special process of education, like that of the formal school period, is that it renders its subject capable of further education: more sensitive to conditions of growth and more able to take advantage of them. Acquisition of skill, possession of knowledge, attainment of culture are not ends: they are works of growth and means to its continuing.[64]

The criterion of an educative experience is simply that it exercise a positive influence on the intellectual, moral, and emotional capacities of personality that facilitate further development of the whole self.

Dewey has been criticized for leaving the definition of growth and an educative experience vague and unclear by not specifying more concretely what constitutes the end of growth. He offers this reply in *Experience and Education* (1931):

> Any experience is mis-educative that has the effect of arresting or distorting the growth of further experience. Any experience may be

such as to engender callousness—it may produce lack of sensitivity and or responsiveness. Then the possibilities of having richer experience in the future are restricted. Again, a given experience may increase a person's automatic skill in a particular direction and yet tend to land him in a groove or rut; the effect again is to narrow the field of further experience. An experience may be immediately enjoyable and yet promote the formation of a slack and careless attitude; this attitude then operates to modify the quality of subsequent experiences so as to prevent a person from getting out of them what they have to give.[65]

Dewey continues:

That a man may grow in efficiency as a burglar, as a gangster, or as a corrupt politician, cannot be doubted. But from the standpoint of growth as education and education as growth the question is whether growth in this direction promotes or retards growth in general. Does this form of growth create conditions for further growth, or does it set up conditions that shut off the person who has grown in this particular direction from the occasions, stimuli, and opportunities for continuing growth in new directions? What is the effect of growth in a special direction upon the attitudes and habits which alone open up avenues for development in other lines? I shall leave you to answer these questions, saying simply that when and ONLY when development in a particular line conduces to continuing growth does it answer to the criterion of education as growing. For the conception is one that must find universal and not specialized limited application.[66]

The overriding concern of education is growth itself, the process of growing, and not any particular end. Growth is an inclusive end which comprehends all the particular intellectual, aesthetic, social, and moral ends that expand, enlighten, and enrich experience.[67] The specific ends will vary according to the educational situation and will be determined in each case by the needs and capacities of the persons involved.

Dewey emphasized that there are no fixed and final ends toward which human growth is evolving. The self is an ongoing process of becoming. The end of human life is not to attain some static ideal state and stop growing. The end of living is to be found in a way of living. The way of truth for Dewey is the way of growth. Criticizing Froebel as well as Hegel, he writes:

The conception of growth and progress as just approximations to a final unchanging goal is the last infirmity of the mind in its transition from a static to a dynamic understanding of life. It simulates the style of the latter. It pays the tribute of speaking much of development, process, progress. But all these operations are conceived to be merely transitional; they lack meaning on their own account.[68]

To assert that activity and growth are a mere means to some end which is a completed static reality is to deny that the very process of growing is itself inherently meaningful. This denial is the idea Dewey wished to uproot. In his evolutionary and dynamic view of life, which rejects all dualisms of ultimate meaning and everyday life, every person—child as well as adult—"lives as truly and positively at one stage as at another, with the same intrinsic fullness and the same absolute claims."[69] In order to realize fully the intrinsic value of life, attention must be focused wholeheartedly on the possibilities of the immediate present and the idea of fixed ends makes this difficult if not impossible.

All intelligent activity involves an end-in-view, but such ends should not be mechanically imposed on a situation from without, and they should not be viewed as fixed. Authentic ends are apprehensions of possibilities accompanying the conditions of the present and their function is to liberate and direct the energies of present activity. They must be open to adjustment, and when achieved they in turn become means to new ends. Dewey does not object if educators use ideas of comprehensive ends of growth and education as a way of broadening the view of present possibilities provided that they are not held rigidly and that when applied they are connected sensitively with the developing experience and abilities of the persons involved.[70]

In line with this approach, Dewey persistently attacked the common practice of conceiving of education as primarily a preparation for the future. For example, in 1894 he wrote:

If I were asked to name the most needed of all reforms in the spirit of education, I should say: "Cease conceiving of education as mere preparation for later life, and make of it the full meaning of the present life." And to add that only in this case does it become truly a preparation for after life is not the paradox it seems. An activity which does not have worth enough to be carried on for its own sake cannot be very effective as a preparation for something else.[71]

In *Democracy and Education,* he points out that with children, emphasis on the future fails to awaken interest and to generate motivation. "Children proverbially live in the present," notes Dewey adding that "that is not only a fact not to be evaded, but it is an excellence."[72] Further, by directing attention to the future it is diverted from the concrete situation, which is the only point to which it can be fruitfully directed.

Dewey, of course, does not deny that education should be preparation for the future, but he objects to attempts to use this idea as the mainspring of educational activity. In *Experience and Education* his position is well stated:

> What, then, is the true meaning of preparation in the educational scheme? In the first place, it means that a person, young or old, gets out of his present experience all that there is in it for him at the time in which he has it. When preparation is made the controlling end, the potentialities of the present are sacrificed to a suppositious future. When this happens, the actual preparation for the future is missed or distorted. The ideal of using the present simply to get ready for the future contradicts itself. It omits, and even shuts out, the very conditions by which a person can be prepared for his future. We always live at the time we live and not at some other time, and only by extracting at each present time the full meaning of each present experience are we prepared for doing the same thing in the future. This is the only preparation which in the long run amounts to anything. [73]

Only in this way does real growth take place. Dewey adds: "Because the need of preparation for a continually developing life is great, it is imperative that every energy should be bent to making the present experience as rich and significant as possible. Then as the present merges insensibly into the future, the future is taken care of."[74] This emphasis on attention to "the full meaning of the present" involves an attitude that is fundamental to what in this study has been identified as Dewey's democratic brand of spiritual practice.

In Dewey's naturalistic theory of the moral life, he asserts that, just as growth is the supreme end of education, so "growth itself is

the only moral 'end.' "[75] Education, as Dewey conceives it, is a process of forming and reconstructing a person's fundamental attitudes
and disposition, that is, the basic beliefs and values which govern
conduct. It involves two closely related objectives: growth in the
direction of ever better, richer, and fuller experience, and ongoing
refinement of those beliefs and values essential to an expanding
democratic community. It is Dewey's argument that the process of
individual moral development is "all one with" this educational
process. The moral life of the individual involves "the continuous
reconstruction of experience," leading to "the continuous passage of
experience from the worse to the better."[76] In situations involving
competing goods, the good chosen by a morally responsible person is
the one that contributes to the ongoing growth of the whole person.

> Wisdom ... is the ability to foresee consequences in such a way that
> we form ends which grow into one another and reenforce one another.
> Moral folly is the surrender of the greater good for the lesser; it is
> snatching at one satisfaction in a way which prevents us from having
> others and which gets us subsequently into trouble and dissatisfac-
> tion.[77]

The greater good is the continuous liberation, enrichment, and harmonizing of experience.

With these ideas in mind, and recognizing the value of moral
principles like the Golden Rule or Kant's categorical imperative,
Dewey endeavors to develop a comprehensive moral principle for a
democratic society. When stated from the point of view of individual
self-development, he formulates the supreme moral principle as "the
injunction to each self on every possible occasion to identify the self
with a new growth that is possible."[78] When stated from the point of
view of the responsibility of society in relation to the individual, the
moral imperative is to organize and manage all social institutions so
that they provide opportunity for growth to all persons regardless of
sex, class, or race.[79]

Why is the injunction to grow a supreme *moral* principle in
Dewey's judgment? In other words, why does the injunction to grow
imply a demand for sympathetic responsiveness, respect for the rights
of others, and justice? As a neo-Hegelian, Dewey had believed that

the person who seeks to grow and realize the ideal self would necessarily be drawn to become a morally responsible person and good citizen, for the ideal self is the universal self. As a naturalist who embraced a social psychology, he continued to believe that commitment to growth and growing means "becoming responsible, that is, responsive to the needs and claims of others."[80] According to Dewey's naturalistic principle of growth, the dynamics of personal development finds its source of vital energy in desire and interest, but the self is dependent upon society for its development. It realizes its identity in and through the give and take of cooperative endeavor. The way to grow, counsels Dewey, is to cultivate shared interests and to contribute to the common good, which includes friendship, citizenship, science, art, education, and manufacture of goods. In brief, personal growth in Dewey's view is intimately related to moral growth. "The *kind* of self which is formed through action which is faithful to relations with others will be a fuller and broader self than one which is cultivated in isolation from or in opposition to the purposes and needs of others."[81]

In Dewey's ethics of growth choice is central. Preserving the voluntarism that was characteristic of his early psychology, Dewey writes that "choice is the most characteristic activity of a self." Choice is something more than spontaneous selection. It involves deliberation, that is, the weighing of opposing values and alternate courses of action. Choice is knowing selection. Dewey further explains its significance.

> Now every such choice sustains a double relation to the self. It reveals the existing self and it forms the future self. That which is chosen is that which is found congenial to the desires and habits of the self as it already exists. Deliberation has an important function in this process, because each different possibility as it is presented to the imagination appeals to a different element in the constitution of the self, thus giving all sides of character a chance to play their part in the final choice. The resulting choice also shapes the self, making it in some degree, a new self. . . . Consequently, it is proper to say that in choosing this object rather than that, one is in reality choosing what kind of person or self one is going to be.

In Dewey's psychology there is no self separate from its interests and acts. There is no faculty of will apart from actual decision making. The self becomes and is what it chooses and does. "Our personal identity is found in the thread of continuous development which binds together these changes."[82]

The critical moral issue concerns the relation of choice to ongoing growth.

> All voluntary action is a remaking of the self. . . . In the strictest sense, it is impossible for the self to stand still; it is becoming and becoming for the better or the worse. It is in the *quality* of becoming that virtue resides. We set up this and that end to be reached, but the *end* is growth itself. To make an end a final goal is but to arrest growth.

Dewey explains further that at every period of life persons find themselves again and again confronted with a choice "between an old, an accomplished self, and a new and moving self, between the static and dynamic self." The old self is identical with formed habits, with established interest and attitudes. There is always a tendency to view "the old, the habitual self . . . as if it were the self—as if new conditions and new demands were something foreign and hostile," but "in this way, we withdraw from actual conditions and their requirements and opportunities; we contract and harden the self." However, this tendency is resisted by the self which has centered its interests in growth and the life of shared experience that fosters growth. It "goes forth to meet new demands and occasions, and readapts and remakes itself in the process." The ethics of growth shifts attention in the moral life from a concern with attainment of certain fixed results to the process of development. The good person is the one who is conscious of the choice to be made between the old habitual self and the growing self and who is "concerned to find openings for the newly forming or growing self." The bad person is anyone, no matter how good he or she has been, who "fails to respond to the demand for growth," that is, to the demands of novel situations and needs in the social environment. In this fashion Dewey's *Theory of the Moral Life* endeavors to rationalize and naturalize the Pauline distinction between the old Adam and the new person in

Christ and the many theological and philosophical variations on this theme.[83]

Democracy as the Way of Freedom and Growth

Discussion of Dewey's moral philosophy of growth provides an opportunity to clarify his view of freedom. He argued that insofar as a human being has the capacity to grow in the sense of ability to purposefully modify his or her habits and character that person is at least potentially free and may sensibly and rightfully be held responsible or accountable for his or her behavior. Persons are held responsible so that they will learn to become responsive and exercise their freedom to grow in positive ways. Actual freedom is realized in and through becoming responsive and growing. Dewey states the relation of freedom and growth as follows:

> Potentiality of freedom is a native gift or part of our constitutions in that we have *capacity* for growth and for being actively concerned in the process and the direction it takes. Actual or positive freedom is not a native gift or endowment but is acquired. In the degree in which we become aware of possibilities of development and actively concerned to keep the avenues of growth open, in the degree in which we fight against induration and fixity, and thereby realize the possibilities of recreation of our selves, we are actually free.[84]

When freedom is so defined as the power to grow, Dewey has no difficulty in reconciling individual liberty and adherence to moral law, that is, freedom and conformity to the imperative to keep growing as a person in one's relationships.

Further insight into Dewey's idea of freedom can be gained by inquiring into the relation of freedom of will and intelligence. Freedom has often been identified with a power of radical freedom of will in the sense of an arbitrary or unmotivated power of choice with which all human beings are endowed at birth. Dewey finds that this idea leads to insoluble philosophical problems regarding the relation of freedom to natural causality, and he abandons it. However, he does closely connect freedom with the power of choice: "What men actually cherish under the name of freedom is that power of varied and flexible growth, of change of disposition and character, that springs from intelligent choice."[85] Freedom is not some original power of arbitrary choice; it is rather an acquired power of intelligent choice. All persons have the potential for freedom but not all realize this potential. The development of intelligence—of the capacity to think and judge clearly and critically—is the way to become free.

In his neo-Hegelian period, Dewey believed that the truth makes a person free, that is, a person becomes free by knowing and living according to what is objectively true, which involves living in a society in which this truth has been institutionalized. As a naturalist, Dewey rejects any notion that this truth exists as something preestablished and fixed, but his thinking adheres to the idea that intelligence and truth are the key to freedom. He writes that "the only freedom that is of enduring importance is freedom of intelligence, that is to say, freedom of observation and of judgment exercised in behalf of purposes that are intrinsically worthwhile."[86] In other words, a free person is one who is able to form his or her purposes intelligently, evaluating desires and goals by the consequences which will result from acting on them, and one who is able to select and order the means necessary to realize chosen ends. This freedom of intelligent choice is in Dewey's view identical with moral or practical freedom, for only with realization of such freedom does a person develop the enlightened self-control and self-direction that leads to the ability to choose the dynamic growing self.

Freedom from restraint is the negative side of this positive freedom and is to be valued only as a means to the latter's realization. Thus Dewey rejects the classical British liberal view and the modern popular idea that persons are made free simply by being emancipated from external social, political, and economic restrictions. Furthermore, the earlier liberalism not only did not perceive the difference between positive and negative freedom; it also failed to recognize that if positive freedom is to be achieved, social conditions must be created that actively foster freedom of intelligence. In Dewey's brand of social liberalism, this becomes the responsibility of every social institution. He writes that in his vision of a reconstructed social order "the main purpose of our schools and other institutions is to develop powers of unremitting and discriminating observation and judgment."[87] Institutions should create living and working conditions that foster attitudes of curiosity, inquiry, initiative, and inventiveness, and encourage deliberation and choice insofar as individual capacity makes possible. "The fundamental defect of the present state of democracy is the assumption that political and economic freedom can be achieved without first freeing the mind," explains Dewey. "Freedom of mind is not something that spontaneously happens. It is not achieved by the mere absence of restraints. It is a product of constant, unremitting nurture of right habits of observation and reflection."[88]

Early in his career Dewey identified democracy as the supreme moral ideal and a way of life characterized by expanding communication, cooperation, and shared experience leading to realization of individual capacity, the reconstruction of society, and the unification of peoples. It may be added that the democratic way of life is for Dewey identical with the process of continuing education, experimental valuation, moral growth, and liberation that has just been described. His educational, moral, and social theories all involve inquiries into the conditions and dynamics of human growth. A democratic society is one that is organized for the purpose of promoting the freedom and growth of its citizens.[89] To have faith in democracy means, then, to pursue the life of freedom and growth as an individual and to work to accomplish a democratic reconstruction of all institutions. Democracy as the way of freedom and growth is Dewey's American secular form of spiritual practice.

Apart from the school, Dewey did not attempt any detailed analysis of how particular social institutions should be reconstructed along democratic lines, but he did offer some further general observations and recommendations. For example, in *Democracy and Education* (1916) he comments that:

> the greatest evil of the present regime is not found in poverty and in the suffering which it entails, but in the fact that so many persons have callings which make no appeal to them, which are pursued simply for the money reward that accrues. For such callings constantly provoke one to aversion, ill will, and a desire to slight and evade. Neither men's hearts nor their minds are in their work.[90]

In Dewey's ideal democratic society people would be liberated from the meaninglessness and alienation that afflicts so many in the modern industrial world. He identified the chief obstacle to realizing this objective as an oppressive dualism of means and ends, and from the late 1880s onwards he hammered away at this dualism. "Every divorce of end from means diminishes by that much the significance of the activity and tends to reduce it to drudgery from which one would escape if he could," writes Dewey.[91] Work is dehumanizing, having the quality of being externally enforced and servile, when the people engaged in it do not share an interest in the end of the work process and do not participate in the direction of it, and when work is only accidentally related to the desired end that the worker has in view such as a wage. Properly understood, means are the constituents of ends, and when ends are valued the activities necessary to achieve these ends become saturated with this meaning. Likewise ends worthy of the name grow out of and are continuous with the activities that produce them. Only when persons working in industrial plants have an active interest in the products that their labor is producing and share in the formation of the policies that govern their industry will modern industrial life be democratized and made an agency of real human progress and welfare. Given these concerns it is readily understandable why Dewey was one of the early supporters of the labor union movement.

In a series of essays for the *New Republic* that appeared in 1929, Dewey set forth a critique of American culture focusing on the plight of the individual and the need for a new unified social faith in democracy and the way of growth. The essays were republished as a book with the title *Individualism, Old and New* (1929). At the outset Dewey explains that "the deepest problem of our time" is "the problem of constructing a new individuality" consonant with contemporary industrial technological civilization and with the social and economic interdependence that characterizes it. He points out that the American people are caught between one culture that is dying and a new civilization that has not yet been fully born. In the absence of "a new center and order of life" consistent with the moving forces of the new age, people continue to espouse ideals and methods inherited from ages past, but these creeds and theories are no longer effective guides and they have little real influence over the way people actually behave and manage their institutions. As a consequence, the

American psyche is divided within itself and people are confused and lost.[92]

Dewey continued to maintain that the major difficulty is not science and the machine, or the American fascination with technique, but rather certain fundamental attitudes of desire and thought that dominate contemporary American culture and govern the way science and technology are used and impact on human experience. He does not deny that industrial society has a tendency to submerge the individual and to depersonalize life through processes of quantification, mechanization, and standardization. He recognizes that in reaction individuals are driven to seek relief in superficial and often reckless activities that provide emotional excitement but no sense of enduring meaning. However, he finds a more fundamental problem. He attacks American society as a "money culture" in which affairs are ultimately controlled by narrow interests and the goal of private profit. He writes of "our religion of prosperity" whose "cult and rites dominate."[93] The older individualism, which imagined the self to be a soul destined to receive the reward of eternal salvation as a separate individual, has been reduced to "the individualism of economic self-seeking." The American tradition of rugged individualism had social value in earlier historical periods characterized by the existence of the frontier and the pioneer life, but it is now invoked by a privileged minority to defend laissez-faire economics and to oppose government regulation of industry.

The result of the growth of America's money culture is a fragmented society of two classes and bewildered, anxious people. Workers live in humiliating dependence, insecurity, and fear at the mercy of economic forces beyond their control and without protection from unemployment insurance or retirement benefits. The leaders of business are negatively affected too, because they deny themselves the kind of deep abiding satisfaction that comes only in and through a sense of shared social purpose. The mind of the businessman lives with a contradiction: "It is divided within itself and must remain so as long as the results of industry as the determining force in life are corporate and collective while its animating motives and compensations are so unmitigatingly private." "The unrest, impatience, irritation and hurry that are so marked in our life," writes Dewey, "are inevitable accompaniments of a situation in which individuals do not find support and contentment in the fact that they are sustaining and sustained members of a social whole."[94]

Dewey points out that the values of this pecuniary culture and the self-seeking individualism associated with it are inconsistent with the ideals of equal opportunity and freedom for all which constitute the genuinely spiritual element in the American democratic tradition and the key to a sound American individualism. The problem of the individual in American technological society can be overcome, believes Dewey, only by abandoning the values now associated with the notion of rugged individualism and by reorganizing society to serve these original democratic ideals. "Can a material, industrial civilization be converted into a distinctive agency for liberating the minds and refining the emotions of all who take part in it?"[95] To use social intelligence to develop a technological culture that truly serves the ideals of freedom and growth for all is the challenge to liberalism. Commitment to this task would generate the sense of shared values and organic interconnection needed to harmonize society and to integrate and set free the personalities of contemporary men and women.

To achieve the ideal of a liberating democratic culture, Dewey returns to a recurrent theme in his social and religious thought contending that there must be a full integration of the spiritual and the material so that the machine and technology themselves become "instrumentalities of a free and humane life." There is no way to halt or turn back the industrial and technological revolution. The hope is that the everyday work of the common people in a new transformed technological civilization will become an instrument of meaningful culture so that "the masses can share freely in a life enriched in imagination and aesthetic enjoyment."

> the unique fact about our own civilization is that if it is to achieve and manifest a characteristic culture, it must develop, not on top of an industrial and political substructure, but out of our material civilization itself. It will come by turning a machine age into a significantly new habit of mind and sentiment, or it will not come at all.[96]

In this vision, which lies at the heart of Dewey's democratic human-ism, there is found the concrete social meaning of his philosophical labors to break down the dualisms of the ideal and the actual, humanity and nature, theory and practice, body and mind.

In pursuit of his objective, Dewey in 1929 put forth a fourfold program of social and economic reform. First, like Charles Beard, Herbert Croly, and Thorstein Veblen, he argued for a planned economy involving the "social control of industry and the use of government agencies for constructive social ends." Dewey was a prophet of the welfare state that emerged with the New Deal and the Great Society. Second, he continued to argue for industrial democ-racy.[97] He favored a decentralized form of democratic socialism involving

> the formation of a genuinely cooperative society, where workers are in control of industry and finance as directly as possible through the economic organization of society itself rather than through any form of superimposed state socialism, and where work ensures not only security, leisure and opportunity for cultural development, but also such a share in control as will contribute directly to intellectual and moral realization of personality.[98]

Third, he proposed that the major criterion of valuation and direction in managing industry be "the effect on the life-experience of the consumer" rather than private profit. Fourth, Dewey reiterated his call for use of the experimental method in developing methods of moral guidance and liberating arts of social planning and control. While some criticize American culture for being overly preoccupied with technique, Dewey argues that "interest in technique is precisely the thing which is most promising in our civilization." "The world has not suffered from absence of ideals and spiritual aims," he explains, "nearly as much as it has suffered from absence of means for realizing the ends which it has prized in a literary and sentimental way.... In the end, technique can only signify emancipation of individuality, and emancipation on a broader scale than has obtained in the past."[99]

Dewey's socialist predilections did not tempt him to become a Communist even though he was at times accused of being one. In

1928, on invitation from the Soviet government, he had joined a group of American educators and visited schools, museums, factories, and related institutions in Moscow and Leningrad. In a series of essays in the *New Republic,* he presented what on balance is a positive picture of the "great experiment" launched by the Russian Revolution. He was critical of Communist ideology and the Bolshevik emphasis on class war and world revolution by violence. However, he was impressed with the energy of the people, the spirit of cooperative and collective action being fostered in the schools, the growth of voluntary cooperative organizations, and the efforts being made to enrich the cultural life of the masses.[100] As the decade of the thirties progressed, he became increasingly critical of the Communists. In a brief essay entitled "Why I am not a Communist" in 1934, he attacked the Communists for their dogmatic philosophy of history, their advocacy of class war as *the* means of social progress, their suppression of civil liberties, and their rejection of the values of fair play and elementary honesty in advancing their own objectives.[101]

Individualism, Old and New concluded with quotations from Emerson and a call for the individual to assume responsibility for creating and integrating his or her personality by embracing the moral faith involved in the democratic ideal. As Dewey puts it in an earlier essay: "Our faith is ultimately in individuals and their potentialities."[102] After noting the flexible and plastic nature of personality and the human situation, he advises: "True integration is to be found in relevancy to the present, in active response to conditions as they present themselves, in the effort to make them over according to some consciously chosen possibility." In framing the ideal possibilities of present conditions for oneself and the larger world with which one is involved and in acting on and reshaping these ideals, "we, who are also parts of the moving present, create ourselves as we create an unknown future."[103] By working to build a unified society founded on the democratic ideals of freedom, equal opportunity, education, and experimental intelligence, the individual in industrial technological civilization will find creative purpose, inner unity, a sense of belonging, and freedom.

It is noteworthy that the emphasis on the critical place of individual initiative and decision grew stronger toward the end of Dewey's career as he faced the rise of totalitarianism and state socialism in Europe during the 1930s. He continued to believe "that the ability of individuals to develop genuine individuality is intimately connected with the social conditions under which they associate with one another." However, Dewey explained: "I should now wish to emphasize more than I formerly did that individuals are the finally decisive factors of the nature and movement of associated life." Writing in 1938 he states:

> It has been shown in the last few years that democratic institutions are no guarantee for the existence of democratic individuals. The alternative is that individuals who prize their own liberties and who prize the liberties of other individuals, individuals who are democratic in thought and action, are the sole final warrant for the existence and endurance of democratic institutions.[104]

"We need a revival of faith in individuality and what belongs to the internal springs and sources of individuality," declares Dewey.[105] In other words, individual choice and initiative, are fundamental in the process of moral and spiritual growth and in the preservation of democracy. This theme in his philosophy culminated in his theory of religious faith, which is set forth in *A Common Faith* (1934).

Before turning to Dewey's idea of the nature and function of religious faith, it is useful to conclude this discussion of his vision of the moral life with a few summary reflections on his understanding of the significance of his experimental theory of moral valuation, which lies at the center of his own unifying moral faith in creative democracy. The discussion in the last two chapters has been centrally concerned with the interrelated problems of the relation between the real and the ideal and between science and values. Addressing these issues, Dewey endeavored to show that properly understood, science does not deny the reality of the valuable qualities of things in nature, and as a method it can be used to unify the ideal and the real in concrete situations. If in Dewey's naturalistic worldview nature as a whole is not governed by a fixed hierarchy of ideal ends, it is nevertheless full of ideal possibilities and idealizable. We live in an open, pluralistic, and changing world that can be shaped and directed by the human mind and will. "While the abolition of fixed tendencies toward definite ends has been mourned by many as if it involved a despiritualization of nature, it is in fact a precondition of the projection of new ends and of the possibility of realizing them through intentional activity."[106] "A natural world that does not subsist for the sake of realizing a fixed set of ends is relatively malleable and plastic; it may be used for this end or that."[107] In this outlook change "loses its pathos, it ceases to be haunted with melancholy through suggesting only decay and loss. Change becomes significant of new possibilities and ends to be attained; it becomes prophetic of a better future."[108] In other words, change means the opportunity for growth.

The decisive factor in achieving growth and realizing the ideal possibilities of existence is intelligent choice, and the key to intelligent choice is the experimental method of knowledge. It provides both the power of discriminating judgment of values and the power of control over the means of realizing chosen goods and eliminating identified evils. In other words, experimental inquiry becomes a way of deepening and refining the human vision of ideal possibilities and of actualizing the ideal. Dewey's philosophy regards "intelligence not as the original shaper and final cause of things, but as the purposeful energetic re-shaper of those phases of nature and life that obstruct social well-being."[109] In short, he rejects both pessimism and wholesale optimism for a doctrine of "meliorism."[110] Experimentalism cannot guarantee a wholesale solution to the problem of unifying the ideal and the actual, but it may be instrumental to freedom, individual growth, and social progress.

Since in Dewey's humanistic naturalism the method of intelligence is the means of identifying the truly good and of making goods secure in existence, it becomes for him a unique good in its own right. "In it, apparent good and real good enormously coincide."[111] Dewey goes further. He makes the experimental method the highest object of his moral faith. *Experience and Nature* closes with these words:

> Because intelligence is critical method applied to goods of belief, appreciation and conduct, so as to construct, freer and more secure goods, ... it is the reasonable object of our deepest faith and loyalty, the stay and support of all reasonable hopes. To utter such a statement

is not ... to assert that intelligence will ever dominate the course of events; it is not even to imply that it will save from ruin and destruction. The issue is one of choice, and choice is always a question of alternatives. What the method of intelligence, thoughtful valuation will accomplish, if once it be tried, is for the result of trial to determine. Since it is relative to the intersection in existence of hazard and rule, of contingency and order, faith in a wholesale and final triumph is fantastic. But some procedure has to be tried, for life is itself a sequence of trials. Carelessness and routine, Olympian aloofness, secluded contemplation are themselves choices. To claim that intelligence is a better method than its alternatives, authority, imitation, caprice and ignorance, prejudice and passion, is hardly an excessive claim. These procedures have been tried and have worked their will. The result is not such as to make it clear that the method of intelligence ... is not worth trying.[112]

To put one's faith in the method of intelligence involves nothing less than "a great change in the seat of authority" in the area of moral, religious, and political beliefs and values, a change which Dewey believes is essential to social progress.[113]

A faith in the method of intelligence is Dewey's chief response to the basic human need that has inspired the philosopher's quest for certainty and that is at least partly responsible for the religious quest for God. "The craving of human beings for something solid and unshakeable upon which to rest is ultimate and unappeasable," acknowledges Dewey. In an evolving pluralistic universe in which there are no fixities, no immutable realities, he counsels depending upon a method of inquiry, a way of thinking and acting, rather than an unalterable scheme of philosophical truths or religious dogmas. In an essay for the *New Republic* entitled "Fundamentals," which was written in 1924 during a renewal of the conflict between science and religion among fundamentalist religious groups, Dewey puts his point clearly.

Those traditionalists and literalists who have arrogated to themselves the title of fundamentalists recognize of course no mean between their dogmas and blank, dark, hopeless uncertainty and unsettlement. Until they have been reborn into the life of intelligence, they will not be aware that there are a steadily increasing number of persons who find security in *methods* of inquiry, of observation, experiment, of forming and following working hypotheses. Such persons are not unsettled by the upsetting of any special belief, because they retain security of procedure. They can say, borrowing language from another context, though this method slay my most cherished belief, yet will I trust it. The growth of this sense, even if only half-consciously, is the cause of the increased indifference of large numbers of persons to organized religion. It is not that they are especially excited about this or that doctrine, but that the guardianship of truth seems to them to have passed over to the *method* of attaining and testing beliefs. In this latter fundamental they rest in intellectual and emotional peace.[114]

This passage suggests the religious value Dewey finds in his moral faith in the experimental method.

Dewey often writes of a faith in experience as well as a faith in intelligence. It should be clear at this juncture that the faith of which he speaks in these two instances is identical. His faith in experience is based on the fact that experience can regulate and guide itself in and through the exercise of experimental intelligence. Whether Dewey speaks of a faith in intelligence or a faith in experience, he is asserting his belief "that actual experience in its concrete content and movement may furnish the ideals, meanings, and values whose lack and uncertainty in experience as actually lived by most persons has supplied the motive force for recourse to some reality beyond experience: a lack and uncertainty that account for the continued hold of traditional philosophical and religious notions which are not consonant with the main tenor of modern life."[115] Dewey is, of course, referring here to the supernatural and transcendental strategies for unifying the ideal and the real, which he rejects as incompatible with the scientific attitude and democracy.

Dewey's faith in intelligence or experimentalism is all one with his faith in education and democracy. His faith in education involves a democratic trust in human nature, including a confidence in the capacity of intelligence to develop the knowledge necessary to guide human growth in liberating creative directions that benefit both the individual and the community. He once commented that "democracy, the crucial expression of modern life, is not so much an addition to the scientific and industrial tendencies as it is the perception of their social or spiritual meaning."[116] The flowering of a democratic moral and social order depends upon a faith in experience and intelligence and adoption of the experimental attitude toward beliefs and values. "Democracy cannot obtain either adequate recognition of its own meaning or coherent practical realization as long as anti-naturalism operates to delay and frustrate the use of methods by which alone understanding of, and consequent ability to guide, social relationships can be attained," Dewey states.[117] The democratic way of life is the embodiment of a spirit of sympathy, open communication, and cooperation joined together with experimentalism and imaginative vision, leading to freedom and ongoing growth for all.

TEN

Religious Humanism

W HEN THE NATION'S economic system broke down with the stock market crash of 1929, the American people were plunged into a prolonged period of confusion and soul searching, and they debated their basic beliefs and values as they have at few other times. As the decade of the twenties had progressed, the economic and social injustice that accompanied the workings of the American capitalist system became increasingly apparent, but as long as the business sector prospered, critics and reformers were voices crying in the wilderness. However, the coming of the Great Depression and the attendant social and psychological bewilderment forced Americans not only to consider major economic reconstruction but also to look beyond Wall Street for the deeper causes of their plight. An unusual quantity of books and journal articles appeared on American moral values, good and evil in human nature, human destiny, the idea of God, and the role of religious faith. Fundamentalists, neo-orthodox conservatives, modernists, and humanists of various stripes and colors battled with each other. Commenting on the situation in 1930 in a volume that searches for answers in the credos of twenty-two intellectual leaders, Dewey noted that "the chief intellectual characteristic of the present age is its despair of any constructive philosophy—not just in its technical meaning, but in the sense of any integrated outlook and attitude." [1]

Dewey, of course, was quietly confident that a philosophy of evolutionary naturalism and democratic humanism offered the American people the kind of creative integrated outlook that was urgently needed. Moreover, as the social and economic crisis deepened, he became increasingly convinced that the minds and hearts of the American people would not be unified around a constructive philosophy such as he proposed unless their religious emotions and commitments were engaged. Only a fresh act of religious faith in widely shared ideals would bring unity and purpose to the life of the individual and inspire the necessary cooperative action on behalf of reform. These concerns led Dewey in the late twenties and early thirties to expand his philosophical vision by clarifying and deepening his own naturalistic reinterpretation of the religious dimension of life.

In his Gifford lectures, published as *The Quest for Certainty* (1929), he began the development of a more coherent theory of religious experience, but the unifying notion in his theory—the idea of the religious quality of experience—was not clearly formulated until the writing of *A Common Faith* in 1934. The theory of the religious dimension of experience set forth in this short, pithy volume is the culmination of Dewey's endeavor as a philosopher to chart a middle way between supernaturalism and a despairing atheistic materialism. It is his argument that a person may give up belief in the supernatural and yet continue to cultivate and enjoy a profoundly meaningful religious life in connection with the human effort to unite the ideal and the actual. It is also important to note that the naturalistic theory of the nature and function of religious faith contained in *A Common Faith* completes Dewey's theory of the self and the dynamics of moral choice and moral faith. In this sense it is to be read as an extension of his *Theory of the Moral Life* and of the social psychology and philosophy in *Individualism, Old and New*.

Given the close connection between Dewey's interests in social reconstruction and religious reconstruction, it is useful to note briefly the extent of his personal social and political involvements at this time in his career. The year that the Great Depression began marked

Dewey's seventieth birthday. In his honor a two-day celebration was held in New York City, involving symposia on education and philosophy. At a great banquet he was presented with a *festschrift* volume. Congratulatory messages came from around the world and Dewey was widely hailed as America's foremost philosopher. In 1932 Harvard University reiterated the praise when awarding him an honorary L.L.D. degree, and on a similar occasion at the University of Paris he was lauded as "the most profound, most complete expression of American genius." During the Depression years, Dewey used the considerable power and influence that came with his achievements to try to marshal and lead the liberal forces in America to institute the social planning and control that he believed were essential to economic recovery and equal justice. In 1930 he retired from his teaching career at Columbia University, which gave him extra time for political activities as well as writing, but he continued to be based at Columbia with the title Professor Emeritus of Philosophy in Residence.[2]

Dewey had joined the League for Industrial Democracy in 1925 and for many years he actively supported the organization's programs of research and education directed at promoting the ideals of a planned economy and social justice. In 1929 he accepted the presidency of the Washington-based People's Lobby, a position he retained until 1936. In this capacity he issued statements to the press and wrote numerous articles for the *People's Lobby Bulletin* applying his philosophy to the economic and social problems of the Depression years. He argued for massive national programs of public works, unemployment insurance, and child relief, and urged new tax laws that would effect a more equitable distribution of the national income.[3] In 1929 Dewey also became the president of the newly organized League for Independent Political Action, which was formed to forge the progressive forces in the nation into an effective political force. In this endeavor Dewey was joined by a diverse group of religious and social liberals, including W.E.B. Du Bois, Reinhold Niebuhr, Paul Douglas, Norman Thomas, Devere Allen (editor of *World Tomorrow*), and Oswald Garrison Villard (editor of the *Nation*).[4] In the early thirties the LIPA set out to organize a new national political party of radical political groups committed to a socialist platform, but the endeavor failed due to a lack of political leadership and popular support.[5] Even after Roosevelt's election in 1932 Dewey remained dissatisfied with the Democratic as well as the Republican party.[6] However, through the work of his Columbia University colleagues, Raymond Moley, Rexford Tugwell, and Adolf Berle, who formed Roosevelt's first brain trust, the ideal of experimental social intelligence influenced in the White House.

Dewey's trip to the Soviet Union in 1928 gave him an insight into the kind of religious transformation that he hoped would take place in America in response to the nation's mounting economic, social, and psychological ills. It was the general spirit of the people rather than the communist ideology that impressed him . Upon his return from Russia, Dewey noted with "a certain envy" how the emergence there of a unified social faith involving "aspiration and devotion" to shared social ideals had brought intellectuals and educators "simplification and integration of life." Their common faith and the work and lifestyle it inspired gave them a sense of being organically related to a living whole, "an organic going movement." Dewey described the social faith of the Russian people as religious in nature, and it is the implication of his comments that this social faith may be termed religious because it had a profoundly unifying effect both socially and psychologically. Furthermore, in Russia he witnessed for the first time "a widespread and moving religious reality," which gave him a sense of "what may have been the moving spirit and force of primitive Christianity."[7] The development of a new unifying social faith with a religious quality consistent with American democratic values and humanistic naturalism was the fundamental objective of Dewey's own religious thinking.

Reflecting on the American religious situation in *Individualism, Old and New* in 1929, Dewey observed that traditional religion no longer serves "as a vitally integrative and directive force in men's thought and sentiments." He also argued that the unification of the individual and of society cannot be achieved by attempts on the part of religious groups at "rejuvenation of the isolated individual soul." Restating a major tenet of his theory of the relation of religious experience and society, he writes:

Religion is not so much a root of unity as it is its flower or fruit. The very attempt to secure integration for the individual, and through him for society, by means of a deliberate and conscious cultivation of religion, is itself proof of how far the individual has become lost through detachment from acknowledged social values. It is no wonder that when the appeal does not take the form of dogmatic fundamentalism, it tends to terminate in either some form of esoteric occultism or private estheticism. The sense of wholeness which is urged as the essence of religion can be built up and sustained only through membership in a society which has attained a degree of unity. The attempt to cultivate it first in individuals and then extend it to form an organically unified society is fantasy.[8]

The "consciousness of connection and union . . . proceeds from being a sustained and sustaining member of a social whole."[9]

Even though Dewey did not believe that religion in the sense of the experience of a deep sense of purpose and belonging can be realized by the self in isolation, apart from social action, he did believe that a shared moral or social faith is essential to creating both a unified society and whole individuals. Moreover, as noted, he calls such a unifying faith religious in quality. It is this kind of religious faith, argues Dewey, that possesses the power to serve as "a vitally integrative and directive force" in the future. "I would suggest," he writes in 1930, "that the future of religion is connected with the possibility of developing a faith in the possibilities of human experience and human relationships that will create a vital sense of the solidarity of human interests and inspire action to make that sense a reality."[10] In the same essay Dewey points out that he has in mind a new faith that will do for democratic America what the faith of the early Christians sought to do for the ancient world: "Primitive Christianity was devastating in its claims. It was a religion of renunciation and denunciation of the 'world'; it demanded a change of heart that entailed a revolutionary change in human relationships."[11] Dewey did not believe that early Christianity had within itself "even the germs of a . . . ready-made solution for present problems," but he admired its spirit of revolutionary social change.

It was social and religious concerns such as these that led Dewey to join a group of thirty-four professors, clergymen, and writers in signing "A Humanist Manifesto" in the spring of 1933. Proclaiming that science and economic change have discredited traditional liberal as well as conservative religious beliefs, the "Manifesto" calls on men and women to unite behind the banner of religious humanism. It goes on to set forth fifteen theses outlining the fundamental tenets of religious humanism. It affirms the worldview of evolutionary naturalism and rejects supernaturalism, deism, theism, personal immortality, and the dualism of mind and body. It adopts a Darwinian and sociological view of the origins of religion and rejects any dualism of the sacred and the secular. It finds the wellspring of religion in the human "quest for the good life," and it asserts that the function of religion is to address human needs. Accordingly the religion of the future should be an endeavor to achieve in the here and now "joy in living," release of human creativity, "complete realization of human personality," and "social well-being" involving "a socialized and co-operative economic order." Traditional religious beliefs, ideals, and practices should be reconstructed in the light of modern knowledge and social developments so as to assist humanity in its struggle to realize these objectives for all. In effect, the "Humanist Manifesto" invites the American people to embrace a new religious faith in shared liberal social values.[12]

The "Manifesto" had been originally drafted by Roy Wood Sellars, a professor of philosophy at the University of Michigan, for the Humanist Fellowship in Chicago. Sellars, who espoused a philosophical naturalism and had an affiliation with the Unitarian Church, was an appropriate choice. In the course of the past decade he had published two books, *The Next Step in Religion* (1918) and *Religion Come of Age* (1928), which championed religious humanism as the next stage in the evolution of the religious consciousness of humanity.[13] Notable among the signers along with Dewey were ten Unitarian ministers, as well as J.H.C. Fagginger Auer (Professor of Church History and Theology at Harvard Divinity School), E.H. Burtt (Professor of Philosophy at Cornell University), A. Eustace Haydon (Professor of Comparative Religions at the University of Chicago), John Herman Randall, Jr. (Professor of Philosophy at Columbia University), Roy Wood Sellars, Robert Morse Lovett (Editor of the *New*

Republic), V.T. Thayer (Educational Director of the Ethical Culture Schools), and Jacob J. Weinstein (a Reformed Jewish Rabbi associated with Columbia University).

The "Manifesto" was initially published in the *New Humanist,* the publication of the Chicago Humanist Fellowship, but it also appeared in the *Christian Century* and the *Christian Register* (a Boston publication of the Unitarian Church).[14] The appearance of the "Manifesto" provoked considerable comment and debate, especially on the subject of the meaning and possibility of religion without God, and it focused public attention on the fact that the philosophy of naturalism and religious humanism had significant support, at least in academic circles and among Unitarians. It also made clear that there were those who identified themselves as humanists but who had nothing in common with the aristocratic and rather negative humanism of Irving Babbitt and Paul Elmer More. In *Humanism and America* (1929), Babbitt and More asserted the dualism of humanity and nature, cast doubt on democracy, condemned science, and preached an attitude of self-discipline and balanced restraint. Protesting their appropriation of the term "humanism" Dewey wrote: "What humanism means to me is an expansion, not a contraction, of human life, an expansion in which nature and the science of nature are made the willing servants of human good."[15]

Believing that the pressing social, psychological, and moral issues facing America were tangled up with religious issues, Dewey became further involved in religious discussions in 1933. He reviewed for the *Christian Century* a book by three philosophers (Douglas Clyde Macintosh, Max Carl Otto, and Henry Nelson Wieman), entitled *Is There A God? A Conversation,* and then found himself caught up in an ongoing debate. This same year he accepted an invitation from President James R. Angell of Yale University to give the 1934 Terry Lectures, which had been established to address the subject of "religion in the light of science and philosophy."[16] Dewey used the occasion to provide an intellectual foundation for his personal faith and religious humanism by setting forth his own naturalistic theory of religious experience coupled with a critique of the American religious situation. The three lectures were published under the title *A Common Faith.* Before turning to an analysis of this volume, which occupies an important place in the history of American religious thought, some further comments about the religious situation in America are in order.

The Religious Situation, 1934

If he was to be successful in spreading the gospel of religious humanism and faith in the democratic way of freedom and growth, Dewey had to counter the appeal of numerous other religious alternatives. If one includes the religious humanists, there were at least five significant approaches to the question of religion and religious faith in competition on the American scene. Major alternative perspectives were offered by the conservatives and fundamentalists, the secular humanists and atheists, the religious liberals or modernists, the religious humanists, and a new brand of postliberal American theology typified by the thought of Reinhold Niebuhr. Dewey's writings on religion in the 1930s are written with these diverse approaches in mind.

First, there was the way of the religious conservatives and fundamentalists, who emphasized the transcendence of God, affirmed supernaturalism, and championed the absolute authority of Biblical revelation and historical creeds. They looked to the past and to external authorities for guidance, and believed in the existence of absolute values and the immortality of the individual person. The writings of the Princeton theologian John Gersham Machen were particularly influential among Protestant conservatives in the 1920s. Machen had an intensely felt need for adherence to historical doctrine as the essence of the Christian tradition. In *Christianity and Liberalism* (1923), he attacked Protestant liberalism, arguing that it "is not Christianity at all," but another new religion.[17] He emphasized the finality and unique nature of biblical revelation and the authority of Christ, insisting that there is no other way to salvation. The modernist ideas that God is immanent in modern culture and revealed in and through individual religious experience were rejected as distortions of Christian truth.

Beginning in the mid-twenties, American religious conservatism began to find support and fresh guidance in the crisis theology of

Karl Barth and Emil Brunner, which emerged in Switzerland and flourished in Germany and Sweden in the wake of the First World War. It is often labelled "neo-orthodoxy," for it is an attempt to return to the main themes of classical Reformation theology with the aid of Søren Kierkegaard's religious existentialism. Barth and his followers were not biblical literalists, but they believed that salvation can be found only through the Word of God as revealed in the Bible. According to Barthian theology, the separation between God in his transcendence and humanity in its sinful condition is so radical that there is no way from humanity to God, from philosophy to saving truth, from culture to God's kingdom. There is not even a way from religion to God. Religion, as defined by the Barthians, is humanity's futile striving to find God, and it is to be carefully distinguished from Christian revelation, where God on his initiative encounters humanity and offers salvation. Barth's dogmatic theology involves a despairing anthropology, but it provided a distracted age with an escape from doubt and anxiety into intellectual certainty through trust in the idea of an absolute historical revelation involving the reconciliation of humanity and God in Christ. The term "crisis theology" is used by the neo-orthodox not only because their theology reflects the crisis situation generated by the war, but also because it seeks to precipitate for the contemporary individual a crisis of choice between the humanist's faith in human goodness, science, philosophy, and social progress, and an authentic Christian faith in the Word of God. In short, the Barthians, like the American conservatives and fundamentalists, were diametrically opposed to what Dewey's philosophy affirmed.

A second kind of response—and one at the opposite extreme—was the approach of the secular humanists and atheists, who rejected all religions and everything religious as a matter of wish-fantasy and illusion. Those who embraced a classical Marxist humanism or who followed Freud's thinking in *The Future of An Illusion* (1928) fall into this category. From the point of view of Marx and Freud, religion is both psychologically and socially repressive as well as delusion and, therefore, should be abandoned by the human race. Marx stressed that such a step is necessary to the forward advance of history, and his atheism was coupled with a dogmatic theory of history and an optimistic view of human destiny that served as a secular substitute for the religious faith he rejected.

The American literary and social critic, Joseph Wood Krutch, also found himself driven to accept atheism and to reject religion as illusion, but he could find no ground for belief in Marx's progressive optimism. In a disturbing and widely read volume entitled *The Modern Temper: A Study and A Confession* (1929), he argued that European and American civilization is entering a period of decline and spiritual malaise having lost its original spontaneous vitality and religious faith. Such, he thought, is the inevitable fate of every advanced civilization. At the root of the problem Krutch identified a fundamental discord and maladjustment between human nature and the natural universe, such that the flowering of what is distinctively human ends in its destruction. As human beings develop their capacities for knowledge, art, and moral order, they find themselves struggling to survive in an alien universe, which eventually overwhelms them with spiritual pessimism and the unthinking animal energy of less-developed peoples.[18] *The Modern Temper* is secular humanism and atheism at its most negative.

Reflecting on western civilization and the fruits of modern science and philosophy, Krutch concludes: "from the universe as we see it both the Glory of God and the Glory of Man have departed." "Science ... does not in any ultimate sense solve our problems," asserts Krutch. It has increased human control over nature, but it has not been an effective source of wisdom and happiness. It also leaves humanity contemplating a universe that is from a human point of view "a vast emptiness." There is no universal moral order, cosmic purpose, ultimate meaning, or God in the world that science describes. In addition, the weakness and depravity of human nature is all too evident. There are no true heroes, and hence no consolation is to be found in the outlook of classical tragedy. Even the Victorian idealization of human love is no longer possible. "Love is becoming gradually so accessible, so unmysterious, and so free that its value is trivial," observes Krutch. Art and aesthetic experience cannot supply the practical guidance and ultimate meaning that have been lost. A new faith is needed, but Krutch finds that "skepticism has entered too deeply into our souls ever to be replaced by faith." The declarations and debates of religious liberals as well as fundamentalists are desperate futile attempts to revive what is dead. "Ours is a lost cause and there is no place for us in the natural universe," argues Krutch with despairing resignation. He then adds defiantly even though a bit weakly: "We are not, for all that, sorry to be human. We should rather die as men than live as animals."[19] Krutch may be seen as a man undergoing the throes of what Nietszche described as the "death of God," but he had no prophecies of a superman who was yet to emerge. If his analysis was correct, Americans in 1929 were threatened by a spiritual as well as an economic Great Depression. Dewey, who had for decades tried to steer clear of such gloomy lines of modern thinking, received an inscribed copy of *The Modern Temper* from the author.[20]

A third way of addressing the religious question was that of the modernist religious liberals. They sought to occupy the middle road between fundamentalism and atheistic secular humanism, and they were constantly under attack from both sides. The spirit of the modernist liberal outlook was manifest during the 1920s and 1930s in the American Jewish Reconstructionist movement led by Mordecai Kaplan, as well as in Reform Judaism. Coming out of the left wing of Conservative Judaism, Kaplan retained a deep commitment to traditional symbols and observances, which he believed operate to provide the Jewish people with a sense of social unity and continuity with historical Judaism. However, drawing heavily on the work of Dewey and Durkheim and defining Judaism as most fundamentally "a civilization" rather than "a religion," he undertook a radical reconstruction of the meaning of traditional religious symbols and beliefs with the objective of bringing them into harmony with science, secularization, and democracy.[21]

The leading defenders of modernism among Protestants in the 1920s and early 1930s were Shailer Mathews (the Dean of the Divinity School at the University of Chicago), Harry Emerson Fosdick (the eloquent preacher at Riverside Church near Columbia University in New York), and Henry Nelson Wieman (a philosophical theologian at the University of Chicago). Mathews put much faith in science and democracy, but he did not believe that these forces by themselves were sufficient to transform society. "When has knowledge meant virtue? After we have learned how to control nature and fully gained social equality and freedom shall we have learned how to live happily and justly?" asks the Chicago theologian in *The Faith of Modernism* (1924).[22] Beyond science and democracy there is a need for a Christian faith in God and the way of love embodied in the life of Jesus. Harry Emerson Fosdick, who was impatient with Christian denomination-alism, believed that the heart of religion is "individual psychological experience," beginning with "devotion to spiritual values" and lead-ing to "peace and power" in communion with God, the creative cosmic "Conserver" of values. Fosdick had respect for the religious life in non-Christian religions, but he found the essence of Christian-ity in a distinctive "reverence for personality" as the supreme spiritual value.[23] Henry Nelson Wieman was representative of a new group of theologians who tried to use the thought of philosophers like Dewey and Whitehead to harmonize empirical naturalism and theism.

As the decade of the 1920s progressed, the social energies of religious liberals became much absorbed in a strategy of restraint involving the outlawry of war, pacifism, and prohibition. As the battle between labor and capital deepened increasing numbers of liberals turned to socialism, giving their support to political leaders such as Norman Thomas. Many cooperated with Dewey in ventures such as the League for Independent Political Action.

Emerging out of the left wing of the modernist liberal movement was yet a fourth way of addressing the problem of religion and modern culture. It was the movement of religious humanism which produced the "Humanist Manifesto" in 1933 and with which Dewey had been associated in spirit for over three decades. Unlike the secular humanists, who rejected everything associated with religion, the religious humanists believed that there is ongoing vital signifi-cance in the religious dimension of life. American religious human-ism has roots in Emerson's attack on religious authoritarianism, bibliolatry, and theism, and in the New England Transcendentalists' vision of a liberating humanitarian religion based upon the divinity of humanity, freedom of inquiry, direct personal religious experience, and moral growth. The Boston Free Religious Association (founded in 1867), the left wing of the Unitarian Church, and Felix Adler's Ethical Culture Society (founded in 1876) all contributed to the further growth of humanistic lines of religious thinking. Ludwig Feuerbach's religious atheism and Auguste Comte's religion of humanity were European precedents that gave support to the development of religious humanism in America. Bertrand Russell's essay, "A Free Man's Worship" (1903), which combined atheistic naturalism and stoic wisdom, with a defiant faith in human dignity and creative idealism, offered another variation on the theme.[24] Russell's view of the universe in relation to humanity is much like Krutch's, but, unlike Krutch, he retained a sense of the "sacredness" of existence and of the heroic possibilities of human nature. The Harvard philosopher George Santayana offered a brilliant reinterpretation of religion as poetry and imaginative moral vision in *Reason in Religion* (1905), and it became a valuable resource for naturalistic humanists with an appreciation of religious values.

Even though the religious humanists rejected the ideas of a personal God and personal immortality, some, recognizing the historic significance of the idea of God, endeavored to reconstruct the concept along nontheistic, naturalistic, and humanistic lines.[25] The thought of Felix Adler, who resented being labelled an atheist, is an interesting early example of this kind of approach. After rejecting the Biblical notion of God as a supreme cosmic monarch as inconsistent with science and democratic values, he continued to employ a reconstructed idea of the divine as integral to his neo-Kantian ethical philosophy. At first he adopted Matthew Arnold's rather vague definition of God as "the Eternal Power, not ourselves, that makes for righteousness."[26] Later he refined his religious vision identifying what he came to call "the godhead" or "the divine life" with the imaginative ideal of a perfect spiritual society extending throughout the universe and made up of an infinite number of unique, interdependent ethical beings.[27] Adler proposed this idea of an infinite ideal community of mutual caring as the best symbol of what is ultimately real and truly divine. In keeping with this view, he taught that the religious life should not focus on worship of a transcendent supreme being but on social reconstruction and on developing interpersonal relations so as to enable all persons to participate ever more fully in what is actually divine, that is, ideal community life. Adler did not believe in personal immortality. However, he did believe that each person is a unique embodiment of ethical energy and, as such, is of absolute worth and that beyond death each person's constructive interrelations with the larger community of life are somehow preserved as an enduring contribution to the inclusive ongoing divine life, which is the eternal spiritual universe. Through compassion and ethical action one can experience this belonging to the divine life now.[28] Adler's philosophical idealism distinguished him from the typical twentieth-century American religious humanist, who was usually a naturalist, but the spirit of his teaching had the effect of encouraging the development of religious humanism among his followers.

The influence of Dewey's thought on the growth of religious humanism is well illustrated by its impact on the Ethical Culture Society. Increasingly during the twentieth century, the majority of Adler's small but dedicated following found his idealist philosophical speculations and religious vision obscure, and many came to fall under the influence of Dewey's naturalistic humanism. When Adler died in 1933 the leadership of the society passed to men like V.T. Thayer and Jerome Nathanson, who championed Dewey's philosophy. Thayer was a signator of the "Humanist Manifesto." One leader of the Society has referred to Ethical Culture as "the movement that Adler built and Dewey, through his followers, so quickly inherited."[29] In short, Adler's Society came to function as a kind of religious humanist fellowship founded upon Dewey's philosophy.

Beginning about 1916 in the Midwest, there developed in the Unitarian Church a strong humanist movement led by the ministers John H. Dietrich and Curtis W. Reese. In the 1920s their cause found vigorous support in the East from Charles Francis Potter. Even though these men did not like to be called atheists because of the negative connotations of the word, they openly confessed that they could find no convincing evidence for the God of theism. They believed that the religion of the future could do without the idea of God—as in the case of Buddhism, for example. They were also agnostics on the subject of immortality. They stressed the development of personality, ethics, and democratic social action as the core of the religious life and were optimists about the possibilities for social progress. In response to a pessimistic vision of the universe, such as Krutch's, they insisted that human creativity can make life sufficiently meaningful to be inherently worthwhile. Their sermons and writings precipitated a heated controversy within the Unitarian Church over "religion without God."[30]

By the late 1920s the controversy had spread beyond the Unitarian fold and engaged the attention of a large number of religious conservatives and liberals. The defense of religious humanism was taken up by philosophers and historians at Cornell, Columbia, Harvard, and the universities of Chicago, Michigan, and Wisconsin. The debate prompted Fulton J. Sheen to respond with a Thomistic critique entitled *Religion Without God* (1928), and Harry Emerson Fosdick defended the moral and religious value of theism from the liberal point of view in an essay published in 1929 under the title "Religion Without God."[31] In *A Preface to Morals* (1929), the social philosopher Walter Lippmann showed respectful appreciation for the role religion had played in human civilization, but he also declared that "the truths of religion are the truths of human experience." "Man creates God in his own image," explained Lippmann, and once a person "knows that he has created the image of God, the reality of it vanishes like last night's dream." Rejecting belief in a superhuman God as no longer possible for the modern mind, he advocated a humanistic "religion of the spirit" based upon a disinterested search for moral wisdom in keeping with both the scientific attitude and the efforts of the great spiritual teachers such as Socrates, Jesus, Buddha, and Confucius.[32] Potter and Reese defended their idea of "religion without God" in the books they separately wrote on *Humanism: A New Religion* (1930) and *Humanist Religion* (1931).[33] Dewey was drawn into the debate in 1933 when he reviewed *Is There a God?* for the *Christian Century*.[34]

As the economic and social crisis of the late twenties and early thirties deepened, another religious movement emerged in America out of modernist religious liberalism. It developed as a reaction against certain liberal ideas and attitudes, especially liberalism's optimistic view of human nature and destiny, and it marked the dawn of a postliberal era in American Protestant thought. This new outlook often combined a shift to the left politically with a return to a more conservative theology. The latter was encouraged in part by the European neo-orthodox revolt against liberalism, but it obscures im-

portant differences to label this new American theology neo-orthodox. The leading figure in this novel American development is
Reinhold Niebuhr. Since it is primarily in and through exchanges
with Niebuhr that Dewey encountered the postliberal reconstruction
of modernism, it is appropriate to concentrate attention on Niebuhr's
thought in describing this fifth religious movement.

Niebuhr emerged on the American Protestant scene in the 1920s
as a spirited, combative champion of modernism and the Social
Gospel. His prophetic voice was regularly heard in pulpits, college
lecture halls, and liberal journals like the *Christian Century* and the
World Tomorrow. He defended his modernist Christian beliefs with
arguments derived from James' pragmatism and urged social reform
on his listeners with appeals to Christian love and respect for justice.
In reaction to the First World War, which he had supported, Niebuhr joined the ranks of the pacifists and eventually became head of
the Fellowship of Reconciliation. As the decade of the twenties
progressed, however, Niebuhr became increasingly uneasy with liberal religion and liberal politics. The Christian ideals of love, conscience, and reason by themselves were proving to be inadequate to
the challenge at hand. The liberal reconciliation of the sacred and the
secular appeared too easy and unrealistic.[35] As his concern with the
inequities of the American capitalist system mounted, Niebuhr began
to seek more radical political solutions. In 1929 he joined the Socialist
Party, and the following year he helped to found the Fellowship of
Socialist Christians. Despite his acceptance of a Marxist analysis of
society, he avoided connections with the Communists. As the 1932
presidential election approached, he joined Dewey and others at the
League for Independent Political Action in exploring the possibilities
for a new national political party built upon a farm-labor coalition
and a socialist platform. In the fall of 1932 Niebuhr ran for Congress
in New York City on the Socialist ticket with Dewey's backing, but
he won little support at the polls.[36]

As Niebuhr's politics became more radical, he simultaneously took
up a more conservative theological stance. In 1928 he joined the
faculty of Union Theological Seminary across the street from Columbia University, and here he found colleagues who shared his growing
disillusionment with liberalism. They were rediscovering classical

Christian thought and listening to the voices of neo-orthodoxy overseas. Niebuhr himself was persistently critical of Barth for his exclusivism, absolutism, and failure to relate the Christian faith meaningfully to human culture. He had lost his progressive optimism, but he had no use for a Barthian social defeatism. At heart Niebuhr retained a modernist's concern to work out some adaptation of religion to the intellectual and social world of the times and a liberal's emphasis on social ethics and social reconstruction. However, the winds of neo-orthodoxy and the influence of the young German theologian Paul Tillich, whom Niebuhr helped to bring to Union Theological Seminary in 1933, led Niebuhr to a reexamination of St. Augustine and classical theology.[37] The result was a new appreciation of the traditional doctrines of the transcendence and sovereignty of God, the sinful condition of human nature, and ultimate salvation by faith and grace. The heart of his attack on liberal religion became centered on rejection of the notion that human beings are basically rational and well-meaning and that reason, science, education, and moral suasion can by themselves solve society's problems. To believe such, he argued, is sentimental idealism. In the light of the war, the Depression, and the rise of fascism, Niebuhr developed a new brand of Christian realism that emphasized the distorting and corrupting presence of pride and egoism in all that men and women do. Returning to the insights of Paul, Augustine, and Luther, he contended that the human will mysteriously exists in a condition of bondage to evil. He resisted all attempts to reduce the problem of sin to a problem of creaturely finitude, the strength of natural impulse, or a lack of education and knowledge.

Deeply frustrated by the moral complacency and social inertia of western industrial society, Niebuhr now searched for a political strategy that would precipitate dramatic social and economic change. His new Christian realism guided his reflections. In *Moral Man and Immoral Society* (1932), an acute and powerful book of political and ethical analysis that shocked his liberal and pacifist friends, he argued that the use of coercive force is a necessity in the struggle for equal justice and that violent revolution may under certain circumstances be ethically justifiable. He did not, however, recommend revolutionary violence as a wise strategy for the foreseeable future in the industrial West given the political and military situation. A search for other nonviolent methods of coercion was recommended. The secular and religious liberals were sharply attacked as naive, confused, and ineffectual. Singling Dewey out for special criticism, Niebuhr writes: "The most persistent error of modern educators and moralists is the assumption that our social difficulties are due to the failure of the social sciences to keep pace with the physical sciences which have created our technologies." Reason, experimental science, and moral idealism by themselves cannot tame the forces of injustice at work in modern industrial society. "Reason is always, to some degree, the servant of interest in a social situation," argues Niebuhr, and progress is only achieved in and through social conflict when oppressed peoples challenge the power of the ruling classes with power.[38] Religious and educational idealists falsely believe "that an entire nation can be educated toward a new social ideal when all the testimony of history proves that new societies are born out of social struggle. . . . No amount of education or religious idealism will ever persuade a social class to espouse a cause or seek a goal which is counter to its economic interest."[39]

Further developing his Marxist outlook, Niebuhr contends that an oppressed class of industrial workers can be motivated to act only by use of "the right dogmas, symbols and emotionally potent oversimplifications."[40] Such nonrational forces are what move people as distinct from scientific knowledge. In this regard Niebuhr argues that the religious imagination has an important role to play, and developing a theme from James' "The Will to Believe" he writes:

> Furthermore there must always be a religious element in the hope of a just society. Without the ultrarational hopes and passions of religion no society will ever have the courage to conquer despair and attempt the impossible; for the vision of a just society is an impossible one, which can be approximated only by those who do not regard it as impossible. The truest visions of religion are illusions, which may be partially realised by being resolutely believed. For what religion believes to be true is not wholly true but ought to be true; and may become true if its truth is not doubted.[41]

Niebuhr concludes these observations by returning to his main point. The critical issue for the religious prophet with a vision of the good society is to learn "how to use force in order to establish justice."

Niebuhr criticized Dewey for ignoring the role of class interest, class conflict, and coercive force in political affairs and for overestimating the role intelligence and education can play in social change. From one point of view his criticisms seem overstated and unfair. First of all, Niebuhr's outlook was very close to Dewey's in many ways. He opposed defeatism in social affairs, attacked moral absolutism, knew the need for social intelligence, and often employed pragmatic methods of moral valuation. Also he and Dewey shared a similar socialist vision of economic justice. Second, many of Niebuhr's criticisms of liberal thinking and much of what he had to say about the political necessity of coercive force had been stated by Dewey himself in his essays on force, coercion, and violence in 1916 and 1917, as well as elsewhere. Dewey certainly had no illusions about the powerful influence of class interest. In other words, the Dewey that Niebuhr attacks is something of a straw man which Niebuhr set up for polemical purposes.[42]

Third, it hardly made sense for Niebuhr to disparage efforts on behalf of the method of intelligence and education, because without them there was no hope of realizing the socialist reconstruction of society to which he was committed. As Dewey put it in a response to Niebuhr in the *New Republic:* "What are the alternatives? Dogmatism, reinforced by the weight of unquestioned custom and tradition, the disguised or open play of class interests, dependence upon brute force and violence." Dewey warned that to discredit use of the method of intelligence plays into the hands of those whose economic interests lead them to defend the status quo. Further, those who downplay the potential contribution of social science only "strengthen the forces that will introduce evil consequences into the result of any change, however revolutionary it may be, brought about by means into which the method of intelligence has not entered." If one is going to have a religious faith that inspires and guides action, argues Dewey, is not faith in the method of intelligence worth a trial? Responding directly to Niebuhr's notion of religious visions as helpful illusions, he asks: "In view of the influence of collective illusion in the past, some case might be made out for the contention that even if it [the method of intelligence] be an illusion ... this particular one may be better than those upon which humanity has usually depended." Dewey goes on to criticize Niebuhr for "a deplorable vagueness about what needs to be done." It is Dewey's position that only a union of thought and action such as is involved in his experimentalism will be able to develop an idea of the social ideal toward which radicals should strive and an understanding of the means to its realization. This brand of liberalism, asserts Dewey, bears little resemblance to the sentimental liberalism that Niebuhr criticizes.[43]

Toward the end of his career in the 1960s Niebuhr acknowledged "that he and Dewey had more in common than his earlier polemical writings might suggest," and he regretted the harshness of his attack on Dewey.[44] However, the two men were clearly divided on a substantive religious issue. It concerned the new theological perspective that Niebuhr embraced and especially his doctrine of sin. It is this issue that underlies Niebuhr's criticisms of Dewey and liberalism generally. Just because Niebuhr himself remained a modernist liberal in many respects, he had to distance himself aggressively from the older liberals in order to establish his new outlook as a distinct position and to take possession of the center stage in what had been the old liberal theological arena. It is useful to consider further Niebuhr's postliberal religious thought because it is an alternative to Dewey's approach that would exercise an increasingly wide influence among people with roots in the liberal tradition.

Niebuhr argues that the essence of human nature is freedom, by which he means a power of self-transcendence and self-determination beyond all the limits and necessities of nature, history, and the laws of reason. In other words, he adheres to the idea of a radical freedom of will, a power of arbitrary choice, which is an idea that Dewey rejected. However, since human beings are finite creatures of nature, Niebuhr acknowledges that their freedom is not absolute. Human freedom is limited, but it can be expanded endlessly as human capacities are developed. This freedom of spirit constitutes the unique dignity of human beings and is the source of their creative power. It is in the exercise of this freedom of spirit that sin manifests itself according to Niebuhr. In short, the evil in human nature lies at the center of the self in the freedom of the will. This is the offense of Biblical faith to rationalism and optimistic humanism. Niebuhr used the term "sin" to refer to a universal human condition of spiritual bondage involving a tendency to act in ways that obstruct the healthy growth of personality and cause social injustice. When writing about sin he is especially concerned to emphasize the existence of this spiritual condition involving the estrangement of the self from its essential nature as opposed to specific sins, which proceed from this condition. He does not deny that psychology and social science may find various social causes that contribute to certain forms of destructive and unethical human behavior, but beyond all such causes there lies this deeper problem of evil involving the condition of the human will itself.[45]

Niebuhr explains that the occasion for sin is the anxiety of human beings about their finitude. "We fall into sin by trying to evade or to conquer death or our own insignificance, of which death is the ultimate symbol."[46] However, finitude and death are not to be understood as the cause of sin, because human beings sin in their freedom. Reflecting on the universality of sin, Niebuhr, therefore, states that sin is inevitable but not necessary. Herein lies the mystery of sin to which the mythical notions of original sin and the Fall point. The Biblical story of the Fall is to be taken seriously but not literally. It is a symbol of the human condition and of human responsibility for it. One cannot explain why, in the final analysis, the human will inevitably fails to achieve the ideal ethical possibilities that lie before it, but Niebuhr insists that this is the case and empirical observation of human nature will bear out the truth of this classical Christian teaching.

> Prophetic religion attributes moral evil to an evil will rather than to the limitations of natural man. The justification for such an emphasis lies in the fact that human reason is actually able to envisage moral possibilities, more inclusive loyalties, and more adequate harmonies of impulse and life in every instance of moral choice than those which are actually chosen. There is, therefore, an element of perversity, a conscious choice of the lesser good involved in practically every moral action; and certainly there are some actions in which this conscious perversity is the dominant force.[47]

What this means is that the expansion of human knowledge, power, and freedom will always involve some new distortions and injustices as well as realization of novel creative possibilities. Failure to recognize this fact, according to Niebuhr, accounts for the liberals' sentimental and overly optimistic views of human destiny.[48]

It is only by faith and divine grace that the problem of sin as well as death can be overcome, asserts Niebuhr. The problem of sin and evil will never be resolved in history. The taint of pride cannot be purged in a final way from the human spirit. This is true of saints as well as sinners, and it is especially true of human groups and nations. However, it is possible for faith, in response to the Word of God, to appropriate God's forgiveness now and to look forward to eternal life and a realization of the kingdom of God by divine grace beyond history. Insofar as faith takes root in the human heart, it can quiet the anxiety that tempts the human spirit to fall into the sin of pride or to escape into sensuality. Through faith and repentance individual spiritual growth may occur. Never losing the spirit of a social reformer, Niebuhr's realism and Biblical faith did not lead him to counsel quietism. The problem of sin cannot be eliminated, but some wrongs can be righted, some distortions of self-interest can be corrected, and new structures of justice can be created. Niebuhr urges men and women, therefore, to engage themselves in the social struggle, knowing that ultimately they are justified by faith not works and recognizing that such progress as can be made requires a realistic understanding of human nature. Humanity's creative capacities for goodness make a free society possible, reasons Niebuhr, but given the universal problem of sin, he finds much wisdom in the American democratic system which maintains a separation of government powers and has criticism built into the system.

A Common Faith contains Dewey's response to Niebuhr's fresh emphasis on sin as well as to the fundamentalist's rejection of modernity, the liberal's effort to reconcile Christianity and culture, Krutch's despairing atheism, and the debate over religion without God. The remainder of this chapter and the following chapter explore the main ideas in this book and Dewey's other writings from the 1920s and 1930s which develop his naturalistic theory of religious experience.

The Religious Quality of Experience

The comprehensive problem with which Dewey concerned himself as a philosopher was the uniting of the ideal and the actual in the context of a democratic technological culture and an evolving universe. His philosophy of religion develops the implications for religion of his naturalistic and instrumentalist approach to this problem. Adopting the way of experimental intelligence and social action, he sought to idealize the world, not just by speculative philosophical vision or by chance intense emotional experiences, but by the "deliberate quest for security of the values that are enjoyed by grace in our happy moments." A religion consistent with this approach, reasons Dewey, would be "a religion devoted to inspiration and cultivation of the sense of ideal possibilities in the actual."[49]

In *The Quest for Certainty,* Dewey argues that "the religious attitude" which complements and harmonizes with naturalism, experimentalism, and democracy is "a sense of the possibilities of existence and . . . devotion to the cause of these possibilities." Religious faith in this view is "devotion to the ideal" understood as a possibility of nature rather than an actuality such as the God of theism. So defined, religious faith "would surrender once for all commitment to beliefs about matters of fact, whether physical, social or metaphysical." It would recognize that such matters fall within the province of scientific inquiry. When the religious attitude is conceived as faith in the ideal possibilities of natural existence, there is, then, no reason for a conflict between religious faith and science. Dewey makes a further critical point in this connection:

> But religious devotees rarely stop to notice that what lies at the basis of recurrent conflicts with scientific findings is not this or that special dogma so much as it is alliance with philosophical schemes which hold that the reality and power of whatever is excellent and worthy of supreme devotion, depends upon proof of its antecedent existence, so that the ideal of perfection loses its claim over us unless it can be demonstrated to exist in the sense in which the sun and stars exist. . . . The claims of the beautiful to be admired and cherished do not depend upon ability to demonstrate statements about the past history of art. The demand of righteousness for reverence does not depend

upon ability to prove the existence of an antecedent Being who is righteous.

Dewey asserts that a religious faith, as he conceives it, would not substitute a fixed belief in certain values or ideals for a fixed belief in a divine Being. However, a religious faith consistent with an evolutionary naturalism would be unalterably committed to one basic value: the "value of the worth of discovering the possibilities of the actual and striving to realize them." Experimental inquiry in such matters would over time cause the reconstruction of the particular object of faith, but it would not disturb the basic nature of the religious attitude.

> Whatever is discovered about actual existence would modify the content of human beliefs about ends, purposes and goods. But it would and could not touch the fact that we are capable of directing our affection and loyalty to the possibilities resident in the actualities discovered. An idealism of action that is devoted to creation of a future, instead of to staking itself upon propositions about the past, is invincible.

A religious faith in the ideal possibilities existing in nature coupled with an idealism of action involves a religious attitude fully adaptable to the challenges of life in an evolving universe and a democratic technological culture.[50]

Dewey's discussion of the religious attitude and religious faith in *The Quest for Certainty* involves a problem. As a naturalist he completely separates religious faith from belief in the supernatural or transcendental and from belief in some eternal unity of the ideal and the real such as is involved in classical theism or absolute idealism. His notion of religious faith in the ideal seems to reduce religious faith to what Matthew Arnold called "morality touched by emotion."[51] This raises a critical issue. If religious faith is basically moral faith, why use the word religious at all? What is distinctively religious about Dewey's concept of religious faith? In the context of a thoroughgoing naturalism, is there in the final analysis any place for religion and does the adjective "religious" possess a distinct meaning and denote a unique aspect of experience? In his essay on "Religion and Our Schools" (1908) and other writings in the area of social philosophy, Dewey had argued that the forces of communication, shared experience, and moral faith possess religious meaning and value insofar as they create social unification and a sense of belonging to a whole. In *Human Nature and Conduct,* Dewey wrote about "religion as sense of community and one's place in it," and in *The Quest for Certainty* he indicated that the religious attitude involves a certain natural piety and sense of dependence and that aesthetic experiences may acquire a certain religious mystical quality. All of these statements on religious experience indicate that for Dewey the religious dimension of experience involves more than morality even though it is intimately connected with the moral life. However, it was not until 1934 and publication of *A Common Faith* that his thinking on this matter was fully clarified.

In *A Common Faith,* Dewey at the outset seeks to give the adjective "religious" a definite meaning distinct from other adjectives like "moral" and "aesthetic." In and through his reconstruction of the meaning of the term "religious," which is heavily influenced by his biological, functional, and instrumentalist modes of thought, he develops the basic idea around which he is able to organize his thinking on the subject of religion and the distinct nature of religious experience.

It seems probable that Dewey's early psychology of religion exercised a certain influence on the direction his thinking takes. In the *Psychology* (1886), for example, he had noted that religious experience involves certain distinctive qualitative feelings such as a sense of dependence, peace, and joy, and he had associated religious experience with the unification of the self around the ideal and the complete adjustment of the self in relation to the world. In all likelihood, however, it was William James' Gifford Lectures on Natural Religion, delivered in Edinburgh, Scotland, in 1901–1902, that crystallized Dewey's thinking in his efforts to formulate a naturalistic redefinition of the meaning of the term "religious." James' lectures focus on the nature and meaning of personal religious experience, and when published they were aptly entitled *The Varieties of Religious Experience.* In this work James assembled an impressive mass of empirical data. His lectures sparkle with fresh formulations, distinctions, and insights, and his philosophical reflections on his empirical investigations in the psychology of religion continue to challenge thoughtful minds. Dewey recognized James' genius in the area of the study of religion, and a comparison of his thought with that of James indicates that in a general way he followed James' approach to the subject.

At the outset of his study James makes it clear that he is primarily interested in personal religious experience, which he views as the heart of religion, as distinct from religious institutions, ceremonies, and creeds, which are considered secondary religious phenomena. Dewey agrees with this distinction. Second, contradicting a theory popular among nineteenth-century liberals since Schleiermacher, James argues that there is no unique, separate religious feeling or emotion, but rather there are many religious emotions which are natural emotions reflecting the varied responses of the human organism to whatever men and women may consider to be divine, the religious object. James, then, makes an observation that may have been very suggestive to Dewey. He writes: "As there thus seems to be no one elementary religious emotion, but only a common storehouse of emotions upon which religious objects may draw, so there might conceivably also prove to be no specific and essential kind of religious object, and no one specific and essential kind of religious act."[52] James in the final analysis puts forth the speculative hypothesis that there is a specific religious object, which is God, but he leaves this as an open question. Third, James makes an observation that probably provided Dewey with the key to the naturalistic way of thinking about religious experience for which he was searching. James argues that "the essence of religious experiences, the thing by which we finally must judge them, must be that element or quality in them which we can meet nowhere else."[53] This unique quality is "the practically important *differentia*" of religious experiences. In other words, from a scientific point of view one cannot assume that there is one specific essential religious object, emotion, or act that defines a religious experience, but what does characterize it empirically is a certain distinct quality.

In line with his biological and functional point of view, James suggests that this quality is to be defined with reference to the way religious experiences function in helping the human organism adjust to life in the universe. James goes on to identify the function that differentiates an experience as religious with an "added dimension of emotion," a certain "faith-state." The religious attitude has to do with a person's "total reaction upon life," the manner in which he or she accepts and relates to the larger universe and the power and truth which is supreme in the universe. In describing the faith-state, James is much influenced by the experiences of "the sick soul" or "divided self" and the great mystics, and he understands it to involve a particular kind of unification of the self and adjustment to life that is more free, enthusiastic, affirmative, and glad than Stoic resignation or "the athletic attitude" of the moralist.[54] What is especially impressive from Dewey's point of view with James' analysis of the varieties of religious experience is the demonstration that by adopting an empirical and functional approach and by defining what is distinctly religious about an experience with reference to its consequences and quality, it is possible to develop a naturalistic theory of religious experience which does not necessarily require the idea of the supernatural or presuppose one special object, emotion, or kind of action that is uniquely religious.

In the first lecture in *A Common Faith,* Dewey endeavors to distinguish the adjective "religious," to which he wishes to give fresh positive meaning as designating a distinct and important quality of human experience, from the noun "religion." He means by "religion" the institutional religions, and he defines a religion as a body of beliefs and practices bound up with the idea of the supernatural and associated with some form of institutional organization. The religions are many and varied, involving a diverse set of metaphysical and moral beliefs relative to the social cultures in which they occur. A person who embraces one particular form of religion is inevitably led to reject on intellectual and moral grounds much that is identified with religion as a whole. Dewey wishes to push this process to a more radical conclusion. He seeks "to emancipate the religious quality" of experience, which is a natural phenomenon in his view, from any necessary connection with the historic religions or any new institutional religion.[55] Whereas some conservative theologians following Barth have distinguished between Christian revelation and religion and others like Bonhoeffer have spoken of "religionless Christianity,"

Dewey proposes to free the religious from a necessary identification with religion and to speak about the possibility of religionless religious experience.

In explaining what he means by the adjective "religious" and the idea of the religious quality of experience, Dewey makes it clear that he rejects the kind of theory found in Rudolf Otto's highly influential book *The Idea of the Holy* (1920), which contends that religious experience is something sui generis, separate from all other kinds of experience and involving a distinct religious reality or object—the sacred—which is utterly separate from all natural realities. The religious quality of experience, as Dewey understands it, is not dependent on interactions with any particular thing or object, and it does not necessarily involve adopting any one particular set of beliefs or practices. It is not, strictly speaking, a particular kind of experience separate from other kinds of experience. On the contrary Dewey has in mind a quality of experience which may be realized in the midst of secular activities and may come to "belong" to a person's aesthetic, scientific, political, social, and moral experience. Dewey's point is that under certain conditions various experiences which people undergo have what he describes as a religious "force," "function," "effect," or "value," and when this occurs, under whatever circumstances, a person's life acquires a religious quality.[56]

Experiences with a religious function are those that bring about "a better, deeper and enduring adjustment in life" involving "an orientation that brings with it a sense of security and peace." Such experiences provide a person with "the sense of values which carry one through periods of darkness and despair." What Dewey means by a deep adjustment goes beyond accommodation to, or submissive acceptance of, particular conditions in the environment that cannot be changed, and it involves more than adaptations to the environment that entail modifying certain conditions so that they harmonize better with human needs. The kind of deep enduring adjustment in life that is religious in quality is one that involves "our being in its entirety," and it includes "a composing and harmonizing of the various elements of our being such that, in spite of changes in the special conditions that surround us, these conditions are also arranged, settled, in relation to us." In other words, what Dewey has in mind is "a thoroughgoing and deepseated harmonizing of the self with the Universe (as a name for the totality of conditions with which the self is connected)." Dewey notes that even though there is an element of submission involved in a religious adjustment, a person whose life has been imbued with a religious quality manifests an attitude that is "more outgoing, more ready and glad" and "more active" than Stoic resignation.[57]

In *Art as Experience* (1934), Dewey describes human experience as involving "the rhythm of loss of integration with environment and recovery of union." Happiness and joy are experienced when the realization of harmony involves "a fulfillment that reaches to the depths of our being—one that is an adjustment of our whole being with the conditions of existence." Having realized such a harmony of self and world there abides in the self through future "phases of perturbation and conflict . . . the deep-seated memory of an underlying harmony, the sense of which haunts life like the sense of being founded on a rock." It is just such experiences of profound adjustment that Dewey identifies in *A Common Faith* as possessing religious value.[58]

The unification of self and self and world that gives life a religious quality is not in Dewey's view externally imposed; it is voluntary. However, he notes that it is not the consequences of a particular act of will: "It is a change *of* will conceived as the organic plenitude of our being, rather than any special change *in* will." Reflecting explicitly on William James' exploration of the unconscious sources of religious experience and on theological theories which attribute a religious change in attitude to the intervention of divine grace, Dewey notes that "an 'adjustment' possesses the will rather than is its express product."[59] In other words, while it is possible to nurture the processes of spiritual growth, the maturation of religious experience has its own times and seasons which cannot be forced in a mechanical fashion.

With reference to George Santayana's identification of religion with imaginative poetic vision that penetrates deeply into life shaping values and purposes, Dewey argues that imagination plays a critical role in experiences that have a religious force and unify the self. The ideas of a whole self and of the whole universe are not attained through observation and analytical thought, and unification of self and of self and world are not ever perfectly achieved as a practical matter.[60] The ideas of a completely unified self and of the harmonizing of self and world, therefore, operate only through the imagination. It is in and through the workings of imaginative vision nurtured by poetry, philosophy, and moral faith that a deep enduring adjustment possesses the self. Dewey also notes that the self achieves unification only in and through relation to that "mysterious totality of being the imagination calls the universe," because the self cannot exist and grow in isolation and "the self is always directed toward something beyond itself." The unification of the self, then, depends upon "the idea of the integration of the shifting scenes of the world into that imaginative totality we call the universe."[61]

Dewey's general idea of the religious quality of experience is similar in many respects to that of James. However, in contrast with Dewey's account, James' description of the faith-state is more extensive and is more heavily influenced by mysticism and extraordinary religious experiences such as one finds in the lives of Augustine, Luther, and Tolstoy. In addition, James asserts that not every unification of the self is to be identified as religious in nature. He criticizes the French psychologist R. Murisier for seeming to regard inner unification as unique to religion. James observes that "*all* strongly ideal interests, religious or irreligious, unify the mind and tend to subordinate everything to themselves."[62] Dewey would want to argue that from an empirical point of view unification of self and adjustment are what define experience as religious in quality. However, he also insists that to be called truly religious in quality, a unification of self must be of a deep enduring nature and be characterized by the emotions of peace and gladness. Dewey, like James, then, does not identify psychological unification of personality as of religious value without qualification. Finally, it is important to note that James' empirical inquiries in the area of religious experience lead him in the final analysis to speculate about the reality of a divine spiritual realm, which is at once beyond and continuous with the natural world, and to explore a new brand of evolutionary theism.[63] Dewey sticks more rigorously to James' basic naturalistic and functional approach.

Dewey recognizes that religions claim to produce a reorientation of personality having a religious effect and that many people associate achieving of a deep enduring adjustment with their involvement with a religion and with supernatural agencies such as the God of theism. He, however, sees at most only an accidental connection between any institutional religion and the process of adjustment. He argues that supernatural explanations of the cause of it are "not inherent in the experience itself." They are "adventitious to the intrinsic quality of such experience." Theological and supernatural interpretations vary from culture to culture, and all of them simply reflect various traditional ways of thinking involving uncriticized beliefs and assumptions. He firmly believes that an experience with a religious force is the work of natural conditions and causes. Furthermore, achievement of the kind of complete adjustment that gives a person's life a religious quality, may come about in a variety of ways. For example, Dewey writes:

> It is sometimes brought about by devotion to a cause; sometimes by a passage of poetry that opens a new perspective; sometimes as was the case with Spinoza—deemed an atheist in his day—through philosophical reflection.

The conditions and causes that produce the effect that is religious in quality vary, and they are often totally unrelated to institutional religion.[64]

This last statement by Dewey quoted above has an autobiographical ring to it. Indeed, the fundamental inspiration for Dewey's interpretation of the nature of religious experience is his own religious experience and the evolution of his personal religious consciousness. At the outset of his career, his interests were guided by a passionate quest for unity and adjustment, which was intimately related to a religious quest. He identified God with the principle of organic unity in the self and in the universe at large. Through the study of Wordsworth's poetry and Hegel's philosophy he began to realize the unity and religious sense of meaning and value that he craved. Most importantly, Dewey found that as his moral faith in unifying social ideals matured, his personal adjustment in relation to his world deepened and his life gained in religious quality. When he abandoned belief in the God of theism and absolute idealism, he found that the religious quality of his life experience was not lost. On the contrary, through the ongoing power of philosophical vision, moral faith, community life, and aesthetic and mystical intuitions, his own experience of inner unity and adjustment with the world deepened. There were times of trial and stress, especially during the war years (1916–1918), as is revealed in his poetry and letters. However, he found natural means of handling "the phases of perturbation and conflict" in his own experience, and as the years passed, his life continued to gain in those qualities which he had identified from very early with distinctly religious values. In the final analysis he had to conclude that his experience with the institutional church had been more of an obstacle than a help in his own religious development. For him the religious quality of experience had come basically in and through natural processes of interacting with his world involving imaginative philosophical vision, poetic feeling, and an idealism of action guided by a moral faith in democracy and intelligence.

Dewey's notion of the religious quality of experience becomes more concrete in *A Common Faith* when he further clarifies his idea of the nature of religious faith, explaining the way in which a moral faith in the ideal may have a religious effect.

Moral and Religious Faith

In the history of religion it is possible to distinguish two major aspects of religious experience, and having this distinction in mind helps to clarify the way in which Dewey goes about developing his understanding of the religious dimension of experience.[65] On the one hand, religion involves an encounter with the ideal as that which ought to be and as the supreme good which human nature aspires to realize. In this regard the divine is identified with what is good and right, the law of human well-being. It stands in judgment of what is, demands realization, and promises fulfillment. The moral types of religious faith make this aspect of religious experience their central concern. Moral types of faith usually recognize the unfinished nature of the battle to overcome suffering and evil, and they emphasize practical reason and will. On the other hand, religious experience involves more than moral striving to achieve the ideal. It also involves the direct personal experience of the presence of saving truth and power, a sense of being one now with the divine and the ideal. This aspect of religious experience brings consolation, liberation, harmony, and peace in the face of the conflicts, evil, and suffering in life. It is the predominant concern of sacramental and mystical types of religions. Where this aspect of religious experience is central, special emphasis is put on the heart, the feelings, and transrational intuition. In all religious traditions, both aspects of religious experience are present and they are interrelated, but the tendency is for one aspect to dominate.

From early in Dewey's life, both aspects are at work in his personal religious experience and both find expression in his philosophy of religion. The moral aspect tends to be dominant in both his early ethical idealism and his religious humanism, but there is also a noteworthy current in his thought that emphasizes the role of feelings of belonging, harmony, and peace. By considering first Dewey's idea of religious faith and then his concepts of natural piety and the aesthetic and mystical dimensions, of experience, it is possible to appreciate the way in which these two major aspects of religious experience find expression in his mature thought. Both aspects, of course, contribute to development of the religious quality of experience, and they are interconnected.

On several occasions Dewey indicated that Samuel Taylor Coleridge and James Marsh had a lasting influence on his religious thinking and on the ideas in *A Common Faith*.[66] Only a few years before writing *A Common Faith*, he had an opportunity to refresh his mind on their thought. He returned to the University of Vermont to deliver the James Marsh lecture in commemoration of the centenary of the publication of Marsh's edition of Coleridge's *Aids to Reflection* (1829), and he entitled his lecture "Coleridge, Marsh and the Spiritual Philosophy."[67] There are dramatic differences between the spiritual philosophy of Coleridge and Marsh on the one hand and Dewey's naturalistic philosophy of religion on the other, but it does seem clear that Dewey's idea of religious faith is to a significant extent a naturalized version of the idea of faith he encountered as a youth in the thought of these men. In the religious philosophy of Coleridge and Marsh, which is based on a reconstruction of Kant's theory of pure reason and practical reason, the essence of human nature is understood to be spirit, or rational will, and self-determination. A religious faith is conceived to involve direct insight into and wholehearted commitment to the supreme ethical ideal governing all rational beings. The religious life is most fundamentally a life of ethical action in devotion to the common good. Dewey's exposure to neo-Hegelian idealism with its notions of moral and religious will reinforced the conviction that a religious faith is in a fundamental sense a unifying act of the will involving the whole self and commitment to the supreme practical ideal governing the individual and society. He never seriously questioned throughout his career that such an inclusive moral faith is basically religious in nature and gives to a person's life a religious quality.[68] He also came to believe, in the light of his own personal experience, that wholehearted devotion to great ethical and social ideals is the chief way in which a person's life may acquire a religious quality, even though other factors also contribute.

The neo-Hegelians, whom Dewey followed during his years as an ethical idealist, made a distinction between moral will, which affirms the ideal as what ought to be, and religious will, which affirms the actual identity of the ideal and the real as the deeper truth of the self and the universe. As a naturalist, Dewey, of course, could not any longer accept the neo-Hegelian definition of religious will or faith. How then did he as a naturalist define what is distinctively religious about a moral faith?

First of all, he clarifies what he means by faith. It is not basically a form of intellectual belief involving assent to propositions pertaining to the actual existence of some being or the occurrence of events about which there is a lack of empirical evidence. Faith is belief in the sense of moral conviction. "Conviction in the moral sense signifies being conquered, vanquished, in our active nature by an ideal and it signifies acknowledgement of its rightful claim over our desires and purposes." Dewey further explains that "such acknowledgement is practical, not primarily intellectual. It goes beyond evidence that can be presented to *any* possible observer.... The authority of an ideal over choice and conduct is the authority of an ideal, not of a fact, of a truth guaranteed to intellect...."[69] In other words, moral faith involves being possessed by an imaginative vision of ideal possibilities.

Second, when a moral faith has a distinctively religious function, it may then—and only then—be termed a religious faith.

> What has been said does not imply that all moral faith in ideal ends is by virtue of that fact religious in quality. The religious is "morality touched by emotion" only when the ends of moral conviction arouse emotions that are not only intense but are actuated and supported by ends so inclusive that they unify the self. The inclusiveness of the end in relation to both self and the "universe" to which an inclusive self is related is indispensable.[70]

Again, Dewey gives this account of "the faith that is religious:"

> I should describe this faith as the unification of the self through allegiance to inclusive ideal ends, which imagination presents to us and to which the human will responds as worthy of controlling our desires and choices.[71]

Dewey adds:

> Any activity pursued in behalf of an ideal end against obstacles and in spite of threats of personal loss because of conviction of its general enduring value is religious in quality. Many a person, inquirer, artist, philanthropist, citizen, men and women in the humblest walks of life, have achieved, without presumption and without display, such unification of themselves and of their relations to the conditions of existence. It remains to extend their spirit and inspiration to ever wider numbers.[72]

Dewey's notion of religious faith as a moral faith with a unifying function is an example of what Paul Tillich had in mind when he put forth the general definition of religious faith as the state of being grasped by an ultimate concern. An ultimate concern, explains Tillich, is one that possesses the whole personality—heart, mind and will—demanding total surrender, promising total fulfillment, and leading to an integration of personality.[73]

Unlike Tillich, Dewey does not wish to assert that there is any necessary connection between a religious faith or ultimate concern and what is absolute in being. He prefers to explain the dynamics of faith in terms of natural interactions between the whole self and the larger world of nature and society with which the self is connected.

Since a faith experience involves being possessed from beyond oneself by a great social ideal, and since it is dependent upon the workings of unconscious processes of growth that cannot be forced, it has often been explained with reference to supernatural or transcendental powers. However, Dewey prefers to view it as the product of natural interactions and consummations that have their own season in the course of human events. One can create conditions favorable to the growth of faith, but then one must trust to nature including the deeper resources of the individual to bring it forth.

In the present secular democratic scientific age, Dewey would have men and women become fully conscious that the true positive essence of religious faith in all cultures with a developed moral concern has been and is similar in form to what he has described as a moral faith in a unifying vision of the ideal possibilities of nature, self, and society. This he describes as "the common faith" of the human race. The content of this common faith, of course, continues to evolve. He believes that recognition and acceptance of this perspective on religious faith coupled with his theory of the religious quality of experience would pave the way for a complete integration of the religious aspect of life with the everyday secular existence of men and women thus overcoming the biggest problem with which modern culture seems to confront religion.

The growth of secularism has dramatically altered the social place and function of religion. "The essential point is not just that secular organizations and actions are legally or externally severed from the control of the church, but that interests and values unrelated to the office of any church now so largely sway the desires and aims of even believers."[74] The social significance of organized religion has steadily declined. Dewey concludes: "This change either marks a terrible decline in everything that can justly be termed religious in value, in traditional religions, or it provides the opportunity for expansion of these qualities on a new basis and with a new outlook."[75] Dewey believes that the latter alternative is possible and that it is also necessary to the well-being of contemporary society. To accomplish this revitalization and fresh expansion of the religious dimension of experience, however, requires recognition that there is no necessary connection between religious values on the one hand and religion or the supernatural on the other, and there is no inherent dualism between the religious and the secular or the religious and the natural. Stated more positively, human experience may naturally acquire a religious quality and this is brought about most often by what has been the common faith of humanity, that is, a unifying moral faith in the ideals and values that guide the ongoing development of human relations and culture.

Reiterating his belief in a theory of the social origins of traditional religion, he contends that religious symbols, ceremonies, and creeds are to a large extent symbols of the moral, aesthetic, intellectual, and political values of a particular social group. However, one can distinguish three stages in the evolution of human consciousness regarding the origin and meaning of religious values. In the first stage, human nature is viewed as so weak and corrupt that only with supernatural revelation, guidance, and inspiration can the human situation be rectified. Religious values are believed to be derived from a transcendent divine source and to be distinct from the values natural to human beings in their sinful condition. Dewey identifies the second stage with the outlook of the modern theological liberals, who acknowledge that religious values are akin to the values discovered by human beings in and through their natural relations with each other. He would take this realization one step further, arguing for recognition "that in fact the values prized in those religions that have ideal elements are idealizations of things characteristic of natural association, which have then been projected into a supernatural realm for safe-keeping and sanction." It is Dewey's position that in actual fact "all significant ends and securities for stability and peace have grown up in the matrix of human relations" and "that goods actually experienced in the concrete relations of family, neighborhood, citizenship, pursuit of art and science, are what men actually depend upon for guidance and support." Dewey would have men and women become fully aware of the natural and social origins of the values in which they actually put faith.[76] Such an approach integrates religious faith with secular life. Secular experience would gain a religious quality and religious values would be understood to pervade the world of human relations.

For Dewey the great significance of this naturalistic and humanistic reconstruction of religious values is that it promises not only to revitalize religious life, but it also has the potential to liberate human life in the broadest sense by releasing fresh energy for the endeavor to realize the ideal possibilities potential in human relations. In Dewey's view, one cannot introduce spiritual values into the world of human relations by trying to impose them from the outside. Progress "can only come from a more intense realization of values that inhere in the actual connections of human beings with one another," coupled with deliberate and intelligent efforts to cultivate these ideal possibilities in their natural setting.[77] By leading people to recognize that religious values are ideal possibilities inherent in human relations and that religious faith is commitment to these ideals in desire and action, Dewey seeks to harmonize the religious impulses of men and women in the most fundamental way with the cause of social reconstruction and liberation.

Dewey's naturalistic theory of religious experience and his idea of a common faith did not lead him to become completely negative about the institutional church and related organizations. He was not personally interested in the church or any other institutional religion. For example, even though he might send his children to Felix Adler's school and sign the "Humanist Manifesto," he did not join the Ethical Culture Society or some humanist fellowship organization. In his own life the religious was completely integrated with his secular activities. However, regarding his idea of a common faith and the churches, in 1930 he wrote: "If our nominally religious institutions learn how to use their symbols and rites to express and enhance such a faith, they may become useful allies of a conception of life that is in harmony with knowledge and social needs."[78] In *A Common Faith* Dewey took a similar position:

> The transfer of idealizing imagination, thought and emotion to natural human relations would not signify the destruction of churches that now exist. It would rather offer the means for a recovery of vitality. The fund of human values that are prized and that need to be cherished, values that are satisfied and rectified by *all* human concerns and arrangements, could be celebrated and reinforced, in different ways and with differing symbols, by the churches. In that way the churches would indeed become catholic.[79]

The churches, asserts Dewey, should "take a definite stand upon such questions as war, economic injustice, political corruption," but they must also be willing to participate on "a natural and equal human basis" with others in efforts on behalf of such causes. This means giving up supernaturalism and "the surrender of claims to an exclusive and authoritative position" regarding social values.

Before leaving this discussion of Dewey's idea of faith, it is important to comment further on the intimate connection in his thinking between faith and moral virtue. In his *Psychology* (1886), he had indicated that the moral life finds its fulfillment in the life of religious faith, which brings deeper commitment, greater unity of purpose, and fresh energy to a person's moral strivings. Dewey makes a comparable point in his naturalistic moral and religious philosophy. In *Theory of the Moral Life* (1932), he defined virtue as love of the ideal in the sense of wholehearted interest in and devotion to the ideal resulting in complete union of self and those actions demanded by the ideal. *A Common Faith* indicates that such virtue is the fruit of being "vanquished ... in our active nature" and possessed by the ideal. In other words, for Dewey the moral life finds its completion in a religious faith, that is, in being possessed in the center of one's being by a great unifying ideal. The moral life is perfected by choice and action guided by sympathy and intelligence, but what makes this possible in the final analysis is a faith that is religious in function, that is, unifying. Only a religious faith that possesses the deeper active center of personality—"the organic plenitude of our being"—can generate the love, the interest, the devotion, to the values of democracy and intelligence that will ensure the control of intelligent sympathy over conduct.

There are many statements in Dewey's philosophy that seem to affirm the Socratic teaching that virtue is knowledge or practical wisdom. However, Dewey's ideas on moral virtue and faith cause one to recognize that there is also a different emphasis and that one must be careful as to how one interprets him in this matter. Intelligence and knowledge are essential to the good life, but intelligence has the power consistently to govern conduct only if and when it is supported by a religious faith in its value. In this sense, faith is more fundamental than knowledge. If one understands that the Platonic idea of knowledge encompasses an imaginative vision of the human ideal in which the aspiring human heart and the ideal become one, then it would not be incorrect to assert that Dewey agrees with the Platonic teaching that virtue is knowledge. However, it is perhaps more to the point to recognize that, in the final analysis, Dewey's humanistic understanding of virtue has a decidedly Christian emphasis. Virtue is religious faith and wholehearted love, which are in a real sense gifts of grace—natural grace from Dewey's point of view to be sure, but nonetheless gifts of grace, "unforced flowers" as he once put it.[80]

Reflections on Sin and Death

One of the common criticisms directed against Dewey's idea of faith, and specifically his faith in intelligence, is the view that he has not adequately addressed the problem of sin and evil, and consequently his reconciliation of the religious and the secular is too easy. Dewey addressed this issue in *A Common Faith* responding to what he described as "a revival of the theology of corruption, sin, and need for supernatural redemption." With Reinhold Niebuhr's *Moral Man and Immoral Society* much in mind, he attacked this new theological movement as an obstacle to the development of social intelligence and reform. He was particularly critical of the attempt to explain social evils by reference to "general moral causes" such as the sinfulness of the human will.

> The sinfulness of man, the corruption of his heart, his self-love and love of power, when referred to as causes are precisely of the same nature as was the appeal to abstract powers (which in fact only reduplicated under a general name a multitude of particular effects) that once prevailed in physical "science," and that operated as a chief obstacle to the generation and growth of the latter. Demons were once appealed to in order to explain bodily disease and no such thing as a strictly natural death was supposed to happen. The importation of general moral causes to explain present *social* phenomena is on the same intellectual level. Reinforced by the prestige of traditional religions, and backed by the emotional force of beliefs in the supernatural, it stifles the growth of that social intelligence by means of which

direction of social change could be taken out of the region of accident...[81]

The appeal to supernatural agencies for help in the face of radical
evil also has the effect of retarding the kind of careful empirical
investigation that would be helpful, notes Dewey.

Reiterating an argument he made in his attack on religious sentimentalism in his 1917 essay on "Progress," Dewey also points out
that in human beings there is a natural passion for liberation from
oppression and most people are well enough endowed with impulses
toward justice, kindliness, and order. What is needed is scientific
knowledge of social ills and of how to reconstruct society in positive
directions so that these emotions and impulses can be channeled in
creative directions. The negative behavior of individuals can be altered to a large degree by changing the social environment, including
the schools. The major problem is not a lack of kindly feelings or the
corruption of the will but ignorance, a lack of social planning, and
the absence of a strong unifying moral faith in intelligence. Dewey's
idealism of action calls for "a marriage of emotion with intelligence"
resulting in "passionate intelligence," that is, "devotion, so intense as
to be religious, to intelligence as a force in social action."

> There already exists, though in a rudimentary form, the capacity to
> relate social conditions and events to their causes, and the ability will
> grow with exercise. There is the technical skill with which to initiate
> a campaign for social health and sanity analogous to that made in
> behalf of physical public health. Human beings have impulses toward
> affection, compassion and justice, equality and freedom. It remains to
> weld all these things together.... The point to be grasped is that,
> unless one gives up the whole struggle as hopeless, one has to choose
> between alternatives. One alternative is dependence upon the super-
> natural; the other, the use of natural agencies.[82]

In the 1930s Dewey made no sweeping claims for his approach. If
society were to put its faith in intelligence as a moral guide, he
promised no abrupt and complete transformation, but "the disorder,
cruelty, and oppression that exist would be reduced." "I make no
claim to knowing how far intelligence may and will develop in
respect to social relations," writes Dewey. We will never know, he

adds, unless we undertake the challenge to find out by trying the experiment.[83]

In evaluating the Dewey-Niebuhr debate over the problem of sin and evil, it is, first of all, well to keep in mind that the doctrine of sin —the idea that the human will is so corrupt that no amount of knowledge and insight into the human good by itself can liberate the will to act according to reason and the good—is an unprovable hypothesis. It may be correct, but no amount of observation of human behavior can either prove or disprove in a decisive fashion the idea that the deeper human problem is sin rather than, for example, ignorance. If this Christian teaching is true, it is as Kierkegaard clearly pointed out, a revealed truth lying beyond the reach of natural knowledge.[84] If it is to be accepted, it must be accepted on faith. In his denunciations of liberal thought, Niebuhr often seemed to assume that the classical Christian doctrine of sin is demonstrably true, which is to overstate the case.

Second, the doctrine of sin should not be used to belittle the efforts of persons like Dewey who employ experience and reason to address specific problems of evil and suffering and who seek to reconstruct the school and society so as to create an environment more conducive to the growth of moral virtue and a unifying social faith. Dewey's approach to problems of suffering and evil is multifaceted and highly constructive. He is concerned with both the education and liberation of the individual on the one hand and the reconstruction of society on the other and also with the dynamic interaction of the individual and society in the processes of individual growth and social change. His approach involves experimental inquiry, social reform, progressive education, the Alexander Method, an empirical method of moral valuation, the cultivation of moral vision, and the awakening of a unifying social faith in moral democracy.

Third, history teaches that the problem of moral evil is immensely complicated and that it is a persistent problem such that freedom and justice can only be protected and advanced by never-ending vigilance. At its best the Christian doctrine of sin may be used as a symbol to point to the deep roots in personality and society of the dark side of human behavior and the complexities and obscurities that accompany this problem. Dewey might have acknowledged this more explicitly than he did. Given the historical association between the doctrine of sin and theories of the necessity for supernatural redemption, it is clear why he chose to abandon use of the word "sin." However, he did not develop an entirely convincing explanation of human evil as it has manifested itself in the twentieth century, and he might have probed more deeply into the problem.

Fourth, the deeper, more complex aspects of the problem of moral evil become apparent when it is recognized that the problem can only be addressed in a profound and lasting way by the awakening of what Dewey calls "a religious faith in the ideal." Further, such faith cannot be awakened simply by giving an individual information about the ideal or by the deliberate strivings of an individual aided by technique. Information and technique may be vitally important as means of preparation, but they are not sufficient. Dewey acknowledges this when he points out the fundamental role of individual decision in the process of moral growth and then goes on to argue in line with what he had learned from Coleridge that a unifying moral faith in the ideal is not a product of a particular act of will. It is the result of being possessed or "vanquished" by the ideal in the deeper center of the self, engaging the whole self—heart, mind, and will. The great problem involved in trying to get at the roots of moral evil concerns the enormous difficulty most individuals and societies have in awakening to the ideal on this deeper spiritual level, which is called the heart in the Bible and the heart-mind in much Asian religious literature. Even when such an awakening occurs, it tends to remain partial and incomplete. Recognizing that a person who has not been possessed by the ideal cannot by self-effort achieve union with the ideal, classical Christian theology declares that it is by grace —a power of goodness from beyond the self—that humans are saved from sin. William James has shown that such claims have a certain psychological truth, and Dewey does not wish to deny this. However, as noted earlier, he chooses to think in terms of natural rather than supernatural grace. He views faith and love as flowers that bloom naturally when all the conditions are right—conditions of body, mind, and environment. Human beings should concentrate on using their intelligence to improve the natural conditions of moral and spiritual growth like diligent gardeners who trust their seeds, fertile soil, and the sun. His approach assumes the immanence of a divine creativity in nature, including human nature.

Fifth, the Christian doctrine of sin is concerned to assert that all human beings bear some responsibility for the condition of estrangement in which they find themselves, and hence there is a need for divine forgiveness as well as the power to overcome the condition of sin. Dewey does not deal explicitly with this problem in *A Common Faith,* but the way he would respond to this issue seems clear. In "The Value of Historical Christianity" (1889), he had argued that the individual who wholeheartedly seeks "union with humanity and humanity's interests, and surrenders individual desires" will find liberation from sin and guilt and reconciliation with God, for God is "the living spirit" of the human community.[85] The Hegelian theology is gone in *A Common Faith,* but otherwise the spirit of the teaching is similar. There is no solution to the problem of individual guilt and forgiveness as long as the individual is treated as an isolated entity. However, through a religious faith in unifying social ideals such as democracy and experimentalism an individual's experience may acquire a religious quality, including a deep sense of belonging, harmony, and peace. By repenting of past choices that have hampered the growth of the self, and by wholeheartedly choosing to pursue the democratic life guided by the spirit of intelligent sympathy, one will come to participate in the healing and liberating power of "the miracle of shared life and shared experience."[86]

The problem of death and immortality is often an issue when religious liberals as well as conservatives challenge the adequacy of a philosophy of humanism and naturalism. Some theologians would contend that a belief in an afterlife in heaven or hell is necessary to support and make sense out of the moral life. Others would assert that it is anxiety about death that tempts people to fall into sin or that the problem of death threatens to deny the ultimate meaning of life. With such problems in mind, it may be argued that a religious faith must involve belief in some form of immortality, if it is to help human beings overcome the problems of sin and despair. Dewey does not directly discuss the question of death and immortality in *A Common Faith.* However, in response to a *New York Times* survey of personal beliefs about immortality published on Easter Sunday in

1928, he indicated agnosticism on the subject of life after death. He noted that the psychical researchers had not come up with significant scientific evidence in support of the idea.[87]

A few years later a book by Corliss Lamont entitled *The Illusion of Immortality* (1935), which is based on Lamont's doctoral dissertation written for the philosophy department at Columbia University, seems to have convinced Dewey to drop his agnosticism and to affirm openly that he did not believe in immortality in the sense of "future life." In a very favorable review of Lamont's book entitled "Intimations of Mortality," he accepted Lamont's conclusion that belief in immortality is an illusion and humanity would do well to give the idea up. Lamont was commended for showing "the inconsistency of the argument for immortality that bases itself on the need for rectification of the ills of this life, on the futility and meaninglessness of this life without immortality, while at the same time deriving from this very mortal state all the values with which it endows a future existence." The major criticism Dewey makes of the idea of immortality is that it has "the morally and socially injurious consequences of putting preoccupations with another world in place of active interest in this one." He agrees with Marx on this matter: "Of belief in immortality more than of any other element of historic religions it holds good, I believe, that 'religion is the opium of peoples.' "[88] Moreover, it was Dewey's conviction as expressed in his naturalistic theory of the religious quality of experience that men and women could abandon belief in an afterlife and still find a sustaining sense of meaning, purpose, and joy in their present life.

In conclusion, reconstructing and synthesizing ideas derived from a variety of sources including Coleridge, the neo-Hegelians, and James, Dewey created a theory of the religious quality of experience and of religious faith that constitutes a substantial contribution to the development of both a naturalistic philosophy of religious experience and an American democratic spirituality. Rejecting the idea of a necessary connection between the religious and the supernatural, and the religious and religion, he offered a fresh understanding of the nature of religious experience and of what it means to be a religious person. The result is an approach that overcomes the conflict between religious faith and natural science and reconciles religious life and secular life. With reference to his overall philosophical vision, his theory of religious faith and the religious quality of experience completes his understanding of the way of liberation–the way the individual and society may advance the creative process of overcoming the separation of the ideal and the real. He identified what is religious in value with experiences that have a profoundly unifying effect on the self and on the self in relation to its world. According to *A Common Faith,* a person realizes a religious quality in life most fundamentally in and through a unifying moral faith in the ideal, but other types of experience such as philosophical reflection and poetic intuition may support such faith and contribute to the deep enduring adjustment that generates the religious quality of experience. One may distinguish between Dewey's general theory of the nature of a religious moral (or social) faith and the specific content of his own personal faith involving the ideals of democracy, experimentalism, and education. Dewey's general theory, however, was constructed to make fully intelligible the religious meaning and value that he found in these great liberal ideals.

It remains to consider further Dewey's thinking on the origins of religious emotion, the idea of God, and the problem of ultimate meaning.

ELEVEN

Nature, God, and Religious Feeling

W HILE IN CHINA, Dewey wrote that a true conception of
the spiritual ideal would include both the western "ethical
ideal of service" and concern for social progress on the one hand, and
the eastern ideal of "esthetic appreciation and meditation" on the
other.[1] From Dewey's perspective, China and Japan had much to
learn from what his Chinese disciple Hu Shih approvingly called
"the religion of democracy." But Dewey found in the cultures of
these nations a "quiet, calm appreciation of the beauties of nature,
literature and art" and "a peaceful cultivation of the mind in meditation and contemplation" that are needed to counterbalance the
hurried activism of the West.[2] As Dewey's writings on the religious
dimension of experience make clear, he well understood that achievement of a deep, enduring adjustment in life involves more than a
moral faith and ethical activism fundamental as these are in his view.
Other factors as well may have a unifying effect on a person's
experience. The feelings of harmony, belonging to a whole, and peace
that are characteristic of the religious quality of experience may be
nourished by philosophical insight, natural piety, aesthetic experience,
and mystical intuition.

The role of philosophical reflection and mystical intuition had a religious or unifying effect in Dewey's experience beginning early in his career. As a young thinker he identified God with the organic unity of the world, and Hegel's philosophy had a profound religious impact on him for it accomplished what he described as "an immense release" from dualism. As a result of his early enjoyment of nature and study of Wordsworth's poetry, there was awakened in Dewey an element of Romantic feeling, including a mystical sense of belonging to the larger whole, that stayed with him and sustained him over the years. During his early career, it was tempered—to be sure—by his passion for logical understanding and his social activism. However, it was also complemented and even fostered by the antidualism in his Hegelian philosophy and by ethical mysticism associated with it.

Even though Dewey as a mature thinker abandoned Hegel's panentheism and ceased to take the metaphysics of Wordsworth's poetic pantheism literally, his philosophy continued to be a method for overcoming dualism, and of Romantic feeling persisted as an important factor in his personality. Consequently, both philosophical reflection and aesthetic and mystical feeling retained a religious meaning and value in his experience and thinking.

Dewey clarified his views on this subject in his correspondence with Scudder Klyce. In the spring of 1927 Dewey wrote to Klyce that "I have had no emotional disturbances for many years, since substantially I am resting on bed rock."[3] Employing well-known Biblical language, several months later he states: "Now as to emotions. As a matter of fact I enjoy the peace which passes understanding." The rhythms of his ups and downs "are long and gentle," he comments.[4] When asked to explain how he came to realize this inner peace, Dewey responded as follows:

> I believe that the related many, the many in their relationships or continuity, when perceived as such, inevitably tend to make persons respond with a sense of One, God if you please. I believe that the great obstacles are the multitude of matters, mind and body, man and the world, mechanism and purpose, facts and meaning, matter and mind, science and art, individual and universal, psychology and logic, etc. in which the man of action and the thinker have cooperated however unconvincingly in setting up fixed barriers. I have done what

I could to break down these barriers by showing that facts show there are no such separations and that they lead to false conclusions and harmful results, the most seriously harmful results in actual life, going far into those who have no interest in philosophy. Upon the whole I think the men of action, especially through politics, business and the church have taken the lead in fostering these fixities—I say this not to relieve the thinker; it is rather his reproach, for he has followed tamely after and "rationalized" what he has done. I believe that I could do the best I can do by means of helping people to see the continuities and the movement of connections where in the mind of most, men of action as well as thinkers, divisions and fixities exist. And I repeat I am convinced, by experience as well as by emotional predilection, that when this is gained, the perception and emotion of unity and totality [will follow] by the very constitution of man—so much so that I am not especially anxious about what form it takes— especially what verbal form, as long as the reality is attained. You ask me, in effect, how I got the experience of oneness which is the source of emotional peace. Well, I got it first by "Intuition" based on experience, a few typical ones. Then I got it by discriminating thought, hard work too, in examining in large number the current dualisms and resolving them into "dynamic" continuities.[5]

In *Art as Experience* Dewey used the term "intuition" to refer to emotional experiences of a mystical nature. His reference to such experiences in the passage above indicates that following the Oil City mystical experience in the early 1880s he had other such experiences. This is confirmed by descriptions in two of his poems, especially "Last night I stood upon the hill."[6] In short, his correspondence with Klyce indicates that both rigorous philosophical reflection focused on breaking down dualisms and emotional intuitions of a poetic and mystical nature contributed over the years to his sense of emotional peace.

Even though Dewey in his letter to Klyce linked the term "God" to the "One," that is, the universe as a whole, he himself generally preferred not to use the term "God" in this way. As discussed earlier, he explained this to Klyce in a letter in 1915, and he made his position clear in *A Common Faith*. Also when Dewey referred to the One, a term which he did not use in his published writings as a naturalist, he did not have in mind the One of Plotinus or the neo-Hegelian idea of a cosmic organic unity in which the ideal and the real are one. For him as a naturalist the "continuity of the many implies oneness." "Do the reality of the many—as continuous and interrelated—and of the one hang together? Santayana denies it; I assert it."[7] Dewey is an infinite pluralist who emphasized the idea of continuity and interconnection leading to a sense of oneness and peace.

As has been indicated, the element of romantic mystical feeling in Dewey is closely associated in his thinking with aesthetic experience, which became increasingly important to him as his naturalistic philosophical system matured. With the assistance of Albert Barnes he concentrated much attention on the nature and function of the aesthetic dimension of experience during the 1920s. His labors culminated in 1932 in a series of lectures on art and aesthetic experience, which inaugurated the William James memorial lectures at Harvard University. It is significant that at the very time that Dewey was deeply involved in trying to shape a new enlightened coalition of liberal political forces and was constructing a theory of a religious social faith, he was also passionately engaged in exploring the role of art in civilization and the continuity between aesthetic experience and everyday life. The James lectures were published as *Art as Experience* in 1934, the same year that *A Common Faith* appeared. This fact is symbolic of the breadth and complexity of Dewey's philosophic vision and also of significance for an understanding of his philosophy of religious experience.

In order to appreciate fully the religious function of intellectual insight and romantic feeling in Dewey's later thought, it is helpful to give attention first to his doctrine of natural piety, which shows the strong influence of George Santayana. Then it is necessary to consider his theory of mystical intuition, which deepens his natural piety, taking it beyond anything that one might find in Santayana. Further, the mystical feelings of the Romantic poet in Dewey often seem to fuse with something of the spirit of his early neo-Hegelian ethical mysticism that lived on in him in connection with his democratic idealism of action. An explanation of these aspects of Dewey's theory of religious experience provides a deeper understanding of the attitudes and feelings he associated with the religious quality of experience. In his writings on these matters, one finds Dewey addressing questions about meaning, joy, trust, belonging, harmony, and peace that have traditionally been considered distinctively religious issues. Following consideration of these factors, attention will be given to Dewey's proposal for a naturalistic reconstruction of the idea of God or the divine.

Natural Piety

Dewey's concept of natural piety grew out of his philosophical understanding of the continuity or interdependence of humanity and nature and the ideal and the real. It is also closely related to his idea of a religious moral faith in natural possibilities, and it finds support in his intuitive sense of harmony with nature. The attitude of piety toward nature involves a sense of belonging to nature including feelings of dependence and vital support. Dewey defined the attitude of natural piety as religious because it introduced perspective into the piecemeal and shifting episodes of life contributing to realization of a deep enduring adjustment and the religious quality of experience. "Whatever introduces genuine perspective is religious," states Dewey.[8] The term "natural piety" is borrowed from Wordsworth, and Dewey's idea of piety toward nature shows the influence of Schleiermacher's notion of religion as the feeling of dependence.[9] However, the decisive influence in leading Dewey to develop his idea of natural piety was probably Santayana's concepts of piety and spirituality as set forth in *Reason in Religion* (1905), which is the third volume in *The Life of Reason; or The Phases of Human Progress.*[10]

The highest human ideal is for Santayana found in what he called "the Life of Reason," which comprehends humanity's quest to envisage, unify, and expand the meanings and values which make life worthwhile. According to Santayana's humanistic and naturalistic interpretation, there is reason in religion, but the truth of religion is expressed imaginatively in poetic and symbolic forms. This truth concerns the meaning of the natural world we live in and is not information about another reality. It involves understandings of the nature of human experience as it actually is or as it should be. "True religion," writes Santayana, "is entirely human and political, as was that of the ancient Hebrews, Romans, and Greeks. Supernatural machinery is either symbolic of natural conditions and moral aims or else is worthless." In short, for Santayana what truth there is in religion is found chiefly in its "practical and moral meaning." However, he had little interest or faith in democracy and liberalism, and he emphasized the contemplative enjoyment of this meaning as an intrinsically valuable activity superior to practical action.[11]

Santayana contended that a "rational religion" has two major aspects: piety and spirituality. "Piety, in its nobler and Roman sense, may be said to mean man's reverent attachment to the sources of his being and the steadying of his life by that attachment." The objects of piety, according to Santayana, "are those on which life and its intervals really depend: parents first, then family, ancestors, and country, finally humanity at large and the whole natural cosmos." It involves a consciousness that "the human spirit is derived and responsible, that all its functions are heritages and trusts," which brings with it "a sentiment of gratitude and duty." Santayana further explained that "religion has a second and a higher side, which looks to the end toward which we move as piety looks to the conditions of progress and to the sources from which we draw our energies." This higher side is what Santayana called spirituality. It is "life in the ideal." It involves the imaginative "ideal synthesis of all that is good" and "devotion to ideal ends." "A man is spiritual when he lives in the presence of the ideal, and whether he eats or drinks does so for the sake of a true and ultimate good." "Piety drinks at the deep, elemental sources of power and order: it studies nature, honours the past, appropriates and continues its mission. Spirituality uses the strength thus acquired, remodelling all it receives, and looking to the future and the ideal." "Spirituality is nobler than piety," asserts Santayana, "because what would fulfill our being and make it worth having is what alone lends value to that being's source." In his view the ideal only is worthy of being called divine.[12]

Dewey's idea of a religious moral faith is an expression of what Santayana called spirituality, but Santayana and Dewey differ in that the former depreciated the practical dimensions of spirituality and exalted poetic vision as a supreme end in itself. Dewey's concept of natural piety seems to have been influenced especially by Santayana's notion of "cosmic piety" in *Reason in Religion*. The latter described cosmic piety as "a philosophical piety which has the universe for its object" and as "this feeling, common to ancient and modern Stoics," which has "an obvious justification in man's dependence upon the natural world." In explaining the attitude of piety toward nature Santayana writes:

> The universe, so far as we can observe it, is a wonderful and immense engine; its extent, its order, its beauty, its cruelty, makes it alike impressive. If we dramatise its life and conceive its spirit, we are filled with wonder, terror, and amusement, so magnificent is that spirit, so prolific, inexorable, grammatical, and dull. Like all animals and plants, the cosmos has its own way of doing things, not wholly rational nor ideally best, but patient, fatal, and fruitful. Great is this organism of mud and fire, terrible this vast, painful, glorious experiment. Why should we not look on the universe with piety? Is it not our substance? Are we made of other clay? All our possibilities lie from eternity hidden in its bosom. It is the dispenser of all our joys. We may address it without superstitious terrors; it is not wicked. It follows its own habits abstractedly; it can be trusted to be true to its word. Society is not impossible between it and us, and since it is the source of all our energies, the home of all our happiness, shall we not cling to it and praise it, seeing that it vegetates so grandly and so sadly, and that it is not for us to blame it for what, doubtless, it never knew that it did? Where there is such infinite and laborious potency there is room for every hope.[13]

This passage can be read as expressing a keen sense of the continuity of the ideal and the actual as well as the interconnection of humanity and nature. This is the way Dewey originally interpreted Santayana, and so understood it is fair to assert that the attitude of Santayana's cosmic piety became Dewey's too, as his major works demonstrate. However, Santayana's later writings reveal that he did not believe that the ideal has its origin in nature even though nature does embody certain ideals and gives to human nature the power to know the ideal. There emerged in Santayana's thought a sharp distinction between the natural world of existence, which is nature and the sphere of practical action, and the realm of essences, which is the object of contemplation and the source of the mind's greatest happiness. This dualism Dewey rejected.[14]

Dewey first explicitly introduced the concept of natural piety into his writing in 1908 in his essay on "Religion and Our Schools," where it is defined as "the sense of the permanent and inevitable implication of man and nature in a common career and destiny."[15] The study of Hegel left Dewey with a deep sense of the interrelationship of the individual and society, and familiarization with Darwinian biology added to this a deep appreciation of the continuity between culture and nature. Dewey had no use for doctrines which conceive the individual to exist in isolation from other persons or nature. He was critical of both supernaturalism and militant atheism for being preoccupied with humanity in isolation from its natural environment, and he rejected the related view that "apart from man, nature is . . . either accursed or negligible."[16] The defiant atheism that one finds in Bertrand Russell's "A Free Man's Worship" or the pessimistic despairing atheism that characterizes Joseph Wood Krutch's *The Modern Temper* exercised no appeal.

Pursuing his middle way, Dewey adhered to the doctrine of the continuity of the ideal and the real, and his doctrine of natural piety served as a corrective to the extremes of atheistic pessimism.

> Militant atheism is also affected by lack of natural piety. The ties binding man to nature that poets have always celebrated are passed over lightly. The attitude taken is often that of man living in an indifferent and hostile world and issuing blasts of defiance. A religious attitude, however, needs the sense of a connection of man, in the way of both dependence and support, with the enveloping world that the imagination feels is a universe.
>
> The essentially unreligious attitude is that which attributes human achievement and purpose to man in isolation from the world of physical nature and his fellows. Our successes are dependent upon the cooperation of nature.

Natural piety does not involve a romantic idealization of nature, for nature does frustrate human effort as well as support it; but it avoids a sense of isolation and pessimism by recognizing that humanity is continuous with and dependent upon nature and when it strives for and realizes ideals it does so "as a cooperating part of a larger whole."[17]

There is an intimate connection between Dewey's naturalistic concept of a religious moral faith in the ideal and his idea of natural piety.

> Religious faith which attaches itself to the possibilities of nature and associated living would, with its devotion to the ideal, manifest piety toward the actual. It would not be querulous with respect to the defects and hardships of the latter. Respect and esteem would be given to that which is the means of realization of possibilities, and to that in which the ideal is embodied if it ever finds embodiment.... Nature and society include within themselves projection of ideal possibilities and contain the operations by which they are actualized. Nature may not be worshiped as divine even in the sense of the intellectual love of Spinoza. But nature, including humanity, with all its defects and imperfections, may evoke heartfelt piety as the source of ideals, of possibilities, of aspirations in their behalf, and as the eventual abode of all attained goods and excellences.[18]

Thus for Dewey natural piety supports and grows with a moral faith that is grounded in an empirical understanding of the natural origin and function of ideals. Such piety for Dewey involves reverence or respect for all the sources of human well-being, including history as well as the larger world of nature.

The depth and quality of feeling involved in Dewey's natural piety is suggested by his use of the mother image in describing nature. In 1884 he had spoken of "the mother soil of experience," whence "the Antaeus of humanity derives its strength and very life."[19] In his naturalism, experience is of as well as in nature, and he speaks of nature as a mother. Writing about pragmatic instrumentalism in 1908, he asserts that philosophy is "love of wisdom that is nurse, as nature is mother, of good."[20] In *Art as Experience* he declares that "nature is the mother and habitat of man, even if sometimes a stepmother and an unfriendly home. The fact that civilization endures and culture continues—and sometimes advances—is evidence that human hopes and purposes find a basis and support in nature."[21]

In 1922, shortly after his return from China, Dewey asserted that he found in the Chinese Taoist tradition "a remarkable exhibition of piety towards nature," and he viewed it as having some important lessons to teach the West. He briefly summarizes his understanding of the central doctrine of Lao Tzu, the founder of Taoism, as follows:

The important thing is the doctrine of the superiority of nature to man, and the conclusion drawn, namely, the doctrine of non-doing. For active doing and striving are likely to be only an interference with nature. The idea of non-doing can hardly be stated and explained; it can only be felt. It is something more than mere inactivity; it is a kind of rule of moral doing, a doctrine of active patience, endurance, persistence while nature has time to do her work. Conquering by yielding is its motto. The workings of nature will in time bring to naught the artificial fussings and fumings of man. Give enough rope to the haughty and ambitious, and in the end they will surely be hung in the artificial entanglements they have themselves evolved.[22]

Employing his genetic method of analysis, Dewey argues that these teachings of Lao Tzu had been adopted by the Chinese because they express attitudes and approaches to nature which the Chinese over thousands of years have learned are essential to their survival as an agricultural people dependent upon the land. The Chinese "laissez-faire reverence for nature and their contempt for hurried and artificial devices of man's contriving" are rooted in their agrarian experience. "While western peoples have attacked, exploited and in the end wasted the soil, they have conserved it. The results are engraved upon both Chinese and western psychologies. The Chinese have learned to wait for the fruition of slow natural processes. They cannot be hustled because in their mode of life nature cannot be hustled."[23]

Dewey recognizes that the Taoist way fosters a certain fatalism and conservatism that may be a major obstacle to social progress: "Non-doing runs easily into passive submission, conservation into stubborn attachment to habitudes so fixed as to be 'natural,' into dread and dislike of change." He further notes that popular Taoism and the related art of geomancy are linked with many superstitious beliefs. However, he also points out that Taoism and geomancy involve a significant expression of piety toward nature that has many beneficial consequences. The Chinese piety toward nature has prevented a shortsighted selfish exploitation of the land. It fosters attitudes of "conserving the resources of nature" and of calm patient working with nature from which the West has much to learn. It also generates in the Chinese their "laissez-faire, contented, tolerant, pacific, humorous and good humored attitude toward life." Dewey concludes that "the Chinese philosophy of life embodies a profoundly valuable contribution to human culture and one of which a hurried, impatient, over-busied and anxious west is infinitely in need."[24] Dewey did not explicitly develop this Taoist emphasis in his later writings on natural piety, but it remained consistent with his mature idea of a sense of dependence on nature and his words in 1922 were prophetic. In another fifty years large numbers of Americans would begin to realize the urgent importance of the attitudes and values Dewey described as the positive contribution of Taoism.

Mystical Intuition and The Religious Emotions

There are a number of passages in Dewey's writings from the 1920s and 1930s where his natural piety seems to intensify and to pass into a mystical sense of belonging to the larger whole. In these passages he does not actually use the term "natural piety," and what he describes clearly involves a communion with nature that transcends what Santayana intended by the term "piety." Here it seems that the influence of Wordsworth and Whitman is an important factor. Prior to the First World War, in his correspondence with Scudder Klyce and related writings, Dewey had begun to formulate his views as a naturalist on the mystical intuition of "the vast vague continuum" which is the universe.[25] In 1920 he observed that Bergson's philosophy enjoyed a wide following and was able to satisfy the religious needs of many people in a way that pragmatism did not, because it combined pragmatism with mysticism.[26] In his subsequent publications it seems that Dewey quite deliberately, even though very cautiously, endeavored to rectify this perceived weakness of his naturalism by showing that it grants a significant place and function to mystical experience provided that it is understood within the framework of a naturalistic theory of religious experience.

The major significance of mystical intuition in Dewey's philosophy is that it serves as an inherently valuable experience contributing to the generation of feelings that are fundamental to a deep enduring adjustment and the religious quality of life. More specifically, these religious feelings include a trust in the meaningfulness of life and a sense of freedom, peace, and joy. The core of these religious emotions for Dewey is an abiding vital sense of "unity with the universe," "of belonging to the larger, all-inclusive, whole which is the universe in which we live."[27] As a neo-Hegelian idealist at the outset of his career, he could explain and justify a sense of ultimate meaning, cosmic trust, and inner peace with reference to his metaphysical belief in the identity of the ideal and the real. Dewey came to believe, however, that one could reject neo-Hegelian idealism and all other traditional Western ways of formulating the ground of such emotions and still retain a profound sense of cosmic trust and meaning. Some examples will illustrate his point.

In *Human Nature and Conduct* (1922), Dewey identifies "religious consciousness" with the sense of belonging to and being interconnected with a vast enduring enveloping whole, which is "the totality of natural events." This infinite totality is to consciousness "a vague whole, undefined and undiscriminated" and "incapable of objective presentation." Thought cannot grasp the totality of events, but this vast reality is quietly present in every experience and is apprehended in emotional "appreciations and intimations" that bring feelings of "freedom and peace."[28] *Human Nature and Conduct* is an essay on ethics, and when Dewey discussed "the sense of the whole" in this volume, he had in mind both a sense of belonging to the continuous human community and to the larger natural universe. Given his idea of the continuity of nature and culture, the actual and the ideal, the sense of human community shades off into a sense of cosmic community. He writes, for example: "Infinite relationships of man with his fellows and with nature already exist. The ideal means ... a sense of these encompassing continuities with their infinite reach. This meaning even now attaches to present activities because they are set in a whole to which they belong and which belongs to them." He further explains the spiritual meaning of this interdependence with nature:

> In a genuine sense every act is already possessed of infinite import. The little part of the scheme of affairs which is modifiable by our efforts is continuous with the rest of the world. The boundaries of our garden plot join it to the world of our neighbors and our neighbors' neighbors. That small effort which we can put forth is in turn connected with an infinity of events that sustain and support it. The

consciousness of this encompassing infinity of connections is ideal. When a sense of the infinite reach of an act physically occurring in a small point of space and occupying a petty instant of time comes home to us, the *meaning* of a present act is seen to be vast, immeasurable, unthinkable. This ideal is not a goal to be attained. It is a significance to be felt, appreciated.[29]

Dewey adds that even though this consciousness of interconnection with the larger whole may not be intellectualized, it is nourished by imaginative philosophical thinking.

A sense of the whole may sustain a person "in the midst of conflict, struggle or defeat," and this is an important part of its religious function.

> Some philosophers define religious consciousness as beginning where moral and intellectual consciousness leave off. In the sense that definite purposes and methods shade off of necessity into a vast whole which is incapable of objective presentation this view is correct. But they have falsified the conception by treating the religious consciousness as something that comes *after* an experience in which striving, resolution and foresight are found. To them morality and science are a striving; when striving ceases a moral holiday begins, an excursion beyond the utmost flight of legitimate thought and endeavor. But there is a point in *every* intelligent activity where effort ceases; where thought and doing fall back upon a course of events which effort and reflection cannot touch. There is a point *in* deliberate action where definite thought fades into the ineffable and undefinable—into emotion. If the sense of this effortless and unfathomable whole comes only in alternation with the sense of strain in action and labor in thought, then we spend our lives in oscillating between what is cramped and enforced and a brief transitory escape. The function of religion is then caricatured rather than realized. Morals, like war, is thought of as hell, and religion, like peace, as a respite. The religious experience is a reality in so far as in the midst of effort to foresee and regulate future objects we are sustained and expanded in feebleness and failure by the sense of an enveloping whole. Peace in action not after it is the contribution of the ideal to conduct.[30]

Here again one finds Dewey trying to break down the dualism of the spiritual and the natural, enduring meaning and everyday life, the peace which passes understanding and worldly action.

In the Christian tradition, religious faith is thought to liberate a person from an oppressive sense of moral responsibility. Dewey argues that "religion as a sense of the whole" effectively performs this function quite apart from any distinctively Christian theological belief.

> Yet every act may carry within itself a consoling and supporting consciousness of the whole to which it belongs and which in some sense belongs to it. With responsibility for the intelligent determination of particular acts may go a joyful emancipation from the burden for responsibility for the whole which sustains them, giving them their final outcome and quality. There is a conceit fostered by perversion of religion which assimilates the universe to our personal desires; but there is also a conceit of carrying the load of the universe from which religion liberates us. Within the flickering inconsequential acts of separate selves dwells a sense of the whole which claims and dignifies them. In its presence we put off mortality and live in the universal.[31]

In this fashion Dewey's religious humanism and naturalism seeks to infuse everyday existence with a sustaining sense of freedom and peace.

In order "to enhance and steady" the sense of belonging to the whole, Dewey observes, "this consciousness needs, like every form of consciousness, objects, symbols." In the concluding lines of *Human Nature and Conduct* he states: "The life of the community in which we live and have our being is the fit symbol of this relationship. The acts in which we express our perception of the ties which bind us to others are its only rites and ceremonies."[32] In the final paragraphs of *A Common Faith,* Dewey returns to this notion, making it clear that when he writes of "the life of the community in which we live and have our being," he has in mind the entire "community of causes and consequences in which we, together with those not born, are enmeshed," that is, "the mysterious totality of being."[33] The imaginative idea of "the continuous human community" interconnected with the larger evolving world of nature "is the embodiment for sense and thought of that encompassing scope of existence the intellect cannot grasp." It is "the widest and deepest symbol" of "the matrix within which our ideal aspirations are born and bred." To contemplate this vast reality and one's life as a link in its ongoing existence generates in Dewey a profound sustaining sense of harmony with the larger infinite whole.

In a harsh attack on institutional religion reflecting his own democratic loyalties, Dewey charges that "the office of religion as sense of community and one's place in it has been lost." Historically, religious symbols often provided the individual with a sense of the whole, but "religion has lost itself in cults, dogmas and myths" that foster sectarianism, divisiveness, and intolerance rather than a liberating sense of community.

> In effect religion has been distorted into a possession—or a burden—of a limited part of human nature, of a limited portion of humanity which finds no way to universalize religion except by imposing its own dogmas and ceremonies upon others.... Instead of marking the freedom and peace of the individual as a member of an infinite whole it has been petrified into a slavery of thought and sentiment, an intolerant superiority on the part of the few and an intolerable burden on the part of the many.[34]

Dewey's answer is to reconstruct the idea of the religious life along humanistic and naturalistic lines focusing on the human community and nature as the source and abode of human values. He hastens to add that he does not regard the human community as something to be worshipped, however.[35] His views on this latter point will become clearer in the light of his idea of God, which will be considered shortly.

The best-known passage in Dewey's writings on natural piety is found in the final pages of *Experience and Nature* (1925). Here he articulates a deep sustaining sense of relationship with the larger universe. This sense seems to arise out of his philosophical labors in support of a naturalistic worldview that affirms the continuity of nature and experience and the ideal and the actual. It also reflects the positive spiritual effects of his own moral faith and activism, and it is tinged with a poetic mystical sensitivity.

> Men move between extremes. They conceive of themselves as gods, or feign a powerful and cunning god as an ally who bends the world to do their bidding and meet their wishes. Disillusionized, they disown the world that disappoints them; and hugging ideals to themselves as

their own possession, stand in haughty aloofness apart from the hard course of events that pays so little heed to our hopes and aspirations. But a mind that has opened itself to experience and that has ripened through its discipline knows its own littleness and impotencies; it knows that its wishes and acknowledgments are not final measures of the universe whether in knowledge or in conduct, and hence are, in the end, transient. But it also knows that its juvenile assumption of power and achievement is not a dream to be wholly forgotten. It implies a unity with the universe that is to be preserved. The belief, and the effort of thought and struggle which it inspires are also the doing of the universe, and they in some way, however slight, carry the universe forward. A chastened sense of our importance, apprehension that it is not a yardstick by which to measure the whole, is consistent with the belief that we and our endeavors are significant not only for themselves but in the whole.

Fidelity to the nature to which we belong, as parts however weak, demands that we cherish our desires and ideals till we have converted them into intelligence, revised them in terms of the ways and means which nature makes possible. When we have used our thought to its utmost and have thrown into the moving unbalanced balance of things our puny strength, we know that though the universe slay us still we may trust, for our lot is one with whatever is good in existence. We know that such thought and effort is one condition of the coming into existence of the better. As far as we are concerned it is the only condition, for it alone is in our power. To ask more than this is childish; but to ask less is a recreance no less egotistic, involving no less a cutting of ourselves from the universe than does the expectation that it meet and satisfy our every wish. To ask in good faith as much as this from ourselves is to stir into motion every capacity of imagination, and to exact from action every skill and bravery.[36]

It is important to note that while Dewey acknowledges in this passage that the human venture is a transient occurrence in the universe, he also states that it is "not a dream to be wholly forgotten" and involves "a unity with the universe that is to be preserved." This passage also involves an affirmation of trust in the enduring meaning of existence in language borrowed from the King James Version of Job 13:15: "though he [God] slay me, yet will I trust in him." For Dewey as a naturalist, this sense of unity and meaning is the implication of his ideas of continuity and interconnection, and his reflections suggest that humanity is intimately related to a larger universe that is infinite in space and time.

In passages such as that quoted above it becomes difficult to distinguish Dewey's piety toward nature and feeling of unity with the universe from what is usually called religious faith in the sense of a trust in the ultimate meaning of existence.[37] The Biblical God and the Hegelian Absolute have been excluded from the worldview set forth in *Experience and Nature,* but the sense of trust and the sense of being a cooperating part of a larger whole often associated with these ideas remains. Dewey seems to recognize this when, in a letter to Klyce cited earlier, he identifies "the experience of oneness" with an experience of "God if you please." In other words, the social and natural world still retains for Dewey much of the halo of meaning and value cast around it by the romantic poets and Hegelian philosophy.

While imaginative philosophical reflection can awaken such a sense of the whole in some, Dewey asserts: "It is the office of art and religion to evoke such appreciations and intimations; to enhance and steady them till they are wrought into the texture of our lives."[38] In explaining the power of poetry and painting to awaken a sense of the whole, he argues that these arts only intensify and heighten awareness of what is actually implicit in everyday experience. "Things, objects, are only focal points of a here and now in a whole that stretches out indefinitely."[39] The margins of this indeterminate setting shade off into that vague expanse which imagination calls the universe. In every normal experience there is some dim sense of this vague whole and of continuity with the whole. In our use of language specific things are discriminated and related but all statements about things take for granted and imply the larger total setting. Dewey contends that it is the implied larger total setting which supplies meaning, intelligibility, to all that is explicit, stated, named and pointed at.[40] "The sense of an extensive and underlying whole is the context of every experience and it is the essence of sanity. For the mad, the insane, thing to us is that which is torn from the common context and which stands alone and isolated."[41]

In his Gifford lectures, Dewey drew a close connection between intense aesthetic experiences and religious experience. He explains that an experience is properly called aesthetic when it is final, complete in itself, and "arouses no search for some other experience." He then comments:

> The fine arts have as their purpose the construction of objects of just such experiences; and under some conditions the completeness of the object enjoyed gives the experience a quality so intense that it is justly termed religious. Peace and harmony suffuse the entire universe gathered up into the situation having a particular focus and pattern.

In other words, at certain moments from the perspective of certain situations the meaning of the universe is beauty and harmony, even if this unification of the ideal and the real is not characteristic of all situations and is not something fixed once and for all. Dewey also asserts that an experience in which the aesthetic quality of completeness is particularly intense is to be identified with "a mystic experience."[42]

Art as Experience provides a more complete account of the way painting and poetry foster mystical intuitions and contribute to religious experience. In his *Psychology* (1887), Dewey had used the word "intuition" for the supreme cognitive act of grasping intellectually all the relations which constitute the organic unity of ultimate wholes such as the self, the world, and God, but in *Art as Experience* the term "intuition" is reserved for the noncognitive awareness of the distinctive qualitative unity that permeates a work of art rendering it an organic unity. Dewey writes:

> Not only must this quality be in all "parts," but it can only be felt, that is immediately experienced. I am not trying to describe it, for it cannot be described nor even be *specifically* pointed at—since whatever is specified in a work of art is one of *its* differentiations. I am only trying to call attention to something that everyone can realize is present in his experience of a work of art, but that is *so* thoroughly and pervasively present that it is taken for granted. "Intuition" has been used by philosophers to designate many things—some of which are suspicious characters. But the penetrating quality that runs through all the parts of a work of art and binds them into an individualized whole can only be emotionally "intuited." The different elements and specific qualities of a work of art blend and fuse in a way which physical things cannot emulate. This fusion is the felt presence of the

same qualitative unity in all of them. "Parts" are discriminated, not intuited. But without the intuited enveloping quality, parts are external to one another and mechanically related.

The felt presence of this pervading and enveloping qualitative unity, which Dewey calls "the spirit of the work of art," renders the work an organic whole leaving the perceiver with a keen sense of the "quality of being a whole" and a "sense of totality."[43]

Dewey goes on to point out that this undefined qualitative unity functions as "the background" in an aesthetic experience that qualifies everything distinguished as a part of the whole. In addition, the experience of this qualitative background as an undefined enveloping whole awakens in the perceiver a sense of being a part of the larger inclusive whole which is the universe. He further asserts that "there is something mystical associated with the word intuition, and any experience becomes mystical in the degree in which the sense, the feeling, of the unlimited envelope becomes intense—as it may do in experience of an object of art."[44] For Dewey, then, all strong intimations of the all are mystical in nature.

Dewey summarizes his position as follows, pointing out that the mystical element in aesthetic experience is also to be identified as a religious feeling.

A work of art elicits and accentuates this quality of being a whole and of belonging to the larger, all-inclusive, whole which is the universe in which we live. This fact, I think, is the explanation of that feeling of exquisite intelligibility and clarity we have in the presence of an object that is experienced with esthetic intensity. It explains also the religious feeling that accompanies intense esthetic perception. We are, as it were, introduced into a world beyond this world which is nevertheless the deeper reality of the world in which we live in our ordinary experiences. We are carried out beyond ourselves to find ourselves. I can see no psychological ground for such properties of an experience save that, somehow, the work of art operates to deepen and to raise to great clarity that sense of an enveloping undefined whole that accompanies every normal experience. This whole is then felt as an expansion of ourselves. For only one frustrated in a particular object of desire upon which he had staked himself, like Macbeth, finds that life is a tale told by an idiot, full of sound and fury, signifying nothing. Where egotism is not made the measure of reality and value, we are citizens of this vast world beyond ourselves, and any intense realization of its presence with and in us brings a peculiarly satisfying sense of unity in itself and with ourselves.

Dewey adds that this mystical sense of the including whole "rather than any special purgation, is that which reconciles us to the events of tragedy."[45]

These comments about mystical intuition in *Art as Experience* add a dimension of understanding and appreciation that is missing in Dewey's rather restrained discussion of mysticism in *A Common Faith*. In the latter he is primarily concerned to reject the attempt of liberal theologians to use religious experience, and especially mysticism, as empirical evidence in support of supernaturalism, transcendentalism, or theism. Dewey does not question the existence of mystical experiences. "On the contrary," he writes, "there is every reason to suppose that, in some degree of intensity, they occur so frequently that they may be regarded as normal manifestations that take place at certain rhythmic points in the movement of experience." He also points out that the evidence suggests that the term "mysticism" is used to cover a great variety of types of experience. Dewey's chief objection is that "interpretations of the experience have not grown from the experience itself with the aid of such scientific resources as may be available. They have been imparted by borrowing without criticism from ideas that are current in the surrounding culture." Christians in medieval Europe use one set of assumptions regarding a personal God to interpret mystical experiences and Taoists in China use another. Dewey wishes to approach mystical experiences with no assumptions other than the idea that they are natural phenomena, the cause of which should be explored with the aid of appropriate scientific methods, if we wish to understand them. He rejects any return to a dualism of a phenomenal and noumenal realm and a corresponding split between scientific and spiritual methods of knowledge of causal relations. If it is suggested that a mystical experience itself provides immediate spiritual knowledge of its cause and reveals that this cause is a transcendental reality, Dewey responds that "there is no more reason for converting the experience itself into an immediate knowledge of its cause than in the case of an experience of lightning or any other natural occurrence."[46]

Dewey's wariness about the dangers of a preoccupation with mysticism, which he describes as having "sometimes added a dimension of value to human experience—and ... sometimes worked for obscurantism and degradation," was expressed in an exchange he had in 1935 with the empirical theologian Bernard Meland. In an essay on "Mystical Naturalism and Religious Humanism," Dewey agreed with Meland that a keen appreciation of the interdependence of human life and nature is essential to a healthy religious humanism. Natural piety can help to prevent humanism from falling into what Meland described as an inordinate "exaltation of man" and "a man centered order of existence," leading to the exploitation of nature and the abuse of other life forms. However, Dewey questioned Meland's contention that a "mystical naturalism," that is, a mystical sense of belonging to nature, is the primary source of natural piety and the only safeguard against "anthro-inflation." He acknowledged that a mystical sense of nature may be of value in the case of some people, but he was not willing to assert that it was "a necessary and imperative part of religious humanism." Such comments by Dewey indicate his concern to avoid a one-sided emphasis on mysticism in a philosophy of religion and to keep the place of moral faith, intelligence, and social relations central.[47]

Dewey did not clarify in a systematic fashion the relation between the religious and the aesthetic dimensions of experience. However, as has been suggested, in this discussion of mystical intuition, these two qualities of experience are closely interconnected in his thought. It is clear that experiences with a religious quality are consummatory in nature, fulfillments, involving immediately enjoyed meanings, and in this sense they are aesthetic in quality. Furthermore, the aesthetic possibilities of life are not fully realized until experience has gained a profound religious quality. Works of art such as paintings, poems, and music, as well as unifying moral ideals and philosophic visions may have a religious effect. Even though Dewey does not explicitly discuss the idea of religious faith in *Art as Experience*, it is the implication of that work as of *A Common Faith* that achievement of a unifying faith in the ideal is essential to perfection of the art of life and that the kind of imaginative vision operative in the arts is of critical importance to the formation of an inspiring religious social faith.[48]

In connection with Dewey's theory of natural piety, mystical intuition, and the religious feelings of trust, interdependence, meaning, and peace, it is important to note that while he views these emotions as religious in value, he does not use the term "religious faith" in his published writings when describing them. According to Max Eastman, he did in an interview equate religious faith with a mystical sense of belonging, but in his publications he employs the concept of religious faith exclusively in connection with a moral or social faith in a unifying ideal. A religious moral faith is, of course, the chief source of a deep enduring adjustment in life, and it does help to foster the feelings of harmony and peace by unifying personality and giving a person a sense of his or her place in the social whole. The point is that Dewey does not directly identify these religious feelings, or the natural piety and mystical intuitions that deepen them, with faith. In other words, the comprehensive idea in Dewey's philosophy of religious experience is not the idea of faith but the idea of the religious quality of experience generated by all the factors contributing to a deep enduring adjustment. A unifying moral faith, natural piety, and mystical intuition contribute to development of the religious quality of experience and the religious feelings of harmony, trust, and peace associated with it. As noted earlier, some confusion over the use of language arises because when Dewey describes the mystical sense of the whole from which trust and peace flow, it is as if his experience has deepened into something close to what has traditionally been identified with a vital aspect of religious faith.

The Idea of God

When Dewey began work on the Terry Lectures for Yale, which were published as *A Common Faith*, he had just finished a debate in the pages of the *Christian Century* on the idea of God with two modernist liberals, Douglas Clyde Macintosh of Yale Divinity School and Henry Nelson Wieman of the University of Chicago. William Ernest Hocking, the Harvard philosopher and author of *The Meaning of God in Human Experience* (1912), and John Wright Buckham, a childhood companion of Dewey and a professor at the Pacific School of Religion, had entered into the debate. Charles Clayton Morrison, editor of the journal and a leader among Protestant liberals, hailed the exchange between Dewey and Wieman, who were both empirical naturalists, as "the most crucial and radical discussion of the idea of God which could possibly be carried on for our generation."[49] The excitement for Morrison was the possibility of identifying scientific evidence for the reality of the God of traditional Christian faith. In his Terry Lectures, Dewey tried to clarify his views on the subject. However, when his reflections were published in *A Common Faith*, they caused the debate to resume and another Chicago philosopher, Charles Hartshorne, got involved. Wieman, Buckham, and A. Eustace Haydon (an historian of religion at the University of Chicago), carried the discussion into the pages of the *Journal of Religion*. Dewey's contributions to these exchanges on the idea of God are illuminating expressions of the nature and spirit of his religious orientation as a naturalist and humanist.

Toward the end of the 1890s Dewey had ceased using the idea of God in expounding his own developing brand of humanistic naturalism, and the concept does not reappear in *Reconstruction in Philosophy, Experience and Nature,* or *The Quest for Certainty.* However, Dewey's poetry, most of which seems to have been written between 1911 and 1918, indicates that the word "God" had retained a certain symbolic power in his imagination. The poetry and his letters to Scudder Klyce also establish that he was pondering new naturalistic ways of using the term. He commented in 1915 that he prefers to use the word "God" as a preferential term "to denote those forces which at a given time and place are actually working for the better," and he explained that he does not like to use it to refer to the universe as a whole. In the conclusion of *Human Nature and Conduct,* Dewey did make a passing poetic reference to "the one God," using the word "God" as a symbol for the whole.[50] However, in this particular discussion he proposes that the most appropriate symbol for the whole and the individual's interconnection with it is to be found simply in the idea of the continuing life of the comprehensive community "in which we live and have our being."

Over a six month period in 1932, the *Christian Century* had sponsored a debate on the idea of God involving Macintosh, Wieman, and Max Carl Otto, all of whom were deeply influenced by the empirical method and pragmatism. Macintosh and Wieman argued in diverse ways in favor of two very different forms of empirical theism and Otto defended a nontheistic brand of naturalism. Morrison edited the essays and published them as a book entitled *Is There a God?* He then persuaded Dewey, who had been his ally in a number of liberal social causes, to review the volume. In his review and in the exchanges with Macintosh and Wieman that followed, Dewey rejected theism as incompatible with his brand of humanistic naturalism. However, he indicated his openness to a naturalistic reconstruction of the idea of God or the divine along nontheistic lines. He also comments that "I do not of course deny the logical possibility of the existence of a personal will which is causative and directive of the universe and which is devoted to the promotion of moral ends." He is doubtful that empirical evidence for such a being will ever be found, and is convinced with Otto that the beneficial moral effects of theism in the past "have been, to put it mildly, much exaggerated." [51]

The critical perspective and assumptions with which he entered any discussion of the idea of God are explained by Dewey as follows:

> Separating the matter of religious experience from the question of the existence of God (as for example those as far apart from one another as the Buddhists and the Comtean Positivists have done), I have found —and there are many who will corroborate my experience by their own—that all of the things which traditional religionists prize and which they connect exclusively with their own conception of God can be had equally well in the ordinary course of human experience in our relations to the natural world and to one another as human beings related in the family, friendship, industry, art, science, and citizenship. *Either then the concept of God can be dropped out as far as genuinely religious experience is concerned, or it must be framed wholly in terms of natural and human relationship involved in our straightaway human experience.* [52]

With these concerns in mind Dewey found Otto's position in general accord with his own. Macintosh, who claimed to employ an objective empirical approach, ends up with an idea of God close to that of classical theism. Dewey found his Kantian line of reasoning in support of belief in God unsound and his appeals to Christian religious experience unconvincing.

Emphasizing that "God is the source of meaning in the whole scene of things," W.E. Hocking expressed his support for Macintosh's general idea of God and contended that the true source of the knowledge of God is not found in empirical investigations or theoretical arguments but in "direct insight into the nature of things" and "an immediate sense of God" of a "simple and primitive sort."[53] Buckham wrote in defense of this later point.[54] Dewey chose not to take up this issue in the *Christian Century*, but in *A Common Faith* he gave his answer in his discussion of religious experience and mysticism, which has already been considered. In his *Christian Century* essays he concentrated most of his attention on Wieman, who he believed came close to adopting a sound naturalistic reconstruction of the idea of God.

Wieman identifies God with those conditions and forces in nature and society that promote human well-being, which Dewey can accept, but Dewey charges that Wieman goes beyond the empirical evidence when he asserts that God is an organic unity and in some sense a unitary object, a single being. "I can but think that Mr. Wieman's God rests upon hypostatization of an undeniable fact, experience of things, persons, causes, found to be good and worth cherishing, into a single objective existence, *a* God." Dewey rejects the notion that "the forces and factors which make for good" possess inherent unity; they "are a collection of forces, unified only in their functional effect: the furtherance of goods in human life."[55] This functional unity is not grounds for arguing for the existence of a prior organic unity of all these forces. Insofar as this collection of forces is organized and integrated, it is as a result of the work of "human thought and action" and not of some unified reality greater than humanity working in and through humanity.[56] This is the point where Dewey draws the boundary between his brand of religious humanism and Wieman's attempt at a naturalistic theism.

Dewey's major criticism of Macintosh and Wieman is that their philosophies of empirical theism remain too much influenced by the ideas and practices of traditional Christianity, which tie authentic religious values to "limited and exclusive organs, channels and objects." Consequently they fail to appreciate fully the religious value to be found in everyday interests and activities that have no necessary connection with any particular religious institution or traditional creed including belief in theism. In short, they do not understand the true nature and source of what Dewey, in *A Common Faith,* came to call the religious quality of experience. Like modernist liberals in general, they have taken important steps in moving away from identification of the divine and religious experience narrowly with the objects and practices of an exclusive historical tradition. However, their theism is an indication that they have not gone far enough.

Dewey acknowledges that Wieman in particular is close to understanding the religious value to be found in the ordinary course of human experience, but he "is held back from realizing its full implications because in the end he is overmastered by emotional overtones derived from the Biblical idea of God." In short, Wieman as well as Macintosh is caught in a contradiction. On the one hand he, tries to articulate a genuinely common faith consistent with a thoroughgoing empirical humanistic naturalism; on the other hand, he seeks to defend the faith of a particular tradition which leaves him still influenced to one degree or another by the old supernaturalism, theism, and exclusivism. This problem makes the position of Protestant theological liberalism "one of intrinsic unstable equilibrium," declares Dewey, who later comments that he wrote *A Common Faith* in part "for the 'liberals' to help them realize how inconsistent they are." [57]

As presented in *A Common Faith,* Dewey's naturalistic concept of God has two aspects. First of all, he connects his notion of God with the object of a religious social faith: "the word 'God' means the ideal ends that at a given time and place one acknowledges as having authority over his volition and emotion, the values to which one is supremely devoted, as far as these ends, through imagination, take on unity." In other words, the idea of God is "one of ideal possibilities unified through imaginative realization and projection." Dewey emphasizes that " 'God' represents a unification of ideal values that is essentially imaginative in origin," and in his view God is not a particular being in whom an integration and a unification of all ideal ends has already been realized.[58]

To identify God with the imaginative vision of "the unity of all ideals arousing us to desire and actions" does not mean in Dewey's mind that God is just a matter of wish-fantasy or that God is an illusion. One does not need to believe in supernaturalism or theism to believe in the reality and authority of authentic ideals. "The aims and ideals that move us are generated through imagination. But they are not made out of imaginary stuff. They are made out of the hard stuff of the world of physical and social experience." In addition a vision of ideal possibilities possesses "its own inherent meaning and value."

> The ideal itself has its roots in natural conditions; it emerges when the imagination idealizes existence by laying hold of the possibilities offered to thought and action. There are values, goods, actually real-ized upon a natural basis—the bonds of human association, of art and knowledge. The idealizing imagination seizes upon the most precious things found in the climacteric moments of experience and projects them. We need no external criterion and guarantee for their goodness. They are had, they exist as good and out of them we frame our ideal ends.

Dewey adds that "the reality of ideal ends as ideals is vouched for by their undeniable power in action." "Aims, ideals, do not exist simply in 'mind'; they exist in character, in personality and action. One might call the role of artists, intellectual inquirers, parents, friends, citizens who are neighbors, to show that purposes exist in an *operative* way." In and through "human embodiment" ideals exist as "forces" that shape the world.[59]

In earlier cultures dominated by supernaturalistic ways of thinking it was in a sense natural to hypostatize ideals leading to polytheism and theism, explains Dewey. However, "the power and significance in life of traditional conceptions of God are ... due to the ideal qualities referred to by them," and given the changed intellectual situation it is advisable to separate the object of a religious moral faith—these "ideal qualities"—from the idea of an existing being, a

God. The latter notion has become problematic for modern men and women; it is also not necessary to belief in the authority and value of authentic human ideals. With the idea in mind of separating faith in the ideal from faith in the God of theism Dewey writes:

> The dislocation frees the religious values of experience once for all from matters that are continually becoming more dubious ... The reality of ideal ends and values in their authority over us is an undoubted fact. The validity of justice, affection, and that intellectual correspondence of our ideas with realities that we call truth, is so assured in its hold upon humanity that it is unnecessary for the religious attitude to encumber itself with the apparatus of dogma and doctrine. Any other conception of the religious attitude, when it is adequately analyzed, means that those who hold it care more for force than for ideal values—since all that an Existence can add is force to establish, to punish, and to reward.[60]

These last comments appear to be directed at the moral concerns that lead Macintosh as well as Kant to posit the existence of God. Dewey's concerns pertaining to the negative moral and practical consequences of preoccupation with theism and transcendentalism have already been noted.

Santayana had identified the divine solely with the human vision of the ideal, but for Dewey the idea of God encompasses more than an integrated and unified vision of ideal possibilities. "A humanistic religion, if it excludes our relation to nature, is pale and thin," asserts Dewey with his doctrine of natural piety in mind. The second aspect of his idea of God is closely connected with his idea of the continuity of human values and nature. It reflects his appreciation of the intimate connection between the imaginative vision of ideal ends and the natural conditions in human nature and nature at large that promote and support it. These natural conditions include physical materials and energies and human capacities. Fresh creative visions of the ideal arise in and through interaction with these conditions, involving imaginative reconstructions of the possibilities at hand. Further, the process of forming visions of the ideal is an ongoing experimental process that develops with the evolution of civilization. Dewey reasons that the term "God" should, therefore, be expanded to comprehend all the actual conditions and processes "that promote the growth of the ideal and that further its realization."[61]

These reflections lead Dewey to his final conception of God as the "active relation between ideal and actual." Like many other ideas in his mature philosophy, this idea of God is a naturalistic reconstruction of a neo-Hegelian idea—in this case the idea of God as the unity of the ideal and the real. Under the impact of his naturalistic evolutionary view of reality, Dewey redefines the word "God" to denote the ongoing active process of "uniting . . . the ideal and actual." The idea of God comprehends all the natural conditions and all the human capacities and activities in and through which the world is creatively idealized. God is not anything supernatural and does not transcend the natural world. God is a finite evolving reality wholly immanent in nature and includes only those forces and processes in individuals, society and the larger world that are involved in the realization of the intellectual, moral, aesthetic, and religious values that guide human life toward well-being and fulfillment. Since God is not a being or a person or a transcendent reality, Dewey suggests that it may be best to use the term "the divine" rather than "God."[62]

One reason why Dewey found it appropriate to speak of God or the divine with reference to the active process of uniting the ideal and the actual is that he hoped it would help to "protect man from a sense of isolation [from nature] and consequent despair or defiance." Dewey never referred to himself as an atheist and did not like being labelled one. He felt that the word "atheism" carries negative connotations that do not accurately characterize his worldview. Using the term "God" or "the divine" can help to foster a healthy sense of natural piety and a more balanced perspective than is usually associated with militant atheism. His idea of God points to the presence in nature of that which is divine from the human point of view, and it is this presence in nature that makes piety toward nature appropriate.

However, Dewey is careful to point out that, when he uses the word "God" or "the divine," "the meaning is selective," and it does not imply an indiscriminate worship of nature in general or of human nature and humanity as a whole. "It selects those factors in existence that generate and support our idea of good as an end to be striven for. It excludes a multitude of forces that at any given time are irrelevant to this function." Dewey also notes that "a humanistic religion ... is presumptuous, when it takes humanity as an object of worship." "The 'divine' is thus a term of human choice and aspiration" involving only the ideal and what supports it and actualizes it.[63]

Dewey summarizes his principal reasons for introducing the word "God" in *A Common Faith* as follows:

> The *function* of such a working union of the ideal and actual seems to me to be identical with the force that has in fact been attached to the conception of God in all the religions that have a spiritual content; and a clear idea of that function seems to me urgently needed.

This statement reflects Dewey's Protestant Christian religious background, but insofar as God or the divine has been historically identified with a creative reality that supports and promotes the good and leads humanity to realize it in history he has a valid point. Focusing attention on and generating a religious commitment to participate in this process of uniting the ideal and the actual in society is the chief concern at work in Dewey's naturalistic reconstruction of the idea of God. He explains this concern more fully as follows:

> But the facts to which I have referred are there, and they need to be brought out with all possible clearness and force. There exist concretely and experimentally goods—the values of art in all its forms, of knowledge, of effort and of rest after striving, of education and fellowship, of friendship and love, of growth in mind and body. These goods are there and yet they are relatively embryonic. Many persons are shut out from generous participation in them; there are forces at work that threaten and sap existent goods as well as prevent their expansion. A clear and intense conception of a union of ideal ends with actual conditions is capable of arousing steady emotion. It may be fed by every experience, no matter what its material.[64]

In short, Dewey identifies the reality of God in today's world with the creative democratic life and with all the natural conditions that support it. His use of the word "God" as a naturalist is a kind of poetic or symbolic device for unifying interests and energies, generating emotion, and inspiring action in connection with what is supremely important and meaningful—the human struggle for freedom, equal justice, and well-being. In short, he believes that use of the word "God" properly understood, can help to inspire the kind of religious faith in democracy and intelligence and the piety toward nature that make up the chief components of a vital religious attitude in the contemporary world.

In the *Christian Century* debate preceding the writing of *A Common Faith,* Dewey several times indicates that if a person wishes to use the term "God" in a fashion consistent with a sound empirical naturalism and religious humanism he does not object. He recognizes that "in a time of transition and disturbance many persons will find it helpful and consoling to continue to use the *word* 'God.' "[65]

> The important thing is the fact, the reality, namely, that certain objective forces, of a great variety of kinds, actually promote human well-being, that the efficacy of these forces is increased by human attention to and care for the working of these forces, so that if Mr. Wieman or any one else gets contentment and energy by naming them God as they function to promote welfare, let him do so—*provided* it is clear *what* it is to which is given the name God.[66]

In *A Common Faith,* Dewey makes it clear that "personally I think it fitting to use the word 'God' to denote that uniting of the ideal and the actual. . . ." In the present "distracted age," he advises that others may find it appropriate also, but he writes that "I would not insist that the name *must* be used."[67] He leaves it up to the reader to decide whether or not the word is personally helpful.

Sidney Hook, who assisted Dewey in preparing the manuscript for *A Common Faith,* objected to Dewey's introduction of the word "God" into a naturalistic theory of the religious, and he questioned Dewey closely as to why he wished to do it. Hook gives this account of Dewey's response:

> He argued that the term had no unequivocal meaning in the history of thought; that there was no danger of its being misunderstood (in which he was shortly proved wrong); and that there was no reason why its emotive associations of the sacred, profound and ultimate should be surrendered to the supernaturalist, especially since for him not religion but the religious experience is central. All this seemed to me to be legitimate if not sufficient grounds. But then he added something which men like Russell or Cohen would never have dreamed of saying: "Besides there are so many people who would feel bewil-

dered if not hurt were they denied the intellectual right to use the term 'God.' They are not in the churches, they believe what I believe, they would feel a loss if they could not speak of God. Why then shouldn't I use the term?"[68]

Dewey sympathizes with the people to whom he refers in this statement because he knows from personal experience their situation. His poetry as well as the tenor of his discussion of God in *A Common Faith* indicate that he himself got a certain personal satisfaction and consolation in being able to speak about God or the divine within the framework of his naturalism. It was another way of affirming for himself toward the end of his career that he had radically reconstructed but not rejected the living truth at work in of the Christian tradition at its best. Writing to Max Otto in 1935, Dewey comments that "my book was written for the people who feel inarticulately that they have the essence of the religious with them and yet are repelled by the religions and are confused—primarily for them."[69]

Horace Kallen has written that it was the writings of Edward Scribner Ames which "I am sure enabled Dewey to accept and use the word 'God' with a good conscience."[70] As a professor of philosophy at the University of Chicago for over three decades, Ames employed a functional psychology and closely associated himself with Dewey's brand of empirical naturalism and democratic social ethics. His intellectual labors were concentrated on working out the implications of this psychology and philosophy for an understanding of religion. Building on the research of such intellectual pioneers as James, Hall, Coe, Mead, Starbuck, Durkheim, and Levy-Bruhl, Ames himself did pioneering work in the psychology of religion early in his career and set forth a fully developed naturalistic philosophy of religion in his major work, *Religion,* which appeared in 1929. In the latter, he emphasized the social origin and function of religion, and he presented a theory of religious faith and a naturalistic concept of God that in broad outline are close to the position Dewey adopted in the 1930s. Ames applied and experimented with his philosophy of religion at the University Church of Disciples of Christ where he served as the minister throughout his academic career. His approach to religious and ethical values was summarized in an essay in the *festschrift* volume prepared in Dewey's honor in 1929. Writing to express his appreciation to Ames, Dewey states: "I need not say that I am in general sympathy with the position that you have taken in your essay. . . ."[71] Dewey had a copy of *Religion* in his personal library. It is very likely that he was encouraged by Ames' theology to believe that the idea of God can be employed responsibly in a naturalistic and humanistic philosophical context, and he probably found Ames' work helpful in the writing of his Terry Lectures.[72]

Over thirty reviews of *A Common Faith* were written in English-language journals and newspapers, and the debate over the idea of God was resumed in the *Christian Century*.[73] Most reviewers welcomed the clarification of Dewey's views on religion, but he was also criticized from both the left and the right. For example, the humanist Corliss Lamont entitled his critique in the *New Masses* "John Dewey Capitulates to 'God'," and the Marxist Norbert Guterman lamented in the *New Republic* that Dewey had not totally rejected everything to do with the religious as well as religion.[74] Professor A. Eustace Haydon, who had signed the Humanist Manifesto, praised Dewey's book as presenting "a religion for the citizens of the new universe," but doubted that the continued use of the word "God" would help humanity in the task of realizing the ideal.[75] John Wright Buckham, who had remained faithful over the years to H.A.P. Torrey's theology, lamented the fact that Dewey did not recognize the need for a personal, transcendent God to explain the origin of the ideal.[76]

Writing for the *Nation*, Reinhold Niebuhr found that Dewey's "credo comes closer than Dr. Dewey is willing to admit to the primary tenets of prophetic religion."

> Dr. Dewey may insist that he does not believe in the ideals as "antecedently existing actualities," but he does believe in a world in which the possibility of realizing ideals exists. He believes in appreciating the world of nature as a realm of meaning even where it does not obviously support man's moral enterprise but is in conflict with it. This is the kind of faith which prophetic religion has tried to express mythically and symbolically by belief in a God who is both the creator and the judge of the world, that is, both the ground of its existence and its *telos*.
>
> It is questionable whether the supernature against which Dr. Dewey protests, a realm of being separate from the natural world and inter-

fering in its processes, is really the kind of supernature about which really profound prophetic religion speaks. Its God is not a separate existence but the ground of existence. Prophetic religion contrives to express in its paradoxes faith both in a meaningful universe and in a dynamic one which has not exhausted the meaning suggested in its actual realities. This kind of faith is not arrived at by a scientific observation of the detailed facts of existence. It is an a priori involved in all knowledge and action, since both knowledge and purposeful action presuppose a meaningful world. To use Dr. Dewey's own phrase, "the *imagination feels* that [the world] is a universe." [77]

Niebuhr's comments are representative of those liberal theologians who found much of value in Dewey's religious thinking but who felt something was missing in the way of a metaphysical foundation. For them, Dewey's naturalistic idea of God was not sufficient.

Wieman greeted *A Common Faith* in the *Christian Century,* warmly proclaiming that "the religious function will not come again to the earth to fill human life with passionate devotion to God until we discover God operating in the practical, everyday concerns of human living in some such way as Dewey indicates." "Some of us have known for a long time," writes Wieman, "that he [Dewey] was a deeply religious man." [78] According to Wieman, Dewey had finally rejected a "non-theistic humanism" and adopted the kind of American empirical naturalistic theism which Wieman championed. In this view, God is an organic unity involving a superhuman system of interacting activities which function together in nature to unite progressively the ideal and the actual. God works "in and with the human" but "is more than personality, mind or intelligence." [79] What Wieman did in interpreting Dewey's idea of God was to focus on the latter's emphasis on the continuity between human values and nature. He arrived at the conclusion that Dewey has identified God with the process of interaction itself, and he contended that this process of interaction is a unified operative reality greater than humanity to which humanity should give its supreme devotion as the living source of all good. The divine reality is superhuman, added Wieman, because humanity cannot actually control it—rather "man must be mastered by it in order to receive the sustenance, development and high fulfillment that it can bring." [80]

Wieman's review prompted the editors of the *Christian Century* to publish a further discussion entitled "Is John Dewey a Theist?" Edwin Ewart Aubrey, Wieman's colleague at the University of Chicago, doubted that Wieman had understood Dewey aright, but Wieman defended his interpretation.[81] At this juncture Dewey corroborated Aubrey's observations, commenting that Wieman "has read his own position into his interpretation of mine." Restating his own position Dewey writes:

> What I said was that the union of ideals with *some* natural forces that generate and sustain them, accomplished in human imagination and to be realized through human choice and action, is that to which the name God might be applied. . . . I thought the *word* might be used because it seems to me that it is this union which has actually functioned in human experience in its religious dimension.

Whereas Wieman argued that the unification of ideals and of ideals and the actual is the work of a creative superhuman complex of activities, Dewey asserts that the unification is "the work of human imagination and will."[82]

In response, Wieman acknowledged the error in his interpretation of Dewey, but insisted that Dewey has failed "to follow through to the inevitable implications of his position."[83] He endeavored to clarify further his argument that the reality which Dewey asserts may be called God actually possesses inherent unity. However, his reasoning is not entirely clear and in the final analysis his conclusion seems speculative. Nevertheless, Morrison gave editorial support to Wieman's theistic interpretation of the meaning of Dewey's own statements.[84] In a letter to the editor, Charles Hartshorne, another philosopher at the University of Chicago, acknowledged that "while I do not altogether follow Professor Wieman's exposition of his thesis that Professor Dewey is implicitly a theist, or would be a theist if he thought through his position, I feel that there is something to be said for the thesis," and he went on to give his own arguments in support of the idea.[85]

Replying to an invitation from Morrison to respond to Wieman's final statement and to Hartshorne, Dewey observes that Hartshorne "makes some points rather more clearly than Mr. Wieman does . . . ," but he declined to engage further in the debate.[86] As he explained in a letter to Max Otto: "I didn't want to get further drawn into the *Christian Century* discussion, because their assumption is that I am primarily interested—as they are—in 'God' when in fact my reference to it was purely incidental."[87] Dewey was becoming discouraged with the confusion generated by his use of the word "God." In July 1935, retreating somewhat from what he had said in *A Common Faith,* he confided to Corliss Lamont, one of his critics in the matter: "The meaning in my mind was essentially: If the word 'God' is used, this is what it *should* stand for; I didn't have a recommendation in mind beyond the proper use of a word."[88] This seems to have been Dewey's last written comment on the subject.[89]

Others continued to press the issue. A few years later, for example, in *Beyond Humanism* (1937), Hartshorne fully developed his critique of Dewey's philosophy of religion and concludes: "It is possible that, somewhat indirectly at least, he [Dewey] may prove a principal creator of what may appear as the twentieth century's supreme theoretical discovery—theistic naturalism."[90] It was just such a possibility that had so fascinated Morrison with the Dewey-Wieman debate. In later works such as *The Source of Human Good* (1946) and *Man's Ultimate Commitment* (1958), Wieman endeavored to refine his position, moving somewhat closer to Dewey's humanism in that he comes to identify the reality of God chiefly with the processes of creative human interchange. Among Wieman's followers the debate with Dewey goes on.[91]

It is also to be noted that the naturalistic theology of Ames, Wieman, and Dewey had an impact on the Jewish theological community, primarily in and through the work of Rabbi Mordecai M. Kaplan, who was the founder and leader of the only distinctively American Jewish movement, Reconstructionism.[92] Kaplan tried to do for Judaism something similar to what Ames had attempted for Protestant Christianity, except that Kaplan was far more concerned than Ames with maintaining historical observances. He freely reconstructed the traditional beliefs associated with the old forms, but he saw the latter as fundamental to the preservation of Jewish civilization.[93] In such works as *The Meaning of God in Modern Jewish Religion* (1937), he interpreted salvation in terms of this-worldly fulfillment writing about integration of personality, ethical goodness, and democracy. Accordingly, God is identified with the creative processes immanent in the universe that make for salvation.[94] Kaplan's idea of God is in many respects similar to that of Ames and Dewey. However, his sympathies probably were with Wieman in the *Christian Century* debate, for he argued that, even though God is not an entity or a person, God is a creative teleological process in nature that guarantees not only "that whatever ought to be can be" but also that it "ultimately will be, realized."[95] There is a kind of evolutionary optimism and faith in progress here that goes beyond what Dewey affirmed in his later works. While rejecting traditional ideas of the supernatural, Kaplan also later introduced the somewhat obscure notion of the "transnatural" in explaining his view of the reality of God. The transnatural is a dimension of reality that lies beyond verification by a strictly empirical method, but it provides humanity with confirmation of the ultimate meaningfulness of its striving for the good.[96]

Humanistic Naturalism and Ultimate Meaning

In concluding this exploration of Dewey's philosophy of religious experience, it is useful to inquire into how he addresses the problem of ultimate meaning. This will provide an opportunity to summarize the interrelation of the various ideas at work in his theory of the religious quality of experience and to put his naturalistic approach in further perspective in relation to Christian theology and the history of religious thought. It is noteworthy that others besides Wieman, Morrison, and Hartshorne believed that there is, underlying Dewey's thought or implied in it, a religious reality that is not fully acknowledged by Dewey himself. For example, labelling Dewey's position "half-hearted" naturalism, Santayana argued that Dewey's philosophy is governed by "social and ethical mysticism" and constitutes a kind of "transcendental moralism."[97] The literary critic Waldo Frank, in his portrait of Dewey for the *New Yorker* in 1926, described him as "at heart a Christian" in his attitude toward life and "a poet" whose "driest work is builded on a mystic faith."[98] Reinhold Niebuhr found that Dewey's religious moral faith and natural piety "comes closer than Dr. Dewey is willing to admit to the primary tenets of prophetic religion." Two points are to be made about these observations of admirers and critics. On the one hand, religious liberals were constantly trying to claim Dewey's philosophy as consistent with or supportive of their own diverse positions, and Dewey and his followers like Sidney Hook resisted all such overtures and claims. On the other hand, there are problems in Dewey's philosophy of religion that raise puzzling questions and evoke criticism from naturalists like Santayana and unwanted praise from theologians like Wieman. This latter point warrants further discussion.

Addressing a problem that had been high on the agenda of religious liberals ever since the days of Schleiermacher and Hegel, Dewey set out in his philosophy of religion to break down completely the old dualism of sacred and secular, of religious life and modern culture. Working his way out of the neo-Hegelian integration of the spiritual and the material and using his own empirical naturalism to dissolve all dualisms, he asserted continuity between nature and religious values and unified the democratic life and the religious life. It is a powerful fresh vision that offers modern men and women a way of overcoming the disheartening split in modern culture between spiritual life and everyday existence. It is interesting to compare Dewey's approach with that of Martin Buber, whose little book *I and Thou* (1927) also seeks to address this same problem and has become one of the most influential religious statements of the twentieth century.

In seeking to overcome the dualism of sacred and secular, Buber chose to retain the word "God." Even though for the most part he refused to do theology, arguing that one cannot speak *about* God, he does preserve a general panentheistic framework for his philosophy, claiming that one can listen and speak *to* God. The reality of God is encountered chiefly in and through a person's relations with other persons and things, whenever they are addressed as a "Thou" or "You" as opposed to an "it," that is, something that can be objectified, conceptualized, and used. Making the point that God cannot be found when one looks for him, as if he were an object or a being, Buber declares: "One does not find God if one remains in the world; one does not find God if one leaves the world." However, with the right attitude toward the persons and things in one's world, one can find God in the midst of everyday life: "Whoever goes forth to his You with his whole being and carries to it all the being of the world, finds him whom one cannot seek."[99] By retaining a panentheistic frame of reference, Buber has no difficulty explaining why he believes I-Thou relationships are supremely important and provide men and women in the midst of their secular existence with a sense of religious value, that is, ultimate meaning, including a liberating feeling of harmony and peace.

There are some parallels between Dewey's notion of acting wholeheartedly with love or complete interest and Buber's idea of an I-Thou relationship, and one might compare Dewey's distinction between the aesthetic and instrumental phases of experience with certain aspects of Buber's distinction between I-Thou and I-it encounters. Like Buber, he also wishes to affirm that, by adopting the right attitude, a liberating and sustaining sense of religious meaning and value may be realized in and through everyday relationships with other persons and the larger world of nature. The difficulty involved in his philosophy from the point of view of the history of religious thought is that while he affirms the religious meaning and value to be found in experience, he rejects all traditional theological and philosophical ideas used to express it as inconsistent with his empirical naturalism. For example, even though Dewey uses the word "God" as a symbol for the religious meaning he finds in life, the point is that, unlike Buber and Wieman, he does not wish to embrace any traditional idea of God. The religious meaning and value that Dewey affirms includes most fundamentally a sense of ultimate meaning. He generally avoids using the adjectives "ultimate" and "unconditional," but his statements indicate that he believes ultimate meaning is there to be realized in life. This is the crux of the problem. On what basis can Dewey, given his naturalistic worldview, affirm the reality of ultimate meaning?

Dewey did not believe that there is such a thing as *the* meaning of life in the sense of a fixed ultimate purpose or a static absolute good. He rejected such notions, and this is not the issue. Some concrete examples from material already considered will make clear what is meant by his sense of ultimate meaning. Using Biblical language from the Book of Job in *Experience and Nature* , he asserts: "we know that though the universe slay us still we may trust, for our lot is one with whatever is good in existence." Borrowing a phrase from the Apostle Paul's epistle to the Philippians (4:7), he confesses in a letter: "I enjoy the peace which passes understanding." He is probably also influenced by Biblical imagery when in *Art as Experience* he explains the positive effects of achieving a deep enduring adjustment of self and world that is religious in quality: "through the phases of perturbation and conflict, there abides the deep-seated memory of an underlying harmony, the sense of which haunts life like the sense of being founded on a rock."[100] To confess a trust in the meaningfulness of life which is not disturbed by anxiety about defeat and death and to speak about the peace which passes understanding and being founded on a rock is to affirm the presence of ultimate meaning in life.

By introducing in *A Common Faith* the supreme biblical symbol for religious meaning and value, the word "God," Dewey acknowledges that he is concerned to help people ward off pessimism and despair. In the final analysis it seems that he turns to use of the word "God," which he personally had never entirely let go in the world of his own poetic imagination, precisely because he wishes to affirm that there is ultimate meaning to be realized in life. His concept of God directs the attention of the person who would seek and find meaning to the human community and to shared experience in the course of the struggle to realize the ideal. It is clear that, for Dewey, the sense of the meaningfulness of existence is closely tied to hope regarding the possibilities for personal growth and social progress. His definition of the word "God" points to the ground of this hope in the continuity of the ideal and the actual, the experimental method of knowledge, and the progressive possibilities of the future. However, as Dewey's paraphrase of Job's words indicates, he also believes that it is possible in life to realize a sense of ultimate meaning that can carry one through times of failed hope.

Dewey explains his understanding of the source and nature of cosmic trust, ultimate meaning, hope, and peace in various ways. In *A Common Faith* he describes how a moral faith and natural piety may generate a religious quality of experience which involves a deep enduring sense of harmony with one's self and with the universe at large. *Reconstruction in Philosophy* and *Experience and Nature* assert that communication and shared experience may have an emotional "mystic force" that generates a profound sense of belonging. In *Human Nature and Conduct* and personal letters, he states that philosophical insight into the continuity and interconnections of things coupled with intuitions of a poetic and mystical nature awaken a consciousness of belonging to the whole, the vast unfathomable totality of events that is the universe. He also points out that this sense of a vague, larger, all-inclusive context or whole "is implicit, in some degree of intensity, in every experience;" and even though it is "strictly ineffable" it supplies meaning and coherence to every experience and to all that is formulated in language and stated.[101] The essence of insanity is a sense of isolation, a loss of the sense of being interrelated with a larger enveloping totality. In short, an intuition of the whole underlies the human sense of meaning according to Dewey. It sustains and consoles a person in the face of defeat and tragedy and liberates the compassionate conscientious person from an oppressive feeling of moral responsibility for the larger whole. In *Art as Experience* he explains that art objects may generate an immediate experience of an enveloping qualitative unity pervading all their parts, and they consequently operate to deepen and intensify the human mystical awareness of being intimately related to an enveloping whole. Such mystical intuitions of the whole provide the self with a sense of expansion, unity, and meaning.

It is reasonable to conclude that the sense of ultimate meaning that pervades Dewey's attitude toward life adds a special depth of concern to his sense of moral responsibility and commitment to the ideal. He is a relativist only in the sense that he believes the good in any situation is determined by the situation, but he argues that there are objective distinctions to be made between good and bad in any situation. His moral outlook seems to be pervaded by a profound belief in the absolute value inherent in the process of endeavoring to identify and realize the good. His moral faith in the ideal becomes a form of religious faith involving a sense of ultimate concern. This quality of Dewey's moral thinking and faith is rooted in his sense of there being an underlying meaningfulness in life, and it is this quality that in part leads philosophers like Santayana to refer to Dewey's "social and ethical mysticism." In addition, Dewey emphasizes that an attitude of sympathy is fundamental to the process of sound moral deliberation, and even though he did not make the connection explicit, it is fair to assume that his own compassionate nature was fed by his deep abiding sense of belonging to the larger community of being.

Dewey's account of the way in which philosophical, aesthetic, mystical, moral, and social experience may grace and sustain life with a religious quality is illuminating and persuasive. Furthermore, given the evidence, there is no reason to doubt that Dewey in his personal life enjoyed a deep realization of the religious sense of meaning, peace, trust, hope, and freedom about which he writes. The question which may legitimately be raised about his concept of religious experience concerns its relationship to his naturalistic interpretation of the nature of reality. Does Dewey's naturalistic view of the world make intelligible how ultimate meaning is possible? In other words, does his account of the religious dimension of experience have implications for an understanding of reality that are not fully articulated in his metaphysics and idea of the divine? Does Dewey's own religious experience point to a depth dimension of reality that is not adequately expressed in his philosophical language?

When men and women realize a sense of ultimate meaning and the peace which passes understanding they have found in their hearts a resource that enables them to overcome fear and despair in the face of evil, suffering, and death. To affirm the possibility of realizing ultimate meaning is to affirm the possibility of transcending the most radical threats posed by the problem of death and evil. In Dewey's evolving universe, growth, novel creation, and progress occur but everything that comes to be also passes away. The human community and all that constitutes human civilization may be totally destroyed and human history may be completely forgotten, leaving no trace. In *Experience and Nature* Dewey asserts that the human presence will not be forgotten in the universe, but he cannot mean this literally for he does not assert the existence of conscious intelligent life outside of humanity and he rejects theism. Just what Dewey means is quite vague when he says that humanity's efforts result in "a unity with the universe that is to be preserved." Furthermore, even though he seems to believe that nature will exist forever and thus will forever retain some effect of humanity's striving, it may well be that the natural world will be totally destroyed as the universe collapses back upon itself. In the face of the possibility of such annihilation—of such nothingness—how can there be a sense of ultimate meaning? Unless there be some eternal truth beyond or within the nothingness, the source or foundation of ultimate meaning is not made intelligible. The point is that Dewey's own experience of cosmic trust and meaning seems to point to participation in some such dimension of reality, but he avoids articulating such a notion.

In his letter to the *Christian Century* in the course of the Dewey-Wieman debate, Hartshorne presents questions of the kind raised here. When asked to reply, Dewey excused himself from further participation in the debate and in his own writings he does not meet this problem head on. He rather tries to smooth over the rough edges in his thought created by this dilemma, charting a middle way between idealism and naturalism, and reconstructing the ideas of nature and the religious. What seems to have happened is something like this. Aided by Coleridge, Wordsworth, Vermont Transcendentalism, and Hegel, Dewey as a young man acquired an abiding sense of the religious meaning and value of life, and despite some dark hours during his early years and some painful losses including the deaths of two gifted children, he never lost this sense. Over time he learned that a trust in the democratic way of freedom and growth, a faith in intelligence, and an understanding of ideals as natural possibilities can be a valid liberating religious way in its own right. It gave his life hope, purpose, and unity. His poetic and mystical intimations provided this way added vital support, deepening his sense of belonging, community, and meaning. He resisted all invitations to adopt some new form of theism or transcendentalism, because he feared a return to otherworldliness, dogmatism, and sectarianism. He was opposed to any idea that might weaken the will in people to take responsibility for their situation and that could draw their attention away from the world of natural relationships and shared experience where meaning may actually be realized. These are valid concerns.

Dewey's position has great appeal as a way of reconciling the secular and sacred, but the difficulties posed for a naturalistic worldview by the problem of ultimate meaning cannot be removed as easily as he imagined. The issue as it presents itself in Dewey's thought can be stated in the form of a paradox, which itself points to what may well be profoundly true about human existence: there is only one world, the world of nature, which is an open pluralistic evolving universe where ideals are possibilities but not fixed realities, where there are times of fulfillment but there is nothing permanent to hold onto, where there are endless possibilities for growth but existence is precarious and death follows life; and yet in this changing impermanent world where life at best is a mixture of joy and sorrow it is possible for persons to realize an enduring sense of freedom and ultimate meaning by living wholeheartedly in a caring and intelligent fashion, creatively responsive to the needs of this changing world, each according to his or her own unique capacities. The paradoxical nature of this view of things becomes fully evident only when one faces squarely the problem of death and nothingness, which Dewey's writings avoid doing. It is the paradox of being able to realize ultimate meaning in a changing world where nothing is fixed and where nothingness is always underfoot. As a practical matter Dewey's life experience as expressed in his writings is an example of how this can be done. The possibility and truth of such a realization is not being questioned. The objective here is to call attention to the paradox and to point out that when it is faced it indicates that there is a source of ultimate meaning in the midst of this impermanent world hidden in the mystery of its being.

The problem at issue can perhaps be further clarified by stating the paradox in another way, putting special emphasis on the problem of evil. We live in a world where evil and suffering are frighteningly real and where the best human victories over the forces of division and darkness are never complete or final; and yet in the midst of the struggle and in the face of terrible loss and tragedy a person may be sustained by a sense of "an underlying harmony" and "the peace that passes understanding." From one point of view the truth of life is an ongoing battle against chaos and evil; from the other the deeper truth is harmony, wholeness, peace. It is the empirical and naturalistic perspective that emphasizes the first part of the paradox. It is the mystical perspective that introduces the second part. Human experience testifies that both parts of the paradox are true. If in affirming one part, the other is denied, then one is left with a one-sided restrictive view. For example, if in asserting the reality of eternal peace one declares evil and suffering to be simply an illusion, one is in danger of falling into quietism and denying the testimony of common experience and the compassionate heart.

As one who founds his worldview on empirical naturalism, Dewey does not wish to make statements in interpretation of the meaning of the second part of the paradox that contradict the first, but he goes farther than many naturalists and humanists in acknowledging the mystical dimension of life. Further, it is because he is a compassionate empirical naturalist, who sees clearly the reality of social injustice and knows the struggle required to unite the ideal and the real, that his personal religious outlook puts the greatest emphasis on moral faith rather than mystical faith. Persons who are primarily concerned with the truth of ultimate meaning and the reality of spiritual peace tend to develop world views that emphasize a mystical faith and that contradict the naturalistic perspective, as, for example, in the case of theists or absolute idealists. Insofar as they do so, however, their positions are just as problematic as that of the tough-minded naturalist, even though in the opposite way. In his attacks on supernaturalism and transcendentalism, Dewey identifies the problems involved. Given these problems there is a certain wisdom in Dewey's reluctance to get drawn into lengthy discussions with theists and to remain relatively silent on such matters. Rather than worry about theological complexities, Dewey advises modern men and women to adhere to a naturalistic worldview and to live compassionately and intelligently, tending to the concrete practical problems of everyday life; the problem of meaning will then take care of itself. The problem of meaning in his view is most fundamentally a problem of right attitude and right practice rather than an intellectual problem which can be solved by philosophy and theology. Again, there is sound practical wisdom in this teaching, and for some, especially some of those whom James called the healthy-minded, it is sufficient.

However, Dewey himself has acknowledged that some people need and can benefit from a powerful religious symbol like the word "God," and some in the face of doubt, death, and great evil need a stronger affirmation of a ground of ultimate meaning than is provided by Dewey's idea of God. Furthermore, it is being argued that Dewey's own life and thought point to the presence in experience of such a source of ultimate meaning. If his view of the divine could be deepened without returning to theism or absolute idealism and without undermining his account of spiritual practice as the democratic life of compassion, intelligence, and growth, something might be gained for those who can benefit by a more explicit affirmation of the presence in the world of an eternal ground of meaning and value.

The problem of ultimate meaning and nothingness gains special urgency in an age of nuclear weapons and horrendous human evil, the most frightening example of which is the Holocaust. The human race now lives in a time when it knows that it may destroy itself and life on planet Earth. Moreover, even if human civilization is not terminated by nuclear war or some other man-made environmental catastrophe, how can human beings trust in the meaning of their existence in the face of the abyss of great evil that has manifested itself in history? These questions are not of minor import. If contemporary civilization does not have an answer to them, its creative energies will be sapped by pessimism and it will lose its sense of direction and coherence.

This essay is not the place to explore at length a reconstruction of Dewey's idea of God. Here only a few brief comments will be made in the spirit of adding yet another point of view to the ongoing debate started in the *Christian Century* in 1933 and in the hope of putting Dewey's experience and thought in some better perspective in relation to the history of religion. First, Dewey's idea of God as the uniting of the ideal and the real can be understood as a naturalized version of what Stoic philosophy called the Logos or what Christian theology under the influence of Greek as well as ancient Hebrew thought identified as the Cosmic Christ. As John Wright Buckham points out, Dewey's idea of God is a naturalized version of the Christ reality conceived as the Word of God, the principle of order, creativity, and goodness immanent in the universe.[102] In opposition to Wieman, Dewey of course, thoroughly naturalized and humanized this Logos reality denying to it any inherent unity apart from human spirituality and moral action.

Second, the philosophy of mysticism as developed by thinkers such as Walter Stace and Keiji Nishitani offers a language for talking about the foundation of ultimate meaning in human experience and reality that can enrich Dewey's philosophical language and vision without denying the truth in his naturalism and undermining his reconciliation of the natural and the spiritual.[103] It seems that Dewey's mystical intuition of the whole involves an intimation of that dimension of reality which mystical theologians like Dionysius the Areopagite and Meister Eckhart have called the Godhead and distinguished from God understood as a divine person. What Dewey calls a sense of the whole and of interdependence may also be related to what Mahāyāna Buddhists call absolute nothingness or emptiness and symbolize with an empty circle. Dewey himself acknowledges that mystics and idealist philosophers have all built their religious philosophies on an experience of the whole. He criticizes such thinkers for converting words like the absolute or the all into terms of discrimination and statement when they are properly understood as symbols of this inexpressible awareness. However, the Godhead of Christian mystics like Eckhart or the absolute nothingness of the Mahāyāna philosophers is recognized to symbolize a dimension of experience and reality which in the final analysis cannot be fully conceptualized. It transcends the dualism of subject and object, and it is ineffable. It is not a fixed or static reality, and it is not to be identified with a being existing either separate from or within the world. Paradoxically, this reality can be said to be both absolutely immanent and absolutely transcendent. It is the beyond in the midst. It cannot be identified simply with any thing or all things taken together, but at one and the same time it and each thing, and it and the world as a whole, are not two. It transcends the world in the sense that evil, death, and nothingness cannot overcome it. It is the final source of ultimate meaning and the eternal ground of the Great Yes to life. It is this dimension of reality that Dewey does not seem to have acknowledged adequately in his idea of the divine. He approaches it when he describes how the individual is interconnected in an infinite number of ways with the larger whole and that whole is present in and with the individual, or when he emphasizes dynamic continuities rather than hard and fast dualisms.

Developing the implications of Dewey's own mystical intuitions, it may be argued, then, that there is a depth to the divine reality which involves what may be called the eternal One, immanent in and yet transcending nature as he describes it. One might then expand and deepen his idea of God or the divine to include this principle of nondualism, which overcomes even the dualism of life and death, being and nothingness. It could then be argued that when a person participates in what Dewey actually calls God, which is a reconstructed version of the classical idea of the divine Logos, and which he identifies with all the forces making for a compassionate intelligent democratic life, a person also encounters and is upheld by this deeper reality of the divine life, the Godhead or absolute nothingness, which is mysteriously present in and with this evolving universe. In line with this way of thinking one would have to recognize that Dewey's piety toward nature deepened by mystical intuition develops into an attitude that is more than natural piety, becoming a form of what has traditionally been called a religious faith in the divine presence.

The danger in pursuing this kind of reconstruction of Dewey's idea of the divine is that some will use it to reassert all the old dualisms of ideal and real, natural and spiritual, religion and culture that Dewey devoted his life to overcoming and that are fraught with negative consequences. However, this can be avoided if one keeps clearly in mind that the eternal One is not a being, an it, an object. It may be identified as the ground of personality and the wellspring of human goodness and ultimate meaning, and employing symbolic language, it may be addressed in personal terms, but it is not *a* person. Since this divine reality is not an object and may be realized in and through a person's everyday relations with the world, Dewey's concern to emancipate the religious from any necessary connection with institutional religion has merit, and his concept of the religious quality of experience stands as a valuable intellectual tool for developing an empirical understanding of religious life. A person realizes religious meaning and value not primarily by relating to a being called God, dwelling outside the world, but by relating to the persons and things of this world with the right attitude. According to Dewey this attitude includes wonder, openness, sympathy, a will to share, wholehearted attention, experimental thoughtfulness, and moral faith. The intellectual, social, moral, and aesthetic interactions that follow will spontaneously reveal the divine presence in the form of the grace that manifests itself as the religious quality of experience. What is this divine presence? It cannot be objectified and conceptualized. In that sense it is elusive and mysterious. Nevertheless, it can be experienced on the level of the heart by living according to the democratic way of freedom and growth.

One further observation is in order by way of amplifying what has been stated about the advantages of undertaking a reconstruction of Dewey's idea of the divine along the lines suggested. While leaving the religious dimension of experience free of a necessary connection to institutional religion, it opens up Dewey's thought to a greater appreciation of the positive values that may be found by some people in symbols and rituals associated with the institutional religions. Dewey was so intent upon integrating fully the energies of the religious life with the democratic life that he had little use for what seemed to him to be religious beliefs and practices associated with earlier forms of social life and utterly separate from the affairs of contemporary civilization. His criticisms of the exclusivism and divisiveness generated by many traditional institutional religions is certainly justified. However, in many human beings there is a natural impulse to express their religious feelings in rituals with symbols. In religious rituals, social and moral as well as aesthetic and mystical sensitivities are at work. Furthermore, religious rituals may under the right circumstances intensify a person's religious consciousness. Dewey did not wish to deny this, but he did not explore fully the ritual aspect of the religious life as a natural mode of expression and sharing and the ways in which it may become part of the democratic life.

In conclusion, Dewey's vision of the meaning and value of the democratic way of uniting the ideal and the actual culminates in his philosophy of the religious dimension of experience. It is his thesis that philosophy, natural piety, art, and mystical intuition as well as an active moral faith in an inclusive ideal may advance the process of unification of self and self and world, leading to development of a religious quality of experience that includes liberating feelings of interdependence, belonging, harmony, trust, meaning, and peace. He employs the idea of God or the divine in a poetic fashion to refer to all those factors in nature and society that contribute to the unifying of the ideal and the real and that generate a sense of religious meaning and value. This naturalistic reconstruction of the idea of God was a final step in his endeavor to integrate completely the spiritual and the natural, the life of faith and everyday life, the religious way and the democratic way. To participate wholeheartedly in the life of a community governed by natural piety and the democratic ideal is to participate in a shared creative life where that which is divine in meaning and value is at work and may be directly realized.

TWELVE

"A Gift of Grace"

A S A YOUNG MAN Dewey's mind and heart had been filled with an intense craving for a synthesis of ideas that would promote unification of self, of self and world, and the ideal and the real. By the mid 1930s he had worked out in his own original fashion what he had left Vermont half a century earlier to accomplish. With publication of *A Common Faith* and *Art as Experience* the main components of Dewey's mature philosophical system had been set forth. It was a loosely constructed system designed to be constantly adjusted in response to new situations and discoveries, but it was nevertheless a coherent naturalistic and humanistic vision of experience, nature, and the way to freedom and community. Throughout the remainder of his life, Dewey continued to clarify his philosophy, responding to critics and applying his thought to the changing situation in America and overseas. The result was scores of new essays and five new books in the areas of logic, education, and social philosophy.

Continuing the Reconstruction, 1935–1952

Some of the major ideas set forth in Dewey's writings published after 1934 have been discussed in the preceding exposition of his philosophy, but a few further comments are in order to complete this account of his career. Beginning during the Chicago years Dewey had published a number of essays and books designed to accomplish an instrumentalist reconstruction of logic in the light of the experimental method employed by the natural sciences. This work in the method of creative intelligence, which he viewed as his most important technical contribution to philosophy, culminated in 1938 with a major treatise entitled *Logic: The Theory of Inquiry*. Dewey was not much interested in the formal rules of deductive reasoning and the kind of quasi-mathematical problems that have engaged most twentieth century logicians. However, his work has helped to establish the validity of a different view of logic—logic as the theory of productive inquiry—and his studies in logical theory have been a major contribution to an understanding of the function of logical principles and concepts in that experimental process. Dewey believed that the standpoint from which his logic was written "is ... thoroughly sound," but he recognized that his own theoretical work would have to be revised and further developed.[1] During the 1940s he kept at the task, undertaking cooperative research with Arthur F. Bentley, a philosopher concerned with social science, mathematics, and linguistic analysis. Their joint efforts were eventually published in *Knowing and the Known* (1949), the year Dewey turned ninety.

Responding to attacks against liberalism from the left and the right in the mid-thirties, he wrote a short volume entitled *Liberalism and Social Action* (1935), which offered a concise history of liberalism and a lucid summary of his own approach to reconstructing and revitalizing the liberal tradition in the light of current problems. Throughout the thirties Dewey also devoted much time and energy to defending his philosophy of education, which remained central to his own vision of democratic social progress. He battled to correct what he perceived as the excesses in many progressive education programs as well as the deficiencies in traditional approaches. His views were succinctly set forth in *Experience and Education* (1939), which may also serve as an excellent short introduction to his general approach as a philosopher.

Among the more extraordinary of Dewey's activities during the thirties was his chairing of the Commission of Inquiry into the charges brought against the Bolshevik leader Leon Trotsky, during the Moscow Trials of 1936 and 1937. The hearings were held in the home of the celebrated Marxist artist, Diego Rivera, outside Mexico City during the spring of 1937. The testimony from the hearings and the Commission's report, which found Trotsky innocent, filled over one thousand pages. Dewey, like many American radicals who once held high hopes for the Russian communist experiment, was deeply disillusioned by the corrupt practices and brutal tactics employed by Stalin's government in the Moscow Trials. He joined the Trotsky Commission because he believed the truth about Russian communism should be fully exposed. The experience of the Trotsky hearings deepened Dewey's conviction that only democratic means truly serve democratic ends. "The dictatorship of the proletariat has led, and I am convinced, always must lead to a dictatorship over the proletariat and over the party," Dewey stated.[2]

In the face of the mounting threat to freedom posed by the rise of totalitarianism in Europe, Russia, and Japan, Dewey in 1939 undertook an inquiry into the meaning of freedom and the foundations of democracy, which was published as *Freedom and Culture*. It is Dewey's argument that political freedom can be sustained only by a vital social faith in democracy that issues in creation of a "free culture," that is, a society in which all human relations and institutions are governed by democratic attitudes and methods. "The struggle for democracy has to be maintained on as many fronts as culture has aspects: political, economic, international, educational, scientific and artistic, religious." The most serious threat to democracy in America is not the emergence of foreign totalitarian states: "It is the existence within our own personal attitudes and within our own institutions of conditions similar to those which have given a victory to external authority, discipline, uniformity and dependence upon the Leader in foreign countries."[3] Dewey's concern over the threat to liberal democratic values both nationally and internationally, led him in 1939 to help form and chair the Committee for Cultural Freedom, which was dedicated to exposing and challenging the repression of human rights and intellectual freedom at home and abroad.

During Dewey's stay in Mexico for the Trotsky hearings, he regularly wrote letters to Roberta Lowitz Grant. He had known

Roberta as a small child in Chicago where her father had been a school teacher, and they met again some time after Alice Dewey's death.[4] Their letters reveal that by early 1937 they had established a warm friendship.[5] Roberta, an outgoing woman with a good mind and a gentle sense of humor, was then thirty-two and John was seventy-seven. In the course of the next nine years Dewey, who lived together with one or another of his children in his own apartment in New York City, continued this relationship, often spending much time with Roberta. In December 1946 they were married in the Dewey apartment by Jerome Nathanson, a leader of the New York Society for Ethical Culture. Prior to the marriage Roberta had adopted a four-year-old Canadian boy, who was named John, and after the marriage the Deweys adopted the little boy's older sister Adrienne.[6] Dewey delighted in the company of his new wife and enjoyed being once again with young children. The family continued to go to his summer home in Hubbards, Nova Scotia, as well as to Roberta's farm in Pennsylvania. During the winter months John and Roberta spent much time in Florida, living in either Key West or Miami Beach.[7]

During the 1940s Dewey remained intellectually engaged in a wide range of social and philosophical issues, writing over fifty essays and book reviews. In addition to efforts directed at clarifying technical points in the fields of logic, metaphysics, and the theory of valuation, he is found revisiting the philosophy of William James with fresh appreciation, warning against war propaganda that denied the evil in Stalin's totalitarianism, reasserting his views on war and peace, and reaffirming his faith in social science and education. He joined the NAACP and the ACLU in appealing to the Supreme Court to rehear the case of Odell Waller, a black sharecropper who appeared to have been unjustly convicted of first degree murder in the killing of a white landlord.[8] In the early 1940s Dewey and the Committee for Cultural Freedom devoted considerable time and energy to defending the academic freedom of Bertrand Russell in a case that Dewey viewed as a critical battle in the struggle against the forces of reaction, dogmatism, and intolerance. As a result of a legal suit, Russell was denied the right to teach at the City College of New York by a state Supreme Court judge, who found Russell's published views on the subject of sexual ethics to be morally unacceptable. Certain conservative groups within both the Protestant and Catholic churches had led the attack on Russell, and Dewey believed that Russell's thought had been grossly distorted and unfairly criticized by them. With Dewey's assistance a lectureship was secured for Russell at the Barnes Foundation. Dewey and Horace Kallen collected and edited a series of essays on the case, and in his contributions Dewey gave special attention to the need for the scientific study of sexual ethics and informed public discussion.[9]

In his last years, Dewey published three noteworthy essays that focus attention on religion: "Religion and Morality in A Free Society" (1942), "Anti-Naturalism in Extremis" (1943), and a contribution to a symposium on the theme of "Religion and the Intellectuals" (1950). In all of these essays Dewey was reacting to the rise of totalitarianism overseas and to a resurgence of supernaturalism, absolutism, and authoritarianism in the United States. In this regard he was particularly concerned about attacks against naturalism and humanism. Theologians and philosophical idealists, argued that these intellectual movements were undermining the values essential to a free society, including belief in the dignity of humankind. Dewey found his critics looking for "some centre and authority entirely outside nature" as a necessary foundation for human values and as a regulative principle in human conduct. In addressing this outlook Dewey identified two basic issues. First, he points out that a "skeptical, even cynical and pessimistic, view of human nature is at the bottom of all the assertions that naturalism is destructive of the values associated with democracy."[10] Rather than seek some supernatural foundation for values, he argued that the critics of humanistic naturalism should recognize that "the worth and dignity of men and women" is "founded in human nature itself, in the connections, actual and potential, of human beings with one another in their natural social relationships."

Second, Dewey notes that anti-naturalism and pessimism about human nature is the cause of "systematic disrespect for scientific method," leading to authoritarianism and absolutism in morals.[11] Again and again Dewey reasserted his conviction that the choice in moral matters is not, as often imagined in the public debate, a matter of deciding between absolutism and subjective relativism, authority or anarchy. A sound empirical method of moral valuation offers a middle way that provides grounds for objective moral judgments, making possible liberating social reconstruction. For Dewey the danger in the revival of anti-naturalism is clear. It is "loss of confidence and faith" in human nature and human intelligence and a return to the rule of uncriticized tradition and arbitrary authority, obstructing free inquiry, open communication, and social progress.[12] Some critics of Dewey's faith in social science as an instrument of moral guidance and social planning point out that this faith in experience and intelligence has been tried and found inadequate. In the last half of the twentieth century the federal government and the university have undertaken the massive cooperative research that Dewey called for throughout his career, and the results, it is argued, have not produced either intellectual agreement or clear moral direction. Dewey would respond that significant social progress is being made, the experiment has just begun, and there is no more promising alternative.

In spite of his strong feelings on the subject of supernaturalism and the behavior of certain conservative church groups, Dewey did —consistent with his liberal values—strongly support toleration in matters of religious belief. He also urged an openness to learn from the various points of view represented by the different religious traditions.[13] Moreover, he writes: "Genuine toleration includes active sympathy with the struggles and trials of those of other faiths than ours and a desire to cooperate with them in the give-and-take process of search for more light." He also points out that this search and interfaith cooperation may itself become a source of religious experience:

> Search for ever more and more wisdom and insight may become intense enough to have religious quality. And this religious quality is strengthened and deepened by realization that discovery of the truth that governs our relations to one another in the shared struggles, sorrows and joys of life is our common task and winning it our common reward. . . . There will be differences on many points. But we may learn to make these differences a means of learning, understanding that mere identity means cessation of power of growth.

Dewey urged all the religions to find unity in the midst of their diversity by committing themselves to the cause of a free society and by embracing the democratic humanistic spirit that is essential to its realization. He defined this spirit as involving: "faith in the possibility of continued growth; search for new truth as a condition of growth, and that mutual respect and regard which constitute charity as the inspiration of peace and good will among men." [14]

Insofar as a religion emphasizes theistic supernaturalism, a fixed and final historical revelation, and an authoritarian approach to morals, it will not be able to accept fully Dewey's humanistic, naturalistic, and experimental approach to morals and the religious dimension of experience. However, insofar as the religions are committed to the values of compassion and peace, they cannot escape the challenge of democratic humanism, which calls on all peoples to devote themselves to the task of cooperatively building a harmonious world of equal opportunity, freedom, and justice as the supreme moral and spiritual challenge. Democratic humanism critically evaluates a religion in the light of the consequences that follow from its faith and practice in this regard, giving special attention to the moral and religious quality of experience it generates. Most religions have a fundamental concern with the overcoming of evil and suffering; and insofar as they do they are humanistically oriented and recognize the impact of religion on human growth and well-being as an important criterion of evaluation. Dewey would make this concern central, rejecting reliance on supernatural solutions in this or another world and emphasizing humanity's responsibility for its own advancement.

Philosophy and Faith

The celebration of Dewey's ninetieth birthday was an extraordinary event, symbolic of the significance of his life's work. In twelve countries, including India, Israel, Japan, Mexico, and Turkey, universities and educational organizations arranged special programs. Personal messages were sent to Dewey from President Harry S. Truman and from the presidents and prime ministers of six other nations. Newspapers and journals published editorials and feature articles. Organized by the League for Industrial Democracy, a great birthday party was held in New York City, and 1500 people from all segments of the community attended. The speakers included representatives from the worlds of philosophy, the university, the schools, labor, and public affairs. In addition, Hu Shih, the former ambassador from China to the United States, and Jawaharlal Nehru, Prime Minister of India, paid tribute to Dewey. Nehru spoke of Dewey's "ripe wisdom" and commented that "there are few Americans ... who had exercised so much influence on my own thinking and, I suppose consequently on my action." The Consul General from Chile presented Dewey with the Order of Merit.[15]

When it was Dewey's turn to respond he emphasized two points. First, he observed that throughout his career he had been "first, last, and all the time engaged in the vocation of philosophy," and he reaffirmed his commitment to an instrumentalist approach to philosophy. Second, living in a world that had experienced two world wars and that was in the grip of a cold war, he identified the most fundamental issue facing civilization as the conflict between the attitudes of fear and faith. He expressed hope that his philosophical investigations had "helped to liberate my fellow human beings from fear" and to foster in them "faith in democracy as a moral and human ideal."[16] Dewey's view of the task of philosophy and his reflections during his later years on the interconnections between philosophy and the issues of fear and faith explore themes that lie at the heart of his understanding of the purpose and significance of his life's work.

Dewey's idea of the role of philosophy in the human quest for freedom and unity may be clarified by addressing an important issue. While some critics argue that Dewey had an overly optimistic view of the possibilities for human transformation, others raise the objection that he did not develop a method of transformation that adequately addresses the deeper dimensions of the problem. The first point to make in this regard is that he stands in the tradition of Socrates and Plato—"the dramatic, restless, co-operatively inquiring Plato of the *Dialogues*."[17] Dewey was keenly aware of the need for liberation from "bondage to ignorance and prejudice" and for growth of the whole person, and as in the case of these Greek thinkers, he viewed philosophy—critical thought applied to the search for wisdom—as a potent method for promoting growth and transformation. It was the process of education become fully self-conscious and experimental. Like Socrates and Plato, he believed that "tradition and custom are pretty well broken down as dependable resources in guiding our activity."[18] He pursued philosophy both as a method of criticizing the habits of mind—the ideas and values—that obstruct liberation and as a method of imaginative reconstruction, generating light and fresh guidance.

The second point to be made regarding Dewey's idea of the method of transformation is related to what he had learned as a youth from Vermont Transcendentalism and the neo-Hegelian idealism of G. S. Morris. He acquired from these traditions the view that the way of liberation, which they identified with Christianity, is not most fundamentally a theory or a philosophy but a way of living, involving a certain character orientation in relation to the world. True religion, they taught, is experimental religion; one comes to a genuine understanding of saving truth by embodying it and testing it in action. As a humanistic naturalist, Dewey retained the idea that the method of learning and growth is found in the final analysis in a way of individual life. In clarifying this way he radically reconstructed rather than abandoned what he regarded as the essential values of Christianity, and his reconstruction of Christianity came to a focus around the democratic ideal. He conceived of the democratic way of life in all its everyday concreteness as a method of intellectual, moral, and spiritual growth in which thought and action, the spiritual and the material, the individual and society, person and work, art and everyday life, the religious and the secular, are fully integrated. In this approach philosophy has creative transformative power insofar as it is intimately related to the democratic life, contributing to its preservation and development.

A Darwinian concept of the nature and function of mind coupled with a profound appreciation of the experimental method of knowledge reinforced Dewey's view that philosophy serves as an effective method of transformation when it is intimately related to the process of creative living. From his own experience he recognized that for some intellectuals a philosophical synthesis of ideas could provide a sense of psychic wholeness and aesthetic enjoyment, contributing to a sense of religious fulfillment, but he rejected the Hegelian conception of thinking and philosophy as in the final analysis an end in itself with direct access to ultimate reality and the ideal. As an empirical thinker he became very critical of the "intellectualistic fallacy," that is, the tendency in Western philosophy to reduce the real to the known and to view the unification of the ideal and the real as basically an intellectual task, a quest for certainty. He abandoned the idealist's metaphysical search for some absolute truth and wholesale solution to human problems. He came to think largely in biological and social categories, emphasizing the ideas of process, interaction, continuity, communication, participation, growth, and adjustment. As a Darwinian, he viewed the mind chiefly as a problem-solving instrument and ideas as guides to action. Knowledge, he argued, provides an understanding of the interrelations and causal connections between things, and consequently it is of great instrumental value. It is, however, direct or immediate experience that reveals those values which are ends in themselves, giving to life aesthetic quality—a sense of intrinsic worth. Direct experience of the values inherent in actual situations awakens the human vision of the ideal. Ideals are properly understood as desirable possibilities of nature apprehended by intelligence and imagination. With these reflections in mind, Dewey contended that the supreme end of life is not thinking about life but the process of living itself. The full meaning and value of this process may be achieved, believed Dewey, by engaging wholeheartedly with the aid of intelligence in creative relations with others and the larger world of nature, transforming experience into art in pursuit of the ideal. In experience as art, instrumental knowledge and aesthetic enjoyment are joined, culminating in experience with a religious quality.

Dewey's appreciation of philosophy as a method of transformation is rooted in his conviction regarding the profound importance of independent critical thought in the process of human liberation. In his tribute to Dewey at his ninetieth birthday celebration, the Harvard philosopher Ralph Barton Perry well summarized Dewey's outlook:

> His humanism, his democracy, his progressivism in education and elsewhere, his moral code, all rest on his belief that man's dignity lies in his capacity to think for himself. This capacity is not limited, in

Dewey's view, to a class of intelligentsia or to professional investigators; he would have it recognized throughout all walks of life, and through all ages of man, beginning in the kindergarten, if not in the cradle. Thinking, thinking for oneself, thinking freshly, learning from one's own experience, drawing one's own inferences, applying thought to one's own problems—all in association and interaction with one's fellows—this is the distinguishing prerogative of man, his indefeasible right, and the only guarantee of the advancement of mankind.[19]

Awakening to the capacity for autonomous critical thought and intelligent choice is in Dewey's view the most essential factor in the development of human personality and the achievement of freedom. He interpreted the democratic ideal of equality as most fundamentally a guarantee to all of equal opportunity for development of the powers of independent thought and judgment. In his liberal social philosophy, it was the first responsibility of all social institutions to create conditions that are educative and foster freedom of intelligence. Philosophy is a refined development of humanity's capacity for intellectual freedom, having a special interest in criticizing methods of inquiry as well as applying them.

The individualism—the emphasis on autonomous thought and choice—in Dewey's perspective is counterbalanced by an equal emphasis on the common good, and he maintained that philosophy should be grounded in the needs and problems of the common life. This was not due to a lack of concern for the needs of the individual, but rather an expression of his firm belief in the organic connection of the self and society. Self-realization and social development are interrelated, argued Dewey. Several statements he made toward the end of his career in correspondence with Trigant Burrow, an American psychoanalyst and pioneer in the field of group therapy, clearly set forth his position regarding the interconnection of individual well-being and social reconstruction.

> While I appreciate, I hope, all that psychiatry can do for disturbed and more or less disordered individual persons, it seems to me that it is what I have called socio-cultural conditions that have to be the central and final point of attack in dealing with the spread of disordered personality.

I think profound *institutional* changes are the precondition of any widely and enduringly successful attempt to deal with the neurotic state of present day man.[20]

It was Dewey's conviction that human beings come to an abiding understanding of ideas and values only by living them in their relations with other persons and nature at large. Therefore, the social conditions that shape human attitudes and behavior go far in determining the understanding and self-realization that people are able to achieve.[21] For example, developing in society at large an appreciation of freedom of intelligence requires institutions that foster certain specific attitudes and habits of mind. Consequently, the search for the social ideal and social reform are fundamental to the process of human transformation and well-being; and if people do not have the benefit of living now in the ideal society, they can participate in that reality through imaginative vision and an active faith in the ideal. In line with this outlook, Dewey contended that philosophy should be centrally concerned with understanding the basic value conflicts in society, clarifying the ideal, and furthering the process of social reconstruction.

Dewey did not think that philosophy could by itself solve human problems, "since they can only be solved by and in action." The philosopher's "criticisms and constructions may however aid in the practical and human solving by making clear what the problem is and by propounding a hypothesis as to the way to proceed in the action which alone can effect actual resolutions."[22] In the work of identifying the origins and nature of human problems, "it is possible for philosophers to make good their claim that they go below the surface; go behind ways in which things appear to be."[23] Dewey never tired of emphasizing that in pursuing creative reconstructions that help society overcome problems, philosophy's task is "to interpret the conclusions of science with respect to their consequences for our beliefs about purposes and values in all phases of life."[24] Using a Platonic metaphor and adopting a characteristic prophetic perspective, Dewey described the task of philosophy in 1946 as "the act of midwifery": "There is no phase of life, educational, economic, political, religious, in which inquiry may not aid in bringing to birth that world which Matthew Arnold rightly said was as yet unborn."[25]

The key to the free world and the fulfillment that Dewey envisioned is the democratic faith. His discussions of fear and faith and their bearing on human happiness well summarize many of the attitudes and values that he associated with the democratic ideal. Dewey took up the subject of the democratic faith in addresses prepared for dinners in his honor at his seventieth, eightieth, and ninetieth birthdays, and issues of fear and faith were explored on the first and last of these occasions. Reflecting in 1929 just prior to the stock market crash on the conditions of human fulfillment, he began by pointing out that "the great enemy to what is attainable in happiness in the life of human beings is the attitude of fear."[26] He explained that he means by fear in this context, not something consciously felt in emergencies, but rather "an unconscious attitude which runs through and pervades everything of which we are conscious." More specifically, "it is an attitude of withdrawal, an attitude of exclusiveness which shuts out the beauties and troubles of experience as the things from which we alone can really learn and go on growing." In 1949 Dewey returned to this issue, focusing on the way fear obstructs social progress. He observed that if people are not guided by cooperative intelligence, their tendency is to act either mechanically following custom or impulsively out of fear. He then added:

> Living as we now do in what is almost a chronic state of crisis, there is danger that fear and the sense of insecurity become the predominant motivation of our activities ... For more than anything else, the fear that has no recognized and well-thought-out ground is what both holds us back and conducts us into aimless and spasmodic ways of action, personal and collective.[27]

In this attitude of fear, which can lead to despair and a reliance on brute force rather than cooperative intelligence, lies the deeper spiritual malaise that Dewey as a philosopher worked to overcome.

"This attitude of fear cannot be abolished by any direct attack," asserted Dewey in 1929; "It can be expelled only by the power of another and more positive attitude and emotion."[28] This positive attitude is fundamental to the way of life Dewey associated with faith in the democratic ideal. Speaking about the democratic spirit as the antidote to fear and the source of personal fulfillment, Dewey explained that it involves open-mindedness and sympathy. By this he meant the "positive attitude of interest, so far as one's limitations do at times permit, in all of the concerns of our common humanity." He urged his audience to abandon "the armorplate of prejudice, of convention" that prevents one "from sharing to the full in the larger and even the more unfamiliar and alien ranges of the possibilities of human life and experience."[29] Dewey went on to observe that "the most easily attained source of happiness in what we call a specialized intellectual class, is found simply in this broadening of intellectual curiosity and sympathy in all the concerns of life." Such an attitude promotes the continuing growth of the self, stimulating the sense of well-being.

Dewey also pointed out that the democratic way of life involves a character orientation that puts the emphasis on being rather than having. With this in mind, he concluded his remarks in 1929 with a call for "a revival of faith in individuality." In this connection Dewey deplored the "externalism" in American culture, which he identified as the cause of much anxiety and a major obstacle to "realizing the possibilities of life."

> External opportunities so abound in our American life that instead of nurturing the sources of happiness we tend to make happiness a direct pursuit; and the direct pursuit of happiness always ends in looking for happiness in possessions, in possessions of what is external, in having something whether in having a good time, having money, having a multitude of material things, or having someone else to lean upon for our ideas. We pursue happiness in these external things because, I suppose, we do not really possess our own souls. We are impatient; we are hurried; we are fretful because we try to find happiness where it cannot be got.... Without knowing it, we distrust the slow processes of growth, and we do not tend the roots of life from which a lasting happiness springs.[30]

Liberal democracy is often identified with a self-seeking individualism and consumerism, but Dewey regarded this idea as a perversion of the true meaning of this tradition.

Americans will find the meaning and peace they seek, argued

Dewey, only when they cease to be anxiously focused on getting and having and become centrally concerned with being and sharing.

> Our present American ideal seems to be, "Put it over—and make it snappy while you do it." I do not imagine the state of things will endure forever. Mere fatigue and sheer disappointment will bring it to an end sometime. But in the meantime we need a revival of faith in individuality and what belongs to the internal springs and sources of individuality. Only a return to that individuality, which after all is what each of us is, will bring calm, repose, and a sense of beauty in the multitude of distractions of our modern life and action.
>
> The world is either a wonderful scene or a dismal one according to whether we bring wonder with us to it or whether we bring with us the desire to possess as much of it as possible in as short a time as possible. What we bring to the world in which we live always has and always will, at last, go back to the depths of our own being.

While these remarks may in part reflect Dewey's appreciation of the contemplative aspects of Japanese and Chinese culture, they also spring from a deep conviction formed early in his career that the educational process and the ethical life are centrally concerned with the quality of a person's self or character.

In his *Ethics* (1932) Dewey clarified the relation between the democratic way and achievement of a deep enduring happiness or sense of well-being—what Aristotle called *eudaimonia*. "Happiness is a matter of the disposition we actively bring with us to meet situations, the qualities of mind and heart with which we greet and interpret situations," explains Dewey. It involves a "contentment of character and spirit which is maintained in adverse circumstances." However, happiness cannot be realized by making it itself the object of desire and interest. It is rather "an end-product, a necessary accompaniment," of a certain mode of being or condition of the self. It is the spontaneous fruit of an "interest in objects that are enduring and intrinsically related to an outgoing and expansive nature."[31] It is, in other words, the product of a self that is more concerned with being than having and that has adopted the attitude of the open mind and sympathy—a self engaged in the democratic way of growth. The person who makes a commitment to the democratic ideal, choosing to become an ever-growing self, achieves a unique and lasting kind of happiness—what Dewey in the *Ethics* called "the final happiness." He had this final happiness in mind when he described the religious quality of experience in *A Common Faith*. In the *Ethics*, he writes:

> The final happiness of an individual resides in the supremacy of certain interests in the make-up of character; namely, alert, sincere, enduring interests in the objects in which all can share. It is found in such interests rather than in the accomplishments of definite external results because this kind of happiness alone is not at the mercy of circumstances. No amount of outer obstacles can destroy the happiness that comes from lively and ever-renewed interest in others and in the conditions and objects which promote their development. To those in whom these interests are alive (and they flourish to some extent in all persons who have not already been warped) their exercise brings happiness because it fulfills the self.[32]

Dewey emphasizes that such interests fulfill the self because the self has chosen to identify with these interests. The quality of choice determines the quality of happiness which a person realizes. However, Dewey is careful to point out that the kind of interests which involve this "final happiness" are chosen because they express the kind of self a person elects to *be* and not because they give greater happiness.

Such is Dewey's naturalistic and democratic reconstruction of the nineteenth century, neo-Hegelian, Christian ideal of the universal man or woman. In this connection it is also noteworthy that Dewey did not conceive of the final happiness—experience with a religious quality—as necessarily excluding sadness and pain, for it arises with the growth of compassion.

> As George Eliot remarked in her novel, *Romola,* "It is only a poor sort of happiness that could ever come by caring very much about our own narrow pleasures. We can only have the highest happiness, such as goes along with being a great man, by having wide thought and much feeling for the rest of the world as well as ourselves; and this sort of happiness often brings so much pain with it, that we can only tell it from pain by its being what we would choose before everything else, because our souls see it is good."[33]

Dewey found that in the midst of conflict and sorrow there can be an abiding sense of meaning and peace, provided a person approaches the situation with the right disposition.

At his ninetieth birthday party Dewey again reflected on the power of the democratic faith to counteract the fear and despair that threaten to overwhelm people in the contemporary world. On this occasion he chose to emphasize faith in human nature as fundamental to the democratic spirit. "When we allow ourselves to be fear-ridden and permit it to dictate how we act," remarked Dewey, "it is because we have lost faith in our fellowmen—and that is the unforgiveable sin against the spirit of democracy."[34] Democracy as a social method is a "an educative process"—"a continued process of open and public communication" in and through which an "interchange of facts and ideas exposes what is unsound and discloses what may make for human well-being." The whole process "is based upon faith in human good sense and human good will as it manifests itself in the long run when communication is progressively liberated from bondage to prejudice and ignorance." Dewey goes on to point out that living together in the democratic spirit has the effect of "increasing faith in the humaneness of human beings" and of developing an understanding of human relations "that expels fear, suspicion, and distrust." His faith in human nature is not an unqualified trust in human beings regardless of the situation, but a confidence that if sound education is provided and an environment of free communication is created, such trust is justified.

For Dewey, then, the corrective to the attitude of fear and the suffering it engenders is a faith in the democratic way of life, involving a belief in the possibilities of human nature, a concern for the quality of one's own individuality, wonder, the open mind, sympathy, and sharing. These values joined with equality of opportunity, progressive education, experimental inquiry, free communication, voluntary association, cooperative effort, and nonviolence are what the democratic ideal meant to Dewey. In this ideal he found the key to individual growth and freedom, social reconstruction, and world peace. It is in the context of living the democratic life in search of freedom and community that Dewey found philosophy to be an effective transformative method. He also, of course, appreciated the way therapeutic methods, such as the Alexander technique, as well as aesthetic experience and mystical intuition, could contribute to the process of human growth and enrich the democratic life.

Dewey has been criticized for failing to appreciate fully the depth of the contradictions that divide certain social groups and for not recognizing the need for "confrontational politics and agitational social struggle" as a necessary aspect of the process of social reconstruction.[35] While there may be some validity in such observations, it must also be pointed out that Dewey's approach remains fundamental, for without experimental inquiry and evaluation confrontation is without intelligent purpose, and without effective communication and a spirit of cooperation the peace of authentic community will never be more than a dream. In supporting the Women's International League for Peace and Freedom in the mid-forties, Dewey wrote: "The measure of civilization is the degree in which the method of cooperative intelligence replaces the method of brute conflict."[36] Here lies the basic issue from the perspective of democratic humanism, and where this point is not appreciated—and this applies especially to those in positions of power—democracy as a way of life has little chance of full realization.

By arguing that the process of social reform is dependent upon the faith of individuals, Dewey underlined the pivotal significance of individual decision in a democratic society. Sound institutions may be necessary to foster autonomous and responsible individuality, but the exercise of this individuality is in the final analysis an individual matter. By employing the term "faith" for the decision to commit the self to the democratic ideal, Dewey also indicated that this decision proceeds from a transformation of character involving the whole feeling, thinking, willing self. He viewed a moral faith in the democratic ideal as religious insofar as it was wholehearted and involved the unifying of personality and the harmonizing of self and world. Dewey recognized that such a religious faith in the ideal could not be forced, but he also believed that individuals and societies can tend the conditions of its growth. As a philosopher, teacher, reformer, father, and friend, this had been his overriding purpose.

Going Home

A week after Dewey's ninetieth birthday celebration in New York City, he journeyed back to his boyhood world to be honored by the city of Burlington and the University of Vermont. It was his third return visit since his departure in the 1880s. During the day he visited many places including the old family home, the First Congregational Church, Mount Mansfield, and his parents' grave site. Addressing an audience of faculty and students, Dewey commented: "My heart and mind are both very full of memories. It is good to come back to the town where I was born and brought up, where my parents lived, and even find some old friends of my childhood. I spent four happy years on this campus."[37] In the evening he was feted at a dinner hosted by the university, and at the end of the affair, he once again rose to his feet to speak. He spoke of his pride in being a native Vermonter and of the democratic spirit that he had experienced in Vermont community life. He concluded by reading a passage from the writings of Liberty Hyde Bailey, a ninety-one-year-old Cornell University horticulturist and the author of fifty books including *The Holy Earth.* The passage is significant because it reveals how Dewey's piety toward nature and his Darwinian naturalistic modes of thought were leading him in 1949 to embrace the spirit embodied in the kind of ecological worldview that was to become popular in the 1970s and 1980s under the impact of a worldwide environmental crisis. George Dykhuizen, who was present at this event, reports that the Bailey statement read by Dewey "describes the planet Earth as a wonderful and beautiful place to live, where man can fashion a happy and worthwhile life provided he tends the earth and its resources with care and reverence and its inhabitants with intelligence and good will."[38]

Throughout most of his adult life Dewey had tried to forget the painful aspects of his early life, and he developed a philosophy that emphasizes living in the present and working to create a better future. However, at the age of ninety, he had long ago overcome the dualisms with which Vermont culture had once burdened him, and his return to Vermont was a homecoming in the most heartwarming sense. In a letter from New York expressing his gratitude to President Elias Lyman of the University of Vermont, he comments: "Of course, the dinner here on the 20th was a wonderful occasion but the home coming last night had something that went deeper."[39] In and through this return a final note of reunion, wholeness, and completion was added to Dewey's life experience.

During his last two and a half years, Dewey's health was on the decline. Nevertheless, he continued to read, answer letters, and write essays for publication. He also began planning a revised edition of *Experience and Nature*. At the age of ninety-two he broke his hip in a fall while staying in his New York apartment, and recovery was slow and difficult.[40] Then in late May 1952, he came down with a case of pneumonia. His condition worsened during the day of June 1. Early in the evening he told Roberta that something had changed within him in a way he had not felt before, intimating his awareness of the approach of death.[41] Shortly thereafter, he lost consciousness and died peacefully.[42]

Roberta Dewey chose to have Dewey's funeral held at the Community Church in New York. The statement of purpose at the Community Church was in harmony with the democratic ideals expressed in *A Common Faith*, and it was very similar to the statement of purpose that Edward Scribner Ames had used over the years as pastor of the University Church in Chicago. In spite of his impatience with most institutional religion, Dewey respected the work of the Community Church as well as that of Ames. Eulogies at the funeral service were given by Reverend Donald Herrington of the Community Church and Professor Max C. Otto of the University of Wisconsin, a philosophical humanist with whom Dewey had maintained a warm friendship and an extensive correspondence during his later years. Dewey's body was cremated, and Roberta Dewey kept the urn with his ashes until her death in 1970. Subsequently, and in keeping with Roberta Dewey's wishes, the urn with Dewey's ashes and an urn with her ashes were given to the University of Vermont to be interred there.[43] In a quiet location adjacent to the Ira Allen Chapel, the university created a Dewey memorial. It seems appropriate that Dewey's final resting place is in Vermont where his quest began and where the people's motto is Freedom and Unity.

In the midst of his career, Dewey in 1915 described himself as "something of a John the Baptist," a "forerunner" with a vision of a new world that was the ideal possibility and deeper meaning of the creative forces at work in America and the larger emerging modern world.[44] Instead of going into the church pulpit with his message, he, like Emerson, turned to philosophy, the essay, and the lecture hall in a sustained effort to convert the intellectual community and the larger public. His career coincided with the emergence in America of the secular university as a powerful center of research and graduate study, and he based himself in the university and helped to define its mission. His vision had deep roots in the Protestant Christian tradition, and even though he rejected Hegel's metaphysical system, he was profoundly inspired by Hegel's grand attempt to understand the great conflicts of history as a dialectical process by which the human spirit progressively moves to a new and higher synthesis to be worked out in the social, intellectual, moral, aesthetic, and religious life of society.

Dewey enthusiastically embraced the forces of the Enlightenment, evolutionary biology, social science, secularization, and liberal democracy. Working through and resolving the value conflicts these movements engendered became for him the chief spiritual challenge of the age. Even though these forces of change inevitably caused a loss of faith in certain cherished old moral and religious ideas, he did not believe they meant the destruction of human values. To the contrary, he believed that they opened the door for the first time to the birth of a genuinely free world, and he joined the attack on all the old ideas that seemed to obstruct the process of liberation.

However, he always sought a middle way, endeavoring to avoid the dangerous tendencies of modern life that issue in materialism, atheism, pessimism, atomistic individualism, and totalitarianism. He labored to create a new synthesis of the old and the new, reason and experience, the ethical and the scientific, the aesthetic and the practical, faith and intelligence, the religious and the secular. He accomplished this task in a revolutionary fashion on a new empirical and naturalistic basis. His philosophy was pervaded by the conviction that "our democratic tradition is a gift of grace" and our task is to develop that tradition creatively in response to the new problems that have been generated by modern civilization.[45] It was a melioristic philosophy based on faith, hope, and intelligent sympathy. Its objective was creation of a free world order, beginning with transformation of the school and the liberation of children.

Dewey did not doubt that there is religious—ultimate—meaning and value to be realized in life. He did not, however, believe that the self could participate in the reality of the divine except in and through relation to other persons and the larger world of nature. From his perspective the idea of God as an all-powerful perfect being dwelling apart from the world is an illusion just as the idea of the self as a being which can develop itself and find fulfillment in itself as an isolated ego is an illusion. As a mature religious thinker he adopted an organic and holistic approach seeking to break down completely any dualism between the divine and the ideal possibilities of nature, the spiritual and the material, the individual and society, religious life and everyday life, the religious quest and the search for social liberation. He understood as few others have that, if men and women in contemporary civilization are to find the wholeness, meaning, and inner peace that are the fruit of a healthy religious life, and if the violent conflict and suffering of twentieth-century history are to be overcome in the social sphere, then religious life and social life must not only be reconstructed, they must also be fully integrated. The divine, he taught, is to be identified with a unified vision of the ideal, the common good, and with those forces and processes in nature and human culture that make for the actualization of the ideal. God—if one chooses to use this traditional symbolic language—is the mind, heart, and body of authentic community, which finds its highest expression in the contemporary world in creative democracy. To those who in faith give themselves wholeheartedly to the life of creative democracy, this life reveals itself spontaneously as divine in significance through the grace that is the religious quality of experience.

During the 1940s and the decades immediately following Dewey's death, philosophy narrowed its focus, becoming for the most part absorbed in highly technical and formal issues of logical analysis. With a few notable exceptions philosophers and theologians lost interest in Dewey's vision, which they tended to label—often with little firsthand acquaintance—as a dated product of an overly optimistic liberal imagination nurtured by an earlier time of innocence in American history. It seemed impossible to maintain Dewey's progressive faith and hope in the face of world war, totalitarianism, economic oppression, class conflict, and persistent racism and sexism. "Where there is no vision the people perish," William James once remarked, and the comment suggests one fundamental reason why Dewey's thought continues to be profoundly relevant and a new generation of philosophers are beginning to develop a fresh appreciation of his contribution.[46] It is also well to keep in mind Albert Schweitzer's admonition that "if humanity is not to perish" in this age of nuclear weapons, it must cultivate the "faith in humanity" and the ethical ideals that inspire all peoples to work cooperatively together in building a world order that will issue in the "reign of peace" historically identified with the kingdom of God.[47] Dewey's philosophy addresses these concerns. Furthermore, it does so by speaking directly to the issues raised by the worldwide struggle for freedom, which has been the most influential ideal in nineteenth- and twentieth-century history. Everywhere women and men yearn for liberation from oppression, and they face the challenge of building the institutions and ordered social life that make the achievement of authentic freedom a real possibility. It is difficult to imagine how this work of creating freedom and peace for all can be accomplished in a pluralistic technological civilization on a small fragile planet apart from a philosophy of life that emphasizes individual self-realization, human responsibility, a sense of interdependence with nature, the organic connection of self and world, a process view of reality, experimental intelligence, an empirical method of moral valuation, progressive education, and a shared faith in the democratic way of living and growing together.

Dewey, who as a process philosopher and experimentalist rejected any notion of fixed ideas, would be the last to regard his system as complete and finished. The testing of ideas and the debate continues as with Dewey's understanding of the problem of ultimate meaning and God, which has been examined closely earlier in this study. Furthermore, change is constant, and new opportunities and problems arise. The work of inquiry and reconstruction never ends. For example, while Dewey had a keen sense of belonging to the larger universe and well understood the close interconnection between human culture and nature, it has become necessary in the light of the deepening environmental crisis to include the nonhuman world of nature in our concept of community in a way that is not fully developed in Dewey's thought. However, the direction in which he oriented the process of reconstruction in terms of both methods and ideals is sound. His orientation points the logician, the psychologist, the social philosopher, and the religious thinker in directions they must go, if the ideals of freedom and community are to become realities in the twenty-first century.

In the closing lines of *A Common Faith,* the spirit of Dewey's democratic humanism and faith is eloquently expressed. It is fitting to conclude with these words:

> The ideal ends to which we attach our faith are not shadowy and wavering. They assume concrete form in our understanding of our relations to one another and the values contained in these relations. We who now live are parts of a humanity that extends into the remote past, a humanity that has interacted with nature. The things in civilization we most prize are not of ourselves. They exist by grace of the doings and sufferings of the continuous human community in which we are a link. Ours is the responsibility of conserving, transmitting, rectifying and expanding the heritage of values we have received that those who come after us may receive it more solid and secure, more widely accessible and more generously shared than we have received it. Here are all the elements for a religious faith that shall not be confined to sect, class, or race. Such a faith has always been implicitly the common faith of mankind. It remains to make it explicit and militant.[48]

Notes

Prologue

1. Herbert W. Schneider, *A History of American Philosophy* (New York: Columbia University Press, 1946), pp. 218–19.

2. Sidney E. Ahlstrom, *A Religious History of the American People* (New Haven: Yale University Press, 1972), p. 356.

3. Paul F. Boller, Jr., *American Transcendentalism, 1830–1860* (New York: Putnam, 1974), pp. 44–54.

4. Ralph Waldo Emerson, "The Over-Soul," in *Essays: First and Second Series* (Mount Vernon, N.Y.: Peter Pauper Press, n.d.), p. 138.

5. Octavius Brooks Frothingham, *Transcendentalism in New England: A History* (Philadelphia: University of Pennsylvania Press, 1959), p. 356. First published in 1876.

6. March Edmund Jones, *George Sylvester Morris: His Philosophical Career and Theistic Idealism* (New York: Greenwood Press, 1968), pp. 32, 208–10.

7. For accounts of the controversy over evolution in the American religious community see: Ahlstrom, *A Religious History of the American People,* pp. 766–72; John Herman Randall, Jr., "The Changing Impact of Darwin on Philosophy," *Journal of the History of Ideas* (October-December 1961) 22:435–62; and Ira V. Brown, *Lyman Abbott: Christian Evolutionist* (Cambridge: Harvard University Press, 1953), pp. 139–49.

8. Israel Scheffler, *Four Pragmatists* (New York: Humanities Press, 1974), pp. 13–14.

9. William James, "Philosophical Conceptions and Practical Results," in John J. McDermott, ed., *The Writings of William James*, pp. 347–48 (Chicago: The University of Chicago Press, 1977).

10. Dorothy Ross, *G. Stanley Hall: The Psychologist As Prophet* (Chicago: University of Chicago Press, 1972), pp. 33–34.

11. John Dewey, "From Absolutism to Experimentalism," in LW 5:155.

12. John Dewey, *The Quest for Certainty*, in LW 4:240–41.

O N E: *A Quest for Unity*

1. A.M. Hemenway, ed., *The Vermont Historical Gazetteer* (Burlington, 1867), vol. 1, pp. 1:5, 491, 518–19.

2. Levi Smith, "A Masterpiece In Living," in *The Very Elect: Baccalaureate Sermons and Occasional Addresses of Matthew Henry Buckham, D.D., LL.D., President of the University of Vermont, 1881–1910* (Boston: Pilgrim Press, 1912), p. 6.

3. *Vermont Historical Gazetteer*, 1, 536–51, 721.

4. John Dewey, "James Marsh and American Philosophy," in LW 5:193–194.

5. Jane Dewey, ed., "Biography of John Dewey," pp. 4, 6. Jane Dewey's biographical essay was written with the close cooperation of her father, John Dewey. See "Biography of John Dewey," p. 3.

6. Dykhuizen, *John Dewey*, p. 328, n. 8.

7. Jane Dewey, ed., "Biography of John Dewey," p. 3.

8. *Ibid.*, pp. 7–8.

9. Sidney Hook, *John Dewey: An Intellectual Portrait*, pp. 5–6.

10. Lewis O. Brastow, *The Work of the Preacher* (Boston: Pilgrim Press, 1914), p. 25.

11. Matthew Henry Buckham, "The Baccalaureate Discourse, 1879," in *Orations and Addresses, The University of Vermont, 1806–1880*, vol. 3.

12. Matthew Henry Buckham, "Christianity and Social Reform," in *The Very Elect*, p. 229.

13. *Ibid.*, p. 508; Dykhuizen, *John Dewey*, pp. 1–2.

14. Jane Dewey, ed., "Biography of John Dewey," p. 7.

15. *Ibid.*, pp. 5–6; Feuer, "H.A.P. Torrey and John Dewey," pp. 51–52.

16. Jane Dewey, ed., "Biography of John Dewey," p. 7.

17. Hook, "Some Memories of John Dewey," pp. 109–10. See also Corliss

Lamont, ed., *Dialogue on John Dewey* (New York: Horizon Press, 1959), pp. 39, 43.

18. Sidney Hook, *Education and the Taming of Power* (La Salle, Ill.: Open Court, 1973), p. 141.

19. Jane Dewey, ed., "Biography of John Dewey," p. 6.

20. *Ibid.* Hook, "Some Memories of John Dewey," pp. 102–03.

21. *The Directory of the First Church* (January 1889), John Dewey Papers, coll. 102/1/2, Special Collections, Morris Library, Southern Illinois University, Carbondale.

22. M.F.P., "Mrs. Lucina A. Dewey, An Appreciative Tribute to Her Worth," *Burlington Daily Free Press,* March 28, 1899, as quoted in *The Adams Mission Monthly* (April 1899), John Dewey Papers, coll. 102/1/2.

23. Sarah P. Torrey, "Women's Work in the First Church," in *Hundreth Anniversary of the Founding of the First Church, Burlington, Vt.*, pp. 62–3 (Burlington, 1905).

24. Jane Dewey, ed., "Biography of John Dewey," p. 7.

25. Dykhuizen, *John Dewey,* pp. 7, 329, n. 28. Information on Lucina Dewey and the Rich family may be found in Jane Dewey, ed., "Biography of John Dewey," p. 7. Laura Chasin has written an excellent psychological analysis of John Dewey with reference to his Vermont experience. Her insights into Lucina's personality and young John's response to her have been helpful to me. Private collection of Laura Chasin.

26. Dykhuizen, *John Dewey,* p. 6; John E. Goodrich, "Historical Discourse," in *Hundreth Anniversary of the Founding of the First Church, Burlington, Vt.*, pp. 35–36.

27. Dykhuizen, *John Dewey,* pp. 6, 329, n. 25.

28. John Dewey to Joseph Ratner, October 7, 1946. Joseph Ratner Correspondence, coll. 142, Special Collections, Morris Library, Southern Illinois University, Carbondale, Illinois.

29. Poems #36, 47, 64, 71, 91 in *The Poems of John Dewey.*

30. Hook, "Some Memories of John Dewey," p. 102.

31. Dykhuizen, *John Dewey,* p. 6.

32. John Dewey, "The Place of Religious Emotion," in EW 1:91.

33. Hook, "Some Memories of John Dewey," p. 102.

34. John Dewey, "Religious Education as Conditioned by Modern Psychology and Pedagogy," in MW 3:211.

35. Unpublished manuscript by Laura Chasin on Dewey's personality and early experience. Private collection of Laura Chasin.

36. Dykhuizen, *John Dewey,* pp. 4–5; Jane Dewey, ed., "Biography of John Dewey," pp. 7, 9.

37. *Ibid.*, p. 17.

38. Eastman, "My Teacher and Friend," pp. 254–55. John Dewey to Joseph Ratner, October 4, 1946, Joseph Ratner Correspondence. Dewey told both Eastman and Ratner that he joined the church early in his college career. Dykhuizen does not mention this, because he assumed that Dewey's letter requesting membership at age eleven contradicted Dewey's own account. It seems that two separate incidents were involved here.

39. Marjorie Perrin, "Historical Notes: Concerning the First Congregational Church, United Church of Christ, Burlington, Vermont, 1805–1965," in the collections of the First Congregational Church. See also Feuer, "H.A.P. Torrey and John Dewey," p. 40; and Eastman, "My Teacher and Friend," p. 255.

40. Brastow, *The Work of the Preacher,* pp. 23, 32.

41. Archibald Dewey to John Dewey, October 16, 1882, John Dewey Papers, coll. 102/1/6.

42. Brastow, *The Work of the Preacher,* p. 24.

43. *Ibid.*, p. 27.

44. *Catalogue of the Officers and Students of the University of Vermont and State Agricultural College. With a Statement of the Several Courses of Instruction* (Burlington, Vt., 1875–1876), p. 10; *Ibid.*, 1878–1879, p. 7; *Organization of the University of Vermont and State Agricultural College, 1791–1959* (Burlington, Vt.), p. 8.

45. *The Laws of the University of Vermont and State Agricultural College* (Burlington, Vt.: Free Press, 1874), pp. 7–8. According to *The Laws of the University of Vermont,* students were required to be present at chapel services led by the faculty each weekday morning and to attend a local church of their choice on Sundays. They were also "earnestly advised . . . to become a member of a Bible Class."

46. Henry W. Hill, *Delta Psi Goodrich Memorial,* p. 19, Special Collections, Bailey/Howe Library, University of Vermont, Burlington, Vermont.

47. *Ibid.,* pp. 19, 62–63.

48. *In Memoriam Henry A.P. Torrey, LL.D., Marsh Professor of Intellectual and Moral Philosophy in the University of Vermont, 1868–1902,* Addresses at the Annual Meeting of Associate Alumni, June 23, 1903 (Burlington: University of Vermont, 1906), p. 23.

49. Buckham, "The Baccalaureate Sermon, 1878," in *Orations and Addresses.*

50. Buckham, "The Baccalaureate Discourse, 1879," in *Orations and Addresses.*

51. Buckham, "The Baccalaureate Sermon, 1878," in *Orations and Addresses*.

52. *Ibid*. In this statement Buckham adds a religious factor to Kant's idea of moral motivation and reconstructs Matthew Arnold's definition of religion.

53. Buckham, "Address to the Graduating Class, 1879," in *Orations and Addresses*.

54. Dykhuizen, *John Dewey*, p. 11.

55. H.A.P. Torrey to Daniel C. Gilman, April 5, 1883, Daniel Coit Gilman Papers, Ms. 1, Special Collections, Milton S. Eisenhower Library, The Johns Hopkins University, Baltimore, Maryland.

56. Matthew Henry Buckham to Daniel C. Gilman, April 3, 1883, Daniel C. Gilman Papers.

57. John Dewey, "From Absolutism to Experimentalism," in LW 5:153.

58. John Dewey to Joseph Ratner, October 15, 1946, Joseph Ratner Correspondence.

59. See Poems #36 and #43 in *The Poems of John Dewey*, pp. 24, 28. See also discussion of these poems and this issue in chapter 7.

60. Jane Dewey, ed., "Biography of John Dewey," pp. 7–8; Eastman, "My Teacher and Friend," pp. 154, 263.

61. Jane Dewey, ed., "Biography of John Dewey," pp. 7, 16.

62. Eastman, "My Teacher and Friend," p. 254.

63. John Dewey, "From Absolutism to Experimentalism," p. 153.

64. John Dewey, *Psychology*, in EW 2:347. Jane Dewey, ed., "Biography of John Dewey," p. 17.

65. John Dewey, "Religious Education as Conditioned by Modern Psychology and Pedagogy," p. 213.

66. Dykhuizen, *John Dewey*, pp. 10, 331, n. 43.

67. John Dewey, "The Place of Religious Emotion," pp. 91–92.

68. John Dewey, *Psychology*, p. 290.

69. H.A.P. Torrey to Daniel C. Gilman, April 5, 1883, Daniel C. Gilman Papers.

70. John Dewey, *Psychology*, p. 260.

71. *Ibid.*, pp. 78, 201.

72. *Ibid.*, p. 98.

73. John Dewey, "From Absolutism to Experimentalism," p. 153.

74. *Ibid.*, p. 150.

75. John Dewey, *Problems of Men*, pp. 184–85.

76. John Dewey, *Psychology*, p. 202.

77. John Dewey, "From Absolutism to Experimentalism," p. 153.

78. *Ibid.*

79. John Dewey, *Leibniz's New Essays Concerning the Human Understanding,* in EW 1: 255, 263.

80. Jane Dewey, ed., "Biography of John Dewey," pp. 10–12. Dykhuizen, *John Dewey,* pp. 10–18.

81. John Dewey, "From Absolutism to Experimentalism," p. 154.

82. John Dewey, "Poetry and Philosophy," in EW 3:112.

83. John Dewey, "Religious Education as Conditioned by Modern Psychology and Pedagogy," p. 213.

84. H.A.P. Torrey to Kant Centennial committee, *Journal of Speculative Philosophy* (July 1881), 15:300.

85. John Dewey, "From Absolutism to Experimentalism," p. 148.

86. John Dewey to H.A.P. Torrey, November 17, 1883, John Dewey Papers, coll. 102/1/7.

87. Feuer, "H.A.P. Torrey and John Dewey," pp. 41–44.

88. John Dewey to Jerome Nathanson, August 9, 1949, private collection of Jerome Nathanson.

89. Julian Ira Lindsay, "Coleridge and the University of Vermont," *Vermont Alumni Weekly* (January-February 1936),15:8–9.

90. *In Memoriam Henry A.P. Torrey,* pp. 21–22, 35.

91. G. G. Atkins, "An Estimate of Professor Torrey's Christian Life," *Ibid.*, pp. 26, 34. Reverend Atkins was Torrey's pastor during the latter part of his life.

92. Address by Edward H. Griffin in *In Memoriam Henry A.P. Torrey,* pp. 8–9. Reverend Griffin was pastor of the First Church in Burlington from 1868–1872, that is, during Torrey's first four years as a professor at the University of Vermont. Griffin later became Dean of the College at Johns Hopkins University.

93. For information pertaining to the philosophy courses of Joseph and H.A.P. Torrey, see *Catalogue of the Officers and Students of the University of Vermont and State Agricultural College, With a Statement of the Several Courses of Instruction* (Burlington, Vt., 1848–80); and Jane Dewey, ed., "Biography of John Dewey," p. 11.

94. Dewey himself defined "Intuitionalism" in this way in *The Universal Cyclopoedia,* 1900, p. 321. There he states that intuitionalism is "the theory, in its broader sense, that fundamental principles of being are known directly without intervention of either sense-experience or discursive logical processes; in its narrower sense, the theory that moral distinctions are known in this direct fashion." Torrey himself states in the announcement for his

course on moral philosophy in the course catalogue that "the intuitional theory is taught." *Catalogue of the Officers and Students of the University of Vermont, 1878–1879,* p. 18. John Buckham, the son of President Buckham and a student of Torrey's from the class of 1885, asserts that Torrey was an "intuitionist" in the tradition of James Marsh. See "A Group of American Idealists," *The Personalist* (April 1920), 1:25–26. Torrey's intuitionalism is made explicit in his essay, "The 'Theodicee' of Leibniz," *Andover Review* (July-December 1885), 4:509–11.

95. John Dewey, "From Absolutism to Experimentalism," p. 149.

96. Buckham, "A Group of American Idealists," pp. 24–25. President Buckham articulated the principle doctrine of Burlington intuitionalism clearly in a Baccalaureate Sermon in 1873. Regarding the first truths of religion, he states:

> Its prime truths, its essential and in some respects its most important truths, are out of reach of demonstration. This is not saying that they are irrational, but that the spiritual reason which apprehends them is a different faculty from the logical understanding, and works by different methods. That the whole is equal to the sum of all its parts, and that infinity is greater than the sum of all finite generalities, I know by intuitive reason. That the Supreme Being is holy and Good and that the supreme good for man is to be like him, I know, at least I recognize and approve, by my spiritual reason. For it is not meant that because of this power of spiritual vision we can dispense with revelation, but that we can perceive the truth as revealed without the intervention of any logical demonstration.

See *Orations and Addresses.*

97. John Dewey, "From Absolutism to Experimentalism," p. 149.

98. John Dewey in a letter to the editor, *The University* (January 9, 1886), p. 18. This brief statement is signed J.D. and it is indicated as an article by John Dewey, Davis Rich Dewey Papers in Joseph Ratner Papers, coll. 142, Morris Library, Southern Illinois University, Carbondale, Illinois.

99. John Dewey to Jerome Nathanson, August 9, 1949, private collection of Jerome Nathanson.

100. John Dewey as quoted by Herbert Schneider in Corliss Lamont, ed., *Dialogue on John Dewey,* p. 15. See also Herbert Schneider, "Reminiscences About John Dewey at Columbia, 1913–1950," p. 5, typewritten manuscript, Special Collections, Morris Library, Southern Illinois University. Jane Dewey mentions the influence of Coleridge and Marsh on Dewey at the University of Vermont in her "Biography of John Dewey," p. 12. Dewey mentions the

general historical significance of Marsh's edition of *Aids to Reflection* in "From Absolutism to Experimentalism," but Herbert Schneider's recollections of Dewey's comments are the only record of the major influence that book exercised on Dewey's own religious outlook. Schneider's accounts of these comments deal with three separate occasions when he heard Dewey refer to Coleridge and Marsh. Schneider mentions Dewey's comments about their influence on five occasions. See notes 102 and 105. In all these accounts Schneider quotes Dewey, but his renderings of Dewey's statements are made from memory of events that occurred many years before and there is some variation in exactly what he remembers Dewey to have said. However, Schneider's accounts do not contradict each other and all the accounts seem to agree on the general points which are discussed in the text of this book. Schneider must be regarded as a reliable source of information on Dewey. He was Dewey's colleague in the Department of Philosophy at Columbia University for a decade, is the author of *A History of American Philosophy* (1946), and has written extensively on American religious thought. Further, the thesis that Marsh's edition of *Aids to Reflection* exercised an important influence on Dewey fits well with the known facts about Dewey's development and later thought. However, Dewey's comments to Schneider and Schneider's own interpretation of the influence of Coleridge on Dewey overstate the case when it is suggested that Dewey actually arrived consciously in the 1880s at the ideas of the religious dimension of experience and a common faith which Dewey formulates as a naturalist in *A Common Faith* in 1934.

101. John Dewey, "The Marsh Lecture," Special Collections, Bailey/Howe Library, University of Vermont Library, Burlington, Vt. *The Vermont Cynic* (November 30, 1929), 48:1, 4. See John Dewey, "James Marsh and American Philosophy," pp. 178–96. Jo Ann Boydston, "Textual Commentary," in LW 5:514–15.

102. John Dewey as quoted by Herbert Schneider in Oral History Interview, June 29, 1967, Special Collections, Morris Library, Southern Illinois University, Carbondale, Illinois.

103. *Ibid.*

104. John Dewey, "From Absolutism to Experimentalism," p. 150.

105. Schneider reports that when he was beginning research on his *History of American Philosophy,* Dewey handed him a copy of Marsh's *Remains* with the comment: "This was very important to me in my early days and is still worth reading." See "John Dewey: A Talk Delivered by Professor Herbert W. Schneider in the Ira Allen Chapel, the University of

Vermont, on October 26, 1949, at the Celebration of John Dewey's Ninetieth Birthday Anniversary," typewritten manuscript, p. 5. Archives, Bailey/Howe Library, University of Vermont. Schneider also quotes Dewey as saying: "I admired Marsh as a teacher and philosopher; he had a big influence on me." See unpublished review by Herbert Schneider of George Dykhuizen, *John Dewey*, p. 3. Archives, Bailey/Howe Library, University of Vermont.

106. John Dewey, "James Marsh and American Philosophy," p. 182.

107. Samuel Taylor Coleridge, *Aids to Reflection,* in *The Complete Works of Samuel Taylor Coleridge* (New York: Harper, 1853), vol. 1, p. 115.

108. *Ibid.*, p. 117.

109. James Marsh, "Preliminary Essay," in Coleridge, *Aids to Reflection,* p. 77.

110. Jeremy Taylor as quoted in *Aids to Reflection,* p. 321.

111. Coleridge, *Aids To Reflection,* p. 173.

112. Marsh, "Preliminary Essay," pp. 77–78.

113. *Ibid.,* p. 68.

114. John Dewey, "What is the Demonstration of Man's Spiritual Nature?" in *The University* (January 4, 1886): 43–44. This article is signed "J.D." and is indicated as an article by John Dewey, Davis Rich Dewey Papers in Joseph Ratner Papers.

115. Marsh, "Preliminary Essay," p. 10.

116. *Ibid.*, p. 90.

117. Coleridge, *Aids to Reflection,* vol. 1, pp. 134, 241–42, 246, 263, 275, 367. Marsh, "Preliminary Essay," p. 90. Coleridge, *Statesman's Manual* in *The Complete Works of Coleridge,* vol. 1, p. 456.

118. Coleridge, *Aids to Reflection,* pp. 134, 215, 241–42, 367. See Walter Johnson Bate, *Coleridge* (New York: Macmillan, 1968), pp. 221–22; James D. Boulger, *Coleridge As Religious Thinker* (New Haven: Yale University Press, 1961), p. 92. Thomas McFarland likens Coleridge's idea of faith to Paul Tillich's concept of ultimate concern. See *Coleridge and the Pantheist Tradition* (New York: Oxford University Press, 1969), pp. 230–31.

119. Coleridge, *Statesman's Manual,* p. 433.

120. John Dewey, "James Marsh and American Philosophy," p. 181.

121. Marsh, "Preliminary Essay," p. 82.

122. John Dewey, "James Marsh and American Philosophy," p. 181. Coleridge himself states: "Faith is properly a state and disposition of the will, or rather of the whole man, the I." (*The Complete Works of Coleridge,* vol. 5, p. 91.)

123. James Marsh, *The Remains of the Rev. James Marsh, D.D., Late*

President and Professor of Moral and Intellectual Philosophy in the University of Vermont; with A Memoir of His Life, (Burlington, Vt.: Chauncey Goodrich, 1845), pp. 382–90, 404–16, 445, 472, 477, 520–21, 530, 543–44.

124. Coleridge, *Aids to Reflection,* p. 134.

125. *Ibid.*; Coleridge, *Stateman's Manual,* p. 455.

126. Marsh, *The Remains,* p. 548.

127. *Ibid.,* pp. 376, 383, 395, 482, 486.

128. Coleridge, *Aids to Reflection,* p. 242.

129. John Dewey, "The Place of Religious Emotion," p. 92.

130. John Dewey, "President Porter's 'Moral Science'," *Index* (February 28, 1885). This review of Porter's *Elements of Moral Science, Theoretical and Practical* is not signed by Dewey, but is included among the Davis Rich Dewey Papers as an article by Dewey. The quotations cited are in complete accord with the views set forth in Dewey's *Psychology* (1887).

131. In a letter to Alice Chipman dated December 30, 1885, Dewey writes: "While in a store down town this evening I picked up Coleridge's *Biographia Literaria.* Did you ever read any of Coleridge? The University of Vermont (where perhaps you may know, I graduated) used to rest its fame mostly on its teaching of philosophy which was that of Coleridge, never having bowed the knee to the Baal of Locke or the Scotch School and I have always felt as if it were a filial duty I owed to read him up some time ..." John Dewey Papers, coll. 102/1/8.

132. Notes of George Dykhuizen on Dewey's early reading based on the University of Vermont Library records of books borrowed from the library during the years 1881 and 1882. Archives, University of Vermont. The original records have been lost. See also John Dewey, "From Absolutism to Experimentalism," pp. 148–49.

133. Eastman, "My Teacher and Friend," pp. 255–57, 261–62.

134. Marsh, *The Remains,* p. 466.

135. John Dewey, "The Obligation to Knowledge of God," in EW 1:60–63.

136. John Dewey to Alice Chipman, April 13, 1886, John Dewey Papers, coll. 102/1/11.

137. Frederick Copleston, S.J., *A History of Philosophy* (Garden City, N.Y.: Image Books, Doubleday, 1965), vol. 7, part 1, pp. 33–34.

138. *The Complete Poetical Works of Wordsworth* (Boston: Houghton-Mifflin, 1932), pp. 91–93, 353–56. Regarding the influence of Wordsworth on the Transcendentalists see Octavius Brooks Frothingham, *Transcendentalism in New England* (Philadelphia: University of Pennsylvania Press, 1972), pp. 6–103.

139. John Dewey, *The Quest for Certainty,* in LW 4:240–41.

140. Jane Dewey, ed., "Biography of John Dewey," p. 8.

141. John Dewey to Alice Chipman, June 25, 1885, John Dewey Papers, coll. 102/1/8. John Dewey to John Wright Buckham, December 9, 1929, John Dewey Papers.

142. John Dewey, *Psychology,* p. 174.

143. Dykhuizen, *John Dewey,* pp. 18–21.

144. Eastman, "My Teacher and Friend," pp. 255, 257.

145. *The Complete Poetical Works of Wordsworth,* p. 91.

146. Eastman, "My Teacher and Friend," p. 257.

147. The statement was made by Anna L. Byington to George Dykhuizen, July 17, 1938. See Dykhuizen, *John Dewey,* p. 25.

148. Dewey began reading *The Journal of Speculative Philosophy* early in 1881 while he was still in Oil City, if not earlier, for he was in correspondence with the editor, W.T. Harris, in the spring of 1881. See Dykhuizen, *John Dewey,* p. 22. According to George Dykhuizen's notes on Dewey's reading during the winter of 1881–1882, Dewey took ten of the fourteen volumes of the *Journal of Speculative Philosophy* out of the University of Vermont library. Archives, University of Vermont.

149. *Journal of Speculative Philosophy* (April 1882), 16:208–13. See EW 1:3–8.

150. Coleridge, *Aids to Reflection,* p. 362. Joseph Torrey, "A Memoir," in *The Remains of the Rev. James Marsh,* p. 124.

151. Torrey, as quoted by John Dewey, "From Absolutism to Experimentalism," p. 148.

152. John Dewey, "The Pantheism of Spinoza," in EW 1:9, 10, 18.

153. John Dewey, *The Quest for Certainty,* p. 240. John Dewey, "Self-Realization as the Moral Ideal," in EW 4:44.

154. John Dewey, "From Absolutism to Experimentalism," p. 150. John Dewey to Joseph Ratner, October 15, 1946, Joseph Ratner Correspondence.

155. Ralph Barton Perry, *The Thought and Character of William James* (Boston: Little, Brown, 1935), vol. 2, *Philosophy and Psychology,* p. 518.

156. Jane Dewey, ed., "Biography of John Dewey," p. 14. John Dewey, "From Absolutism to Experimentalism," p. 149.

157. *Ibid.*, p. 153.

158. *Ibid.*

T W O: *Neo-Hegelian Idealism and the New Psychology*

1. John Dewey to W.T. Harris, January 17, 1884. Dykhuizen, *John Dewey*, pp. 29–30.

2. John Dewey, *Logic: The Theory of Inquiry*, in LW 12:17,n.1.

3. G. Stanley Hall, *Life and Confessions of a Psychologist* (New York: D. Appleton, 1923), p. 245.

4. *Ibid.*, p. 250.

5. *Ibid.*, p. 245; Dorothy Ross, *G. Stanley Hall: The Psychologist As Prophet* (Chicago: University of Chicago Press, 1972), p. 135.

6. Marc Edmund Jones, *George Sylvester Morris: His Philosophical Career and Theistic Idealism* (New York: Greenwood Press, 1968), p. 32.

7. *Ibid.*, pp. 186, 208–10.

8. George Sylvester Morris, *Kant's Critique of Pure Reason* (Chicago: S. C. Griggs, 1882).

9. Hall, *Life and Confessions of a Psychologist*, pp. 196–97.

10. John Dewey, "From Absolutism to Experimentalism," in LW 5:153.

11. John Dewey, "The Late Professor Morris," in EW 3:6. Dewey commented on the qualities of Morris's character on three separate occasions in 1889, 1915, and 1930.

12. *Ibid.*, p. 13.

13. John Dewey, "From Absolutism to Experimentalism," p. 152.

14. John Dewey as quoted in Robert M. Wenley, *The Life and Work of George Sylvester Morris* (New York: Macmillan, 1917), p. 313.

15. *Ibid.*, p. 319.

16. John Dewey, "The Late Professor Morris," p. 12.

17. George Sylvester Morris, *Philosophy and Christianity* (New York: Robert Carter, 1883), pp. 11–22, 266, 268.

18. Morris, *Kant's Critique*, p. 12. Morris, *Philosophy and Christianity*, p. 36.

19. Morris, *Philosophy and Christianity*, pp. 20–21, 48.

20. John Dewey as quoted in Wenley, *George Sylvester Morris*, pp. 316–17.

21. *Ibid.*, p. 316.

22. Morris, *Philosophy and Christianity*, pp. 22, 37. Morris, *Kant's Critique*, pp. 20–23.

23. *Ibid.*, p. 28.

24. *Ibid.*, pp. 20, 23, 47, 49.

25. *Ibid.*, p. 4.

26. John Dewey, "The Late Professor Morris," p. 8.

27. Morris, *Philosophy and Christianity,* pp. 52–53, 137.

28. *Ibid.,* pp. 206–07, 209, 214, 218, 229.

29. *Ibid.,* pp. 233, 245, 249.

30. *Ibid.,* pp. 223, 250.

31. John Dewey, "The Late Professor Morris," p. 10.

32. John Dewey as quoted in Wenley, *George Sylvester Morris,* p. 320.

33. John Dewey, "The Late Professor Morris," p. 13.

34. John Dewey, Williston S. Hough, Frederick C. Hicks, and Alice H. Graves, "Memorial of Professor Morris," in the George Sylvester Morris Papers, 1857–1935, Michigan Historical Collections, University of Michigan, Ann Arbor, Michigan.

35. Morris, *Philosophy and Christianity,* pp. 57, 91, 100, 143–47, 207–08, 258–59.

36. *Ibid.,* pp. 237, 249–50, 270–71.

37. *Ibid.,* p. 9.

38. John Dewey, "Kant and Philosophic Method," in EW 1:35, 38–46. First published in *Journal of Speculative Philosophy* (April 1884), 28:162–74.

39. Ross, *G. Stanley Hall,* pp. 3–81.

40. *Ibid.,* pp. 103–38.

41. G. Stanley Hall, "The New Psychology," *Andover Review* (February 1885), 3: 127.

42. Dewey, "From Absolutism to Experimentalism," p. 8.

43. Hall, "The New Psychology," p. 134. Hall, "The New Psychology," *Andover Review* (March 1885), 3:242, 244.

44. *Ibid.,* (February 1885), 3:134.

45. Ross, *G. Stanley Hall,* pp. 109–10, 122, 141.

46. Hall, *Life and Confessions of a Psychologist,* p. 184.

47. John Dewey, "The New Psychology," in EW 1:48.

48. *Ibid.,* pp. 56–60. Neil Coughlan has identified some parallels between Dewey's essay on "The New Psychology" and the writings of the Andover Seminary theologian Newman Smyth. Coughlan argues that Smyth exercised an important influence on the development of Dewey's early psychological thought and his effort to fuse the new psychology with idealism. There may have been some influence here, but Dewey does not mention Smyth as an influence and much in Dewey's thought that Coughlan traces to Smyth can better be traced to Hall and to Morris. See Coughlan, *Young John Dewey,* pp. 42–53, 56–60.

49. *Ibid.,* pp. 51, 60.

50. *Ibid.,* p. 60.

51. "In Memoriam A. H. H.," section 55. Regarding his spiritual quest

during his twenties, Hall explains that in religious matters "the poets helped me to clarity, most of all Tennyson. My cheap volume being badly soiled and worn and the 'In Memoriam' almost committed to memory." Hall, *Life and Confessions of a Psychologist,* p. 185.

52. John Dewey, "From Absolutism to Experimentalism," p. 11.

53. Jane Dewey, ed., "Biography of John Dewey," p. 21.

54. John Dewey, "The Psychological Standpoint," in EW 1:122–24, 128, 130–31.

55. *Ibid.*; John Dewey, "Psychology as Philosophic Method," in EW 1:144–45, 162–63.

56. John Dewey, "The Psychological Standpoint," pp. 141–42.

57. John Dewey, "Psychology as Philosophic Method," pp. 148–49, 157, 160–61.

58. *Ibid.,* pp. 149, 157, 161.

59. *Ibid.,* p. 157.

60. *Ibid.,* p. 158.

61. Shadworth Hodgson, "Illusory Psychology," in EW 1:xli–lvii. First published in *Mind* (October 1886), 9:478–94.

62. John Dewey, "Psychology as Philosophic Method," p. 153.

63. *Calendar of the University of Michigan* (Ann Arbor: University of Michigan, 1884–1885), pp. 50–51; *Ibid.,* 1885–1886, pp. 54–55; *Ibid.,* 1886–1887, pp. 50–52; *Ibid.,* 1887–1888, pp. 49–50.

64. John Dewey, *Psychology,* in EW 2:3–4.

65. John Dewey to H.A.P. Torrey, February 16, 1886, as quoted in Dykhuizen, *John Dewey,* p. 46.

66. John Dewey, "Soul and Body," in EW 1:112–15. In the *Psychology,* p. 217, Dewey writes that "the self, taken in its lowest terms, is the organic body, fitted out with a nervous system."

67. John Dewey, *Psychology,* pp. 7, 8, 18, 254, 318–20. The terms "soul," "self," and "spirit" all signify generally the same thing in young Dewey's writings, but the different terms each have their own special emphasis. The term "self" is the term Dewey uses most frequently to designate in a general way all that constitutes and is involved in the essential human nature. He uses the term "soul" less frequently than the term "self." He explains in the *Psychology* that "soul is a term which calls to mind the distinction of the self from the body, and yet its connection with it. Psychical is an adjective used to designate the facts of self, and suggests the contrast with physical facts of nature. . . . Spirit is a term used, especially in connection with the higher activities of self, and calls to mind its distinction from matter and mechanical modes of action." The term "mind" is also closely related in significance to

the term "spirit" in young Dewey's vocabulary, and it "suggests especially the fact that the self is intelligent." *Ibid.,* p. 7. A person, as Dewey understands the concept, is identical with a self. The spiritual capacities of human nature constitute personality.

68. John Dewey, *Leibniz's New Essays Concerning the Human Understanding,* in EW 1:290–91.

69. John Dewey, *Psychology,* p. 13.

70. Quoted by F. N. Scott, "John Dewey," in *The Castalian* (Ann Arbor: University of Michigan, 1891), p. 26.

71. *Ibid.* A student journal commented in 1890 that the *Psychology* "fills a long felt need for a distinct, logical and comprehensive text-book upon this important and interesting subject, and it well deserves the high commendary notices of the press and the great popularity which it has won with both students and educators throughout the country." "John Dewey, Ph. D.," *The Chronicle* (May 1890), 21: 327.

72. Dykhuizen, *John Dewey,* p. 55.

73. John Dewey, *Psychology,* pp. 200–02, 208.

74. *Ibid.,* pp. 209–10, lxxviii-lxxix.

75. *Ibid.,* pp. 205–06, 211–12, 361.

76. John Dewey, *Leibniz's New Essays,* p. 395.

77. John Dewey, *Psychology,* p. 212.

78. John Dewey, "The Value of Historical Christianity," *The Monthly Bulletin* (November 1889), 11:34. See LW 17:529–34.

79. John Dewey, "Christianity and Democracy," in EW 4:4–7.

80. John Dewey, *Psychology,* pp. 211–12, 261.

81. *Ibid.,* p. 243.

82. *Ibid.,* p. 259.

83. John Dewey, "The Place of Religious Emotion," in EW 1:91–92.

84. John Dewey, *Outlines of a Critical Theory of Ethics,* in EW 3:249–89. First published in 1891 by Register Publishing Company, Inland Press, in Ann Arbor, Michigan.

85. John Dewey, *Psychology,* pp. 237–38, 253–54, 309, 315.

86. *Ibid.,* pp. 318, 319.

87. *Ibid.,* pp. 342–46, 349–52.

88. *Ibid.,* pp. 283, 285–87, 289.

89. *Ibid.,* pp. 294, 295.

90. *Ibid.,* p. 288–90, 296.

91. *Ibid.,* pp. 296–97.

92. Dewey, *Psychology,* p. 297.

93. John Dewey, *The Ethics of Democracy,* in EW 1:243. On the relation

between law and desire, see John Dewey, *Outlines of a Critical Theory of Ethics,* p. 337.

94. *Ibid.,* p. 244.

95. John Dewey, *Psychology,* p. 355.

96. John Dewey, *Psychology,* pp. 357–58, 360. Already in the *Psychology* the distinction between the desired and the desirable is suggested. In *Leibniz's New Essays* (1888) Dewey begins to discuss the evaluation of desires on the basis of conditions and consequences (see pages 298–99), and this approach is developed at considerable length in his *Outline of a Critical Theory of Ethics* (1891).

97. John Dewey, "Relation of Morality and Religion," *The Monthly Bulletin,* Students' Christian Association, University of Michigan (March 1891), 12: 94.

98. Reprint, (Glasgow: James Maclehose , 1901), pp. 280–89.

99. John Dewey, *Psychology,* pp. 290–91.

100. *Ibid.,* pp. 360–61.

101. John Dewey, "Relation of Morality and Religion," p. 94.

102. John Dewey, *Psychology,* pp. 292, 360.

103. *Ibid.,* pp. 360, 361, 363. Dewey never defined freedom very precisely in the *Psychology,* but in his *Outlines of a Critical Theory of Ethics* he offers a definition that is consistent with his use of the term in the *Psychology.* "The *capacity* of freedom lies in the power to form an ideal or conception of an end. *Actual* freedom lies in the realization of that end which actually satisfies. An end may be freely adopted, and yet its actual working-out may result not in freedom, but in slavery. It may result in rendering the agent more subject to his passions, less able to direct his own conduct, and more cramped and feeble in powers. Only that end which executed really effects greater energy and comprehensiveness of character makes for actual freedom. In a word, only the good man, the man who truly realizing his individuality, is free, in the positive sense of that word." See EW 3:343–44.

104. *Ibid.*

105. John Dewey, "What is the Demonstration of Man's Spiritual Nature?" *The University* (January 23, 1886), p. 43.

106. John Dewey, "The Revival of the Soul," *The University* (December 5, 1885), p. 7.

107. John Dewey, *Psychology,* pp. 245–46, 292.

108. *Ibid.,* pp. 229, 231, 237–38, 245, 291–92, 361.

109. *Ibid.,* pp. 174, 244–45, 272–73, 359. For an in-depth treatment of Dewey's early and later views on aesthetics, see Alexander, *John Dewey's Theory of Art, Experience and Nature.*

110. John Dewey, "The Lesson of Contemporary French Literature," in EW 3:36–42.

111. Dewey, *Leibniz's New Essays,* pp. 267, 269, 281, 285, 292, 297.

112. *Ibid.,* 295, 413, 414.

113. *Ibid.,* 415–22.

114. John Dewey, "The Place of Religious Emotion," p. 91.

115. John Dewey, *Psychology,* pp. 318–19, 359.

116. For Dewey's defense of T. H. Green's idealism against the charge of pantheism, see "The Philosophy of Thomas Hill Green," in EW 3:23.

117. See, for example, John A. T. Robinson, *Exploration into God* (Stanford: Stanford University Press, 1967), pp. 86f.

118. John Dewey, *Psychology,* p. 259.

T H R E E: *Christian Liberalism and Social Action*

1. Theodore T. Munger, *The Freedom of Faith* (1883) as quoted in Robert Ferm, ed., *Issues In American Protestantism: A Documentary History From the Puritans to the Present* (Garden City, N.Y.: Doubleday, 1969), p. 227.

2. Lyman Abbott, *The Evolution of Christianity* (Boston: Houghton, Mifflin, 1892), pp. iii–iv.

3. Ira V. Brown, *Lyman Abbott, Christian Evolutionist: A Study in Religious Liberalism* (Cambridge: Harvard University Press, 1953), pp. 99–113.

4. Sidney E. Ahlstrom, *A Religious History of the American People* (New Haven: Yale University Press, 1972), p. 776.

5. Daniel Day Williams, *The Andover Liberals* (New York: King's Crown Press, 1941), pp. 65f, 255–76.

6. John Dewey to Joseph Ratner, October 4, 1946, John Dewey Papers, Special Collections, Morris Library, Southern Illinois University. In a recent study by Bruce Kuklick, *Philosophers and Churchmen: From Jonathan Edwards to John Dewey,* it is argued that the Andover Seminary theologians "shaped" Dewey's thought and that he understood his early philosophical labors as providing a "conceptual basis for" and "defense of" their Progressive Orthodoxy (see pp. 243, 247, 251, 255). This overstates the influence of the Andover liberals and Dewey's interest in Christian theology as a distinct discipline. The very existence of the movement of Progressive Orthodoxy at a respected Congregational seminary gave support and encouragement to Dewey as a liberal in the church. However, in none of his philosophical or autobiographical essays does Dewey single out the Andover theologians for mention as a strong influence on his philosophical development.

7. Martin L. D'Ooge, "The Religious Life of the University," *Religious Thought at the University of Michigan* (Ann Arbor: Register Publishing Co., Inland Press, 1893), pp. viii-ix.

8. Students' Christian Association, University of Michigan, *The Monthly Bulletin* (March 1887), 8:101.

9. Students' Christian Association, *Students' Handbook* (Ann Arbor: Registry Printing House, 1886), p. 12.

10. D'Ooge, "The Religious Life of the University," p. x.

11. *Ibid.,* p. 17; *Calendar of the University of Michigan* (Ann Arbor: University of Michigan, 1893–1894), p. 273.

12. DeWitt H. Parker and Charles B. Vibbert, "The Department of Philosophy," in Wilfred B. Shaw, ed., *The University of Michigan Encyclopedic Survey,* part 4, pp. 668–73(Ann Arbor: The University of Michigan Press, 1944), as cited in Willinda Savage, *The Evolution of John Dewey's Philosophy of Experimentalism as Developed at the University of Michigan.* Doctoral Dissertation Series, publication no. 1999 (Ann Arbor: University Microfilms, 1950), pp. 7–8.

13. John Dewey to Alice Dewey, July 5, 1894, John Dewey Papers, coll. 102/2/6.

14. *Monthly Bulletin* (November 1884), 6:23–25. See EW 1:61.

15. G.W.F. Hegel, *Reason In History: A General Introduction to the Philosophy of History,* trans. by Robert S. Hartman (New York: Bobbs-Merrill Company, 1953), p. 16. This same theme appears in Hegel's *Lectures on the Philosophy of Religion.* See, for example, G.W.F. Hegel, in J. Glenn Gray, ed., *On Art, Religion and Philosophy: Introductory Lectures to the Realm of Absolute Spirit* (New York: Harper & Row, 1970), pp. 160–61.

16. *Monthly Bulletin* (November 1884), 6:28.

17. Congregational Church Membership Roll, 1887–1906, Michigan Historical Collections, University of Michigan, p. 16. According to this record, Dewey joined the church on November 2, 1884.

18. *Monthly Bulletin* (November 1884), 6:20–21.

19. *Students' Handbook,* 1889–1894.

20. *Ibid.,* 1886, p. 12.

21. *Ibid.,* p. 13.

22. *Monthly Bulletin* (April 1885), 6:112–13; *Ibid.* (November 1885), 7:20. See also Savage, *The Evolution of John Dewey's Philosophy,* p. 137.

23. Interview with Jessie Phelps, January 19, 1950, as quoted in Savage, *The Evolution of John Dewey's Philosophy,* pp. 137–38.

24. *Monthly Bulletin* (January 1886), 7:56.

25. *Ibid.* (November 1886), 8:23–25. See EW 1:90–92.

26. *Ibid.* (February 1887), Supplement:47.

27. *Ibid.* (December 1887), 9:47.

28. *The Michigan Argonaut* (June 16, 1888), 6:249.

29. *Monthly Bulletin* (November 1889), 11:31–36.

30. *Ibid.* (March 1891), 12:94–95.

31. *Ibid.* (November 1891), 13:33; *Ibid.* (December 1891), 13: 41.

32. *Religious Thought at the University of Michigan* (Ann Arbor: Inland Press, 1893), pp. 60–69. See EW 3:3–10.

33. *Monthly Bulletin* (June 1894), 15:149–56. See EW 4:96–105.

34. John Dewey, "The Church and Society," in *The University* (December 26, 1885): 7.

35. John Dewey, *Psychology,* in EW 2:295.

36. Dykhuizen, *John Dewey,* p. 50.

37. *Monthly Bulletin* (November 1887), 9: 24.

38. *Ibid.* (March 1890), 11:93. See also "Ancient Life and Thought in Relation to Christianity: Topics for the Students' Class at Congregational Church Conducted by John Dewey," Davis Rich Dewey Papers in Joseph Ratner Papers, collection 142, Morris Library, Southern Illinois University, Carbondale, Illinois.

39. *Students' Handbook,* 1892–1893, p. 19.

40. *Ibid.,* p. 18.

41. *Ibid.,* 1893–1894, p. 20; *Monthly Bulletin* (October 1893), 15:14–15; *Ibid.* (June 1894), 15:157.

42. *Calendar of the University of Michigan,* 1892–1893.

43. John Dewey to Thomas A. Davidson, October 9, 1892, Thomas Davidson Papers, Manuscripts and Archives, Yale University, New Haven, Connecticut.

44. *Monthly Bulletin* (March 1891), 12:92–94. On the size and purpose of the Ministerial Band, see *Monthly Bulletin* (February 1889):68–69; *Ibid.* (November 1890), 12:18; and *Students' Handbook,* 1890–1891, p. 13; 1891–1892, p. 13.

45. *Monthly Bulletin* (January 1893), 14:66–68. See EW 4:365–68.

46. *The Ann Arbor Argus,* May 22, 1891.

47. *Monthly Bulletin* (November 1892), 14:45, as cited in Dykhuizen, *John Dewey,* p. 65.

48. Savage, *The Evolution of John Dewey's Philosophy,* pp. 28, 138.

49. *Monthly Bulletin* (April 1893), 14:171, as cited in Dykhuizen, *John Dewey,* p. 342.

50. *Monthly Bulletin* (June 1894), 15:147, as cited in Dykhuizen, *John Dewey,* p. 65.

51. John Dewey to Alice Dewey, May 14, 1894, John Dewey Papers, coll. 102/2/2.

52. Walter Stace, *The Philosophy of Hegel* (New York: Dover, 1955), pp. 485–88, 509–10, 515–18.

53. John Dewey, "The Relation of Philosophy to Theology," in EW 4:366.

54. John Dewey, review of *Studies in Hegel's Philosophy of Religion,* in EW 3:188–89. See also John Dewey, "What is the Demonstration of Man's Spiritual Nature?" Letter to the Editor, *The University* (January 23, 1886): 43–44.

55. John Dewey, "The Late Professor Morris," in EW 3:8.

56. Jane Dewey, ed., "Biography of John Dewey," pp. 10–11. Library records indicate that Dewey read Herbert Spencer more than any other author in the University of Vermont Library. See Lewis Feuer, "John Dewey's Reading at College," *Journal of the History of Ideas* (June 1958), 20:420.

57. John Dewey, "The Philosophical Work of Herbert Spencer," in MW 3:199–208.

58. John Dewey, "A Clergyman's View of Evolution" (review of *Evolution and Christianity,* by Benjamin Tefft), in *Index* (March 21, 1885), p. 313.

59. This statement was made by Professor Fred Newton Scott, who knew Dewey well at the University of Michigan (See chapter 4 of this book). See F.N. Scott, "John Dewey," in *The Castalian*, p. 26 (Ann Arbor: University of Michigan, 1891). This is also mentioned in "John Dewey, Ph.D.," *The Chronicle* (May 1890), 21:327–28. Both these publications were student journals at the University of Michigan. Dewey is not listed as a member of the editorial staff in the *Christian Union* itself, but the paper had an editorial section of several pages and may have depended on periodic contributions from people who, like Dewey, lived outside New York City in different parts of the country. Dewey did contribute one signed article to the *Christian Union* in 1889, "The Lesson of French Literature," and the Davis Rich Dewey Papers attribute three unsigned pieces in that paper during the 1880s to Dewey, including a book review and two essays entitled "The Dramatic Instinct in Social and Political Life" and "The Higher Criticism and the Highest." See Davis Rich Dewey Papers.

60. John Dewey, "Soul and Body," in EW 1:102–3.

61. John Dewey, "Ethics and Physical Science," in EW 1:207–26.

62. *Ibid.,* pp. 205–7.

63. Ahlstrom, *A Religious History of the American People,* pp. 772–73.

64. John Dewey, "Reconstruction," in EW 4:103.

65. John Dewey, "The Higher Criticism and the Highest," *Christian Union* (February 7, 1889), p. 34. This article was not signed by Dewey, but it is contained in the Davis Rich Dewey Papers as an essay by him.

66. *Ibid.,* p. 92.

67. John Dewey, "The Philosophy of Thomas Hill Green," in EW 3:34.

68. Dewey, "The Relation of Philosophy to Theology," p. 367. On Hegel's interpretation of Jesus and Christian doctrine see Stephen Crites, "The Gospel According to Hegel," *Journal of Religion* (April 1966), 46:246–263.

69. John Dewey, "What is the Demonstration of Man's Spiritual Nature?" in *The University* (January 23, 1886), p. 43.

70. John Dewey, "The Philosophy of Thomas Hill Green," pp. 34–35.

71. "Memorial of Professor Morris," George Sylvester Morris Papers, 1840–1889, Michigan Historical Collections, University of Michigan, Ann Arbor.

72. John Dewey, "The Relation of Philosophy to Theology," pp. 366–67.

73. John Dewey, "Education and the Health of Women" and "Health and Sex in Higher Education," in EW 1:64–80.

74. John Dewey, "The Church and Society," *The University* (December 26, 1885), p. 5.

75. *The Michigan Argonaut* (May 18, 1886), 4:224.

76. Dewey adds: "However, of course, it is not so much so as philosophy so I shall continue my dabbles in the latter." John Dewey to Alice Chipman, April ?, 1886, John Dewey Papers, coll. 102/1/11.

77. John Dewey to Alice Chipman, March ?, 1886, John Dewey Papers, coll. 102/1/10.

78. Savage, *The Evolution of John Dewey's Philosophy,* p. 128.

79. Savage, *The Evolution of John Dewey's Philosophy,* pp. 14, 34–35, 40–42; Jane Dewey, ed., "Biography of John Dewey," p. 21.

80. Max Eastman, "My Teacher and Friend," p. 265.

81. John Dewey to Alice Chipman, December 31, 1885, John Dewey Papers, coll. 102/1/8.

82. John Dewey to Alice Chipman, December 22, 1885, John Dewey Papers, coll. 102/1/8.

83. John Dewey to Alice Chipman, September 20, 1886, John Dewey Papers, coll. 102/1/11.

84. John Dewey to Alice Chipman, April 11, 1886, John Dewey Papers, coll. 102/1/11.

85. John Dewey to Alice Chipman, December 31, 1885, John Dewey Papers, coll. 102/1/8.

86. John Dewey to Alice Chipman, December 24, 1885 and January 1, 1886, John Dewey Papers, coll. 102/1/8.

87. Alice Chipman to John Dewey, December 28, 1885 and January 1, 1886, John Dewey Papers, coll. 102/1/8.

88. Eastman, "My Teacher and Friend," p. 257.

89. Jane Dewey, ed., "Biography of John Dewey," p. 26.

90. John Dewey, "In Response," in LW 5:420.

91. Savage, *The Evolution of John Dewey's Philosophy,* ch. 3; Dykhuizen, *John Dewey,* pp. 49–51, 65–66.

92. "John Dewey, Ph.D.," *The Chronicle* (May 1890), 21:327–28.

93. Memorandum, James H. Tufts to William Rainey Harper, as quoted in Dykhuizen, *John Dewey,* p. 74.

94. Dewey, "In Response," p. 422.

95. Jane Dewey, ed., "Biography of John Dewey," p. 21.

96. John Dewey, "From Absolutism to Experimentalism," in LW 1:151.

97. Jane Dewey, ed., "Biography of John Dewey," p. 21.

98. John Dewey, "The Philosophy of Thomas Hill Green," p. 16.

99. John Dewey, *Liberalism and Social Action,* in LW 11:20–21, 26.

100. John Dewey, "The Philosophy of Thomas Hill Green," p. 31.

101. G.W.F. Hegel, "America Is Therefore the Land of the Future," in William H. Goetzmann, ed., *The American Hegelians,* p. 20 (New York: Knopf, 1973).

102. *The Nation,* as quoted in Herbert Schneider, *A History of American Philosophy* (New York: Columbia University Press, 1946), pp. 170, 173; Elijah Mulford, *The Republic of God* (Boston: Houghton-Mifflin, 1881), p. 168.

103. *The Republic of God,* pp. 67, 76.

104. John Dewey to Alice Dewey, April 6, 1887, John Dewey Papers, coll. 102/1/13.

105. Walt Whitman, *Specimen Days,* in Mark Van Doren, ed., *Walt Whitman,* p. 610 (New York: Viking, 1945).

106. Whitman, "Preface to Leaves of Grass, 1855," in *Walt Whitman,* p. 6.

107. *Ibid.,* p. 15; Whitman, "Song of Myself," in *Walt Whitman,* p. 55.

108. Whitman, "A Backward Glance O'er Travel'd Roads," in *Walt Whitman,* pp. 298–99.

109. Whitman, *Democratic Vistas,* in *Walt Whitman,* p. 365.

110. *Ibid.,* p. 375; Whitman, "A Backward Glance O'er Travel'd Roads," p. 310.

111. Whitman, *Democratic Vistas,* p. 323.

112. *Ibid.,* p. 324.

113. John Dewey, *Leibniz's New Essays Concerning the Human Understanding,* in EW 1:295–96.

114. John Dewey, *The Ethics of Democracy,* in EW 1:228, 232, 239–40, 248.

115. *Ibid.,* pp. 244–46, 248.

116. *Ibid.,* pp. 244, 246, 248.

117. *Ibid.,* pp. 237, 242–44.

118. John Dewey, "Emerson—the Philosopher of Democracy," in MW 3:190–91.

119. John Dewey, *Outlines of a Critical Theory of Ethics,* in EW 3:320–22.

120. John Dewey, *The Ethics of Democracy,* pp. 246–47.

121. *Ibid.,* p. 248.

122. *Ibid.,* pp. 248–49.

123. John Dewey, "The Value of Historical Christianity," *Monthly Bulletin* (November 1889), 11:31–32. See LW 17:529–34.

124. *Ibid.,* p. 31.

125. *Ibid.,* p. 32. A good summary of Hegel's views on the nature of genuine and false religion, which most probably influenced Dewey's "The Value of Historical Christianity," may be found in Emil W. Fackenheim, *The Religious Dimension In Hegel's Thought* (Boston: Beacon Press, 1967), pp. 119–24.

126. John Dewey, "The Value of Historical Christianity," pp. 529–34.

127. *Ibid.,* p. 35.

128. *Ibid.,* pp. 35–36.

129. John Dewey, "The Relation of Philosophy to Theology," p. 367.

FOUR: *"The Truth Shall Make You Free"*

1. John Dewey, "Experience, Knowledge and Value: A Rejoinder," in EW 14:79.

2. Charles Frankel, "John Dewey's Social Philosophy," in Steven M. Cahn, ed., *New Studies in the Philosophy of John Dewey,* pp. 10–11 (Hanover, N.H.: University Press of New England, 1977).

3. John Dewey, "Preface," in George R. Geiger, *The Philosophy of Henry George,* p. xiii (New York: Macmillan, 1933). See LW 9:299–302. On George's religious views, see *The Philosophy of Henry George,* pp. 336–43.

4. Ira V. Brown, *Lyman Abbott, Christian Evolutionist: A Study in Religious Liberalism* (Cambridge: Harvard University Press, 1953), pp. 101–02.

5. "The American Institute of Christian Sociology," *Monthly Bulletin,*

Students' Christian Association, University of Michigan (January 1893), 14:68–69.

6. *Religious Thought at the University of Michigan* (Ann Arbor: Register, Inland Press, 1893), pp. vi, 29–51.

7. Lawrence A. Cremin, *American Education: The Metropolitan Experience, 1876–1980* (New York: Harper & Row, 1988), pp. 153–55.

8. Franklin Ford, *Draft of Action* (1893), as quoted in Neil Coughlan, *Young John Dewey,* p. 96.

9. For Dewey's outline of Ford's thinking, see: Letter and Memorandum, John Dewey to Henry Carter Adams, April 29, 1889, Henry Carter Adams Correspondence, April to June 1889, Michigan Historical Collections, University of Michigan, Ann Arbor; also Letter of John Dewey to William James, June 3, 1891, in Ralph Barton Perry, *The Thought and Character of William James* (Boston: Little, Brown, 1935), vol. 2, pp. 517–18.

10. Corydon Ford, *The Child of Democracy* (Ann Arbor: John V. Sheehan, 1894), p. 174.

11. John Dewey, "From Absolutism to Experimentalism," in EW 1:154.

12. John Dewey, "Health and Sex in Higher Education," in EW 1:80.

13. John Dewey to William James, June 3, 1893, in Perry, *The Thought and Character of William James,* vol. 2, p. 518.

14. John Dewey, *Outlines of a Critical Theory of Ethics,* in EW 3:239.

15. John Dewey to William James, June 3, 1893, in Perry, *The Thought and Character of William James,* vol. 2, p. 518.

16. John Dewey, "Is Logic a Dualistic Science," in EW 3:75. First published in *Open Court* (January 16, 1890), 3:2040–43.

17. John Dewey, "The Present Position of Logical Theory," in EW 3:133. First published in *Monist* (Oct. 1891), 2: 1–17.

18. John Dewey, "Poetry and Philosophy," in EW 3:113, 122–23.

19. John Dewey, "The Present Position of Logical Theory," pp. 125–26, 137–39.

20. *Ibid.,* pp. 127, 140–41.

21. John Dewey, "Poetry and Philosophy," pp. 123–24.

22. John Dewey, "Green's Theory of the Moral Motive," in EW 3:172–73.

23. John Dewey, "Poetry and Philosophy," pp. 123–24.

24. John Dewey, "Two Phases of Renan's Life," in EW 3:174–79. John Dewey, "Renan's Loss of Faith in Science," in EW 4:11–18.

25. Jo Ann Boydston, "A Note on the Text," in EW 4:liii–liv.

26. John Dewey, "Renan's Loss of Faith in Science," p. 18.

27. Edwin Spencer Peck Class Lecture Notes, October 6, 1891 to June 16, 1892, Michigan Historical Collections, University of Michigan.

28. John Dewey, *Outlines of a Critical Theory of Ethics,* pp. 319–20.

29. John Dewey, "From Absolutism to Experimentalism," p. 156.

30. John Dewey, "Moral Theory and Practice," in EW 3:95. First published in *International Journal of Ethics* (January 1891), 1:186–203.

31. John Dewey, *Outlines of a Critical Theory of Ethics,* p. 361.

32. John Dewey, "Moral Theory and Practice," pp. 105, 106.

33. John Dewey, *Outlines of a Critical Theory of Ethics,* pp. 304, 335.

34. John Dewey, "Moral Theory and Practice," pp. 102–04.

35. John Dewey, "The Chaos in Moral Training," in EW 4:115. First published in *Popular Science Monthly* (August 1894), 45: 433–43.

36. John Dewey to Thomas Davidson, March 14, 1891, Thomas Davidson Papers, Manuscripts and Archives, Yale University, New Haven, Connecticut.

37. John Dewey, "Moral Theory and Practice," p. 109.

38. John Dewey to William James, May 10, 1891, in Perry, *The Thought and Character of William James,* vol. 2, p. 517.

39. John Dewey to William James, June 3, 1891, in *Ibid.,* p. 519.

40. John Dewey to Alice Dewey, June 6, 1891, John Dewey Papers, Special Collections, Morris Library, Southern Ilinois University, coll. 102/2/1.

41. John Dewey to Alice Dewey, August 14, 1891, John Dewey Papers, coll. 102/2/1.

42. John Dewey to William James, June 3, 1891, in Perry, *The Thought and Character of William James,* vol. 2, pp. 518–519.

43. John Dewey, "The Scholastic and the Speculator," in EW 3:149, 153. First published in the *Inlander* (University of Michigan) (December 1891), 2:145–148; (January 1892), 2:186–88.

44. Willinda Savage, *The Evolution of John Dewey's Philosophy of Experimentalism as Developed at the University of Michigan.* Doctoral Dissertation Series, publication no. 1999 (Ann Arbor: University Microfilms, 1950), p. 143.

45. Fred Newton Scott, "Christianity and the Newspaper," in *Religious Thought at the University of Michigan,* pp. 70–85.

46. *Religious Thought at the University of Michigan,* pp. vi-vii.

47. John Dewey, "Fred Newton Scott," in EW 4:119–21.

48. Savage, *The Evolution of John Dewey's Philosophy,* pp. 20, 129–30; Dykhuizen, *John Dewey,* pp. 64, 341; Coughlin, *Young John Dewey,* p. 107.

49. Coughlin, *Young John Dewey*, pp. 126, 130, 145.

50. Scott, "Christianity and the Newspaper," pp. 77–78.

51. *Ibid.*, p. 79.

52. *Ibid.*, pp. 79–85.

53. The full text of the press release is printed in Coughlin, *Young John Dewey*, p. 102.

54. *Ibid.*, p. 105.

55. *Ibid.;* Savage, *The Evolution of John Dewey's Philosophy*, p. 147.

56. John Dewey, "Christianity and Democracy," in EW 4:3–4.

57. *Ibid.*, p. 4–5.

58. *Ibid.*, p. 6.

59. John Dewey, "Green's Theory of the Moral Motive," p. 171.

60. John Dewey, "Christianity and Democracy," p. 7.

61. *Ibid.*, p. 5. See also Dewey, "Green's Theory of the Moral Motive," p. 171.

62. John Dewey, "The Relation of Philosophy to Theology," in EW 4:367.

63. John Dewey, "Christianity and Democracy," pp. 8–9.

64. *Ibid.*, pp. 7–8.

65. John Dewey, *The School and Society*, in MW 1:24.

66. John Dewey, "The Challenge of Democracy to Education," in LW 11:182–85.

67. John Dewey, "Christianity and Democracy," pp. 9–10.

68. Coughlin, *Young John Dewey*, p. 105.

69. John Dewey to Willinda Savage, May 30, 1949, in Savage, *The Evolution of John Dewey's Philosophy*, p. 150.

70. Dewey told Horace Kallen that he had discovered Ford was a "scoundrel." See Lewis Feuer, "America's Medicine Man" (review of *Young John Dewey*, by Neil Coughlin), *Times Literary Supplement* (December 3, 1976): 1507.

71. John Dewey, *The Public and Its Problems*, in LW 2:350.

72. Neil Coughlin has given an extensive account of young Mead's spiritual quest as disclosed in his correspondence during the 1880s and 1890s, and I have followed his interpretation. See *Young John Dewey*, pp. 113–33, 145–48. On the influence of Mead on Dewey regarding his break with idealism, see also R.W. Sleeper, *The Necessity of Pragmatism*.

73. George Herbert Mead to Mr. and Mrs. Samuel Castle, June 18, 1892, as quoted in Coughlin, *Young John Dewey*, p. 146.

74. *Ibid.*, p. 148.

75. Mead to Mr. and Mrs. Samuel Castle, August 21, 1892, June 29, 1892, and June 18, 1892, as quoted in Coughlin, *Young John Dewey,* pp. 146–48.

76. John Dewey to Professor H. Robet, May 2, 1911, John Dewey Papers. Dewey's letter to Robet gives a valuable summary of the factors leading him from absolute idealism to pragmatism and naturalism during the 1890s. He mentions the influence of James, his work on the scientific method of inquiry, his effort to work out "a more organic connection between thought and action" in moral theory, and the effect of his work in education at Chicago. This letter should be read together with his comments in "From Absolutism to Experimentalism."

77. John Dewey, "From Absolutism to Experimentalism," pp. 157–58. Andrew J. Reck has given an excellent account of James' influence on Dewey between 1890 and 1903. See "The Influence of William James on John Dewey in Psychology," *Transactions of the Charles S. Peirce Society* (1984), 20:87–117. In an unconvincing essay, Michael Buxton tries to show that James' influence was not the major factor in Dewey's shift from absolutism to experimentalism, which Dewey himself repeatedly says that it was over almost a forty-year period. Buxton also incorrectly asserts that "Dewey ceased to be an idealist in any meaningful sense in 1891." Dewey's writings evidence the influence of idealist metaphysics up through 1892. See M. Buxton, "The Influence of William James on John Dewey's Early Work," *Journal of the History of Ideas* (1984), 45:451–63. See also R.W. Sleeper's account of the early influence of Peirce as well as James in *The Necessity of Pragmatism,* ch. 3.

78. John Dewey, "Self-Realization as the Moral Ideal," in EW 4:44.

79. *Ibid.,* p. 53; Dewey, *The Study of Ethics: A Syllabus,* in EW 4:257, 261–62.

80. John Dewey, *The Study of Ethics,* pp. 258, 264.

81. John Dewey, "Self-Realization as the Moral Ideal," p. 43.

82. John Dewey, *The Study of Ethics,* p. 262.

83. *Ibid.,* p. 244.

84. *Ibid.,* pp. 245, 293.

85. John Dewey, "Self-Realization as the Moral Ideal," p. 51.

86. *Ibid.,* p. 52.

87. *Ibid.,* p. 234.

88. *Ibid.,* p. 293.

89. *Ibid.,* p. 293. Dewey makes a related point about peace and action in *Human Nature and Conduct* (1922). See MW 14:180–81.

90. John Dewey, *The Study of Ethics,* p. 226.

91. *Ibid.,* p. 297.

92. John Dewey, *The Study of Ethics,* p. 361.

93. John C. Maraldo, "The Hermeneutics of Practice in Dōgen and Francis of Assisi: An Exercise in Buddhist-Christian Dialogue," *Eastern Buddhist* (1981), 14:22–46.

94. Jane Dewey, ed., "Biography of John Dewey," p. 30.

95. Herbert W. Schneider, *A History of American Philosophy* (New York: Columbia University Press, 1946), p. 393.

96. John Dewey to Thomas A. Davidson, October 9, 1892.

97. Jane Dewcy, ed., "Biography of John Dewey," p. 30.

98. Schneider, *A History of American Philosophy,* pp. 394–95.

99. Benny Kraut, *From Reform Judaism to Ethical Culture: The Religious Evolution of Felix Adler* (Cincinnati: Hebrew Union College Press, 1979), pp. 56–57, 222–23.

100. Lawrence A. Cremin, *American Education ,* pp. 75–78.

101. John Dewey to Jane Addams, January 27, 1892, Rockford College Archives, Rockford, Illinois.

102. Anne Firor Scott, "Introduction" in Jane Addams, *Democracy and Social Ethics,* pp. vii-xxiii (Cambridge, Mass.: Harvard University Press, 1964).

103. See Christopher Lasch, ed., *The Social Thought of Jane Addams* (Indianapolis: Bobbs-Merrill, 1965), pp. 28–43.

104. *Ibid.,* p. 29.

105. Compare *Ibid.,* pp. 40–41 with Dewey, "Christianity and Democracy," pp. 4 and 7. Addams picks up the themes that Jesus had no set of special truths labeled religious, that Christianity is revelation, and that "action is the only medium man has for receiving and appropriating truth."

106. John Dewey to Alice Dewey, October 9, 1894, John Dewey Papers, coll. 102/2/9.

107. John Dewey, "The Realism of Jane Addams," in Jane Addams, *Peace and Bread in Time of War: Anniversary Edition* (New York: Kings Crown Press, 1945).

108. Addams, *Democracy and Social Ethics,* p. 276.

109. Dykhuizen, *John Dewey,* p. 74.

110. John Dewey, "Reconstruction," in EW 4:98–100.

111. *Ibid.,* pp. 100–101.

112. *Ibid.,* p. 102.

113. *Ibid.,* p. 104.

114. *Ibid.,* p. 105.

115. John Dewey to Alice Dewey, July 9, 1894, John Dewey Papers, coll. 102/2/6.

116. John Dewey to Alice Dewey, August ?, 1894, John Dewey Papers, coll. 102/2/7.

117. Dykhuizen, *John Dewey,* pp. 74, 100.

118. *Ibid.,* p. 100.

119. John Dewey, "Self-Realization as the Moral Ideal," pp. 49–50.

120. John Dewey, "Reconstruction," p. 102.

F I V E: *Democracy, Education, and Religious Experience*

1. David W. Noble, *The Progressive Mind 1890–1917* (Minneapolis: Burgess Publishing, 1971), chs. 1–2 and pp. 154–56. Eric Goldman, *Rendez-vous with Destiny* (New York: Vintage Books, 1956), chs. 6–8.

2. Dykhuizen, *John Dewey,* pp. 77–78, 80–81.

3. Darnell Rucker, *The Chicago Pragmatists* (Minneapolis: University of Minnesota Press, 1969), p. 107.

4. As quoted in Goldman, *Rendez-vous,* p. 123.

5. Lawrence A. Cremin, *American Education: The Metropolitan Experience, 1876–1980* (New York: Harper & Row, 1988), p. 154.

6. Dr. J. M. Rice, *The Public-School System of the United States* (New York: Century, 1893), pp. 6, 10–11, 20–21, 220–21, 229–30.

7. Cremin, *American Education,* pp. 223–29.

8. Dykhuizen, *John Dewey,* pp. 86–91, 107–15.

9. Jane Dewey, ed., "Biography of John Dewey," pp. 29–30. Jo Ann Boydston, "John Dewey and the New Feminism," *Teachers' College Record* (February 1975), 3:444.

10. John Dewey to Alice Dewey, September 23, 1894, John Dewey Papers, coll. 102/2/8, Special Collections, Morris Library, Southern Illinois University.

11. Jane Addams, "The Objective Value of a Social Settlement," in Christopher Lasch, ed., *The Social Thought of Jane Addams,* pp. 59–60 (Indianapolis: Bobbs-Merrill, 1965), Jane Addams, "John Dewey and Social Welfare," in *John Dewey: The Man and His Philosophy,* pp. 140–41 (Cambridge: Harvard University Press, 1930). See also Lewis S. Feuer, "John Dewey and the Back-to-the-People Movement in American Thought," *Journal of the History of Ideas* (October-December 1959), 20: 545–68.

12. John Dewey, "In Response," in LW 5:421–22.

13. John Dewey to Alice Dewey, July 9, 1894. Max Eastman and George Dykhuizen mistakenly assert that Morris went to Europe with Alice.

14. John Dewey to Alice Dewey, October 7, 1894. The title of the picture that Dewey associates with young Morris is not clearly written in his letter. The word seems to be "Sistine," and it may well refer to Michelangelo's "The Doni Madonna," which, even though it is not in the Sistine Chapel, is done in a style that anticipates the painting of the Sistine Chapel. See Valerio Mariani, *Michelangelo, the Painter* (New York: Harry N. Abrams, 1964), plate 3.

15. Jane Dewey, ed., "Biography of John Dewey," p. 24, and Eastman, "My Teacher and Friend," p. 268.

16. Jane Dewey, ed., "Biography of John Dewey," p. 35.

17. Dykhuizen, *John Dewey*, pp. 109–15.

18. John Dewey, *The Poems of John Dewey*, pp. xviii, 30. It is possible that another poem, entitled "To Death" (No. 44) may also have been written by Dewey to Morris or Gordon.

19. Eastman, "My Teacher and Friend," pp. 278–80.

20. Dykhuizen, *John Dewey*, pp. 149 and 382, n. 31.

21. John Dewey, "From Absolutism to Experimentalism," in LW 5:156.

22. John Dewey, *Democracy and Education*, in MW 9:336.

23. John Dewey, "My Pedagogic Creed," in EW 5:93–94. See also John Dewey, *Democracy and Education*, pp. 338–42.

24. John Dewey, "Education as a Religion," in MW 13:318.

25. John Dewey, "My Pedagogic Creed," p. 94. John Dewey, "Education as Religion," p. 319.

26. John Dewey, *Democracy and Education*, pp. 337–39.

27. John Dewey, "The Need of an Industrial Education in an Industrial Democracy," in MW 10:139.

28. John Dewey, "My Pedagogic Creed," p. 95.

29. John Dewey, "Education as a Religion," pp. 318–19.

30. *Ibid.*, pp. 319–21. John Dewey, "Education as Engineering," in MW 13:327–28.

31. Jane Dewey, ed., "Biography of John Dewey," pp. 17–18. See also Dewey, *Democracy and Education*, p. 64.

32. John Dewey, *The School and Society*, in MW 1:69.

33. John Dewey, "My Pedagogic Creed," p. 84.

34. John Dewey, "The Need of an Industrial Education in an Industrial Democracy," pp. 137–38.

35. John Dewey, "Creative Democracy—The Task Before Us," in LW 14:226–27.

36. John Dewey, "The Need of an Industrial Education in an Industrial Democracy," p. 138.

37. John Dewey, *Democracy and Education*, p. 7. John Dewey, "The One World of Hitler's National Socialism," in MW 8:443–44, 446.

38. John Dewey, *Democracy and Education*, pp. 103–05. See also Dewey, "The One World of Hitler's National Socialism," pp. 445–46.

39. John Dewey, *Reconstruction in Philosophy*, in MW 12:196.

40. John Dewey, *Experience and Nature*, in MW 1:132, 144–45, 157–59.

41. John Dewey, *Reconstruction in Philosophy*, p. 191.

42. *Ibid.*, p. 186. See also John Dewey and Goodwin Watson, "The Forward View: A Free Teacher in a Free Society," in LW 11:538–40.

43. *Ibid.*, p. 199.

44. John Dewey, *Ethics*, in LW 7:251–52.

45. John Dewey, *Democracy and Education*, p. 129.

46. John Dewey, *Individualism, Old and New*, in LW 5:68.

47. John Dewey, *Reconstruction in Philosophy*, p. 201.

48. *Ibid.*, p. 199.

49. John Dewey, "Creative Democracy," p. 226.

50. John Dewey, *Democracy and Education*, pp. 127–28, 130.

51. John Dewey, *Ethics*, pp. 251–52, 270, 299–300.

52. John Dewey, "Creative Democracy," pp. 226–27.

53. *Ibid.*, p. 227.

54. Reinhold Niebuhr, *The Children of Light and the Children of Darkness* (New York: Scribner's, 1944), pp. xii–xv.

55. John Dewey, "Creative Democracy," p. 228.

56. Hook, "Some Memories of John Dewey."

57. John Dewey, *Reconstruction in Philosophy*, p. 201. The phrase taken from Wordsworth is a line in the "Elegiac Stanzas": "The light that never was, on sea or land." Wordsworth is referring to a celestial light which may be perceived in the imaginative vision of the artist and poet and which transfigures the natural world rendering it a scene of tranquility, harmony, and bliss.

58. John Dewey, *Experience and Nature*, pp. 159–60.

59. Randall, "The Religion of Shared Experience."

60. *Ibid.*, p. 245.

61. John Dewey, "The Significance of the Problem of Knowledge," in EW 5:22. For a brief discussion of the issue raised by this quotation, see Darnell Rucker, "Introduction," in MW 3:xi–xii.

62. John Dewey, "My Pedagogic Creed," p. 85. Dewey, *Ethics*, p. 290.

63. John Dewey, *The Child and the Curriculum*, in MW 2:278.

64. *Ibid.,* p. 291.

65. John Dewey, "My Pedagogic Creed," p. 86.

66. John Dewey, "The Democratic Faith and Education," in LW 15:258–60.

67. John Dewey, *Democracy and Education,* p. 183.

68. John Dewey, "The Challenge of Democracy to Education," in *Problems of Men,* p. 49.

69. John Dewey, "My Pedagogic Creed," p. 84.

70. *Ibid.,* p. 87.

71. John Dewey, *Democracy and Education,* p. 26.

72. John Dewey,"My Pedagogic Creed," pp. 87–88. See also John Dewey, "Self-Realization as the Moral Ideal," in EW 4:50–51; John Dewey, *Experience and Education,* in LW 13:29–30; Dewey, *The School and Society,* pp. 12, 24–25.

73. John Dewey, "My Pedagogic Creed," p. 89.

74. *Ibid.,* pp. 10, 68–70.

75. John Dewey, *The School and Society,* pp. 55, 74.

76. John Dewey, "The Need of Industrial Education in an Industrial Democracy" and "Learning to Learn: The Place of Vocational Education in a Comprehensive Scheme of Public Education," in MW 10:138–41, 149.

77. John Dewey, *Democracy and Education,* p. 252.

78. *Ibid.,* p. 245.

79. *Ibid.,* p. 247.

80. *Ibid.,* pp. 246–47. See also Dewey, *Experience and Nature,* p. 159.

81. John Dewey, *Democracy and Education,* p. 22.

82. John Dewey, "My Pedagogic Creed," p. 93.

83. *Ibid.,* p. 88.

84. John Dewey, *Democracy and Education,* p. 243.

85. John Dewey, *Experience and Education,* p. 53.

86. *Ibid.,* p. 54.

87. John Dewey, "Is Co-Education Injurious to Girls?" in MW 6:159–62.

88. Cremin, *American Education,* p. 174.

89. *Ibid.,* pp. 187–92. John Dewey, "Class Struggle and the Democratic Way," in LW 2:382–86. First published in *Social Frontiers* (May 1936), 2: 241–42.

90. Robert Maynard Hutchins, *The Higher Learning in America* (New Haven: Yale University Press, 1936).

91. John Dewey, "President Hutchins' Proposals to Remake Higher Education," in LW 2:382–86. First published in *Social Frontiers* (January 1937), 3:103–04.

92. See John Dewey, "Rationality in Education," in LW 2:391–96. First published in *Social Frontiers* (December 1936), 3:71–73. Robert Maynard Hutchins, "Grammar, Rhetoric and Mr. Dewey," in LW 2:592–97. First published in *Social Frontiers* (February 1937), 3:137–39. John Dewey, "The Higher Learning in America," in LW 2:401–07. First published in *Social Frontiers* (March 1937), 3:167–69. See also Cremin, *American Education,* pp. 192–95.

93. On contemporary social science and moral development, see Karen J. Winkler, "Experts on Moral Development Find Common Ground," *Chronicle of Higher Education* (October 26, 1988):A4, A8. See also William Damon, *The Moral Child: Nurturing Children's Natural Moral Growth* (New York: Free Press, 1988).

94. "A Call For A Convention to Effect a National Organization For The Improvement of Religious and Moral Education Through the Sunday School and Other Agencies," Official Document No. 1 and 2. It was "the Council of Seventy Directing the American Institute of Sacred Literature," of which Harper was the Principal, which issued the "call" for the convention where the REA was actually brought into being.

95. John Dewey, "Religious Education as Conditioned by Modern Psychology and Pedagogy," in MW 3:210–15.

96. Martin E. Marty, *Modern American Religion,* vol. 1: *The Irony of It All, 1893–1919* (Chicago: University of Chicago Press, 1986), pp. 264–67.

97. Dorothy Ross, *G. Stanley Hall, The Psychologist as Prophet* (Chicago: The University of Chicago Press, 1972), pp. 416–17. G. Stanley Hall, "A New Universal Religion at Hand," *Metropolitan* (December 1901), 14:778–80.

98. John Dewey, "Religion and Our Schools," in MW 4:165–77.

99. Ames, *The Psychology of Religious Experience* (Boston: Houghton Mifflin, 1910), pp. 249–50.

100. John Dewey, "Religion and Our Schools," p. 168.

101. *Ibid.,* pp. 165–66, 176.

102. John Dewey, "From Absolutism to Experimentalism," p. 153.

103. John Dewey, *Reconstruction in Philosophy,* p. 200.

104. *Ibid.,* p. 201.

105. John Dewey, "Religion and Our Schools," pp. 167–68.

106. *Ibid.,* p. 169.

107. *Ibid.,* p. 175.

108. Dykhuizen, *John Dewey,* p. 295. John Dewey, "Implications of S.2499," in LW 15:284–85.

s i x: *Pragmatism, Progressivism, and the War*

1. John Dewey to Scudder Klyce, May 13, 1915, Scudder Klyce Papers, Manuscript Division, Library of Congress, Washington, D.C.

2. William R. Hutchinson, *The Modernist Impulse in American Protestantism* (Cambridge, Mass.: Harvard University Press, 1976), pp. 165–73; Eric Goldman, *Rendezvous With Destiny: A History of Modern American Reform* (New York: Vintage Books, 1956), pp. 84–85; Henry F. May, *The End of American Innocence: A Study of the First Years of Our Time, 1912–1917* (New York: Knopf, 1959), pp. 9–29; Martin Marty, *Modern American Religion,* vol. I, *The Irony of It All, 1893–1919* (Chicago: University of Chicago Press, 1986), pp. 25–31, 283–91.

3. John Dewey, "Progress," in MW 10:236.

4. Marty, *The Irony of It All,* pp. 291–97.

5. David H. Shannon, *The Progressive Era* (Chicago: Rand McNally, 1974), p. 100.

6. Hutchinson, *The Modernist Impulse,* pp. 196–98.

7. Marty, *The Irony of It All,* pp. 198–207.

8. John H. Randall, Jr., "The Department of Philosophy," in Jacques Barzun, ed., *A History of the Faculty of Philosophy: Columbia University,* pp. 124–25 (New York: Columbia University Press, 1957); Dykhuizen, *John Dewey,* pp. 118–22.

9. Horace L. Freiss, in Fannia Weingartner, ed., *Felix Adler and Ethical Culture: Memories and Studies,* pp. 2, 7, 47–59, 121–22, 127, 215–17 (New York: Columbia University Press, 1981); Randall, "The Department of Philosophy," pp. 121–22.

10. Hook, "Some Memories of John Dewey," p. 102.

11. Eastman, "My Teacher and Friend," pp. 282–83; Randall, "The Department of Philosophy," p. 128; Corliss Lamont, ed., *Dialogue on John Dewey* (New York: Horizon Press, 1959), pp. 39–40, 43.

12. Irwin Edman, *Philosopher's Holiday* (New York: Viking, 1938), p. 140.

13. Hook, "Some Memories of John Dewey," p. 112.

14. Randall, "The Department of Philosophy," pp. 129–30.

15. Ottoline Morrell Papers, #1008, 22.3.14, Humanities Research Center, University of Texas at Austin. Quoted in Jo Ann Boydston, "Textual Commentary," in MW 7:496.

16. Hook, "Some Memories of John Dewey," p. 112.

17. Eastman, "My Teacher and Friend," p. 283; Edman, *Philosopher's Holiday,* p. 19. Eastman received a Ph.D. in Philosophy from Columbia in 1913.

18. Edman, *Philosopher's Holiday,* p. 19.

19. Eastman, "My Teacher and Friend," p. 283.

20. Hook, "Some Memories of John Dewey," pp. 111, 113.

21. David W. Noble, *The Progressive Mind, 1890–1917* (Minneapolis: Burgess, 1981), pp. 27–35.

22. Goldman, *Rendezvous,* pp. 96–99, 119, 122–23.

23. May, *The End of American Innocence,* pp. 314–17, 322–27; Dykhuizen, *John Dewey,* pp. 165–66.

24. John Dewey, "Is Nature Good? A Conversation," in MW 4:16–17.

25. It is likely that Dewey read Bergson prior to 1910 given Bergson's reputation as an evolutionary philosopher. In 1913 Bergson was a visiting professor in the Department of Philosophy at Columbia, and Dewey wrote an introduction to a Bergson bibliography published that year. In 1920, Dewey chose Bergson along with William James and Bertrand Russell for a series of lectures delivered in Peking, China, on "Three Contemporary Philosophers." He commented directly on the role of mysticism in Bergson, finding the latter's popularity to arise from the way he combined pragmatism and mysticism. John Dewey, "Introduction," in Isadore Gilbert Mudge, *A Contribution to a Bibliography of Henri Bergson,* p. xiii (New York: Columbia University Press, 1913). Reprinted in MW 7:204. Regarding the role of the intellect as a principle of division, see "Introduction à la Métaphysique," *Revue de la métaphysique et de morale* (January 1903), 11:1–36. An English translation appeared in 1913. Dewey, "Three Contemporary Philosophers," in MW 12:227–28.

26. John Dewey, "Is Nature Good?" pp. 26–27.

27. *Ibid.,* pp. 16, 20, 27.

28. *Ibid.,* pp. 17–18.

29. *Ibid.,* p. 19.

30. *Ibid.,* pp. 28–29.

31. Reviewing *The Two Sources of Morality in Religion* in 1935, Dewey acknowledged that one may "learn a great deal from Bergson's clear and informed discussion of these matters," but he found that Bergson overestimated the creative power of mystical intuition and did not adequately appreciate the constructive role of social intelligence. See "Bergson on Instinct," in LW 11:428–31.

32. John Dewey, "The Need for a Recovery of Philosophy," in MW 10:46.

33. *Ibid.*

34. *Ibid.,* p. 48.

35. John Dewey, "Introduction" to 1948 reprint of *Reconstruction in*

Philosophy, in MW 12:266. See also John Dewey, "The Need for Social Psychology," in MW 10:62–63.

36. John Dewey, "Introduction" to *Reconstruction in Philosophy,* p. 269.

37. John Dewey, "The Influence of Darwin on Philosophy," in MW 4:3–4, 7, 13.

38. John Dewey, "An Added Note As to the 'Practical,' " in *Essays in Experimental Logic,* in MW 10:366.

39. Mary V. Dearborn, *Love in the Promised Land: The Story of Anzia Yezierska and John Dewey* (New York: Free Press, 1988), pp. 72, 75, 92–95. Eastman, "My Teacher and Friend," pp. 288–89.

40. Dykhuizen, *John Dewey,* pp. 145–46, 169–70.

41. John Dewey, "Introductory Address to the American Association of University Professors," in MW 8:98f; John Dewey, "The Case of the Professor and the Public Interest," in MW 10:164–67.

42. John Dewey, "Professorial Freedom," in MW 8:407–08. First published as a letter to the editor in *New York Times,* October 22, 1915; John Dewey, "Professional Organization of Teachers," in MW 10:169–70.

43. Jo Ann Boydston, "John Dewey and the New Feminism," in *Teachers College Record* (February 1975), 3:441–48; Dearborn, *Love in the Promised Land,* pp. 90–91; Jane Dewey, ed., "Biography of John Dewey," p. 30.

44. Dykhuizen, *John Dewey,* pp. 149–50.

45. *New York Times,* August 9, 1912, in MW 7:409.

46. John Dewey, "A Symposium on Woman's Suffrage," in MW 6:153–54.

47. Dearborn, *Love in the Promised Land,* pp. 90–91; Boydston, "John Dewey and the New Feminism," p. 441.

48. John Dewey to Scudder Klyce, July 5, 1915. Scudder Klyce Papers. In "John Dewey and the New Feminism," Jo Ann Boydston quotes extensively from the Dewey-Klyce correspondence on this subject.

49. Dewey to Klyce, May 8, 1920, Scudder Klyce Papers.

50. Dewey to Klyce, July 5, 1915, Scudder Klyce Papers.

51. Dewey to Klyce, May 8, 1920, Scudder Klyce Papers.

52. James M. McPherson, "Introduction," in *Proceedings of the National Negro Conference, 1909* (New York: Arno Press and the *New York Times,* 1969).

53. John Dewey, "Address to National Negro Conference," in MW 4:156–57. First published in *Proceedings of the National Negro Conference,* pp. 72–73.

54. John Dewey, "Nationalizing Education," in MW 10:204.

55. *Ibid.,* pp. 202–10.

56. John Dewey, "Racial Prejudice and Friction," in MW 13:242–54. First published in *Chinese Social and Political Science Review* (1922), 6:1–17. John Dewey, "A Philosophical Interpretation of Racial Prejudice," in MW 13:437–40. First published in *Dewey Newsletter* (July 1969):13–17 as an abstract from an article Dewey published in Japanese in 1921 in the Japanese journal *Kaizo*. See Jo Ann Boydston, "Textual Commentary," in MW 13:506.

57. Herbert Croly, in Arthur M. Schlesinger, Jr., ed., *The Promise of American Life*, pp. 20–24, 453–54 (Cambridge, Mass.: Harvard University Press, 1965). See also Schlesinger, "Introduction."

58. Croly, *The Promise of American Life,* pp. 214, 400–12, 431.

59. Sidney Hook, *Education and the Taming of Power* (LaSalle, Ill.: Open Court, 1973), p. 141.

60. Charles F. Howlett, *Troubled Philosopher: John Dewey and the Struggle for World Peace* (Port Washington, N.Y.: Kennikat Press, 1977), pp. 71–74.

61. John Dewey, "Force, Violence and Law," in MW 10:212. First published in *New Republic* (1916), 5:295–97.

62. *Ibid.,* pp. 213–14.

63. *Ibid.,* p. 213.

64. See untitled, undated, unpublished Dewey essay on Leo Tolstoy, in a Columbia University envelope, John Dewey Papers, Special Collections, Morris Library, Southern Illinois University. Reprinted in LW 17:381–92.

65. Morton White, *Social Thought in America; The Revolt Against Formalism* (New York: Oxford University Press, 1947), pp. 161–66.

66. Hook, "Some Memories of John Dewey," pp. 106–07.

67. John Dewey, "Force and Coercion," in MW 10:246–48, 251. First published in *International Journal of Ethics* (1916), 26:359–67.

68. John Dewey, "Force, Violence and Law," pp. 214–15.

69. *Ibid.,* p. 213.

70. John Dewey, "Force and Coercion," p. 251.

71. John Dewey, "Force, Violence and Law," p. 213.

72. John Dewey, "Force and Coercion," pp. 249, 251.

73. White, *Social Thought in America,* p. 165.

74. John Dewey, "Force, Violence and Law," pp. 214–15.

75. *Ibid.,* pp. 213–14.

76. *Ibid.,* pp. 214–15. John Dewey, "Progress," pp. 238–39.

77. Dewey, "Force, Violence and Law," p. 215.

78. John Dewey, "The Future of Pacifism," in MW 10:266.

79. John Dewey, "Conscience and Compulsion," in MW 10:262.

80. John Dewey, *Reconstruction in Philosophy,* p. 192.

81. John Dewey, "Progress," pp. 238, 239, 240.

82. John Dewey, *Human Nature and Conduct,* in MW 14:19–20.

83. Aeschylus, *The Eumenides,* in *The Orestes Plays of Aeschylus,* tr. by Paul Roche, pp. 175–202 (New York: New American Library, 1962).

84. John Dewey, *Ethics,* in LW 7:259–60.

85. John Dewey, "Conscience and Compulsion," pp. 262, 264.

86. *Ibid.,* pp. 262–64. Dewey's essay prompted Norman Thomas to write "War's Heretics: A Plea for the Conscientious Objector" (New York: American Union Against Militarism, 1917), in which he argued that a concern for inner purity in matters of conscience is the best method for maintaining a moral social system.

87. See unpublished manuscript on Tolstoy, John Dewey Papers. Reprinted in LW 17:390.

88. John Dewey to Scudder Klyce, May 29, 1915, Scudder Klyce Papers.

89. John Dewey, *Ethics,* in MW 5:293–94; Dewey, *Ethics,* in LW 7:268–72. Dewey published both editions of *Ethics* in cooperation with James Hayden Tufts, but Dewey wrote the sections noted above.

90. John Dewey, *German Philosophy and Politics,* in MW 8:151, 152.

91. Jo Ann Boydston, "Textual Commentary," in MW 8:486.

92. Eastman, "My Teacher and Friend," p. 285.

93. John Dewey, *German Philosophy and Politics,* pp. 147–52, 164–65. For further clarification of Dewey's critique of Kant, see John Dewey, "Kant After Two Hundred Years," in MW 15:10–13.

94. John Dewey, "The One-World of Hitler's National Socialism," in MW 8:421–46; see also Sidney Hook, "Introduction," in MW 8:xxx-xxxx.

95. John Dewey, "In a Time of National Hesitation," in MW 10:258–59. First published in *Seven Arts* (1917), 2:3–7.

96. John Dewey, "The Discrediting of Idealism," in MW 11:180–81. First published in *New Republic* (1919), 20:285–87.

97. Harold Stearns, *Liberalism in America: Its Origin, Its Temporary Collapse, Its Future* (New York: Boni and Liverwright, 1919), pp. 3, 7.

98. Dykhuizen, *John Dewey,* pp. 161–62, 168; Howlett, *Troubled Philosopher,* pp. 33–34; Goldman, *Rendezvous,* pp. 197–200.

99. *New York Times,* February 14, 1917, p. 5; see Howlett, *Troubled Philosopher,* pp. 33, 56.

100. John Dewey, "Conscription of Thought," in MW 10:278–80. First published in *New Republic* (1917), 12:128–30.

101. John Dewey, "In Explanation of Our Lapse," in MW 10:295. First published in *New Republic* (1917), 13:17–18.

102. Howlett, *Troubled Philosopher,* pp. 33–34.

103. Dykhuizen, *John Dewey,* pp. 171–73.

104. Randolph Bourne, "Twilight of Idols," in James Oppenheim, ed., *Untimely Papers,* pp. 117–34 (New York: B. W. Huebsch, 1919). For other discussions of Dewey and Bourne, see M. White, *Social Thought in America,* pp. 169–72, and Coughlan, *Young John Dewey,* pp. 158–62.

105. Bourne, "Twilight of Idols," pp. 130–32, 134–35.

106. Oppenheim, "Foreword," in *Untimely Papers,* pp. 6–7.

107. Randolph Bourne, "Making Over the Body," Review of *Man's Supreme Inheritance* (New York: E.P. Dutton, 1918) in *New Republic* (1918), 15:28–29. Reprinted in MW 11:359–60. For Dewey's reply to Bourne, see "Reply to a Reviewer," in MW 11:353–54. First published in *New Republic* (1918), 25:55.

108. Lamont, *John Dewey,* pp. 25, 30; Howlett, *Troubled Philosopher,* p. 37.

109. Stearns, *Liberalism in America,* ch. 8.

110. White, *Social Thought in America,* p. 172.

111. Eastman, "My Teacher and Friend," p. 285.

112. John Dewey, "Progress," pp. 236–38.

113. John Dewey, "The Discrediting of Idealism," pp. 181–82.

114. Hutchinson, *The Modernist Impulse,* pp. 146–47, 169, 193, 215, 221–23, 226–31.

115. John Dewey, *Reconstruction in Philosophy,* pp. 153–55.

116. Howlett, *Troubled Philosopher,* pp. 6–7, 84, 92, 108, 112–13.

117. For examples of Dewey's positions on the outlawry of war, see John Dewey, *Outlawry of War: What It Is and Is Not* (Chicago: American Committee for the Outlawry of War, 1923), which is reprinted in MW 15:115–27; John Dewey, "Afterword," in Charles Clayton Morrison, *The Outlawry of War: A Constructive Policy for World Peace* (Chicago: Willett, Clark & Colby, 1927), which is reprinted in LW 3:348–58; and John Dewey, "Outlawry of War," in LW 8:13–18. See Howlett, *Troubled Philosopher,* pp. 75–127, 140, 143, and Sidney Ratner, "Introduction," in LW 6:xx-xxi.

118. John Dewey, "Democratic Ends Need Democratic Methods for their Realization," in LW 14:367–68. See also John Dewey, "Democracy is Radical," in LW 11:298. and John Dewey, *Freedom and Culture,* in LW 13:187.

119. John Dewey, "Freedom," in LW 11:252.

120. John Dewey, "No Matter What Happens—Stay Out," in LW 14:364. First published in *Common Sense* (March 1939), 8:11.

SEVEN: *Poems, Letters, and Lessons*

1. Jo Ann Boydston, ed., *The Poems of John Dewey,* poem #3, p. 4. All subsequent poetry citations are from this text and will be cited by poem number and page number.

2. #36, p. 24; #43, pp. 28–29; #50, pp. 37–38.

3. #43, pp. 28–29.

4. Jo Ann Boydston has undertaken a very thorough study of the origin and date of the poems. See her "Introduction," in *The Poems of John Dewey,* pp. ix-lxvii.

5. #42, p. 28.

6. #27, p. 19

7. #28, p. 19; #43, pp. 28–29.

8. #46, pp. 30–31.

9. #6, pp. 5–6; #13, pp. 9–10; #22, pp. 14–17.

10. #43, pp. 28–29; see also #28, p. 19.

11. #70, pp. 50–51.

12. #22, pp. 14–17.

13. #29, p. 20; #60, pp. 42–43.

14. #60, pp. 42–43.

15. #29, p. 20.

16. #73, pp. 53–54.

17. #44, p. 29.

18. #46, pp. 30–31.

19. #22, pp. 15–16.

20. John Dewey to Scudder Klyce, October 21, 1927, Scudder Klyce Papers, General Correspondence: John Dewey, Manuscript Division, Library of Congress, Washington, D.C.

21. #29, p. 20. This is the only poem which was found preserved among the Dewey Papers. See Jo Ann Boydston, "Description of the Text," in *The Poems of John Dewey,* p. 91.

22. #58, pp. 40–41.

23. John Dewey to his family, April 14, 1919, John Dewey Papers, Morris Library, Special Collections, Southern Illinois University, Carbondale.

24. #36, p. 24.

25. #8, pp. 6–7; #27, p. 19; #30, pp. 20–21.

26. #82, pp. 60–61.

27. #46, pp. 30–31; #67, p. 49; #81, p. 59; #89, p. 66.

28. #46, pp. 30–31.

29. #89, p. 66.

30. #50, pp. 37–38.

31. #67, p. 49.

32. #35, p. 24.

33. #80, pp. 58–59.

34. #65, p. 48.

35. #74, p. 54.

36. #19, p. 13.

37. #77, p. 56.

38. #22, p. 15.

39. #9, pp. 7–8.

40. #34, p. 23. See Exodus 3:1–6.

41. #18, p. 13.

42. #66, p. 48.

43. #81, pp. 59–60.

44. #47, pp. 35–36.

45. Boydston, "Introduction," pp. liv–lv.

46. Klyce to Dewey, April 4, 1915. Center for Dewey Studies, Southern Illinois University, Carbondale.

47. Hook, "Some Memories of John Dewey," p. 104.

48. Dewey to Klyce, May 11, 1915, Scudder Klyce Papers.

49. Dewey to Klyce, May 13, 1915, Scudder Klyce Papers.

50. Klyce to Dewey, May 29, 1915.

51. Klyce to Dewey, April 19, 1915, and May 29, 1915.

52. Dewey to Klyce, May 29, 1915, Scudder Klyce Papers.

53. Klyce to Dewey, May 22, 1915.

54. Dewey to Klyce, May 29, 1915, Scudder Klyce Papers.

55. Dewey to Klyce, May 13, 1915, Scudder Klyce Papers.

56. Dewey to Klyce, May 29, 1915, Scudder Klyce Papers.

57. Dewey to Klyce, June 19, 1915, Scudder Klyce Papers. Dewey adds: "But I am grateful for having the infinite part of the pluralism made obvious. I find plenty of places where I had criticized certain things and the principle of the criticism is that the thing involved a finite pluralism, but I had never generalized it . . . having the thing formulated here increases my confidence."

58. Dewey to Klyce, May 4, 1915, Scudder Klyce Papers.

59. Dewey to Klyce, April 22, 1915, Scudder Klyce Papers.

60. Dewey to Klyce, April 6, 1915, Scudder Klyce Papers.

61. Dewey to Klyce, April 16, 1915, Scudder Klyce Papers.

62. Dewey to Klyce, May 29, 1915, Scudder Klyce Papers.

63. John Dewey, *Essays in Experimental Logic,* in MW 10:324–25.

64. John Dewey, "Introduction" to S. Klyce, *Universe;* typed, hand-corrected manuscript written in Nanking, China, and mailed to S. Klyce, March 6, 1920, Scudder Klyce Papers. See also "First Introduction to *Universe,*" in MW 13:412–20.

65. John Dewey, "First Introduction to *Universe,*" p. 416. In 1916 Dewey observed that "mysticism doubtless roots in this fact" that "thinking is set in a continuum which is not an object of thought." He also asserts: " 'Intuition,' mysticism, philosophical or sophisticated monism, are all of them aberrant ways of protesting against the consequences which result from failing to note what is conveyed by words which are not terms." *Essays in Experimental Logic,* pp. 324–25.

66. John Dewey, "First Introduction to *Universe,*" p. 416.

67. Dewey to Klyce, April 23, 1915, Scudder Klyce Papers.

68. Dewey to Klyce, April 16, 1915, Scudder Klyce Papers.

69. Dewey to Klyce, April 23, 1915, Scudder Klyce Papers.

70. Dewey to Klyce, June 19, 1915, Scudder Klyce Papers.

71. Dewey to Klyce, April 23, 1915, Scudder Klyce Papers.

72. Dewey to Klyce, October 18, 1927, Scudder Klyce Papers.

73. Klyce to Dewey, May 29, 1915.

74. Dewey to Klyce, July 5, 1915, Scudder Klyce Papers.

75. Dewey to Klyce, May 29, 1915, Scudder Klyce Papers.

76. Dewey to Klyce, March 24, 1927, Scudder Klyce Papers. See also June 19, 1915.

77. Dewey to Klyce, June 19, 1915, Scudder Klyce Papers.

78. Wilfred Barlow, *The Alexander Technique* (New York: Warner Books, 1973), pp. 3–4. Alexander gives an account of how he developed his technique in chapter 1 of his book *The Use of the Self: Its Conscious Direction in Relation to Diagnosis, Functioning and the Control Reaction* (New York: E. P. Dutton, 1932).

79. Randolph Bourne, "Making Over the Body," *New Republic* (1918), 15:28–29. Reprinted in MW 11:360.

80. Barlow, *The Alexander Technique,* p. 213.

81. Eric David McCormack, *Frederick Matthias Alexander and John Dewey: A Neglected Influence.* A thesis submitted in conformity with the requirements of the degree of Doctor of Philosophy in the University of Toronto, 1958.

82. Corliss Lamont, ed., *Dialogue on John Dewey* (New York: Horizon Press, 1959), p. 27.

83. F. Matthias Alexander, *Constructive Conscious Control of the Individual* (London: Methuen, 1923), pp. 189–90.

84. See Eastman, "My Teacher and Friend," pp. 285–86; Dykhuizen, *John Dewey,* pp. 181–82.

85. John Dewey, "Introduction," in F.M. Alexander, *The Use of the Self,* in LW 6:317, 319.

86. John Dewey, "Introductory Word," in MW 11:350–52. First published in F. Matthias Alexander, *Man's Supreme Inheritance* (New York: E.P. Dutton,1918), pp. xiii-xvii. See also John Dewey, "Reply to a Reviewer," in MW 11:353–54. First published in *New Republic* (1918), 15:55.

87. John Dewey, "Introductory Word," in *Man's Supreme Inheritance,* pp. 351–52; John Dewey, "Introduction," in *Constructive Conscious Control of the Individual,* in MW 15:316, 318.

88. John Dewey, "Introduction," in *The Use of the Self,* p. 317.

89. *Ibid.,* p. 319.

90. John Dewey, "Introduction," in *Constructive Conscious Control of the Individual,* p. 314.

91. *Ibid.,* pp. 308, 314. Dewey affirmed existence of the "subconscious" and argued that "making it right depends upon its bodily conditions being right." John Dewey, "A Sick World," in MW 15:45. First published in *New Republic* (1923), 33:217–18.

92. *Ibid.,* p. 309.

93. John Dewey, "Introduction," in *The Use of the Self,* p. 319.

94. John Dewey, *Human Nature and Conduct,* in MW 14:15, 21–22, 31–32.

95. *Ibid.,* pp. 25–26.

96. *Ibid.,* pp. 25–26, 28–29.

97. *Ibid.,* pp. 18–19.

98. *Ibid.,* pp. 27–28.

99. John Dewey, "Introduction," in *Constructive Conscious Control of the Individual,* pp. 310–11.

100. Jane Dewey, ed., "Biography of John Dewey," pp. 44–45.

101. Frank Pierce Jones, *Body Awareness In Action: A Study of the Alexander Technique* (New York: Schocken Books, 1976), pp. 103–05.

102. John Dewey, "Introduction," in *Constructive Conscious Control of the Individual,* pp. 313, 315.

103. John Dewey, "Introduction," in *The Use of the Self,* p. 315.

104. John Dewey and Alice Chipman Dewey, in Evelyn Dewey, ed., *Letters From China and Japan* (New York: E. P. Dutton, 1920), pp. 30, 36,

94. Soyen Shaku in his lectures to westerners explicitly taught a kind of "panentheism" and philosophical idealism, and he used the term "God" on such occasions to refer to the Buddhist idea of ultimate truth and reality, noting that Buddhists did not normally use the term. At this early stage in the dialogue between Zen and western culture, Zen Buddhists rarely discussed actual meditation practice, because they did not think that westerners were interested in it. This did not change until the late 1950s and 1960s. See "The God Conception of Buddhism" and other essays in the Rt. Rev. Soyen Shaku, *Sermons of a Buddhist Abbot,* tr. by Daisetz Teitaro Suzuki (New York: Samuel Weiser, 1906, 1971).

105. Eastman, "My Teacher and Friend," p. 286.

106. John Dewey to Joseph Ratner, July 24, 1946, John Dewey Papers. Dewey adds: "Dr. 'Hunger' Meyer of Karlsbad doubtless helped some on the personal side of keeping me here."

107. John Dewey, "Introduction," in *Constructive Conscious Control of the Individual,* pp. 310–11. See also John Dewey, "A Sick World," pp. 42–46. In this essay Dewey criticizes techniques and therapies that simply eliminate symptoms and do not foster the conditions of human well-being and growth. He also praises the contribution of Alexander.

108. Irwin Edman, *Philosopher's Holiday* (New York: Viking, 1938), p. 140.

109. Henry Hart, *Dr. Barnes of Merion* (New York: Farrar, Strauss and Cooper, 1963), p. 66; William Schack, *Art and Argyrol* (New York: Thomas Yaseloff, 1960), p. 102.

110. John H. Randall, Jr. "The Department of Philosophy," in Jacques Barzun, ed., *A History of the Faculty of Philosophy: Columbia University* (New York: Columbia University Press, 1957), p. 128; Lamont, *Dialogue on John Dewey,* pp. 47, 49; Edman, *Philosopher's Holiday,* pp. 138ff.

111. Hook, "Some Memories of John Dewey," pp. 108–09; Lamont, *Dialogue on John Dewey,* p. 46.

112. Dykhuizen, *John Dewey,* pp. 221–22. See also Schack, *Art and Argyrol.*

113. John Dewey, *Art as Experience,* in LW 10:8.

114. Louise Levitas Henriksen, "Afterword," in *The Open Cage: An Anzia Yezierska Collection* (New York: Persea, 1979), pp. 254, 257–59; Boydston, "Introduction," in *The Poems of John Dewey,* pp. xxiii-xxvi. Boydston has undertaken an extensive inquiry into the relationship of John Dewey and Anzia Yezierska as revealed by his poems and her stories and novels. See also Louise Levitas Henriksen, with assistance from Jo Ann Boydston, *Anzia Yezierska: A Life* (New Brunswick and London: Rutgers University

Press, 1988), and Mary V. Dearborn, *Love in the Promised Land: The Story of Anzia Yezierska and John Dewey* (New York: Free Press, 1988), chapters 2, 4. Building on the work of Boydston and Levitas, Dearborn has undertaken a further searching critical account of the Dewey-Yezierska relationship. Regarding the immigration of Jews to America, there were roughly a quarter million Jews in the United States in 1881 and most had come from Germany. By 1920 that number had jumped to four million, and the majority had immigrated from Eastern Europe. See Lawrence A. Cremin, *American Education: The Metropolitan Experience, 1876–1980* (New York: Harper & Row, 1988), pp. 138–40.

115. Henriksen, "Afterword," p. 259.

116. Schack, *Art and Argyrol,* p. 102.

117. Yezierska, *Red Ribbon on a White Horse* (New York: Scribner's, 1950), pp. 107, 112; Boydston, "Introduction," pp. xxiv-xxix, xl, xliv.

118. Anzia Yezierska, "Prophets of Democracy," *Booksman* (February 1921), 52:496, and Anzia Yezierska, *All I Could Never Be* (New York: Brewer, Warren & Putnam, 1932), pp. 70–71.

119. Henriksen, "Afterword," pp. 259–60.

120. #4, pp. 4–5.

121. "Wild Winter Love," *Century* (February 1927), 113:489–90.

122. #22, p. 15.

123. #1, p. 3. See Boydston, "Introduction," p. xxxiv.

124. #10, p. 8.

125. #22, pp. 15–16. See Boydston, "Introduction," pp. xxx, xxxix-xl.

126. #22, p. 14.

127. #22, pp. 14–16; #6, p. 6.

128. #25, p. 18; #40, pp. 26–27; #13, pp. 9–10.

129. See, for example, Boydston, "Introduction," pp. xliv-xlvi, and Dearborn, *Love in the Promised Land,* pp. 128–31, 153–58.

130. Hart, *Dr. Barnes of Merion,* p. 65. Dewey's involvement in the Polish-American study has become controversial. For a brief introduction to the more recent debate, see Dearborn, *Love in the Promised Land,* pp. 103–06, 122–26.

131. John Dewey, "Confidential Report of Conditions Among the Poles in the United States," in MW 11:259–60. In August 1918, U. S. Military Intelligence requested Dewey to submit a report on his findings regarding the American Polish community, and the result was three confidential memoranda. See MW 11:248–330.

132. John Dewey to Alice Dewey, July 13, 1918, John Dewey Papers.

133. #22, p. 14.

134. Boydston, "Introduction," p. xlvi.

135. #8, pp. 6–7.

136. John Dewey, *Reconstruction in Philosophy*, in MW 12:201.

137. Henriksen, "Afterword," p. 260; Boydston, "Introduction," pp. xxiii-xxiv, xxxvi-xlvii. Henriksen cites Yezierska's novels, *All I Could Never Be* (1932) and *Red Ribbon on a White Horse* (1950), as containing autobiographical accounts of her relationship with Dewey. Boydston mentions two short stories, "To the Stars" (1921) and "Wild Winter Love" (1927), as also describing the relationship. See also Dearborn, *Love in the Promised Land*, pp. 137–38. Mary Dearborn has unfairly criticized Dewey for having "seduced and betrayed" Yezierska and for showing a failure of nerve in not pursuing the relationship. Such criticisms oversimplify the situation ignoring Yezierska's own role in initiating the relationship, the substantive personal problems she had throughout her life in maintaining relationships (which Dearborn describes), and Dewey's responsibilities to Alice Dewey, about which he was clear with Yezierska from early on. Further, the limited evidence does not justify the charge that Dewey in "cavalier" fashion dismissed Yezierska "refusing to explain." He was unwilling to communicate with her after the relationship ended, but to assume, as Dearborn does, that this was due to cowardice and hard-heartedness is conjecture and does not fit with what is known about Dewey's character. See *Love in the Promised Land*, pp. 6, 119–39, 158.

138. See #22, p. 15, and Boydston, "Introduction," pp. xxxii, xliii-xliv.

139. "Prophets of Democracy," *Booksman* (1921), 52: 496–97.

140. "Philosophy," in Harold E. Stearns, ed., *Civilization in the United States: An Inquiry by Thirty Americans* (Westport, Conn.: Greenwood Press, 1922), p. 176.

141. Henry F. May, *The End of American Innocence: A Study of the First Years of Our Own Time, 1912–1917* (New York: Knopf, 1959), p. 393.

E I G H T: *Nature, Science, and Values*

1. Jane M. Dewey, ed., "Biography of John Dewey," p. 42.

2. *Ibid.*, pp. 40–42.

3. Hu Shih, "John Dewey in China," in Charles A. Moore, ed., *Philosohy and Culture East and West* (Honolulu: University of Hawaii Press, 1962), pp. 762–69. Robert W. Clopton and Tsuin-chen Ou, trans. and eds., "Introduction," in *John Dewey: Lectures in China, 1919–1920*, pp. 3–25 (Honolulu: University Press of Hawaii, 1973).

4. Eric Goldman, *Rendezvous with Destiny* (New York: Vintage Books, 1956), pp. 223–41.

5. John Dewey, "A Sick World," in MW 15:45. First published in *New Republic* (1923), 33:217–18.

6. Carl Cohen, "Introduction," in MW 15:xiii-xix; Jo Ann Boydston, "Textual Commentary," in MW 15:427–30.

7. Dykhuizen, *John Dewey*, p. 232.

8. John Dewey, "In Response," in LW 5:420.

9. John Dewey to E.A. Burtt, August 14, 1927, John Dewey Papers, Special Collections, Morris Library, Southern Illinois University, Carbondale, Illinois.

10. Dykhuizen, *John Dewey*, p. 233.

11. John Dewey, "What I Believe," in LW 5:277.

12. John Dewey, *Experience and Nature*, in LW 1:4.

13. John Dewey, "What I Believe," p. 267.

14. John Dewey, "The New Psychology," in EW 1:59.

15. John Dewey, *Experience and Nature*, p. 17.

16. *Ibid.*, p. 18.

17. *Ibid.*, p. 20.

18. John Dewey, *Democracy and Education*, in MW 9:173.

19. John Dewey, *Experience and Nature*, pp. 11–13.

20. John Dewey, *Democracy and Education*, pp. 146–47. John Dewey, *Reconstruction in Philosophy*, in MW 12:128–30.

21. John Dewey, *Experience and Nature*, p. 29.

22. *Ibid.*, p. 28.

23. John Dewey, *Democracy and Education*, in MW 9:146, 151–52, 173. Dewey, *Reconstruction in Philosophy*, pp. 129–30.

24. John Dewey, "Experience, Knowledge and Value: A Rejoinder," in LW 14:10–19, 28–29.

25. John Dewey, *Democracy and Education*, pp. 151–52.

26. John Dewey, *Experience and Nature*, p. 55.

27. John Dewey, "What I Believe," in LW 5:268.

28. John Dewey, *The Quest for Certainty*, in LW 4:3, 7–12, 203–04.

29. *Ibid.*, pp. 27–28, 186–87.

30. John Dewey, *Experience and Nature*, pp. 56–57.

31. John Dewey, *The Quest for Certainty*, p. 240. See also John Dewey, *A Common Faith*, in LW 9:31.

32. John Dewey, *Reconstruction in Philosophy*, p. 94.

33. John Dewey, *The Quest for Certainty*, pp. 5, 7.

34. *Ibid.*, p. 14.

35. John Dewey, "The Influence of Darwin on Philosophy," in MW 4:12.

36. John Dewey, *The Quest for Certainty,* pp. 28–29, 31, 240.

37. John Dewey, *Experience and Nature,* p. 51. John Dewey, *Human Nature and Conduct,* in MW 14:178–79.

38. John Dewey, *A Common Faith,* pp. 31–32; John Dewey, *The Quest for Certainty,* pp. 28–29.

39. John Dewey, *The Quest for Certainty,* pp. 7–8, 26–27.

40. John Dewey, "Anti-Naturalism in Extremis," in LW 15:48, 55.

41. John Dewey, *A Common Faith,* p. 48.

42. John Dewey, *Experience and Nature,* pp. 40–41.

43. John Dewey, "Anti-Naturalism in Extremis," p. 58; John Dewey, "Religion and the Intellectuals," p. 133.

44. John Dewey, "Anti-Naturalism in Extremis," pp. 58–59.

45. John Dewey, "The Influence of Darwin on Philosophy," p. 14.

46. William James, "The Will to Believe," in Joseph Ratner, ed., *The Will to Believe and Other Essays in Popular Philosophy* (New York: Longmans, Green, 1896); William James, *The Varieties of Religious Experience* (New York: University Books, 1963), chapter 20 and postscript.

47. White, *Science and Sentiment in America,* pp. 166–69.

48. See John Herman Randall, Jr., "The Changing Impact of Darwin on Philosophy," *Journal of the History of Ideas* (October-December, 1961), 22:437, 439–41, 446–48.

49. John Dewey,"The Subject Matter of Metaphysical Inquiry," in MW 8:3–6. First published in *Journal of Philosophy, Psychology and Scientific Methods* (1915), 12:337–45.

50. John Dewey, *Experience and Nature,* pp. 52, 308.

51. John Dewey, "Half Hearted Naturalism," in LW 3:75–76. First published in *Journal of Philosophy* (1927), 24:57–64. For a critique of Dewey's approach to metaphysics, see Rorty, *The Consequences of Pragmatism,* pp. 72–88; Alexander, *John Dewey's Theory of Art, Experience and Nature,* pp. 57–118; and Boisvert, *Dewey's Metaphysics.*

52. John Dewey, "The Influence of Darwin on Philosophy," pp. 3–4.

53. John Dewey, "What I Believe," in LW 5:271.

54. John Dewey, *Reconstruction in Philosophy,* p. 260.

55. John Dewey, *Experience and Nature,* pp. 63, 66.

56. John Dewey, *Reconstruction in Philosophy,* p. 114.

57. John Dewey, *Experience and Nature,* pp. 49–50.

58. John Dewey, "The Philosophic World of Herbert Spencer," in MW 3:209. First published in *Philosophical Review* (1904), 13:159–75.

59. John Dewey to Scudder Klyce, June 19, 1915, John Dewey Papers. Dewey provided a useful clarification of what the term "pluralism" meant to him in 1902, in his entry on this topic in James Mark Baldwin, ed., *Dictionary of Philosophy and Psychology* (New York: Macmillan, 1902), vol. 2. He notes that "James has probably done more than anyone else to give it [pluralism] currency" and that "the needs which pluralism endeavors to serve are (1) the possibility of real change . . .; (2) the possibility of real variety . . .; (3) the possibility of freedom, as a self-initiating and moving power inherent in every real *qua* real." Reprinted in MW 2:204.

60. John Dewey, *Reconstruction in Philosophy,* pp. 110, 114.

61. John Dewey, "Force, Violence and Law," in MW 10:212. First published in *New Republic* (1916), 5:295.

62. John Dewey, *Reconstruction in Philosophy,* p. 113.

63. For a full discussion of the problems with Dewey's writings on contingency, see Robert E. Dewey, *The Philosophy of John Dewey.*

64. John Dewey, *The Quest for Certainty,* p. 195.

65. John Dewey, *Experience and Nature,* p. 47.

66. John Dewey, *The Quest for Certainty,* pp. 160–62.

67. *Ibid.,* pp. 184–85, 198–99.

68. John Dewey, *Experience and Nature,* p. 67.

69. John Dewey, *The Quest for Certainty,* p. 199.

70. *Ibid.*

71. John Dewey, *Experience and Nature,* pp. x-xi, 54–55, 60–63, 66–68.

72. John Dewey, *Experience and Nature,* pp. 138, 162, 186–87.

73. John Dewey, *The Quest for Certainty,* pp. 186, 191.

74. John Dewey, *Experience and Nature,* pp. 48, 207.

75. *Ibid.,* pp. 198, 200, 208, 212.

76. John Dewey, *The Quest for Certainty,* pp. 20, 33.

77. *Ibid.,* pp. 17–18, 20, 175.

78. John Dewey, *Experience and Nature,* p. 28.

79. *Ibid.,* pp. 26–29. Dewey, *The Quest for Certainty,* pp. 33–36, 175, 201.

80. John Dewey, *Experience and Nature,* p. 27.

81. *Ibid.,* p. 82. Dewey seems to be asserting that the right brain as well as the left brain apprehends real qualities of things.

82. John Dewey, *The Quest for Certainty,* pp. 187, 190–91.

83. John Dewey, *Experience and Nature,* p. 295.

84. *Ibid.,* pp. 74–75, 75–76, 81–82, 93. Dewey, *The Quest for Certainty,* p. 187. For a careful discussion of the issues involved in Dewey's theory of immediate quality, see Alexander, *John Dewey's Theory of Art, Experience and Nature.*

85. John Dewey, *Experience and Nature,* pp. 87, 94–95.
86. *Ibid.,* pp. 28–29.
87. *Ibid.,* p. 6.
88. John Dewey, *The Quest for Certainty,* pp. 175–76.
89. John Dewey, *Experience and Nature,* pp. 5–6, 74–75, 81–83.
90. John Dewey, *The Quest for Certainty,* p. 191.
91. John Dewey, *Experience and Nature,* pp. 83, 93.
92. *Ibid.,* pp. 85–88.
93. *Ibid.,* pp. 310–11. John Dewey, *The Quest for Certainty,* pp. 238–39; John Dewcy, *Reconstruction in Philosophy,* pp. 147–48, 149–50; John Dewey, *A Common Faith,* pp. 32–33.
94. John Dewey, *The Quest for Certainty,* pp. 241, 243.
95. John Dewey, *Experience and Nature,* pp. 268–69. See also John Dewey, *Reconstruction in Philosophy,* in MW 12:152.

N I N E: *The Moral Life in an Evolving World*

1. John Dewey, "Creative Democracy—The Task Before Us," in LW 14:227.
2. John Dewey, *Experience and Nature,* in LW 1:298.
3. John Dewey, *The Quest for Certainty,* in LW 4:241.
4. *Ibid.,* p. 211.
5. John Dewey, *Experience and Nature,* pp. 298, 301–02.
6. John Dewey, *The Quest for Certainty,* pp. 180–81.
7. *Ibid.,* pp. 235–36; John Dewey, *Reconstruction in Philosophy,* in MW 12:164, 165.
8. John Dewey, *The Quest for Certainty,* p. 232.
9. *Ibid.,* p. 110.
10. Regarding the distinctive contributions of Dewey in comparison with Peirce and James in the area of theory of knowledge and logic, see R.W. Sleeper, *The Necessity of Pragmatism,* and Stephen Toulmin, "Introduction," in LW 4:vii–xxii.
11. John Dewey, *Reconstruction in Philosophy,* pp. 169–70.
12. John Dewey, *The Quest for Certainty,* pp. 110, 157. For a discussion of the way Dewey's theory of knowlege parallels that of Martin Heidegger and Ludwig Wittgenstein, see Richard Rorty, *Philosophy and the Mirror of Nature* (Princeton: Princeton University Press, 1979), and Toulmin, "Introduction," in LW 4:vii–xxii.
13. John Dewey, *Reconstruction in Philosophy,* p. 663.
14. See John Dewey, *How We Think,* ch. 5, in MW 6:224–32; Dewey,

The Quest for Certainty, p. 189. See also Hook, *John Dewey: An Intellectual Portrait,* pp. 95–97.

15. John Dewey, *The Quest for Certainty,* pp. 230–31.

16. *Ibid.,* p. 213.

17. John Dewey, *Experience and Nature,* p. 297.

18. *Ibid.,* pp. 296–97, 300–05, 315–20.

19. John Dewey, *The Quest for Certainty,* pp. 204–06.

20. *Ibid.,* p. 208.

21. *Ibid.,* p. 212.

22. John Dewey, *Theory of Valuation,* in LW 13:213. First published as vol. 2, no. 4, *International Encyclopedia of Unified Science* (Chicago: University of Chicago Press, 1939).

23. *Ibid.,* pp. 246–49.

24. John Dewey, *Individualism, Old and New,* in LW 5:112.

25. John Dewey, *The Quest for Certainty,* pp. 221–22.

26. John Dewey, *Ethics,* in LW 7:271–72; John Dewey, *Human Nature and Conduct,* in MW 14:130–31.

27. John Dewey, *Theory of Valuation,* pp. 249–50.

28. John Dewey, *Ethics,* p. 268.

29. John Dewey, *Human Nature and Conduct,* pp. 176, 177.

30. John Dewey, *Ethics,* p. 269.

31. John Dewey, *Human Nature and Conduct,* pp. 147–48, 149–51; Dewey, *Ethics,* pp. 273–74.

32. John Dewey, *Ethics,* pp. 268–70.

33. *Ibid.,* pp. 273–74, 278, 279.

34. *Ibid.,* pp. 242, 271.

35. *Ibid.,* pp. 267–68, 271.

36. *Ibid.,* pp. 251–52, 270, 299–300.

37. John Dewey, *Reconstruction in Philosophy,* pp. 173–74.

38. John Dewey, *Ethics,* p. 298.

39. John Dewey, *Art as Experience,* in LW 10:349–51.

40. *Ibid.,* pp. 255–59, 290. For a further discussion of the fundamental role of love in morals, see also *Art as Experience,* pp. 351–52.

41. John Dewey, *Reconstruction in Philosophy,* p. 172.

42. John Dewey, "What I Believe," in LW 5:271.

43. John Dewey, *Reconstruction in Philosophy,* pp. 174–77. John Dewey to Scudder Klyce, May 6, and May 15, 1915. Scudder Klyce Papers, General Correspondence: John Dewey, Manuscript Division, Library of Congress, Washington, D.C.

44. John Dewey, *Theory of Valuation,* pp. 231–33.

45. John Dewey, *Reconstruction in Philosophy*, p. 173.

46. *Ibid.*, pp. 176, 180.

47. John Dewey, *Ethics*, p. 279.

48. *Ibid.*, pp. 257, 275–83.

49. John Dewey, *Experience and Nature*, pp. 308, 311, 321.

50. John Dewey, *Reconstruction in Philosophy*, p. 181.

51. George Santayana, "Dewey's Naturalistic Metaphysics," in LW 3:370. First published in *Journal of Philosophy* (1925), 22:673–88.

52. John Dewey, "Half-Hearted Naturalism," in LW 3:80–81. First published in *Journal of Philosophy* (1927), 24:57–64.

53. John Dewey, *Individualism, Old and New*, p. 121.

54. John Dewey, *Human Nature and Conduct*, pp. 95–98.

55. John Dewey, *Democracy and Education*, in MW 9:49.

56. John Dewey, *Experience and Education*, in LW 13:19.

57. John Dewey, *Ethics*, p. 170.

58. John Dewey, *Human Nature and Conduct*, pp. 196–97.

59. John Dewey, *Ethics*, pp. 285–92, 295.

60. *Ibid.*, pp. 287, 295.

61. *Ibid.*, pp. 170–71.

62. John Dewey, *Democracy and Education*, pp. 49–54, 82–83.

63. *Ibid.*, p. 59.

64. John Dewey, *Reconstruction in Philosophy*, p. 185.

65. John Dewey, *Experience and Education*, pp. 11–12.

66. *Ibid.*, pp. 19–20.

67. Sidney Hook, *Education and the Taming of Power* (LaSalle, Ill.: Open Court, 1973), p. 25.

68. John Dewey, *Democracy and Education*, p. 61.

69. *Ibid.*, p. 56.

70. *Ibid.*, pp. 107–17.

71. John Dewey, "Self-Realization as the Moral Ideal," in EW 4:50.

72. *Ibid.*, p. 59.

73. John Dewey, *Experience and Education*, pp. 29–30. See also Dewey, "Self-Realization as the Moral Ideal," p. 50.

74. John Dewey, *Democracy and Education*, p. 61.

75. John Dewey, *Reconstruction in Philosophy*, pp. 181, 184.

76. *Ibid.*, pp. 184–86.

77. John Dewey, *Ethics*, pp. 210–11.

78. *Ibid.*, p. 308.

79. John Dewey, *Reconstruction in Philosophy*, pp. 185–86.

80. John Dewey, *Ethics*, p. 304.

81. *Ibid.*, p. 302.

82. *Ibid.*, pp. 285–87, 306.

83. *Ibid.*, pp. 306–08.

84. *Ibid.*, p. 306.

85. John Dewey, "Philosophies of Freedom," in LW 3:111.

86. John Dewey, *Experience and Education*, p. 39.

87. John Dewey, "Philosophies of Freedom," p. 113.

88. John Dewey, "Science, Belief and the Public," in MW 15:51.

89. John Dewey and Goodwin Watson, "The Forward View: A Free Teacher in a Free Society," in LW 11:538–40. See earlier discussion of the democratic ideal in chapter 5.

90. John Dewey, *Democracy and Education*, pp. 326–27.

91. *Ibid.*, p. 113.

92. John Dewey, *Individualism, Old and New*, pp. 45–47, 56, 66–75.

93. *Ibid.*, pp. 45–46, 84–85.

94. *Ibid.*, pp. 52–85.

95. *Ibid.*, p. 100.

96. *Ibid.*, pp. 74, 100.

97. *Ibid.*, pp. 96–98, 104–05.

98. John Dewey, "Unity and Progress," in EW 9:72. First published in *World Tomorrow* (March 8, 1933), 16:232–233.

99. John Dewey, *Individualism, Old and New*, pp. 54–55, 105–08.

100. John Dewey, *Impressions of Soviet Russia*, in LW 3:203–50. Dewey's essays on the Soviet Union first appeared in the *New Republic* in November and December 1928. They were published in 1929 by the *New Republic* in book form under the title *Impressions of Soviet Russia and the Revolutionary World: Mexico-China-Turkey*. See also Dykhuizen, *John Dewey*, pp. 235–39.

101. John Dewey, "Why I Am Not a Communist," in LW 9:91–95. First published in *Modern Monthly* (April 1934), 8:135–37.

102. John Dewey, "A Critique of American Civilization," in LW 3:144. First published in *World Tomorrow* (1928), 11:394–95.

103. John Dewey, *Individualism, Old and New*, pp. 121, 123.

104. John Dewey, "What I Believe, Revised," in LW 14:91–92.

105. John Dewey, "In Response," in LW 5:422.

106. John Dewey, *The Quest for Certainty*, p. 82.

107. John Dewey, *Reconstruction in Philosophy*, p. 120.

108. *Ibid.*, p. 146.

109. *Ibid.*, p. 108.

110. *Ibid.*, pp. 181–82.

111. John Dewey, *Experience and Nature*, p. 304.

112. *Ibid.,* pp. 325–26.

113. John Dewey, *Reconstruction in Philosophy,* p. 171; John Dewey, *The Quest for Certainty,* pp. 226–28.

114. John Dewey, "Fundamentals," in MW 15:7.

115. John Dewey, *The Quest for Certainty,* p. 86.

116. John Dewey "Intelligence and Morals," in MW 4:39.

117. John Dewey, "Anti-Naturalism in Extremis," in LW 15:49.

T E N: *Religious Humanism*

1. John Dewey, "What I Believe," in LW 5:276–77.

2. Dykhuizen, *John Dewey,* pp. 243–45, 271.

3. *Ibid.,* pp. 229–30. Sidney Ratner, "Introduction," in LW 6:xviii–xix. For Dewey's articles in the *People's Lobby Bulletin,* see LW:5, LW:6, LW:9.

4. Dykhuizen, *John Dewey,* pp. 223, 251–52; Charles F. Howlett, *Troubled Philosopher: John Dewey and the Struggle for World Peace* (Port Washington, N.Y.: Kennikat Press, 1977), pp. 121–22.

5. "John Dewey Assails the Major Parties," *New York Times,* October 14, 1929, p. 2. See LW 5:442. "Dewey Asks Norris to Lead New Party," *New York Times,* December 26, 1930, p. 1. See LW 5:445.

6. John Dewey, "Imperative Need: A New Radical Party," in LW 9:76–80. First published in *Common Sense* (September 1933), 2:6–7.

7. John Dewey, "The Great Experiment and the Future," in LW 3:245–46. First published in *New Republic* (December 19, 1928), 57:134–37.

8. John Dewey, *Individualism, Old and New,* in LW 5:71–72.

9. *Ibid.,* p. 83.

10. John Dewey, "What I Believe," pp. 273–74.

11. *Ibid.,* p. 273.

12. "A Humanist Manifesto," in *The New Humanist* (1933), 6:1–4.

13. Mason Olds, *Religious Humanism in America: Dietrich, Reese and Potter* (Washington, D.C.: University Press of America, 1978), pp. 21, 34.

14. *Ibid.,* p. 21.

15. John Dewey, "What Humanism Means to Me," in LW 5:266.

16. Jo Ann Boydston, "Textual Commentary," in LW 9:448.

17. John Gersham Machen, *Christianity and Liberalism* (New York: Macmillan, 1923), pp. 6–8.

18. Joseph Wood Krutch, *The Modern Temper: A Study and A Confession* (New York: Harcourt, Brace, 1929), pp. 44–54, 233–38, 246–49.

19. *Ibid.,* pp. 63, 99, 101, 141, 182–83, 207, 247–49.

20. *John Dewey's Personal and Professional Library: A Checklist,* compiled

by Jo Ann Boydston, Bibliographical Contributions, no. 10 (Carbondale: Southern Illinois University Press, 1982), p. 60.

21. Mordecai M. Kaplan, *Judaism as a Civilization: Toward a Reconstruction of American Jewish Life* (New York: Macmillan, 1935), pp. 173–85, 311–49. See also Joseph L. Blau, *Modern Varieties of Judaism* (New York: Columbia University Press, 1966), pp. 167–72.

22. Shailer Mathews, *The Faith of Modernism* (New York: AMS Press, 1924, 1969), p. 8.

23. Harry Emerson Fosdick, *As I See Religion* (New York: Harper and Brothers, 1932), pp. 6, 11, 21, 26–27, 40, 48; William R. Hutchinson, *The Modernist Impulse* (Cambridge, Mass.: Harvard University Press, 1976), pp. 274–86.

24. Bertrand Russell, "A Free Man's Worship," in *Mysticism and Logic,* pp. 46–57 (London: Longmans, Green, 1918).

25. Olds, *Religious Humanism in America,* p. 157. See also Raymond F. Bulman, " 'The God of Our Children': The Humanist Reconstruction of God," in Maurice Wohlgelernter, ed., *History, Religion and Spiritual Democracy: Essays in Honor of Joseph L. Blau,* pp. 35–52 (New York: Columbia University Press, 1980).

26. Benny Kraut, *From Reform Judaism to Ethical Culture: The Religious Evolution of Felix Adler* (Cincinnati: Hebrew Union College Press, 1979), pp. 69, 101–22. *Ibid.,* p. 69. The quotation is from Matthew Arnold's *Literature and Dogma: An Essay towards a Better Apprehension of the Bible* (New York: Macmillan, 1874), pp. 57–58, 322, 330, 336.

27. Horace L. Freiss, in Fannia Weingartner, ed., *Felix Adler and Ethical Culture: Memories and Studies,* pp. 8–10, 229–31, 252–53. (New York: Columbia University Press, 1981).

28. *Ibid.,* pp. 229–32, 248, 250–52.

29. Edward L. Ericson, "Ethical Culture Since Felix Adler: An Afterword," in Freiss, *Felix Adler and Ethical Culture,* pp. 258–59.

30. Olds, *Religious Humanism in America,* pp. 30–52.

31. *Ibid.,* pp. 1–3.

32. Walter Lippmann, *A Preface to Morals* (New York: Time, Inc., 1964), pp. 33–34, 305–09.

33. Charles Potter, *Humanism: A New Religion* (New York: Simon and Schuster, 1930); C.W. Reese, *Humanist Religion* (New York: Macmillan and Co., 1931). See also Charles F. Potter, *Humanizing Religion* (New York: Harper, 1933).

34. John Dewey, "A God or The God?" in LW 9:213–22. In this essay Dewey reviews Henry Nelson Wieman, Douglas Clyde Macintosh and Max

Carl Otto, *Is There a God? A Conversation* (Chicago: Willett, Clark, 1932). The essays in this volume originally appeared in the *Christian Century* between February 10, and August 24, 1932. See Jo Ann Boydston, "Textual Commentary," in LW 9:446–47.

35. Richard Wightman Fox, *Reinhold Niebuhr: A Biography* (New York: Pantheon Books, 1985), chs. 3–6; "Intellectual Autobiography of Reinhold Niebuhr," in *Reinhold Niebuhr: His Religious, Social and Political Thought,* in Charles W. Kegley and Robert W. Bretall, eds., *The Library of Living Theology,* vol. 2, pp. 7–8 (New York: Macmillan, 1956).

36. Fox, *Reinhold Niebuhr,* pp. 129–35.

37. "Intellectual Autobiography of Reinhold Niebuhr," pp. 8–9; Fox, *Reinhold Niebuhr,* pp. 117, 160–61.

38. Reinhold Niebuhr, *Moral Man and Immoral Society; A Study in Ethics and Politics* (New York: Scribner's, 1932), pp. xiii–xv.

39. Reinhold Niebuhr, "After Capitalism—What?" *World Tomorrow* (March 1, 1933), 16:203–05. Reprinted in LW 9:403–4.

40. Niebuhr, *Moral Man and Immoral Society,* p. xv.

41. *Ibid.,* p. 81.

42. Fox, *Reinhold Niebuhr,* pp. 164–66. Fox writes of "Niebuhr's almost willful failure to do justice to the liberal tradition." He comments that "Mill and Dewey were his intellectual comrades-in-arms in the campaign to root human values securely in a scientific era. They were his colleagues in toppling all absolutisms, whether imposed by defenders of the past or created by worshippers of the future" (p. 166).

43. John Dewey, "Intelligence and Power," in LW 9:108–11. First published in *New Republic* (April 25, 1934), 78:306–07.

44. Note, Professor James A. Martin, Jr. to SR, March, 1989. Interview with James A. Martin, Jr., November 21, 1988. Martin's comments are based on recollections of a conversation with Niebuhr at the home of Professor Roger Shinn in the early- or mid-1960s.

45. Reinhold Niebuhr, *An Interpretation of Christian Ethics* (New York: Meridien Books, 1958), pp. 74, 87. This volume was first published in 1935, and it contains Niebuhr's first systematic attempt to restate the classical Christian doctrine of sin. See also Reinhold Niebuhr, *The Nature and Destiny of Man: A Christian Interpretation* (New York: Scribner's, 1941), pp. 3–4, 13–17, 269–70.

46. "Intellectual Autobiography of Reinhold Niebuhr," p. 6.

47. Niebuhr, *An Interpretation of Christian Ethics,* p. 75.

48. *Ibid.,* p. 92. Niebuhr, *Faith and History: A Comparison of Christian and Modern Views of History* (New York: Scribner's, 1949), pp. 122–23.

49. John Dewey, *The Quest for Certainty,* in LW 4:240–41, 248.

50. *Ibid.,* pp. 242–44.

51. Matthew Arnold, *Literature and Dogma,* p. 21. Arnold writes: "Religion, if we follow the intention of human thought and human language in the use of the word, is ethics heightened, enkindled, lit up by feeling; the passage from morality to religion is made when morality is applied emotion. And the true meaning of religion is thus not simply *morality,* but *morality touched by emotion.* And this new elevation and inspiration of morality is well marked by the word 'righteousness' " (pp. 20–21).

52. William James, *The Varieties of Religious Experience,* Joseph Ratner, ed. (New Hyde Park, N.Y.: University Books, 1963), p. 28.

53. *Ibid.,* p. 45.

54. *Ibid.,* pp. 51–52.

55. John Dewey, *A Common Faith,* in LW 9:4–9.

56. *Ibid.,* pp. 8–11.

57. *Ibid.,* pp 10–14.

58. John Dewey, *Art as Experience,* in LW 10:20–23.

59. John Dewey, *A Common Faith,* pp. 12–14.

60. *Ibid.* Dewey may have derived this idea originally from his understanding of Kant's distinction between the functions of the understanding and reason. For example, in an exposition of Kant's philosophy he writes: "While Reason furnished ideals of unity and complete totality, which go beyond the scope of the understanding, they are for us unrealizable ideals" ("James Marsh and American Philosophy," in LW 5:185).

61. John Dewey, *A Common Faith,* pp. 14, 56.

62. James, *Varieties of Religious Experience,* pp. 349, n. 1, 175–76.

63. *Ibid.,* pp. 508–19, 523–25.

64. John Dewey, *A Common Faith,* pp. 10–13.

65. Paul Tillich, *The Dynamics of Faith* (New York: Harper & Brothers, 1957), pp. 55–69. In this work Tillich provides a very helpful analysis of the two major elements in religious experience

66. See chapter 1.

67. Jo Ann Boydston, "Textual Commentary," in LW 5:514–15.

68. Corliss Lamont, ed., *Dialogue on John Dewey* (New York: Horizon Press, 1959), pp. 15–16, 20.

69. John Dewey, *A Common Faith,* p. 15.

70. *Ibid.,* p. 16.

71. *Ibid.,* p. 23.

72. *Ibid.,* p. 19.

73. Tillich, *The Dynamics of Faith,* pp. 1–8, 105–11.

74. John Dewey, *A Common Faith,* p. 44.

75. *Ibid.,* p. 55.

76. *Ibid.,* pp. 28–29, 40–41, 47–49.

77. *Ibid.,* p. 53.

78. John Dewey, "What I Believe," p. 274.

79. John Dewey, *A Common Faith,* pp. 54–55.

80. John Dewey, *Reconstruction in Philosophy,* in MW 12:201.

81. John Dewey, *A Common Faith*, pp. 51–52.

82. Dewey, *A Common Faith,* p. 54. See also John Dewey, *Freedom and Culture,* in LW 13:65–98.

83. *Ibid.,* pp. 32, 51.

84. Søren Kierkegaard, *Sickness Unto Death,* tr. by Walter Lowrie (Princeton: Princeton University Press, 1941, 1954), p. 226.

85. John Dewey, "The Value of Historical Christianity," *Monthly Bulletin* (November 1889), 11:33–35. See LW 17:529–33. See chapter 3 for a discussion of this essay.

86. John Dewey, *Reconstruction in Philosophy,* p. 201.

87. *New York Times,* April 8, 1928, sec. 9, p. 1, col. 2.

88. John Dewey, "Intimations of Mortality," in LW 11:425–27. See also Corliss Lamont, *Yes to Life* (New York: Horizon Press, 1981), pp. 33, 47, 82.

ELEVEN: *Nature, God, and Religous Feeling*

1. John Dewey, "Some Factors in Mutual National Understanding," in MW 13:265–66.

2. *Ibid.;* Hu Shih, "The Civilizations of the East and the West," in Charles A. Beard, ed., *Whither Mankind: A Panorama of Modern Civilization,* p. 37 (New York: Longmans, Green, 1928).

3. John Dewey to Scudder Klyce, May 13, 1927, Scudder Klyce Papers, General Correspondence: John Dewey: Manuscript Division, Library of Congress, Washington, D.C. In *Art as Experience* Dewey equates achievement of a deep enduring adjustment that gives life a religious quality with "the sense of being founded on a rock." See LW 10:23.

4. John Dewey to Scudder Klyce, October 18, 1927.

5. John Dewey to Scudder Klyce, October 21, 1927.

6. Poem #29 in Boydston, ed., *The Poems of John Dewey,* p. 20. See discussion of this poem in chapter 7.

7. John Dewey to Scudder Klyce, April 30, 1927.

8. John Dewey, *A Common Faith,* in LW 9:17.

9. John Dewey, *The Quest for Certainty,* in LW 9:244–46.

10. Randall, "The Religion of Shared Experience," pp. 241–47.

11. George Santayana, *Reason in Religion,* vol. 3 of *The Life of Reason; or the Phases of Human Progress,* 5 vols. (New York: Scribner's, 1905), pp. 6–13, 43, 213, 176–277.

12. *Ibid.,* pp. 179, 184, 190, 193–95, 212, 276. "There is one other phase or possible overtone of religion," explains Santayana, which is mysticism. He denies to mystical experience a place at the summit of spiritual experience: "Mysticism is the most primitive of feelings, and only visits formed minds in moments of intellectual arrest and dissolution." However, it is not without a certain elemental importance, for it involves "the ancient, overgrown feelings of vitality, dependence, inclusion" that constitute "primordial assurances" and "rudimentary joys" on which the Life of Reason builds and which it refines. *Ibid.,* pp. 277, 279.

13. *Ibid.,* pp. 191–92.

14. John Dewey, "Philosophy as a Fine Art," in LW 3:287–89. First published in *New Republic* (1928), 53:352–54.

15. John Dewey, "Religion in Our Schools," in MW 9:176.

16. John Dewey, *A Common Faith,* p. 36.

17. *Ibid.,* pp. 18, 36.

18. John Dewey, *The Quest for Certainty,* p. 244.

19. John Dewey, "The New Psychology," in EW 1:51.

20. John Dewey, "Intelligence and Morals," in MW 4:46.

21. John Dewey, *Art as Experience,* p. 34.

22. John Dewey, "As the Chinese Think," in MW 13:222.

23. *Ibid.,* pp. 222–24.

24. *Ibid.,* pp. 222–24, 227.

25. See chapter 7.

26. John Dewey, "Three Contemporary Philosophers," in MW 12:227.

27. John Dewey, *Experience and Nature,* in LW 1:313. Dewey, *Art as Experience,* p. 199.

28. John Dewey, *Human Nature and Conduct,* in MW 14:180–81, 226.

29. *Ibid.* See Randall, "The Religion of Shared Experience," p. 252.

30. Dewey, *Human Nature and Conduct.,* pp. 180–81.

31. *Ibid.,* p. 227.

32. *Ibid.*

33. John Dewey, *A Common Faith,* pp. 56–57.

34. John Dewey, *Human Nature and Conduct,* pp. 226–27.

35. Reply to Aubrey and Wieman in "Is John Dewey a Theist?" in LW 9:295.

36. John Dewey, *Experience and Nature,* pp. 313–14.

37. John Herman Randall, Jr. makes the following comment about the statement under discussion from *Experience and Nature:* "These paragraphs, a classic example of natural piety, attest that Dewey has been able to find in the perception of man's oneness with nature the sources of as deep and profound a religious feeling as others have gained from more traditional attachments" ("The Religion of Shared Experience," p. 253).

38. John Dewey, *Human Nature and Conduct,* p. 180.

39. John Dewey, *Art as Experience,* p. 197.

40. John Dewey, "First Introduction to *Universe,*" in MW 13:412–20.

41. John Dewey, *Art as Experience,* p. 198.

42. John Dewey, *The Quest for Certainty,* p. 188.

43. John Dewey, *Art as Experience,* p. 196. For an excellent account of Dewey's theory of art, see Alexander, *John Dewey's Theory of Art, Experience and Nature.*

44. *Ibid.,* p. 197.

45. *Ibid.,* pp. 198–99.

46. John Dewey, *A Common Faith,* pp. 9–11, 25–27.

47. John Dewey, "Mystical Naturalism and Religious Humanism," in LW 11:84–85. See also Bernard Meland, "Mystical Naturalism and Religious Humanism," in LW 11:583–87.

48. John Dewey, *Art as Experience,* pp. 350–52.

49. Morrison, "Dewey and Wieman," in *Christian Century* (April 5, 1933), 50:448.

50. John Dewey, *Human Nature and Conduct,* p. 226.

51. John Dewey, "A God or The God?" in LW 9:213–28; "Dr. Dewey Replies," in LW 9:227–28.

52. "Dr. Dewey Replies," p. 224.

53. William Ernest Hocking, "What If God is Gone?" Review of *Is There a God? A Conversation* in *Christian Century* (March 8, 1933), 50: 330–31.

54. John Wright Buckham to Editor, *Christian Century* (March 8, 1933), 50:330–31.

55. John Dewey, "A God or The God?" pp. 219–21.

56. "Dr. Dewey Replies," pp. 226–27.

57. John Dewey, "A God or The God?" pp. 215–18, 221–22. John Dewey to Max Carl Otto, January 14, 1935, Otto Papers, as quoted by Jo Ann Boydston in "Textual Commentary," LW 9:455.

58. John Dewey, *A Common Faith,* pp. 29–30, 34.

59. *Ibid.,* pp. 29, 32–34.

60. *Ibid.,* pp. 30–31.

61. *Ibid.,* pp. 33–34, 36.

62. *Ibid.,* pp. 34–36.

63. *Ibid.,* p. 36.

64. *Ibid.,* p. 35.

65. John Dewey, "A God or The God?" pp. 220–21.

66. "Dr. Dewey Replies," p. 225; see also pp. 224, 226.

67. John Dewey, *A Common Faith,* pp. 35–36.

68. Hook, "Some Memories of John Dewey, 1859–1952," p. 114.

69. John Dewey to Max Otto, January 14, 1935, Max Otto Papers as quoted by Jo Ann Boydston, "Textual Commentary," in LW 9:455. John Herman Randall, Jr. reports that Dewey "has himself been willing, in private, to claim a fair share of the 'Christian spirit'; few would deny that rather ambiguous claim" ("The Religion of Shared Experience," p. 249).

70. Horace M. Kallen to Van Meter Ames, July 21, 1958, Van Meter Ames papers. Kallen adds in this letter: "Dewey has been a very great borrower and far less generous in his acknowledgements with far greater cause to be generous than James. I am sure your father must have been aware that Dewey had learned something from him, in its domain as significant as what he has learned from James. . . ."

71. Dewey to E.S. Ames, November 11, 1929, Edward Scribner Ames Papers, Southern Illinois University Archives, Collection 351. Edward Scribner Ames, "Religious Values in Perspective," in *Essays in Honor of John Dewey On the Occasion of His Seventieth Birthday,* pp. 23–35 (New York: Octagon Books, 1970).

72. *John Dewey's Personal and Professional Library: A Check List,* compiled by Jo Ann Boydston (Carbondale: Southern Illinois University Press, 1982), p. 4. Ames devoted five chapters in *Religion* to developing an idea of the nature of God consistent with empirical naturalism and social science. Reflecting on the meaning of the idea of God from an historical perspective he writes:

From such a survey, the lesser gods, and the great gods of all religions, are seen to be the life-process itself, idealized and personified. Every god bears the marks of the habits and moral character of his worshippers, and he undergoes the changes and transformations that profoundly affect his people. When they are militant, so is he; when they are peaceful, so is he; when they have a monarchy, he is a monarch; when they become democratic, he becomes friendly, renounces external authority and rules by reason and justice. God is shown to be the spirit of a people, and in so far as there is a world of humanity, God is the soul of social values, the embodiment of ideals, the reality of the good and the beautiful, the meaning of the world.

Regarding his own theology, Ames explains that "the reality to which the term God applies . . . is . . . the reality of a social process belonging to the actual world. . . . The word God is not properly taken to mean a particular person, or single factual existence, but the order of nature including men and all the processes of an aspiring social life." The reality of God is not identical with all of nature; rather it includes "the reality of the world in certain aspects and functions." God is to be identified with the order and beauty found in nature and with the functions of intelligence, imaginative vision, and love wherever they manifest themselves in the life of individuals and institutions. "Reality conceived as friendly, as furnishing support for men's existence and for the realization of ideal ends, is God." Even though Ames did not conceive of God as a person, he, nevertheless, argued that since reality includes persons and the aspiration to realize personality, it is appropriate to call the reality of God personal in nature. God is in a real sense the Spirit of a people, the Oversoul, and the being of God is found in their shared consciousness and values. From this point of view God may be symbolized as a person, and prayer retains meaningful psychological and social functions, the chief of which is fostering in people the attitudes necessary for actualizing the ideal and the divine. The idea of God is a central concept in Ames' philosophy and he developed the idea much more fully than Dewey did. He also used traditional theological language more freely than Dewey, as, for example, when he refers to God as personal in nature. The root of the chief differences between Ames and Dewey is that Ames was for forty years a practicing minister. Chicago was full of liberal experiments, and Ames used his church to try to develop a religious community life consistent with the values of scientific inquiry and creative democracy. His philosophy of God reflects the concerns and interests of a man who had an ongoing commitment to a religious institution and a greater appreciation of the role of religious rituals and symbols than Dewey. However, Ames formulated the ideals of his church in a fashion that Dewey could well appreciate: "This church practices union; has no creed; seeks to make religion as intelligent as science; as appealing as art; as vital as the day's work; as intimate as the home; as inspiring as love." It was probably the example of churches like that of Ames as well as the Ethical Culture Society that led Dewey in *A Common Faith* to argue that his approach to religious life need not mean "the destruction of churches that now exist" but "would rather offer the means of a recovery of vitality." See Edward Scribner Ames, *Religion* (New York: Henry Holt, 1929), pp. 132–84, 241; Ames, "Theory in Practice," in Vergilius Ferm, ed., *Contemporary American Theology: Theological Autobiographies,* second series, p. 10 (New York: Round Table Press, 1933).

73. For a bibliography of reviews of *A Common Faith,* see Jo Ann Boydston, "Textual Commentary," in LW 9:452–53, n. 38.

74. Corliss Lamont, "John Dewey Capitulates to 'God'," in *New Masses* (July 31, 1934), 12:23–24. See also Corliss Lamont, "The Right Reverend Re-Definer," *New Masses* (October 2, 1934), 13:39. Norbert Guterman, "John Dewey's Credo," in LW 9:423–25. First published in *New Republic* (February 20, 1935), 82:53.

75. A. Eustace Haydon, "Mr. Dewey on Religion and God," *Journal of Religion* (January 1935), 15:22–25.

76. John Wright Buckham, "God and the Ideal: Professor Dewey Reinterprets Religion," in *Journal of Religion* (January 1935), 15:1–2, 5–7. See also J.W. Buckham, "Religious Experience and Personality; A Reply to Professor Wieman," *Journal of Religion* (January 1935), 15:309–15.

77. Reinhold Niebuhr "A Footnote on Religion," *Nation* (September 26, 1934), 139:358–59.

78. Henry Nelson Wieman, "John Dewey's Common Faith," in LW 9:426, 434. First published in *Christian Century* (November 14, 1934), 51:1450–52.

79. Wieman to Editor in "Is John Dewey a Theist?" *Christian Century,* (December 5, 1934), 51:1552–53.

80. Wieman, "John Dewey's Common Faith," p. 433.

81. Aubrey to Editor in "Is John Dewey a Theist?" in LW 9:435–37. First published in *Christian Century* (December 5, 1934), 51:1550. Henry Nelson Wieman to Editor in "Is John Dewey a Theist?" in LW 9:439. First published in *Christian Century* (December 5, 1934), 51:1550–51.

82. John Dewey to Editor in reply to Aubrey and Wieman in "Is John Dewey a Theist?" in LW 9:294. First published in *Christian Century* (December 5, 1934), 51:1551–52.

83. Wieman to Editor in reply to Aubrey and Dewey in "Is John Dewey A Theist?" in *Christian Century* (December 5, 1934), 51:1552–53.

84. Morrison, "The Philosophers and God," *Christian Century* (December 12, 1934), 51:1582–84.

85. Charles Hartshorne to Editor in *Christian Century* (January 9, 1935), 52:51–52.

86. See note by the Editor on Dewey's personal letter to Morrison in

"Three Questions for Professor Dewey," *Christian Century* (January 9, 1935), 52:52.

87. John Dewey to Otto, January 14, 1935, Otto Papers as quoted in Jo Ann Boydston, "Textual Commentary," in LW 9:455.

88. John Dewey to Corliss Lamont, July 28, 1935, as quoted in *Yes to Life: Memoirs of Corliss Lamont* (New York: Horizon Press, 1981), p. 81.

89. Jerome Nathanson, who became the leader of the New York Society for Ethical Culture, recalls Dewey saying to him some time after 1942 that he would omit the word "God," if he were to write another book along the lincs of *A Common Faith*. Dewey made this remark in the context of a conversation in which Nathanson told him that John L. Elliott, an early disciple of Felix Adler and a leader in the Ethical Culture Society, had once said: "I will never forgive John Dewey for using the word God in *A Common Faith*." Interview SR and Jerome Nathanson, July 26, 1972, New York City.

90. Charles Hartshorne, *Beyond Humanism: Essays in the Philosophy of Nature,* p. 56.

91. See, for example, *The Source of Human Good* (Carbondale, Ill.: Southern Illinois University Press, 1946), pp. 194–95, and Marvin C. Shaw, "Wieman's Misunderstanding of Dewey: The *Christian Century* Discussion," *Zygon* (March 1987), 22:7–19. For an example of the way the naturalistic tradition in theology of Ames, Dewey, and Wieman is being developed in the late twentieth century, see Gordon Kaufman, *Theology for a Nuclear Age* (Philadelphia: Westminster, 1985).

92. Horace M. Kallen to Van Meter Ames, July 21, 1958, Private collection of Van Meter Ames. Kallen writes about Edward Scribner Ames: "I was particularly impressed by his *Psychology of Religious Experience* which I know underlies Mordecai Kaplan's Judaist Reconstructionism . . ."; Bernard Martin, "Mordecai M. Kaplan and Reform Judaism," *Judaism* (Winter 1981), 3:73.

93. Mordecai M. Kaplan, *The Future of the American Jew* (New York: Macmillan, 1948), pp. xvii, xix, 284, 516. See also Joseph L. Blau, *Modern Varieties of Judaism* (New York: Columbia University Press, 1966), pp. 167–72.

94. Mordecai M. Kaplan, *The Meaning of God in Modern Jewish Religion* (New York: Reconstructionist Press, 1962), pp. 26–31, 40f, 54, 76, 89, 297.

95. *Ibid.,* pp. 29, 320–25.

96. Kaplan, *The Future of the American Jew,* p. 183. See Jacob B. Agus, "God in Kaplan's Philosophy," and William E. Kaufman, "The Transna-

tural Theology of Modecai M. Kaplan," *Judaism* (Winter 1981), 30:30–35, 45–52.

97. George Santayana, "Dewey's Naturalistic Metaphysics," *Journal of Philosophy* (1927), 22:673–88. See LW 3:375, 377, 380. It is also noteworthy that some critics like Benedetto Croce and Stephen Pepper have argued that Dewey's aesthetics involve certain Hegelian idealist strands of thought that are inconsistent with his naturalism and pragmatism. For a description of the controversy, see T. M. Alexander, *John Dewey's Theory of Art, Experience and Nature*, pp. 1–15.

98. Waldo Frank, "The Man Who Made Us What We Are," in *The New Yorker* (May 22, 1926), 2:15–16.

99. Martin Buber, *I and Thou*, tr. by Walter Kaufmann (New York: Scribner's, 1970), p. 127.

100. John Dewey, *Art as Experience*, p. 23.

101. See discussion of Dewey's exchanges with S. Klyce on this matter in chapter 7 and Dewey, "First Introduction to *Universe*," pp. 412–20. See also *Art as Experience*, pp. 197–99.

102. Buckham, "God and the Ideal: Professor Dewey Reinterprets Religion," p. 6 and "Religious Experience and Personality," pp. 312–13.

103. Walter T. Stace, who sought to combine empirical naturalism and mysticism, developed a concept of God along the lines being suggested. See W.T. Stace, *Religion and the Modern Mind* (New York: J.B. Lippincott, 1952) and *Mysticism and Philosophy* (New York: Macmillan, 1960). The philosphical naturalist John Herman Randall, Dewey's colleague at Columbia, found in Stace's work "a suggestive recognition of what I have called the religious dimension of experience." John Herman Randall, Jr., *Nature and Historical Experience: Essays in Naturalism and the Theory of History* (New York: Columbia University Press, 1958), p. 128, n. 10; Keiji Nishitani, *Religion and Nothingness*, tr. by Jan Van Bragt (Berkeley: University of California Press, 1982). See also Steven C. Rockefeller, "Nishitani Keiji and John Dewey's Naturalistic Humanism," in *The Religious Philosophy of Nishitani Keiji*, Taitetsu Unno, ed., pp. 201–56 (Berkeley: Asian Humanities Press, 1989).

TWELVE: *"A Gift of Grace"*

1. John Dewey, *Logic: Theory of Inquiry*, in LW 12:5. For a succinct overview of Dewey's contribution and related ongoing controversies regarding his work in logic, see Ernest Nagel, "Introduction," in LW 12:ix–xxvii.

2. "John Dewey, Great American Liberal, Denounces Russian Dictatorship," *Washington Post,* December 19, 1937.

3. John Dewey, *Freedom and Culture,* in LW 13:67–68, 97–98, 152, 185–88.

4. Dykhuizen, *John Dewey,* pp. 313–14.

5. See letters of John Dewey to Roberta Lowitz Grant, January 6, 1937; April 5, 1937; April 12, 1937; June 6, 1937; June 10, 1937; June 13, 1937. John Dewey Papers, Special Collections, Morris Library, Southern Illinois University.

6. John Dewey to Max Otto, March 5, 1947. Max C. Otto Papers, Division of Archives and Manuscripts, State Historical Society of Wisconsin, Madison, Wisconsin.

7. Dykhuizen, *John Dewey,* pp. 233–34, 313–14.

8. "The Case of Odell Waller," in LW 15:356–58. First published in *New York Times* (May 15, 1942), p. 18.

9. John Dewey, "The Case for Bertrand Russell," in LW 14:231–34; John Dewey, "Introduction," in *The Bertrand Russell Case,* in LW 14:357–59; John Dewey, "Social Realities versus Police Court Fictions," in LW 14:235–48.

10. John Dewey, "Anti-Naturalism in Extremis," in LW 15:54.

11. *Ibid.,* p. 56.

12. John Dewey, Contribution to "Religion and the Intellectuals," in LW 16:390–91.

13. It was not only the role of religious conservatives in public controversies that generated some strong feelings in Dewey. For example, he confided to a friend the following: "I got a rise out of a Catholic once who was concerned about the salvation of my soul by inquiring if what he wrote was a manifestation of Christian charity and telling him that though I had enough Christian *spirit* to forgive him personally his moral arrogance I couldn't forgive the Institution that had it as a result." John Dewey to Max Otto, July 19, 1947. Max C. Otto Papers.

14. John Dewey, "Religion and Morality in a Free Society," in LW 15:183.

15. Harry W. Laidler, ed., *John Dewey at Ninety: Addresses and Greetings on the Occasion of Dr. Dewey's Ninetieth Birthday Dinner, October 20, 1949* (New York: League for Industrial Democracy, 1949), pp. 4–30. Dykhuizen, *John Dewey,* p. 314.

16. John Dewey, "John Dewey Responds," in LW 17:86.

17. John Dewey, "From Absolutism to Experimentalism," in LW 5:155.

18. "John Dewey Responds," p. 86.

19. Ralph Barton Perry, "Dewey as Philosopher," in Laidler, ed., *John Dewey at Ninety,* p. 17.

20. Trigant Burrow, *Science and Man's Behavior: The Contribution of Phylobiology* (New York: Greenwood Press, 1953), pp. 46–47.

21. Toward the end of his career Dewey found what he believed to be further scientific confirmation for this viewpoint in the work of Adelbert Ames, Jr. and Hadley Cantril, whose experimental research in visual perception seemed to demonstrate that "our basic habits of perception are formed and framed in terms of our relations with our fellow human beings," which provide an inclusive and underlying frame of reference. See John Dewey to Max Otto, July 19, 1947. Max C. Otto Papers. Ames and Cantril adopted in their psychological studies the transactional point of view worked out by Dewey and Bentley. See "The Nature of Scientific Inquiry," in Albert C. Cantril, ed., *Psychology, Humanism and Scientific Inquiry; The Selected Essays of Hadley Cantril* (New Brunswick, N.J.: Transaction Books, 1988), pp. 3–10.

22. John Dewey to Max Otto, April 18, 1940. Max C. Otto Papers.

23. "John Dewey Responds," p. 85.

24. John Dewey, *The Quest for Certainty,* in LW 4:250.

25. John Dewey, "Introduction," in *Problems of Men,* in LW 15:169.

26. John Dewey, "In Response," in LW 5:421.

27. "John Dewey Responds," p. 86.

28. John Dewey, "In Response," p. 421.

29. *Ibid.*

30. *Ibid.,* pp. 422–23.

31. John Dewey, *Ethics,* in LW 7:197–99.

32. *Ibid.,* p. 302.

33. *Ibid.,* pp. 198–99.

34. "John Dewey Responds," p. 86.

35. Cornel West, *The American Evasion of Philosophy: A Genealogy of Pragmatism* (Madison: University of Wisconsin Press, 1989), pp. 101–07.

36. Unsigned statement in John Dewey's handwriting on a fund raising card prepared by the Women's International League for Peace and Freedom, Washington, D.C. John Herman Randall, Jr. Papers, Special Collections, Columbia University Libraries, New York, N.Y.

37. "Burlington, Vermont, Fetes John Dewey," *New York Times,* October 26, 1949, pp. 29, 40.

38. Dykhuizen, *John Dewey,* p. 317.

39. John Dewey to Elias Lyman, October 27, 1949, Special Collections, Bailey/Howe Memorial Library, University of Vermont. See Dykhuizen, *John Dewey,* p. 318.

40. Roberta Dewey to Max and Rhoda Otto, March 4, 1952, Max C. Otto Papers.

41. Interview with George Dykhuizen, June, 1971. Dykhuizen reported to this author what Roberta Dewey had told him regarding John Dewey's last words to her.

42. Dykhuizen, *John Dewey,* pp. 319–20.

43. *Ibid.,* pp. 320–22. John Haynes Holmes, who had been the Pastor of the Community Church and Chairman of the American Civil Liberties Union, was one of the speakers at Dewey's ninetieth birthday dinner in 1949. The statement of purpose used by E.S. Ames at the University Church may be found in chapter 11, note 72, of this book. See also letter of Van Meter Ames to George Dykhuizen, February 1, 1975, regarding E.S. Ames' use of this statement. George Dykhuizen Papers, Special Collections, Bailey/Howe Memorial Library, University of Vermont, Burlington, Vermont. The Community Church statement is printed in Dykhuizen, *John Dewey,* pp. 320–21.

44. John Dewey to Scudder Klyce, May 29, 1915, Scudder Klyce Papers, General Correspondence: John Dewey, Manuscript Division, Library of Congress, Washington, D.C.

45. John Dewey to Max Otto, December 19, 1939, Max C. Otto Papers. See also John Dewey, "Creative Democracy—The Task Before Us," in LW 14:224–25.

46. William James, *A Pluralistic Universe* (Cambridge, Mass.: Harvard University Press, 1977), p. 77.

47. Albert Schweitzer, "The Problem of Peace in the World of Today," The Nobel Peace Prize Address, Oslo, Norway, November 4, 1954," in *Albert Schweitzer: Yesterday's Man for Today's World* (Glastonbury, Conn.: Albert Schweitzer Memorial Foundation, Inc., 1988). Schweitzer, "The Conception of the Kingdom of God in the Transformation of Eschatology," in Walter Kaufmann, ed. *Religion From Tolstoy to Camus* (New York: Harper Torchbooks, 1961), pp. 420, 427.

48. John Dewey, *A Common Faith,* in LW 9:57–58.

Bibliography

Chronological Listing of Works by John Dewey on Religious Issues

Note: As a general rule, this bibliography notes only the first place of publication and publication in *The Works of John Dewey*. However, reference is also made to certain important collections of Dewey's essays published during his lifetime, including *The Influence of Darwin on Philosophy* (1910), *Characters and Events*, I & II (1929), and *The Problems of Men* (1946).

"The Pantheism of Spinoza." *Journal of Speculative Philosophy* (July 1882), 16:249–57. Reprinted in EW 1:9–18.

"The New Psychology." *Andover Review* 2 (September 1884): 278–289. Reprinted in EW 1:48–60.

"The Obligation to Knowledge of God." *The Monthly Bulletin,* Students' Christian Association, University of Michigan (November 1884), 6:23–25. Reprinted in EW 1:161–63.

"A Clergyman's View of Evolution." Review of *Evolution and Christianity* by Benjamin F. Tefft. *Index* (March 21, 1885), p. 313. (Not signed by Dewey but identified as a Dewey essay by his brother Davis Rich Dewey, in Joseph Ratner Papers, collection 142, Morris Library, Southern Illinois University).

"The Church and Society." *The University* (December 26, 1885), p. 7. Reprinted in LW 17:19–20.

"Science and The Idea of God." Review of John Fiske, *The Idea of God as Affected by Modern Knowledge.* Boston: Houghton, Mifflin, 1885. *The University* (January 2, 1886), pp. 5–6. Reprinted in LW 17:93–97.

"The Revival of the Soul." *The University* (December 5, 1885), pp. 6–7. Response by H.S. Swift, *The University* (January 9, 1886). Reply by Dewey to Swift, "What is the Demonstration of Man's Spiritual Nature." *The University* (January 23, 1886), pp. 43–44. Dewey and Swift exchange reprinted in LW 17:10–14, 531–33.

"The Psychological Standpoint." *Mind* (January 1886), 11:1–19. Reprinted in EW 1:122–43.

Review of *The Social Philosophy and Religion of Comte* by Edward Caird. *The Christian Union* (April 1, 1886), 33:22–23. (Not signed by Dewey but identified as a Dewey essay by his brother Davis Rich Dewey, in Joseph Ratner Papers, collection 142, Morris Library, Southern Illinois University).

"Psychology as Philosophic Method." *Mind* (April 1886), 11:153–73. Reprinted in EW 1:144–67.

"Soul and Body." *Bibliotheca Sacra* (April 1886), 43:239–63. Reprinted in EW 1:93–115.

"The Place of Religious Emotion." *The Monthly Bulletin* (November 1886), 8:23–25. Reprinted in EW 1:90–92.

Psychology. New York: Harper & Brothers, 1887. Reprinted in EW 2.

"Ethics and Physical Science." *Andover Review* (June 1887), 7:573–91. Reprinted in EW 1:205–26.

Leibniz's New Essays Concerning the Human Understanding. A Critical Exposition. In George Sylvester Morris, ed., *Grigg's Philosophical Classics,* vol. 7. Chicago: S.C. Griggs and Company, 1888. Reprinted in EW 1:253–435.

The Ethics of Democracy. University of Michigan Philosophical Papers, Second Series, no. 1. Ann Arbor: Andrews & Company, 1888. Reprinted in EW 1:227–49.

"The Higher Criticism and the Highest." *The Christian Union* (February 7, 1889), 39:165. (Not signed by Dewey but identified as a Dewey essay by his brother Davis Rich Dewey, in Joseph Ratner Papers, collection 142, Morris Library, Southern Illinois University).

"The Late Professor Morris." In The College Fraternities at the University of Michigan, eds., *The Palladium* (1889), 31:110–18. Reprinted in EW 3:3–13.

"The Philosophy of Thomas Hill Green." *Andover Review* (April 1889), 11:337–55. Reprinted in EW 3:14–35.

"The Lesson of Contemporary French Literature." *The Christian Union* (July 11, 1889), 9:38–39. Reprinted in EW 3:36–42.

"The Value of Historical Christianity." *The Monthly Bulletin* (November 1889), 11:31–36.* Reprinted in LW 17:529–34.

Review of *The Critical Philosophy of Immanuel Kant* by Edward Caird. *Andover Review* (March 1890), 13:325–27. Reprinted in EW 3:180–84.

Review of *Studies in Hegel's Philosophy of Religion* by James MacBride Sterrett. *Andover Review* (June 1890), 13:684–85. Reprinted in EW 3:187–189.

"I had rather speak five words with my understanding than ten thousand words in an unknown tongue." *The Monthly Bulletin* (March 1891), 12:92–94.*

"Relation of Morality and Religion." *The Monthly Bulletin* (March 1891), 12:94–95.*

"Poetry and Philosophy." *Andover Review* (August 1891), 16:105–16. Reprinted in EW 3:110–24.

"Green's Theory of the Moral Motive." *Philosophical Review* (November 1892), 1:593–612. Reprinted in EW 2:155–73.

"Two Phases of Renan's Life: The Faith of 1850 and the Doubt of 1890." *Open Court* (December 29, 1892), 6:3505–06. Reprinted in EW 3:174–79.

"Christianity and Democracy." In *Religious Thought at the University of Michigan*, pp. 62–69. Ann Arbor: Inland Press, 1893. Reprinted in EW 4:3–10.

"The Relation of Philosophy to Theology." *The Monthly Bulletin* (January 1893), 14:66–68. Reprinted in EW 9:365–68.

"Renan's Loss of Faith in Science." *Open Court* (January 5, 1893), 7:3512–15. Reprinted in EW 4:11–18.

"Self-Realization as the Moral Ideal." *Philosophical Review* (November 1893), 2:652–64. Reprinted in EW 4:42–53.

The Study of Ethics: A Syllabus. Ann Arbor: Register Publishing Company, 1894. Reprinted in EW 4:219–362.

*"The Value of Historical Christianity" (1889), "I had rather speak five words" (1891), and "Relation of Morality and Religion" (1891), which all appear in the *Monthly Bulletin*, present remarks or addresses made by Dewey, but it is not clear whether they involve a transcription of what he said or are copies of a written text supplied by Dewey. The length of "The Value of Historical Christianity" indicates that it is a reprint of a Dewey manuscript.

"Reconstruction." *The Monthly Bulletin* (June 1894), 15:149–56. Reprinted in EW 4:96–105.

"My Pedagogic Creed." *School Journal* (January 16, 1897), 54:77–80. Reprinted in EW 5:84–95.

Review of *The World and the Individual* (Gifford Lectures, First Series: The Four Historical Conceptions of Being) by Josiah Royce. *Philosophical Review* (May 1900), 9:311–24. Reprinted in MW 1:242–56.

Review of *The World and the Individual* (Gifford Lectures, Second Series: Nature, Men and the Moral Order) by Josiah Royce. *Philosophical Review* (July 1902), 11:392–407. Reprinted in MW 2:120–37.

Contributions to *Dictionary of Philosophy and Psychology,* James Mark Baldwin, ed. New York: Macmillan, 1902, vol. 2. Reprinted in MW 2:139–269.

Studies in Logical Theory, by John Dewey, with the Co-operation of Members and Fellows of the Department of Philosophy. University of Chicago Decennial Publications, Second Series, vol. 11. Chicago: University of Chicago Press, 1903. Dewey's four essays reprinted in MW 2:293–375.

"Emerson—The Philosopher of Democracy." *International Journal of Ethics* (1903) 13:405–13. Reprinted as "Ralph Waldo Emerson." In Joseph Ratner, ed., *Characters and Events,* vol. 1, 69–77. New York: Henry Holt, 1929. Reprinted in MW 3:184–92.

"Religious Education as Conditioned by Modern Psychology and Pedagogy." In *Proceedings of the First Annual Convention of the Religious Education Association.* Chicago, 1903, pp. 60–66. Reprinted in *Religious Education* (January-February 1974), 69:6–11. Reprinted in MW 3:210–15.

"Religion and Our Schools." *Hibbert Journal* (July 1908), 6:796–809. Reprinted in Joseph Ratner, ed., *Education Today,* pp. 74–86. New York: G. P. Putnam's Sons, 1940. Reprinted in MW 4:165–77.

"Is Nature Good? A Conversation." *Hibbert Journal* (July 1909), 7:827–43. Reprinted as "Nature and Its Good: A Conversation." In *The Influence of Darwin on Philosophy,* pp. 20–45. New York: Henry Holt, 1910. Reprinted in MW 4:15–30.

"Darwin's Influence Upon Philosophy." *Popular Science Monthly* (July 1909), 75:90–98. Reprinted as "The Influence of Darwinism on Philosophy." In *The Influence of Darwin on Philosophy,* pp. 1–19. Reprinted in MW 4:3–14.

"Some Thoughts Concerning Religion." Address delivered to the Philosophical Club, Columbia University, New York, March 17, 1910. Reprinted in LW 17:374–80.

"Dr. Dewey Replies." Letter in *New Republic* 2 (May 22, 1915), 2:72. Reply to "Parochial School Education," letter of Charles P. Megan, *Ibid.* Reprinted in MW 8:416–17, 471–72.

Democracy and Education. An Introduction to the Philosophy of Education. In Paul Monroe, ed., Text-Book Series in Education. New York: Macmillan, 1916. Reprinted in MW 9.

"Progress." *International Journal of Ethics* (1916), 26:311–22. Reprinted in Joseph Ratner, ed., *Characters and Events,* vol. 2, pp. 820–30. New York: Henry Holt, 1929. Reprinted in MW 10:234–43.

"Conscience and Compulsion." *New Republic* (1917), 2:297–98. Reprinted in *Characters and Events,* vol. 2, pp. 576–80. Reprinted in MW 10:260–64.

"H.G. Wells, Theological Assembler." Review of H.G. Wells, *God the Invisible King. Seven Arts Magazine* (July 1917), 2:334–39. Reprinted as "H.G. Wells." In *Characters and Events.* vol. 1, pp. 78–82. Reprinted in MW 10:310–14.

"The Future of Pacifism." *New Republic* (July 28, 1917), 40:358–60. Reprinted in *Characters and Events,* vol. 2, pp. 581–86. Reprinted in MW 10:265–70.

"George Sylvester Morris: An Estimate." In Robert Mark Wenley. *The Life and Work of George Sylvester Morris,* pp. 313–21. New York: Macmillan, 1917. Reprinted in MW 10:109–15.

Untitled and unpublished manuscript on Leo Tolstoy's philosophy. Dewey Papers, Special Collections, Morris Library, Southern Illinois University. Date unknown. Reprinted in LW 17:381–92.

Reconstruction in Philosophy. New York: Henry Holt and Company, 1920. Reprinted in an enlarged edition with new introduction by John Dewey. Boston: Beacon Press, 1948. Reprinted in MW 12:77–202, 256–77.

"Three Contemporary Philosophers." [James, Bergson and Russell] First published in Chinese in *Peking Morning Post,* 1920. Translated into English by Robert W. Clopton and Tsuin-chen Ou and reprinted in MW 12:205–50.

"First Introduction." In Scudder Klyce. *Universe,* pp. iii–v. Winchester, Mass.: S. Klyce, 1921. Reprinted in MW 13:412–20.

"Some Factors in Mutual Understanding." *Kaizo* (1921), 3:17–28. Reprinted in MW 13:262–71.

Human Nature and Conduct. An Introduction to Social Psychology. New York: Henry Holt, 1922. Reprinted in MW 14.

"Education as a Religion." *New Republic* (September 13, 1922), 32:63–65. Reprinted in *Education Today* (1940), pp. 144–49. Reprinted in MW 13:317–22.

"As the Chinese Think." *Asia* (1922), 22:7–10, 78–79. Reprinted as "The

Chinese Philosophy of Life." In *Characters and Events,* vol. 1, pp. 199–210. Reprinted in MW 13:217–227.

"Introduction." In F. Matthias Alexander. *Constructive Conscious Control of the Individual,* pp. xxi-xxxiii. New York: E.P. Dutton, 1923. Reprinted in MW 15:308–15.

"Fundamentals." *New Republic* (February 6, 1924), 37:275–76. Reprinted in *Characters and Events,* vol. 2, pp. 453–58. Reprinted in MW 15:3–7.

"Science, Belief and the Public." *New Republic* (April 2, 1924), 38:143–45. Reprinted in *Characters and Events,* vol. 2, pp. 459–64. Reprinted in LW 15:47–52.

Experience and Nature. Chicago: Open Court, 1925. Reprinted in a revised edition. New York: W.W. Norton, 1929. Reprinted in LW 1.

"Church and State in Mexico." *New Republic* (August 25, 1926), 48:9–10. Reprinted in *Characters and Events,* vol. 1, pp. 352–57. Reprinted in LW 2:194–98.

"Bishop Brown: A Fundamentalist Modernist." *New Republic* (November 17, 1926), 48:371–72. Reprinted as "William Montgomery Brown." In *Characters and Events,* vol. 1, pp. 83–86. Reprinted in LW 2:163–66.

"Half-Hearted Naturalism." *Journal of Philosophy* (February 3, 1927), 24:57–64. Reply to George Santayana, "Dewey's Naturalistic Metaphysics," *Ibid.* (December 3, 1925), 22:673–88, and Frank Thilly, "Contemporary American Philosophy," *Philosophical Review* (November 1926), 35:522–38. Reprinted in LW 3:73–81, 367–400.

The Public and Its Problems. New York: Henry Holt, c. 1927. Reprinted in LW 2:235–372.

"The Integration of a Moving World." Review of *Purposive Evolution: The Link between Science and Religion* by Edmund Noble. *New Republic* (May 25, 1927), 51:22–24. Reprinted in LW 3:299–304.

"Philosophies of Freedom." In Horace M. Kallen, ed., *Freedom in the Modern World,* pp. 236–71. New York: Coward-McCann, 1928. Reprinted in LW 3:92–114.

"The Great Experiment and the Future." *New Republic* (December 19, 1928), 57:134–37. Reprinted in *John Dewey's Impressions of Soviet Russia and the Revolutionary World: Mexico—China—Turkey.* Intro. William W. Brickman. New York: Bureau of Publications, Teachers' College, Columbia University, 1929. Reprinted in LW 3:242–50.

"Personal Immortality: What I Believe." *New York Times* (April 8, 1928): sec. 9, p. 1. Reprinted with the title "On Immortality" in LW 17:126.

The Quest for Certainty. New York: Minton, Balch, 1929. Reprinted in LW 4.

"James Marsh and American Philosophy." *Journal of the History of Ideas* (April 1941), 2:131–50. Reprinted in *Problems of Men,* pp. 357–78. New York: Philosophical Library, 1946. Reprinted in LW 5:178–96.

Individualism, Old and New. New York: Minton, Balch, 1930. Reprinted in LW 5:41–123.

"An Organic Universe: The Philosophy of Alfred N. Whitehead." Review of *Process and Reality* by A.N. Whitehead. *New York Sun* (October 1929), 26. Reprinted in LW 5:375–81.

"From Absolutism to Experimentalism." In George Plimpton Adams and William Pepperell Montague, eds., *Contemporary American Philosophy: Personal Statements,* vol. 2, pp. 13–27. New York: Macmillan, 1930. Reprinted in LW 5:147–60.

"In Response." In *John Dewey, The Man and His Philosophy: Addresses Delivered in New York in Celebration of His Seventieth Birthday,* pp. 173–81. Cambridge: Harvard University Press, 1930. Reprinted in LW 5:418–23.

"What I Believe." *Forum* (March 1930), 83:176–82. Reprinted in *Living Philosophies: A Series of Intimate Credos by Twenty-Two Modern Thinkers,* pp. 21–35. New York: Simon and Schuster, 1931. Separately published under the title *A Credo.* New York: Simon and Schuster, 1931. Reprinted in LW 5:267–78.

"Religion in the Soviet Union: An Interpretation of the Conflict." *Current History* (April 1930), 32:31–36. Reprinted in LW 5:355–62.

"What Humanism Means to Me." *The Thinker* (June 1930), 2:9–12. Reprinted in LW 5:263–66.

Ethics. Revised edition, with James Hayden Tufts. New York: Henry Holt, c. 1932. Reprinted in LW 7.

"A Humanist Manifesto." *New Humanist* (May-June 1933), 6:1–5. Signed by John Dewey and thirty-three leading United States philosophers, writers, and clergymen. Reprinted in Charles Francis Potter, *Humanizing Religion,* pp. 6–15. New York: Harper, 1933.

"A God or The God?" *Christian Century* (February 8, 1933), 1:193–96. Review of *Is There a God?—A Conversation* by Henry Nelson Wieman, Douglas Clyde Macintosh, and Max Carl Otto. Response by Wieman and Macintosh. "Mr. Wieman and Mr. Macintosh 'Converse' with Mr. Dewey." *Ibid.* (March 1, 1933), 1:299–302. Reply by Dewey. "Dr. Dewey Replies," *Ibid.* (March 22, 1933), 1:394–95. Dewey, Weiman, and Macintosh exchange reprinted in LW 9:213–28, 412–22.

Art as Experience. New York: Minton, Balch, 1934. Reprinted in LW 10.

"The Liberation of Modern Religion." *Yale Review* (June 1934), 23:751–70. Reprinted in *A Common Faith* (1934) with title "Faith and Its Object."

A Common Faith. New Haven: Yale University Press, 1934. Reprinted in LW 9:1–58. Review by Henry Nelson Wieman. "John Dewey's Common Faith." *Christian Century* (November 14, 1934), 51:1450–52. Response to Wieman by Edwin Ewart Aubrey. "Is John Dewey a Theist?" *Ibid.* (December 5, 1934), 51:1550. Reply to Aubrey by Wieman, *Ibid.* Reply to Aubrey and Wieman by Dewey, *Ibid.,* 1551–52. Dewey, Wieman, and Aubrey exchange reprinted in LW 9:294–95, 426–40. Reply to Dewey by Wieman. *Christian Century* (December 5, 1934), 51:1552–53. Editorial comment, "The Philosophers and God," *Ibid.* (December 12, 1934), 51:1582–84. Review by Norbert Guterman. "John Dewey's Credo." *New Republic* (February 20, 1935), 82:53. Reply by Dewey. "Religions and the 'Religious.' " *Ibid.* (March 13, 1935), 82:132. Dewey and Guterman exchange reprinted in LW 9:293, 423–25. Reply by Guterman and letter of Irvin Kelley. *New Republic* (March 20, 1935), 82:161.

"Philosophy." In *Encyclopedia of the Social Sciences.* eds. Edwin R.A. Seligman and Alvin Johnson. New York: Macmillan, 1934, vol. 12, pp. 118–29. Reprinted in LW 8:19–39.

"Future of Liberalism." *People's Lobby Bulletin* (February 1935), 4:1–2. Reprinted in LW 11:258–60.

"Intimations of Mortality." Review of *The Illusion of Immortality* by Corliss Lamont. New York: G.P. Putnam's Sons, 1935. *New Republic* (April 24, 1935), 82:318. Reprinted in LW 11:425–27.

"Mystical Naturalism and Religious Humanism." *The New Humanist* (April–May 1935), 8:74–75. Response to article under same title by Bernard Meland, *Ibid.,* 72–74. Dewey and Meland exchange reprinted in LW 11:84–85, 583–87.

Liberalism and Social Action. New York: G.P. Putnam, 1935. Reprinted in LW 11:1–65.

"Bergson on Instinct." Review of *The Two Sources of Morality and Religion* by Henri Bergson. *New Republic* (June 26, 1935), 83:200–01. Reprinted in LW 11:428–31.

"One Current Religious Problem." *Journal of Philosophy* (June 4, 1936), 33:324–26. Reply to Percy Hughes. "Current Philosophical Problems." *Ibid.* (April 9, 1936), 33:212–17. Reprinted in LW 11:115–17.

"Religion, Science and Philosophy." Review of *Religion and Science* by Bertrand Russell. *Southern Review* (Summer 1936), 2:53–62. Reprinted in *Problems of Men,* pp. 169–79. Reprinted in LW 11:454–63.

"The Philosophy of William James." Review of *The Thought and Character of William James,* by Ralph Barton Perry. *Southern Review* (Winter 1937), 2:447–61. Reprinted in LW 11:464–78.

"Freedom." In National Education Association, *Implications of Social-Economic Goals for Education: A Report of the Committee on Social Economic Goals of America,* pp. 99–105. Washington, D.C.: National Education Association, 1937. Reprinted in LW 11:247–55.

"Democracy is Radical." *Common Sense* (January 1937), 6:10–11. Reprinted in LW 11:296–99.

Experience and Education. New York: Macmillan, 1938. Reprinted in LW 13:1–62.

"What I Believe, Revised." In Clifton Fadiman, ed., *I Believe: The Personal Philosophies of Certain Eminent Men and Women of Our Time,* pp. 347–54. New York: Simon and Schuster, 1939. Reprinted in LW 14:91–97.

Freedom and Culture. New York: G.P. Putnam, 1939. Reprinted in LW 13:63–188.

"Democratic Ends Need Democratic Methods for their Realization." *New Leader* (October 21, 1939), 22:3. Reprinted in LW 14:367–68.

"Experience, Knowledge and Value: A Rejoinder." In Paul Arthur Schilpp, ed., *The Philosophy of John Dewey,* pp. 517–608. Volume I of *The Library of Living Philosophers.* Chicago: Northwestern University, 1939. Reprinted in LW 14:8–91.

"The Basis for Hope." *Common Sense* (December 1939), 8:9–10. Reprinted in LW 14:249–51.

"Creative Democracy—The Task Before Us." In Sidney Ratner, ed., *The Philosophy of the Common Man. Essays in Honor of John Dewey to Celebrate His Eightieth Birthday,* pp. 220–28. New York: Putnam's, 1940. Reprinted in LW 14:224–30.

"Presenting Thomas Jefferson." In Alfred O. Mendel, ed., *The Living Thoughts of Thomas Jefferson,* pp. 1–30. New York: Longmans, Green, 1940. Reprinted in LW 14:201–23.

"The Meaning of The Term: Liberalism." *Frontiers of Democracy* (February 15, 1940), 6:135. Reprinted in LW 14:252–54.

"Art as Our Heritage." From an April 25 radio address over WMAL, Washington, D.C. Reprinted in *Congressional Record,* 76th Congress, 3rd session, April 29, 1940, 86, pt. 15:2477–78. Reprinted in LW 14:255–57.

Review of *The Human Enterprise: An Attempt to Relate Philosophy to Daily Life,* by Max C. Otto. *Journal of Philosophy* (May 23, 1940), 37:303–05. Reprinted in LW 14:289–92.

Review of *Social Religion* by Douglas Clyde Macintosh. *Review of Religion* (March 1940), 4:359–61. Reprinted in LW 14:286–88.

"The Basic Values and Loyalties of Democracy." *American Teacher* (May 1941), 25:8–9. Reprinted in LW 14:275–77.

"Religion and Morality in a Free Society." Address at Hollins College Centennial, May 18, 1942. University of Virginia Library, Manuscript Division, Charlottesville, Virginia. Reprinted in LW 15:170–83.

"William James and the World Today." In *William James, the Man and the Thinker. Addresses Delivered at the University of Wisconsin in Celebration of the Centenary of His Birth.* Madison, University of Wisconsin Press, 1942, pp. 91–97. Reprinted in LW 15:3–8.

"Anti-Naturalism in Extremis." *Partisan Review* (January-February 1943), 10:24–39. Reprinted in Yervant H. Krikorian, ed., *Naturalism and the Human Spirit,* pp. 1–16. New York: Columbia University Press, 1944. Reprinted in LW 15:46–62.

"Statement on Jefferson." From a typescript in the Jerome Nathanson Papers, Society for Ethical Culture, New York City; prepared for press release for conference on The Scientific Spirit and Democratic Faith, May 29–30, 1943. Repinted in LW 15:366.

"The Democratic Faith and Education." *Antioch Review* (June 1944), 4:274–83. Reprinted in *The Problems of Men,* pp. 22–33. Reprinted in LW 15:251–60.

"The Crisis in Human History: The Danger of the Retreat to Individualism." *Commentary* (March 1946), 1:1–9. Reprinted in LW 15:210–23.

"Comment on 'Religion at Harvard'." *Harvard Alumni Bulletin* (March 8, 1947), 49:450. Response to Harold R. Rafton, "Religion at Harvard," *Harvard Alumni Bulletin* (January 11, 1947), 11:330. Rafton and Dewey statements reprinted in LW 17:135, 545.

"Implications of S.2499." *Nation's Schools* (March 1947), 39:20–21. Reprinted in LW 15:281–85.

"William James' Morals and Julien Benda's: It Is Not Pragmatism That Is Opportunist." *Commentary* (January 1948), 5:46–50. Reprinted in LW 15:19–26. First published as a reply to Julien Benda, "The Attack on Western Morality: Can European Schools Survive?" *Commentary* (November 1947), 4:416–22. Benda's essay is reprinted in LW 15:381–92.

"John Dewey Responds." In Harry W. Laidler, ed. *John Dewey at Ninety: Addresses and Greetings on the Occasion of Dr. Dewey's Ninetieth Birthday Dinner October 20, 1949 at the Hotel Commodore, New York.* New York: League For Industrial Democracy, 1949. Reprinted in LW 17:84–87.

"Religion and the Intellectuals." *Partisan Review* (February 1950), 17:129–33. Reprinted in *Religion and the Intellectuals: A Symposium,* pp. 53–57. New York: Partisan Review, 1950. Reprinted in LW 16:390–94.

"Modern Philosophy." In Frederick Burkhardt, ed., *The Cleavage in Our*

Culture: Studies in Scientific Humanism in Honor of Max Otto. Boston: Beacon Press, 1952, pp. 15–29. Reprinted in LW 16:407–19.

The Poems of John Dewey. Jo Ann Boydston, ed. Carbondale: Southern Illinois University Press, 1977.

Selected Bibliography of Books and Essays

Alexander, Thomas M. *John Dewey's Theory of Art, Experience and Nature: The Horizons of Feeling*. New York: SUNY Press, 1987.

Ames, Van Meter. "Dewey and Zen." In his *Zen and American Thought*, pp. 214–35. Honolulu: University of Hawaii Press, 1962.

Blewett, John, S.J. "Democracy as Religion: Unity in Human Relations." In John Blewett, S.J., ed., *John Dewey: His Thought and Influence*, pp. 33–58. New York: Fordham University Press, 1960.

Boydston, Jo Ann. "Introduction." In Jo Ann Boydston, ed., *The Poems of John Dewey*, pp. ix–lxvii. Carbondale: Southern Illinois University Press, 1977.

Boisvert, Raymond. *Dewey's Metaphysics*. New York: Fordham University Press, 1988.

Coughlan, Neil. *Young John Dewey: An Essay in American Intellectual History*. Chicago: University of Chicago Press, 1975.

Dewey, Jane Mary, ed. "Biography of John Dewey." In Paul Arthur Schilpp, ed., *The Philosophy of John Dewey*. Evanston, Ill.: Northwestern University Press, 1939, pp. 3–45. Reprinted, with the bibliography extended to 1950 by Muriel Murray. New York: Tudor, 1951. Reprinted again, LaSalle, Ill.: Open Court, 1970.

Dewey, Robert E. *The Philosophy of John Dewey: A Critical Exposition of His Method, Metaphysics and Theory of Knowledge*. The Hague: Martinus Nijhoff, 1977.

Dykhuizen, George. *The Life and Mind of John Dewey*. Jo Ann Boydston, ed. Carbondale: Southern Illinois University Press, 1973.

Eastman, Max. "John Dewey: My Teacher and Friend." In his *Great Companions*, pp. 249–98. New York: Farrar, Strauss, & Cudahy, 1959.

Feuer, Lewis Samuel. "H.A.P. Torrey and John Dewey: Teacher and Pupil." *American Quarterly* (Spring 1958), 10:34–54.

Feuer, Lewis Samuel. "John Dewey and the Back-to-the-People Movement in American Thought." *Journal of the History of Ideas* (October-December 1959), 20:545–68.

Feuer, Lewis Samuel. "Introduction," in LW 15:xi-xxxiv.

Feuer, Lewis Samuel. "The Standpoints of Dewey and Freud: A Contrast and Analysis." *Journal of Individual Psychology* (November 1960), 16:119–36

Frank, Waldo [Search-Light]. "The Man Who Made Us What We Are." *New Yorker* (May 22, 1926), pp. 15–16. Reprinted in *Time Exposures* (by Search-Light), pp. 121–27. New York: Boni and Liveright, 1926.

Hartshorne, Charles. "Dewey's Philosophy of Religion." In his *Beyond Humanism: Essays in the Philosophy of Nature,* pp. 39–57. Gloucester, Mass.: Peter Smith, 1975.

Hook, Sidney. *John Dewey: An Intellectual Portrait.* New York: John Day, 1939.

Hook, Sidney. "Some Memories of John Dewey, 1859–1952." In his *Pragmatism and The Tragic Sense of Life,* pp. 101–14. New York: Basic Books, 1974.

Hook, Sidney. "Introduction," in MW 9:xi-xxiv.

Korvitz, Milton, "Introduction," in LW 9:xi-xxxii.

Kuklick, Bruce. *Churchmen and Philosophers: From Jonathan Edwards to John Dewey.* New Haven: Yale University Press, 1985.

Nathanson, Jerome. *John Dewey: Reconstruction of the Democratic Life.* New York: Frederick Unger, 1951.

Randall, John Herman, Jr. "The Religion of Shared Experience." In Beth J. Singer, ed., *Philosophy After Darwin: Chapters for the Career of Philosophy, Volume III, and other Essays,* pp. 241–67. New York: Columbia University Press, 1977. First published in Horace M. Kallen, ed., *The Philosopher of the Common Man: Essays in Honor of John Dewey to Celebrate His Eightieth Birthday,* pp. 106–45. New York: G.P. Putnam's, 1940.

Ratner, Joseph. "Introduction." In William James, *The Varieties of Religious Experience: A Study in Human Nature,* pp. v-xxxiv. Hyde Park, N.Y.: University Books, 1963.

Rockefeller, Steven C. "John Dewey: The Evolution of A Faith." In Maurice Wohlgelernter, ed., *History, Religion, and Spiritual Democracy: Essays in Honor of Joseph L. Blau.* pp. 5–34. New York: Columbia University Press, 1980.

—— "John Dewey's Theory of the Religious Quality of Experience." In William J. Hynes and William Dean, eds., *American Religious Empiricism: Working Papers, Volume I,* pp. 41–74. Denver: Regis College Press, 1988.

—— "Nishitani Keiji and John Dewey's Naturalistic Humanism." In *The Religious Philosophy of Nishitani Keiji* Taitetsu Unno, ed., pp. 201–56. Berkeley: Asian Humanities Press, 1989.

—— "John Dewey, Spiritual Democracy, and the Human Future." *Cross Currents* (Fall 1989), 39 (3):300–21.

Rorty, Richard. *Consequences of Pragmatism*. Minneapolis: University of Minnesota Press, 1982.

Roth, John K. "William James, John Dewey, and the 'Death-of-God'." *Religious Studies* (1971), 7:53–61.

Roth, Robert J., S.J. "John Dewey and Religious Experience." In Robert J. Roth, ed., *American Religious Philosophy,* pp. 85–108. New York: Harcourt, Brace & World, 1967.

Rucker, Darnell. *The Chicago Pragmatists*. Minneapolis: University of Minnesota Press, 1969.

Schaub, Edward L. "Dewey's Interpretation of Religion." In Paul Schilpp, ed., *The Philosophy of John Dewey,* pp. 3–45. Evanston, Ill.: Northwestern University Press, 1939. Reprinted, with the bibliography extended to 1950 by Muriel Murray. New York: Tudor, 1951. Reprinted again, LaSalle, Ill.: Open Court , 1970.

Shaw, Marvin C. "Wieman's Misunderstanding of Dewey: The *Christian Century* Discussion." *Zygon* (March 1987), 22:7–19.

Shea, William M. *The Naturalists and the Supernatural*. Macon, GA: Mercer University Press, 1984.

Sleeper, R.W. *The Necessity of Pragmatism: John Dewey's Conception of Philosophy*. New Haven: Yale University Press, 1986.

Sleeper, R.W. "Introduction," in LW 14:xi-xxiv.

Westbrook, Robert B. *John Dewey and American Democracy*. Ithaca, N.Y.: Cornell University Press, 1991.

White, Morton. *Science and Sentiment in America: Philosophical Thought from Jonathan Edwards to John Dewey*. New York: Oxford University Press, 1972.

Index